Corporation with $70,000 in venture capital.

Committee on Data Systems Languages. Hopper invents a compiler that makes COBOL run on many types of computers.

1962

Computer industry revenues reach the $1 billion mark.

1958 to 1964

Second generation computers are characterized by transistors and magnetic tape drives.

1961

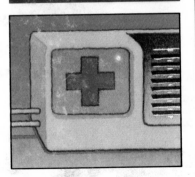

The first patient monitoring system is implemented at the National Health Institute Clinic in Maryland.

1965

BASIC (Beginner's All-Purpose Symbolic Instruction Code) language is created by Tom Kurtz and John Kemeny of Dartmouth.

1959

COBOL, for Commercial and Business-Oriented Language, based on Grace Hopper's Flow-Matic, is created by the

WORLD OF COMPUTING

WORLD OF COMPUTING

RONALD E. ANDERSON
University of Minnesota

DAVID R. SULLIVAN
Oregon State University

HOUGHTON MIFFLIN COMPANY   **BOSTON**

Dallas   *Geneva, Illinois*   *Palo Alto*   *Princeton, New Jersey*

Cover Photography by Ralph Mercer Photography

Art credits: Part I Opener Mark Antman/Stock Boston/Figure 1.3 photo by
Liane Enkelis; Figure 1.4 Courtesy of Comdisco, Inc.; Figure 1.5 Courtesy
of Texas Instruments; Figure 1.6 Courtesy of Electronic Data Systems,
Dallas, Texas; Figure 1.7 Photo Researchers/Catherine Ursillo; Figure 1.8
Courtesy of Northern Telecom Inc.; Figure 1.9 Courtesy of Commodore
Electronics Ltd.; Figure 1.10 Federal Aviation Administration; Figure 1.11
Courtesy of International Business Machines Corporation; Figure 1.12
Courtesy of Apple Computer, Inc. Credits continue on page C-1.

Library of Congress Catalog Card Number: 87-81964

ISBN: 0-395-43554-4

ABCDEFGHIJ-RM-9543210-8987

Software Solutions Series

The World of Computing *is augmented
by the Houghton Mifflin Software
Solutions Series. This innovative series
of remarkably affordable tutorial
manuals keyed to leading commercial
application software products is designed
to accompany* The World of Computing.

Contents in Brief

Contents

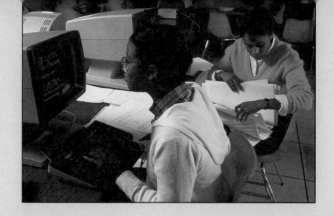

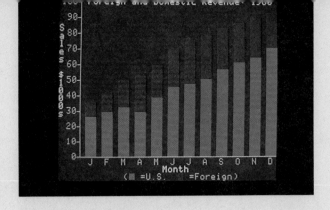

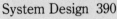

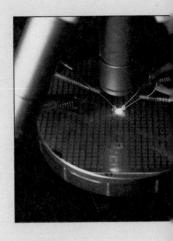

Preface

The Purpose of *The World of Computing*

This book has four main objectives:

- To teach why it is important for most people in our society to be knowledgeable about computers.
- To provide a thorough treatment of how all types of computers work.
- To explain principles and concepts from a user's perspective and emphasize practical applications.
- To present the broader issues of how computer systems are developed and what their role is in our society.

The content and organization of *The World of Computing* is well suited to a variety of introductory courses in computing. It can be used in a campus-wide computer literacy course for non-technical as well as technical students; or in a modern first-course in business data processing.

Organization of the Book

The World of Computing is designed to accommodate a variety of course formats. Its four major parts have been kept as independent as possible. After completing Part I, the remaining parts can be studied in any order.

Part I describes the basics of computing. After reviewing the importance of computers and computer literacy in Chapter 1, Chapters 2 through 4 describe the inner workings of computers from their central processing engines to their input and output devices. Finally, Chapter 5 describes how to operate a computer by explaining the purpose and function of an operating system and by illustrating the use of visual and textual user interfaces.

Part II deals with the concepts underlying the major types of application software. Chapter 6 describes the most pervasive use of computers: word processing.

Chapter 7 introduces spreadsheet analysis, including the concept of an electronic worksheet and the methods used to store numbers, text, and formulas. It also touches on the more advanced features of spreadsheet programs, leading to the realm of modelling and the development of professional-quality spreadsheet templates. Chapter 8 begins with a discussion of file management programs, the simplest form of data management software. It concludes by extending the file management concepts to include the database management systems used on mainframes, minis, and micros. Chapter 9 discusses the burgeoning fields of telecommunications and computer networking. Chapter 10 shows how the graphical capability of computers can be used to make bar charts, line graphs, and other types of presentation graphics. It also discusses the powerful graphics systems used to design airplanes, computers, and buildings. This introduction to computer graphics sets the stage for Chapter 11, the final chapter in Part II, which discusses how desktop publishing is used to assemble a printed page from text and graphics files.

Part III focuses on the design of new systems. Chapter 12 covers the system analysis approach to defining and solving data processing problems, complete with data flow charts and structured design methodology. Chapter 13 is an overview of programming in general. It compares features of different programming languages and should be read prior to studying the appendix on BASIC programming. Chapter 14, the last in this section, overviews the field of artificial intelligence and goes into some depth about how an expert system is developed.

Part IV examines the evolving role of computers in work, organizations, and society's institutions. Chapter 15 begins with office automation and management information systems and moves into a review of how the computer is used by industry and by particular professions: law, medicine, and journalism. Chapter 16 reviews how computers are used in government, education, art, and science. Chapter 17 extends the discussion by raising grave issues concerning privacy, pirating of software, security, and the general topic of ethics in computing. Finally, Chapter 18 traces the computer revolution from its roots to contemporary society. It provides the usual coverage of the generations of mainframe computers, includes a unique treatment of the development of personal computers, and concludes with some projections about the future.

Coverage of Productivity Software

The ancient proverb "May you live in interesting times," is especially appropriate for instructors of computing. It would be far easier to teach calculus—at least the basic assumptions and techniques of calculus wouldn't continually change.

The world of computing refuses to stand still, which raises questions about how to teach and learn about it. The computer that a freshman uses today is likely to be obsolete by the time that graduation day arrives. $5\frac{1}{4}$-inch floppy disks are headed to a place in the computer graveyard next to punched cards and paper tape. Software is undergoing even more dramatic changes. Programs are becoming more graphic. Desktop publishing is transforming the ordinary word processor into a tool that breaks down the traditional barriers between thinking, writing, presenting, and publishing. Typed commands are giving way to user interfaces that rely on icons, pull-down menus, windows, and dialog boxes. The list of recent and important evolutionary changes goes on and on.

One less than satisfying response to all this turmoil would be for a text to resort to generalizations about the Information Age and the Computer Revolution. Relying too heavily on such generalizations could lead to a dull treatment of what is an exciting and practical field. Accordingly, we have strived to include in this book as many realistic examples and explanations of current trends as we could fit between the covers.

There is no universally accepted definition for what computer literacy means, or what a computer literacy text should contain, but it could boil down to teaching students to use particular application programs. The value of learning to write, manage lists, perform calculations, and prepare graphs with a computer is undeniable and must be addressed in any text today. But this approach to computer literacy might run into a bit of trouble if the mechanics of using a particular program are allowed to overwhelm larger considerations. Imagine what would happen if other academic disciplines suddenly began to do this. Statistics texts, for example, would no longer take time to explain when to use the various types of statistical tests or why the tests work. Instead they would jump right into the details of controlling statistics programs. It would be unfortunate if too many students simply memorize facts like "WordStar requires you to press [Ctrl]–K–B to mark the beginning of a block of text" without also learning the differences between various word processing programs or when to use the available features. Such an approach seems especially risky in the field of computers, where today's refrigerator is tomorrow's oak-sheathed ice box.

There are thousands of programs available. Each has its own characteristics, command structure, and user interface. In writing this text it was a challenge to see beyond the superficial differences among programs and find the essence of word processors, spreadsheets and other productivity software. For example, moving a paragraph is conceptually identical in all word processors; organizing a file of data is conceptually similar in different data management systems. Knowing these concepts will serve the user well no matter which computer or productivity software package is selected. Familiarity with these principles builds a basis for learning to use any program and understanding much about computing in general.

Supplementary Materials

A full set of supplementary materials is available to accompany *The World of Computing*. These supplements include:

- A carefully developed study guide. The study guide provides students with a list of objectives for each chapter. In addition, one of the unique features of this guide is that all the multiple choice and true/false questions are keyed to the objectives to make studying easier.

- Microstudy, an electronic study guide. The study guide is also available on disk for students to use in a lab environment. This interactive program allows students to view and answer the questions in the study guide.

- A combined instructor's manual and test bank. The manual gives valuable teaching suggestions for the course. In addition, some student lab exercises are also provided. The test bank contains more than 1700 true-false, matching, and multiple choice test questions.

- Disks containing the test questions from the Test Bank and the BASIC programs from the BASIC appendix for IBM equipment.

- A set of forty-eight acetate overhead transparencies.

- Software solution series. The series currently consisting of seven inexpensive tutorial manuals explicitly designed to offer solutions to the problems encountered by countless numbers of educators who wish to include as a component of courses they teach, instruction on popular commercial application software programs. Educational versions of the actual program disks to accompany many of these manuals are available without charge to adopters.

- GPA: Grade Performance Analyzer. A software program designed to aid users of the text in maintaining student test scores.

Acknowledgments

We would like to thank Professor Tim Sylvester of the College of DuPage for his important contribution to Chapter 15, "Computers in Business, Industry, and the Professions." Barry Shane should also be acknowledged for the material he wrote on expert systems for the Artificial Intelligence and Expert Systems chapter. His expertise about developing expert systems is evident in that chapter.

We would also like to thank the following reviewers:

Tim Sylvester, *College of DuPage*
Barry Kolb, *Ocean County College*
David Wen, *Diablo Valley College*
Abolfazl Sirjani, *Washington State University*
Hugh L. McHenry, *Memphis State University*
John R. Talburt, *University of Arkansas, Little Rock*
Dennis Kochis, *Suffolk Community College*
Myron Mandiak, *Monroe Community College*
Ron Browning, *Niagara County Community College*
Richard Manthei, *Joliet Junior College*
Albert Polish, *Macomb Community College*
Marianne Johnson, *Western Michigan University*
Peter Irwin, *Richland College*
Dorothy B. Reiss, *Manchester Community College*
Virginia Jones, *Central Connecticut State College*
Seth A. Hock, *Columbus State Community College*

Charlotte Peterson, *Community College of Allegheny County*
David F. Harris, *College of the Redwoods*
Gretchen L. Van Meer, *Central Michigan University*
Leonard Presby, *William Patterson State College*
Harvey Blessing, *Essex Community College*
John Avitabile, *Rutgers University*
James Buxton, *Tidewater Community College*
E. Gladys Norman, *Linn-Benton Community College*
William O'Hare, *Prince George's Community College*
John Rezak, *Johnson County Community College*

Ron Anderson
David Sullivan

WORLD OF COMPUTING

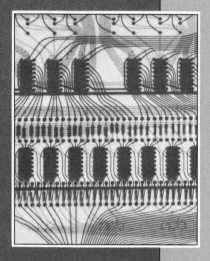

PART I
BASIC CONCEPTS
OF COMPUTING

Never before has a generation been privileged to witness the introduction of such startling inventions as atomic power, space travel, genetic engineering, and personal computing. Incredibly, all of these have been introduced within the last 50 years. Computing ranks among the most profound inventions of our time and even surpasses the others in one respect: it allows the ordinary citizen to participate in revolutionary discovery.

Steady declines in cost and improvements in performance have moved computers and machine intelligence from data processing centers to homes, offices, shopping centers, even cars. Now the average person has within reach a powerful agent for change. But what are people going to do with these easily available and powerful machines? Only two facts are clear: computers are pervasive, and they are capable of revolutionizing nearly every area of life.

The pervasiveness of computers presents a problem: how should you learn to evaluate and use them? Our answer is to introduce you to some fundamental computing concepts, to make it easy for you to acquire a working knowledge of such important applications as word processing, communications, and graphics. Mastery of the concepts presented in this first part of the book will increase your chances of success in using a computer in your own specialty. Knowing the basic principles and terminology will also make it easier for you to stay abreast of issues and evaluate the ways in which society puts its computers to work.

Part I takes the first step in preparing you to understand and evaluate the computer world by teaching you some basic computer concepts. In Chapter 1, we survey the world of computers, define some terms common to all of computing, and identify some of the issues raised by computerization. Chapter 2 outlines and discusses the anatomy of a computer system. Chapter 3 explains how the "thinking" part of a computer—the central processing unit—and storage devices work together to execute the series of instructions known as a program. In Chapter 4, you will find details on how information enters and leaves computers. Then, in Chapter 5, we discuss computer programs, emphasizing the operating system, which is the master program that manages the computer. ∎

1 The World of Computing

T he computer is the most important invention of the twentieth century. Computers are touching every part of our lives because of the rapidly decreasing cost of personal computers, the increasing dependence of large organizations on large computers, and modern society's need to make decisions quickly and accurately. Meanwhile, computer systems are becoming more "intelligent" as scientists learn more about how to automate human thinking processes. This process has promoted the spread of computers into activities that were once the preserve of people—activities such as forecasting future events from past trends, controlling production processes in factories, and managing the collection and distribution of information in organizations. To some this is threatening; to others, exciting.

However you feel about them, computers are altering modern institutions. For this reason, you need a general understanding of what computers are and how they work, in order to fully understand how our world works and how it may change. In this chapter, you'll see why it is important to acquire some experience with computers; you'll review how the computer has become part of the fabric of society; and you'll confront some of the questions that you should ask to evaluate the computer's role in today's society.

COMPUTER LITERACY IN AN INFORMATION AGE

The computer has been the major force moving society from an Industrial Age into what has come to be known as the Information Age—an age in which the collection, modification, and distribution of information becomes a primary enterprise. Some of the differences between the Industrial Age and the Information Age are shown in Table 1.1. The Industrial Age was characterized by the construction of mechanical machines for cutting, stamping, moving, and producing. These machines enabled farmers and blue-collar workers to be more productive. Today our economy is driven by electronic instead of mechanical innovations. The Information Age is characterized by the development of information systems to help us think, communicate, manage, and control. The technology of the Information Age promises to make "knowledge workers"—office workers, managers, educators, architects, scientists, lawyers, and other professionals—more productive.

To be productive and to participate fully in the Information Age, individuals must become computer literate. There has been some debate, particularly in educational circles, over what computer literacy is and how students and others

Table 1.1 Characteristics of the Industrial Age and the Information Age

Industrial Age	Information Age
Primarily mechanical tools that augmented our physical capabilities	Primarily electronic tools that augment our mental capabilities
Slowly changing technology	Rapid technical innovation
Output rated in physical terms: units sold, tons produced, and so on	Output judged by intangibles: value added, timeliness, accuracy, service, flexibility, usefulness
Rapid growth in domestic markets for goods	A world economy with mature markets for most goods
Simple tools designed for specific tasks	Complex tools supporting numerous tasks
Tools used on a standalone basis	Tools form highly integrated and sophisticated networks
Inventions built by entrepreneurs using custom tools	Innovations occur in research environments providing ample access to machine intelligence

should be prepared for a society that is entering an Information Age. Should students learn to write computer programs? Do students need to know how to operate a computer but not how to write programs? How much does a computer-literate person need to understand about the role of computers in society?

This text defines **computer literacy** as the ability to use computer-based tools for writing, communicating, and processing data, as well as the ability to evaluate the personal and social consequences of computerization. Our fundamental premise is that, to achieve computer literacy, you need three things:

- a general understanding of what computers are and what they do
- experience working with computer-based "information tools," such as word processors and spreadsheets
- the ability to evaluate the consequences of computerization and to understand the variety of social issues that have arisen with this new technology

In a society like ours, with a complex division of labor, not everyone needs to be computer literate to the same degree. An airline agent, for example, needs much more computer knowledge than does a custodian. Increasingly, however, society will depend on computers, and those who are not computer literate may be held back.

THE COMPUTER IN PERSPECTIVE

The first component of computer literacy is an understanding of what computers are and how they are generally used. Without a knowledge of what a computer is, it is easy to be misled into believing that computers are "electronic brains" that have somehow become more intelligent than their creators. Similarly, if you don't fully understand how computers are used, you can be deceived or feel powerless when faced with a computer-related problem. For example, people who don't realize that most computer-produced letters contain at least one piece of "personal" data—often a name, age, or address—might believe that a piece of junk mail was written to them personally and is therefore important. Likewise, people who aren't aware that most billing errors are caused, not by computers, but by the people who enter the data can be intimidated when billing problems arise.

The Essential Computer

Our understanding of computing devices and their capabilities has grown substantially over the past four decades. This is reflected in the varied ways in which people have described the essence of the computer. Table 1.2 lists some examples. A **computer** is essentially an information-handling device. When we use the term *computer* in this book, it refers to a **computer system**: that is, an interconnected set of devices for entering, sending, and storing data. Typical devices in a computer system include keyboards for entering data, printers, and storage units (see

Table 1.2 Evolving Characterizations of the Computer

"A person employed to make calculations in an observatory, in surveying, etc."
The Oxford English Dictionary, *1940*

"A computer is a piece of equipment that can be made to follow a predetermined plan or to obey a spell you cast on it. That's the good news. The bad news is that creating such a plan, casting such a spell, is much harder than you'd think."
Ted Nelson

"A computer is a machine that handles patterns. It takes them in and sends them out. We think of these patterns as words or numbers, but computers handle them as words of their own language."
Lee Felsenstein, designer of the Sol and Osborne I computers

"A computer is a book. No, a computer is an encyclopedia. No, a computer is a whole damned library."
Ray Bradbury

"Just as the camera is an extension of the eye and the wheel the extension of the foot, the computer could qualify as the extension of, not the brain or mind, but the *ego*."
Doug Colligan, senior editor, Omni *magazine*

"An electronic device for performing high-speed arithmetic and logical operations."
Webster's New World Dictionary of Computer Terms copyright © 1983 by Simon & Schuster, Inc. Reprinted by permission of Simon & Schuster.

"A computer is a device which manipulates data according to a series of instructions stored in its memory. By changing the instructions the computer can be made to do a completely different task. Thus the computer is probably the most general-purpose machine yet invented. It is important to note that both the instructions and the data are stored in the same memory and that both can be manipulated by the computer with equal ease. The individual operations performed by the modern, electronic computer are very simple, but it does them at the rate of thousands per second, enabling complex tasks to be finished in a remarkably short time."
John Prenis, The Computer Dictionary *(Philadelphia: Running Press, 1983)*

Figure 1.1). Controlling or monitoring this information-processing equipment is a *central processing unit* that initiates the transformation and transmission of data. This central unit contains the electronics that basically compare two chunks of data to see if they match. If a match is found, then a different sequence of commands will be followed than if a match does not occur. This ability to act on the result of data matches is the essence of the computer's decision-making power.

A computer is not a "mathematical brain." It can, however, perform lengthy or complicated calculations at an amazing speed. When a computer is used in this way, it is sometimes called a "number cruncher." One of the most exotic computers designed primarily to crunch numbers is the Cray X-MP (see Figure 1.2), which can perform 600 million calculations per second.

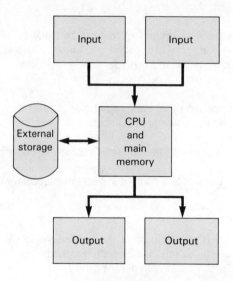

Although computers do have remarkable computational capabilities, they are also used for other complicated tasks, such as the storage of large quantities of information for long periods of time (see Figures 1.3 and 1.4). Computers can retain, process, rearrange, calculate, display, and report new information, which may, in some cases, be derived from older information. In other words, computers have both memory and data processing power. This combination provides a startling ability to augment human decision making and to improve communication with others.

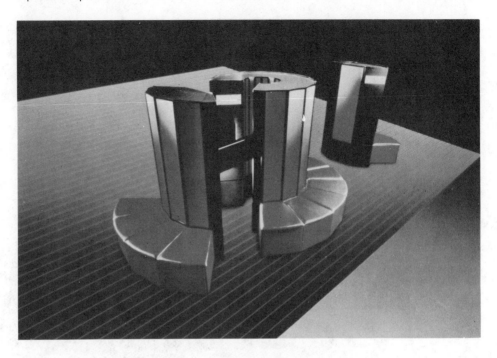

Consider, for example, a small construction company called Buildco, which competes against several other companies for building contracts. To prepare a bid for a contract, the owner must estimate the labor, materials, and time required to complete a project. The company with the lowest bid will win the contract, but if the bid is too low, the company that does the work will lose money. Buildco installed a computer to do the calculations and print the reports needed to prepare a bid. A computer can act like a fast adding machine, but it can also function as a more general information machine. Buildco started using the computer to estimate what competitors would bid on new construction projects. The company collected data from past projects and past estimates by competitors and stored this data in the computer. The computer's logical capability enabled it to find patterns in the other contractors' bids. For example, one company always bid very high on tall buildings, perhaps because it did not own a crane. Such information helped Buildco to win more contracts and earn greater profits. As the company grew, it found the computer more and more useful, especially in planning and managing projects. The complexity of construction work (see Figure 1.5) requires that supplies and subcontractors be scheduled well ahead of time but be available at just the right time. With its computer system, Buildco was able to schedule work much more precisely, increase its control over inventory, and reduce wasted time and resources.

Figure 1.3 A magnetic tape library in a large government agency or a company contains hundreds of tape reels, each with millions of stored characters or numbers, which can become input into a computer for processing at a later time.

Figure 1.4 A typical disk storage unit attached to a large computer system stores over a billion characters of information. Computers "remember" vast amounts of information by keeping track of where it is stored.

Buildco's computer could perform calculations, store factual information, and make logical decisions. Computers can also help people communicate over very long distances. Computer-controlled satellites (see Figure 1.6) are one example of how computers help us communicate. Still another example is illustrated in Figure 1.7, where an analyst in a stock brokerage firm is using a computer. The analyst uses the memory and calculating ability of her personal computer to track prices of stocks and bonds. Potentially the most important function of her computer, though, is to communicate her ideas to others. She uses the computer to do this in at least three ways. First, she constructs graphs of stock and bond prices measured over time in three colors on her computer screen. If she had to do this by hand, she might never have the time. Second, she uses the computer to outline a report, to write it and incorporate graphs as needed, and to check her spelling. Finally, she uses the computer to send a copy of her report to 250 clients, many of whom might need the information faster than they could receive it via the postal service. To speed up the delivery of the report, she sends the text and graphics over the telephone the same evening, using her personal computer, a telephone connection, and a program that runs the computer automatically in her absence.

Figure 1.6 Earth station antennas follow satellites across the sky. Communications satellites and computers have extended the reach of global communications by many orders of magnitude.

Figure 1.7 Almost every stockbroker has a computer terminal on his or her desk to access the latest market reports as well as to complete buy and sell orders for clients.

Figure 1.8 Telephone systems and personal computers are rapidly being merged into integrated electronic office systems.

The examples of the builder and the stock analyst show clearly that computers are more than just adding machines. Computers are capable of storing information in various forms—as numbers, text, and pictures. They can not only perform calculations on information contained in their memories, but also rearrange the information in new and interesting ways, find patterns, and ultimately influence human decisions. And once information has been processed, the computer can help disseminate it quickly to people and to other computers (see Figure 1.8).

The Pervasive Computer

The computer's ability to recall facts, process those facts, and disseminate the results to all corners of the world is the key reason why computers have become so important and pervasive in modern society. Everyone in the industrialized world uses computers either directly or indirectly. When you cash a check, pay a bill, or use a credit card, the transaction is quickly converted into an electronic form that is processed by a computer. Every year, millions of Americans depend on computers operated by the Internal Revenue Service (IRS) to process income tax returns. Figures 1.9 and 1.10 show some of the other ways computers are used. Without large, powerful computers running 24 hours a day, banking as we know it today would be impossible, the stock market would fail, and international trade would come to a halt.

Figure 1.9 Personal computers are used extensively in schools to teach everything from arithmetic to history.

We find computers closer to home as well. In many grocery stores, an electronic scanner reads the prices of goods directly from coded labels and sends this information directly into a computer system. The workings of most modern cars, cameras, and telephones are controlled by an *embedded microprocessor*—a unit similar to the central processor of a microcomputer. For all practical purposes, these embedded microprocessors function like computers; the difference is that they are preset to perform only one set of tasks. Embedded microprocessors in a car, for example, can adjust the flow of fuel, provide safe braking, and display information on the dashboard about how the car is operating. Many household appliances—microwave ovens, digital clock radios, and videocassette recorders, to name a few—also depend on such internal computing devices for control of their operation.

Computers are also making communication easier and faster. For years, people throughout the world have been able to communicate with one another by telephones controlled by computers. Recently, however, people have begun to communicate with others directly from the keyboards of their personal computers via **electronic mail,** or messages sent and received by computers. Most newspapers and magazines are produced from text stored in computer systems, and television shows are now edited with computers.

Figure 1.10 On November 9, 1979, air traffic controllers across the nation, after receiving a message on their computer screens of a Soviet missile launch, ordered all flights to prepare to land. Air traffic control computers are linked to the North American Air Defense Command (NORAD), which that day had a mechanical malfunction.

Perhaps the most controversial uses of computers occur in the workplace. Computers are rapidly changing the way we work; from the mailroom to the boardroom, corporate America is highly computerized. For example, in a manufacturing company, orders for goods are entered into the company's computer system, after which the computer produces reports that are used by many employees for many purposes. The shipping department fills orders from the SHIP-TO report; the vice president of finance uses the INVENTORY report to estimate how much money is tied up in inventory, how much demand there is for the company's products, and how long customers must wait to receive their orders. Incoming orders are also relayed directly to the factory floor, where other computers control the operation of *numerically controlled machines*—production tools that accept numerical commands. These machines enable computers to automate entire factories (see Figure 1.11), working much more quickly and accurately than any group of people could.

We all depend on computers, large and small, to entertain us, to assist us in our work, to control other machines, and to communicate with one another over great distances. Modern society could not function without computerized control, communication, and automation. Is it any wonder that our era is becoming known as the Information Age?

Figure 1.11 Robots are rapidly taking over manufacturing jobs in industry. Here, an IBM robot capable of precision to 20-millionths of an inch automates the production of computers.

USING INFORMATION TOOLS

It may be possible to be computer literate without understanding the **hardware**—the physical devices—of a computer system, but the ability to work with software is essential. **Software**—the computer programs—is the most important part of any computer system, because it determines what the computer will do and how the user will communicate with the computer. This section provides an overview of the most frequently used types of software and then summarizes the obstacles to using these information tools.

Software comes in several forms. Two of the most important are *system software* and *application software*. **System software** does not perform practical tasks outside the computer; instead, it helps to manage the way in which the computer system operates. **Application software** performs practical or specific tasks for the users of a computer. When people talk about working with a computer, they are usually talking about working with one of the most frequently used types of application software.

Application Software

The category of application software includes such information tools as **word processors**, which are programs used to prepare the text for letters, memos, reports, and books; **spreadsheet programs**, which are programs that display and manipulate numbers in an electronic worksheet and are used for forecasting, modeling, and analysis; **database management systems (DBMS)**, which help maintain collections of logically related data; **graphics packages**, which help users depict ideas through graphs and other types of drawings; and **communications programs**, which set up and manage connections between two or more computers. These five types of software are the most frequently used applications in business and education.

Why are application software packages so useful? Here are a few answers.

- Writers find that word processing helps change thoughts into words on paper.
- Analysts find that spreadsheet programs open up new ways to create mathematical models and make financial forecasts.
- Researchers find that one type of database management system, bibliographic retrieval programs, reduces the frustration associated with locating appropriate books, journals, and other reference materials.
- With graphics software, a graphically untrained analyst can create new ways to share and effectively present information from large collections of data.
- Desktop publishing packages give someone without publishing experience the tools to combine text and pictures into polished, typeset-quality documents.
- Electronic mail helps distribute information far faster and at less expense than conventional mail. Voice-store-and-forward systems record messages and replay them later, which changes the rules of "telephone tag" to everyone's benefit.

We could easily list many more benefits provided by application software. Looking at even this brief list of benefits, you might wonder why more people haven't embraced the computer wholeheartedly and taken full advantage of application software. For a partial answer to this question, we need to look at some of the obstacles to using computers and application software.

Obstacles to Using Computers

There has always been a mystique surrounding the computer. The computer has been thought of as both exceedingly powerful and at the same time extremely fragile; computers could do amazing things, but they were often "down" for extended periods of time. According to conventional wisdom, computers were difficult to work with, and anyone who planned to do so required an extensive education. In Table 1.3, you'll find a summary of many of the concerns that have caused new users to be wary of computers.

Table 1.3 Fears and Their Underlying Misconceptions

■ **I might get electrocuted.** This particular anxiety was a favorite among our forefathers, who trotted it out when they were confronted by inventions like the light bulb and telephone. Rest assured: the computer keyboard's electrical current, about equal to that of a cordless electric shaver, is just too low to cause harm.

■ **I'll never understand how to operate a computer.** Nowadays, turning on the machine usually involves no more than flipping a switch and loading in a program. And in place of those undecipherable symbols that trigger long-forgotten fears of fractions, most programs now use English as the means of communication. Many of them also have pick-and-choose menu formats to guide you through available choices.

■ **I might break it.** You can't get that rough with a computer simply by typing on it and turning it on or off. Home computers are akin to any store-bought item: they vary in durability according to manufacturer, model, and wear and tear, and they have to be treated with a bit of respect. I have no sympathy for the user who douses his machine with coffee and complains when it prints out Martian dialect.

■ **The machine might lose my work.** Wiping out a sentence or two is always a possibility, as is destroying everything you've entered over the last five years. But you can guard against such losses by watching your delete commands and taking proper care of your floppy disks. Most important is that well-known data processing axiom: "Back it up." It takes no time at all to copy a program or data from one disk to another, thus assuring yourself of the ability to restore any work that gets lost along the way.

■ **I might lose the privacy of my data.** If you have the traditional stand-alone system, with no outside machines attached, your data is as safe as it would be on a piece of paper. For added security, don't let anyone read over your shoulder when you enter your data or password and remove the disk when your session is finished. If your computer is hooked up via modem and telephone line to a friend's machine, and if you happen to be paranoid about wiretapping, you can invest in encryption hardware or software to encode and decode your communications. As for the suspicion that someone will phone your computer and search through your disk-based data while you sleep, just keep the power turned off; no one has yet found a way to turn on a computer by remote control.

■ **Computers have more capability than I need.** This is also true of pencils, but how many people worry about not using them to draw works of art or create literary masterpieces? Personal computers range from relatively inexpensive units to quite elaborate affairs and offer a wide array of functions. Chances are, as you and your computer get used to each other, you'll expand your horizons and purchase software packages that increase your machine's versability.

■ **Using a computer will lower my status.** This illusion circulates among office personnel who are actually afraid of looking silly as they try to master the new technology. If computers are that alien to you, especially if you're older or set in your ways, a gradual introduction is probably best. Sympathetic private tutoring can prevent loss of face before co-workers and convince you that business computers may enhance your status.

■ **I might lose the ability to do things on my own.** A computer is not an electrode-studded brain sapper, nor is it a device that turns users into Einsteins. As a tool, the computer simply helps you accomplish your work with maximum efficiency and expands rather than hinders your own capabilities. Erasing typewriter errors by hand, for example, impedes the creative act of writing, whereas correcting text on a personal computer is a pleasure. As for mathematics, is it more productive to hunt for a multiplication error or to be freed to explore new formulas?

■ **A computer is mathematical and not for creative types.** This view is held by artistes, literary denizens, and just plain folks with a morbid fear of numbers. The good news about computers is that if you don't want to play with accounting or physics, you can buy a word processing program to help with your writing, a music package to aid in composing, or a knee-slapping outerspace game to match your wits against.

Source: Digital Deli, edited by Steve Ditlea. © 1984 by Steve Ditlea. Reprinted by permission of Workman Publishing. All rights reserved.

Basic Concepts of Computing

The advent of the personal computer has to some extent changed this situation. Personal computers are small, relatively inexpensive machines; they aren't as threatening as their larger predecessors. The advertising for personal computers, however, went perhaps too far in creating the notion that a computer could be used by someone with virtually no training. People came to expect that they could master the computer in just a few quick, easy steps. In its own way, this assumption is as erroneous as were the earlier fears about computers. More than one person has tried to harness the computer's power with no training or assistance, only to give up in frustration and disillusionment. In 1986 a special report published in *The Wall Street Journal* concluded that "computers still require far more effort, special knowledge, and expense to operate properly than any other popular home technology. . . . Just setting up the [computer] can be a frustrating, infuriating nightmare. And reaping the benefits of fast-moving changes in hardware or software capabilities can require a whole new effort."

Although it is almost certain that hardware and software manufacturers over the next few years will attempt to make it easier for beginners to use their products, it is likely that people will still need specialized knowledge and experience to take full advantage of the computer. There are at least two interrelated reasons why you should not expect the computer to be as easy to use as an appliance. First, compared to devices like the photocopier, the videocassette recorder, or the automobile, the computer is much more "active." When different programs are used, it displays the changeability of a chameleon. Second, software developers are under constant pressure from users to add features to their programs. Although these new features make programs more powerful, they also make them more complex and hence more difficult to learn. It seems apparent that computer users will need to invest a fair amount of time learning to use applications in order to reap the full benefits of the new technology.

What, then, does it take for you to learn how to use computers effectively? What is the best route to computer literacy? There are many routes to this goal but all of them include both an understanding of basic principles and hands-on experience. The basic principles of computing apply to all computers, large and small; once you understand them, you need not limit yourself to personal computers. But your emphasis should be on practical experience with computers. Without this experience, you're likely to forget within a few weeks any concepts and procedures you hear or read about.

Taking a course is generally an effective way to obtain this required knowledge and experience, especially if computers are available and accessible and if human consultants are close at hand (see Figure 1.12). You'll find that your hands-on experience with computers will be more valuable if it is based on a sound understanding of the concepts on which the computer is based. This book is designed to provide a conceptual framework that can guide your experience and help you overcome the obstacles to computer literacy.

Figure 1.12 One of the best ways to learn how to use computers and computer software is to take a laboratory class or workshop where each student runs programs on his or her microcomputer while the instructor guides them through the steps.

EVALUATING COMPUTERIZATION

The third component of computer literacy is the ability to recognize the implications and consequences of computerization and to evaluate what they mean to individuals and society. Why is this sort of evaluation necessary? Simply put, we cannot afford to adopt without examination every new application of information technology. We need to evaluate each new computing alternative to determine if the cost of the alternative will provide sufficient benefits to justify additional investments of time or changes in the way we work. Society, too, needs to monitor the impact of computerization to determine if the resulting changes in organizational and cultural values are likely to be beneficial.

When machines replaced workers during the Industrial Age, the resulting changes came to be known as *automation*. Because human considerations were often neglected, the concept of automation acquired many negative connotations. With the introduction of electronic machines into production plants, the term *computerization* came to be used synonymously with automation and therefore to take on some of the same connotations. In this book, however, *computerization* refers simply to any application of computers. This is the broadest possible interpretation, and we use it in order to avoid asserting judgments about the effects of computers. Our intention is to provide the tools you need to make your own judgments about whether computerization exerts a positive or a negative influence on individuals and society.

Evaluating computerization can be tricky. During the Industrial Age, it was relatively easy to evaluate inventions and technological advances. The benefits were objective and observable: faster production, better yields, lower costs, and so forth. Innovations in the Information Age, however, often bring less tangible benefits. What, for example, is the value of more timely information or a more thorough analysis of a problem? Such questions don't yield answers that can be expressed in dollars and cents—but then neither does the question of the value of a college education. What, after all, is the value of a more informed mind? It is clear that we cannot afford to ignore new developments in computing, because they provide tools to enhance the thought processes of an educated mind. Yet neither should we applaud without question all technological advances.

To evaluate computerization, you should begin by taking a position between these two extremes. Evaluation is a process that brings together relevant considerations to appraise value. Whenever possible, all relevant facts should be brought to bear on the appraisal. Throughout this book, we will attempt to provide enough information about how computers are used to enable you to identify the values and issues that need to be investigated. As a starting point, we'll identify some of the personal aspects and social impacts of computerization that warrant consideration.

Personal Aspects

You should carefully evaluate your decisions about involvement with computers. In the paragraphs that follow, we have listed some issues that we feel should be resolved when you make these choices. But it will be up to you to consider your own values and decide how an involvement with computers will affect your goals.

Evaluating the Appropriateness of Using a Computer

The development of a computer application requires that several conditions be met. There must be a problem to be solved; specific activities must be able to resolve the problem; and techniques must be available that can perform the activities. Many problems are not readily solved by a computer, and some activities do not result in efficient solutions. It would be ridiculous, for example, to use a database management system to keep track of the chairs you own—unless you are in the furniture business. But if you were not aware of what a database management system does, you might reach this conclusion only after investing a considerable amount of money and effort.

To make sound decisions about computers, you must first identify the project you wish to complete. Next, you need to evaluate how a computerized solution might help you to complete the project. Computerization may increase costs; these costs, in turn, should be measured against the benefits received. If you don't understand how computerization works and what options are available, you may make a decision that leads to error, waste, or even the failure of an entire project.

Once you've established that you need to use a computer, you must select a program that will meet the need. This decision can be affected by such factors as the availability of software or, in some cases, the cost of computer time. If you've had experience with several programs, learning to use a new program should be quicker and easier than if you're starting from scratch. After working with several programs on a particular computer, you can usually transfer your learning to other programs or to different computers without taking additional courses.

A serious problem associated with computerization is the tendency to view computer-produced output as absolute truth. This tendency, which is sometimes called the *computer mystique,* stems largely from ignorance about the potential sources of effort in computing. To avoid this sort of uncritical thinking, you need a working knowledge of the general steps that a computer system follows in processing data.

The output produced by a computer may look reasonable and accurate—and be riddled with errors. Within programs there are numerous steps where problems can develop and eventually distort results. For example, a spreadsheet program will produce inaccurate results if you select an incorrect subset of data as a basis for calculation, if you enter a formula that is incorrect for its intended purpose, or if you label a row improperly. Or you might enter the data into the computer file incorrectly. An experienced, computer-literate user anticipates these kinds of errors and checks both the input to the program and the details of the printed output. This double-checking can dramatically reduce inaccurate output.

Monitoring Your Computer Usage

If you start spending lots of time with a computer, you should also evaluate how the machine fits into the rest of your life. How much time do you spend working with a computer, and have your feelings about other aspects of your life changed? Most of us have heard at least one anecdote about people who use the computer to escape from problematic relationships or from people in general. You should also keep in mind that computing activities have brought many people together because of their common interest and have provided great pleasure and personal satisfaction to many. As you become involved with computers, try to maintain the self-awareness that will allow you to keep your use of the computer consistent with your goals and inner values.

Societal Impacts

Dozens of books have been written about the positive and negative effects of computers on society. This is not another such book. Although the last few chapters describe how computers are being used in society, they do not emphasize whether computerization has been good or bad for society.

This text is optimistic, because we believe that on balance computerization has been, and will continue to be, more a positive than a negative force in society. But, like every other social trend, it has not been uniformly beneficial; one person's increased status or productivity may be another person's technological nightmare. You should evaluate computerization on the basis of the issues and the evidence and come to your own conclusions. We'll suggest some of the important factors to consider in order to evaluate how the computer fits into society.

Productivity and Economic Value

There seems to be general agreement that computerization leads to increased productivity. In rare cases, a computer system will be judged inefficient, and an organization will return to doing things the way they were done before the computer entered the picture. More often, the system is refined until there is evidence that it produces results justifying its cost. It is usually a mistake, however, to focus on measurable costs. The greatest benefits provided by a computer system may not be easily quantifiable. An emergency management system, for example, may save lives or avert disasters. These outcomes certainly have an economic value, but it is not easily expressed in dollars and cents.

Working Conditions and Employment

Much of the academic research on the effects of computerization has focused on whether specific computer systems have caused jobs to become *deskilled;* that is, downgraded so that they require less expertise. Although some jobs have been deskilled, many have been upgraded or enhanced by the computer. For example, computerized payroll systems calculate and print paychecks, relieving accounting clerks of many routine activities and freeing them to perform a wider range of tasks.

Computerization *has* been responsible for the displacement or replacement of some workers. But, often, automation and the replacement of employees receives much more public exposure and scrutiny than does the creation of new employment opportunities. For example, in the 1960s and 1970s, the introduction of computerized phototypesetting eliminated the need for over 40,000 Linotype operators. This change received extensive news coverage, as publishers, employees, and unions debated how or when the transition to the new technology should occur. Less publicity was given to the new jobs which were made possible by increased production of printed documents and decreased setup costs. Despite many decades of automation and despite fears of cutbacks, employment has generally remained constant.

Political Control and Equality

A computer system may be installed for the purpose of tightening one group's control over another. For example, managers may seek to measure and reduce the time that clerical workers take to complete routine tasks. Obviously, this effort can increase intergroup conflict. Greater control over employees may in some cases be needed, but the benefits of increased control should be weighed against the costs of damage to morale.

Another potential consequence of computerization is the widening of gaps between large social groups. If computing opportunities are available to the rich but not to the poor, the rich might tend to get richer and the poor, poorer. But it is also possible that the personal computer—like the personal car, the wristwatch,

A WORD ABOUT
HOME-BASED WORKERS WATCH AS EXPLOITATION DEBATE FLARES

An estimated 300 U.S. corporations employ data entry and word processing clerks who work at home, but a national debate has erupted over whether those home-based workers are exploited and whether the practice should be banned by the government.

Unions say businesses can easily exploit home-based workers, turning telecommuting into an electronic sweatshop that should be banned. The U.S. Department of Labor, however, last week proposed to repeal the existing ban on homework in six garment industries, a move that observers said makes it highly unlikely that a ban on home-based computer workers will be added.

"The Labor Department move on garment workers is a tremendous symbolic action for telecommuters in the data processing field and elsewhere," commented Gil E. Gordon, a Monmouth Junction, N.J.–based consultant on corporate telecommuting.

Nevertheless, the department's proposal has renewed the debate over whether businesses exploit home-based workers, and Congress is putting pressure on federal agencies to increase enforcement of existing laws that protect home workers.

Firm statistics are not available, but Gordon estimates there are roughly 300 U.S. corporations with telecommuting programs, and Congress' Office of Technology Assessment estimates there are 3,000 to 5,000 home workers using computers for outside employers or clients.

J.C. Penny Co., for example, since 1981 has run an experimental program with 20 telephone sales associates who work at home with terminals to take incoming catalog orders and transmit them to IBM hosts.

Proponents of telecommuting say it boosts productivity, reduces office space requirements and transportation problems, and retains valued employees who stay home to care for children. Carl Kirkpatrick, who manages J.C. Penny's telecommuting program for the Milwaukee office, said his firm has very good relations with its home workers because it treats them like office employees.

"There's only one way to go, and that's to treat them like any other associate in our telephone sales centers. They don't pay for any equipment, they are paid the same salary, they have the same benefits and vacations," he said.

Paul Edwards, cofounder of the Association of Electronic Cottagers in South Pasadena, Calif., said exploitation is very rare. He added that the vast majority of home workers like their working conditions and that union attempts to ban telecommuting would "throw the baby out with the bathwater."

In a 1983 resolution, the AFL-CIO called for a ban on computer homework on grounds that employers may deny home workers fringe benefits and minimum wages and pay piece rates rather than salaries. The dispersed nature of homework means that federal and state officials cannot protect workers from unfair labor practices, the union warned.

Dennis Chamot, associate director of the AFL-CIO's professional employees department, said that the ban against homework in the garment industries was instituted 44 years ago because of horrendous sweatshop conditions and that the union is concerned that such conditions could occur in the 1980s as well.

"If we're seeing these problems with the very tiny numbers that are involved in computer homework today, then surely the potential for more serious problems grows year by year," Chamot warned. "With no regulation at all, the marketplace sometimes tends to drift to the lowest level," he said.

Source: Mitch Betts, *Computerworld,* 25 August 1986, p. 2.

and the television—might bring greater equality, because most people can afford one. Affordable personal computers that provide access to computerized libraries and other databanks might help to equalize opportunities to use information and consequently contribute to a balance of power among social groups.

Crime and Human Rights

Hundreds of articles and many books have examined computer-related crimes, especially those in which computing devices are instruments of crime. The magnitude of the problem attests to the significance and power of the computer today. New ways of using the computer—for example, computerized listening devices—may create social risks. Malfunctions and misuse add to these risks. It is equally significant that computerized information systems have strengthened society's capacity to detect and deter crimes of all types. Very rapid computer searches of relevant case histories can greatly increase the chances of identifying legitimate suspects. On the other hand, inaccurate criminal records can harm the reputation of innocent citizens. Such complex tradeoffs involve difficult choices. To date, public concern for potential invasions of personal privacy has curtailed the establishment of a single, integrated national databank of personal information, even though it might improve law enforcement. Preserving privacy while supporting the efforts of law enforcement is a major public policy challenge.

Communication and Culture

The computer may restructure social communication more than any other facet of society. Computer-mediated networks have become a major mode of social interaction for hundreds of thousands of people. Electronic mail can facilitate both friendship and data sharing across national boundaries, racial groups, and social classes. Breaking down such barriers between people could yield cultural changes that are impossible to visualize now. Certainly we will see more and more evidence of the computer's influence on our language, thinking patterns, and culture in general.

The Freedom to Innovate

The foregoing considerations for evaluating computerization identify negative as well as positive changes in our society. Computer crime, deskilling of jobs, and other negative consequences of computerization are public problems that evoke calls for new legislation, regulation, or policies to curtail further computerization. Of course, we must have laws that prohibit the theft of computer-based information and policies that guard the privacy of personal data, but it is important that these regulations not undermine other fundamental values, such as the freedom to create technological innovations.

Computer-based information is critical to the functioning of modern society, and developments in this area need encouragement. One way to expand benefits while guarding against abuses is to have an informed electorate that can evaluate the issues surroundir ; each new problem. If we invest in thorough and insightful evaluations of computerization issues, we should be able to control the way computers shape our world.

Computing today is about where the automobile industry was in 1920. There were many car manufacturers then, and there was little interchangeability among the parts for different cars. The performance and efficiency of cars varied greatly, and few people were trained to use or repair the new technology—let alone to find new applications for it. The automobile industry was changing so rapidly in 1920 that few (if any) people could accurately predict its future.

Today it is very difficult to predict what will happen to computers and information technology. Looking toward the future, we should keep in mind that, although inventions seem to drive society, it is in fact people who determine how new technologies are used and where they will lead.

SUMMARY

There seems to be little argument that our society is moving into an Information Age—an age in which the collection, modification, and distribution of information becomes a primary enterprise. To function effectively in this new era, you will need some degree of computer literacy. We define this capability as an understanding of what a computer is and how computers are used, the ability to work with information tools (application software), and the ability to evaluate computing's effect on society.

A computer is essentially an information-handling device consisting of a central processing unit, data storage capabilities, and devices for the entry and output of data. Computers are used throughout society in a variety of ways. Under the control of elaborate software, computer systems can perform billions of calculations at high speeds, develop forecasts, make decisions, and model complex systems. They also control the functions of other electronic and mechanical devices, such as cameras, videocassette recorders, telephones, and automobiles. Without computers, many aspects of our daily lives would be more difficult, and some forms of business and commerce—banking and the stock market, for example—would probably collapse.

The use of information tools, usually in the form of application software, is a crucial component of computer literacy. Included in the category of application software are such tools as word processors, spreadsheet programs, database management systems, graphics packages, and communications programs. The best way to learn to work with these programs is to develop a sound understanding of how computers work and then to acquire hands-on experience, ideally in an environment in which people are available to help you.

Another key component of computer literacy is the ability to evaluate the various consequences of computerization. Some of these consequences are personal;

you need to evaluate the appropriateness of using a computer, select appropriate applications, evaluate the accuracy of computer-produced output, and monitor the amount and quality of time spent working with a computer. The societal impact of computerization also needs to be evaluated. We need to be aware of both the economic and the social consequences of computerization and to develop an understanding of the degree to which computers can be abused. Guided by our personal and social values, ongoing evaluations of computerization will help to ensure that our future technological surroundings remain in harmony with our aspirations.

KEY TERMS

application software

communications program

computer

computer literacy

computer system

database management system (DBMS)

electronic mail

graphics package

hardware

software

spreadsheet program

system software

word processor

DISCUSSION QUESTIONS

1. Literacy is the ability to read, write, and effectively communicate with language. What, then, is computer literacy?
2. Why does the description "Information Age" better characterize our society today than society during the first half of the twentieth century? Does your answer suggest the need for changes in the educational system?
3. What is electronic mail, and how is it different from ordinary mail?
4. How can you distinguish software from hardware?
5. What makes computers more difficult and challenging to use than video-cassette recorders and televisions?
6. Is there a computer mystique? If so, how does it manifest itself, and how might it be changed?
7. When a computer system is installed in a fast-food restaurant to communicate orders to the cooks, what changes are likely to take place in the jobs, the organization, the distribution of power, and the communication patterns there?
8. What personal or social values do you think are promoted or threatened by computerization?

EXERCISES

1. Gather evidence that we live in an Information Age. List and describe the evidence that directly affects your work or school environment and other aspects of your life.

2. Contact an on-line data service such as CompuServe or The Source. Explore and describe the information resources available.

3. Draw a map showing the computer facilities for students on your campus. List the number and type of computers in each location.

4. Find out what plans, if any, your college has for acquiring more computers. Also try to find out your college's policies regarding computer education.

5. List all the embedded microprocessors in your residence.

6. Find a small business that has installed a computer within the past five years. Interview someone there who uses the computer and find out how he or she feels the computer has changed working conditions.

7. Evaluate the personal and social consequences of installing a particular computer. If possible, report on one with which you are familiar. List all the benefits and costs.

8. What computer-related legislation was considered during the past year by your state legislature?

2 Anatomy of a Computer

Computers accept information (input), manipulate information (processing), retain information over time (storage), and present the results of processing (output). At this level, every computer—from the multimillion-dollar mainframe to hand-held models—works the same way. Once you understand the relationships among the parts of a computer, the mystery about how computers operate will diminish. This chapter discusses the hardware and software components that make up a computer system. Throughout the chapter, we will compare the power and features of large, medium, and small computers.

But just understanding what the parts are is not enough. You also need to know how these parts interact to perform useful work. For this reason, the chapter closes with a sample computer session, which illustrates how the components of a computer system work together.

29

A computer is actually a complete *system,* composed of many interacting parts. For example, we saw in Chapter 1 that computer systems are made up of hardware and software. The *hardware* is the physical equipment you can see and touch, such as the disks and the display screen. *Software* is the total of all the programs that can be run on the computer system, the intangible "control" that governs the computer. A **program** is a set of instructions that the computer hardware follows. Programs tell the hardware how to behave and thus give the computer system its "personality."

If a computer were a component stereo system, we might imagine the music to be the software and the record player to be the hardware. In a stereo system, information is recorded on the surface of a disk, entered into the stereo through a stylus or needle, and sent to the speakers to be converted to sound. In a computer system, information is recorded on the surface of magnetic tape, magnetic disks, and other devices; it is entered through a keyboard or other special equipment attached to the computer; and it is sent to a display screen or other device designed to accept electrical signals and convert them into human-readable form. A printer, for example, converts electrical signals into intelligible text. Figure 2.1 shows the similarity between a stereo system and a computer system. Both systems receive some type of input, process it, and then produce some kind of output.

Despite these similarities, computer systems differ in a significant way from stereos or any other kind of mechanical system. Every time a particular record is played, the stereo system repeats exactly the same tune; it can play whatever is on the record, but it cannot create new music. In contrast, a computer system can produce different, possibly surprising, results each time it is run. The software of a computer system provides the "intelligence" a computer system needs in order to "play back a different tune." Thus, software is the "mind" of a machine, whereas hardware is its "body." Without the mind, the body does not know what to do.

HARDWARE COMPONENTS

Every computer system has hardware components that perform four basic functions: input, processing, storage, and output. Thus, even a minimal computer has

- an *input device,* such as a keyboard
- a *central processing unit (CPU)* for processing data
- a short-term memory, called *primary memory,* to hold programs and data temporarily while they are being used
- a long-term memory, called *external storage* or *secondary storage,* to read and write permanently stored programs and data. The most common secondary storage units are magnetic tape and disks

Figure 2.1 Stereo and computer systems are somewhat analogous.

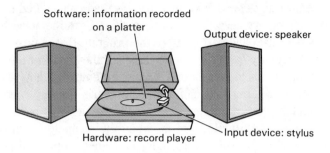

Software: information recorded on a platter

Output device: speaker

Hardware: record player

Input device: stylus

(a) A stereo system

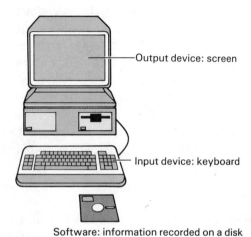

Output device: screen

Input device: keyboard

Software: information recorded on a disk

(b) A computer system

- an *output device,* such as a display screen or monitor (and most likely a printer)

An **input device** senses events in the computer's environment (such as pressure on a key) and converts them into electrical signals that the CPU can process. Input devices perform much the same function as human sensory organs, which receive information, convert it into a new form, and then send it to the brain. Keyboards, digital thermometers, and speech recognition units are examples of input devices.

The **central processing unit (CPU)** contains electronic circuitry that performs arithmetic, logical comparisons (such as deciding which of two numbers is larger), and data-moving operations. In addition, the CPU must be able to temporarily hold programs and the information that is to be processed in its memory while it is working. The memory in a CPU is often called **primary memory**, **main memory**, or **RAM**. *RAM* is short for *r*andom-*a*ccess *m*emory, meaning that the content of any memory location can be read or modified independently of that in all other memory cells. Think of it as short-term memory that temporarily holds fragments of data and part or all of the program that controls the computer. The capacity of primary memory helps determine the "size" of the computer. For example, a programmable calculator's primary memory might store only a few hundred numbers, whereas a mainframe computer's primary memory can store millions of numbers, letters of the alphabet, and elements of pictures.

Primary memory is **volatile**; that is, when the computer is turned off, the information is lost. Another form of memory is needed to provide permanent storage of programs and data. This memory is obtained by storing copies of both program and data *outside* the computer, on external magnetic media, such as a tape or a disk like that shown in Figure 2.1. Magnetic storage devices generally have a larger capacity than primary memory but are slower and transfer information in larger blocks. Because magnetic media retain information even after the computer is shut off, they are not volatile. Thus, you can remove tapes and disks from the computer, store them for months at a time without losing information, and then put them back into the tape or disk drive to be used by the computer system.

An **output device** accepts electrical signals from the CPU and converts them into a new form. For example, a plotter converts electrical signals to a pictorial form on paper. For personal computers, the most common output devices are printers and display units or monitors. Other output devices include the warhead on a cruise missile, the air vents of a computer-controlled building, and a telephone line driven by a speech synthesis unit. Collectively, input and output devices are known as **I/O devices**.

Peripheral is a generic term for any external device attached to a computer. Thus, tape and disk drives are peripherals, as are all I/O devices.

Storing Data in Memory

All computer systems are limited in what they can store. The computer is a **digital** device—a device that is restricted to storing and handling discrete *binary* values. In contrast, **analog** devices have *continuous* values. For example, the volume control of your television is an analog device, because it allows you to adjust the volume in one smooth, continuous action. But the channel selector on the television set is a digital device, because it restricts you to a discrete set of channels; you cannot, for example, select channel 3.14159. Unlike your channel selector, digital computers work with just two alternatives. Like a light switch, a computer can "remember" an "on" or an "off," but nothing in between. To store numbers, letters of the alphabet, and graphical images, the computer must encode all information in switches that can have only one of two discrete values. For convenience, we assign a 0 or a 1 to indicate whether a switch is on or off. Each 0 or 1 is one **bit** (*bi*nary dig*it*) of information. *All information in a computer is represented by a pattern of 1s and 0s.* It takes a very large number of fast on-off switches to encode and store numbers, letters, and graphical images, so the switches of a computer are made of millions of tiny magnetic spots or very small electrical circuits, which can be switched on and off very quickly. These magnetic and electrical switches use the principle that the presence of an electrical charge can be interpreted as a binary 1 and the absence of a charge, as a binary 0.

A number containing only two kinds of digits—0 and 1—is called a **binary** number. (This is why modern electronic computers are often called *binary computers.*) Binary numbers are just like decimal numbers, except for one important difference: they build numbers from the numerals 0 and 1 instead of the numerals 0 through 9. For example, 0100 is the binary number equivalent to the decimal number 4. Appendix A, "How Computers Process Information," covers binary numbers in more detail.

Groups of 1s and 0s are stored in the computer's memory as binary numbers. A binary number formed from an 8-bit grouping is called a **byte**. Early personal computers worked on only 1 byte of information at a time. Larger computers work on 16-, 32-, or 64-bit *words* at a time. A **word** is a fixed-length packet of bits that is handled as a unit by the computer. A computer's **word length** is detemined by the size of its storage cells in memory. For example, an IBM mainframe word consists of 32 bits, or 4 bytes.

Each of the 8 bits of a byte can be either on (1) or off (0). Thus, there are 256 possible patterns of on-off settings in a byte. (The patterns are 00000000, 00000001, . . . 11111111.) These 256 patterns form the basis of a numerical code that represents the letters of the alphabet, numerals, special symbols, and any other character of information stored in a computer's memory. Whether the information is a collection of numerical facts, alphabetic text, program instructions, or a graphical display, a computer stores it in memory as a group of encoded numbers.

Types of Computers

Computers come in all shapes and sizes, as Figures 2.2 through 2.4 illustrate. They are usually classified into three broad categories: mainframes, minicomputers, and microcomputers.

Mainframes are the largest, fastest, and most expensive multiuser computers. They are found in banks, insurance companies, large corporations, and government organizations. Very large mainframes are called *supercomputers* and are used primarily for the analysis of scientific and engineering problems. Usually mainframes serve many users and many functions; they are considered *general-purpose machines.* They are particularly good for problems requiring extensive mathematical calculations or for sharing large volumes of information among many people. Like a television network, they provide valuable and important services in bulk, but their users have little control over these services.

Minicomputers, or **minis**, are a smaller version of mainframes; they are slower and cheaper than mainframes. Often minicomputers are used in research labs, universities, and manufacturing plants. Compared with mainframes, minicomputers usually provide more specialized, well-defined services; they are said to

Figure 2.2 An Amdahl mainframe computer system consisting of two central processing units and attachments for storage and communications. Many simultaneous users (not shown here) are supported by such machines.

Figure 2.3 A Digital Equipment Corporation (DEC) VAX minicomputer. Whether used for dedicated applications or as general-purpose computer systems, minicomputers offer economies of scale in the middle of the cost/performance range.

be *dedicated* to specific applications. For example, minicomputers may be used to control an assembly line in a factory, to record data in a research laboratory, to help programmers develop programs for other computers, or to process specific types of data for building contractors or doctors.

Both mainframes and minicomputers are **timesharing** systems, which means that they can divide their attention simultaneously among many users. With a timesharing system, some users might be entering data while other users are receiving output. The simplest way to implement timesharing in a computer is to allocate short periods of processing (known as *time slices*) to each user's program in a round-robin fashion. If the time slices are short enough, then from any particular user's perspective, it may seem as if the computer is responding instantly. For billing purposes, timesharing systems must also keep track of who is using the system and for how long.

To illustrate how timeshared mainframes and minicomputers give the illusion of simultaneous use, consider how a juggler appears to toss three balls into the air at the same time. A juggler actually holds only one ball at a time; but while one ball is in the left hand, another ball is in the air between hands, and the third ball is in the air above both hands. Each ball is given a turn to be tossed into the air. Most of the time, the juggler is doing nothing! A timesharing computer system juggles programs by keeping all but one program "in the air." Only one program is ever run-

Figure 2.4 A personal computer system with a detached keyboard, a printer, a video display, and a system unit (underneath the display) containing two microfloppy disk drives.

ning at any time; but because the computer is so fast, you never notice that each program spends most of its time waiting to be "tossed in the air" by the CPU.

Microcomputers, or **micros**, are the smallest, least powerful, least expensive computers, based on microprocessors. They frequently take the form of **embedded microprocessors** in other devices—for example, in cars, clock radios, burglar alarms, toys, microwave ovens, greeting cards, or space vehicles. They also take the form of **personal computers**—computers that are designed to be used by one person. They are even more specialized than minicomputers. Microcomputers offer to computer users advantages and disadvantages somewhat like those provided to television watchers by a videocassette recorder: although you must purchase the personal computer or videocassette recorder and purchase or rent disks or cassettes, you have complete control over how you use these pieces of equipment.

Actually, there is no clear line dividing one type of computer from another. All three types may be used in similar ways. For example, one or two people might use a mainframe to solve a very specialized program in much the same way one person might use a personal computer. Or, instead of using a mainframe computer, a corporation might connect minicomputers together to handle all of the company's record keeping.

Even though there are no absolute dividing lines among the types of computers, however, there are vast differences between small and large computers. If the CPU of an Apple II could carry out the same instructions as an IBM mainframe at the same speed, IBM would lose a lot of business. Instead, the CPUs of different types of computers vary greatly in how fast they process instructions, in which instructions they can carry out, and in how many different instructions they can handle. These differences determine the "power" of a computer and whether a computer can execute a given program or not.

Because each instruction is extremely simple, completing a useful task takes hundreds, thousands, or even millions of primitive operations. Obviously, a CPU must work quickly to be useful. Most computers operate at speeds measured in fractions of a second. A *nanosecond* is one-billionth of a second; there are 1 million *microseconds,* or 1,000 *milliseconds,* in a second. Microcomputers operate in the microsecond range, whereas minicomputers and mainframes operate in the nanosecond range.

The collection of instructions that a certain computer's CPU can perform directly is called its **instruction set**. Large computers have large instruction sets, and small computers have smaller instruction sets. Besides the number of instructions in a computer's instruction set, the capability of each instruction is important. A mainframe computer has very powerful instructions, whereas a microcomputer has simple instructions. For example, a mainframe computer might have a single instruction for multiplying two 64-bit numbers, but it might take a microcomputer 30 instructions to compute the same multiplication. Clearly, the power of a computer's instruction set influences how fast the computer can process data.

Because computers differ in both the size of the instruction set and the power of instructions, it is difficult to compare one computer with another. A general measure of performance is the **MFLOP** (*million floating-point operations per second*). A 1-MFLOP computer can perform 1 million floating-point operations per second. (A **floating-point number** has two parts, a fractional part and an exponent, and is used in mathematical or scientific calculations.) If we accept the MFLOP measure of "power," then Figure 2.5 succinctly summarizes the cost versus the performance of all classes of computers. At the low end, calculators cost less than $100, but their MFLOP rating is so small that it does not register on the scale shown in Figure 2.5. Microcomputers operate at 0.01 to 0.04 MFLOP and range in cost from about $400 to over $5,000. Professional workstation computers cost more but deliver additional performance.

Figure 2.5 also groups all computers into three general classes: personal, shared, and central. A *personal computer* has a single operator. A *shared computer* divides its attention among a group of people; a minicomputer that supports 10 to 50 users is an example. A *central computer* is timeshared in a large organization and may support up to 1,000 users simultaneously. The category of central com-

Figure 2.5 A comparison of the cost, performance, and class of current computers.

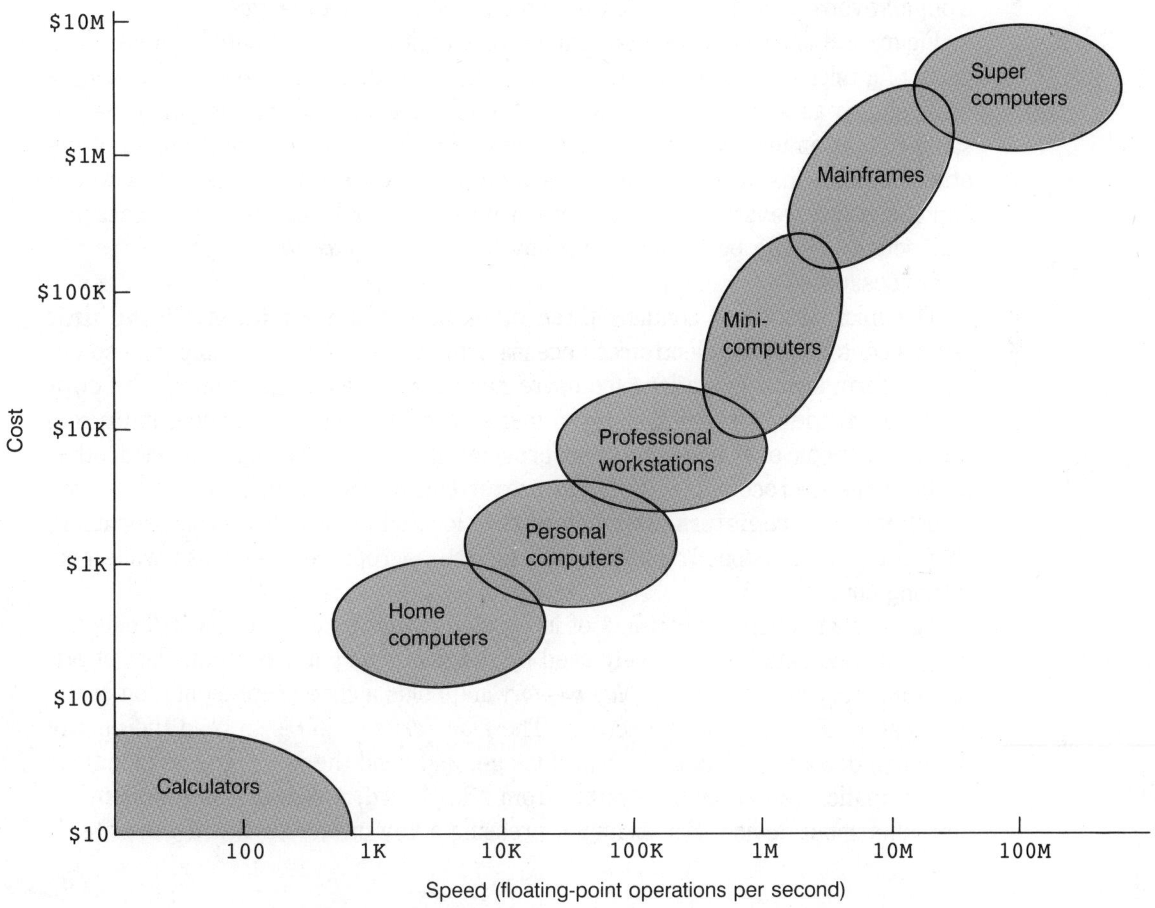

puters includes mainframes and supercomputers. They generally cost more than $1 million. Central computers are so expensive that it is difficult to imagine anyone being able to justify one, but central computers are extremely cost effective when speed and capacity are required. For example, a Cray X-MP supercomputer, which costs $5 million, delivers 6.6 floating-point operations per second per dollar, whereas a DEC VAX-11/780 minicomputer, which costs $200,000, delivers only 1.65 floating-point operations per second per dollar. A $6,000 IBM AT with a floating-point coprocessor is about as cost effective as a Cray X-MP, at 6.7 floating-point operations per second per dollar.

Despite the tremendous differences in speed and capacity between microcomputers and mainframe computers, the way their hardware components are organized is remarkably similar. In the next two sections, we will examine the hardware of both types of computers.

The Hardware of a Microcomputer

A microcomputer is a small computer that uses a single integrated circuit called a **microprocessor** as the basis for its central processing unit. Usually a microcomputer costs less than $5,000, uses disk drives for secondary storage, accepts data from a keyboard, and displays output on a screen called a *monitor*.

Figure 2.6 illustrates the organization of a typical microcomputer system. The parts of a microcomputer are tied together by a set of parallel conductors called a **bus,** shown as colored lines in the center of Figure 2.6. The bus performs the same role as an intercom; it allows any device to broadcast messages to all of the other devices. Just as in an intercom system, rules govern who gets to talk when, and there are ways to interrupt normal messages with high-priority messages. The activity on the bus is moderated by the *bus interface unit,* a part of the microprocessor.

The microprocessor contains three other parts. The **arithmetic/logic unit (ALU)** contains all the electronics necessary to calculate (add, multiply, and so on) and perform logical operations (compare numbers and make decisions). The **control unit** retrieves instructions from memory in the proper sequence, interprets the instructions one at a time, and provides the arithmetic/logic unit and other parts of the microcomputer with the proper control signals to implement the instructions. The **registers** are memory cells located on the microprocessor itself; they act as a high-speed "scratch pad" for the microprocessor to use while performing computations.

The primary memory consists of integrated-circuit memory chips. It holds the programs and data being actively used by the microcomputer system. Part of primary memory is called the *display memory* and holds a coded representation of the information to appear on the screen. The *video driver*'s job is to read the display memory, decode its data into a visual image, and send the image to the monitor.

Information can enter the system from a keyboard, a disk drive, a modem, or any other input device. For example, pressing a key on the keyboard generates a

Figure 2.6 The organization of a typical microcomputer system.

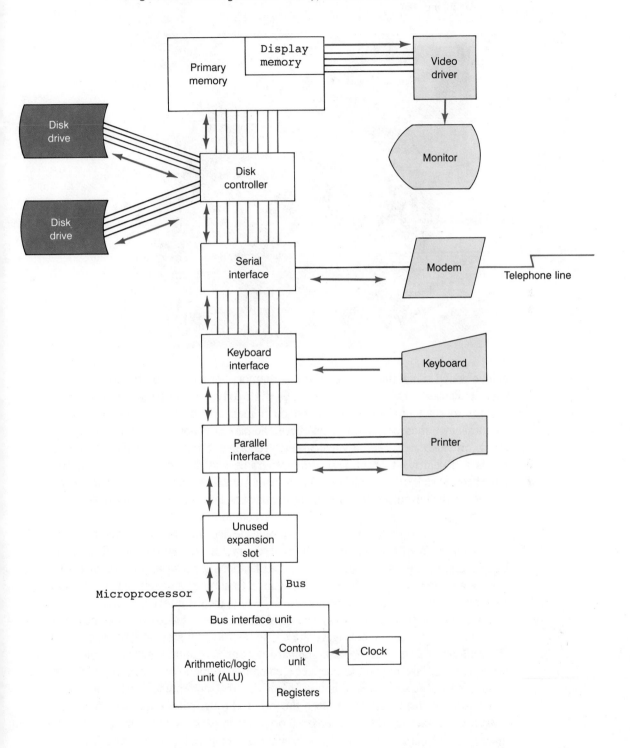

unique coded signal that can be stored in memory, processed by the microprocessor, or displayed by the video driver. A **disk drive** enables the microcomputer system to read or write information on a magnetic disk. The analogy with a videocassette recorder is very close here. To play or record a television show or a movie on video, you need a videocassette recorder. Similarly, the microcomputer needs a disk drive to read and write programs and data on a disk. A **modem** (short for *mo*dulator-*dem*odulator) is an input-output device that converts (modulates) the digital pulses generated by computers into analog signals that can be sent through the telephone system to other computers.

Every input, output, and external storage device in a microcomputer system must have its own connecting electrical circuitry, or **interface**, linking it to the bus. The interface may conform to the specifications for a *standard interface,* or it may be a *custom interface* like the one required to support a special-purpose device such as a video disk player (see Figure 2.7). A standard interface, which is often called an **I/O port**, makes it easy and reliable to connect pieces of equipment that adhere to the standard (see Figure 2.8). The best-known standard interface is the **RS-232** *serial port.* The RS-232 standard defines the timing and other electrical properties that are needed to connect a computer to modems, printers, and other serial devices. A *serial device* is any I/O device that communicates by sending or receiving a string of bits one after the other through one data line. A *parallel device,* in contrast, sends or receives information in packets all at once, over many (usually eight) data lines. The industry standard for parallel interfaces is the *Cen-*

Figure 2.8 Devices can be connected to standard I/O ports by plugging cables into the back of a microcomputer.

tronics parallel interface, developed by the Centronics Corporation and used by many other manufacturers. Parallel interfaces can send and receive data faster than serial interfaces because they send more bits in each time segment, but both the RS-232 and the Centronics interface will work faster than most printers or modems.

An **expansion slot** is a connector inside the microcomputer where a custom interface, or *adapter card,* can be plugged into the system. This is illustrated in Photos 16, 17, and 18 of Window 2. An **adapter card** is a circuit board that contains special I/O interface circuits; color graphics adapters and disk controller cards are examples. A *combination card* integrates many functions on a single card. For example, one combination card might include extra RAM, serial and parallel ports, and a system clock; another might include a disk controller or color graphics adapter along with extra RAM. Expansion slots are used to extend the hardware by adding extra primary memory, more disk drives, modems, and so forth.

The Hardware of a Mainframe

The basic functional organization of a mainframe, shown in Figure 2.9, is similar to that of a microcomputer, shown in Figure 2.6. In both figures, the CPU contains an arithmetic/logic unit, a control unit, and registers. Just as in a microcomputer, the data transfers in a mainframe's CPU travel through a bus. But the bus structure of the mainframe computer is not apparent in Figure 2.9, because the bus is hidden inside the CPU and is not directly available to peripheral devices.

For a mainframe, the equivalent of an expansion slot is a channel. A **channel** is actually a limited-capacity computer that takes over input and output tasks in order to free the general-purpose mainframe to handle internal processing tasks. Many devices can be attached to a channel, including disk drives, printers, plotters, and

Figure 2.9 The organization of a typical mainframe computer.

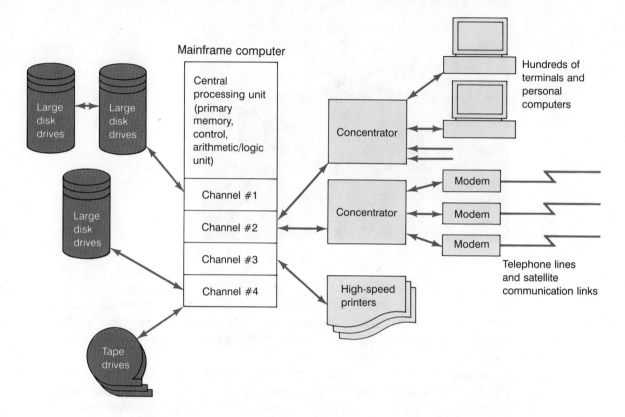

terminals. Channels play an important role in helping a mainframe manage the interactions among hundreds or even thousands of peripherals. By relieving the CPU of the need to communicate directly with peripherals, channels make it possible for input, output, and internal processing operations to occur at the same time. Each channel receives and transmits data independently of the others. Several types of channels exist. A *daisy-chain channel* is one in which many devices are connected like pearls in a necklace. Information is sent along the daisy chain to be picked off by the destination device. Some channels are designed to accept information from many low-speed devices that transmit only one byte at a time. Other channels accept longer chunks of data, known as *blocks* of data, in each transmission. These are typically used in conjunction with high-speed storage devices.

The fast CPUs of mainframes and minicomputers allow many users to share access to the hardware through stations called **terminals**. A typical terminal has a keyboard, display screen, and wire that connects the terminal to the computer system. Most terminals do very little data processing themselves. Data is entered on the keyboard and sent to the mainframe for processing, and anything received from the mainframe is displayed. Sometimes the terminal is connected via telephone and may be located thousands of miles away from the computer.

Microcomputers may look like terminals; they have a keyboard and a display screen, just like a terminal. In addition, however, a microcomputer has a general-purpose CPU hidden inside. As a result, microcomputers are very flexible and can run virtually any type of program.

SOFTWARE COMPONENTS

We have seen that the organization of a computer includes input and output devices, external storage units, and a central processor with its associated memory. This structure is simple, even trivial. But how does it work? In this section, we explore how software controls the hardware.

First we will examine two basic concepts that lie behind all computer programs: the idea of storing instructions inside the same machine that executes the instructions and the idea of using codes to represent information in electrical and magnetic memories. These two techniques give modern computers their power and versatility. Then we will explore the events that occur in a typical computer session, from turning on the machine to loading programs, processing data, and ending the computer session.

The Stored-Program Concept

The most profound concept in all computing goes back to the dawn of modern science. In the mid-1800s—when Darwin was formulating the theory of evolution, when electromagnetism was being discovered, and when the Industrial Revolution was in full swing—Charles Babbage was attempting to build the first stored-program computer. A **stored-program computer** is a machine controlled by software stored within the hardware. The controlling software is called a *stored program* because the machine holds the program in its memory while the program is guiding the actions of the hardware.

One hundred years passed before Babbage's idea was rejuvenated and used in modern stored-program computer systems. (Chapter 18 gives a brief history of computing.) Today the operation of all computers depends on a memory that contains instructions in the form of a program and facts in the form of data. Stored programs are essential to modern computing, because they are held within the computer machinery itself, making a computer self-contained and automatic.

A CPU's circuits can execute a limited number of different instructions. Each instruction is assigned a pattern of binary bits. For example, one pattern might instruct the CPU to compare two numbers and store the location of the larger number in a particular register. Another pattern might tell the CPU to multiply the number in one register by the number in another. Thus, a modern computer executes programs constructed of long sequences of 1s and 0s.

Although computers understand only binary instructions, programmers try to avoid writing in binary code, because it is tedious and error prone. Instead, programmers express their logic in more understandable ways. Usually they begin by organizing their ideas in a well-structured outline (known as *pseudocode*) or by creating a flowchart similar to Figure 2.10(a). This helps them to organize their

Figure 2.10 Software controls a computer system. The flowchart (a) describes one part of an accounts receivable system. It acts as a blueprint from which the program fragment (b) is developed.

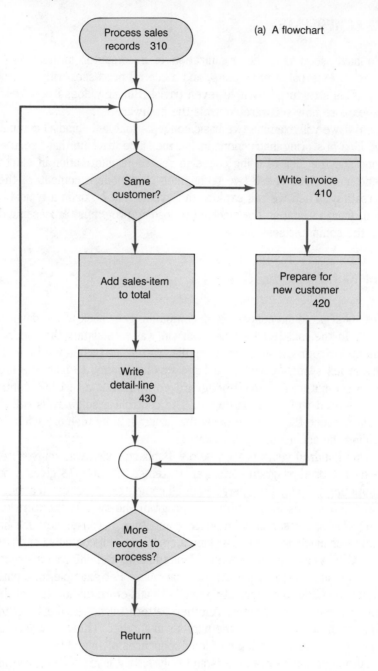

(a) A flowchart

Figure 2.10 continued

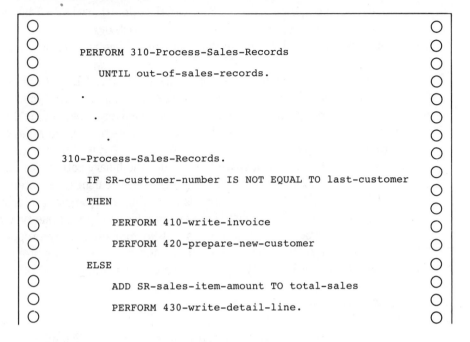

```
        PERFORM 310-Process-Sales-Records
           UNTIL out-of-sales-records.

             .

               .

                 .

     310-Process-Sales-Records.
        IF SR-customer-number IS NOT EQUAL TO last-customer
        THEN
             PERFORM 410-write-invoice
             PERFORM 420-prepare-new-customer
        ELSE
             ADD SR-sales-item-amount TO total-sales
             PERFORM 430-write-detail-line.
```

(b) A program fragment

thoughts before writing instructions in a programming language, such as the COBOL instructions shown in Figure 2.10(b). (*COBOL* is the most widely used business programming language.) COBOL allows the programmer to use English-like statements to describe processing instructions to the computer.

This raises an interesting question: How does the computer execute a program written in COBOL? Clearly, the computer's circuits cannot execute a COBOL program directly, because COBOL statements are not written in the computer's binary instruction code. The answer is that the COBOL program must be translated into binary instructions. This step is accomplished with the help of a *compiler* or an *interpreter,* two broad classes of programs that translate other programs into binary instructions.

Representing Information

We have seen that a binary code is used to represent instructions, numbers, letters of the alphabet, and graphical information. How is this possible? The secret is in *representation* and *interpretation* through binary encoding.

Representation and interpretation of text are often misunderstood, perhaps because a variety of codes are used to store text. The *ASCII* (American *S*tandard

Code for Information Interchange) code is used in microcomputers, and other codes, such as *EBCDIC* (*E*xtended *B*inary *C*oded *D*ecimal *I*nterchange *C*ode), are used in larger computers. The **ASCII code** establishes a 7-bit pattern for each printable character on the keyboard. Thus, each of the letters of the alphabet, the numerals 0 through 9, and special characters, such as $, &, and %, is defined by a 7-bit ASCII pattern.

For example, the uppercase alphabetic characters (*A, B, C,* and so on) are represented by 7-bit binary patterns that are the equivalent of decimal numbers 65 to 91. The binary pattern 01000001 (the decimal equivalent is 65) is thus the encoded representation of the letter *A*. Lowercase alphabetic characters (*a, b, c,* and so on) range from the binary equivalents of 97 to 123. A ? is stored as the binary equivalent of 63. Even a blank space has a code: the binary pattern for 32.

The same ASCII pattern may have different meanings; the interpretation of the pattern depends on what the CPU is expecting. If a computer interprets a number as a character, an ASCII character as a graphical image, or one type of information as another type, the wrong results will be computed. Only proper programming can prevent such misinterpretation of information in a computer. The computer does not automatically "know" one type of information from another.

The Events in a Computer Session

On the surface, the events in a personal computer session might seem straightforward. You start the computer by turning on the power and placing a disk in the disk drive. The CPU causes a program to be transferred from the disk into primary memory, where a program takes control of the CPU. Acting under the program's control, the CPU shifts data back and forth between primary memory and the disk in order to process it. Data cannot be directly processed while it is on disk; it must be brought into primary memory to be totaled, compared, displayed, printed, and so forth. The program allows you to control its operation by typing commands on a keyboard or by using another input device. Eventually the program gives up control of the computer and ceases to operate. When this happens, you must tell the computer what to do next. No matter what directions you give the computer, however, the same pattern is followed: a program is transferred into memory, where it takes control; it processes data; and finally it terminates. This three-part process is called *program execution.*

After a bit of thought, however, the events in a computer session may not seem so clear. For example, when the CPU requires information from a magnetic disk, it must first read the information from the disk into primary memory, because only information stored in primary memory is directly accessible to the CPU. But the CPU can do nothing without the intelligence of software. If the software is not permanently stored in the primary memory, then how does the computer hardware "know" how to get information when it is turned on? This knowledge comes from two features not discussed so far. First, a small amount of nonvolatile memory is built into the computer. Called **ROM** (*r*ead-*o*nly *m*emory), it retains information permanently, even when the computer is off, and can be read, but not changed.

Second, the program in ROM instructs the CPU to read another program from a disk, thus performing a self-helping startup when the computer is first turned on. This process is called **booting** the computer, a reference to "pulling yourself up by your bootstraps."

The notion of including software inside the computer to help run other software is basic to all computer systems. The special software that controls the running of other software is called *operating system software*. An **operating system** is a master set of programs that control the operation of the computer itself. Through the CPU, the operating system programs control all I/O devices, such as the keyboard, display screen, printer, disk drives, and every other device connected to the computer.

There are many different kinds of operating systems; some are for large mainframe computers, some for minis, and still others are suited for microcomputers. Mainframe and minicomputer systems typically use a timesharing operating system, whereas microcomputer systems typically use a single-user operating system. A *timesharing operating system* controls several programs that run alongside each other. This allows several people to use the computer system simultaneously; to each person it seems as if no one else is using the computer. In contrast, a *single-user operating system* is simpler because it manages only one program at a time and does not need to monitor computer usage for billing purposes.

For example, all application programs, or application software, are supervised by the operating system. The operating system is like an air traffic controller at a busy airport and the application programs, like airplanes. The controller determines what each airplane is allowed to do, and when it is permitted to do it. Similarly, the operating system tells when each application program is allowed to run on the CPU.

Most computer sessions involve the use of application programs, which perform various tasks for people. Programs that solve mathematical equations or manage payrolls, as well as programs that process words, display graphs, manage data, and play games, are all examples of application software. Application software temporarily converts a general-purpose computer into a special-purpose machine that does exactly what you want done. A general-purpose microcomputer, for example, becomes a video arcade machine when it runs a game program, a serious tool for the designer when it runs an architectural layout program, and a tool for the accountant when it runs a general ledger program.

We can classify application software into two broad categories: vertical software and horizontal software. **Vertical software** is specialized application software designed to serve a particular discipline or activity. Examples include medical billing systems, project estimation systems for building contractors, and information storage for breeders of thoroughbred horses. **Horizontal software** is software designed to serve a wide group of users, who must, in turn, tailor the programs to their own needs. Examples of horizontal software are word processors, spreadsheet programs, and programs to set up and manage *databases,* which are collections of logically related data. We will, for the most part, concern ourselves with horizontal programs because of their general applicability to a wide variety of

Figure 2.11 Visual user interfaces like GEM DESKTOP from Digital Research simulate a real desktop with sheets of paper, icons, and menus.

users. But you should know that horizontal software may be cumbersome and inefficient compared with vertical software, specifically designed for special needs.

To use any application program, you must operate it through the keyboard or some other kind of input device. To guide its users, every program employs a **user interface**—a protocol for communicating between the computer and the user. A *friendly user interface* is one that is easily understood and does not intimidate users. Since computers are sophisticated machines, nearly everyone is intimidated by a user interface at some time. But once you understand the logic and underlying model employed by the interface, using a computer can be as easy and comfortable as driving a car. There are two main types of interfaces: text-oriented and visual. A *text-oriented user interface* displays messages on the screen in words; a *visual user interface* employs pictures called **icons**, which symbolize different computer functions. Figure 2.11 shows an example of a visual interface. Our examples in the next section will illustrate a text-oriented interface.

A SAMPLE COMPUTER SESSION

We can illustrate the interaction between software and hardware in a computer system by walking through a typical session with a personal computer. Because using a personal computer is much like using a large timeshared computer via a terminal, this illustration can be used to introduce you to whatever computer you are likely to use. (The principal difference is that you must **log on** to a mainframe computer, or identify yourself by typing an account number and a password which identify you for purposes of billing.)

Booting the Computer

If the computer is turned off, you must first find a copy of the operating system disk and insert it into the disk drive. Then flip the power switch on to boot the operating system into primary memory. Recall that a permanent bootstrap program is read from ROM; it instructs the computer to read the operating system program from the disk into primary memory, thus bringing the computer to "life."

Some disks contain both a copy of the operating system and an application program. These disks may also contain instructions that cause them to load the operating system into memory and immediately proceed to load the application program into another part of memory. This can be convenient, because the computer will immediately begin to run an application program, such as a word processing program or a game. Nearly all program disks for Apple II computers are configured this way. Thus, if you use an Apple II, you will not need to perform separate steps to boot the computer with the operating system and to begin running an application program. Instead, both of these steps occur automatically when you turn on the computer with the appropriate program disk in the disk drive.

With most computers, the first message shown on the display screen comes from the operating system. The message varies depending on the model of computer. The message may be the computer's operating system prompt. (In computer jargon, a **prompt** is any signal that tells you that the computer is waiting for you to enter an answer, supply it with needed information, or respond to a message.) Here are some likely prompt lines:

```
Ok?
A >
:
?
```

These cryptic messages tell you that the computer is waiting
for you to give it a command. A **command** is an instruction that tells the computer what you want it to do next.

Loading a Program

Suppose, for purposes of illustration, that we want to use the computer to run a word processing program in order to enter and print a short letter. (For more details on word processing, see Chapter 6.) Before you can run a program, you must load it into the computer. To load a program, you typically, enter its name as a command to the operating system. For example, suppose you respond to the prompt A > by typing the command WP (your response is shown in color).

```
A > WP
```

This command might cause a program called WP to be copied from the diskette into primary memory and executed. The CPU *executes* a program by performing each instruction, one at a time.

Next, the WP program will prompt you for input. For example, the first WP prompt may request a name.

Enter the name of the document to type or edit: MYLETTER

Typing MYLETTER and pressing the key marked [Return] or [Enter] causes the word processing program to fetch the text previously stored on disk under the name MYLETTER or, if no text under that name exists, to create a new document called MYLETTER.

If MYLETTER is new, the word processor clears the display screen and waits for you to type text, just as if the computer were a typewriter. For example, you might enter the following letter:

February 12, 1848

Mr. Wilkins Micawber
Care of Mr Namby's
Coleman Street

Dear Mr. Micawber:

I regret that I am forced to write you in the matter of a loan you have failed to repay when due. You and I have had more than one such business dealing.

If the sum of 24 pounds, 7 shillings, 9 pence (principle, interest, and penalty) has not been received by this office before the close of business on Monday the 20th of this month, the matter will be turned over to my solicitors, Kenge and Carboy of Lincoln's Inn.

Ralph Nickleby

After the letter is entered, you can store it, print it, or correct it by editing the text displayed on the screen. These operations require you to give commands to your computer.

Entering Commands

Terminals and personal computers have special keys on their keyboards that simplify many operations. One of the most important is the *control key,* which is labeled [Ctrl] on most computer keyboards. (Apple computer keyboards have a key marked with a small apple.) To enter many commands, you press this key and hold it down while pressing another key. For example, suppose you want to save your sample letter. *Saving* a document means copying it from the primary memory to the disk, thus making a permanent copy on the disk. The exact command for doing so varies from one word processing program to another, but with some programs, you press [Ctrl] and [S] simultaneously to direct the program to save a document.

The keyboard has other special keys to help you operate various programs and give commands easily. For example, a word processing program may also use keys marked [Ins] (for inserting material), [Del] (for deleting material), and [PgDn] (for paging down through the document). These keys are likely to take on other meanings when you run other programs on the computer.

Quitting

Sometimes the most difficult command to discover is the one that will make a program stop running. Usually, if you remember just a few commands, you can ask the program to tell you what the other commands are, including the command that will stop a program and return control to the operating system. Suppose pressing [Ctrl] and [L] causes a list of choices to appear on the screen, such as

        P = Set page parameters
        G = Get another document
        X = Exit this program

Pressing [X] at this point takes you out of the word processor program. The operating system takes control of the computer, displays its prompt, and waits for you to enter a command.

If you are running a mainframe or minicomputer, you must tell the operating system that you are leaving, through a process called **logging off**. Often, logging off is as simple as typing

        A > logoff

Because a personal computer serves only one user at a time, you need not log off. Simply turning the power off suffices.

SUMMARY

All computers have the same basic functional organization: input devices capture information in a machine-processable format; the CPU processes information stored in primary memory; storage units provide long-term storage of data; and output devices present the processed information in a usable format.

Computers come in three sizes: mainframe, mini, and micro. Each has its role in society. Mainframes are found predominantly in large organizations, and minicomputers are used in more dedicated applications in factory automation, universities, and medium-sized organizations. Both mainframes and minis are timesharing systems for multiple users. Micros are used as personal computers or in household appliances.

All computers also use software. Software is classified according to its purpose. Application software is designed to solve real-world problems such as found in the fields of accounting, engineering, or factory control. System software, on the other hand, is designed to control the computer itself, such as the various kinds of operating systems. Timesharing operating systems allow many people to "simultaneously" use the same computer. Single-user operating systems are typically found in personal computers.

KEY TERMS

adapter card	mainframe
analog	main memory
arithmetic/logic unit (ALU)	MFLOP
ASCII code	microcomputer (micro)
binary	microprocessor
bit	minicomputer (mini)
boot	modem
bus	operating system
byte	output device
central processing unit (CPU)	peripheral
channel	personal computer
command	primary memory
control unit	program
digital	prompt
disk drive	RAM
embedded microprocessor	register
expansion slot	ROM
floating-point number	RS-232
horizontal software	stored-program computer
icon	terminal
input device	timesharing
instruction set	user interface
interface	vertical software
I/O device	volatile
I/O port	word
log off	word length
log on	

1. What are the two main components of a computer system? Explain how they work together.

2. What are the differences among micro, mini, and mainframe computers? How are they alike?

3. What is the "mind" of a computer, and what is its "body"? Can computers think?

4. Suppose a movie projector, camera, and film are compared with a computer system. What is the computer's equivalent of film? Of the projector? Is this a good analogy?

5. Computers communicate over the telephone. Is the telephone an I/O device?

6. An RS-232 interface is used for serial communication, whereas a Centronix interface is used for parallel communication. Which does your computer use to communicate with your printer?

7. When a computer is first turned on, what causes the CPU to transfer a program from disk into primary memory?

8. What is the relationship between application software and operating system software?

9. How does a timesharing operating system run many programs at the same time? What is the difference between timesharing and a single-user operating system?

10. What is the difference between vertical and horizontal software? What programs might fall between the two?

11. What are the two principal kinds of user interface? Which kind do you think is the easiest to learn? to use?

EXERCISES

1. Who makes computers? List all the computer manufacturers you can think of, then compare your list with the *Datamation* 100, a listing of the top 100 computer companies given in one of the June issues of *Datamation* magazine each year.

2. Cars are vehicles for moving people; computers are vehicles for moving information. Prepare a report on the kinds of information computers are capable of moving over communication lines.

3. Is a medical billing program considered vertical or horizontal software? How about a tax preparation program? How about games like PacMan?

4. Examine the keyboard of your terminal or personal computer. Which keys are used to give commands, and which ones are used to enter data into the computer? Can you tell the difference?

3

The CPU and Storage

I n Chapter 2 we explained how information is coded and represented in the memory of a computer. Now we will examine how information is processed in the heart of all computers: the central processing unit (CPU). Close interaction between the CPU and primary memory, with its stored programs, is responsible for the "reasoning power" of computers. Because external memory is also closely tied to the CPU, we will also examine the role of external storage in the overall computer system and the exchange of information between external and internal memory, which is called *file access*. Throughout the chapter, we will compare the cost, speed, and reliability of various memory technologies.

Figure 3.1 shows a useful way of thinking about the parts of a CPU. Primary memory is shown divided into a large number of storage cells. You can think of them as somewhat like the safe deposit boxes in a bank vault or as post office boxes. Each box or cell has its own unique electronic **address**—a number identifying its location in memory—and each is the same size. However, unlike post office boxes, locations in computer memory can hold only numbers.

Recall that the *arithmetic/logic unit (ALU)* in the CPU does all the computing; it can add two numbers, subtract, multiply, and divide. It can compare two numbers

Figure 3.1 Parts of a CPU. Primary memory is like a collection of post office boxes; each one is numbered and stores a small amount of information. For example, box 98 holds the number 07. The control unit fetches numbers from memory locations and interprets them as instructions. The ALU performs arithmetic on the numbers stored in memory.

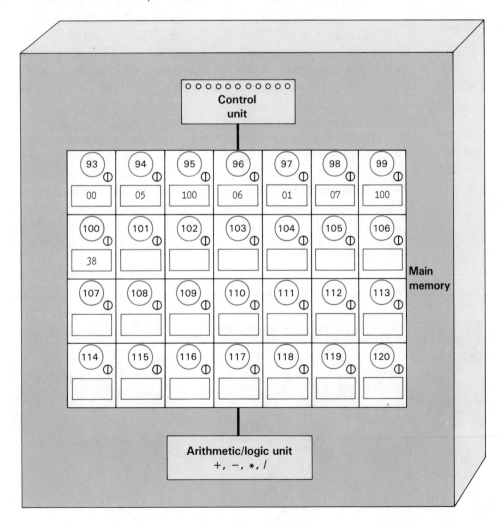

to determine which is larger, move bits from one place to another, and keep track of time. The ALU works exclusively on encoded binary numbers. It takes its order from binary-encoded instructions stored like any other information in primary memory. The *control unit* is the supervisor of the CPU; it fetches numbers from memory and interprets them as instructions. The control unit dissects each instruction and then directs the flow of information through the ALU, input/output devices, and main memory.

The physical appearance of CPUs differs more than their logical structure. A mainframe's CPU fills a large box and requires many circuit boards, or ceramic chip-carrying modules. In contrast, a microcomputer's CPU is often mounted on a single plastic circuit board and can be hidden inside the keyboard or monitor. In every microcomputer, the control unit and ALU are combined on a single circuit board or chip. Because this component is so small, it is called a *microprocessor*.

Designing a microprocessor is an expensive proposition, so there are only a few hundred microprocessor models. Of these models, only a few are used in personal computers. Each model has a name that sounds like the model number for a sports car. For example, the Apple II uses the Mostek 6502; the IBM PC uses the Intel 8088; and the Apple Macintosh uses the Motorola 68000. Figure 3.2 shows two views of the Motorola 68000. Programs for one CPU will not run on another unless they are rewritten or translated from one instruction set to the other. Depending on how a program was written, translating a program can be as much work as writing it from scratch.

In both types of CPUs, the components operate quickly, though the parts of a mainframe are quicker. To the extent possible, components are designed to operate independently. For example, the ALU might be multiplying two numbers while the control unit is "looking ahead" to read the next instruction. This technique, in which several instructions can be working their way simultaneously through the parts of the CPU and be in various stages of completion, is known as **pipelining**. Until the most recent generation of microprocessors, it was safe to say that mainframe computers made more use of pipelining than microcomputers. Now there

Figure 3.2 The Motorola 68000 microprocessor, before (left) and after (right) packaging.

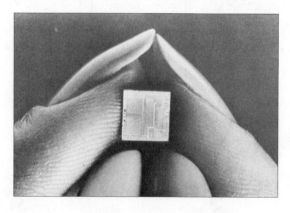

are single-chip microprocessors with hundreds of thousands of circuits and the ability to run several programs concurrently. The gap between the performance of a mainframe's CPU and that of a microprocessor has been shrinking consistently over the last ten years.

A microprocessor has a limited and simple instruction set compared with that of a mainframe's CPU. Four factors influence a CPU's power. First, how many bits of data are processed in one operation? (An analogy is the size of the scoop on a steam shovel.) This depends on

1. The number of bits processed internally in each operation. A 6502 processes 8 bits in each operation, an 8088 processes 16 bits, and a 68000 handles 32.

2. The number of bits transferred between the microprocessor and primary memory at once—8 bits with a 6502 or 8088, but 16 bits with a 68000.

Second, how many instructions are in the instruction set, and how powerful are they? (An analogy is the number of useful attachments for a tractor.) Third, how long does it take to complete an instruction? (An analogy is the time it takes a steam shovel to dump each scoop.) This depends on

1. The **clock rate**, the speed for all the operations in the CPU. Clock rate is measured in **megahertz (MHz)**, or millions of cycles per second. For example, an IBM PC has a 4.77 MHz clock rate, which means that there are 4,770,000 ticks (called *clocks)* of the CPU's clock each second.

2. The number of clocks per instruction. It takes an IBM PC 4 clocks to transfer one byte from primary memory to the microprocessor, and it can take more than 100 clocks to multiply two 16-bit numbers.

Fourth, how much primary memory can the CPU manage? The maximum amount of primary memory is limited by the length of each memory address. (As an analogy, consider the number of telephones that can be dialed with a seven-digit telephone number.) This factor can be quite important, because it determines the largest program the CPU can load into memory at once and execute.

A microprocessor uses a 16-, a 20-, a 24-, or a 32-bit memory address. For example, the 6502 uses a 16-bit memory address, which limits it to 2^{16}, or roughly 65,000, locations for primary memory. The 8088 uses a 20-bit address, for a maximum of slightly over 1 million addresses. The 68000 uses a 24-bit address, for a maximum of about 16 million addresses. The newest microprocessors use 32-bit addresses; the maximum amount of memory they can manage is effectively unlimited.

Most computers do not have as much physical memory as their CPU can address. This makes it possible to add memory to the computer later. If a program asks the CPU to retrieve information from a nonexistent memory location, however, a processing error is likely to occur, as when you dial a nonexistent telephone number.

A computer's raw processing power is not important for most applications, just as the size of a car's engine is not important for stop-and-go driving. It is much better to have a system in which the software makes full use of a processor with rather limited capabilities than to have poor software running on a potentially powerful processor. However, some scientific problems would take years to solve with a microprocessor. When this is the case, a mainframe or supercomputer is needed.

Primary Memory

The primary memory of a computer is composed of **integrated circuits**. These high-speed electronic circuits are capable of quickly saving and retrieving information. In today's technology, they are printed on small chips cut from thin slices (or wafers) of silicon crystals (see Window 8). They are thus called **memory chips**. Figure 3.3 shows several memory chips in various stages of packaging.

It is easiest to build and use memory chips that have a round binary number of storage cells, which in decimal numbers means 2, 4, 8, and so on. Current memory chips tend to have between 2^{18} and 2^{20} cells; this is 262,144 to 1,048,576 bits of storage. A more convenient unit of measurement for memory uses the symbol K. In the metric system, K is the symbol for 1,000, but when memory is being measured, K is the symbol for 2^{10}, or 1,024. Thus, a memory chip with 16,384 binary storage cells is called a 16K-bit chip. Similarly, **kilobit** means 1,024 bits of memory, and **kilobyte (KB)** means 1,024 bytes.

To designate the memory capacities of mainframe computers and hard disk drives, we need even larger units. A **megabyte (MB)** is 1,024KB, or 2^{20} bytes, which is roughly 1 million characters of storage. Primary memory sizes of 16MB are common in large computer installations, but 1MB is considered a lot of mem-

Figure 3.3 Several 64K-bit memory chips in various stages of packaging.

ory in a personal computer. A **gigabyte** is 1,024MB, roughly 1 billion characters. Large mainframe disk drives hold a few gigabytes of information, but personal computers are more likely to have hard disk drives that can hold just 10 to 40 megabytes or to use even smaller floppy disk drives.

The amount of memory the computer has is important in determining what the computer can do. A computer with less than 16KB of memory is limited to trivial applications, because it can execute only tiny programs. Such a machine might be able to play video games or balance a checkbook, but it will not run a full-featured word processing program. To be useful for most professional or business applications, a computer must have at least 64KB of memory.

Memory Management Techniques

When you purchase software for a personal computer, it is important to match the software's requirement for main memory with the amount of memory in your computer. A 512KB program cannot run on a 256KB personal computer. Mainframe computers, however, are equipped with **virtual memory**—a feature allowing them to accommodate programs that are larger than the main memory. In a computer with virtual memory, the hardware simulates a very large primary memory by automatically moving parts of a running program from internal to external (disk) memory as the program runs. Thus, a 1MB memory might appear to be 100MB in size when running a very large program.

Microcomputers are sometimes programmed to approximate the virtual memory of their larger cousins by the use of **program overlays**. This technique partitions a large program into many shorter segments. Each segment is *swapped* from external storage into main memory as it is needed and removed from main memory when it isn't needed. In this way, a small computer can "act like" a big computer, but at the expense of processing speed. Program overlays have another disadvantage as well. They require extra work by the programmer, who must break the program into segments and write instructions specifying when each segment is to be swapped in or out. In contrast, virtual memory is said to be **transparent** to the programmer, because it is built into the hardware and operates automatically, without requiring the programmer's attention.

Virtual memory and program overlays were invented to compensate for the high cost of main memory, but over the last 20 years, manufacturing techniques have lowered the cost of memory chips. A reliable rule of thumb has been that, every 3 years, the number of bits per chip quadruples, whereas the cost per chip stays constant. As a result, the price of memory has been dropping about 30 percent each year for nearly two decades. Perhaps the computers of the future will have sufficiently large main memories that virtual and physical memory sizes will be the same.

ROM and RAM

The two major types of primary memory are ROM and RAM. ROM (read-only memory) is memory that is manufactured to store a fixed set of information permanently. This book is similar to ROM because its information can be read but not changed. RAM is the acronym for random-access memory. **Random access** implies that any piece of information can be read in approximately the same time, regardless of its location. In fact, the term *RAM* is misleading, because both ROM and RAM are random-access memories. The real difference between ROM and RAM is this: information that is stored in RAM can be changed. RAM is the computer's scratch pad; you can write new information into it, and it allows the computer to store information quickly for later reference.

In most computers, RAM holds

- The active parts of the operating system, the master program that controls the computer's operation
- The application program that is being executed (for example, a word processing program)
- Part or all of the data used by the application program (for example, a letter being written with the word processing program)
- A representation of the data being shown on the video display
- Anything else that is likely to change frequently (for example, the time of day in the computer's clock or information about the disk in external storage)

Most RAM is *volatile*—even a short interruption in the computer's power supply erases RAM, giving it a case of total amnesia. Obviously, it isn't wise to store the only copy of important work in RAM. In contrast, ROM is *nonvolatile,* because when you turn the computer off, the contents of ROM are not changed.

Because ROM is somewhat cheaper than RAM, as well as nonvolatile, manufacturers use ROM for permanent storage of frequently used programs in the main memory of the computer. The ROM chips containing these programs are included in the computer when it is purchased. For example, in all personal computers, ROM stores the instructions that tell the computer what to do when the power is turned on. A simple version of the BASIC programming language is usually included in a personal computer's ROM. In addition, portable computers can compensate for their limited (or nonexistent) external storage by using ROM to store application programs, such as a word processor. And the microprocessors in cars, microwave ovens, calculators, and video games are instructed to perform their special-purpose, fixed functions by a program stored in ROM.

Instructions

The control unit and primary memory work in concert: the control unit fetches instructions one at a time from memory, fetches the data to be processed from primary memory, and feeds the data to the ALU for processing. Each instruction is a simple operation, such as adding the number in one memory location to the number in another location, moving a character from the keyboard to memory, or deciding where to find the next instruction.

Figure 3.4(a) illustrates how the control unit directs the CPU to execute a simple program to add two numbers. (We have converted the contents of memory to

Figure 3.4 (a) The control unit fetches the instruction LOAD 110 from locations 100 and 101, temporarily holds the LOAD instruction in the instruction register while it is being processed, and directs the ALU to copy 38 from location 110 into the accumulator. (b) After the control unit has executed each instruction one at a time, the results are stored back in primary memory.

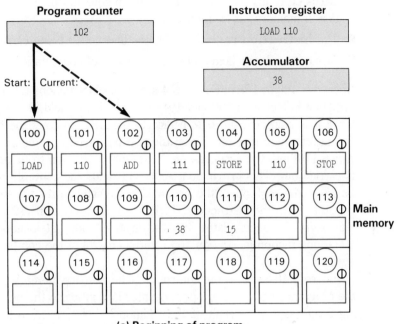

(a) Beginning of program

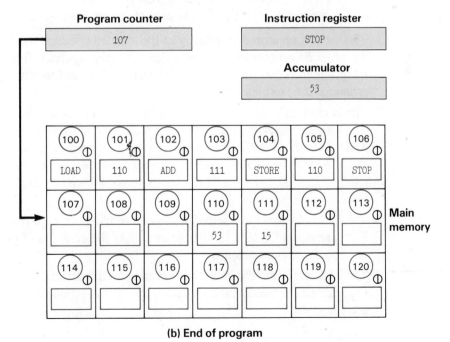

(b) End of program

words and decimal numbers to make the figure easier to read, but keep in mind that all information in a computer is stored as encoded binary numbers.) The figure shows three registers, which are special storage cells in the control unit:

- The **program counter** holds the address of the next instruction to be plucked from memory. In Figure 3.4(a), the instruction from locations 100 and 101 is currently executing; the program counter "points to" the next instruction in memory, at location 102.
- The **instruction register** holds the instruction being carried out.
- An **accumulator** holds temporary results of computations inside the ALU.

Locations 100 to 106 in Figure 3.4 store four instructions from a program. The instruction in locations 100 and 101, LOAD 110, is held in the instruction register while it is being carried out. It directs the CPU to copy the contents of location 110 into the accumulator. Thus, the first instruction copies 38 (the contents of location 110) into the accumulator. Next, the instruction from locations 102 and 103 is carried out. This instruction, ADD 111, adds the contents of location 111 (that is, 15) to the contents of the accumulator (38) and stores the sum back in the accumulator. Then the instruction STORE 110, from locations 104 and 105, copies the sum from the accumulator into the main memory at location 110. Finally, the STOP instruction in location 106 returns control of the computer to the operating system.

Figure 3.4(b) shows the control unit and primary memory as they appear after the program stops. The program counter is pointing to the next instruction following STOP, and the result of the addition (53) is stored in location 110. At this point, the operating system determines what to do next.

We can generalize from this simple example to all computers.

1. The instruction stored in memory at the location specified by the contents of the program counter is copied into the instruction register. The contents of the program counter are increased to point to the next instruction, in preparation for the next instruction cycle.

2. The control unit interprets the instruction stored in its instruction register. The *op-code* (operation code) tells the ALU what is to be done; for example, ADD, LOAD, STORE. This part of the instruction is "stripped off" and sent to the ALU. The *operand address* (the address specified in the instruction) is also stripped off and used by the control unit to fetch the data from memory to be processed by the ALU.

3. The data stored at the operand address is fetched and copied into a register. For example, a LOAD 110 instruction causes the contents of location 110 to be copied into the accumulator.

4. The ALU performs the indicated operation on the data and produces a result. For example, if the operation is ADD, the sum is produced and stored in the accumulator.

5. The control unit repeats the cycle starting with step 1.

Both the program (instructions) and the data (letters, decimal numbers, ages, colors, and so on) are stored in memory as numbers. Whether the CPU interprets a number as a program step or as data depends on what it is expecting. When the ALU needs an instruction, it fetches the contents of the memory address that is supposed to contain the next instruction. It treats whatever number is at that address as an instruction and acts accordingly. If things get fouled up and the ALU interprets a letter as an instruction, the results are just as unpredictable as if you dialed a social security number on the telephone.

Types of Programming Languages

A program that can be loaded into memory and executed immediately is called a *machine language program.* Every computer has its own **machine language**—the set of binary codes that the circuits in the ALU can execute. It is exceedingly tedious to write programs as a series of binary numbers, so no one writes programs in machine language. Instead, programmers write programs in a *programming language,* a human-oriented language for telling the computer what to do. There are hundreds of programming languages, and they differ dramatically.

The programming language that is closest in spirit to machine language is assembly language. In a simple **assembly language** program, each instruction in the program corresponds to an instruction that the circuits of the computer can perform. For example, here is what the program shown in Figure 3.4 might look like as an assembly language program:

```
MOV     110,ACC     'Copy the contents of 110 into the accumulator
ADD     111,ACC     'Add the contents of location 111 to the
                     accumulator
MOV     ACC,110     'Copy the sum in the accumulator to location 110
END                  'Stop this program
```

As you can see, assembly language is a convenient way of expressing machine language. Assembly language provides instructions and addresses with names instead of using binary numbers as in machine language, and it encourages programmers to place comments in the program explaining how the program works.

Before the computer can execute an assembly language program, the program must be translated into machine language. This translation is done by another program called an **assembler,** which accepts an assembly language program as its input and creates an equivalent machine language program as its output. Among other things, the assembler must translate assembly language verbs, such as MOV, into their binary-code equivalents.

Assembly language is considered a *low-level language,* because it requires an intimate knowledge of the computer's inner workings to program in assembly language. Most programmers choose to write programs in a *high-level language,* such as BASIC, COBOL, Pascal, or FORTRAN. High-level languages are easier to understand and produce results more quickly than assembly languages.

EXTERNAL STORAGE

External storage is the place outside the CPU where programs and data are stored when the power is turned off. The most common external storage units are magnetic tapes and disks. External storage has three advantages in all computer systems.

1. Because they do not need a constant supply of power to "refresh" themselves (as most RAM chips do), tapes and disks are *nonvolatile.* This means that the tape or disk can be removed from the computer system, set aside, and used again later. As a result, tapes and disks are used in libraries of information called *archives.* An *archival copy* of information is any information that is set aside for later use. Word processor documents, large databases, and accumulated information are all candidates for archival storage.

2. External memory is *cheaper* per unit of storage than primary memory. A rough rule of thumb is that a tape or removable disk can store 1 million characters per dollar, whereas primary memory can store only 1,000 characters per dollar. Thus, magnetic storage devices are 1,000 times less expensive than electronic memories per stored character.

3. Because of the nonvolatility and low cost of magnetic media, most external storage can be *removed* and replaced with additional media. A disk can be replaced by another disk, thus extending the computer's effective storage capacity. The fact that a disk drive can be replenished with "empty" disks is a major factor in making personal computers useful in the office.

The three most common forms of magnetic media are magnetic tapes, floppy disks, and hard disks. Tapes and disks store information as magnetic spots on magnetic oxide surfaces. A tape or disk drive reads and writes on tapes and disks by moving them past a **read/write head** (see Figure 3.5). The head reads their magnetized surfaces, converting the information into the electrical impulses that it sends to the computer. On a given drive, a magnetic north pole might represent a binary 1, and a magnetic south pole, a binary 0. Hence, magnetic storage devices employ a binary-encoding scheme similar to that used in primary memory.

All of these devices can be erased and recorded on again and again. As new information is written, it automatically overwrites whatever was there before. To avoid accidental erasure, both tapes and floppy disks can be **write-protected.** That is, they can be marked so that you can neither write to nor change any information on them. This is usually accomplished by removing a plastic ring or tab from the tape's reel or case or by covering up a notch on the floppy disk's jacket.

The Computer Itself: The Central Processor and Storage

Although a supercomputer has thousands of times the speed and storage of a personal computer, they both perform four basic functions: input, output, processing, and storage. This photo essay illustrates the processing and storage components of modern computer systems.

1. Row after row of integrated circuits are visible in this view of three circuit boards that form a high-speed graphics processor. The brown connectors on the circuit boards are used to plug the graphics processor into a DEC VAX minicomputer. The graphics processor outperforms a VAX 780 by as much as 50 times for graphics tasks such as rotating a model or changing a perspective.

INSIDE THE SYSTEM UNIT

Personal computers are housed inside a system unit containing a CPU, primary memory, and—in most systems—disk storage.

2.   Inside this Macintosh you can see the CRT in front of a circuit board containing analog electronics. The microfloppy disk drive is a metal box below the CRT. Both the CPU and primary memory are hidden on a digital circuit board below the floppy disk drive.

3.   This early IBM PC has two floppy disk drives. The power supply and fan are housed in the black box at right, and four optional circuit boards are standing at left.

4–5.   At the left is an IBM AT; on the right is a Compac 386. Both have the same basic organization: the disk drives are at the right-front; behind them are the power supply and fan; and on the left is room for optional circuit boards.

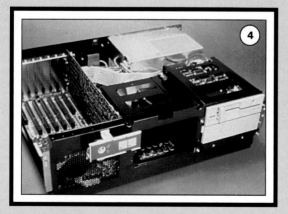

THE SYSTEM BOARD

At the heart of most personal computers is a system board. It is a large flat circuit board that lies across the bottom of the system unit.

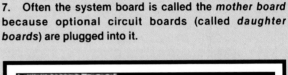

6. The system board of an Apple IIc contains nearly all the electronics for the entire computer.

7. Often the system board is called the *mother board* because optional circuit boards (called *daughter boards*) are plugged into it.

8. The "brain" of many IBM and compatible personal computers is the Intel 80286 microprocessor, the large gray integrated circuit at the center of this photo. Depending on the speed of the computer's clock, its operations are paced at speeds of 6 to 12 million cycles per second. The microprocessor receives and sends data in 2-byte chunks. Theoretically, it can manage 16 megabytes of internal memory, but few machines have that much actual memory.

9. Also on the system board is memory. In this photo the author has removed a 256-kilobit memory chip from an IBM AT-clone. The larger chips to the left are ROM chips containing a portion of the MS-DOS operating system.

EXTERNAL STORAGE

Long-term memory requires some form of external storage. The most common external storage devices are floppy and hard disk drives.

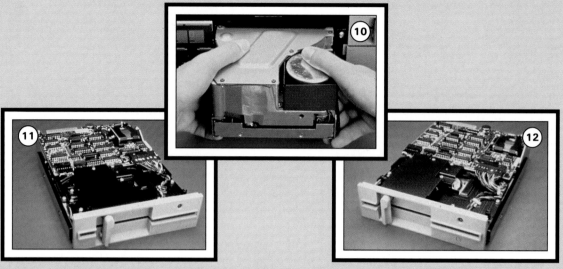

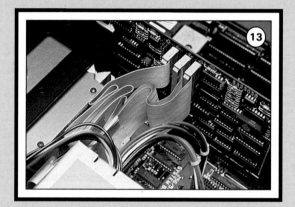

10–12.   Here are three types of external storage. On the top is a 20MB (megabyte) hard disk; on the bottom are 1.2MB and 360KB floppy disk drives. Both floppy disk drives look identical from the front.

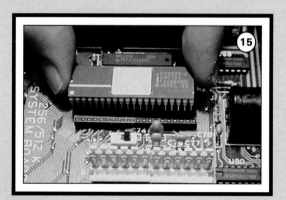

13.   The blue ribbon cables of this IBM AT connect the disk drives to a disk-controller circuit board, which in turn plugs into the system board.

14.   This shows the installation of a 40MB hard disk drive. It stores the equivalent of about 13,000 pages of single-spaced typed text.

15.   An optional math coprocessor is installed in an IBM AT by pushing it into an empty socket on the system board. For programs that perform extensive mathematical operations, this can increase the processor's speed by a factor of ten or more.

ADDING OPTIONS

The basic capabilities of a personal computer can often be expanded by adding chips or circuit boards.

16.   The yellow arrow points to a circuit board that provides two interfaces (or *ports*) for controlling peripheral devices such as printers, plotters, monitors, or mice.

17.   The capabilities of most computers can be increased by shoving optional circuit boards into *expansion slots*. This photo shows the addition of a multifunction board that provides an additional megabyte of memory and several interface ports.

18.   This rear view of the IBM AT-clone shows eight expansion slots filled with four cards: a disk-controller card, an EGA (enhanced graphics adapter) display card, a multifunction card with memory and two interface ports, and a mouse-controller card. The three gray cables lead to a color display, a laser printer, and a mouse.

DISK STORAGE

Storage on disks provides fast and reliable access to large quantities of data.

20. Even a tiny particle of dust can scratch the surface of a spinning hard disk, so manufacturing is done in ''clean rooms'' to reduce the number of airborne particles.

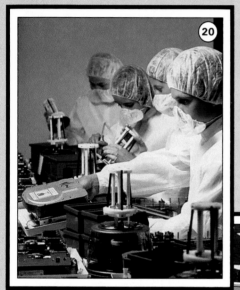

19. Hard disks store data on rapidly spinning metal platters that are coated with magnetic oxides. Each platter is polished to a mirror finish to provide a uniform surface for extremely dense storage of data.

21. Large-capacity hard disks are created by stacking a number of disk platters into one disk drive assembly, called a disk pack. The read/write heads of the disk drive move in and out between the disk platters, storing data on both sides of most platters.

22. A disk drive assembly is loaded with contamination-free precision by a special-function industrial robot.

24. In this photo an IBM 3380 disk drive is being assembled in Vimercate, Italy. Model 3380 disk drives are among the most powerful of IBM's disk drives. Each 3380 disk pack can store 2.5 gigabytes (a gigabyte is roughly one billion characters) and has a data transfer rate of 3MB per second.

23. These 5 1/4-inch hard disk drives fit in the same space as a standard 5 1/4-inch floppy disk drive and feature from 20 to 40MB of storage, a data transfer rate that exceeds 1/2MB per second, and an average access time of 40 milliseconds (less than 1/20th of a second).

25. A disk pack is inserted in a disk drive. Removable disk drives are slightly more expensive and are more likely to be damaged by dust particles than fixed disks. In a fixed disk the disk platters are permanently sealed inside a housing at the factory. The obvious advantage of a removable disk drive is that more than one disk pack can be purchased for each drive, enabling data to be stored inexpensively on off-line disk packs.

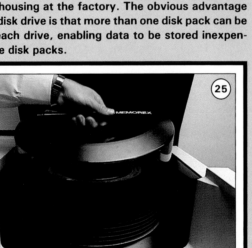

26. Optical disks hold the promise of providing very large amounts of storage. For example, this removable 12-inch disk can record 1.2 gigabytes (1,200 megabytes) per side. Over 140 of these cartridges can be mounted in a jukebox system, replacing roughly five million pages of data that would fill more than 500 4-drawer file cabinets.

window 2

TAPE STORAGE

28. Increasingly, mainframe computer centers are switching to magnetic tape cartridges, which are easier to load and require less storage space.

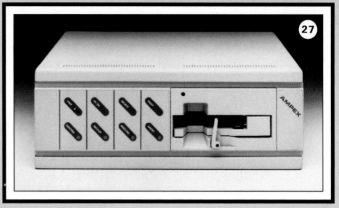

27. This small storage unit is designed for personal computer systems. It combines a 20MB fixed disk with a 25MB tape drive for backing-up the fixed disk. The tape drive accepts 1/4-inch tape cartridges and can find any file on the tape in 92 seconds.

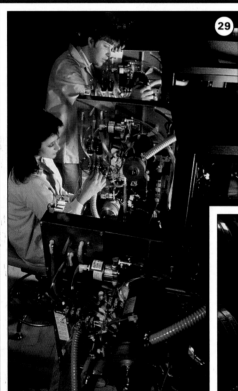

29. Large commercial tape drives use vacuum systems to start and stop loops of tape quickly without placing excessive stress on the tape. Here, data cables are being attached to tape drives made by Storage Technology Corporation.

30. Magnetic tape is an excellent medium for inexpensive, long-term data storage. Because tapes provide sequential data storage, they are rarely used when data is being processed. Instead, they are used to back-up hard disks and to store infrequently used data.

Figure 3.5 When a tape containing magnetic spots moves through an electrical field, a 1 or a 0 is sensed by the read/write head. A 1 or a 0 is written on the tape by energizing the electromagnetic field to induce a charge (1) or not (0).

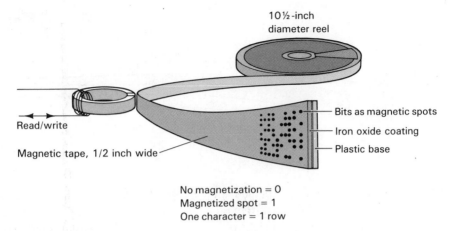

10½-inch
diameter reel

Bits as magnetic spots

Iron oxide coating

Read/write

Plastic base

Magnetic tape, 1/2 inch wide

No magnetization = 0
Magnetized spot = 1
One character = 1 row

Tape recorders and floppy disk drives will not write on write-protected media. Most hard disks cannot be write-protected.

Tapes

Computer information is stored on tapes very similar to the tapes used to store stereo music at home, but information is stored on them differently. Your home stereo tapes probably store music as a continuous signal, much like the continuous stream of water from a kitchen tap. The information stored on a computer tape is **digitized**, so that it can be processed by the computer; each piece of information is a bit whose value is either a 0 or a 1.

Tape density is measured by the number of bits per inch (bpi) recorded on the tape. Mainframes typically use 1,600-bpi tapes, but some tapes store 6,250 characters per inch or more. Since typical reel-to-reel tapes are 2,400 feet long, a 1,600-bpi tape can store approximately $2,400 \times 12 \times 1,600 = 46$ million characters of information. Most mainframe computer tapes are $\frac{1}{2}$ inch wide and 400 to 3,200 feet in length. Microcomputer systems tend to use cartridge tapes that are $\frac{1}{4}$ inch wide.

The bits on a tape are typically arranged in 9-bit bytes across the width of the tape. The extra, ninth bit, called a **parity bit**, is used to detect and correct single-bit errors. The bytes recorded on tape are grouped together to form **fields**, as shown in Figure 3.6. Furthermore, groups of related fields are combined into **records.** For example, all fields pertaining to customer Jim Smyth of Portland constitute a single record.

Tapes provide **sequential storage**; that is, information is recorded in se-

Figure 3.6 Tapes are sequential storage media because information is stored as a series of records. To get to any one record, the computer must read the tape from the beginning record up to the one desired.

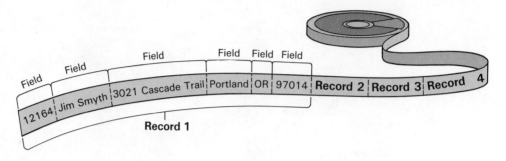

quence, one record behind another. As a result, reading and writing from tapes is slow. To read the last item on a tape, you must wind the tape past all the previous items. The time it takes to begin reading the desired information from a storage device is called the device's **access time**. The rate at which data are read once information transfer has begun is the **data transfer rate**. Typical mainframe tapes move at speeds ranging from 25 to 200 inches per second. Thus, a tape running at 200 inches per second transfers data at $200 \times 1,600 = 320,000$ characters per second. This may sound fast, but compared with a disk drive, tapes are slow.

Despite their slow performance, tapes have several uses. Because tape has been around since the earliest days of modern computing, almost every mainframe and minicomputer can read $\frac{1}{2}$-inch reel-to-reel tapes produced by any other computer. Hence, tapes are used for exchanging and coverting information. In mainframe computer centers, the low cost of tape makes it a good medium for the long-term storage of large quantities of data. For example, the social security files, income tax returns, and census data kept by the U.S. government are all stored on tape. The most frequent use of tape is for archival storage of infrequently used data in tape libraries. In minicomputer operations, tapes are used to transfer information from one site to another. A 40-megabyte file can be stored cheaply on a single reel of tape and sent across the country by postal delivery for a few dollars. Electronic transmission of 40 megabytes of data would take about a day on a common telephone line and cost $500 for the phone call. Tapes are also useful if you are using a microcomputer with a hard disk drive. Small, high-speed **streaming tape drives** using $\frac{1}{4}$-inch cartridge tapes can make backup copies of the hard disk. If the hard disk fails, thousands of records of information can be lost; backing up the hard disk with streamer tapes can save many days of anguish.

Disks and Disk Drives

A *disk drive* is a mechanical device that converts magnetic spots on the surface of a magnetic disk into electrical signals understandable to a computer. Since mag-

TAKING CARE OF MAGNETIC MEDIA

You need to follow some simple precautionary rules whenever you use tapes or disks, because magnetic media are not as reliable as paper-based storage. It is difficult to erase all the writing from a piece of paper, but a magnetic disk can be erased by any strong magnetic field.

Your first line of defense against accidental erasure of magnetic media should be to take good care of tapes and disks. Treat them as you would treat yourself. Avoid extreme temperatures and dusty or dirty environments. Don't let anything touch the recording surface, including your fingers, which deposit an oily film on everything they contact. Be very cautious near electrical devices. Tapes can lose information if they are placed above the motors in a tape drive. The ringer in a telephone can create a strong enough magnetic field to erase data from floppy disks under the phone.

But the most important rule—one that should be followed religiously—is to keep two copies of any information you don't want to lose. Then if one of the copies turns out to be unusable, you still have a duplicate, a **backup copy**.

Backing up a floppy disk is more convenient if you have two disk drives. You place the original disk in one drive, the back-up disk in the other, and give a COPY command, which completes the process in one step. Backing-up a floppy disk on a single drive system is more complicated. You swap the original and back-up disks in and out of the drive while the CPU copies portions of the original disk into RAM and then writes them on the back-up disk. Eventually the computer will tell you that the copy has been made, but this might be after eight or ten swaps. The number of swaps depends primarily on the relative sizes of RAM and the disks.

Backing up a hard disk is both more important and more difficult because of its larger storage capacity. The cheapest back-up method is to copy the contents of the hard disk onto floppy disks. This is slow and uses up many floppy disks. For example, a 40MB hard disk holds the same amount of information as thirty-four 1.2MB floppies. One back-up method is to buy two hard disk units. Another solution is to buy a streaming tape drive, a cartridge tape system especially designed to back-up and restsore the information on hard disks.

netic fields must be in motion before they can be sensed by the drive, magnetic disks must rotate. The floppy disks in microcomputers rotate at 300 rpm (rotations per minute); hard disks typically rotate at 3,600 rpm. Disk drives are therefore subject to wear and tear. In fact, the most common failures in computer systems occur in mechanical devices, such as keyboards, printers, and disk drives.

Figure 3.7 shows how information is organized on a magnetic disk. Think of each disk as a collection of short tapes, with each tape corresponding to a concentric arc on the disk. In Figure 3.7, a **track** is equivalent to one imaginary short tape. Each track is in turn divided into pie-shaped wedges called **sectors**, so that the disk drive can quickly access a piece of the track. When information is requested of the disk drive, the rotating disk first positions the requested sector un-

Figure 3.7 Organization of a disk. A *track* is one complete rotation of the disk. A *sector* is a piece of a track. Each sector stores a fixed number of bytes.

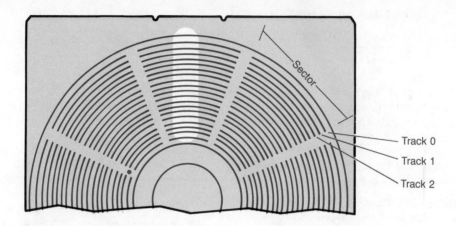

der the read/write head; then the information from that sector is copied into main memory. The smallest amount of *accessible information* on a disk is the sector.

Each sector contains a fixed number of bytes—typically 256 bytes for a floppy disk and up to 8,000 bytes for a mainframe disk. These bytes are encoded in the binary number system, just as if they were in main memory. When converted into electrical signals, they represent a group of eight 0 or 1 bits.

Floppy Disks

The most common external storage device for personal computers is the floppy disk drive. It reads magnetic spots from the surface of a rotating circular magnetic disk sealed inside a square jacket, as shown in Figure 3.8(a). The disk is called a **floppy disk** because it has a flexible base, made of Mylar (plastic). This base supports the magnetic oxide recording surface. Unless ·a floppy disk is encased in a hard plastic protective shell, it can be bent (mildly!) without damage.

Unlike tape devices, floppy disk systems are random-access storage devices. (Recall that a random-access device is any storage device that can retrieve information in roughly the same amount of time, no matter where that information is stored on the device.) The read/write heads of floppy disk drives can move in and out to quickly access a sector of information on any part of the disk, as shown in Figure 3.8(b). Because of this, disks are preferred over tapes, even though they are more expensive.

In several ways, floppy disk systems are like stereo record players. In both systems, a mechanical arm rubs against the disk in order to sense the information recorded on the surface of the disk. But the analogy breaks down quickly. Floppy disks store data in concentric tracks; records store songs in spiral grooves. The pickup arm of a record player is guided by the groove in a record, but the read/ write head of a floppy disk unit must be positioned over a magnetic track on a smooth recording surface. The difficulty of actively locating a narrow magnetic

Figure 3.8 (a) Floppy disks are low-cost, low-density storage media for microcomputers. (b) Reading and writing from a floppy disk is done by a drive. It holds the floppy in place, spins the disk inside the protective jacket, and either records or senses the magnetic spots on the surface of the disk.

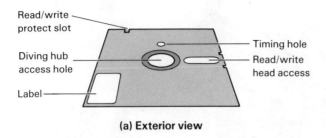

(a) Exterior view

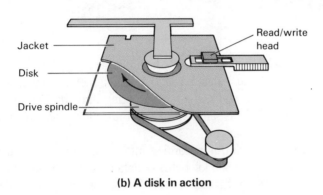

(b) A disk in action

track rather than passively following a physical groove is the major reason why floppy disk drives cost more than record players. Furthermore, record players are read-only devices; you cannot use them to add information to a record. Floppy disk drives are true input/output units: you can write information on the disk, or you can read from it.

Floppy disks come in three standard sizes—8-inch, $5\frac{1}{4}$-inch and $3\frac{1}{2}$-inch—as well as several less popular sizes. IBM developed the original 8-inch floppy disks to load test programs into their mainframe computers. Soon the disks became popular among users of small business computers, because floppy disk drives cost less than hard disk drives. The 8-inch size is still used, mainly for office computers. Improvements in manufacturing techniques led to the availability of $5\frac{1}{4}$-inch disks— sometimes called *minifloppy disks*—with almost the same storage capacity and reliability as 8-inch disks. A majority of the disks in use today are $5\frac{1}{4}$-inch disks. Both 8-inch and $5\frac{1}{4}$-inch disks are wrapped in a stiff cardboard envelope to protect the disk from dirt, body oils, and scratches. An oval slot in the envelope leaves some of the recording surface exposed, allowing the read/write head of the disk drive to get to the recording surface.

Figure 3.9 compares a $5\frac{1}{4}$-inch minifloppy with a $3\frac{1}{2}$-inch disk, which is some-

times called a *microfloppy disk*. Each 3$\frac{1}{2}$-inch disk is housed in a rigid plastic shell and can be carried safely in a shirt pocket. A sliding metal cover protects the read/write slot. These 3$\frac{1}{2}$-inch disks are rapidly eating into the market for minifloppy disks, because they offer the same storage but are more convenient and use drive units that are only half as large.

There are few standards for recording information on floppy disks. One personal computer might store 800 kilobytes of data on a disk, whereas another might store only 270 kilobytes on the same disk. Of course, there is also a lack of standards for typing on paper. The number of lines of text per page, the size of the type, and whether text is typed on both sides of the page depend on the typist and the typewriter, not on the paper. But whereas humans can easily read text in a wide variety of formats, personal computers are less flexible. Although sometimes you can purchase special programs that will translate between formats, microcomputers normally read and write disks in only one format.

Floppy disks can be removed and stored for later use. You can purchase as many floppy disks as it takes to store your information, keeping in mind that only one disk can be **on-line** (connected to the CPU) per disk drive.

Hard Disks

Hard disks use rigid aluminum platters to support a highly polished, magnetic oxide recording surface. Like a floppy disk system, a hard disk system is a random-access storage device. Hard disks were invented before floppy disks, however. Since the 1960s, they have been the primary external storage device for large computers. During this time, their size has shrunk, their price has dropped, the denisty of data stored has grown, and they have become more reliable. Hard disk prices are constantly falling; in 1985 hard disks cost about one dollar for each 20,000 characters of storage. Figure 3.10 compares an obsolete hard disk platter with a more recent hard disk drive.

Figure 3.10 Hard disks. The obsolete hard disk platter on the left is now used as a coffee table. On the right is a modern hard disk drive, which is the size of a standard $5\frac{1}{4}$-inch floppy disk drive. It stores 760 megabytes of information—over 100 times the capacity of the obsolete platter on the left.

 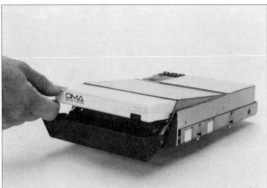

Modern hard disks for mainframes and minicomputers store much more information than floppy disks can. The hard disk units used by mainframe computers can store gigabytes; the hard disks attached to personal computers store between 10 and 200 megabytes. Hard disk systems achieve their large storage capacities in two ways. The principal reason is that they are *denser,* that is, they pack more information per square inch. They can do so because aluminum platters are less sensitive than Mylar disks to variations in temperature, humidity, and mechanical stress. This allows the hard disk to have more tracks per radial inch and to write more bits per inch along each track. Another method of packing more information into a hard disk system is to employ more recording surfaces by stacking a number of platters on top of each other, as shown in Figure 3.11. Instead of reading from only 1 track at a time, a multiple-platter hard disk drive can read from 20 tracks. When multiple tracks are stacked one above the other, as shown in Figure 3.11, we call the collection of tracks a *cylinder.*

Hard disks have another advantage: they transfer data faster than floppy disks, for two reasons. First, because they store data more compactly along each track, every revolution of the disk brings more data beneath the read/write heads. Second, hard disks spin faster than floppy disks. The standard speed for $5\frac{1}{4}$-inch floppy disks is 300 rpm. But a $5\frac{1}{4}$-inch hard disk is likely to rotate at least ten times faster, from 3,000 to 5,000 rpm.

The fast spinning of a hard disk makes the environment inside a hard disk drive very windy. The read/write heads are carefully shaped to use the wind in order to float on a cushion of air a few thousandths of an inch above the disk. Maintaining this air gap is important. At 3,000 rpm (approximately 200 mph at the edge) a read/write head in contact with the disk platter would soon become hot and scorch both itself and the platter. Although this doesn't happen often, it happens often

Figure 3.11 (a) Hard disks contain many recording surfaces to increase recording capacity. (b) Mainframe disk drives access entire cylinders of information at a time. (c) Alternatively, a stack of sectors can be accessed by moving a read/write head across all surfaces simultaneously.

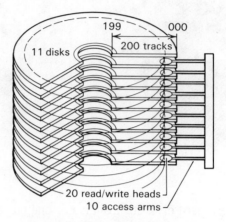

(a) Multiple-platter disk drive

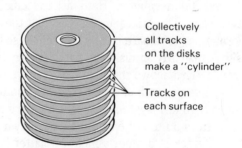

(b) Cylinder organization

(c) Sector organization

enough to have a name: **head crash**. After a head crash, all data on the disk is lost, and the disk drive must be sent back to the factory for extensive repair.

Access times are also faster for hard disks than for floppy disks. Whenever a computer is operating, its hard disk is spinning. This keeps the disk heads floating properly and means that there is no need to wait for the disk to come up to speed. Floppy disks can't afford to turn constantly, because their disk heads rub against the recording surface whenever the disk is turning. Floppy disks have roughly an 80-hour expected life of turning time. This is adequate, as long as the disk is turning only while reading or writing, but it isn't long enough to allow continual rotation. It takes about half a second to bring a floppy disk up to operating speed.

Some hard disk drives accept **removable disk** cartridges called **disk packs**, which are similar to floppy disks. Changing hard disk cartridges takes longer than changing floppy disks, because removable hard disk drives go through an air filtration cycle before beginning operation. Other hard disks called **fixed disks** are built with the disk platter permanently mounted inside an airtight, factory-sealed unit. Fixed disks don't need an air filtration system because there is no way for dirty air to get in. But fixed disks also have a disadvantage. Once a fixed disk becomes full of information, old data must be deleted before new data can be stored.

In short, hard disks offer several advantages over floppy disks. A small hard disk stores 10 megabytes. This is enough space to store 200 useful programs and still leave enough room for the equivalent of several thousand pages of typed text. Every piece of information in the disk is available in an instant; access times are less than one-tenth of a second.

Hard disks also have several disadvantages. Hard disk drives tend to be noisier than floppy disk drives because of their constant, high-speed spinning. More important, though, is their sensitivity. Head crashes can be caused by a bent disk, by dust or cigarette smoke inside the drive, or by a good thump to the side of the drive. Because hard disks operate on extremely precise mechanical tolerances, they are more sensitive to shock than floppy disks. This has retarded their use in portable computers. It is not a good idea to bounce any disk drive on a table, but the consequences can be disastrous if you're using a hard disk.

Disk Storage

The amount of information stored on a disk depends on four factors.

1. The number of tracks (concentric circles) of data from the inside to the outside edge of the disk. Generally, there are between 40 and 80 tracks on a floppy and 200 to 500 on a hard disk.

2. The number of sectors per track. Recall that a sector is the smallest unit of information sent between the disk drive and the CPU.

3. The number of bytes stored in each sector. Generally, disks for microcomputers store between 128 and 512 bytes per sector; disks for large computers, up to 8,000. Double-density disks store twice as many bytes in the same-size sector as single-density disks.

4. Whether data are written on one or both sides of the disk; that is, whether storage is *single-* or *double-sided.* As we have seen, in large systems, multiple platters are used to extend the capacity of a single drive.

For example, the Apple Macintosh records 80 tracks on each side of a double-sided microfloppy disk. Each track has an average of ten sectors; each sector stores 512 bytes. This gives $80 \times 10 \times 512 \times 2 = 819,200$ bytes, or 800KB per disk.

Because the tracks on the outer edge of a disk are longer, the outside sectors of most disks provide the safest storage. Read errors usually occur while reading data stored on the inside tracks, where each sector is shorter. The Macintosh, however, cuts the outside tracks into more sectors than the inside tracks, making each sector approximately the same length. This allows the Macintosh to make better use of a disk's recording capability.

It is easy to get carried away with the technical details of how information is stored on disks. Just as you don't have to know much about a record to play it, you don't have to know much about a disk to store information on it. Your computer automatically handles the details of storing your information, determining which tracks and sectors to use. When the disk becomes full, the computer will not allow you to store new information until you delete some old information. You should know the storage capacity of each disk, but it is not as important to know how this figure relates to tracks and sectors. It is useful, however, to know how the information stored on a disk or tape is organized.

File Storage

The organization of information on a disk can affect how long it takes a computer to retrieve information and how much room it takes to store a file. In this section, we will give a brief introduction to the terminology used to describe file structures.

A **file** is a collection of related records stored on a tape or a disk. Recall from our previous discussion that a record is made up of fields, fields are composed of bytes, and bytes are composed of bits. We need not be concerned about the underlying structure of a file—only that it is composed of records. Think of a disk as a filing cabinet drawer full of manila folders (files), each of which contains records in the form of sheets of paper.

A disk or tape stores many files; thus, a special **directory** file is kept on each disk or tape to keep track of all other files. A directory is like a telephone book; it contains the name and number of every file on the disk. A *file name* is any string of characters assigned to a file, such as PAYROLL.DAT, WORD.HLP, or MYPROG.BAS. The name uniquely identifies each file; it is used by an application program to locate, open, read or write to, and close a file. The *file number* identifies its physical location on the disk; we can let the computer take care of the number and not be concerned with it. Most computer systems employ a *hierarchical directory,* which means that a treelike structure containing many subdirectories is used in place of a single directory. The *root directory* contains the names of files

Optical disks may eventually push hard disks into museums along with 78-rpm phonograph records and buggy whips. But it seems more likely that magnetic storage will continue to dominate, leaving optical storage with applications that require rapid access to large-scale databases made up of permanent or historical records.

Optical disks store large amounts of information on rigid plastic disks that are removable like floppy disks. They use the same laser-based technology as audio *compact disc* (CD) players, which debuted in 1983 and already have higher sales than turntables. An incredible 550 MB of information fits on one side of a CD disc. With the appropriate interface any personal computer can read the digital signals on a CD disc. High-volume production techniques allow many copies of a master disk to be made for less than 5 dollars a copy. This provides a low-cost solution to massive data storage needs, but its usefulness is restricted because the contents of a standard CD disc cannot be altered. For this reason, read-only optical disks are called **CD ROM discs**. The main advantage of CD ROM drives is that they are inexpensive to build because of the vast market for audio CD players. CD ROM drives sell for less than $800, and their price is likely to fall rapidly.

One of the first general applications of CD ROM technology is Microsoft Bookshelf, a $295 disk containing a collection of 10 reference works. The disk offers a potpourri of writer's productivity tools, including complete copies of the *1987 World Almanac and Book of Facts*, the *Chicago Manual of Style, Bartlett's Familiar Quotations,* and the *U.S. Zip Code Directory.* Included with the CD ROM disk is software that allows the disk to work conveniently with a variety of word processing programs.

Some optical disk drives can write on the disk by burning small marks on its surface with a laser. Later, these marks can be sensed by another, lower-power laser. The drives and disks are thus called *write-once read-many* or WORM drives. Although they aren't yet practical for temporary storage of data that must be altered frequently, the drives provide a reliable way to back up hard disks. They also appeal to business users who want to maintain an audit trail of the activity in a computer system: it isn't possible to erase information from a WORM drive.

A $5\frac{1}{4}$-inch optical disk can store from 200 to 800 megabytes of information—about 500 times the amount of information of a similar-sized floppy disk. Larger optical disks have capacities up to 4 gigabytes (4,000 megabytes). Like floppy disks, optical disks are removable and interchangeable. This makes it practical to distribute copies of large databases. For example, a large firm might distribute optical disks containing the firm's parts catalog to branch offices. Each branch office would then have instant access to complete information about the firm's products and prices without having to search through reams of paper or peer at microfiche. In this application the nonerasable nature of the media is an advantage.

and other subdirectories, much as one file folder can be used to group other file folders together. Each *subdirectory* in turn contains the names of files or more subdirectories.

There are different types of files, just as there are different kinds of information. Some files hold text, as in a word processing document, and others hold numbers, pictures, or programs. If a file contains a program, we call it a *binary file,* because programs contain binary information understandable to the hardware. If a file contains pure text, we call it a *text file,* and so forth.

Files can also be categorized according to how their records are accessed (see Figure 3.12). A **sequential file** contains records that can be accessed only as if they were on tape—sequentially. The major advantage of a sequential file is that the records can be of differing lengths. A **direct-access file** contains records that can be accessed directly, without reading all intervening records in the file. Direct-access files must be stored on direct-access devices, such as disks. Obviously, the main advantage of a direct-access file is its access speed. The major disadvantage of a direct-access file is that it cannot store variable-length records. An **indexed file** is actually two or more direct-access files. One file contains the data, and one or more other files contain indexes to the data file (see Figure 3.12). The indexes are used like the index in a book: values called *access keys* are taken from the data file and placed in the indexes in ascending order. Data are retrieved by first consulting the appropriate index; then the "page number" from the index is used to find the desired record in the data file. Indexed files are flexible. Records can be retrieved in a certain order without having to sort them. New information is entered, old information is deleted, and information is retrieved according to its content rather than its position within the data file. Compared to a simple direct-access file, an indexed file requires more disk space (to store the indexes) and takes more processing steps to store data.

Figure 3.12 (a) With a sequential file, access is slow, because intermediate records must be read in order to access a certain record. (b) Direct-access files permit fast access, because intermediate records can be skipped in order to get to a certain record. (c) Indexed files provide flexible access, because records can be retrieved in ascending order by first looking up field values in an index file.

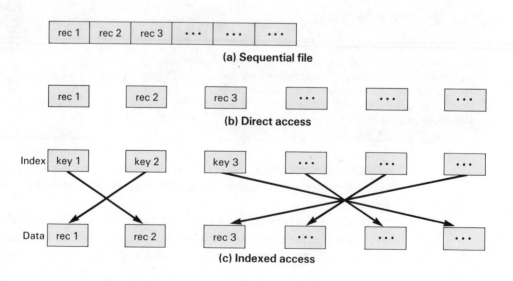

(a) Sequential file

(b) Direct access

(c) Indexed access

Software developers agonize over the selection of a file structure because of the tradeoffs among speed, storage overhead, and flexibility. Sequential files are good for storing text to be sent to another computer by telephone, for programs to be read into memory, or for text created by a word processor. Direct-access files are good for storing frequently accessed and updated information like that found in a data management system or business application. Indexed files are used in a variety of applications ranging from database management systems to accounting applications.

A COMPARISON OF MEMORY SYSTEMS

No one would put up with the slow speed of external storage if primary memory were nonvolatile, removable, and cheap. But, as Table 3.1 shows, each system has its relative merits. Most computer systems, particularly large ones, combine several storage methods in an attempt to blend the best features from each technology.

Examine Table 3.1 carefully. There is an extraordinary range of speeds and costs. Access times and transfer rates vary by many powers of ten. For example, the difference in access time between a floppy disk drive and main memory is greater than the difference in speed between a slug and a jet airplane.

Compare the cost of the access mechanisms with the cost of the removable recording media. The one-time cost of a removable hard disk drive may deter you from buying one, even though each disk pack is relatively inexpensive per unit of storage. Floppy disk drives are ten times more expensive to purchase per byte of on-line storage than the disk drives used by mainframes. But a floppy drive serves the need for a low-cost, direct-access, removable storage device, regardless of its cost per byte.

Numerous storage methods have been developed to serve a special need or to fill a niche of price and performance. For example, a **mass storage unit** is a giant-capacity storage peripheral that uses large numbers of tape cartridges, a jukeboxlike tape-loading mechanism, a hard disk drive, and an intelligent controller to manage many gigabytes of on-line storage. Rapid changes in storage technology are expected to continue.

SUMMARY

All computers—from hand-held models to huge mainframes—have the same functional organization. The four functional units are: the CPU with its primary memory, external storage, input units, and output units. We have discussed the CPU, primary memory, and external storage in this chapter. Input and output units will be discussed in the next chapter.

The CPU has a control unit that supervises the rest of the CPU, including an arithmetic/logic unit that does all calculations and data manipulation. Instructions

Table 3.1 A Comparison of Memory Storage Methods

Storage Type	Access Mechanism		
	Type	*Access Time*	*Cost of Drive ($)*
Microcomputers			
RAM/ROM chips	Random	200 ns	500/MB
3 1/2-inch microfloppy	Direct	0.2–.4 sec	100–400
5 1/4-inch floppy	Direct	0.2–.4 sec	50–200
Cartridge hard disk	Direct	40–90 ms	800–2,000
Fixed disk	Direct	20–90 ms	300–5,000
Streamer tape	Sequential	About 1 min	500–2,000
Optical disk (WORM)	Direct	0.2 sec	1,600–4,000
Optical disk (CD-ROM)	Direct	0.4 sec	500–900
Minis and Mainframes			
RAM/ROM chips	Random	10–150 ns	2,000–10,000/MB
Removable disk	Direct	25 ms	5,000–35,000
Fixed disk	Direct	25 ms	15,000–40,000
Mass storage unit	Combined	1–6 sec	500,000–1,000,000
Tape	Sequential	About 1 min	5,000–20,000

Notes: KB = kilobyte   min = minutes
           MB = megabyte   sec = seconds
           GB = gigabyte   ms = millisecond (thousandth of a second)
                              ns = nanosecond (billionth of a second)

from a stored program are copied from primary memory into the control unit, where they guide the operations of the hardware. For personal computers, the CPU consists of a microprocessor, memory chips, and some timing and support chips, all of which are usually mounted on one circuit board. Personal computers can do the same things larger computers are capable of doing, but they are much slower and can store less information.

The binary instructions a computer can execute are written in machine language. Programmers don't write in machine language; instead, the programs they write are translated into machine language by other programs called assemblers, compilers, or interpreters. Assembly language is fairly close in spirit to machine language and is used for programs that must be exceptionally fast or compact. But most programming is done in high-level languages, such as Basic or Cobol, because they are easier to understand and offer more powerful instructions.

For fast, cheap access to large amounts of information, on-line external storage devices are needed. Direct-access storage devices, such as hard and floppy disk drives, provide fast access to any data they contain. Long-term storage of archival information is achieved by sequential-access, low-cost, permanent media, such as magnetic tape.

Information in external storage is organized in named units called files. To help keep all of the files on a hard disk organized, files can be grouped together in mas-

Table 3.1 continued

		Media		
Capacity	Transfer Rate/Second	Cost of Media ($)	Volatile?	Principal Use
64KB–4MB	1MB–5MB	–	Yes	Mainmemory
400KB–1.6MB	30KB	1–5	No	On-line/archive
400KB–2MB	30KB	1–3	No	On-line/archive
10MB–40MB	0.4MB	90	No	On-line/archive
10MB–200MB	0.4MB–1MB	–	No	On-line
20MB–500MB	60KB	20	No	Back-up/archive
200MB–800MB	0.2MB	50–100	No	On-line/Archive
.5GB–4GB	0.2MB	20	No	On-line ROM
1MB–64MB	4MB–64MB	–	Yes	Mainmemory
100MB–500MB	1MB–3MB	0.5K–1K	No	On-line/archive
0.5GB–5GB	2MB–4MB	–	No	On-line
0.5GB–5GB	3MB	10	No	On-line/archive
100MB–500MB	0.05MB–1MB	10	No	Archive

ter files called directories. Sequential, random, and indexed files use different methods of organizing the information they contain. Each method involves various tradeoffs among storage size, retrieval time, and access flexibility.

Although the range of costs and capacities of external storage devices for mainframe computers overlaps with that of devices for minis and microcomputers, generally there is a hundred- to thousandfold difference in capacity between the two forms of computing.

KEY TERMS

access time	disk pack
accumulator	external storage
address	field
assembler	file
assembly language	fixed disk
backup copy	floppy disk
clock rate	gigabyte
data transfer rate	hard disk
digitize	head crash
direct-access file	indexed file
directory	instruction register

integrated circuit

kilobit

kilobyte (KB)

machine language

mass storage unit

megabyte (MB)

megahertz (MHz)

memory chip

on-line

parity bit

pipelining

program counter

program overlay

random access

read/write head

record

removable disk

sector

sequential file

sequential storage

streaming tape drive

track

transparent

virtual memory

write-protect

DISCUSSION QUESTIONS

1. What is the difference (if any) between a CPU and a microprocessor?

2. Why are there relatively few kinds of microprocessors?

3. What determines the speed of a CPU? Under what circumstances can you say that one CPU is faster than another?

4. Each word of a personal computer's memory is of limited size—8, 16, or 32 bits, depending on the computer. How can a computer represent very large and very small numbers in such small words?

5. Would it make sense to have WOM, write-only memory?

6. When a computer is first turned on, what causes the CPU to transfer a program from a disk into main memory?

7. How does a computer determine whether the contents of a memory word are an instruction or data, such as a number or a letter?

8. Suppose a memory location contains the binary equivalent of the decimal number 66. What might the 66 represent?

9. In truly random-access memory, each word of memory can be located in exactly the same length of time. Is this true for floppy and hard disks? for internal memory?

10. Why is a hard disk drive faster and why does it hold more information than a floppy?

11. What causes a head crash?

12. Compare a disk with a book. What part of a book is analogous to the disk's directory? to the disk's files?

13. What are the relative advantages of sequential versus direct-access file structures?

EXERCISES

1. Look in a reference manual for a microprocessor to find the relative speeds for the various operations for arithmetic and data movement. How much faster is addition than division?

2. Look up the memory size of your personal computer (or any personal computer, if you do not have one) and the memory requirements of some popular application programs.

3. A record player is a read-only device. List some other read-only or write-only devices in your home.

4. Find the number of tracks, the sector size, and the density for the floppy disks on your personal computer. How many bytes of data can be stored on each disk?

5. What is a cylinder? List the reasons why mainframe disks are faster and able to store more information than microcomputer disks.

4 Input and Output

I nput and output devices are the eyes, ears, arms, legs, and mouth of a computer. They allow the computer to communicate and interact with its environment. Without them, computers would be useless.

Input devices are conversion machines that translate information in the computer's environment into digital signals, through a process called *digitizing*. One frequently digitized event is the movement of a key on a keyboard, but the arrival of radio waves at a satellite receiver and the vibration of air pressure at a microphone can also be digitized. In fact, anything that can be sensed electronically is a candidate for computer input. Some input devices convert spoken words into electrical signals so that a computer can "hear"; other devices allow a computer to "see" by converting printed text into electrical signals. These devices are sometimes as sophisticated and cleverly designed as the computer systems they serve. For automobiles, a steering wheel has been found to be the best "input device," but computers use a variety of input devices, including keyboards, light pens, mice, character recognition devices, voice recognition devices, and the infrared sensor in the nose of a heat-seeking missile.

Output devices are also conversion machines, but they convert digital signals into actions. For example, printers accept digital signals and convert them into the placement of ink on paper. Output devices range from printers, plotters, display screens, telephones, and speech synthesizers to the warhead in a missile.

It is important to choose the right I/O device for the task at hand and to use it correctly. This chapter deals with the input and output devices you are most likely to use, giving you the information necessary to do so successfully.

INPUT DEVICES

Keyboards

By far the most common input device is the **keyboard**. This typewriterlike device is standard equipment on virtually every microcomputer and mainframe terminal. Except for specialized applications, such as drawing pictures or pointing at objects on the screen, the keyboard reigns supreme as the primary way to communicate with computers (see Figure 4.1). In the future, keyboards are likely to be replaced by microphones attached to speech recognition units, enabling you to talk to computers (see Figure 4.2). But today, if you want to use a computer effectively, you must have a basic level of skill at keyboard manipulation.

Figure 4.1 Keyboard with separate cursor-movement and numeric keys.

Figure 4.2 This keyboard includes a voice recognition unit that is limited to a vocabulary with at most 160 words. The operator speaks into the microphone, and a processor inside the keyboard analyzes the spoken sounds. Eventually each spoken word is converted into a keystroke or series of keystrokes.

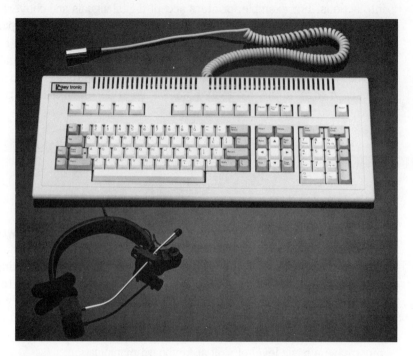

Types of Keyboards

A poor keyboard can make an otherwise reasonable computer hard to deal with. The cheapest keyboards, called **membrane keyboards**, have pictures of keytops drawn on a flat plastic membrane. They rely on pressure to register each keystroke, and they vary widely in sensitivity. On the most sensitive membrane keyboards, you can't rest your fingers lightly on the keys; instead, your fingers must hover over the keyboard. On less sensitive models, it is very difficult to tell when enough pressure has been applied to generate a keystroke. In short, membrane keyboards aren't suitable for extensive typing.

Portable terminals and personal computers often have **compact keyboards**; they have less than full-size keys or reduced spacing between keys. Unless you have small hands, you may find it impossible to touch-type on a compact keyboard. The compact keyboards called **chiclet keyboards** have small rectangular keys like those on hand-held calculators. Although chiclet keys move up and down a bit, they do not depress as far as standard full-stroke keys.

Even among full-size, full-stroke keyboards there is a wide range of options and quality. Some keyboards feel mushy. They do not have a clear point at which the key seems to fall through to the bottom of the stroke. You may find it easier to type if an audible click accompanies each keystroke. But if the click is produced by mechanical key switches, you cannot adjust the volume. Other keyboards generate clicks through a speaker, permitting the sound to be adjusted up for work in a busy office or down for late-night typing at home. Still other computers allow you to adjust the sensitivity of the keyboard as well as the volume of the clicks.

A particularly useful feature is a *keyboard buffer,* it allows you to continue typing even though the CPU is busy doing other tasks. The buffer stores the characters you type until the CPU is ready to accept them. This feature, which is also called *type-ahead,* makes slow programs more bearable. You can begin typing a new command or text while the CPU is still working on the last operation. Keyboard buffers have room for a limited number of characters, from 2 to 20 or more. Characters in the buffer do not appear on the screen until the CPU has accepted them for processing and has echoed them to the screen. If the buffer becomes full, then the keyboard is likely to beep in response to further typing.

For people who must enter a lot of numerical data, it may be wise to use an auxiliary *key pad,* as shown in Figure 4.3. The numeric key pad is shaped and organized like a calculator, which tends to increase both the accuracy and the speed of entering numbers.

Keyboard Layout

The standard layout for typewriter keyboards was developed in the last century. The arrangement is known as the *QWERTY keyboard;* it is named after the order of the keys immediately above where the left hand normally rests on the key-

---

Figure 4.3 A numeric key pad is shaped like a familiar calculator, making entry of numeric information faster and more accurate.

board. The QWERTY keyboard was deliberately designed to slow typing, in order to prevent the hammers on early mechanical typewriters from jamming on their way to the paper. This goal quickly became irrelevant with the invention of improved mechanical typewriters and is of no concern whatsoever with computer keyboards. But the QWERTY layout is still used on nearly all computer keyboards, because typists became accustomed to the layout and didn't want to change. Even minor variations bother touch-typists. For example, a common complaint about the keyboard on the IBM PC is that the location of the [Shift] and [Return] keys differs slightly from that on IBM Selectric typewriters.

Beyond typing normal text, the most common typing operations on computers are entering numbers and moving the cursor. The **cursor** is an indicator on the screen that shows where things will happen next; usually it looks like a blinking rectangle or an underline. The **cursor-movement keys** have arrows on their tops showing in what direction the key moves the cursor. There is no standard location for the cursor-movement keys, but they are easily recognized because they are marked with arrows.

Many other keys can appear on a keyboard. One of the most important is the **control key**, usually labeled [Ctrl]. It operates like the [Shift] key, but instead of creating a capital letter, it generates a *control letter* that has a particular character code. Control letters rarely appear on the screen; instead, they are used to give commands to programs. To type a control letter, you press [Ctrl] and a letter at the same time. The effect will depend entirely on the program being run, but there are conventions that many programs follow. For example, [Ctrl]-[H] usually moves the cursor back one character, and pressing [Ctrl]-[C] often stops execution of the current program. Other keys used to give commands are the **function keys**; these are extra keys that are used for specific purposes and to type text. In some programs, the function keys are *user-programmable;* in other words, you can give them whatever meaning you want while using that program.

Each keyboard has its own quirks. Most computer keyboards have **repeating keys.** This means that pressing a key longer than a second generates a constant stream of characters. Clumsy typists find repeating keys a bother because of the frequent need to delete extra characters. Some keyboards have an "intelligent" shift-lock key; when depressed, it raises all alphabetic keys to upper-case but does not affect punctuation keys or the keys on the top row of the keyboard.

The main thing to remember when using a computer keyboard is that the keys do not have fixed meanings. Hitting the [P] key on a typewriter will always print a *P* on the paper. But striking [P] on a computer keyboard might display a *P* on the screen, print a file, or pull an address out of a list of mailing labels. It all depends on how the program instructs the CPU to interpret the character.

Selection Devices

Many computer operations involve pointing at, selecting, or moving items already on the screen. Often you can perform these tasks more quickly with a pointing device than with the cursor keys on the keyboard. In this section, we discuss several pointing devices: the touch screen, touch-tablet, digitizing pen, mouse, and the puck.

Most people would say that their finger is the most natural pointing device. The **touch screen** shown in Figure 4.4 uses invisible sensors to tell where a finger or pencil touches the surface of the screen. Don't be surprised if the screen in Figure 4.4 looks perfectly normal; the sensors are hidden in the slanted surface surrounding the screen. The accuracy of a touch screen is limited to the nearest character or, even worse, to a group of characters. But then fingers are far too blunt to point to tiny dots on the screen anyway. Touch screens work in a variety of ways. Perhaps the most common mechanism is the *infrared detector.* Infrared rays (heat) scan the surface of the screen. When your finger interferes with the scanning rays, infrared sensors pick up the obstruction and transmit information about the location touched.

A **touch-tablet** is an electronic blackboard that can sense a pencil or stylus on its surface. The touch-sensitive tablet transmits the location of the stylus to the computer whenever it is touched.

Figure 4.5 shows a related pointing device, the *digitizing pen.* Digitizing pens work in a variety of ways. The pencil-shaped **light pen** reads light from the display screen, thus allowing you to point to a spot on the screen. A **sonic pen** uses

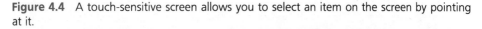

Figure 4.4 A touch-sensitive screen allows you to select an item on the screen by pointing at it.

Figure 4.5 A pen is used to point at an area on a tablet, as shown here, or directly on the display screen.

reflected or emitted sound to determine the pen's position. If you listen closely, you can hear a sonic pen crackle. To use either a light pen or a sonic pen, you aim it at a region of a touch-tablet or screen and then press a button on the pen. The pen reads the location of the region and sends this information to the computer. The computer uses the information to determine what was being pointed at when the pen button was pressed.

Figure 4.6 shows a **mouse**, a hand-operated device. As you drag the mouse across a flat surface, it relays directional information to the computer. Most mice have one or two buttons on top, which are "clicked" when you want the computer to take notice of the cursor's current position on the screen. A **puck** is a pointing device used much like a mouse, but it also has a small magnifying glass with cross-hairs. It is especially good for entering pictorial data from architectural drawings, maps, aerial photographs, blueprints, and medical images. Both mouse and puck can register very small movements, permitting you to point to very precise locations. It takes only a short time to become accustomed to using a puck or a mouse, although most people are skeptical until they have tried one. But if your desk looks like a rat's nest, working with a mouse will be difficult because you need clear desktop space to use it effectively. The major advantages of a mouse over other pointing devices are its accuracy and proven efficiency. Your arm is not likely to tire as quickly when using a mouse as when you use a pen or a touch screen. Furthermore, a mouse is inexpensive and rugged.

Figure 4.6 A mouse is used mostly to point at and select options on the screen.

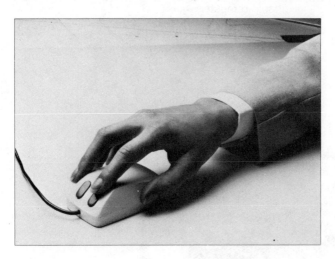

Commercial Devices

Grocery stores, banks, insurance companies, and many other organizations require specialized input devices in order to lower the cost of entering data, increase accuracy, and improve the timeliness of information. Most of these devices are connected to a minicomputer or mainframe running a timeshared operating system. The timesharing software enables the large central computer to juggle hundreds of input devices simultaneously, in order to process transactions. For example, many automatic bank teller machines, as shown in Figure 4.7, are connected to a central computer. When you enter your number and select a command from the machine's list of options, the automatic teller machine sends the information to the timeshared computer. Seconds later, an answer appears on the screen of the teller, or money appears.

Early commercial systems used keypunch machines to prepare punched paper cards that provided the input to computers. A *keypunch machine* is like a typewriter, except that it punches holes in cards rather than printing characters on paper. Keypunch operators produced enormous stacks of cards that were read into the mainframe computer as a batch. The mainframe processed the entire batch of cards in one *processing cycle* before continuing on to the next processing cycle. For example, the computer might read a batch of punched cards indicating all the payments and charges for one day in a medical billing system and then adjust each patient's account before moving on to the next application. This method of periodically processing groups of transactions is known as **batch processing**.

Keypunch machines were eventually replaced by systems that stored information on magnetic media instead of on cards. For example, *key-to-tape* and *key-to-disk* systems generally link a number of workstations (each with a keyboard and a screen) with a dedicated minicomputer and tape or disk storage, as shown in Fig-

Figure 4.7 Whenever you use an automatic teller machine, you are using an input device connected to a mainframe computer.

ure 4.8. They collect input on tape or disk before it is entered into the mainframe system, thus relieving the mainframe computer of a substantial workload. These systems make it easier for people who enter data to fix typing mistakes, eliminate the need to buy blank paper cards, and allow management to monitor performance automatically, through the computer. Despite these advantages, key-to-tape and key-to-disk systems are being replaced by input devices that capture information without the need for typing.

Many other batch input devices are used to collect inventory information, gather production information from workstations on the factory floor, capture shipping invoices for the day, and so forth. For example, video cameras capture graphical information, such as maps, drawings, and photographs. Banks use **MICR** (*m*agnetic *i*nk *c*haracter *r*ecognition) devices to read the numbers printed on the bottom of personal checks. With MICR devices more than 1,000 checks are read per minute.

On-line devices permit a popular alternative to batch input. An *on-line* input

Figure 4.8 Key-to-disk data entry workstations.

device is connected to the computer, so that the computer can process data immediately. Retail stores, factories, and scientific laboratories use a variety of on-line input devices for interactive processing. An **interactive system** is one in which the computer immediately processes its on-line inputs. Not all on-line devices are supported by interactive processing. For example, a time clock might be on-line, but the data from the time clock might be collected only once a week for payroll processing.

Most retail businesses use one or more input devices called *POS terminals* (point-of-sale terminals). Figure 4.9 shows a sales clerk using a POS terminal to verify the amount of a credit card purchase. The computer may be in the next room or thousands of miles away. When the transaction reaches the computer, the machine checks the card number to see if it is stolen, overdrawn, or currently invalid. If the card is approved, the computer sends a validation number back to the POS terminal. By the early 1980s, a person in Australia could use a credit card on an account in New York.

Most grocery stores now use the UPC system shown in Figure 4.10. The *UPC* (Universal Product Code) is a standard way to mark groceries (and any other item in a store). The code involves two numbers: the first represents the manufacturer of the goods, and the second represents the product. The numbers are given in both human-readable and machine-readable form. The machine-readable form is called a **bar code** because it consists of variable-width bars. A bar code reader senses and converts the bar codes into numbers. For example, suppose Dark Red Kidney Beans made by S&W Fine Foods of San Mateo, California, are assigned

numbers 11194 (for S&W) and 38943 (for Red Beans). The can of beans is passed over an optical scanner that reads the bar code printed on the can's label. A "flying spot" scanner reads the bar code by measuring the amount of reflected light bouncing back from the can of beans. The POS terminal deciphers the bar code, sending the numbers 11194 and 38943 to the computer. The computer uses these numbers to look up the current price of the beans, retains in memory the fact that the store has just sold a can of beans, and sends the price information back to the cash register.

Most POS terminals work faster than a human can point or speak. The POS provides speed and accuracy, but that isn't the end of the story. The information provided by a POS terminal can be used to reorder depleted inventory, measure the effects of a sale, and monitor the productivity of clerks.

Commercial input devices capture a lot of information at its source; this is often called *source data automation*. Source data automation systems require more hardware than batch systems, so their initial cost is higher. In contrast, conventional batch processing is people intensive, slow, and inaccurate, because the data must be typed by data entry operators. Because the cost of people is increasing and the

Figure 4.10 The UPC (Universal Product Code) is used to label the package of every item sold in a grocery store with a code that specifies the manufacturer and the product.

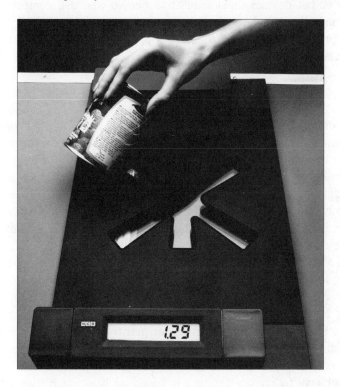

cost of hardware is decreasing, the use of batch processing is likely to continue declining, whereas on-line interactive data entry at the source should increase.

Other-Input Devices

Input devices may be hand held or as large as a 200-inch telescope. They may be on-line and used for interactive data entry, or they may be used to collect data in batches before processing. There is an amazing variety of input devices, each providing a computer with a specific kind of tactile, visual, audible, or other input.

Some input devices go well beyond the abilities of our own senses. Magnetic resonance scanners allow computers to "see" inside our bodies. Temperature-sensing devices collect on-line data about the temperature and humidity of buildings, so that a computer can adjust the climate of a warehouse, factory, or office building. Signals from video cameras in robots on an assembly line allow computers to control the actions of "seeing-eye" robots. Scientific labs use a variety of sensors to collect data from experiments; the data are entered automatically into the computer's memory for processing and graphical display. Obviously, it is wrong to assume that the sensory abilities of computer systems are inherently very limited. This prejudice only discourages the innovative use of computers.

The two output devices most familiar to people who use computer systems are printers and visual display units, such as screen monitors. Printers provide a permanent, printed record of information. Displays provide a quick and inexpensive way to view information.

Printers

Typewriters combine a keyboard for input and paper for output in one device. Personal computers and terminals connected to large computers separate these functions into two units: a keyboard and a printer. Anything typed on a typewriter is printed automatically, because the keyboard and print mechanism are mechanically (or electrically) coupled. But a computer's keyboard is not connected directly to the printer. Instead, the keyboard and the printer are connected separately to the CPU. Characters typed on the keyboard are *not* automatically sent to the printer or display screen unless the program tells the CPU to do so.

There are many ways to classify printers. For example, they can be classified according to whether they use an impact or a nonimpact method of placing ink on the page. Most printers used with personal computers today are **impact printers**. Like typewriters, they form an image by bringing ribbon and paper into physical contact with each other. **Nonimpact printers** are quieter than impact printers, because no print hammer or similar mechanism actually strikes the paper. Examples of nonimpact printers include thermal, ink-jet, and laser printers.

Another way to classify printers is based on how much they print at a time. **Character printers** print only one character at a time by moving the print mechanism back and forth across the page. **Line** and **page printers** print an entire line or page of characters almost simultaneously. Normally, personal computers do not generate enough output to require a line or page printer, except when they are linked in a network. Figures 4.11 and 4.12 show the character printers used with most personal computers and the larger, faster, and more expensive line printers used in a mainframe or minicomputer system.

Still another way to classify printers looks at whether they generate characters by printing a pattern of dots or by printing fully formed, raised images. **Dot matrix printers**, which we'll discuss shortly, create each character by printing dots in a pattern. **Letter-quality printers** create each character by striking an embossed image of a character against an inked ribbon and paper. A letter-quality printer can generate output that is indistinguishable from that of a good typewriter. This means that the edges of each printed character are smooth, or fully formed.

The most common type of letter-quality printer is a *daisy-wheel printer* (see Figure 4.11). A **daisy wheel** is a flat wheel of plastic or metal with 96 or more spokes radiating from the center. On the tip of each spoke is an embossed image of a character. The wheel rotates continuously. As the required spoke moves in front of the print hammer, the spoke is struck onto the ribbon and paper, causing one character to be printed. Daisy-wheel printers generate high-quality output on

Figure 4.11 **(a)** The petals of a daisy-wheel printer create an image by striking the raised image of characters against an inked ribbon. **(b)** Character enhancements available from a daisy-wheel printer.

A.

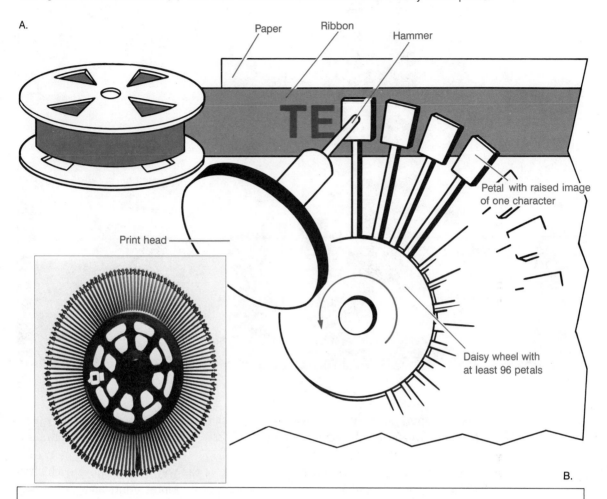

Paper

Ribbon

Hammer

Petal with raised image of one character

Print head

Daisy wheel with at least 96 petals

B.

Bold letters are printed twice, shifted slightly for the second printing.

^{Super}scripts and $_{Sub}$scripts require the paper to be advanced and retracted.

Double-striking is not visible with a quality ribbon, but works with faded cloth ribbons.

<u>Underlining</u> <u>text</u> is used more than ~~striking out passages~~.

Overprinting prints two characters in the same position, as in Ø.

Changing the **pitch** (the number of characters printed per inch) c a n   s t r e t c h   a   l i n e   o u t
or squeeze it together.

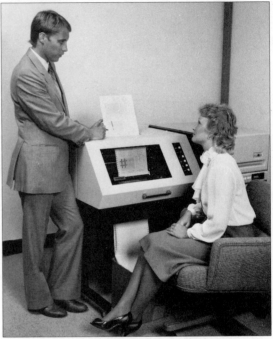

normal paper, but they are slow compared with other printers. Typically they print between 15 and 70 characters per second (cps). And, like other impact printers, daisy-wheel printers are noisy.

Dot matrix printers got their name because of the way they produce each character. Instead of printing a solid letter, a dot matrix printer prints an array of dots in a pattern that only approximates the font of a typewriter. Most inexpensive dot matrix printers use a printing mechanism, called a *print head*, that holds from 9 to 24 short wires or pins. As the print head sweeps back and forth across the paper, the pins shoot forward into the ribbon to create dots on the paper. The number and size of the dots determines the quality of the print (see Figure 4.13). The best dot matrix printers use many small, overlapping dots to build each character. The cheapest dot matrix printers generate crudely shaped characters that are clearly identifiable as computer output. For example, inexpensive 9-pin printers have a resolution of about 75 dots per inch. A high-quality 24-pin printer can have a resolution better than 150 dots per inch. Most manufacturers claim that their 24-pin printers produce letter-quality output, but this claim is debatable.

There are also nonimpact dot matrix printers; examples include thermal printers and ink-jet printers. *Thermal printers* burn dark spots on heat-sensitive paper. The paper is usually expensive, has a shiny surface, and tends to fade over time.

Output: Displaying and Printing

Like everyone else, you use computers to get output. Perhaps you want to look at information in a file. Or maybe you want to print a letter. Or you might need to control a blast furnace. Whatever the application, you need an output device to convert the computer's digital signals into a useful form. This photo essay will give you a better idea of how flexible output systems can be.

1. Printers and monitors vary considerably in size, quality, speed, price, and convenience. It pays to consider options carefully before making a purchase.

VIDEO DISPLAY

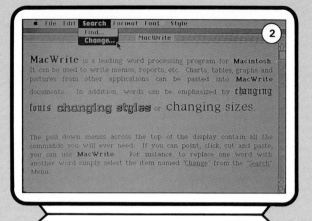

2. The Apple Macintosh uses a monochrome screen with a resolution of 512 by 342 pixels. Here the MacWrite word processing program is displaying several sizes and styles of text.

3. This picture was made with an IBM PC, a Tecmar Graphics Master color adapter card, and a 35-mm slide-maker camera system. Its resolution is 640 by 200 pixels, the same as that on a standard IBM PC color display. Because there are only 8 scan lines for each row, the characters look grainy. The memo in this screen is being edited with WordStar 2000.

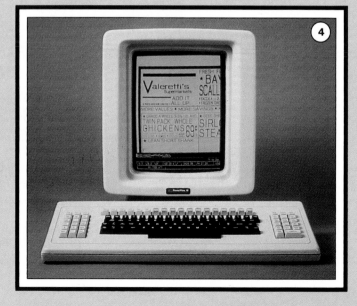

4. The trend in word processing systems is toward what-you-see-is-what-you-get display. This PowerView 10 terminal, produced by Compugraphic, is used to preview work before it is typeset. PowerView processes the screen image with an Intel 80186 microprocessor supported by one megabyte of memory. The screen image can be scrolled horizontally and vertically, reduced in size, or enlarged.

5. This image was produced by the IBM 5080 Graphics System, which is used primarily by design engineers. The screen has a viewing area 11.2 inches square and can display up to 256 colors with a resolution of 1,024 by 1,024 pixels. Today a display of this quality is too expensive for most personal computers—but in the future, who knows?

6. The 9-inch, flat-panel amber display on this portable computer has 512 by 255 pixels and an adjustable viewing angle for easy reading. Built into the top of the computer is a small ink-jet printer. The computer weighs only 25 pounds and costs less than $5,000.

7. Liquid crystal displays are popular for portable computers because they consume little power. For example, the battery in this portable computer can operate up to eight hours without recharging. Hidden in the side of the computer are two 3.5-inch 720KB diskette drives.

PRINTERS

8. Most dot matrix printers can print both text and graphics. Dot matrix printers have captured an increasing share of the market as their cost has fallen and print resolution has increased.

9. This color dot matrix printer has a 24-element printhead that provides 144 dot-per-inch (dpi) resolution. The suggested retail price is less than $270.

10. With daisy-wheel printers, raised images of letters are pressed into an inked ribbon and paper. They produce high-quality letters but are noisy, unable to handle graphics, and slow, printing just 10 to 80 characters per second.

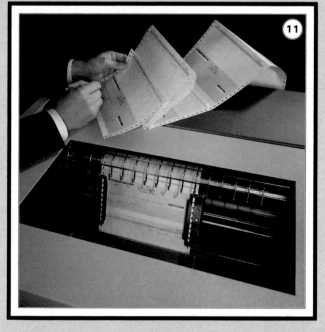

11. Business documents are often created by filling in the blanks in preprinted forms.

12. Like many recently introduced laser printers, Apple's LaserWriter is based on the print engine used in Canon's personal copiers. The printer is controlled by a Motorola 68000 microprocessor supported by 2 megabytes of internal memory. It produces 300-dpi output at rates up to 8 pages per minute, and it comes with a number of built-in fonts in a range of sizes.

13

■RESTAURANT■

GRAND OPENING
C·O·U·P·O·N

This Coupon entitles you to one free glass of wine or one slice of Chocolate Toffee Pie

Cut Here

- -

◆
Our Newest
Watermill Restaurant
is located at 101 Savoy Ave.

The Watermill Restaurant is located between Olmstead St. and Taylor St. on Savoy Ave. Plenty of Free Parking. Open 11am-12pm Mon. thru Sun.

THE WATERMILL
■RESTAURANT■

ANNOUNCING THE OPENING OF
THE WATERMILL RESTAURANT
AT 101 SAVOY AVE.

First Class Mail

G·R·A·N·D O·P·E·N·I·N·G

13. This sample output, which is almost typeset quality, was created using a Macintosh application program and the LaserWriter printer.

PLOTTERS

14. Pen plotters produce smoother lines than dot matrix printers, but they operate much more slowly. This inexpensive six-pen plotter prints by moving the paper back and forth while moving the pen from side to side, with 250 steps per inch. To fill in a region with color the pen must run back and forth many times, which is a slow process.

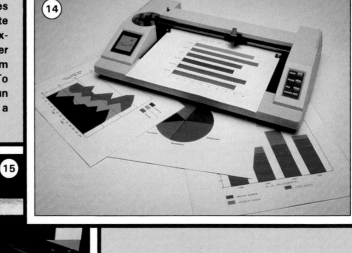

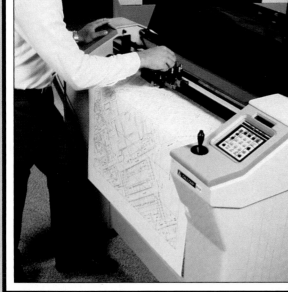

15. Engineering, architecture, and other design applications require large, high-resolution plotters. This drum plotter uses the same basic technology as the small plotter in photo 14, but it is much more accurate.

16. The pen holder of a large commercial flatbed plotter.

17. Sample plot of an integrated circuit from an electrostatic plotter.

18. This stand-alone plotter was designed for drafters, engineers, and architects. From text entered on the keyboard, this system produces wet ink lettering for use on drawings and schematics.

19. This laser-driven photoplotter is accurate to 0.005 of an inch, which is far smaller than can be seen by an unaided human eye.

20. A close-up view of the photoplotter's printhead.

21. High-quality photoplotters have historically been very costly—more than $60,000. This photoplotter costs $25,000. It interfaces with microcomputers, such as the IBM PC/AT shown here, with an RS-232 interface and is used to create the precision artwork for printed circuit boards.

OTHER OUTPUT DEVICES

Anything that can be controlled with electrical signals or motors can be controlled by computer. This page gives three examples of very different types of computer output.

22. Computers are increasingly being called on to perform mechanical tasks. This is an automated testing system that helps ensure the quality of circuits in some of IBM's mainframe computers.

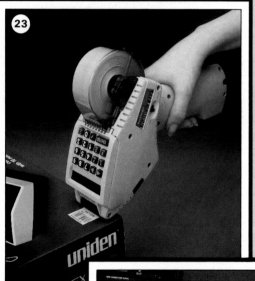

23. This fully portable, electronically controlled printer can produce labels with both bar codes and human-readable information. Because the labels are printed on thermally coated paper with a thermal printhead, no ribbons are required.

24. The electron-beam exposure system shown here etches microscopic patterns on glass plates. The system translates data on a tape into physical form by shooting an intense beam of electrons at a chemically coated glass plate. Eventually the glass plates are used as masks to fabricate integrated circuits.

A WORD ABOUT
PAGE PRINTERS: FOR SPEED AND VOLUME

The printer industry may be the latest example of entropy. As the universe expands, disorder grows.

Choosing a printer is not as easy as it used to be. No longer an insignificant output device at the end of a chain of office automation equipment, today's sophisticated page printers actually generate applications, letting users perform tasks previously done by an outside service—such as typesetting and overhead transparencies—or never performed at all, such as graphics illustrating reports, typeset newsletters, and so on.

This changing market, replete with vendor price/performance battles and overlaps in printer technologies, makes purchasing choices tougher than ever. And because page printers are complex devices with many serviceable components and their own storage, processors, and even programming languages, it is increasingly difficult for data processing managers to treat these devices as commodities or to leave them to end-user departments to specify and service.

The seemingly infinite purchasing possibilities, coupled with the rush of vendors that began selling page printers during the past 12 to 24 months, do have a positive side effect: The page printer segment now edges toward being a buyer's market. After some years of fanfare, this market has finally ripened enough to make it a safe bet for many users.

"The market has changed dramatically, and most of the major players are already involved. We have seen a lot of headway, and we will see more. But products you buy today will not be obsolete tomorrow," says Maureen McManus, product marketing manager at C. A. Pesko Associates, Inc., a consulting firm based in Marshfield, Mass.

Current page printer offerings include low-end models costing from $2,000 and $3,000 up to about $10,000, printing 8 to 12 pages/minute, fitting comfortably on a tabletop and emulating popular impact devices for easy interfacing. High-end models can print 100 to 200 pages/minute, loom as large as a mainframe—one vendor boasts a printing system 16 feet long—and cost several hundred thousand dollars.

Each page printer consists of three subsystems: a printing engine that puts the image on the page, control electronics that determine the imaging capabilities, and software. Vendors vary any of these subsystems to provide a diverse product line. The diversity of models offered means any one company may use page printers for personal computer printing, for departmental output, and for centralized data processing printing.

With the technology for print engines—including laser, LED array, magnetic and ion deposition—remaining fairly stable, the vendors' chief vehicles for innovation and attracting customers lie in the electronic subsystems and printer software. In many instances, users can purchase just the speeds they need and just the features they want, with service contracts to boot.

Touted applications include more sophisticated graphics, dozens of fonts available on-line, mixed text and graphics, plotting, electronic forms overlay, digitized signatures or logos, and what-you-see-is-what-you-get printing. Envelope feed, printing on transparencies plus sorting, collating, and job separation all number among the accessory features.

Across the board, reliability has improved in the past 12 to 24 months. The trend now runs toward user-serviceable print engines with replaceable toner and drum cartridges. Even some of the high-end machines are sold with maintenance kits for in-house servicing. As newer models see more use, vendors raise their conservative mean-time-between-failure ratings and suggested print volumes to match user field experience. Many buying criteria apply to the entire range of page printers as vendors from high end to low end aim to offer the same popular features.

First and foremost, page printers appeal to users because they print high-quality type. Most page printer output is considered letter-quality for business use, although it does not duplicate out-

(continued on p. 98)

put from a typewriter or daisywheel. On the plus side, the fonts produced by many page printers mimic typeset lettering and also allow more type to fit on each page, potentially saving companies money in paper costs.

On the minus side, some users complain that the type produced by laser printers is shiny and somewhat raised—a giveaway that the document was neither typed nor typeset. But in a business environment where highly automated office work has become nearly synonymous with good management, receiving a document produced by a computer may now carry connotations of sleek technology and sound management instead of implying impersonal, form letter correspondence.

Source: Amy Sommerfeld, *Computerworld,* 21 April 1986, P. 45–46.

On the positive side, thermal printers are inexpensive and make only a whispering, crinkly noise as they singe the paper. *Ink-jet printers* work by squirting tiny droplets of ink at the paper. On some systems, magnetic fields deflect each drop to the proper position by acting on the drop's static electricity. The print head shown in Figure 4.14 fires droplets straight at the paper from 12 microscopic nozzles arranged vertically along the print head. In this system, each droplet is ejected by instantly vaporizing a tiny amount of ink behind one of the nozzles, giving momentum to the ink in the nozzle.

If you don't need output that looks as if it just came out of an office typewriter, then matrix printers have several attractive features.

- Matrix printers are cheaper than letter-quality printers. They range in price from under $200 to more than $1,000, instead of from under $400 to more than $2,000.

- Matrix printers are much faster than letter-quality printers. Slow matrix printers print 60 characters per second, but a rate of 200 cps or more is not unusual.

- Most matrix printers are not limited to one size or style of character. Because the characters are formed from dot patterns, the dots can be arranged in Greek, gothic, boldface, or italic fonts with equal ease. Some matrix printers offer many style and sizes of type; others print in only one or two styles.

- Matrix printers can print graphical images as well as text (see Figure 4.14). If the microcomputer has the proper software, a matrix printer can print bar charts, line graphs, company logos, letterheads, your personal signature, and even coarse-grained photographs.

Mini and mainframe computers need much faster printing than can be provided by character printers. The required speed is achieved by *line printers,* which print an entire line at a time, or by *page printers,* which compose a page at a time. Two types of high-speed impact line printers are drum and chain printers. A common type of page printer is the laser printer.

A **drum printer** is a line printer in which the entire set of embossed characters

Figure 4.13 The size and sharpness of a printer's dots determine the quality of the printed image.

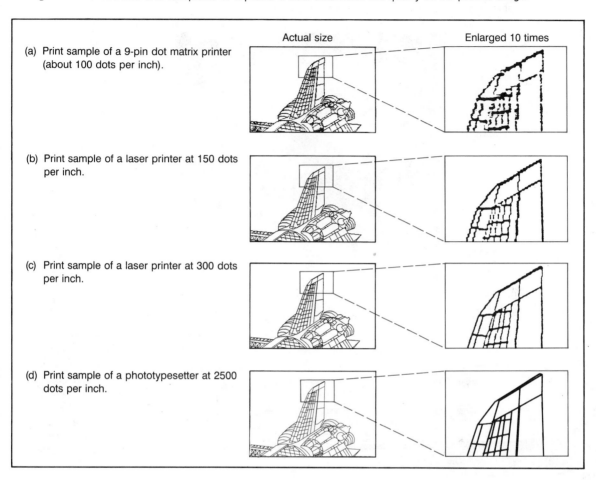

	Actual size	Enlarged 10 times
(a) Print sample of a 9-pin dot matrix printer (about 100 dots per inch).		
(b) Print sample of a laser printer at 150 dots per inch.		
(c) Print sample of a laser printer at 300 dots per inch.		
(d) Print sample of a phototypesetter at 2500 dots per inch.		

is positioned around the circumference of a cylinder or drum. As the drum rotates at high speed, a hammer pushes the paper against the ribbon at precisely the right time. The drum has 132 "rings" along its length, so that a 132-column line can be printed each time the drum completes a single rotation. A **chain printer** is a line printer in which the entire character set is embossed on a rotating chain. As the desired character passes by, a hammer presses the ribbon against the paper to make the imprint. In a typical chain printer, each chain includes five complete character sets, and 132 hammers operate in parallel to increase the printing speed. The major advantage of chain printers over drum printers is that fonts can be changed easily just by changing the chain. Drum and chain printers are fast: they print 600 to over 3,000 lines per minute. They are also expensive, costing $10,000 to $100,000. The ability to print carbon copies is a major selling point of all impact printers.

    Laser printers come in micro and mainframe sizes, but they all work nearly

Figure 4.14 An ink-jet printer. (a) is an inexpensive 150-cps ink-jet printer. (b) is a closeup view of the printer's disposable print head, which contains a rubber pouch of liquid ink.

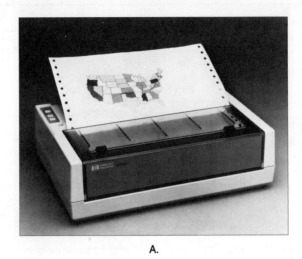

A.

Paper Ribbon From 9 to 24 print wires Print head

B.

the same way (see Figure 4.15). A laser beam traces out the image on a photosensitive drum, which picks up ink particles. The paper rubs the ink particles from the drum, and they are fused to the page. Because the image can be text or pictures and the resolution is excellent, laser printers produce nearly typeset-quality graphics and text.

Small laser printers often use the same print engine as is used in copy machines, except that the light source comes from a laser instead of being reflected

Figure 4.15 A laser printer uses mirrors to direct light to a photosensitive drum. Electrically charged toner particles are attracted to the image, transferred to paper with pressure, and permanently fused in place with heat.

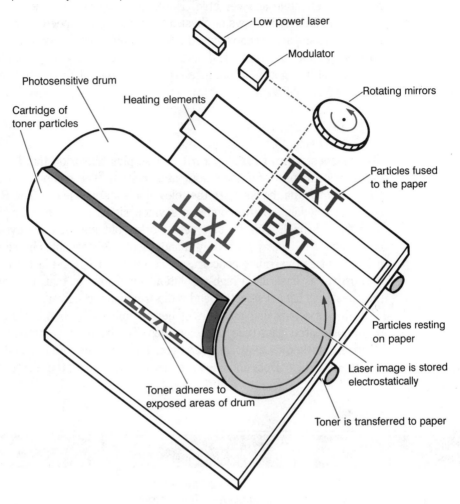

off an original document. Single blank pages are fed in at one end, and printed pages come out the other end. Prices range from less than $2,000 to more than $6,000; typical speeds are eight pages per minute. Large laser printers use continuous-feed paper moving at three to five pages per second through the printer (equivalent to 20,000 lines per minute). Even at this high speed, the quality of these large printers is exceptional.

Since laser printers are nonimpact, they are limited to printing single copies. However, they are fast enough that multiple copies can be made from multiple print runs instead of from carbon copies. The major disadvantage of laser printers, to date, is their high cost. In the next few years, this cost should decline swiftly, making laser printers the dominant printer technology wherever medium- to high-volume printing is required.

Table 4.1 summarizes printer technology. Impact printers are currently the most cost effective and versatile. However, they are not the most reliable, and they are limited by the laws of physics to modest print speeds. The future of printing is in nonimpact technologies. Ink-jet printers will perhaps take over the low-cost end of the spectrum, and laser printer technology may dominate the upper end. For all, the goal is to produce typeset-quality output quietly, while increasing speed and reliability.

Displays

The cheapest **visual display unit** is a surplus television that has been pressed into service as part of a home computer system. The computer is attached to an *RF modulator* that hooks up to the television's antenna leads. The **RF modulator** converts (modulates) the computer's video signal into the *radio frequency* of a television channel. This arrangement works, but not well. Television sets were not designed to display text; they cannot display 80 readable characters per line. If price is not an overriding concern, a video monitor is used instead of a television. A **monitor** is basically a high-resolution television set that has been stripped of the speaker, channel selector, and radio-frequency receiver.

Both televisions and monitors generate images by bombarding the end of a phosphor-coated glass tube with electrons. The beam of electrons is created by an electron gun known as a *cathode;* thus, monitors are often called **cathode ray tubes**, or **CRTs**. Dots and lines are created by turning the electron beam on and

Table 4.1 Some Printer Technologies					
Mechanism	**Quality (dots per inch)**	**Graphics?**	**Speed (per second)**	**Reliability**	**Cost ($)**
Impact					
Typewriter	300–800	N	15 characters	Medium	150–1,000
Daisy-wheel	300–800	N	15–70 characters	Low	400–2,000
Dot matrix	75–200	Y	60–300 characters	Low	200–1,000
Chain/drum	75–150	N	600–3,000 lines	High	10K–100K
Nonimpact					
Thermal	75	N	30–120 characters	Low	20–100
Ink-jet	75–200	Y	200–300 characters	Medium	200–2,000
Laser (micro)	300–600	Y	600 lines	High	1.5K–6K
Laser (main)	300–1,000	Y	21,000 lines	High	50K–300K

off as it sweeps across the surface of the screen. Thus, the image you see is actually a mosaic of glowing spots caused by bombarding a thin layer of phosphors with electrons. To keep a constant image on the screen, the electron beam must redraw the image on the screen 15 to 30 times a second, refreshing the quickly fading phosphors.

Raster Scan and Vector Graphics Displays

The image on a CRT screen can be generated in two radically different ways. In a **raster scan monitor,** the electron beam moves horizontally back and forth across the screen, along what are called *scan lines* (see Figure 4.16). In a **vector graphics monitor,** the electron beam is not limited to traveling along scan lines; instead, it works by drawing straight lines from point to point.

Figure 4.17(a) illustrates the vector graphics method. A circle is constructed by drawing a polygon. Each side of the polygon is a straight line (called a *vector*). If 3 sides are drawn, the result is a triangle; if more straight lines are drawn, an 8-sided or 16-sided polygon is produced. If hundreds of very short straight lines are drawn, the polygon looks like a true circle. Now look at the approximations of a circle shown in Figure 4.17(b); they illustrate the raster scan method. Each box in Figure 4.17(b) represents one position on the screen and is called a **pixel** (an abbreviation of *pic*ture *el*ement), the smallest element on the screen. The raster scan method approximates the circle, not with a collection of straight lines, but by filling in certain pixels. A low-resolution approximation is obtained by filling in a few large pixels. High-resolution images are created with a large number of tiny pixels.

The **resolution** of a picture is a measure of the accuracy or fineness of detail of the graphical reproduction. In a raster scan monitor, the resolution is determined by the number of horizontal rows and vertical columns of pixels. A 640-by-320-pixel monitor has 640 pixels along each scan line and 320 scan lines from the top to the bottom of the screen. The ratio of horizontal to vertical pixels is called the *as-*

Figure 4.16 Color and monochrome raster scan CRTs.

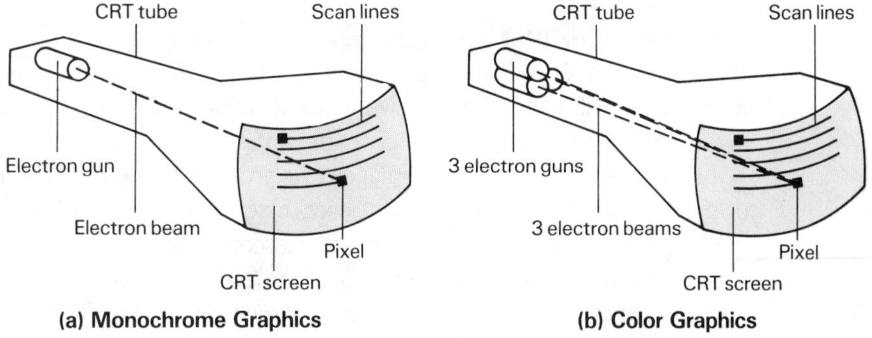

(a) Monochrome Graphics

(b) Color Graphics

Figure 4.17 Vector graphics and raster scan displays.

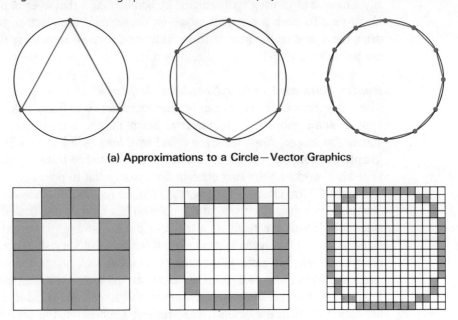

(a) Approximations to a Circle — Vector Graphics

(b) Approximations to a Circle — Raster Scan

pect ratio of the monitor and determines the shape of each pixel. If the aspect ratio is not 1, circles and diagonal lines may be distorted.

Vector graphics monitors produce extremely accurate line drawings. Because it takes more time for the electron gun to draw vectors than to scan the screen horizontally in a fixed pattern, vector graphics monitors are not good at filling in areas of the screen. As a result, an image with many dense objects will cause the screen to flicker noticeably. Vector graphics monitors are used in applications requiring a high-quality graphical display, such as computer-aided design and drafting. Raster scan monitors are less expensive and far more common than vector graphics monitors. All televisions and personal computers use raster scan technology.

Bit-Mapped and Character-Oriented Displays

Before an image can be displayed on a screen, however, it must be stored in RAM. Here will look briefly at two ways of coding and storing this image for raster scan monitors: bit-mapped and character-oriented.

In a **bit-mapped display**, images are produced by coloring each of thousands of pixels and storing the status of each pixel as one or more bits in RAM. This method of storing the screen image in memory is quite simple; each pixel on the screen has a corresponding bit or bits in memory. For a monochrome display, there is a one-to-one correspondence between bits in the bit map and pixels on the screen. A monochrome pixel will be black or white depending on whether its corresponding bit in memory stores a 0 or a 1. Color displays require at least three bits per pixel to specify the pixel's three primary colors: red, green, and blue.

In a **character-oriented display**, the screen image is produced by drawing characters on the screen. Each character to be displayed is assigned a pattern of pixels. The image is stored in RAM as a list of characters to appear on the screen, not as a list of individual pixels. The conversion between the character codes stored in memory and the dot patterns of characters on the screen is peformed by a special circuit called a *character generator*.

A character-oriented display is nowhere near as flexible as a bit-mapped display, for two reasons. First, only a limited set of characters can be displayed, usually less than 256 (see Table 4.2). So there is not likely to be, for example, a character that looks like the mirror image of a question mark. Second, each character must appear in a fixed position on the screen. With a character-oriented display, you

Table 4.2 The IBM PC Character Set

DECIMAL VALUE →	HEXADECIMAL VALUE →	0	16	32	48	64	80	96	112	128	144	160	176	192	208	224	240
		0	1	2	3	4	5	6	7	8	9	A	B	C	D	E	F
0	0	BLANK (NULL)	►	BLANK (SPACE)	0	@	P	`	p	Ç	É	á	░ ¼ Dots On	└	╨	∝	≡
1	1	☺	◄	!	1	A	Q	a	q	ü	Æ	í	▒ ½ Dots On	┴	╤	β	±
2	2	☻	↕	"	2	B	R	b	r	é	FE	ó	▓ ¾ Dots On	┬	╥	γ	≥
3	3	♥	‼	#	3	C	S	c	s	â	ô	ú	│	├	╙	π	≤
4	4	♦	¶	$	4	D	T	d	t	ä	ö	ñ	┤	─	┘	Σ	∫
5	5	♣	§	%	5	E	U	e	u	à	ò	Ñ	╡	┼	╒	σ	∫
6	6	♠	▬	&	6	F	V	f	v	å	û	ª	╢	╞	╓	µ	÷
7	7	•	↨	'	7	G	W	g	w	ç	ù	º	╖	╟	╫	τ	≈
8	8	◘	↑	(	8	H	X	h	x	ê	ÿ	¿	╕	╚	╪	Φ	°
9	9	○	↓	)	9	I	Y	i	y	ë	Ö	⌐	╣	╔	┘	Θ	•
10	A	◎	→	*	:	J	Z	j	z	è	Ü	¬	║	╩	┌	Ω	·
11	B	♂	←	+	;	K	[	k	{	ï	¢	½	╗	╦	█	δ	√
12	C	♀	∟	,	<	L	\	l	|	î	£	¼	╝	╠	▄	∞	η
13	D	♪	↔	—	=	M	]	m	}	ì	¥	¡	╜	═	▌	Ø	2
14	E	♫	▲	.	>	N	^	n	~	Ä	Pts	«	╛	╬	▐	∈	■
15	F	☼	▼	/	?	O	_	o	△	Å	ƒ	»	┐	╧	▀	∩	BLANK 'FF'

Source: Reprinted from the IBM Technical Reference Manual, courtesy IBM Corporation.

cannot shift a letter half a column position left or right. The difference between the coding schemes has important implications for the amount of memory that is required to store a screen image. In most character-oriented systems, each character takes two bytes to store: one byte specifies which symbol should appear in each character position, and the other determines the character's display attributes, such as its color or whether it should blink on and off. Thus, a 25-line-by-80-column screen requires $25 \times 80 \times 2 = 4,000$ bytes of storage space. In contrast, a 640-by-320 pixel color display requires $640 \times 320 \times 3 = 614,400$ pixels or 76,800 bytes to store an entire screen. In short, character-oriented displays require far less memory than bit-mapped displays.

Some computers can generate either a bit-mapped or a character-oriented display. This allows them to store images in the bit-mapped format for graphics programs and to save memory space by storing images in a character-oriented format for text-based programs. Most character-oriented terminals store their character patterns in ROM. As a result, you cannot change the font or size of text unless you modify the hardware. For this reason, many microcomputers allow the character patterns to be stored in RAM, where they can be changed by a running program. In the Macintosh, for example, the character generator takes character patterns from RAM, so it can change fonts and character sets in midstream.

Liquid Crystal Displays

Briefcase-sized computers that run on batteries cannot afford the size or power required for a CRT display. Instead, like digital watches, they often use a liquid crystal display (see Figure 4.18). A **liquid crystal display (LCD)** is a flat panel rather than a bulky tube—an excellent shape for portable or lightweight computers. An LCD does not generate any light itself; rather it depends on reflected light. It has a liquid crystal material and a grid of wires sandwiched between two sheets of polarizing glass. When current is passed between the crossing wires, the crystals shift position, rendering the liquid opaque. The pattern of dark and light produces the image of a character. This works well in some light conditions and poorly in others.

Qualities of a Good Display

A good-quality monitor is very important. No one wants to spend hours peering into a screen filled with blurry characters. Many factors influence a monitor's readability, including

■ The monitor's color. The phosphors in a **monochrome monitor** glow in only one color. The most popular color for monochrome monitors is light green, followed by amber. There are endless debates over which color is best. Apple broke with tradition by choosing a black and white monitor for its Macintosh. **Color monitors** break each pixel into three dots: red, green, and blue. Color monitors create excellent graphics, but their characters are not quite as read-

Figure 4.18   This notebook-sized computer has a 25-line-by-80-column liquid crystal display (640 by 200 pixels).

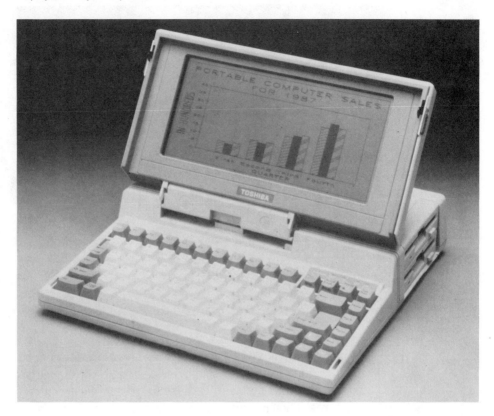

able as those on monochrome monitors, because the extra dots per pixel make each pixel fuzzier.

■ The screen resolution. Resolution is measured horizontally and vertically. The number of scan lines determines the vertical resolution; the number of pixels along each scan line sets the horizontal resolution.

■ The reflective properties of the screen. Glare from reflected light can be very annoying. Etched faceplates, mesh screens, or even simple cardboard shades can be used to reduce unwanted reflections.

Plotters

A **plotter** is a printerlike output device that prints pictures rather than alphanumeric information. Most plotters use a stylus or pen to draw an image on paper (see Figure 4.19). A plotter is used instead of a graphical printer when high-resolution drawings are needed. For example, commercial *flat-bed plotters* can move 10,000 steps per inch. Such machines are indispensable for drawing electronic circuits or making precise mechanical drawings.

Figure 4.19   A plotter converts graphical information into hard copy.

Pen plotters are not well suited for filling areas in a drawing, because they *fill* an image by drawing many lines side by side—a time-consuming process. *Photoplotters* do not have this problem, because they use a light source (often a laser) to draw high-resolution images on photosensitive paper. A special-purpose photoplotter (called a *typesetter*) was used to typeset this book.

Other Output Devices

The most familiar output devices—printers, visual display units, and plotters—use the media of paper or monitors to produce some type of image as output. If you wish to use some other media, chances are there is an output device that will do the job. For example a *COM* (*c*omputer *o*utput *m*icrofilm) device records computer output on microfilm instead of paper. Vast amounts of information can be compactly stored on microfilm. If you need presentation-quality slides, special cameras and slide makers are available, which connect to the display screen of a personal computer or take pictorial information directly from memory and produce developable film. Making presentation-quality slides with these devices is as easy as taking a picture with your Polaroid.

In theory at least, just about anything can be hooked up to a computer and become an output device, even entire factories. For example, most paper products, such as paper plates, tissue paper, cups, and paper towels, are made automatically by computer-controlled machines. The computer senses temperature, moisture, and other characteristics of the pulp and directs the machinery during the paper-making process.

SUMMARY

We have surveyed only a few of the major input and output devices available; there are many more. The keyboard is the most common input unit, although voice recognition devices should become practical in the near future. Printers and visual display units are the most common output units. Most of the input and output devices for microcomputers are smaller versions of those found on mainframes.

To use a computer, you don't need a detailed understanding of its parts, just as you don't need to know how the parts of a car work before learning to drive. But you do need a basic understanding of how the functional units fit together and what they do. Carefully choosing the right I/O device is just as important as selecting the right computer. So keep in mind ease of use, speed, cost, versatility, quality, and reliability when you select I/O devices.

KEY TERMS

bar code

batch processing

bit-mapped display

cathode ray tube (CRT)

chain printer

character-oriented display

character printer

chiclet keyboard

color monitor

compact keyboard

control key

cursor

cursor-movement key

daisy wheel

dot matrix printer

drum printer

function key

impact printer

interactive system

keyboard

laser printer

letter-quality printer

light pen

line printer

liquid crystal display (LCD)

membrane keyboard

MICR

monitor

monochrome monitor

mouse

nonimpact printer

page printer

pixel

plotter

puck

raster scan monitor

repeating key

resolution

RF modulator

sonic pen

touch screen

touch-tablet

vector graphics monitor

visual display unit

DISCUSSION QUESTIONS

1. Can information be sent directly from an input device, such as a keyboard, to an output device, such as a printer?

2. How does the QWERTY keyboard slow a typist down? Does this suggest another type of keyboard? How should this new keyboard be introduced?

3. A touch screen has limited accuracy. What devices would allow you to point to an individual pixel, such as the dot in the letter *i*?

4. What are some of the things a mouse might be used to point at on the screen of a personal computer?

5. If a computer could fully understand spoken commands, why would it still be necessary to have bar code readers, POS terminals, and other types of input devices?

6. Suppose that speech recognition devices are perfected for personal computers and are quite inexpensive. What effect will this have on the use of personal computers in business, education, or elsewhere? Will the impact be different if the devices are expensive?

7. What is meant by the term *letter-quality printing?* Can a dot matrix printer produce letter-quality printing? If so, how small would each dot have to be?

8. An impact printer can be used with multiple-carbon paper to make several copies of the same report. Can an ink-jet printer make multiple copies using carbon-copy paper?

9. Other than speed, what characteristics would you use in comparing printers? Rank these in importance. Is speed the most important?

10. Which peripheral devices are strictly for output? Which are strictly for input? Which perform both input and output functions?

11. Personal computers offer great potential for the handicapped. For various handicaps, such as blindness, describe the special input and output devices that would enable a handicapped person to use a personal computer.

EXERCISES

1. If a 9″ × 9″ touch screen can resolve only the end of a $\frac{1}{4}$″ × $\frac{1}{4}$″ finger, how many points can be located on the screen with a standard finger?

2. Printers are rated according to their speed. If a typical printer for a personal computer can print 120 characters per second, how long will it take to print the contents of a page containing 66 lines of 80 characters each? Assume that the speed rating does not include the time for a carriage return. What effect does this have on the actual time it takes to print the page?

3. Determine how long it would take to print a 15-page report on a letter-quality printer at 30 cps and on a dot matrix printer at 150 cps.

5 Operating Systems and Application Software

The best way to learn about computing is to use a computer. In this chapter, we describe what you need to know about software in order to begin computing. Later chapters will delve into specific applications. What is important now is to get an overall idea of how the programs in a computer system work together and to learn how to perform essential tasks, such as running programs and managing files. If you use a personal computer, you should also know how to perform such maintenance operations as formatting and backing up disks. To use a mini or mainframe computer you must know how to log on and off the computer.

In the first section of the chapter, we describe how the parts of the operating system work together to control the computer system. This part describes how the operating system schedules the tasks to be done, controls interactions with peripheral devices, manages main memory and the storage of files, and provides other useful services. In the next two sections, we explain how you accomplish the most frequently performed tasks by giving commands either through the keyboard or by using a pointing device, such as a mouse. Even though you might use just one of these systems, you should study both. The contrast helps illustrate the difference between form and function in computer programs. In the last section, we discuss application software—the programs that direct a computer to perform specific activities, such as writing a letter, playing Space Invaders, or printing paychecks.

OPERATING SYSTEMS

An *operating system* is the set of programs that governs the operation of a computer. Whenever the computer is running, the operating system provides the computer with the ability to automatically manage the use of its memory, interact with peripheral devices, and execute programs.

In our discussion of operating systems, we will give examples from two specific systems: **PC-DOS** (*Personal Computer–Disk Operating System*) and the Macintosh operating system. PC-DOS is IBM's name for its single-user operating system for the IBM PC family of personal computers. Actually, PC-DOS is a slightly modified version of MS-DOS, an operating system owned and licensed by Microsoft to scores of personal computer manufacturers, including IBM. Several of the figures illustrate screen displays using MS-DOS operating systems. Together, PC-DOS and MS-DOS are the dominant operating systems for 16-bit microcomputers. The Macintosh operating system is a system developed by Apple and available only for the Macintosh.

PC-DOS and the Macintosh operating system have fundamentally different user interfaces. PC-DOS is a **command-line operating system**; commands are given by typing lines including full-word keywords, such as TYPELETTER.JIM. Command-line operating systems are by far the most common type of operating system for all types of computers—micro, mini, and mainframe. Whereas command-line systems accept commands from the keyboard, the **visual operating system** used by the Macintosh accepts commands from a mouse. The commands are given by moving or selecting pictures (called *icons*) and items from ·menus. Thus, a visual operating system is said to use a *visual interface* between the computer and the user. In contrast, command-line systems use a *textual interface*.

Operating System Compatibility

Like most popular personal computer software, PC-DOS is revised about once a year on an entirely unpredictable schedule. Each revision adds new features or removes old **bugs**—program errors or design flaws. For each revision, the operating system is given a new version number, which indicates how extensive the revision is. For example, relatively minor changes were made from PC-DOS 1.0 to PC-DOS 1.1. But PC-DOS 2.0 had many new features, including hierarchical file directories and support for a hard disk. All of the versions of PC-DOS are **upward compatible**; in other words, you can upgrade your operating system to the newest version and still use most of the application software written for older versions. Without upward compatibility, using the new version of the operating system would require buying a whole new set of application software. For large data processing centers, the cost of modifying existing software in order to use a new, upwardly incompatible operating system can be enormous. More than a trillion dollars have been spent developing programs to run on the IBM System/360 series of mainframe computers and its successors. The desire to avoid converting their software led many data processing organizations to commit to only one make of computers.

Major Components

Operating systems vary widely in their size and complexity. Early 8-bit personal computers, such as the Apple II, were limited to 64KB of memory. Because every extra byte in the operating system meant that there was less room for the application program and data, operating systems for these microcomputers provided only the bare essentials for controlling the computer. Because memory is less constrained in 16- and 32-bit machines, their operating systems provide a wider range of functions and more convenience. Still, the operating systems for most personal computers are quite crude by standards of mainframe computers, which use operating systems that occupy megabytes of memory and generally allow the computer to execute concurrent programs, allocate memory among many users, and manage large databases.

Although the specific parts of operating systems vary, all operating systems have components that function as (1) a supervisor, (2) an input/output (I/O) manager, (3) a file manager, and (4) a command processor. You don't have to know how these parts work to use a computer, just as you don't have to know how an engine works to drive a car. But learning what these four basic parts of the operating system do will give you the background necessary to use a computer with more authority and less confusion.

Supervisor

At the heart of all operating systems is the **supervisor**, or *kernel;* it schedules and coordinates the activities of other programs. Think of the supervisor as a traffic cop who signals when each activity is permitted to take place. Whenever a computer is running, its supervisor is loaded in internal memory, directing and controlling everything that's going on.

The supervisor in a mainframe computer's operating system is much more complex than that in a single-user system. Because mainframe computers can have more than 1,000 concurrent users, their supervisors must allocate brief time slices to each user, through the process known as *timesharing.* The supervisor in a multiuser computer must also record who is using which computer resources, so that users can be billed accurately. Finally, the supervisor must ensure that one user's programs cannot affect another user's programs or data.

Input/Output (I/O) Manager

In general, all data transferred to and from peripheral devices is filtered through the **I/O manager**. It insulates the rest of the programs in the computer system from the peculiarities of the peripheral devices. For example, in a microcomputer, the I/O manager might translate the keyboard's character codes into the coding system used by the rest of the computer. In a mainframe computer, the I/O manager might translate the ASCII character codes (described in Chapter 2) that are generated by many terminals into the EBCDIC character codes used for internal processing.

With a good operating system, it is possible to add a hard disk or a faster printer to the computer system simply by modifying the I/O manager, without making changes to any other software. This is called **device independence**. The software that modifies the I/O manager by telling it how the new hardware functions is called a **device driver** and is usually provided free of charge by the vendor of the add-on device.

An operating system can provide an even stronger form of hardware independence, called **machine independence**, which allows application software to be moved from one member of a family of computers to another without programming changes. This can make it possible to replace a small mainframe computer with a larger one overnight, as long as both computers use the operating system. For example, most IBM mainframe computers can be interchanged in this way.

File Manager

As you saw in Chapter 3, everything on disk is stored in a file. Each file has its own name and stores one type of information—for example, a program or data. A *data file* might contain text for a last will and testament, a recipe for banana bread, or a digitized picture. A *program file* might be a BASIC program or a word processor.

Whatever the contents of a file, the **file manager** is responsible for saving, deleting, copying, loading, naming, and renaming files. The file manager also provides a translation between your *logical* view of the file—the file name and the type of data the file stores—and the *physical arrangement* of data on disk. As we saw in Chapter 3, data on a disk is grouped into sectors, with each sector forming part of a track. The file manager provides the translation from file names to storage locations by maintaining a directory and a file allocation table in special areas on the outside edge of each disk. Recall that the *directory* contains a list of the name and number of each file on the disk; the **file allocation table** is an index showing the specific physical locations assigned to each file. Many file managers allow files to be grouped together in a hierarchical manner by setting up subdirectories. In this case, the *root directory* provides a listing of the names of the files in the root directory and the names of the subdirectories.

Suppose the file manager is asked to copy 2,400 bytes from main memory to create a new file named BASEBALL.CAP on a disk with 512 bytes in each sector. Although the exact procedure for storing a file varies somewhat from one operating system to another, in general the file manager must

- Examine the disk's file allocation table to find five unused sectors
- Modify the appropriate directory (or directories) and the file allocation table to include an entry for the new file and to list the sectors it occupies
- Tell the I/O manager to copy the data file from main memory onto the five previously unused disk sectors

Command Processor

The **command processor** (also called a **shell**) communicates between the user and the rest of the operating system. It accepts commands from the user, makes sure they are valid, and then takes the appropriate action. For example, if you ask the computer to copy BASEBALL.CAP and call the new file GOLF.TEE, the shell will translate the command and relay the request to the file manager. If the disk doesn't have enough room to store GOLF.TEE, then the file manager sends a coded error message, which the shell might translate to read: INSUFFICIENT FREE SPACE ON DISK—COMMAND ABORTED. Figure 5.1 gives a rather technical description of how the Unix operating system's shell acts as an intermediary between users and the command processor, or kernel, of the operating system. The Unix operating system was developed by AT&T Bell Laboratories and is available on a wide variety of micros, minis, and mainframes.

Many operating systems have more than one shell available for different types of users. For example, programmers might prefer to use a shell with a command-line interface, whereas casual users might choose to use a shell with a visual interface. From a technical viewpoint, building a shell for an existing operating system is nowhere near as difficult as building a new operating system from scratch.

Sometimes during a computer session, you are bound to say to yourself, "I've typed this same series of operating system commands over and over again." Perhaps you must make a backup copy of a file with one command before you start word processing with another command. You can avoid this sort of repetition if your operating system's shell allows you to establish batch files. A **batch file** is simply a file that contains a series (or batch) of operating system commands. For example, you might build a batch file containing one command to back up the file and another to start word processing. Then you can accomplish the work of two commands with a single command that tells the shell to begin executing the batch file. The shell will address the commands in the batch file one at a time and execute them.

Mainframe operating systems generally provide extensive features for building complicated batch files. These features are collectively known as a **job control language (JCL)**. Programmers use job control languages to link application programs to run one after another. A full-featured job control language can make an

Figure 5.1 The Unix operating system.

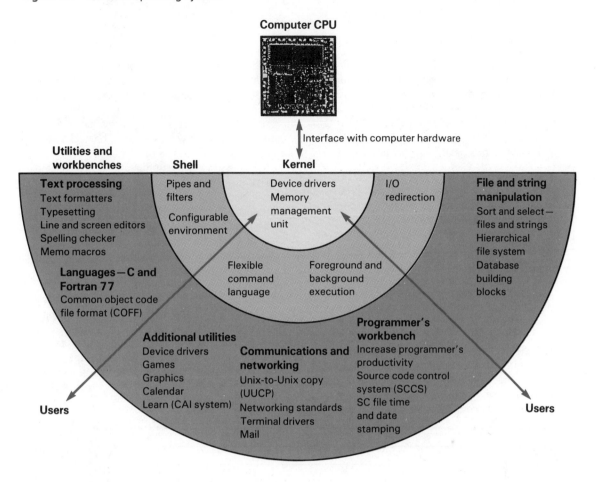

Computer CPU

Interface with computer hardware

otherwise unfriendly operating system seem reasonable to casual users, because all the obnoxious commands can be hidden inside batch files.

Memory Management

In some portable computers, the entire operating system is permanently stored in ROM, but on most computers, the operating system is too large to fit into main memory at once. Instead, the operating system is broken into two parts: resident routines and a set of transient utilities.

The **resident routines** in an operating system are loaded into memory as soon as the computer is turned on. Resident routines always contain the essential routines for controlling the computer and its peripherals and may contain some frills as well. The essentials are the operating system supervisor, the I/O manager, and at least some of the file manager.

A WORD ABOUT DOS SHELLS

"For the beginner, a DOS shell can mean the difference between complete bewilderment and the ability to make a system perform basic functions. For the advanced, user, a DOS shell can either get in the way of normal business or provide a more efficient method to take care of business." —John Walkenbach

For many PC users, having to type "copy a:file c:/path/subdirectory/file" is as pleasant as shaving with cold water. This is especially uncomfortable when there is clearly a better way to do the job.

PC users can bypass DOS via programs called DOS shells, which let users switch back and forth between programs and customize their own integrated packages. While such programs generally cost less than $100, they can be priceless when it comes to improving the user productivity.

Noah Davids, a software developer for Honeywell, in Phoenix, uses the Norton Commander DOS shell extensively. "Almost everything I do is invoked from the Commander itself," he said. "It's reduced the amount of typing, and, as a result, the amount of typos. I use it for everything. I no longer use DOS commands."

Allen Cariker, director of computer systems for the Dallas Cowboys, in Irving, Texas, is a dedicated user of the Xtree hard disk manager. "Xtree gives me the power I need to do all the hard disk management," Cariker said. "It helps me locate a file, determine how many files need to be backed up, and then go through the tree structure."

This is especially useful for Cariker, who has a copy of every software package used in the Cowboy's organization on his hard disk. Anyone in the company with a question about a program comes to him, and he needs a quick way to find the right files.

Cariker agrees that DOS shells flourish because of a perceived deficiency in DOS, and that many of these capabilities should be in the operating system. But he feels "it has more to do with the business acumen of people who have generated them. The Norton Utilities was the first program that gave you control over file notation. Norton saw a business opportunity and filled that need. Xtree is in the same class as the original Norton Utilities, solving an obvious problem in a creative and efficient way."

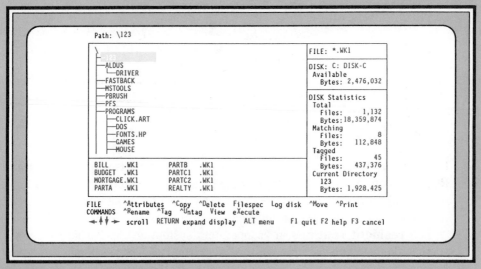

XTREE, a DOS shell that helps show the structure of a hard disk.

The **transient utilities** remain on disk until one of the programs is requested. Then the requested program is transferred into memory. Commands that are resident in one operating system may be transient utilities in another; the choice is made by the operating system designer, not by the user. If a command for a transient utility is given when the computer cannot find that utility program on the disk, an error message is displayed, or on a personal computer, a request for the **system disk** (a disk containing the operating system) is made.

The way an operating system manages memory is best illustrated with a specific example. We will describe how PC-DOS manages a computer session in which a program for a mailing list prints names and addresses onto mailing labels. Figure 5.2 shows how main memory and the disk files might be laid out for this application. On the disk,

■ The two hidden files contain the file and I/O managers of the operating system. A *hidden file* is the same as any other file, except that its name doesn't appear in directory listings of file names.

Figure 5.2 Several transfers of files from disk to memory are necessary before an application program can begin execution. The numbers indicate the sequence of these transfers.

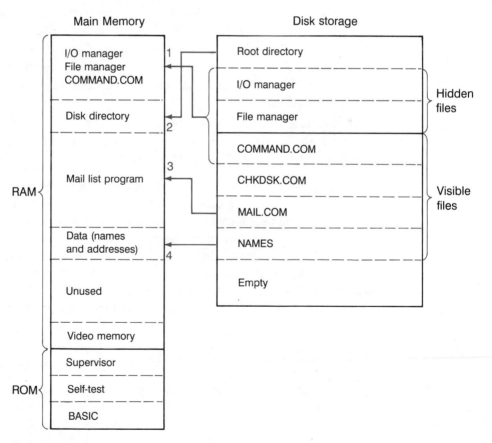

- COMMAND.COM contains the operating system's command processor.
- CHKDSK.COM contains the transient utility program that implements the CHKDSK command (see page 123).
- MAIL.COM contains the mailing list application program.
- NAMES contains the data file of names and addresses to be printed.

Before the machine is turned on, main memory is blank except for programs stored in ROM. In an IBM PC, ROM contains the operating system supervisor, some self-test programs, and a truncated version of Microsoft BASIC. When the computer is turned on, it immediately looks for a system disk. If the system disk is not found, generally the computer responds with an error message and waits. Programs must be in memory before they can be executed. Thus, four transfers from disk to memory are necessary before the mailing list program can print the mailing labels (see Figure 5.2).

1. Loading the I/O manager, the file manager, and the command processor (COMMAND.COM) into memory. This is done by switching on the computer, which activates instructions in ROM that load the resident portion of the operating system from the disk.

2. Loading a copy of the disk's directory into memory. This allows the computer to read files from the disk faster. At this point, the operating system displays a prompt, signifying that it is ready for a command.

3. Loading the mailing list program into memory. You do this by typing MAIL NAMES. This command not only tells the operating system to load MAIL.COM into memory but also tells the mailing list program to use the data file NAMES.

4. Transferring names and addresses from NAMES to memory. MAIL.COM carries out this process, formats the names and addresses to look good on mailing labels, and sends them to the printer.

In this example, you have to give only one command to begin running the application program because the disk has been conveniently configured to store all the programs and data necessary for the application. The movements of data between disk and memory are vastly more complicated in a timeshared operating system with virtual memory. (Recall that a virtual memory operating system automatically moves parts of a program from internal to external memory and makes the computer look as if it has an unlimited amount of main memory.) Fortunately, the increased complexity in memory management is well concealed from the user.

USING A COMMAND-LINE OPERATING SYSTEM

When you begin using a computer, you will find that the tasks you perform most frequently are

- Running application programs
- Copying and deleting files and other file operations
- Formatting new disks, backing up disks, setting the system clock, logging on and off, and other maintenance tasks

In this section, we will explain how to perform these operations on a computer that has a command-line operating system. Although specific commands vary from one command-line operating system to the next, the general approach to using them is fairly standardized.

Command-line interfaces are not easy for beginners to use, because the user must remember commands and type them exactly. The computer prompts a command by displaying a message like ? or A>. Each command is typed on a new line. It begins with a **keyword**—usually a verb, such as TYPE, MOVE or KILL—which is the command's name. Normally a keyword is followed by one or more **parameters** (also called **arguments**), which tell the keyword more specifically what to do. A parameter can be a file name, but it might also be a number specifying how fast to send characters to the printer. A keyword and its parameters must be separated by a **delimiter**, generally a space or a comma, to indicate where one part of the command ends and the next part begins. For example, in the command COPY DATA.OLD DATA.NEW, the keyword is COPY, the two delimiters are the blank spaces, and the parameters are the file names DATA.OLD and DATA.NEW. The number and type of parameters vary depending on the keyword and the action desired.

Running a Program

Becoming proficient with PC-DOS takes time and practice. Each command begins either with the name of a program file or with a keyword. If it begins with a program file name, then the operating system loads the program file into memory and begins executing the program. For example, to execute a word processing program stored on a disk as the file WORD.COM, you type WORD and enter the command by pressing the [Enter] key.

If the command begins with a keyword, then the operating system executes the command. For example, if you type TYPE LETTER.JIM, the file named LETTER.JIM is displayed on the screen. After completing the command, the operating system shows that it is ready for the next command by displaying a prompt, such as B> or A>. Incorrectly typed commands elicit the error message BAD COMMAND OR FILENAME, followed by another prompt.

Besides acknowledging that the computer is ready for the next command, the prompt designates the default drive. Disk drives are named by single letters; the **default** drive is the drive that PC-DOS searches to find a file if it is not told explicitly where the file is stored. If the prompt is A>, for example, then PC-DOS will search drive A to find the file named BASEBALL.CAP, but it will search drive B to find the file B:BASEBALL.CAP. You change the default drive by typing the letter of the new default drive followed by a colon. For example, if the original prompt is B>, then you type A: in order to change the default drive. As a result, the prompt also changes to A>.

Most computer programs rely heavily on default values to reduce the amount of information that must be requested from the user. For example, the disk formatting utility will, by default, make double-sided disks unless you specifically request single-sided disks.

File Names

In PC-DOS, you must follow some rigid rules when you name a file. A file name contains two main parts: a *primary file name* containing one to eight characters and an optional *extension* with one, two, or three characters. For example, you might name three files JIM, INVENT.RPT, and FORMAT.COM. These files might contain a memo to Jim Martin, an inventory report, and the transient operating system utility that formats new disks.

One drawback of magnetic media is that people cannot sense magnetic signals directly and must rely on the computer system to report what a disk or tape contains. The short file names of PC-DOS don't help matters much: a file name like INVENT.RPT may not jog your memory about what is in the file six months after you created the file. This problem is exacerbated if you use a hard disk, because it can contain well over 1,000 files. Fortunately, there are some standard conventions for naming files, which make it easier to determine what is stored in each file. For example, one convention is that any file ending with the extension .COM is a machine language program. Some other conventions are as follows:

- .BAS contains a BASIC language program.
- .BAT is a batch file, containing operating system commands.
- .DOC contains documentation—instructions about how to run or use a program.
- .EXE contains an executable program and is similar to a .COM file.
- .PAS contains a Pascal language program.
- .PIC contains a picture, or graphics, file.
- .SYS contains system parameters used to initialize a program.
- .TXT contains a text file.
- .WKS contains a worksheet created with the Lotus 1-2-3 spreadsheet program.

A complete file name includes two other parts that describe where the file is located. The first part of a complete file name is the name of the drive storing the file. Thus, the file A:ELMER.GLU is stored on drive A. On a two-drive floppy disk system, the left-hand (or upper) drive is usually designated as A, and the right-hand (or lower) drive is designated as B.

The middle part of a complete file name identifies the subdirectories (if any) in which the file is located. Remember that a subdirectory is an index file that contains the names and locations of other files. For example, the file name C:\LETTERS\1985\BIRTHDAY.MOM states that the BIRTHDAY.MOM file is stored inside the subdirectory named 1985, which in turn is located inside the subdirectory named LETTERS, all of which reside on drive C. In this example, the C:\LETTERS\1985 part of the file name is called a *path,* because it describes the route that must be followed to find the file. Subdirectories are particularly important on hard disk systems, because without them, the root directory would contain all of the entries for the disk's files. Imagine trying to find a file in a root directory with over 1,000 file names in it!

File Management

The most important file management operations are

- Examining a root directory or subdirectory to see what files are in it
- Deleting files
- Copying files

We will give examples of each of these operations. In all of the PC-DOS examples in this chapter, characters typed by the user are shown in color, and output generated by the computer is shown in black.

Directory Information

Probably the most frequently used command is DIR. It extracts from a directory a list of file names, file sizes in bytes, and the times when the files were created. Then it formats the list as a report and sends the report to the screen (see Figure 5.3).

CHKDSK (check disk) is a nonresident PC-DOS disk-management utility command. It produces a report about the contents of a disk and the status of memory. In Figure 5.4, the report shows that one of the authors' hard disk drives is about two-thirds full.

Deleting

Erasing files is straightforward. The command ERASE B:DRAWINGS.FEB deletes the file DRAWINGS.FEB from drive B. Actually, the command deletes only the file name from the directories on the disk; the file's content is not affected until a subsequent operation causes another file to occupy its space. But because PC-DOS doesn't provide an UNERASE utility to cancel the deletion, the practical effect is the same as if the file were instantly and permanently erased.

Wild card characters are used to specify a whole category of items. For example, with the asterisk (*), you can indicate several files with just one specification. Thus, the command ERASE LETTERS.* erases every file on the default drive that has the primary file name LETTERS, regardless of the file extension (LETTERS.JIM, LETTERS.SUE, and so on).

Figure 5.3 DIR (directory). This example shows how to request a listing of the file in the root directory of disk drive C.

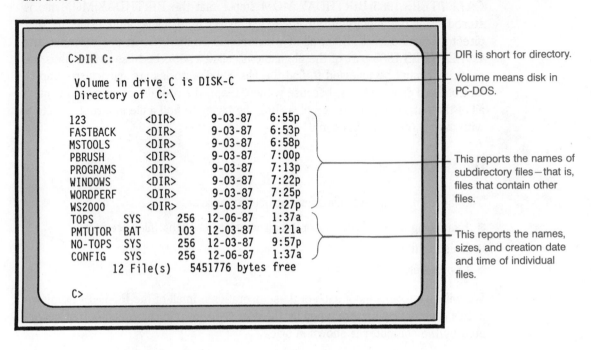

```
C>DIR C:                                            DIR is short for directory.

   Volume in drive C is DISK-C                      Volume means disk in
   Directory of  C:\                                PC-DOS.

   123          <DIR>      9-03-87   6:55p
   FASTBACK     <DIR>      9-03-87   6:53p
   MSTOOLS      <DIR>      9-03-87   6:58p
   PBRUSH       <DIR>      9-03-87   7:00p
   PROGRAMS     <DIR>      9-03-87   7:13p           This reports the names of
   WINDOWS      <DIR>      9-03-87   7:22p           subdirectory files—that is,
   WORDPERF     <DIR>      9-03-87   7:25p           files that contain other
   WS2000       <DIR>      9-03-87   7:27p           files.
   TOPS     SYS     256  12-06-87   1:37a
   PMTUTOR  BAT     103  12-03-87   1:21a            This reports the names,
   NO-TOPS  SYS     256  12-03-87   9:57p            sizes, and creation date
   CONFIG   SYS     256  12-06-87   1:37a            and time of individual
          12 File(s)   5451776 bytes free           files.

   C>
```

Figure 5.4 CHKDSK (check disk). This utility produces a short report about the contents of a disk (in this case a 22MB hard disk) and the amount of memory in the machine.

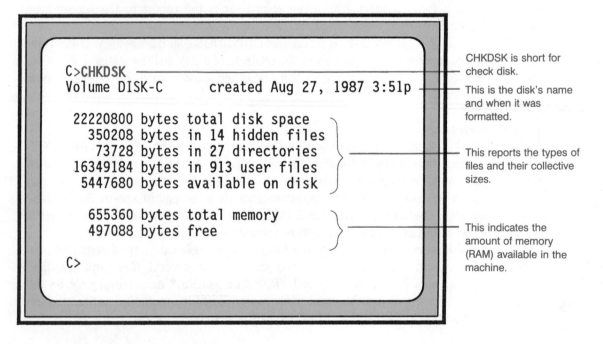

```
C>CHKDSK                                            CHKDSK is short for
Volume DISK-C         created Aug 27, 1987  3:51p   check disk.
                                                    This is the disk's name
                                                    and when it was
   22220800 bytes total disk space                  formatted.
     350208 bytes in 14 hidden files
      73728 bytes in 27 directories                 This reports the types of
   16349184 bytes in 913 user files                 files and their collective
    5447680 bytes available on disk                  sizes.


     655360 bytes total memory
     497088 bytes free                              This indicates the
                                                    amount of memory
   C>                                               (RAM) available in the
                                                    machine.
```

Copying

The COPY command makes copies of specific files. For example, the command COPY A:BASEBALL.CAP B:GOLF.TEE copies. A:BASEBALL.CAP to drive B, forming the file GOLF.TEE. Or, instead of copying one file at a time, you can copy many files with one COPY command by using a wild card character. For example, the command COPY B:*.DOC will take all the files on drive B that have the extension. DOC and copy them to the disk in the default drive.

Maintenance Tasks

The maintenance tasks you perform will depend on the type of computer system you use. On personal computers, you must know how to format new disks and back up used disks. On mainframe computers, the operators are responsible for periodically backing up disk files, so these operations don't concern most users. It is essential for mini and mainframe users to know how to log on and log off, but these operations have no parallels on a single-user system. All of these tasks, however, are important enough to warrant specific examples.

Formatting Disks

Disks come from the manufacturer in a blank, or unformatted, condition; files cannot be stored on unformatted disks. **Formatting** a disk (also called **initializing** a disk) involves erasing the disk and giving it an empty root-directory file. Formatting should therefore be approached with caution. A disk cannot be used until it has been formatted, but formatting a disk by mistake erases its contents completely. Formatting a hard disk by accident can be a major disaster if adequate backup procedures have not been followed.

Figure 5.5 shows the dialog between the user and MS-DOS for disk formatting. The command line begins with the keyword FORMAT followed by the argument A:/S. The A: specifies that the disk to be formatted will be in drive A. The /S is an *option switch,* which tells the format program to initialize the new disk with a copy of the operating system, making it a system disk. **Option switches** are used to override default values. Other option switches for the FORMAT command are /1, to create a single-sided disk, and /V, which allows you to write an electronic name on the disk.

Backing up Disks

It is an excellent idea to periodically copy disks that store letters, reports, spreadsheets, and other data files. Then, if a file is destroyed—either by accidental erasure or by mechanical failure—you'll have a copy of the information on another disk. For very important information, such as business records, you should follow a regular schedule of making backup disks. At least one set of backup disks should be stored away from the computer.

Disks are copied with the DISKCOPY command, a nonresident utility. For example, the command DISKCOPY B: A: causes the operating system to ask for the disk that is being copied to be put in drive B and the target disk to be put in drive

Figure 5.5 Dialog of a typical disk-formatting operation.

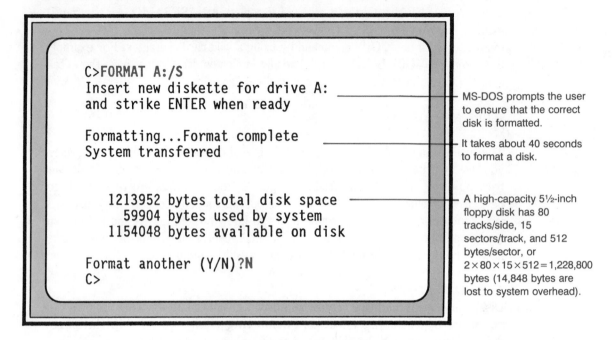

```
C>FORMAT A:/S
Insert new diskette for drive A:
and strike ENTER when ready

Formatting...Format complete
System transferred


   1213952 bytes total disk space
     59904 bytes used by system
   1154048 bytes available on disk

Format another (Y/N)?N
C>
```

MS-DOS prompts the user to ensure that the correct disk is formatted.

It takes about 40 seconds to format a disk.

A high-capacity 5½-inch floppy disk has 80 tracks/side, 15 sectors/track, and 512 bytes/sector, or $2 \times 80 \times 15 \times 512 = 1,228,800$ bytes (14,848 bytes are lost to system overhead).

A. After receiving a confirmation from the keyboard that the correct disks are in the drives, a copy of the disk in drive B is written to the disk in drive A.

Many vendors of software for personal computers have decided to **copy-protect** the disks they sell, in an attempt to prevent users from making unauthorized copies. A copy-protected disk is manufactured with an intentional defect that prevents a normal COPY or DISKCOPY utility from making copies of selected files. As a general rule, only program files are copy-protected. So, even if you use copy-protected programs, you should make backup copies of the data files you create.

Logging On and Logging Off

Before you begin working on a mini or mainframe computer, you must give a command to log on to the computer. Logging on identifies you as a valid user, assigns a job number to your computer session, and starts billing your account. Generally, the log-on command requires a user name (or a user number), a password that corresponds to the user name, and possibly an account number. You should avoid showing or telling your password to others, because it is your private key that provides access to your account. The following example shows a typical log-on sequence for a Digital Equipment Corporation TOPS-20 operating system:

```
Carnegie-Mellon University TOPS-B, TOPS-20
Monitor 4(3352)-2
@LOGIN (USER) LEWIS
```

```
Password:                              <——LEWIS types in his
Job 34 on TTY112 14-Jul-87 10:14:11         password here.
@
```

Although LEWIS types his password into the computer, it isn't displayed on the screen. This makes it harder for others to read LEWIS's password and log on with it later.

Once you have logged on, you can run programs and compute in the same basic way as on a personal computer. When you have finished your computer session, you need to log off to stop the computer from billing your account. Logging off is usually done with a simple one-word command, such as BYE or LOGOFF. For example,

```
@LOGOUT
Killed Job 34, User LEWIS, TTY 112,
at 14-Jul-87 11:34:52 Used 0:01:34 in 1:20:41
```

In this example, LEWIS was logged on for an elapsed time of about 1 hour and 21 minutes but used only 1 minute and 34 seconds of CPU time.

USING A VISUAL OPERATING SYSTEM

Even before games like Pong and PacMan popularized visual interfaces, computer scientists at Xerox Corporation's Palo Alto Research Center were developing a visual interface as the basis of an operating system. They decided to model the interface on a desktop, making the computer screen look like a desk on which papers could be piled on top of each other or placed in in-baskets, out-baskets, file folders, and trash cans. Pictures on the screen represented these objects, as well as printers and pads of blank paper. In 1981 Xerox announced the first commercial computer featuring a visual interface (see Figure 5.6). Immediately recognized by computer professionals as a technical masterpiece, the Xerox Star Information System received little attention from the general public, because a typical workstation cost $30,000. The Apple Lisa, introduced in 1983, used a similar visual system at an introductory price of $10,000. There still were few buyers. Then, in 1984, the introduction of the Apple Macintosh brought the price of a visual operating system down to less than $2,500. Finally the cost of visual interfaces had become competitive with that of textual ones.

To illustrate how a visual operating system works, we will use the Macintosh as an example. All commands to the Macintosh operating system can be made with the mouse or the keyboard. We will explain only the mouse commands. You need to type only when you want to name a new file, rename an old one, or enter information to be stored. The mouse controls an arrow that is used to point at ob-

Figure 5.6 The Xerox 8010 Star Information System. The display had a very high resolution for its visual interface.

jects on the screen. Moving the mouse along a surface causes the arrow to move on the screen.

Running a Program

The first step in running an application program is to switch on the power and slip a disk containing the application program into the drive. The appearance of the screen depends on what disk is inserted. Figure 5.7 shows one example. The gray area of the screen represents the desktop. The three icons represent the system disk in the Macintosh's floppy disk drive (labeled "Start-up w/Tops"), a hard disk connected to the Macintosh via a local area network (labeled "pcmac"), and a trash can sitting on the desk.

The next task is to open the disk to see its contents. The quickest way to do this is to move the mouse until the arrow on the screen points at the disk icon and then to click the button on the mouse twice (a technique called *double-clicking*). This opens a **window**, a rectangular viewing area covering part of the screen, such as the box labeled "Update Disk" in Figure 5.8.

The icons in the Update Disk window tell you what files are on the disk. Those in Figure 5.8 have the following meanings:

- MacWrite is a word processing program.
- MacPaint is a drawing program.

Input:
Entering, Editing, and Sensing

To get useful results from a computer, you must first enter data into it. You might want to enter text, edit a computerized drawing, or have the computer automatically record data from a scientific experiment. Regardless of the task at hand, you will need an input device. If you have the right input device, the task will go smoothly or even effortlessly. The wrong device will make the entire computer system seem unfriendly. This photo essay illustrates how computers can collect data.

1. Inventory records of medical supplies need accurate and timely maintenance. This optical character reader makes the task as easy as passing a wand over a preprinted label.

KEYBOARDS

2–5. Anywhere you find a computer—dorm room, classroom, computer center, or automobile service center—you are likely to find a keyboard. The keyboard is undoubtedly the most common input device. Because of the importance of computers in our society, touch-typing has become a very useful skill.

6. With the appropriate interface you can attach a piano-style keyboard to a personal computer. Here an optional interface card in an IBM Personal System / 2 allows it to control a Musical Instrument Digital Interface (MIDI) keyboard and function as a versatile music synthesizer system.

7. The IBM Personal Computer AT keyboard has two columns of function keys on the left. On the right is a numeric key pad that can also serve as a cursor-movement key pad.

8. The operator is entering data from checks with the help of a cash receipts program. The white text on the screen represents a computerized business form; only the green fields can be modified by the operator. Notice that the operator has entered the word *EASTON* in the customer number field, causing the computer to change the field's color to orange and display an error message on the bottom of the screen.

9. A typical data entry workstation. In the background is a Modular Composition System 8400 phototypesetter, the brand of typesetting machine that created the text you are reading.

SELECTION AND POINTING DEVICES

Steering wheels are standard equipment on cars; so you don't see cars with steering levers or joysticks. The computer industry has fewer standards than the automobile industry; so you can choose how you want to enter data into computers. You can use devices such as a joystick, trackball, light pen, touch screen, mouse, and graphics tablet to select and point.

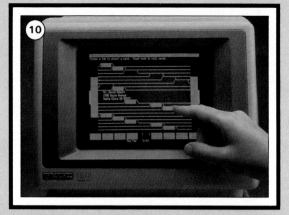

10. This touch screen uses infrared emitters and sensors to determine where a finger or pencil is touching the screen. Here you see a screen image of a card file. Individual cards can be examined by pointing at their tags.

11. Although touch screens appear convenient, they have limitations. Fingers are blunt instruments that leave an oily film on the screen. You cannot see through your finger, and after a while, your arm is likely to complain about using a touch screen.

12. A mouse is a pointing device that relays directional information to the computer as it is dragged across a flat surface. It takes little practice to become a proficient mouse user. Generally, you move the mouse to point or draw; you click a button to select or initiate actions.

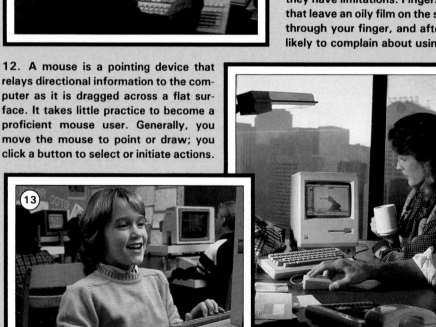

13. An enthusiastic mouse user.

GRAPHICAL DATA ENTRY

Graphics design requires specialized input devices that are capable of digitizing — or tracing — points that indicate the shape of the design.

15. Designs can be digitized by placing the design on a graphics tablet and tracing it with the puck. The key pad on the puck is used to enter specific points and to issue commands.

14. A graphics design workstation. This system includes a joystick for positioning the cursor on the screen and a tablet with a hand-held puck for entering the outline of drawings.

16. A light pen can accurately sense where it touches a CRT screen. The upper and right edges of this screen represent an electronic key pad of commands. With a light pen you can quickly choose commands and draw on the body of the screen.

COMMERCIAL INPUT DEVICES

The market for commercial input devices is characterized by an extreme diversity of data collection equipment.

17. An automatic teller machine (ATM) dispenses cash and conducts banking transactions. Banks have been putting ATM units where the customers are—high-volume retail outlets, airports, and hotels.

18. A fully programmable, portable data collection terminal. With up to 256 kilobytes of memory for data storage, this battery-powered terminal is able to collect extensive amounts of data with its keyboard and optical wand reader. Through a built-in modem, the terminal can send and receive data over ordinary phone lines to a host computer. It is designed for uses such as auditing shelf prices or keeping records of a delivery route—applications that require sophisticated data management by a hand-held unit.

19. Laser-powered bar code readers are able to automatically scan bar codes from as close as three inches, or as far away as three feet.

20. Wherever the movement of products must be recorded quickly and accurately, hand-held optical character readers are useful. These devices help with inventory control in stores, libraries, and assembly lines.

21. This compact OCR makes short work of entering data from utility bills.

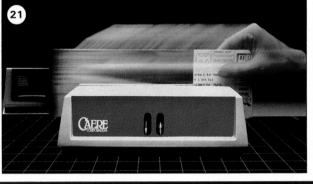

22. Membrane keyboards are inexpensive to manufacture and virtually indestructible. They perform well in harsh environments, such as restaurants where liquids might be spilled on them.

window 4

OTHER INPUT DEVICES

Anything that can be sensed electronically can become input to a computer.

23. Voice input systems are frequently used in applications where the operator's hands are occupied with tasks other than data entry. These systems allow the computer to "listen" to a limited vocabulary of spoken words.

24. You don't need to know how to type to use this pressure-sensitive, battery-operated tablet. Just insert a standard 8 1/2-by-11 inch printed form, pick up a ballpoint pen, and fill out the form. As it recognizes your handwritten characters, they are displayed on the one-line liquid crystal screen and stored in memory. Later the characters can be loaded into any computer with an RS-232 serial port.

25. In the foreground is an optical character recognition reader. Because it can read the text on normal typed pages, it eliminates the need to enter documents manually into the computer system.

Figure 5.7 A nearly empty Macintosh screen display.

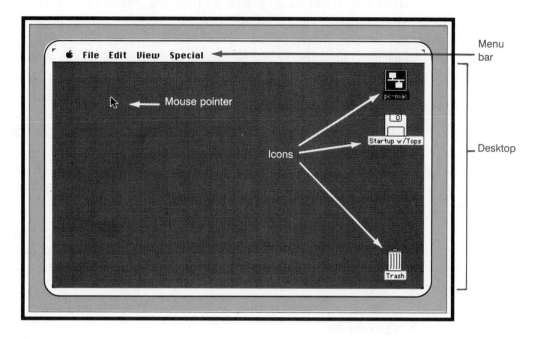

Figure 5.8 Window showing the contents of Update Disk.

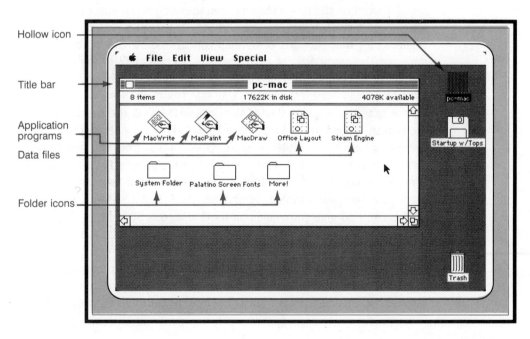

- MacDraw is a line-art drawing program.
- Office Layout and Steam Engine are data files created by MacDraw.
- System Folder is a subdirectory containing files that in turn contain most of the operating system. (Some of the operating system is stored in ROM.) The Macintosh operating system lets you organize the information on a disk by putting files inside folders. Using file folders is important if the disk includes many files because it is difficult to find a specific file if all the files are kept in one large unorganized mess.
- Palatino Screen Fonts is a folder containing various files filled with typeface information.
- More! is a folder containing an outline processor and numerous data files. An outline processor is a type of word processor specifically designed for entering and editing well-formatted lists or outlines.

To run an application program (such as MacPaint or MacWrite), you just move the mouse on the surface of your desk until the arrow on the screen points at the program's icon and then double-click the mouse. Within a few seconds, the screen changes, and you can begin word processing or drawing.

Giving Commands

There is also a slower method of opening a disk, which is worth describing because it illustrates how to give commands by using the Macintosh's two-level menu system. Look again at Figure 5.7. The text at the top of the screen forms part of a **menu bar**; each word on the bar is one item that can be selected. Pointing at a word on the menu bar and then pressing and holding down the mouse button causes a **pull-down**, or **second-level**, **menu** to appear on the screen (see Figure 5.9); that is, a list of options appears below the word. Notice that some items on the menu are not available for selection at this time. For example, if no file has been opened yet, the Close option is unavailable and appears in gray. The available items appear in black. You *select* one of these options by moving the mouse until the arrow points at the desired item on the menu and then releasing the button. Thus, you can also open Update Disk by selecting the File option from the menu bar and then selecting the Open option from the pull-down menu. The pull-down menu vanishes after you use it, leaving the screen as it appeared in Figure 5.8. Although this procedure sounds complicated, with only a few minutes of practice it becomes surprisingly natural.

You can also give commands on the Macintosh by pointing at and moving icons with the mouse. For example, look again at Figure 5.8. To delete System Folder from the Update Disk, you move its icon to the trash can icon. To do this, you point at the System Folder icon, "pick up" the icon by pressing and holding down the mouse button, drag the icon across the screen to the trash can by moving the mouse, and then release the button. When the button is released, the icon for Sys-

Figure 5.9 Second-level menus. These "pull down" from the menu bar.

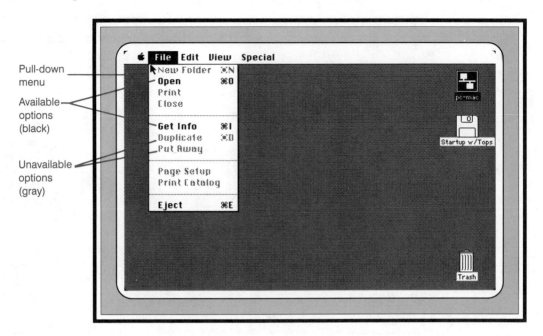

Pull-down menu

Available options (black)

Unavailable options (gray)

tem Folder disappears. This sequence takes many words to describe, but it takes only a second or two to perform.

Window Operations

There are several ways to handle windows in a computer system. The Macintosh uses the most common method: free-form windowing. **Free-form windows** can overlap, as Figure 5.10 shows. The screen looks like a typical, cluttered desktop; its free-form windows look like objects stacked on top of each other. A free-form window can be opened and closed, moved, resized, and scrolled.

- *Opening and closing.* Once a window is opened, it remains open until you close it by clicking the *close* box, a tiny rectangle in the window's upper left-hand margin, or by selecting the Close option from the File menu.

- *Moving.* A window can be moved around on the screen. Pointing at part of a window buried in the pile and clicking the button brings that window to the top (or foreground), so that you can see it and work on its contents. On the Macintosh, windows in the background are deactivated—or frozen in place—until they are activated again. The active window can be moved or dragged by pointing to its upper edge, pressing the mouse button, and dragging the window across the screen.

- *Resizing.* You can make a window larger or smaller by moving its lower right-hand corner.

Figure 5.10 Free-form windows stacked on top of each other.

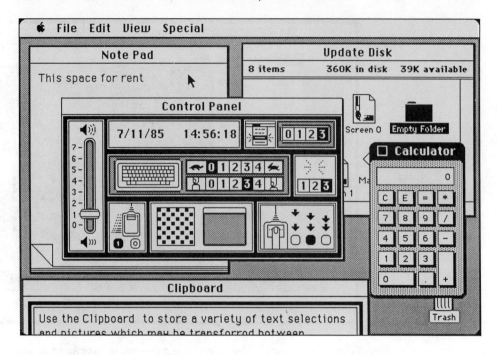

- *Scrolling.* Because a window may not be large enough to display the entire data file, you may have to resort to **scrolling**, which means moving information—in this case, the contents of a window—up, down, left, or right. To scroll, you select one of the arrows in the bars on the side and bottom of the window (see Figure 5.8), or you drag the small box in the bar.

Instead of free-form windows, **tiled windows** are often used on systems in which memory is limited. These windows cannot overlap (see Figure 5.11). Instead, the viewing screen in divided into nonoverlapping regions called *tiles*. Since the tiles do not overlap, the entire rectangular area of each window is visible at all times. Tiled windows can be opened and closed and resized, but in a way different from the methods used with free-form windows.

- *Opening and closing.* To open another window, you must cut an existing window in two. Closing a window causes its "buddy" to fill in the void.
- *Resizing.* An existing window is resized, but not moved, if you move the boundary between two windows.

Windowing requires powerful processors, and using tiled instead of free-form windows conserves processor speed and storage, because the computer does not need to save and then restore a hidden, overlapped part of each deactivated window. Consequently, switching from one tiled window to another is fast and memory efficient.

Figure 5.11 Microsoft Windows creates tiled windows.

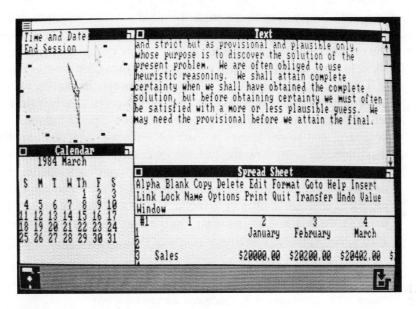

Desk Accessories

The windows in Figure 5.10 illustrate some of the convenient utilities (called *desk accessories*) in the Macintosh operating system.

- *Note Pad* has eight pages on which text notes can be stored. You flip the pages up and down by clicking the upturned corner on the bottom of the pad.

- *Control Panel* adjusts characteristics of the hardware, such as the volume of the speaker and the repeat rate of the keys.

- *Calculator* works like a regular four-function pocket calculator.

- *Clipboard* is not technically a desk accessory, but it is present in most application programs. The clipboard transfers information between programs. For example, if you place a drawing on Clipboard while using MacPaint, you can retrieve it and put it into a letter while using MacWrite.

APPLICATION SOFTWARE

The major categories of software are application software and system software. As we saw in Chapter 1, *application software* performs a specific task, such as word processing, for computer users. *System software* includes all programs designed to help programmers or to control the computer system. Examples include operating systems, as well as the tools programmers use to write new programs—*interpreters, compilers, assemblers, debuggers,* and *editors*. We won't be concerned with system software again until we discuss programming in Chapter 13.

Several layers of software normally insulate a user from a computer's hardware characteristics, as Figure 5.12 illustrates. The innermost layers are occupied by the operating system. The outer layer consists of the programs you use directly. By definition, application software resides on the outer layer of Figure 5.12.

There are some interesting similarities between application software in a computer and the driver of a taxicab. Just as the parts of a taxi (headlights, motor, wheels, and so on) cannot act on their own, so computer hardware (CPU, printer, keyboard, and so on) is inactive without software. As a passenger in a taxi, you don't need to know how the taxi works or even how to drive; you just tell the driver where you want to go. The driver is responsible for getting the cab to your destination. So, too, few computer users know how the computer works or how to program. Instead, they give directions, and the application software translates those directions into instructions for the hardware. Thus, application software adapts the computer to the task you want done.

Figure 5.12 The layers of software in a computer system.

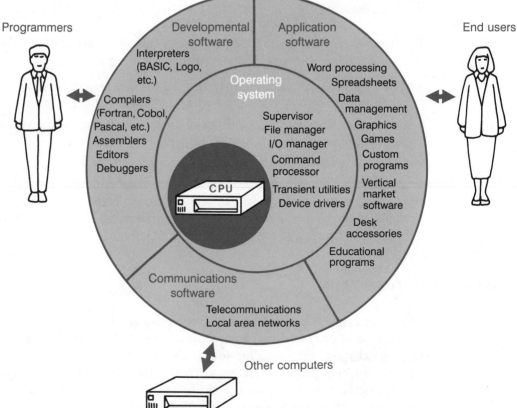

Commercial Application Packages

Thousands of application programs have been written and are available for sale. Each is designed for a particular type of activity. If you cannot find a satisfactory prewritten application program, then you can have a program written to your specifications. For example, a control program for a one-of-a-kind piece of machinery would have to be written from scratch. Although custom programs perform exactly as needed for a specific application, they require expensive and lengthy development. The trend in the computer industry has been away from custom programs and toward commercial application packages that can be purchased and used immediately, with little or no modification. This is particularly true of software for personal computers, where the cost of developing a substantial custom program is likely to exceed the cost of all of the hardware in the system.

Using the right application package for a job is just as important as using the right tools to build a house. Many of the problems that beginners experience can be traced to their using the wrong program. For example, you could write and print a letter with a spreadsheet program, but doing that makes as much sense as cutting a two-by-four in half with a hammer. Choosing the right application program and learning to use it effectively are so important that the bulk of this book is about just that.

Commercial application packages normally include all the materials needed to use the program—instructions, program disks (or tapes), and so forth. For example, Figure 5.13 shows Lotus 1-2-3, a program that combines excellent spreadsheet processing with the ability to produce graphs and manipulate limited amounts of textual data. The package contains

- A notebook of program documentation. **Documentation** is printed material describing what a program does, how to use the program, what error messages a program generates, and so forth.
- Two copy-protected system disks (original and backup)
- Two auxiliary disks filled with less frequently used programs
- A tutorial disk that teaches how to use the package
- A plastic keyboard overlay with definitions for the function keys

Most programs must be *installed* before you can use them the first time. Commercial programs generally come with "cookbook" installation instructions and special installation programs. You must follow these instructions carefully to copy system tracks onto the application disk correctly, configure the program for your particular monitor (color or monochrome), install your printer, and so on. The installation of computer programs for mainframe computers is normally performed by employees of the computer center, thus relieving computer users of this responsibility.

A common problem for new users of application software is confusion about which mode is active. A **mode** is a program state in which only a restricted set of operations can be performed. For example, if a word processor is in the text entry

Figure 5.13 Lotus 1-2-3, a commercial application package.

mode, then any text that is typed on the keyboard is added to the document being created. But if the word processor is in a command mode, then the same keystrokes may be interpreted as commands to erase, move, or reformat text in the document.

Good programs use a number of techniques to help the user switch quickly between modes, recognize which mode is active, and operate effectively within each mode. Some of these techniques are to

- Provide a **help system**—a display of explanatory information—at the touch of the [Help] key.
- Display menus on the screen to prompt the user with choices of available commands.
- Assign commonly used functions to the keyboard's function keys.
- Design the program to operate in a manner similar to that of systems with which most people are already familiar. For example, a file management program might mimic the operations of a Rolodex card file, an integrated package might simulate a clipboard in the way data is transferred among its component programs, and so forth.

- Use windows to display several types of information on the screen at once and to make it easy to switch from one mode to another.
- Permit special selection devices, such as a mouse or touch screen, to be used to enter commands, allowing the keyboard to be reserved for entering data.

Integrated Applications

An **integrated program** is a tightly bundled set of related, specialized programs combined in a unified package that provides a means of transferring data between the programs. For example, an integrated accounting program might combine programs that take care of all the basic accounting systems maintained by a business—accounts payable, accounts receivable, inventory management, payroll, and general ledger. These specialized programs are called *components*. In almost all integrated programs, one component is the central component and the basis for all the others, in two ways.

First, one component is usually the center of communications, the center of data transfers. For example, Figure 5.14 shows two integrated programs, each of which includes spreadsheet, graphics, database management, word processing, and data communications components. An arrow points to a component if data can be transferred to it from another component. In Figure 5.14(a), data can be transferred from the spreadsheet to any other component and from any component to the spreadsheet; but data cannot be transferred directly between the other components. Thus, in this case, the spreadsheet is the central component; this is a *spreadsheet-based integrated program*. Second, the central component may determine the form of the data in all other components and thus exert a strong influence on the other components. For example, if the spreadsheet is the central compo-

Figure 5.14 Relationships among components. Integrated software typically emphasizes one component, called the central component.

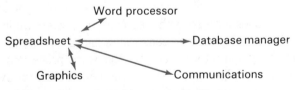

(a) Spreadsheet-based integrated software

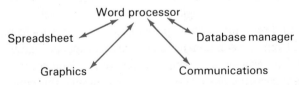

(b) Integrated software based on a word processor

nent, then all other components may adopt the spreadsheet's row-and-column format. The word processor may store text by expanding a spreadsheet column until it is as wide as the printed page, and the fields in the database manager may be basically spreadsheet cells.

Programs are often integrated in one package in order to unify the *user interface*—the communication between the computer and the user. When each program has a common user interface, learning how to operate one part of the package makes learning all the other parts easy, because they share a common mode of operation.

A major advantage of integrated programs is the ease with which data can be transferred from one component to another. For example, if you are writing a letter (word processing) that contains a graph (graphics) illustrating a relationship you discovered with a numerical model (spreadsheet analysis), then an integrated program may work better for you than an assortment of standalone programs. Data can be taken from one program and entered into another by a simple cut-and-paste operation. In contrast, moving data between standalone programs is often time consuming and bothersome. For example, to move part of a Lotus 1-2-3 spreadsheet into a Wordstar word processing document, you must

- Load Lotus 1-2-3 and the worksheet into memory.
- "Print" the portion of the worksheet you want to transfer. Instead of printing to a printer, you must request the print operation to send its output to a disk as a data file.
- Load WordStar and the document into memory.
- Merge (also called *import*) the data file into the document with a BLOCK-READ command.

These four steps are necessary because WordStar cannot directly read Lotus 1-2-3 worksheet files, but it can read files that Lotus 1-2-3 has "printed" to a disk. This type of rigmarole is common when moving data between standalone programs, because they usually store data in their own specialized formats on disk.

Another advantage of integrated programs is the speed with which you can move from one processing activity to another. For example, you may begin a session by preparing a sales forecast with a spreadsheet, as shown in Figure 5.15(a); then use the graphics component to construct a bar graph showing your forecast; and then insert the graph into a memo in the word processing component, as shown in Figure 5.15(b). The most common method of **context switching** (moving from one component to another) is *windowing*. Windowing displays several components, using multiple windows, at the same time. (Recall that a *window* is a region on the screen where a single component is displayed.)

Most integrated programs use a special file—a clipboard—to hold data while it is being moved from one component to another. A clipboard file used in conjuction with windowing can provide powerful methods of merging components. Programs usually provide a *copy-and-paste* operation that removes the data from the source window without destroying the original data. Copy-and-paste operations make

Figure 5.15 Using an integrated program to transfer information from a worksheet to a memo. Sales data in the spreadsheet window (a) are first transferred to a graph window, where they are transformed into a bar graph. Then the bar graph is copied and linked to a memo in a word processing window (b).

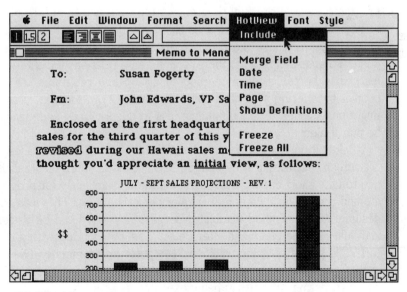

File Edit Window Range Tools Font Style							
	270						
D5							
Monthly Sales Forecast							
	A	B	C	D	E	F	G
1	Sales Forecast						
2	(in thousands)		Inflation=		5%		
3							
4		July	Aug	Sept		Total	
5	Sales	$245	$257	$270		$772	
6	Costs	86	129	135		$350	
7	Profit	159	128	135		$422	
8							
9	Expenses						
10	Auto	24	26	27		$77	
11	Phone	12	13	14		$39	
12	Wages	37	39	41		$117	
13	Taxes	9	10	10		$29	
14	Total	$82	$88	$92		$262	
15							
16	Net	$77	$40	$43		$160	
17							

(a) Worksheet

(b) Word Processing

static ("dead") copies of the original data. If the original version of the data is modified after the copy has been made, the copy remains unchanged. A few of the newest integrated programs allow *copy-and-link* operations that create "live" linkages between components. For example, a portion of the spreadsheet window in Figure 5.15(a) is copied and linked to a graph window to construct a bar chart, which in turn is linked to the memo shown in the word processing window in Figure 5.15(b). Later, if you change the numbers in the spreadsheet, both the bar chart in the graph window and the copy of the bar chart in the word processing window will automatically reflect those changes.

Integrated programs make sense when the programs perform related functions or similar tasks or when they use the same data. Integration tends to make software more powerful, versatile, and complex. Increased power and versatility are certainly commendable, but increasing complexity may make software difficult to use. As software becomes more powerful, it usually requires computers with larger memories and faster disk drives—and more sophisticated users.

Comparing User Interfaces

Not only is there great versatility in computer applications, there is also a wide variety of user interfaces. New users often find this disconcerting because there are few hard-and-fast rules for operating a computer. A command that works in one program is not likely to work in other programs. The meaning of keyboard keys also changes from one program to the next. For example, in one program, pressing [S] might display an *S* on the screen, and in other programs, it might shoot a missile or store a file. Even the on-off switch can have different meanings. On some computers, it immediately disconnects the computer from its power source; on others, it is merely a request for the computer to stop executing application programs, save all work in progress on the disk, and then turn off the power.

Which interface a program uses has a major influence on how long it takes a beginner to learn to use the program and how long it takes an expert to get tasks done. To a certain extent, there is an inverse relationship: the easiest method to learn may be the slowest method to use. Some programs try to sidestep this conflict by offering a combination of methods. For example, common commands might be assigned to function keys; less frequently used commands might have to be put in menus.

It takes little time to become comfortable with visual interfaces like that on the Macintosh, but they can be limiting because visual interfaces usually do not allow you to take short cuts. Command-line interfaces are easy for programmers to create and require little computer memory or processing. They provide the software designer with unlimited flexibility, because any word can be assigned a meaning and built into the command interpreter. Using a program with a command-line interface is similar to doing traditional computer programming. The major difference is that, with computer programming, the commands are accumulated in a file for later processing rather than being executed as soon as they are typed.

Menu-based interfaces are helpful for the novice because all available choices are shown on the screen. *Full-screen menus* fill the entire screen with options. These menus not only show what options are available but also describe briefly what each option means. They are often used in complicated but infrequently run programs, such as end-of-the-month accounting programs. *Menu bars* occupy just one or two lines on the screen, to display the available options. Choosing an option from a menu bar often leads to a subsidiary menu, prompting another choice. Subsidiary menus, like those on the Macintosh, don't obscure the view of the screen until they are needed. This makes them convenient for the user, but they are harder than other menu systems for programmers to create.

Software developers consume much time and energy debating the best user interface for programs. Some argue that a mouse or windows should be used to achieve a consistent interface. Others argue that technological devices are merely gadgets and that the easiest programs to use employ extensive menu systems. Still others argue that making an interface easy to use is less important than creating a responsive system that requires few keystrokes to issue commands. In this book, we show examples of how all of these systems work.

SUMMARY

This chapter has presented the information about software that you need to know to begin computing. We have seen that several layers of software lie between the user and the hardware of a personal computer system.

We described the parts of an operating system and how the operating system controls the computer. Through the command processor of the operating system, you have access to the file manager for manipulating files (copying, deleting, renaming, formatting, and so on) and to the operating system supervisor for loading and executing application programs. The I/O manager handles all data transferred to and from peripherals. Knowing how the operating system manages the computer's resources will help you to understand the progress of any computer session, whether you are involved in word processing, data management, communications, or just playing games.

Every computer program has its own set of commands that must be learned before the program can be used effectively. We have seen several ways of giving those commands: by typing command lines, by manipulating icons, and by choosing options from menu bars and pull-down menus.

KEY TERMS

argument

batch file

bug

command-line operating system

command processor

context switching

copy-protect

default

delimiter	mode
device driver	option switch
device independence	parameter
documentation	PC-DOS
file allocation table	pull-down (second-level) menu
file manager	resident routine
format	scrolling
free-form windows	shell
help system	supervisor
initialize	system disk
integrated program	tiled window
I/O manager	transient utility
job control language (JCL)	upward compatible
keyword	visual operating system
machine independence	wild card character
menu bar	window

DISCUSSION QUESTIONS

1. What is the significance of upward compatibility? Is downward compatibility as important?

2. In a command-line operating system, a batch file stores textual commands. How might a visual operating system store commands in a batch file?

3. What happens if you make a typing mistake in a command-line system? If you make a typing mistake when giving a command, is the result likely to be a valid command?

4. What is a file? What conventions does your computer use for naming files?

5. Suppose the directory of your floppy disk contains the following file names:
   TICTAC.EXE   README.DOC
   ALGEBRA.DAT   DEFAULT.TXT
   STARTUP.BAT
   What do you suppose each file contains? Comment on the importance of choosing meaningful file names.

6. Why are wild card characters convenient? (Think of some tasks that would be easier to perform with wild card characters than without them.)

7. Why are floppy disks sold blank rather than formatted?

8. What is the difference between application software and system software? What kinds of programs might fall in a gray area between the two?

9. What is the difference between device and machine independence?

10. How much on-line help should be provided by an operating system? by an application program?

11. Should an integrated program be based on one basic component, such as a spreadsheet or a database, or should its basis be independent of the components? Why?

12. Describe the features of an ideal, easy-to-use interface for an airline reservation system. How might this interface differ from the ideal interface for a game? for a word processor?

EXERCISES

1. Prepare a list of your computer's operating system commands. Rank the commands according to how often you are likely to use them.

2. Determine which commands in your computer's operating system are resident and which are transient.

3. List the advantages of an integrated program over a collection of individual programs that performs the same tasks. List the disadvantages.

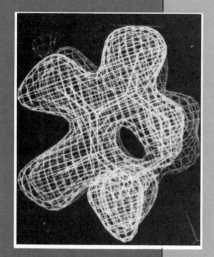

PART II
APPLICATIONS

Before World War II, a computer was a person who performed lengthy calculations. An entire room of human computers was needed to complete the design of a skyscraper, bridge, or airplane; some calculations went on for months. Today a single desktop computer holds the computational power of thousands of human computers. Modern methods of computing, the low cost of electronic computers, and application programs have changed the way people work.

To understand how these changes have occurred, you need to understand software's central role in computing. It is software that adapts a general-purpose computer to a specific task. In Part II, we examine the features of productivity software. These general-purpose application programs—for word processing, spreadsheets, data management, communications, graphics, and desktop publishing—are useful to just about everyone and illustrate concepts relevant to all computer programs.

In Chapter 6, we begin our examination of application areas with word processing, the most popular of all applications. Chapter 6 begins with descriptions of the basic operations necessary to write and print a memo, letter, or other simple document. Then it describes the intermediate and advanced features of today's sophisticated word processors. Chapter 7 introduces you to the power of spreadsheet programs, the second most popular category of productivity software.

Chapter 8 studies the category of software programs designed for data management.

In Part II, we also examine the frontiers of communications and graphics. These are among the most dynamic areas of computing, because no dominant software or standard hardware has emerged. Chapter 9 examines how communications hardware and software are weaving a network of computers into a world-encompassing web the like of which has never before been seen. In Chapter 10, we describe computer graphics—an area that until recently was stunted by the high cost of internal memory and color displays. Today the software for creating graphics is becoming more powerful and easier to use. In Chapter 11, we describe how advances in laser printing technology and page composition software have made desktop publishing the fastest-growing area of computing.

Although Part II covers the most widely used application areas, it is important to remember that these areas account for only a small portion of the software for computers. Software developers have produced programs for virtually every conceivable application. If you are faced with a special or unusual problem, you should be sure to choose software appropriate for the task. Often this involves choosing a special-purpose program rather than adapting a general-purpose program or developing a program from scratch. ■

6 Word Processing

I t's a safe bet that word processing has sold more personal computers than any other application. Writers come to love their word processing systems because they eliminate most of the drudgery associated with traditional, paper-based methods of translating thoughts into printed documents. Moving characters around on the screen allows you to edit words easily before committing them to paper. It's possible to delete text, move whole paragraphs, and lengthen all of the lines on a page with *at most* a few commands.

This chapter will teach you about word processing in several steps. It begins with a comparison of five different word processing programs, to help you understand how important it is to choose your word processor wisely. Next the chapter describes the basic editing processes used in creating memos, letters, and other typical documents. It also describes some functions at the heart of a word processor, such as moving paragraphs, search-and-replace operations, and page design. The chapter concludes with descriptions of some of the "bells and whistles" you can expect in a full-featured word processor.

BASIC CONCEPTS

Word processing is such a big improvement over pencils and typewriters that even a poor word processor can impress a new user. Few people have the time or opportunity to test very many word processing programs; most people choose their word processing program because it came with their computer system or was recommended by friends. As a result, the world is full of people who happily use an inferior word processing program or one that is inappropriate for their needs.

The mistakes people make when they select word processing and desktop publishing programs are amazing. (Word processing programs with the fanciest formatting and page layout features are often called **desktop publishing** programs and are discussed in more detail in a later chapter.) Any bare-bones word processor can handle a one-page letter or memo. But a bare-bones word processor is the wrong product to use if you must create a mailing with hundreds of "personalized" letters; a word processor that can use an electronic mailing list to print the letters automatically is much more efficient. Similarly, a casual user who plans to write short memos does not need the page layout capabilities of a desktop publishing program.

The first step in choosing a program is to define your writing needs. How often will you use it? How important is ease of use versus long-run convenience and advanced features? What types of documents will you create?

After you have answered these questions, you need to know what types of features you can expect to find. One good source of information is the reviews printed in such trade magazines as *InfoWorld* and *Personal Computing*. They provide comparison charts at the end of articles; often these charts go on for page after page, with concise, but cryptic labels for each feature. Today's word processors are full of time savers, writing aids, formatting tricks, and other helpful features. Some make life easier for beginners; others are essential for specific tasks; and still others sound better in advertisements than they work in practice.

Comparing Programs

Table 6.1 compares the features of five popular programs available for IBM PCs: PFS:Professional Write, WordPerfect, WordStar 2000, Microsoft Word, and Ventura Publisher. We chose these particular programs because they illustrate quite different approaches to word processing, ranging from a very simple word processor to a desktop publishing program. Though many of the features listed in Table 6.1 may seem puzzling now, they will become clearer after you read the rest of the chapter.

Table 6.1 A Comparison Chart for Five Word Processing and Desktop Publishing Programs

Feature	PFS:Professional Write	WordPerfect	WordStar 2000	Microsoft Word	Ventura Publisher
Primary user interface	Function keys, pull-down menus, dialog boxes	Function keys, message lines	Control keys, partial-screen menus	Mouse, keyword menus	Mouse, icons, pull-down menus, dialog boxes
Mouse support	No	No	No	Yes	Yes
Edit multiple files at once	No	2	3	8	Many
Newspaper-style columns	No	24	3	Many	Many
Lines per header or footer	2	Unlimited	Unlimited	Unlimited	2
Odd/even page distinctions	No	Yes	Yes	Yes	Yes
On-screen help system	Yes	Yes	Yes	Yes	No
On-screen tutorial system	No	No	Yes	Yes	No
Spelling checker	Yes	Yes	Yes	Yes	No
Automatic hyphenation	No	Yes	Yes	Yes	Yes
On-line thesaurus	Yes	Yes	No	No	No
Avoids widows and orphans	No	If desired	No	Always	If desired
Footnote placement	Manual	Automatic	Automatic	Automatic	Automatic
Movable columns of text	No	Yes	Yes	Yes	No
Document assembly (chaining)	Yes	Yes	Yes	Yes	Yes
Table of contents/indexing	No	Yes	Optional	Yes	Yes
Form letters	Yes	Yes	Yes	Yes	No
Style sheets (format files)	No	No	No	Yes	Yes
Outline processing functions	No	Some	No	Yes	No
User-definable macros	No	Yes	No	Yes	No
Prints proportional spacing	No	Yes	Yes	No	Yes
Prints multiple typefaces	No	Yes	Yes	Yes	Yes
Displays multiple typefaces	No	No	No	Some	Yes
Merges text and graphics files	No	No	No	No	Yes
List price	$199	$495	$495	$450	$895
Minimum memory requirement	320K	320K	320K	192K	512K
Maximum file size	64K	Limited by disk	Limited by disk	Limited by disk	Limited by memory
List price	$199	$495	$495	$450	$895

- *PFS:Professional Write* is a simple word processor designed for easy use by casual users. Its commands are prompted by pull-down menus followed by **dialog boxes**, which contain specific question prompts. As a result, even someone unfamiliar with computers can begin using it productively after just an hour or two of practice.

- *WordPerfect* is perhaps the most popular word processor for IBM PCs. Its commands require frequent use of the function keys. For example, pressing the function key labeled [F3] begins the on-screen help system, and pressing [Ctrl]-[F2] begins the spelling checker that proofs the words in your document against the words in WordPerfect's dictionary. WordPerfect's function-key system takes some time to get used to but is convenient for experienced users.

- *WordStar 2000* is an extensive revision of the original WordStar program. Most of its commands require a combination of keystrokes, such as pressing [Ctrl]-[B] and then [B] to mark the beginning of a block of text. It takes days of practice to become comfortable with the full range of WordStar 2000's commands; but once the commands have been learned, they are far less intrusive and time consuming than the frequent appearance of menus.

- *Microsoft Word* is a state-of-the-art processing program with many innovative features for creating professional-quality documents quickly. Although Microsoft Word's commands can be invoked from the keyboard, it was designed to be used with a mouse. The mouse commands help beginners become proficient quickly with Microsoft Word's many features—but "mousing around" can be distracting if you are a touch-typist, because you must move one hand from the keyboard to use a mouse. Some of Microsoft Word's distinguishing features are that up to eight documents can be edited simultaneously in different windows; an outstanding on-line tutorial system is built into the help system; special format files (known as *style sheets*) standardize and simplify the process of laying out the appearance of documents; and outline processing features help organize ideas into a workable outline.

- *Ventura Publisher* is a screen-oriented *desktop publishing* program. It provides professional page layout features, gives text a typeset appearance, and allows pictures and graphics to be merged with the text on the screen. Although it includes simple text editing abilities, it is more frequently used to format and merge text files created by other word processing programs. Ventura Publisher is discussed in this chapter as well as Chapter 11, "Desktop Publishing," to emphasize the similarities among advanced word processing and desktop publishing programs.

By now it should be clear that all word processors are definitely not alike. Which one is "best" depends on the type of writing to be done.

Steps in a Typical Session

Let's assume that you've selected your word processor and you're ready to begin running the word processing program. On a personal computer, you might do this by turning on the computer, loading the operating system, typing the name of the word processing program, and waiting until the word processing program is loaded into memory and takes control of the computer. On a mainframe computer, you must log in first.

In order to edit an existing document, you must tell the word processor the name of the text file that contains the document. This causes some (or all) of the file to be transferred from disk into memory. Alternatively, you can edit an empty file—in other words, create a new file.

The next step is to type and edit the document. You can correct typing mistakes by deleting, inserting, or replacing characters. Throughout the editing process, it is a good idea to periodically *save* the text—transfer it from memory to the disk. This ensures that a temporary power failure won't create a major problem for you when it erases the contents of memory.

When you're finished editing, you save the text to disk a final time. If you want, you can get a printout by turning on the printer and typing the appropriate command to start the word processor's printing routines. Finally, you end the session either by giving a command to leave the word processing program (thus returning to the operating system) or by turning off the computer.

Understanding the Screen

Figure 6.1 shows a typical screen display while a letter is being entered and edited. Notice that the screen is broken into two parts. The bottom part shows the text that is being edited. The upper part gives the status of the program, such as where the cursor is located, and *help information*, such as how to give commands.

Nearly all word processors reserve part of the screen to display status and help information. Understanding this portion of the screen is a good first step toward mastering any application program. In Figure 6.1, the status and help information includes

- The current location of the cursor (page 1, line 11, column 5), the name of the text file being edited (MEMO), and its location (disk drive A)
- A list of commands. This list includes commands that allow you to move text from one place in the document to another, to print the document on a printer, to quit word processing and begin another task, and to save a copy of the document on a disk.
- The location of the left and right margins (indicated by L and R on line 4 of the screen)
- The positions of the tab stops (indicated by ! on line 4 of the screen)

Figure 6.1 Typical screen display of a word processor while editing a letter.

```
CURSOR: Pg 1  Ln 11  Col 5      EDITING: A:MEMO
COMMAND:  Copy    Delete  Format  Help    Insert
          Move    Print   Quit    Save    Undo
L----!----!----!----!----!----!----!--R
from the desk of . . . MARY SMITH

John Doe
123 Main St.
Anytown, USA

Dear John,

    Thank  you for your interest in my record
collection.   I am tempted to sell  my  1948
Gene  Autry  album, but my cat  cannot  live
without it.

                Yours truly,

                Mary Smith
```

The amount and the kind of status and help information provided vary widely from one word processor to another. A few word processors use a large part of the screen to help you remember what commands are available. Obviously, as more status and help information is displayed on the screen, less room is left to show the text being edited. New users tend to want all the status and help information they can get. Experienced users usually want an uncluttered display showing as much of their text as possible. This conflict is usually resolved in either of two ways: by allowing the user to choose how much of the screen will be devoted to each function or by using pull-down or pop-up menu systems.

Figure 6.2 shows the result of printing the letter shown in Figure 6.1. Although the text in the two figures is identical, the printed letter looks better than the screen version shown in Figure 6.1. This is typical for word processors; often the differences are more dramatic.

For example, the oldest method of electronic word processing—called **off-screen text formatting**—relies on a two-step process to enter and print documents. In the first step you enter special format commands along with the document's text. These commands describe how the text should look when printed. During the editing step the screen shows both the text and the format commands. After all the text and format commands have been entered in a data file, a *text-formatting program* reads the data file, strips the format commands from the text, and uses them as instructions about how to print the text. But because it is time-consuming and error-prone to use text formatters, they are no longer popular for simple word processing tasks. Even so, they are still important to know about.

MICRO OR MAINFRAME WORD PROCESSING: WHICH TYPE TO USE?

An increasingly viable alternative to micro-based word processing is word processing on mainframes.

There are two primary reasons for such a shift back to mainframe word processing. First, many of the users in medium and large companies need to access large data bases that are usually resident on the mainframe computer. Second, a mainframe word processing software package can provide word processing on existing 3270 terminal equipment that is usually available and in many cases paid for, therefore providing a less costly alternative. This also eliminates the need to buy, inventory, and manage the distribution of numerous copies of a given software package as is the case with micro software packages.

One advantage that micros have enjoyed is the tremendous array of fast and flexible office automation application products available such as spreadsheets, graphics, communications, and word processing. Mainframe users have simply not had access to comparable products.

Fortunately, software vendors are responding to this void by developing what used to be considered personal computer—type applications for mainframe systems. These programs are becoming faster, friendlier, and more powerful.

Certain word processing applications for correspondence, proposals, personalized mass mailings, sales letters, custom forms, donor acknowledgements, form letters, contracts, and customer support responses lend themselves particularly well to mainframe systems.

Mainframe word processing can best be utilized in industries such as banking, insurance, utilities, non-profits, education, associations, health care, and government—in fact, anywhere a large number of users share the same computer or have a large data base.

Mainframe word processing solves many of the document distribution and retrieval problems inherent with micros. It allows the user to access the same data and text instantly, regardless if the user is located in an office across the hall or across the country. And depending on the type of software, the user can create a document on one terminal, print it on any printer on the system or send it to any other user's "in box."

Although the best mainframe products are quite interactive, they sometimes do not give the user the immediate feedback of a micro. With micro word processing each keystroke of text is immediately sent to the CPU, and the document instantly appears updated or reformatted on the screen.

Most mainframe systems store entered keystrokes of text in the terminal's memory, so the changes to your document are not permanently updated or reformatted until the operator presses a key to order the document updated on the mainframe. This is a plus in that the mainframe is not interrupted every time a keystroke of text is entered; therefore a large number of users will not degrade the system performance. On the minus side, the user does not always have an exact picture of what the document looks like.

The future promises products that provide horizontal mainframe word processing links to data bases, list management, personal computer—mainframe links, electronic mail, spreadsheets, graphics, and other mainframe applications. In fact, word processing systems without a data base/mail merge interface will probably have little or no market.

Mainframe word processing promises to be a dynamic and evolving market as users continue to demand new features and new links to other existing and new applications.

Source: Bart Carlson, *Computerworld Focus,* 16 October 1986. pp. 41–42.

Figure 6.2 The result of printing the letter shown in Figure 6.1.

---

from the desk of . . . MARY SMITH

John Doe
123 Main St.
Anytown, USA

Dear John,

    Thank you for your interest in my record
collection. I am tempted to sell my 1948 Gene
Autry album, but my cat cannot live without it.

                  Yours truly,

                  Mary Smith

Many of the best scientific word processors, technical documentation systems, and typesetting systems use off-screen text formatting.

The trend in word processing is clearly toward on-screen formatting, known as WYSIWYG (pronounced "wizzy-wig"), an acronym for "*what you see is what you get.*" A **WYSIWYG word processor** attempts to make the text on the screen look just the way it would on paper. It is helpful, especially for a beginner, to see what a document looks like without printing it or using a separate print-previewing operation. But building a perfectly accurate WYSIWYG word processor is an almost impossible technical challenge. One difficulty is the relatively low resolution of monitors—around 75 dots per inch (dpi). Even inexpensive printers provide resolutions from 150 to 600 dpi, so text looks coarser on a screen than on paper. For example, compare the clean-looking text of the printed letter in Figure 6.2 with the on-screen version shown in Figure 6.3. Both versions look identical, except for the resolution of the characters. It takes a good graphics monitor and elegant software to produce the image shown in Figure 6.3, and many computer systems don't have the necessary equipment. Thus, nearly all WYSIWYG word processors make compromises—they attempt to organize the screen like the printed page but reserve some formatting operations for the printing stage. For

Figure 6.3 Typical screen display of a WYSIWYG desktop publishing program.

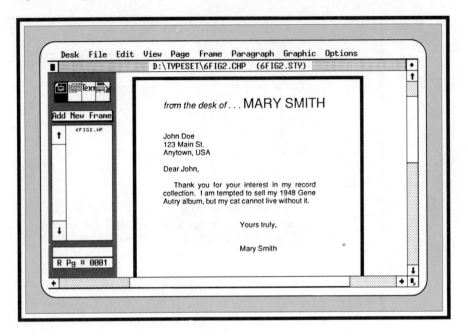

example, the on-screen images of bold, italic, and normal characters may all look the same. Or the lines on the screen may have the same number of characters as they will have when printed, but the spacing between words may be more uniform on paper than on the screen.

Differences between the screen version and the printed document can cause confusion while you're editing. For example, it certainly isn't apparent from Figure 6.1 that the words *from the desk of* in the first line will be printed in italic. Normal and italic characters look the same in Figure 6.1, so how can you tell one from the other? Most word processors answer this sort of question by placing **format codes** in the document. These codes describe how the text will be printed or control how the text will be reformatted if you alter the document—for example, by changing the margins on the page. Usually these codes are hidden so they won't clutter up the screen. But if you have a question about how something will be printed, you can give a command to have them appear on the screen, as shown in Figure 6.4. Because the format codes in Figure 6.4 are shown in color, it is easy to tell them from the text in the document.

The use of format codes hasn't been standardized among word processors. For example, the word processor shown in Figure 6.4 uses the [I] to mark the beginning of italic characters; another might use [ITALIC]; and still another might display italic characters in a different color than normal characters. This sort of varia-

Figure 6.4 Typical screen display of a word processor, showing format codes.

```
CURSOR: Pg 1  Ln 11  Col 5      EDITING: A:MEMO
COMMAND:  Copy   Delete  Format  Help    Insert
          Move   Print   Quit    Save    Undo
L----!----!----!----!----!----!----!--R
[I]from the desk of[i] . . . [18PT]MARY SMITH[HRt]
[2.5 BLANK LINES]
[12PT]John Doe[HRt]
123 Main St.[HRt]
Anytown, USA[HRt]
[HRt]
Dear John,[HRt]
[HRt]
    Thank  you for your interest in my record[SRt]
collection.  I am tempted to sell  my  1948[SRt]
Gene  Autry  album, but my cat  cannot  live[SRt]
with[-]out it.[SRt]
[2 BLANK LINES]
                     Yours truly,[HRt]

[2 BLANK LINES]
                     Mary Smith[HRt]
```

tion among word processors makes people reluctant to switch from one word processor to another; it is time consuming to learn new commands and procedures for the same basic tasks.

WORD PROCESSING BASICS

Editing

Editing is the fun part of word processing. It lets you express your thoughts, by typing them into the computer, so that they can be seen on the screen. If you don't like what you see, then you can use editing operations to quickly insert or delete words or sentences.

To enter and edit a simple document, such as a letter, you need to learn only four editing operations.

1. Moving the cursor to where you want to make changes
2. Scrolling text on the screen so that you can view other parts of the document
3. Deleting characters
4. Adding new characters of text, by inserting or replacing characters

After we have discussed these essential operations, we will describe some of the techniques word processors use to determine how much text to place on each line. Then we will describe two intermediate editing operations that make it much easier to revise a document: block operations and search-and-replace operations. *Block operations* manipulate entire groups of characters at once, as in moving a paragraph, for example. *Search-and-replace operations* allow you to locate numerous occurrences of a group of characters (such as "Smith"), and if you wish, to replace that group of characters with a different group (with "Smythe," for example).

Cursor Control

Recall that the *cursor* is the indicator on the screen that shows where things will happen next. In order to make a change in the text, you must move the cursor to where the change is to be made. Thus, it is important to be able to move the cursor around the screen in an efficient manner.

Most keyboards have cursor-movement keys (also called *arrow keys*). The [←] key moves the cursor one position to the left; the [→] key, one position to the right; the [↑] key, one position up; and the [↓] key, one position down. For example, if you press [→] four times and then press [↓] once, the cursor moves over four columns and down one line, as Figure 6.5 illustrates. To move the cursor all the way to the end of a line, hold down [→]. The cursor will float across the line. When it reaches the last character on the line, it will jump to the beginning of the next line and begin floating across it. You can use the [←] key in the same way, to move right to left across a line. When the cursor reaches the first character on the line, it will jump to the last character on the previous line.

Scrolling

As we mentioned in Chapter 5, *scrolling* moves lines of text up or down on the screen, allowing you to see new parts of the text. It might be useful to think of scrolling as a process similar to that shown in Figure 6.6. That is, scrolling moves

Figure 6.5 Effect of pushing the right-arrow key four times and the down-arrow key once.

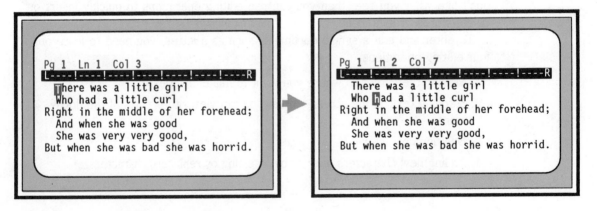

Figure 6.6 Scrolling.

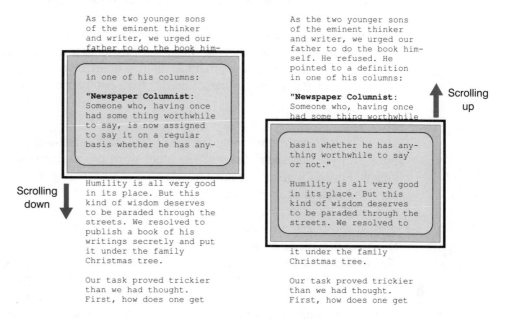

the screen up and down but leaves the document fixed in place. The screen acts as a window, letting you view the document. As you scroll the screen up, lines of text disappear off the bottom of the viewing area, and new lines show up on the top.

Holding down the down-arrow key moves the cursor down the screen until it nears the bottom; then the text on the screen begins to jump up one line at a time. Most word processors begin scrolling the text before the cursor has reached the bottom line (see Figure 6.7). This guarantees that you can see at least one line of text below the line marked with the cursor (unless, of course, the screen is dis-

Figure 6.7 Scrolling two lines by pushing the down-arrow key twice.

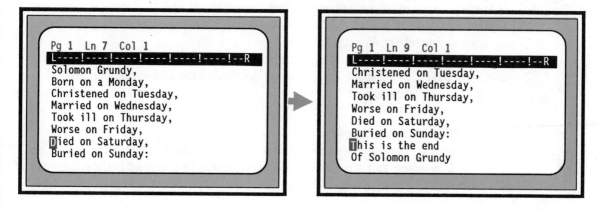

playing the end of the document), which helps you understand the context of the area being edited. Naturally, only the text scrolls on the screen; any status or help information stays put.

You can use the cursor keys to scroll one line at a time to the bottom of a document; but if the document is long, this procedure is time consuming and boring. Full-featured word processing programs offer an alternative: they provide numerous commands that move the cursor quickly from one part of the text to another.

Deleting

You will spend more time using the basic, one-character-at-a-time editing operations than you will spend using all the other word processing commands put together. For this reason, you must have a good understanding of how to delete, insert, and replace characters in a document.

A single character can be erased by moving the cursor to the character to be deleted and typing a *character-delete command.* Although the exact command for this operation varies from program to program, the command itself is always simple. In this discussion, we assume that your keyboard has a key labeled [Del], which is used to delete the character immediately under the cursor.

When you use an eraser or correction fluid to remove characters from paper, blank spaces remain. But when you use a word processor to delete a character, the rest of the line is shifted to the left to fill the void. For most purposes, this is much nicer than having a blank space remain after you erase a character. Holding the [Del] key down continues the erasing and shifting so that entire words and phrases can be deleted. If you want to delete an entire sentence, move the cursor to the beginning of the sentence and hold down [Del]. The characters in the sentence will shift and disappear one by one until the entire sentence has been deleted.

Most word processing programs have two character-delete commands: one for forward deletion and one for backward deletion. We've just described *forward deletion;* it deletes characters in the direction we read. *Backward deletion* deletes the character to the left of the cursor, moves the cursor into the position vacated by the erased character, and shifts the rest of the line left to cover up the hole. Backward deletion is useful when you decide to erase something that you've just typed, because you can do so without moving the cursor to the beginning of what you want to delete. Forward deletion is usually used when you need to go back and edit a document for meaning or style.

Besides deleting individual characters, most word processors also have specific commands for deleting the current word, deleting to the end of the line, and deleting an entire block of text.

Inserting and Replacing

There are two general ways to enter new characters into a document: they can be *inserted,* meaning that they are added between existing characters, or they can *replace* existing characters, meaning that they "type over" existing characters.

Figure 6.8 Three ways to insert text. (a) A word processor in the typeover mode will replace existing text with whatever is typed. (b) A word processor in the insert mode will shove existing characters to the right as new characters are typed. (c) A word processor with dynamic paragraph reforming will automatically shift words from line to line within a paragraph as you type, in order to keep the paragraph within its assigned margins.

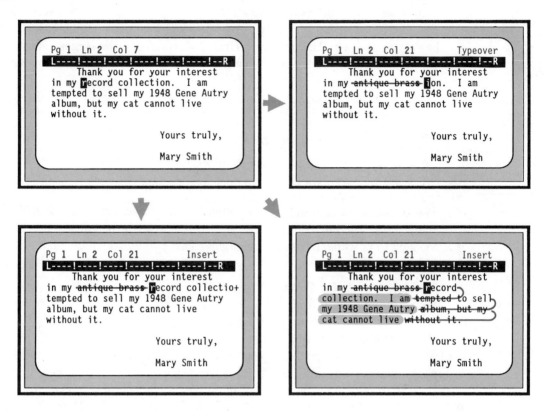

Usually the status portion of the screen indicates which of these methods the program is using, as shown in the upper right-hand corners of the screens in Figure 6.8. When the program is in the **insert mode**, new characters are added within the text as they are typed. When the program is in the **typeover mode**, new characters replace characters already in the text. Most programs begin in the insert mode because it is used more frequently.

The choice between insert and typeover modes is usually made with a toggle switch. Each time a **toggle switch**, which has only two settings, is thrown from one setting to the other, the new value is maintained until the switch is thrown again. Household light switches work this way. If you throw a switch to turn a light on, it stays on until you throw the switch again. Similarly, if you use a toggle switch to give a command to the computer, that command remains in effect until you throw the toggle switch again. Toggle switches are used for many commands in word processing programs. Generally, the same command is used to toggle the switch from one value to another. For example, most word processors on IBM-compatible personal computers use the [Ins] key to toggle between the two modes. Thus, each push of the [Ins] key causes the word processor to alternate between the insert and typeover modes.

For some tasks, such as fixing typing errors, it is quicker to replace characters than to delete the erroneous characters and then insert the correct ones. In general, the typeover mode is convenient when a change does not increase the number of characters in the document. Thus, the typeover mode is more efficient than the insert mode if you are rearranging transposed letters, as in changing *recieve* to *receive*.

When the insert mode is in effect, each character you type causes three things to happen.

1. It pushes the rest of the characters on the line to the right.

2. It inserts the character in the document at the current cursor position.

3. It moves the cursor to the next column position.

These rules explain what happens when you insert characters in the middle of a line of text, but they don't explain what happens when the current line becomes too long to fit within its assigned margins. That is the topic of the next section.

Making Words Fit Within Margins

Word processors provide two features to confine text within its assigned boundaries: *word wrap* and *paragraph reforming*.

A typewriter's bell rings as the carriage nears the end of a line. If the typist doesn't return the carriage, typing soon stops, with the carriage stuck against the right margin. With a word processor, there is no listening for the typewriter bell or peeking to see if the next word will fit on the line. If a word is too long to fit at the end of a line, it is automatically moved to the next line. The [Enter] key is used only to end paragraphs. This feature is called **word wrap**. By eliminating the need to determine where to stop each line, word wrap increases the rate at which you can enter text.

To understand how word wrap functions, it helps to know that words, lines, and paragraphs have different meanings in word processing than in everyday life. In word processing, a *word* is a string of letters or numerals. Words are separated from one another by spaces, punctuation marks, and carriage returns. To a word processor, *R2D2* is as valid a word as any other. A *line* is one row of text on the screen or on paper. At the end of each line is a carriage return, which can be either hard or soft. A *hard carriage return* is a return generated by pressing [Enter] or, on some keyboards, [Return] or [↵]. *Soft carriage returns* are generated automatically by the word wrap feature. When a word extends beyond the maximum line length, word wrap moves the last word on the line to the next line and places a soft return at the end of the old line. A *paragraph* is a string of characters ended by a hard carriage return. Paragraphs can be quite short, and they don't necessarily form a complete thought. For example, if you type "Bananas" and press [En-

Figure 6.9 Breaking a paragraph in two by pressing [Enter] and [Tab].

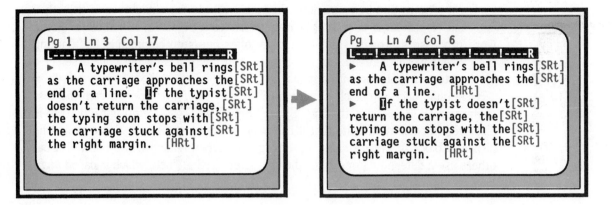

ter], then type "Apples" and press [Enter], and then type "Oranges" and press [Enter], you will place three one-word paragraphs in your document. Some word processors tell you which lines end in a hard carriage return by placing a paragraph symbol (¶) in the rightmost column of the screen. Figure 6.9 illustrates another method of disclosing the same information: each line ends with either a format code of [HRt], indicating a hard return, or [SRt], for soft return.

Figure 6.9 also illustrates how you can break a paragraph in two by pressing [Enter] to insert a hard carriage return in the middle of a paragraph and [Tab] to indent the beginning of the new paragraph. This process is reversible: most word processors allow you to delete format codes in the same way you delete other characters. Thus, you can merge two paragraphs by deleting the hard carriage return at the end of the first paragraph. For example, to move from the right-hand screen of Figure 6.9 to the left-hand screen, you would push [Del] twice to delete the tab and the hard carriage return.

Insertion, deletion, and other editing operations will shorten some lines and lengthen others. On a typewriter, the changed paragraphs would need to be retyped. This is where a word processor shines. **Paragraph reforming** shifts words up to fill shortened lines and moves words down to trim long ones. To reform a paragraph, the word processor first removes the soft carriage returns and any other soft characters previously added by the word processor, such as **soft spaces**, which spread out the line to end squarely with the right margin. Then it determines which words fit on each new line. Finally, it adds soft carriage returns (and possibly other soft characters) at the ends of the new lines.

Block Operations

If you want to move or delete a large number of characters, one-character-at-a-time operations are inefficient. Instead, **block operations** are used to manipulate many characters simultaneously. These usually involve two separate operations: first you mark off the block of characters, then you give a command to manipulate the block.

To mark a block of characters, you must identify both ends of the block. Normally, this involves four steps: (1) moving the cursor to one end of the block; (2) issuing a command to begin marking the block; (3) moving the cursor to the other end; and (4) issuing a command indicating that your selection is complete. Some word processors provide short cuts; they offer one-step commands for marking the current word, sentence, or paragraph. And still others allow you to select a block of text by pointing with a mouse.

Generally, once the block is marked off, it is displayed differently from the rest of the text. For example, the line "Sydney Smith, 1771-1845" in Figure 6.10(b) is displayed in color to indicate that it has been selected as a block. Some programs display a block in *inverse video,* reversing the screen colors in the marked area; others use a different intensity for the characters in the block, which is called *highlighting.*

Deleting Blocks Once you have marked a block, a block-delete command will remove it from the document. Two things can happen to the deleted characters. First, the block may be thrown away permanently. Because a block may contain many pages of text, this method won't seem very "friendly" if you make a mistake. Consequently, most word processors move the block into a separate area of memory, called a **buffer**, *clipboard,* or *scrap area.* You can retrieve a block from the buffer later, but moving something new into the buffer throws away the buffer's previous contents.

Figure 6.10 illustrates the use of a buffer. The status information area of each screen indicates what is stored in the buffer by displaying some of the buffer's contents between curly brackets. Evidently the buffer is empty in the upper right-hand screen, because there are no characters between the brackets. The lower left-hand screen shows that the block has been moved to the buffer by displaying "Sidne. . .-1845" between the brackets.

Cut and Paste Throughout most of this century, newspaper editors cut articles into pieces so that they could paste them together in a different order. Today, word processors let editors "cut and paste" electronically. Needless to say, electronic cutting and pasting is faster and neater than using scissors and glue.

As in deleting a block, the first step in any cut-and-paste job is to mark the block to be manipulated. There are two common ways to move or copy a block.

1. In the simpler method, you place the cursor where the block is to be moved and then give the command to move or copy the block. The command to move the block transfers it from its original position to where the cursor is. This method of moving a paragraph is illustrated by Photos 13 through 16 of Window 5. The command to copy the block leaves the block in its original position and places a copy in the document right after the cursor.

2. The second method follows the cut-and-paste analogy more closely. In the "cut" part, you give a command to move or copy the block into the buffer. For the "paste" part, you place the cursor where the block is to be inserted

Figure 6.10 The steps of a cut-and-paste operation. (a) The first step is to move the cursor to one end of the block of text. (b) Then a block-marking command is given, and the cursor is moved to the other end of the block—in this case, a single line of text. (c) A block-cut command is given to remove the block from the document and place it in a buffer (shown between brackets on the top line). (d) The cursor is moved to a new location, and an insert-from-buffer command is given to place a copy of the block in the document.

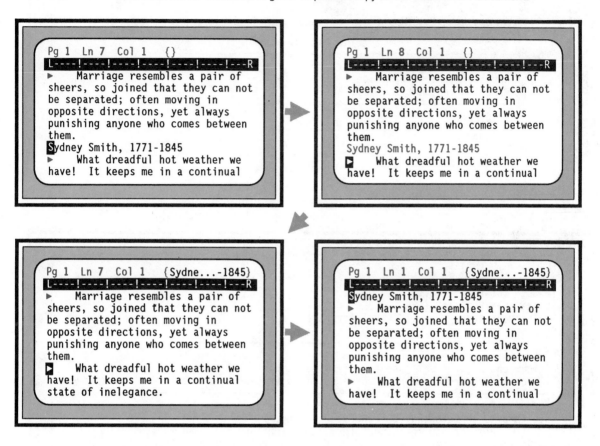

and give a command to restore the block, which copies the buffer's contents back into the document, as shown in Figure 6.10(d).

Search and Replace

Any good word processing program will use **search-and-replace operations** to search a document for a word or phrase and replace it with another. We will use PFS:Professional Write as our example because its search-and-replace operations are easy to understand even though they are not particularly flexible.

Pressing [Ctrl]-[F] begins the search; it produces an empty dialog box similar to the one shown in Figure 6.11(a), but without the colored text. Suppose you are searching for the word *Data*. This is done by typing "Data" after the "Find:" prompt and then pressing [Enter]. Then Professional Write searches the document, beginning at the cursor's location, to find the first occurrence of "Data". Be-

Figure 6.11 Two ways to perform the same search-and-replace operation. (a) PFS:Professional Write uses a simple dialog box to determine the search-and-replace phrases. (b) WordStar 2000 allows more options, such as searches that move backwards from the cursor's current position to the beginning of the file.

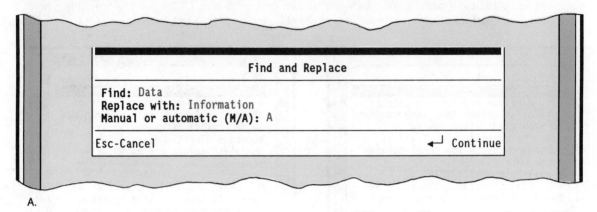

```
                    Find and Replace

Find: Data
Replace with: Information
Manual or automatic (M/A): A

Esc-Cancel                              ↵ Continue
```

A.

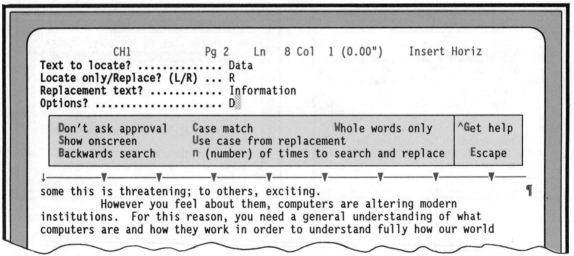

```
         CH1          Pg 2   Ln  8 Col  1 (0.00")    Insert Horiz
Text to locate? .............. Data
Locate only/Replace? (L/R) ... R
Replacement text? ............ Information
Options? ..................... D

 Don't ask approval    Case match              Whole words only   ^Get help
 Show onscreen         Use case from replacement
 Backwards search      n (number) of times to search and replace  Escape

↓──────▼────────▼──────▼──────▼──────▼──────▼──────▼──────▼──
some this is threatening; to others, exciting.                          ¶
        However you feel about them, computers are altering modern
institutions.  For this reason, you need a general understanding of what
computers are and how they work in order to understand fully how our world
```

B.

cause it ignores the difference between upper- and lower-case letters in search operations, the first match it finds might be "DATA" or "data". When a match is found, the program returns to the normal edit mode, with the cursor at the beginning of the phrase it found.

Replacing one word or phrase with another is also a simple operation. Suppose that the easiest way to write a July sales report is to make a copy of the June report and modify it. Rather than searching for "June", this situation calls for replacing every "June" with "July". This is done by

1. Pressing [Ctrl]-[F] to display the Find and Replace dialog box.

2. Typing "June" after the "Find:" prompt.

3. Pressing the [tab] key to move from one prompt to another.

4. Typing "July" after the "Replace with:" prompt.

5. Typing [A] after the "Manual or automatic (M/A):" prompt.

6. Pressing [Enter] to begin the search.

When [Enter] is pressed, Professional Write searches to the end of the document, changes every occurrence of "June" to "July", and positions the cursor after the last occurrence it found. This is called an **automatic search-and-and-replace operation** because the word procesor didn't stop to ask for permission to make the replacement each time it found a match. A **manual search-and-replace operation** pauses after each match is found and asks whether the current match should be replaced or ignored.

The automatic search-and-replace feature is handy, but it can lead to serious problems if the search phrase is more common than you expected. For example, if you replace all occurrences of the word *too* with *to*, the words *tool* and *took* become *tol* and *tok*.

Text Formatting

Most of what you have learned so far about word processing has been about editing—the process of entering, deleting, and reordering characters. This section deals with **text formatting**—controlling the appearance of the document so that it will look good on paper.

The formatting options provided by word processors are adequate for most everyday documents, such as letters or reports. But professional-quality documents, such as newspapers, magazines, and advertisements, may require multicolumn page layouts that combine text and graphics in artistic ways. To produce these documents, it is usually best to use a *page composition program* to arrange the placement of text and graphics on the page. This chapter will discuss the formatting options offered by word processors; page composition will be discussed in Chapter 11.

Formatting activities fall into two interrelated categories: *page design* and *local formatting options.*

- **Page design** determines the *page layout*—the page size and the initial settings for the format and appearance of text on the page. This nearly always involves choosing the top, bottom, left, and right margins of the page. Depending on your word processor, it may also include formatting instructions for items within the document, such as where to place footnotes or how to format different types of paragraphs.

- **Local formatting options** allow you to adjust the appearance of text within a portion of the document. They temporarily override the global page design settings. For example, you might use them to make page breaks, choose a shorter line length for a paragraph, or switch from one type size to another.

Page Design Methods

For a word processor to print correctly, it must know how big each piece of paper is and how large to make the margins. Most full-featured word processors provide page design options like those shown in Figure 6.12. Some of the terms in Figure 6.12 deserve further explanation.

- *Page length* is generally given in number of lines per page. It can be set for standard $8\frac{1}{2}'' \times 11''$ paper or for envelopes, mailing labels, odd-sized pages, or extra-long sheets of paper. The most common setting is 66 lines, which allows 6 lines per inch on 11-inch paper.

- **Headers** and **footers** are the text at the tops and bottoms of pages. They are typed into the file only once; the word processor places them on each page automatically. For example, headers and footers might be used to print the document's title at the top of each page and the page number at the bottom.

- Most programs define the *top* and *bottom margins* as the areas above and below the regular text. These programs print the header and footer lines inside the top and bottom margins, as shown in Figure 6.12. Other programs consider the header and footer to be part of the body of the page.

- Bound documents are usually printed on both sides of the paper; they need different margins on odd and even pages because part of the page is hidden within the binding. The traditional way to accomplish this is to add a *gutter margin* to the right side of even pages and the left side of odd pages.

- The *left margin, right margin, gutter margin,* and *line length* are interrelated because they add up to the *page width.* Some word processors arrive at an implied page width by letting you specify the margins and the line length; others calculate the line length by subtracting the margins from the page width.

With this background about page design terms, we're ready to compare the page design methods of two word processors: PFS:Professional Write and Microsoft Word.

Page Design with PFS:Professional Write Despite its fancy name, PFS:Professional Write is a simple word processor that provides few formatting options. It's worth studying because its features are representative of the capabilities of many easy-to-use word processors.

Figure 6.13 shows the two dialog boxes PFS:Professional Write uses to establish a document's global format specifications. This method is easily learned but quite restrictive, because these two dialog boxes control the page layout for the entire document—few of the global settings can be overridden with local formatting options. Among other things, this means that the top and bottom margins must be the same for every page throughout the document.

The Margins and Page Length dialog box is noteworthy because of the question it *doesn't* ask. For example, it doesn't ask how many columns will be on each page, because Professional Write doesn't create multicolumn documents.

Figure 6.12 Page design terms.

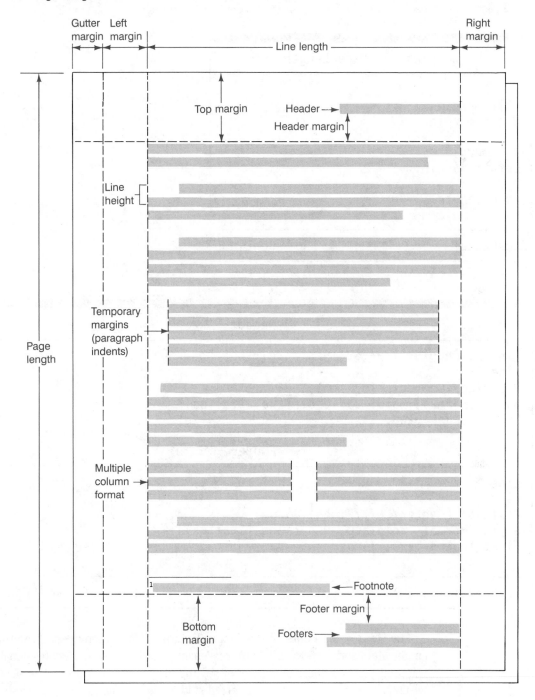

Figure 6.13 Page design with PFS:Professional Write. (a) A simple dialog box establishes the boundaries of the page. (b) Another dialog box is used to set the header and footer lines for the entire file.

```
┌─────────────────────────────────────────────────┐
│ ████████████████████████████████████             │
│                                                   │
│          Margins and Page Length                  │
│ ─────────────────────────────────────────────    │
│                                                   │
│  Left margin   : 10                               │
│  Right margin  : 70                               │
│                                                   │
│  Top margin    : 6                                │
│  Bottom margin: 6                                 │
│                                                   │
│  Page length   : 66                               │
│                                                   │
│ ─────────────────────────────────────────────    │
│  Esc-Cancel              ←┘ Continue              │
└─────────────────────────────────────────────────┘
```
A.

```
┌───────────────────────────────────────────────────────────────┐
│ ████████████████████████████████████████████████████           │
│                         Header                                  │
│ ─────────────────────────────────────────────────────────────  │
│ Line 1: Chapter 2 -- Sally's Misgivings About David             │
│ Line 2:                                                         │
│ Position (Center/Left/Right): C                                 │
│ Style (Normal, Boldface, Underline, Italics): N                 │
│ First header page: 1                                            │
│                         Footer                                  │
│ ─────────────────────────────────────────────────────────────  │
│ Line 1: Page *1*                                                │
│ Line 2:                                                         │
│ Position (Center/Left/Right): C                                 │
│ Style (Normal, Boldface, Underline, Italics): N                 │
│ First footer page: 1                                            │
│ ─────────────────────────────────────────────────────────────  │
│ Esc-Cancel                                     ←┘ Continue      │
└───────────────────────────────────────────────────────────────┘
```
B.

The Header and Footer dialog box collects the information needed to print two-line headers and footers. Like any reasonable word processor, Professional Write will print page numbers as part of either the header or the footer. The position at which page numbers are to be inserted is identified by surrounding a number with asterisks, as in *8*. For example, the dialog box in Figure 6.13 would cause "Page 12" to print in the center of the footer line of page 12 of the document. Professional Write is somewhat unusual, in that it stores the header and footer lines as a global format setting. Consequently, if you want different headers or footers in each part of a document, then you must break the document into parts and store each part in a separate file.

Professional Write doesn't provide a method for automatically distinguishing between odd and even pages, making it difficult to print well-formatted double-sided documents. For example, Professional Write doesn't have gutter margins to reserve space for a binding, and it can't vary the placement of page numbers in headers and footers to fall on the outside edges of opposite pages.

Page Design with Microsoft Word Microsoft Word provides more flexibility for page design. As a general rule, the more sophisticated your word processing program is, the more choices you have to make to determine the document's design. For example, simple word processors don't allow documents to have more than one column per page, but a full-featured word processor may require you to select the number of columns you want to use, specify the line length of each column, and choose the amount of margin to place between columns.

Because it is tedious to lay out the format of each document from scratch, many advanced word processors store your document design choices in a **style sheet**, a file that contains instructions for page and paragraph formatting but does not contain text. With style sheets you can lay out the format of numerous types of documents and store the specifications for each type in a separate file. One file might store the design specifications for letters; another, for legal contracts; and yet another, for financial statements. Whenever you create a new document, the word processor asks you to indicate which file contains the formatting specifications for the document.

Microsoft Word is well known for its extensive and powerful text formatting features. It lets you format a document in two ways: direct formatting or formatting with style sheets. Direct formatting adjusts the appearance of the document by embedding formatting information directly in the document itself. In contrast, a style sheet stores formatting instructions in a file separate from the document. Either method can be used to format a document—even a combination of the two methods can be used. We will explain each method in turn.

Direct formatting attaches formatting instructions directly to selected text by using format commands. It is the simplest method of changing the appearance of a document. Each of Microsoft Word's format commands leads to a menu of formatting choices. For example, the format commands for adjusting paragraphs and divisions (page layouts) produce the menus shown in Figure 6.14. Other format commands control the appearance of characters (bold, italic, and so on), set tab stops, or deal with footnotes or headers and footers.

To illustrate how Microsoft Word's format commands work, suppose you want to give a certain paragraph narrower margins than the standard paragraph style uses. In Microsoft Word, each paragraph can be given a set of attributes that controls how the paragraph is formatted and printed. These attributes are selected

Figure 6.14 Text formatting with Microsoft Word. (a) The FORMAT PARAGRAPH command displays this menu and allows you to adjust the appearance of a paragraph. (b) The FORMAT DIVISION MARGINS menu establishes the page size and margins. (c) The FORMAT DIVISION LAYOUT menu determines the number of columns on the page and the placement of footnotes.

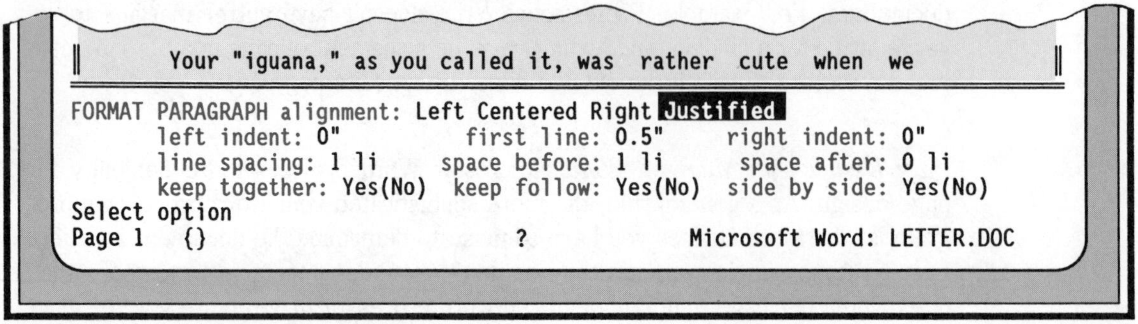

```
        Your "iguana," as you called it, was  rather  cute  when  we

FORMAT PARAGRAPH alignment: Left Centered Right Justified
        left indent: 0"          first line: 0.5"       right indent: 0"
        line spacing: 1 li       space before: 1 li     space after: 0 li
        keep together: Yes(No)   keep follow: Yes(No)   side by side: Yes(No)
Select option
Page 1    {}                          ?              Microsoft Word: LETTER.DOC
```

A.

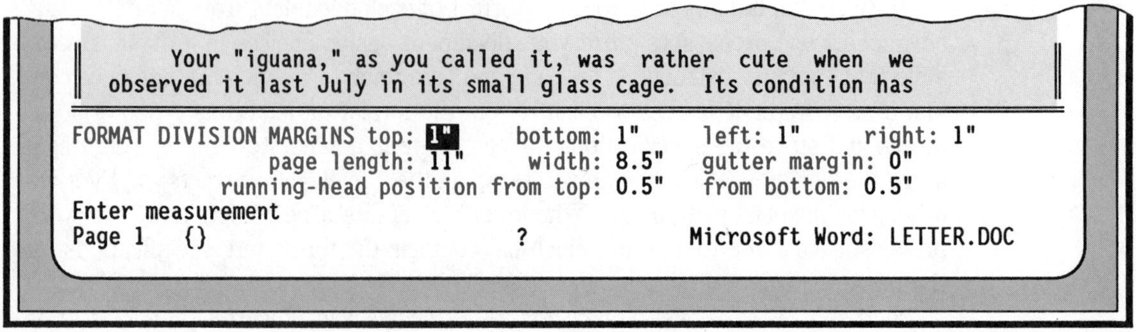

```
        Your "iguana," as you called it, was  rather  cute  when  we
    observed it last July in its small glass cage.  Its condition has

FORMAT DIVISION MARGINS top: 1"        bottom: 1"        left: 1"      right: 1"
                page length: 11"       width: 8.5"       gutter margin: 0"
            running-head position from top: 0.5"      from bottom: 0.5"
Enter measurement
Page 1    {}                          ?              Microsoft Word: LETTER.DOC
```

B.

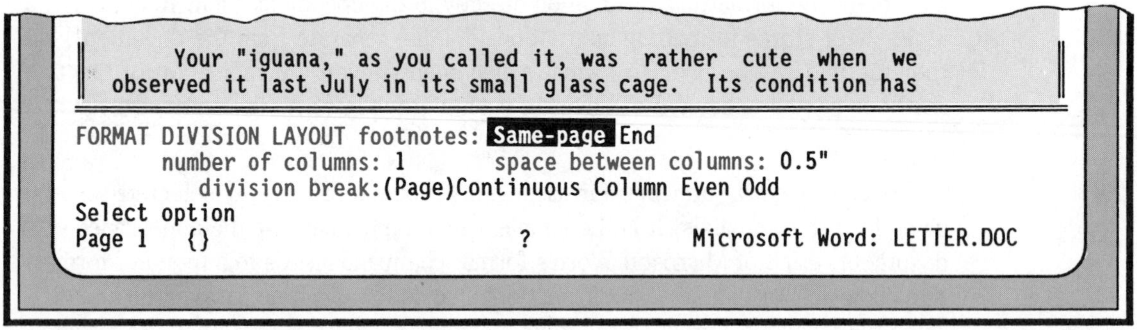

```
        Your "iguana," as you called it, was  rather  cute  when  we
    observed it last July in its small glass cage.  Its condition has

FORMAT DIVISION LAYOUT footnotes: Same-page End
        number of columns: 1         space between columns: 0.5"
            division break:(Page)Continuous Column Even Odd
Select option
Page 1    {}                          ?              Microsoft Word: LETTER.DOC
```

C.

from a menu with choices for line spacing, margins, alignment (left, centered, right, and justified), and so forth. The necessary steps are to

1. Move the cursor to any location in the paragraph.

2. Select the FORMAT PARAGRAPH command from the menu bars on the bottom of the screen. This displays the FORMAT PARAGRAPH menu shown in Figure 6.14(a).

3. Press the [Tab] key to move the "left indent" field of the menu and enter the distance you want to indent the left-hand side of the paragraph.

4. Press the [Tab] key twice to move to the "right indent" field and enter the distance you want to indent the right-hand side of the paragraph.

5. Press [Enter] to complete the command. The paragraph will be reformed immediately to fit within its new margins.

In Microsoft Word, a *division* is a section of a document with the same page format, such as a chapter or a table of contents. Most simple documents need only one division. But because a document can have many divisions, you can change the margins on the page or the size of the page within a document as many times as you like.

The procedure for creating a new division is simple. First, you move the cursor to what will be the first character in the new division. Then you press [Ctrl]-[Enter] to insert a division mark—a line of colons extending across the screen. A *division mark* is a format code (like a hard carriage return) and can be deleted or moved like a normal character. A division's page design and other formatting specifications are adjusted by giving a FORMAT DIVISION command and filling out menus, as shown in the bottom two screens of Figure 6.14.

As noted earlier, a *style sheet* is a file that contains formatting instructions for the various parts of a document. The way formatting instructions are stored in a style sheet varies from one program to another. In Microsoft Word, the style sheet is a list of named definitions for different types of divisions, paragraphs, and characters. Each item in the list is called a *style*. For example, the style sheet in Figure 6.15 lists six styles: two division styles, two paragraph styles, and two character styles. If the style sheet looks confusing, this is understandable. It takes some experience to make sense of the poorly labeled information in a Microsoft Word style sheet. It helps to know that a style has three parts: a name (such as Paragraph 10); a *key code* (such as [Alt]-[Q]), which is used to identify the style quickly; and a definition, which contains the formatting instructions. Here is a partial explanation of two styles shown on the screen:

■ The Division 2 style is invoked by pressing [Alt]-[X], its key code. It formats the pages in a division to have two columns on a normal $8\frac{1}{2}'' \times 11''$ page.

■ The Paragraph 10 style is invoked by pressing [Alt]-[Q]. It causes a paragraph to be preceded by two blank lines and to print in an italic Courier typeface with indented margins.

Microsoft Word is distributed with several sample style sheets. You can create your own style sheets or modify the samples by filling out the same format menus used with direct formatting. For example, the menu at the bottom of Figure 6.15 is in the process of adjusting the page layout instructions of the Division 2 style.

Creating a style sheet for a new type of document can be a substantial job, because decisions must be made about how all the different parts of the document should look. It is often easiest to create a new style sheet by modifying an existing one for a similar type of document.

In organizations, it is desirable to have a consistent appearance among documents produced by different people. This can be achieved by having a person with artistic flair create style sheets for the organization's letters, memos, reports, and other documents. If people are trained to use these style sheets, their documents will have a standardized look.

Creating a style sheet is the tough part; using it is easy. To use a style sheet, you give a format command to "attach" it to the document file—this tells the word processor which style sheet to use. Then you "tag" the parts of your document to tell the word processor where to apply the styles to the text. Tagging text is a two-step process: you select the text (perhaps by pointing and dragging with a

Figure 6.15 Editing a Microsoft Word style sheet.

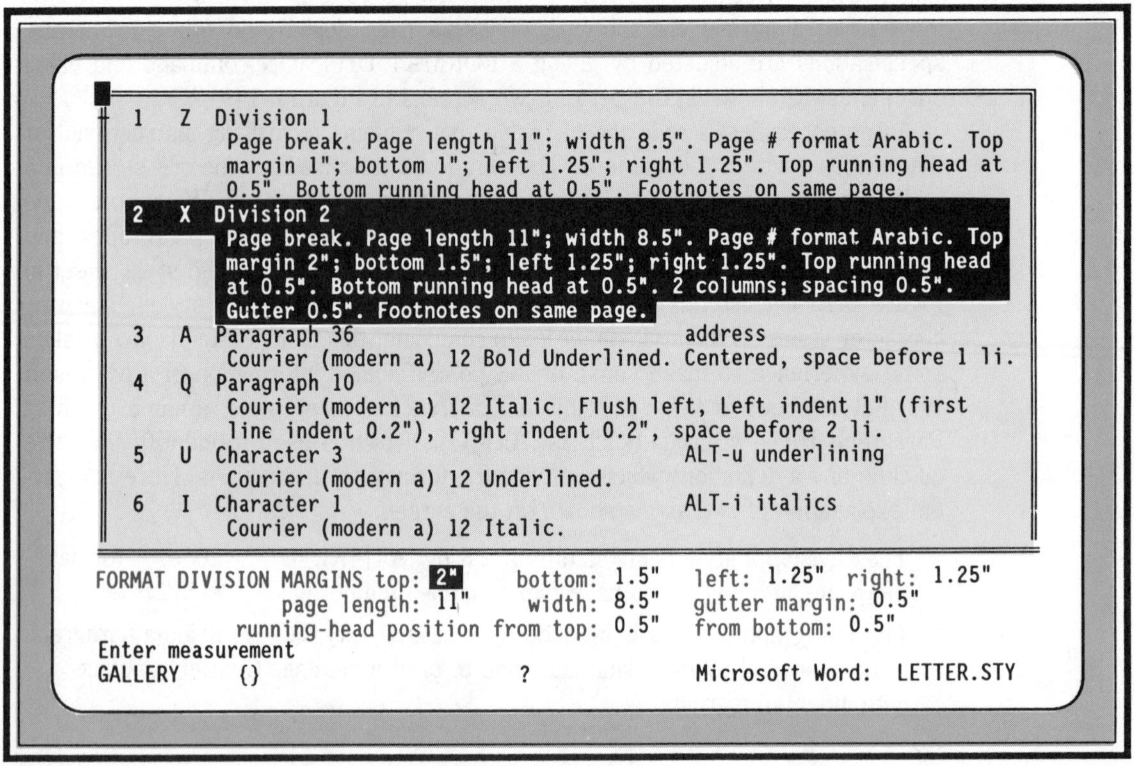

```
  1   Z   Division 1
            Page break. Page length 11"; width 8.5". Page # format Arabic. Top
            margin 1"; bottom 1"; left 1.25"; right 1.25". Top running head at
            0.5". Bottom running head at 0.5". Footnotes on same page.
  2   X   Division 2
            Page break. Page length 11"; width 8.5". Page # format Arabic. Top
            margin 2"; bottom 1.5"; left 1.25"; right 1.25". Top running head
            at 0.5". Bottom running head at 0.5". 2 columns; spacing 0.5".
            Gutter 0.5". Footnotes on same page.
  3   A   Paragraph 36                          address
            Courier (modern a) 12 Bold Underlined. Centered, space before 1 li.
  4   Q   Paragraph 10
            Courier (modern a) 12 Italic. Flush left, Left indent 1" (first
            line indent 0.2"), right indent 0.2", space before 2 li.
  5   U   Character 3                           ALT-u underlining
            Courier (modern a) 12 Underlined.
  6   I   Character 1                           ALT-i italics
            Courier (modern a) 12 Italic.

FORMAT DIVISION MARGINS top: 2"      bottom: 1.5"   left: 1.25" right: 1.25"
                     page length: 11"    width: 8.5"   gutter margin: 0.5"
             running-head position from top: 0.5"   from bottom: 0.5"
Enter measurement
GALLERY        {}                    ?          Microsoft Word: LETTER.STY
```

mouse), then you identify which style definition you want to apply to the text (perhaps by typing the style's key code). As an example, suppose you want to use the style sheet shown in Figure 6.15 to format a paragraph with an italic typeface and indented margins. The Paragraph 10 style matches this description, and its key code is [Alt]-[Q]. So you select the paragraph—in this case, it is sufficient to move the cursor to any location in the paragraph—and then press [Alt]-[Q]. Immediately the paragraph is reformed to fit the new margins and other format instructions contained in the Paragraph 10 style. This illustrates one of the advantages of using style sheets: they provide a quick and easy way to reuse formatting instructions.

Style sheets provide another advantage over direct formatting: they let you change a document's format without editing it—you need only attach a different style sheet. For example, Figure 6.16 shows the effect of switching style sheets on a Ventura Publisher document. It takes just a single command to attach a different style sheet to a document, but the change can give the entire document a completely different appearance. The ability to reformat a document quickly can be a godsend as the document goes through development. For example, it may be useful to edit a draft manuscript in a double-spaced format, send it to reviewers in a single-spaced format, and publish the document in a typeset format.

Local Formatting Options

To give a document a polished appearance, it is often necessary to override the global page design that governs the usual placement of text on the page. For example, you might want to center a title on the page rather than place it flush against the left margin like the rest of the text. Or you might want to reserve an area of blank space where a picture can be pasted in later. You can make this type of format change by giving local formatting commands that temporarily override the global format settings.

Word processors vary considerably in their ability to adjust a document's format from page to page. Advanced word processors are equipped with myriad local formatting options; simple word processors may not even let you change the settings for the margins on the page. In this section, we explain a few of the most important local formatting options and illustrate how they are used.

Adjusting Page Breaks   A **page break** occurs when one page ends and another begins. Page breaks occur automatically when all the lines between the top and bottom margins are filled. A WYSIWYG word processor will show page breaks on the screen in an easily recognized manner; for example, by displaying a line of hyphens or equal signs. But an off-screen text formatter provides no clue during editing about where page breaks will fall.

Adjusting page breaks so that they fall in the right spots can be difficult, especially when a document includes not only paragraphs but also footnotes, tables, figures, and section headings. Sometimes there is no good way to break a page, short of rewriting the text. Two partial solutions offered by word processors are forced page breaks and conditional page breaks.

Figure 6.16 The effect of attaching a different style sheet to a document with Ventura Publisher. Ventura allows paragraph styles to have meaningful names like Chapter Title, First Para, or Body Text. (a) This screen is formatted with the &BOOK-P1.STY style sheet. It centers the Chapter # and Chapter Title on the page and prints text in a single-column format. (b) This screen uses the &BOOK-P2.STY style sheet. It aligns the Chapter # and Chapter Title with the left margin and prints text in a two-column format.

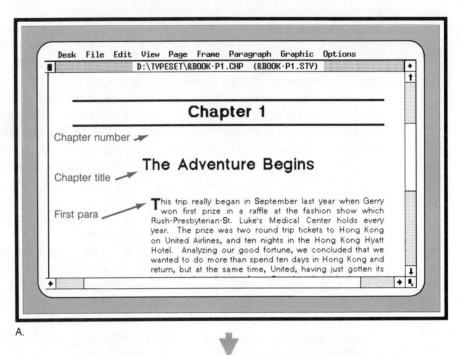

A.

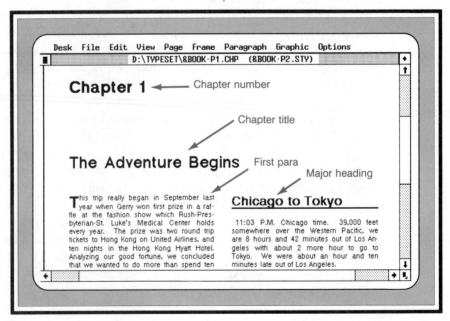

B.

A *forced page break* starts a new page at a specific location rather than fill the rest of the current page. At the end of a chapter, for instance, it is traditional to force a page break. Nearly every word processor provides a method to do this, and some methods work better than others.

You can ask PFS:Professional Write to force a page break by inserting a special format command, *NEW PAGE*, where you want the page break to fall. Normally, Professional Write displays page breaks on the screen in the correct location, but like an off-screen text formatter, it does not consider the *NEW PAGE* command until printing, so all the page breaks after a *NEW PAGE* command are displayed incorrectly.

A more common method of forcing page breaks is to insert a hard page break in the document. A *hard page break* is a format code and is similar to a hard carriage return. A hard page break signals the end of a page and takes effect immediately by displaying a page break on the screen. In contrast, *soft page breaks* are generated automatically by a WYSIWYG word processor and shift to new locations if you edit or reformat the document. Most WYSIWYG word processors let you insert or delete hard page breaks just as you can other format codes. For example, Word-Perfect lets you insert a hard page break in the document by pressing [Ctrl]-[Enter], and you can delete one by moving the cursor immediately before it and pressing [Del].

Adjusting Text Within Paragraphs Suppose you want to distinguish a long quotation from the rest of a document by giving it narrower margins. To do this and similar tasks efficiently, it is important to be able to vary the margins of a paragraph independently from the margins of the page. Most word processors let you do this in conjunction with their ruler line. The *ruler line* is a horizontal line on the screen that displays the position of the cursor, the location of tab stops, and the position of paragraph indents or temporary margins (if any). Figure 6.17 illustrates the ruler lines used by PFS:Professional Write, WordStar 2000, and Microsoft Word. Each of these programs provides a different method of varying the margins of a document.

Professional Write displays its ruler line immediately below the text-editing window (see Figure 6.17a). Its ruler line indicates several types of information.

■ The cursor's position is shown in inverse video.

■ Every tenth column position is indicated by a number.

■ The document's left and right margins are indicated with brackets.

■ A temporary left margin is indicated by a greater-than symbol (>>).

■ Each tab stop is indicated by a T, for a typewriter tab, or a D, for a decimal tab. Typewriter tabs are usually used to align columns of text; decimal tabs align the decimal points in a column of numbers.

To indent a paragraph with PFS:Professional Write, you select the paragraph as a block by means of a pull-down Edit menu, causing the paragraph to appear in inverse video. Then you move the cursor to the column position where you want the

Figure 6.17 The ruler lines of three word processors. (a) PFS:Professional Write's ruler indicates the position of the document's margins with brackets on the ruler. (b) WordStar 2000 allows ruler lines to be inserted in the document to temporarily adjust the margins or tabs. (c) Microsoft Word indicates the current paragraph's margins with brackets on a ruler at the top of the screen.

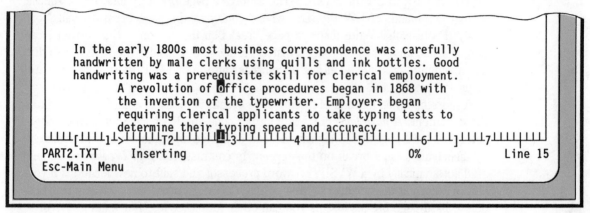

A.

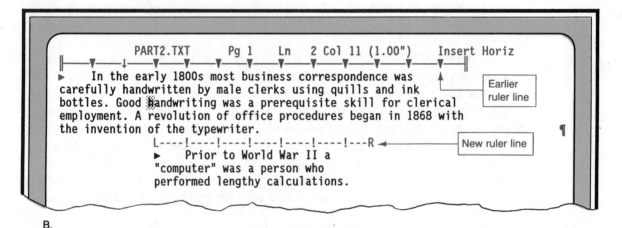

B.

C.

temporary left margin and press [Ctrl]-[N]. The text in the block is immediately reformed to fit with the new left margin. One of PFS:Professional Write's significant limitations is that it doesn't have a corresponding command to indent a paragraph's right margin.

WordStar 2000 displays a ruler above the text-editing window (see Figure 6.17b). In addition, WordStar 2000 lets you adjust the document's margins or change the tab settings by inserting a new ruler in the document. The new ruler is actually a format code, and like other format codes, it can be deleted, moved, hidden, or displayed. Each ruler you place in a document determines the location of tabs and margins until the next ruler. After a ruler is moved, inserted, or otherwise edited, WordStar 2000 reformats the document's text immediately to reflect the changes.

Microsoft Word displays its ruler line at the top of the screen (see Figure 6.17c). This line indicates the current paragraph's margins with brackets. Earlier in this chapter, we saw that Microsoft Word allows you to change the margins of individual paragraphs or the entire page by using the Format menus shown in Figure 6.14 or by attaching new definitions from a style sheet.

Aligning and Justifying Text Almost every word processor has a simple, convenient command for centering a line between the left and right margins (see Figure 6.18). Centering makes titles stand out from the rest of the text.

Handwritten and typed documents have **ragged-right margins**. In other words, the right-hand edge is ragged, or uneven, because the line lengths are uneven. On most word processors, a ragged-right margin is the default value. Occasionally, ragged-left lines are necessary; for example, some letter formats call for the date to be aligned with the right margin, making for a ragged-left line. Most word processors don't have a specific command to create a ragged-left margin, but you can make individual lines ragged left by inserting spaces at the beginning of the line until the end of the line is flush with the right margin.

To **justify** text is to align it within boundaries. *Left-justified* text is placed flush against the left margin. Numbers are usually *right-justified,* so that their decimal points will fall in the same column. The printing in newspapers and books is both left- and right-justified. Because "left- and right-justified" is a mouthful, text with

---

Figure 6.18 Samples of ragged-right, centered, and ragged-left text.

```
L-----------------R
Left-justified text
is placed flush with
the left margin. It
is used for memos
and letters.
```

```
L-----------------R
   Centered text is
  placed between the
     left and right
        margins.
         Titles
   are often centered.
```

```
L-----------------R
     Right justified
text is placed flush
    against the right
margin. It is rarely
               used.
```

Figure 6.19 Text justified with fixed-width spacing, microspacing, and proportional spacing.

```
L--------------R  L--------------R  L--------------R
Fixed-    width   Microspaced text  Proportional spacing
spacing   allows  spreads out the   places letters in fields
text   to    be   gaps between words  with different widths,
justified but can  so that they are   so "MMMM" takes
leave  ugly gaps   less noticeable.   up more room than
between words.                        "iiii."
```

straight left and right margins is said to be simply *justified*. Justified documents look professional, but some studies have shown that documents with ragged right margins are easier to read.

Most word processors have a toggle that turns justification on and off. Text is justified in several ways, but all the methods involve varying the spacing between letters and words.

- **Fixed-width spacing** pads out short lines by inserting full-size spaces between words (see Figure 6.19). This method is often used for on-screen justification, because some monitors are column oriented and cannot shift a character left or right less than a full column position. Even if fixed-width spaces are spread out as evenly as possible, they are noticeable, especially on narrow lines.

- **Microspacing** can make justified text look better by inserting tiny spaces between letters and words. For example, many printers can position the print head in $1/120$-inch increments. If the word processing software and the printer communicate correctly, these printers can spread enough $1/120$-inch spaces between the letters and spaces to fill the line.

- **Proportional spacing** allocates a variable amount of space per character, depending on the width of the character. (For instance, an *M* would have more space than an *i*.) This keeps the space between letters the same, permitting more text to fit on each page without reducing the document's readability.

Setting Character Attributes The appearance of documents produced by a word processing system depends on the combined capabilities of the printer and the software. Buying an expensive, versatile printer is a mistake if the software you plan to use doesn't have commands for selecting different sizes and styles of type. Similarly, there's no sense in acquiring a state-of-the art desktop publishing package, designed for typesetting, if you use a cheap dot matrix printer. Another pitfall to avoid in choosing a printer and software is that, even if the documentation for both the printer and the software claims that they can accommodate a particular printing feature, they might use different coding systems to describe the feature. Because the character codes for ordinary letters and numbers are standardized, getting a printer to work like a simple typewriter is not difficult. But most features, such as shifting from plain text to italic, have not been standardized, so you should check to see that your software and hardware are compatible.

The appearance of a character is influenced by its size, typeface family, and style. Many programs give you control over each of these characteristics; other programs only let you change a character's *style* (boldface, italic, and so on).

Type size is measured in *points,* and the spacing between characters on a line is called the *pitch.* A **point** is $1/72$ inch. Typical point sizes are 10 or 12 points for typewritten characters, 6 to 8 points for the fine print in legal notices, and 24 to 48 points for newspaper headlines. For example, this paragraph is set in $10\frac{1}{2}$-point type. The **pitch** is a measure of how many characters fit within an inch. This measurement makes sense only for fixed-width type; proportionally spaced type is said to have a variable pitch. The pitch of many office typewriters can be set for either 10 or 12 characters per inch. Sometimes dot matrix printers use 17-pitch type to compress a 132-character line onto an $8\frac{1}{2}$-inch-wide page.

The *typeface* determines the shape of each character. For example, Courier is the most common typewriter typeface, Helvetica Bold is often used for headlines, and Times Roman is a popular typeface for the text in books and newspapers. Typefaces are usually designed in "families" that include regular, boldface, and italic styles and may include other styles, such as outline, backslanted, or boldface italic. Technically, a **font** is a set of characters in a particular typeface and size. Thus, the Geneva Bold typeface in 12-point size is one font, and the 14-point size is another. But some word processing vendors use these terms more loosely—for them, the terms *typeface* and *font* appear to mean the same thing.

Some word processing programs may require all characters in a document to be the same size and to come from the same typeface family. For example, PFS:Professional Write limits the options on character styles to regular, boldface and underlined characters. Other programs offer a wider range of character enhancements, including subscripts, superscripts, strikeouts, italics, compressed type, and double-width type. Figure 6.20 illustrates some of the typefaces that can be selected within MacWrite, a fairly simple word processor for the Apple Macintosh. To change the appearance of text with MacWrite, you first select with the mouse the text to be affected, then use the Style menu to choose the typeface and type size.

Many programs allow you to change fonts by inserting format codes in the document. For example, with WordStar 2000, the format code that requests a fixed-width, 12-pitch font looks like: [NON PS 12]. Because the effect of a format code continues until another format code cancels it, you must remember to place format codes both before and after text that is to receive new attributes.

Style sheets provide a different way of selecting fonts. Remember that a style sheet is a list of formatting instructions for the parts of a document. Each part (or style) of the document can be given its own font, and this information can be stored in the style sheet. For example, Figure 6.21 shows the dialog box that Ventura Publisher uses to assign a font to a paragraph. In this illustration, the style

Figure 6.20 Samples of some of the type styles available within MacWrite.

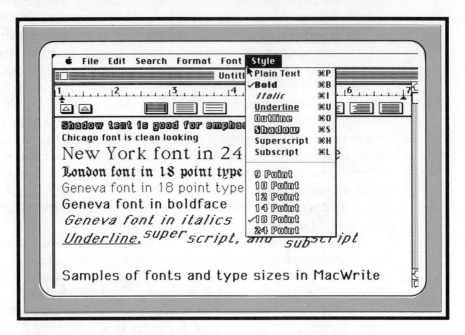

named "Firstpar" is assigned the Times Roman typeface, 10-point type, the normal character style, and black ink. As soon as this selection is made, all of the paragraphs in the document that are tagged with the Firstpar name are displayed with the appropriate font.

Whether character attributes are visible on the screen depends on the capabilities of the display and on the software. For example, if you use an IBM PC with a color monitor, Microsoft Word displays not only underlining but also double-underlining. But, on the same monitor, WordPerfect represents an underlined character by changing its color. Neither program displays different sizes of characters.

Saving and Quitting

Memory Management

Most word processors automatically manage the computer's memory so that you never have to read a message like

FATAL ERROR: MEMORY FULL; PLEASE RE-BOOT

It is nice to know that the system won't crash because you've attempted to enter more text than will fit into memory. Still, this does not mean that you can afford to be ignorant about where your text is being stored. Understanding how your word processor manages memory is important if you want to write a long document—or if you want to recover the last five pages of a document that have been accidentally deleted.

Figure 6.21 (a) A dialog box for selecting the typeface, type size, style, and color of a paragraph's text. (b) Samples of the Times Roman typeface in various sizes.

A.

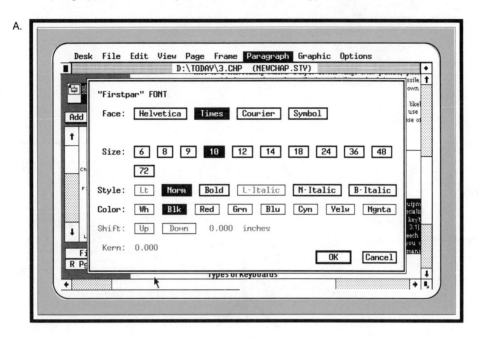

B.

Times Roman (6 point)

Times Roman (12 point)

Times Roman bold (24 point)

Times Roman bold (30 point)

Memory-based word processors require that the entire document fit into memory while it is being edited. If a document becomes large enough to fill the available memory, it must be broken into pieces before more text can be added. Each piece is saved as a separate file on a disk. For example, on an IBM PC with 320KB of main memory, PFS:Professional Write limits each file to 16 pages of text. Other examples of memory-based programs are MacWrite, Ventura Publisher, and Symphony (an integrated program that contains a word processing component).

Editing a long document on a memory-based word processor can be a real chore, particularly if it is necessary to move text frequently from one of the document's files to another. *Disk-based word processors* are more convenient; they can edit files that are too long to fit into memory at once. Figure 6.22 shows how a disk-based word processor loads the text that is being edited into memory, while the rest of the document is stored in temporary disk files. As a result, the size of a

Figure 6.22 Disk-based document editing.

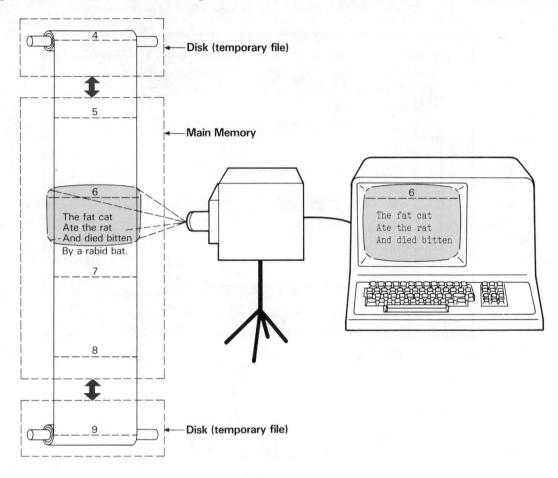

document is limited only by the storage capacity of the disk. Examples of disk-based word processors are WordPerfect, WordStar 2000, MultiMate, and Microsoft Word.

Scrolling through a large document with a disk-based word processor is occasionally interrupted while some of the text in memory is moved to the disk and replaced by new text. As with program overlays (discussed in Chapter 3), the data transfers happen automatically and are noticeable only because of the noise of the drives and the delay. Sometimes the delay can be substantial. On many systems, the command to jump to the bottom of a 100-page document takes over a minute to execute.

Backup Copies

The best defense against a serious loss of data is to have extra backup copies of the file stored on disk. Almost all word processors provide some backup automatically. When you edit a document, the changes alter the contents of memory or temporary disk files, but the changes do not immediately affect the master copy (if any) that is on the disk. If something really drastic happens, it is possible to abandon (*quit*) the current editing session without transferring (*saving*) anything to the disk, leaving the master file unmodified. Abandoning an editing session can be a mixed blessing. You are not likely to be enthusiastic about losing the results of two hours of editing just because you deleted a paragraph by accident.

Sometimes the word processor will abandon the current editing session without asking for your approval. A loss of electricity for a second or more causes this reaction. Less frequently, a bug in the word processing program sends the machine into never-never land until it is rebooted. The way to protect against these problems is to periodically save a copy of the edited text. A few word processors, such as WordPerfect, can be set up to transfer edited text automatically to the disk after a specified length of time (or a specified number of keystrokes), but typically the operator must request that text be saved.

Most word processors retain the original master file as a backup file after the document is saved. For example, assume that you begin by editing a file named A:LETTER, causing a copy of the LETTER file to be transferred from disk drive A to memory. Now assume that, after editing the text in memory, you save the revised text on the disk. Most word processors implement this command by first giving a new name to the old master file (perhaps calling it A:LETTER.BAK) and then saving the new, edited text as the file named A:LETTER.

We would be remiss if we didn't emphasize again that disks are not as reliable a storage medium as paper. Crumpling up a piece of paper, even spilling coffee on it, is not likely to make its contents unreadable. Not so with disks. Important files should always be stored on two disks, and the disks should be stored separately.

ADVANCED WORD PROCESSING

So far, we've described the mechanics of writing, editing, and formatting with a word processor. The rest of this chapter covers some important advanced features provided by most word processors. These features can help you create better-looking documents with much less effort. Any serious writer should understand them.

Outline Processors

Sifting through a jumble of thoughts is easier if you write your ideas down in a list. You can organize your thoughts even more effectively if you arrange them in an *outline*—a hierarchical list of topics and subtopics presented in a logical manner.

Most people find that their outlines undergo considerable refinement: topics are rearranged, edited, split in two, and shifted from one level to another. Doing this on paper inevitably leads to a confusing proliferation of erasures, cross-outs, insertions, and arrows. You can avoid all this mess by using a word processor to enter the outline on a computer screen and to rearrange the topics as necessary with block moves. But an *outline processor* makes the process simpler and less time consuming.

An **outline processor** (also called an *idea processor* or *outliner*) is a program with an array of special-purpose features for creating and manipulating outlines. For example, one generally available feature is a command that collapses the outline so that only the major headings are visible. And nearly all outline processors have single-keystroke commands that change the level of a heading, such as raising a minor heading to major heading status.

There are several types of outline processors.

- *Standalone programs,* with names like ThinkTank, Max Think, and PC Outline, were the first type of outline processor to be developed. Although these programs gained immediate acceptance for organizing thoughts and lists, their limited word processing abilities make them inconvenient for outlining lengthy documents. On the other hand, standalone programs usually provide the most advanced outline processing features. For example, MORE (shown in Figure 6.23) is a standalone outline processor that can quickly switch the display of an outline among three views: an outline view, a tree chart view, and a bullet chart view.

- *Memory-resident outline processors,* such as Ready, Voila, and Pop-Up Partner, are readily accessible when you use other programs. Once they have been loaded into memory, a special keystroke causes them to pop up on the screen—even in the middle of a session with another program.

- The newest versions of many *full-featured word processors* have built-in outline processing commands. These programs blend the easy creation and manipulation of outlines with the capability of fleshing them out into well-organized book-length documents.

Outline processing can be used to create everything from daily "to do" lists to job descriptions, travel itineraries, and outlines of reports and books. This diversity of possible applications has been exploited by Peter Gysegem, the training manager for MS Systems, a computer store in Corvallis, Oregon. He uses Microsoft Word's outline features to organize the topics in his training classes, put together business plans, and structure the logic of the computer programs he writes. "Outline processing is particular useful when I write *pseudo code* [which are English-language notes that programmers use to rough out programs]," says Gysegem. "The indentation shows part of the structure of the program, and is especially important for languages like C and Pascal—languages that are heavily indented. I begin by dividing the program into three or four logical areas (major headings) and then work down to the second level. If something doesn't make sense, I can pop it into another section. Even though you can do all these things with a normal word processor, the tools here are more appropriate and powerful."

An essential feature of an outline processor is the ability to expand a heading to see the text in that section or to collapse the text so that you can see and manipulate the overall organization. For example, an outline processor enables you to reorganize a document by rearranging headings in the outline. These features are illustrated in the four parts of Figure 6.24.

Figure 6.23 Three views of the same outline. (a) The outline view is used to enter and edit topics in the outline. (b) The tree chart view gives a graphical perspective of the relationships among topics. (c) The bullet chart view highlights main headings.

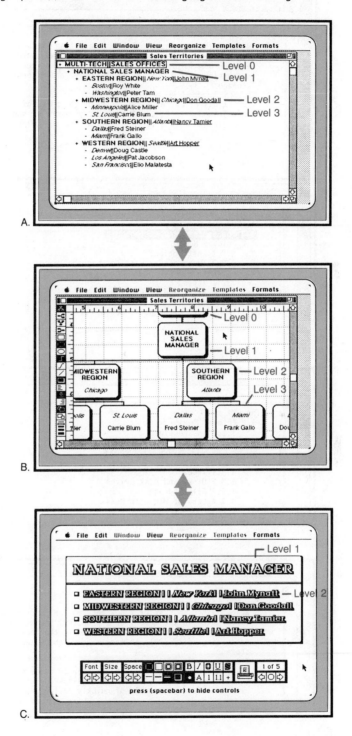

Figure 6.24 Outline processing with Microsoft Word.

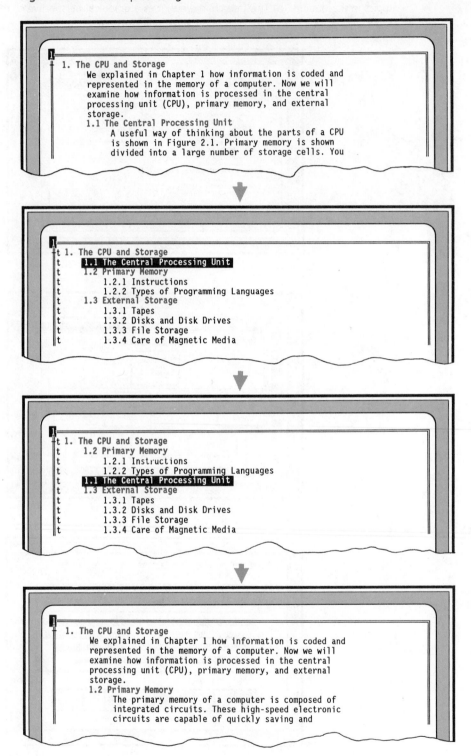

1. The first part shows a document with headings and text. The headings appear in color and are numbered according to their level and position in the hierarchy.

2. The next screen shows the same document in outline form, with only the headings visible. The active heading (the one pointed to by the cursor) is shown in inverse video. Headings that have text hidden beneath them are indicated by a "t" at the left edge of the screen.

3. In the third screen, the active heading has been moved to a new location in the outline; as a result, the headings are temporarily numbered incorrectly. Microsoft Word renumbers headings only when you give it a specific command to do so.

4. The last screen shows the expanded view of the document once more. Because the text in the document is associated with headings in the outline, the text has been rearranged automatically to correspond to the new outline.

Form Letters

Form letters eliminate most of the work associated with printing standard business replies, and the ability to print them is invaluable for producing "personalized" mass mailings. If properly prepared, a computerized form letter is indistinguishable from a manually produced business letter, except possibly by its lack of errors.

A *form letter* is printed by merging data into a partially completed master letter in a primary file. The master letter contains all the text that doesn't change from one letter to the next, as well as special insertion tags to indicate where the missing data will go. Most often, the insertion tags are used to insert names and addresses, but they can receive any information, such as payments received, winning lottery numbers, or dates. The insertion tags can be set up to receive data from the keyboard, from a data file, or from a combination of the two. In the example shown in Figure 6.25, the missing data are supplied by a secondary data file, so we will discuss that case first.

A data file with names and addresses can be created in several ways. If you must print thousands of form letters or if the data file will need frequent maintenance, then you should consider building the data file with the help of a file management program, as described in Chapter 8. But for short, one-shot mailings, it is generally quicker to create a data file by typing information into an empty file with your word processor.

The information in the data file needs to be organized so that the word processor can identify the pieces. Each piece, such as a name or a phone number, is called a *field*. All of the fields related to one form letter are called a *record*. Several methods can be used to identify the ends of the fields and records. For example, Figure 6.25 illustrates the conventions used by WordPerfect: it expects each field to end with ^R and each record to end with ^E. Many word processors expect the fields to be separated from one another by commas. The end of each record is usually indicated by a hard carriage return or a blank line.

Figure 6.25 Producing form letters with WordPerfect. (a) The primary file contains the basic letter and includes insertion tags showing where information will be inserted. (b) The secondary data file contains the information about each individual letter. (c) The finished form letters.

A.

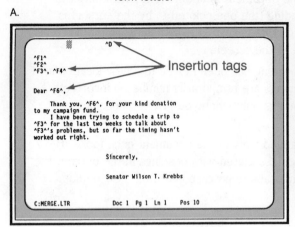

Insertion tags

```
                        ^D
^F1^
^F2^
^F3^, ^F4^

Dear ^F6^,

    Thank you, ^F6^, for your kind donation
to my campaign fund.
    I have been trying to schedule a trip to
^F3^ for the last two weeks to talk about
^F3^'s problems, but so far the timing hasn't
worked out right.

            Sincerely,

            Senator Wilson T. Krebbs


C:MERGE.LTR          Doc 1  Pg 1  Ln 1    Pos 10
```

B.

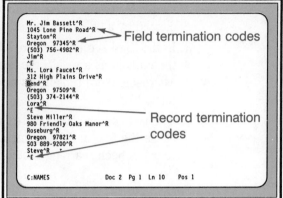

```
Mr. Jim Bassett^R
1045 Lone Pine Road^R
Stayton^R
Oregon 97345^R
(503) 756-4982^R
Jim^R
^E
Ms. Lora Faucet^R
312 High Plains Drive^R
Bend^R
Oregon 97509^R
(503) 374-2144^R
Lora^R
^E
Steve Miller^R
980 Friendly Oaks Manor^R
Roseburg^R
Oregon 97821^R
503 889-9200^R
Steve^R
^E

C:NAMES              Doc 2  Pg 1  Ln 10   Pos 1
```

Field termination codes

Record termination codes

C.

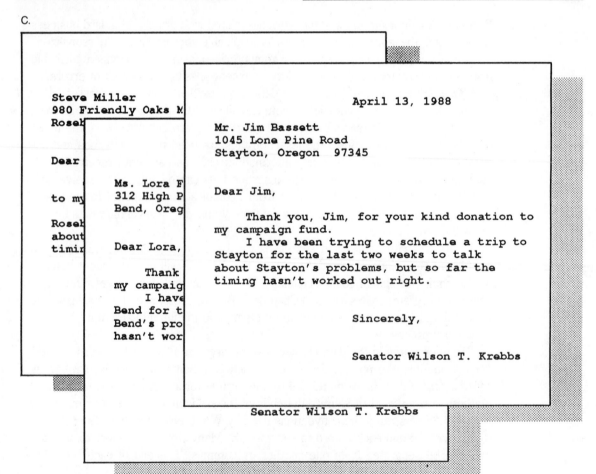

```
Steve Miller
980 Friendly Oaks M
Roseb

Dear

to my

Roseb
about
timin
```

```
Ms. Lora F
312 High P
Bend, Oreg

Dear Lora,

    Thank
my campaig
    I have
Bend for t
Bend's pro
hasn't wor
```

```
                    April 13, 1988

Mr. Jim Bassett
1045 Lone Pine Road
Stayton, Oregon  97345


Dear Jim,

    Thank you, Jim, for your kind donation to
my campaign fund.
    I have been trying to schedule a trip to
Stayton for the last two weeks to talk
about Stayton's problems, but so far the
timing hasn't worked out right.


            Sincerely,


            Senator Wilson T. Krebbs
```

Senator Wilson T. Krebbs

To print the form letters, the word processor needs to know which fields in the data file correspond to which insertion tags in the master letter. To accomplish this, the insertion tags are given names. WordPerfect uses a particularly simple naming convention: insertion tag ^F1^ receives data from the first field of each record in the secondary file, ^F2^ receives data from the second field, and so on. Notice that the fields in the data file do not have to be in the same order as the insertion tags in the primary file. This allows two fields in Figure 6.25 to be used twice in the master letter (fields ^F3^ and ^F6^), and the field containing phone numbers (^F5^) isn't used at all.

If the information to complete the master letter is supposed to come from the keyboard, then each insertion tag causes the word processor to wait for an entry. For example, the dialog for producing the letters shown in Figure 6.25 might proceed as follows (the characters in color are those typed by the user):

```
Enter data for FULL NAME: Mr. Jim Bassett
Enter data for STREET: 1045 Lone Pine Road
Enter data for CITY: Stayton
Enter data for STATE: Oregon 97345
Enter data for FIRST NAME: Jim
Please wait for printing to complete . . .
Enter data for FIRST: STOP
```

The exact procedure for entering data varies from program to program. Most programs have handy features for customizing the prompts or for setting fields (such as the date field) to a fixed value for all copies. For example, ^D is the Word-Perfect insertion tag that retrieves the current date from the computer's clock and places it in the master file.

Spelling Checkers and Electronic Thesauruses

Near every typewriter there is likely to be a pocket dictionary, and within arm's reach of many writers is a thesaurus. For the most part, these books are used mechanically: one looks up a word to verify its spelling or discover its synonyms. Mechanical tasks are what computers excel at, so it shouldn't be surprising that there are electronic dictionaries—called *spelling checkers*—and *electronic thesauruses*. Of the two products, spelling checkers are more important, because they remove most of the drudgery associated with proofreading for typographical errors.

A **spelling checker** performs the most time-consuming part of manual spelling correction: it identifies which words cannot be found in a dictionary. Checking and, if necessary, correcting words that are not in the dictionary still requires human intervention and is the most time-consuming part of computerized spelling checking.

A spelling checker works by comparing the words you type with an electronic dictionary of correctly spelled words. Any word that does not match one of the words in the dictionary list is displayed as a *suspect word*. There are several types of spelling checkers. Some memory-resident programs can check your spelling *as*

A WORD ABOUT
SOFTWARE FOR WRITERS: HELPING THE BAD, HURTING THE GOOD?

Simply processing words is passé.

The latest in personal-computer software tries to help people write better. It fixes misspellings, offers synonyms, catches sexist words, flags clichés and even rates a piece of writing against the Gettysburg Address.

For less-accomplished or careless writers, this software can prevent embarasing—uh, *embarrassing*—mistakes and polish poor prose. "I can't write for people—I had one paragraph that had 81 words in it, in one sentence," says David Englehart, a computer programmer at Ohio Edison Co. in Akron. Thanks to "style-checking" software, he broke up that sentence and otherwise improved a paper for a college course.

But for people who already write well, writing software isn't so good. Style checkers—software that evaluates writing style and syntax—"will make bad writing better but will make good writing worse," says Peter McWilliams, the author of several books on personal computers. Indeed, following rigid rules, the programs spew criticism of the Gettysburg Address and make snide remarks about Mark Twain's "The Adventures of Tom Sawyer."

The problem is that all writing software works in the same simple-minded way. Words or phrases are compared with a list stored in the computer. When the computer sees a phrase that it is programmed to criticize, it does so. Everything else is okay. "It's not artificial intelligence, just a computer program that recognizes certain patterns," says Reference Software Inc. of San Francisco, the maker of Grammatik II, an $89 style analyzer.

"This is a lot of software to tell us stuff that you can pretty well figure out for yourself: Active verbs are better than passive verbs, short words are better than long ones," says William Zinsser, the author of writing guides and the general editor of Time Inc.'s Book-of-the-Month Club. "On the other hand, a lot of people simply don't know these things. If the software can thin out the pomposity of writing in corporations, in bureaucracies, in government, it'll be a public service."

Style analyzers aren't always reliable. *PC Magazine*, a New York biweekly, estimates that the programs catch only 25 percent of the mistakes that a good human editor would find. Grammatik II notices the misuse of "affect" and "effect," but not always. It doesn't like the correct sentence: "He has a flat affect."

But style analyzers do catch common mistakes that are easily fixed. "I learned that I use 'very' too much," says Mr. McWilliams. Walter Davis, a Hollywood screen writer, marvels at the programs' unfailing ability to notice when he inadvertently types the same word twice. F. Ladson Boyle, a University of South Carolina law professor, says the software alerts him when sentences are too long. Also, after six months of using Right Writer, a $95 program by Decisionware Inc. of Sarasota, Fla., Mr. Boyle favors active verbs. "After it jumps you about the passive verbs for about the hundredth time, you start trying to avoid them," he says.

Unfortunately, the software doesn't always know when a writer's style works well. Grammatik pounces on Abraham Lincoln for saying, "Now we *are engaged* in a great civil war," scolding him for using the passive voice which the software dislikes.

The problem lies not with the rules that the software applies. Rather, the programs don't know when to break them. "They don't allow for personal style," says Stephen Levy, a New York nonfiction writer who has experimented with software for writing. Sometimes, he says, a sentence fragment works. Perfectly. But the software doesn't know that.

RightWriter, moreover, never likes negative constructions. It suggests rephrasing Mr. Lincoln's famous sentence: "The world will little note nor long remember what we say here, but it can *never forget* what they did here." Also, according to

Continued on next page

RightWriter: Virginia Woolf had "a strong style" but should have used simpler sentences. John Updike's prose is "complex and may be difficult to read." As for Mark Twain, who used many superlatives, it asks: "Is this appropriate?"

Style analyzers try to measure the quality of writing with all sorts of numbers, but most of them aren't much help in distinguishing good writing from bad. Grammatik calculates that the sentences in this story average 16.4 words and that a reader needs a ninth-grade education to understand this story. Grammatik says that compares with 11th-grade for the Gettysburg Address and fourth-grade for a Hemingway short story. Grammatik likes simple words and short sentences.

The numbers can be ignored. But Charles Spezzano, a Denver psychologist and writer, says the gimmicks of such software can be distracting. He explains, "You become more fascinated with what the programs do than with the writing itself."

you type. If you misspell a word, these programs alert you with a beep of the speaker. This sort of immediate feedback can be disconcerting. Most people prefer to spell-check document files immediately before printing them. This is most conveniently done if your word processor includes a built-in spelling checker.

The dictionaries used by spelling checkers differ from traditional paper-based dictionaries in that they do not have definitions. True electronic dictionaries are available on CD-ROM disks, but they are not in common use because most computers lack a CD-ROM reader. Some dictionary lists have more than 200,000 words. Most include between 80,000 and 140,000 words, so validly spelled words have a good chance of being in the dictionary. For example, in CorrectStar (a portion of WordStar 2000) the main dictionary contains 103,000 words drawn from *The American Heritage Dictionary* and occupies 296KB of disk space—not particularly compact. Still, any program with a dictionary large enough to be useful will require a sizable amount of disk space.

Standard dictionaries do not include many of the words in your written vocabulary, such as the proper nouns you use frequently: your last name, the name of the street you live on, and so forth. Unless the electronic dictionary can be modified, these words will be displayed as suspect words over and over again. Most programs adapt to your vocabulary over time by allowing you to add words to the main dictionary or an auxiliary dictionary.

What do you do when a dictionary program has found a suspect word? The options available for handling suspect words vary from program to program. As Figure 6.26 shows, you can tell WordPerfect to do any of the following:

■ You can type the letter next to any of the words in the replacement list. This causes WordPerfect to replace every occurrence of the suspect word in the document with the suggested replacement and is handy for those pesky words that are consistently misspelled.

■ The *Skip Once* option causes WordPerfect to ignore the current occurrence of the suspect word and continue checking words in the file.

■ When the *Skip* option is selected, the suspect word is ignored for the duration of the spelling correction session.

Figure 6.26 During a spell-check operation, WordPerfect doesn't find the word *flor* in its dictionary, so it provides a list of suggested replacement words.

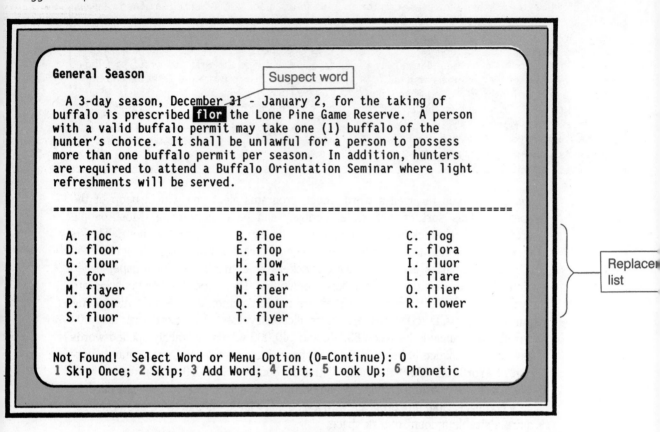

- The *Add Word* option places the suspect word in an auxiliary dictionary, so that the word will never again be classified as a suspect word, in this or any future session.
- The *Edit* option allows you to correct the spelling of the suspect word. When you press [Enter], the program verifies that the replacement is in the dictionary and continues spell-checking.
- The *Look Up* option lets you search through the dictionary for words that match a pattern containing wild card characters. For example, entering "bl*ot" might display "blot", "Blackfoot", and "bloodshot".
- The *Phonetic* option displays a list of replacement words that sound or look like the suspect word. For example, if the suspect word is *sicology*, this choice displays "psychology" and *sociology*.

Dictionary programs are not proofreaders; they cannot tell when correctly spelled words are being used incorrectly. They will not notice "that too errors are inn this quotation." After the dictionary program has caught the misspellings, it is best to read the document carefully for sense.

Application Software: A Professional's Tools

White-collar workers are rapidly abandoning conventional office products in favor of more powerful tools. Typewriters are being replaced by word processors. Pencils, multicolumn paper, and calculators are giving way to electronic spreadsheets. Information in filing cabinets is being moved into hard disks controlled by data management programs. Letters are traveling through electronic mail systems. Graph paper remains unused as graphics programs transform lists of numbers into instant charts and graphs. This photo essay will give you a clearer view of the capabilities of these new software products.

1. In this screen each of six programs is given its own window in which to display information. Windowing makes it easy to switch quickly between different tasks.

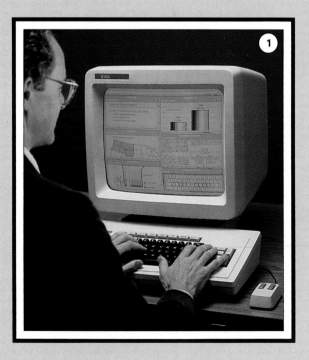

WINDOWS

A window *is a region of the screen dedicated to a particular activity. Programs that use windows give you control over how the area of the screen is to be used.*

2. Two types of windows are in common use: overlapping and tiled. This display shows tiled windows; the viewing area is broken up into nonoverlapping regions called tiles. With tiled windows, if you want to create a new window, you must split an existing window in two. And if you want to make a window larger, you must make one of its neighbors smaller by moving the boundary between them.

3. The Macintosh II—like all Macintosh computers—has support for overlapping windows built into its operating system. But unlike other Macintosh computers, it uses a color display with a 640 by 480 pixel resolution and can accept six expansion circuit boards.

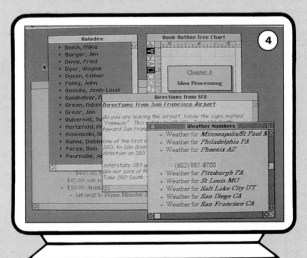

4. Windows appear to sit on this Macintosh screen in the same way pieces of paper can pile up on a desktop. Overlapping windows can be created, moved, or resized without affecting existing windows. You can bring any window to the top of the stack by pointing at it and clicking the mouse button.

VISUAL OPERATING ENVIRONMENTS

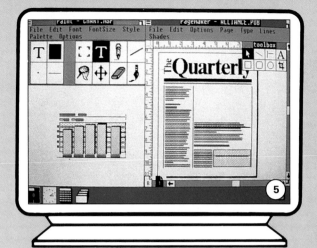

A visual operating environment uses windows, pull-down menus, and icons to create an understandable interface between the user and computer. The features of a visual operating environment can be built into the operating system. Alternatively, they can be added on top of an operating system by another program, such as the way Microsoft Windows or the GEM Desktop add visual capabilities to MS-DOS.

5-6. A visual operating environment can help integrate normally separate programs in two ways. First, it can allow them to appear in different windows so that switching between applications is fast and efficient. Second, it can help move data between applications by providing a *clipboard* or *buffer*. For example, a graph has been prepared in the left window of photo 5, and a newsletter is being laid out in the right window. Then, a copy of the graph is placed on the operating environment's hidden clipboard. The finished newsletter is shown in photo 6, complete with the graph retrieved from the clipboard.

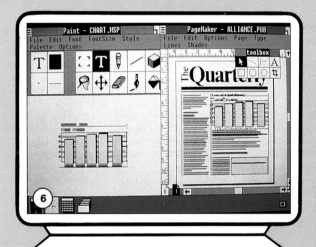

7. Early versions of Microsoft Windows used tiled windows (shown in photo 5 and 6), because they require less memory and processing than overlapping windows. But in late 1987 Microsoft Windows began using overlapping windows (shown here) to give the user more control over the size and placement of windows.

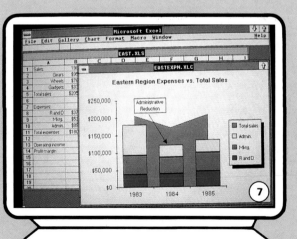

window 5

DESK ACCESSORIES

Desk accessories are readily available tools that can be used even in the middle of a session with another application program. They appear in pop-up windows that lie on top of the primary application program. This page shows how Sidekick, a desk accessories program, might be used while using a word processor.

8–11. While writing a letter, a question arises about what is stored in another file. Instead of closing one file in order to open another, Sidekick's Notepad feature is used to view the second file in a pop-up window. In photo 9 the Notepad is brought to the screen by pressing [Ctrl] and [Alt] at the same time—producing the Sidekick Main Menu—and pressing function key [F2] to select the Notepad. Next, a number in the Notepad window needs to be verified by recomputing it. This calls for another Sidekick feature, the electronic calculator shown in photo 10. In photo 11 a calendar window is opened on top of the other windows to find out what day of the week May 17th falls on in 1988. Eventually, Sidekick's pop-up windows are closed—one at a time—by pressing [Esc] repeatedly.

WORD PROCESSING

12. It is likely that more people have learned to use word processing than any other computer application. Word processing frees writers from the tyranny of paper when making revisions.

13-16.   This sequence shows how a paragraph is moved with WordStar. The first step (photo 13) is to move the cursor to the beginning of the paragraph and to insert a marker in the document. In photo 14 the cursor has been moved to the end of the paragraph and another marker has been inserted, causing the paragraph to turn green on the screen and the first marker to disappear. In photo 15 the paragraph has been transferred to its new location. Finally, in photo 16 the markers are removed.

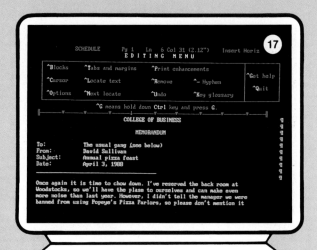

17. A typical WordStar 2000 screen display. WordStar 2000 is an enhanced version of the original WordStar program and is primarily designed for use on personal computers with hard disks.

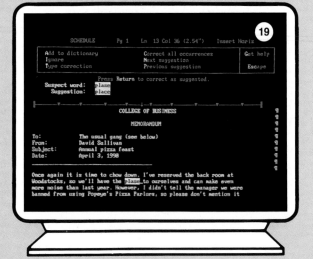

18. Normally WordStar 2000 hides the formatting codes it uses which control how the document will be printed. But in this screen the formatting codes have been made visible so they can be examined or changed. For example, *MEMORANDUM* will be centered on the printed page because it is preceded by the [Center] formatting code.

19. A spelling checker looks up each word in the document in its own dictionary. Words that aren't found in the dictionary are highlighted as suspect words. In this screen the spelling checker can't find the word *plase* in its dictionary, so it suggests the word *place* instead.

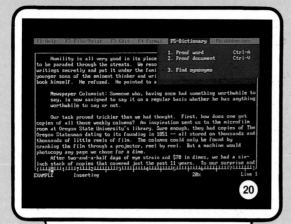

THESAURUS PROGRAMS

A thesaurus program allows you to find synonyms at the touch of a key. You might use one to spruce up your writing with more descriptive words or to verify that you understand the meaning of a word correctly.

20-21. PFS:Professional Write includes a built-in thesaurus program. To use it, you begin by moving the cursor to the word you are curious about. Pressing function key [F5] produces the pull-down menu shown in photo 20. After you select the Find Synonyms option from this menu, a pop-up window containing synonyms appears.

22-23. For word processors that don't have a built-in thesaurus program, you might want to use a *memory-resident program,* such as Turbo Lightning. A memory-resident program is loaded into memory and remains there even when other application pro-

grams are running. To use Lightning to verify the spelling of a word or find a word's synonyms, you can activate Lightning's pull-down menu system (shown in photo 22) by pressing Shift-[F8]. Then you can select an option from one of the pull-down menus. Alternatively, you might use one of Lightning's, short-cut commands to bypass the pull-down menu system. For example, pressing Alt-[F6] provides synonyms for the word containing the cursor, as shown in photo 23.

OUTLINE PROCESSING

An outline processor *is a program with features designed to let you create and revise well-formatted lists quickly.*

24.   Microsoft Word is a full-featured word processor with built-in outline processing features. For example, the chapter and section titles in a report can be "tagged" as headings in an outline. Then, with a simple command, the text in the report can be collapsed so that only the headings are visible.

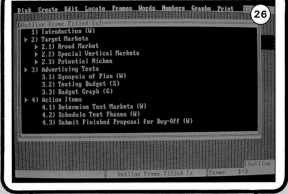

25–27.   Framework is an integrated program with word processing, data management, spreadsheet, graphics, and communications components. It stores information in windows called *frames*. Framework uses outline processing as the basis for organizing the information created by its components. A new frame can be created with the pull-down menu system, as shown in photo 25. The outline frame shown in photo 26 lists the frames it contains; word processing frames are labeled with a (W), spreadsheet frames with (S), and graphics frames with (G). In photo 27 a graphics frame overlaps a spreadsheet frame and an outline frame.

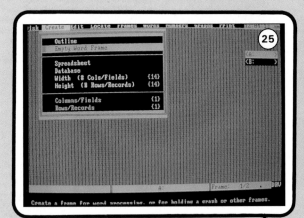

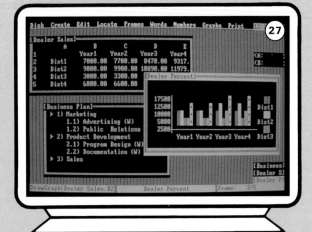

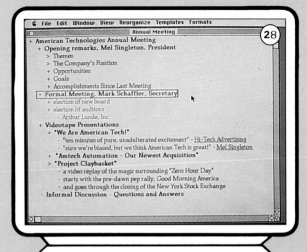

The photos on this page were created with MORE, a stand-alone outline processor with the ability to transform an ordinary outline into a tree chart or a bullet chart.

28. This is the normal text-editing view used to enter and edit the headings in an outline. Headings can be rearranged, deleted, promoted (raised to a higher level in the outline), or demoted to reorganize an outline.

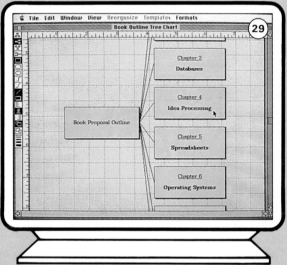

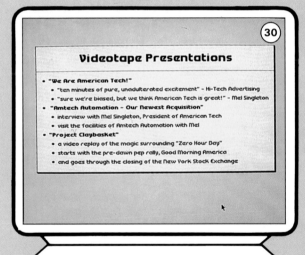

29. The tree chart view changes an outline instantly into a tree diagram. The icons along the left edge of the screen determine what kind of tree chart MORE creates.

30. The bullet chart view can turn an outline into professional-quality overhead transparencies or slides.

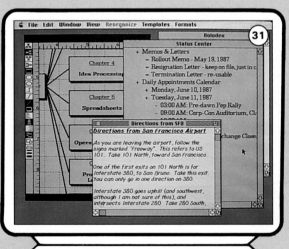

31. Several MORE windows can be open on the screen at the same time.

DESKTOP PUBLISHING

Desktop publishing takes simple word processing several steps further by giving the user control over the size and style of type as well as merging graphics with text on a page. It is one of the hottest areas in computing.

32. A complete desktop publishing system is likely to include a laser printer (foreground), a scanner (middle), and a fast personal computer with a high-quality display.

33–35. Virtually any type of document can be produced with desktop publishing. However, the color separations of photographs still need to be prepared with traditional equipment.

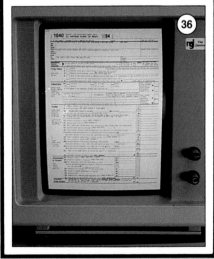

36. With a high-resolution display you can preview a full page and still read the small type sizes. For example, this tax form is displayed on a monitor with 736 by 1008 pixels.

PAGE COMPOSITION PROGRAMS

A page composition program combines text and graphics from various sources to form a finished page. They are an essential part of a complete desktop publishing system.

37.   Aldus PageMaker was one of the first personal computer-based page composition systems to provide an interactive display of what the final page layout would look like. This facing-pages view allows the user to determine whether a two-page spread will look balanced. The text in this screen is *greeked*—represented by straight lines—to save time while redrawing the screen.

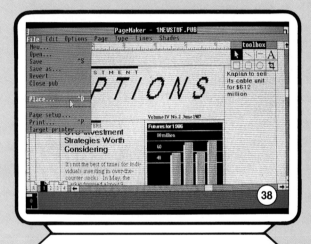

38–39.   The IBM version of PageMaker, introduced in 1987, uses Microsoft Windows to provide the same sort of visual operating environment found on the Macintosh version. Commands are selected from pull-down menus. The icons in the toolbox provide tools for cropping graphics, entering text, and drawing boxes, lines, and circles.

ELECTRONIC SPREADSHEETS

Electronic spreadsheet programs automate the process of editing and manipulating worksheets containing numbers. Spreadsheets have evolved through several generations since Visicalc, the first spreadsheet program, was introduced in 1979.

40. Visicalc was so important to the early success of the Apple II computer that some people called it the Visicalc machine. By today's standards Visicalc had very crude features. For example, it displayed numbers without commas and had no on-line help system. Despite Visicalc's shortcomings, it ushered in an entirely new way to manipulate numbers.

41. Visicalc soon had scores of copycat competitors, known as "Visi-clones." Most of these products offered better features, a lower price, or both. This screen shows SuperCalc, one of Visicalc's strongest competitors in 1981. SuperCalc introduced an excellent help system and can be displayed in color.

42. Multiplan won *InfoWorld* magazine's 1982 Software Product of the Year award. Multiplan provided a host of improvements including complete words in its menu, the ability to establish up to eight windows on the screen, and a way to link numbers between worksheets so that changes in one worksheet would automatically affect other worksheets.

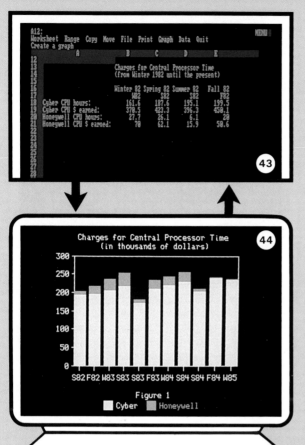

43. Lotus 1-2-3 became the best-selling personal computer program within a few months of its introduction in late 1982. Its instant success resulted from combining an excellent spreadsheet with limited graphics and data management in one easy-to-use package.

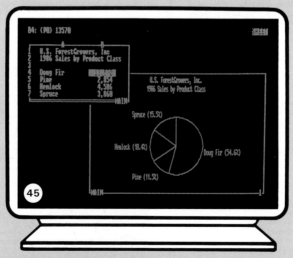

44. A Lotus 1-2-3 bar chart. Once numbers are in a 1-2-3 worksheet, it takes only a few keystrokes to convert them into a simple pie chart, bar chart, or line graph. To create a graph, you must point out which numbers are to be graphed, and you need to select the type of graph you want. Although 1-2-3 can't display a graph and the worksheet simultaneously on one screen, it takes only five keystrokes to switch from the worksheet to the graph and back to the worksheet again.

45. In mid-1984 Lotus Symphony combined Multiplan's windowing abilities with an improved version of 1-2-3's spreadsheet. Also included in the package are simple graphics, record management, word processing, and telecommunications. This screen shows a small spreadsheet window and a larger graph window. If a number in the spreadsheet window is changed, the graph is immediately redrawn to reflect the change.

DATA MANAGEMENT SOFTWARE

46. Businesses rely heavily on data management systems to do their record keeping. Most data management systems allow business forms to be displayed on the screen, making it easy to enter, revise, or query data about a particular transaction.

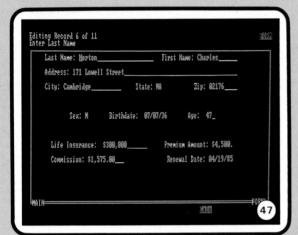

47. Lotus Symphony provides single-file data management but not database management. This means Symphony can manipulate information in one file conveniently but cannot extract or process information from several files at once. This sort of simple data management system is well suited for such everyday tasks as keeping a calendar of appointments, maintaining a Christmas card mailing list, or recording the names, addresses, and phone numbers of clients.

48. SuperCalc4 is another spreadsheet-based integrated program with single-file data management abilities. In this example, SuperCalc4's ability to store and execute commands in *macros* has been used to create a customized data management system for maintaining the inventory in a wine cellar. Notice how the menus at the bottom of the screen apply specifically to managing an inventory of wines.

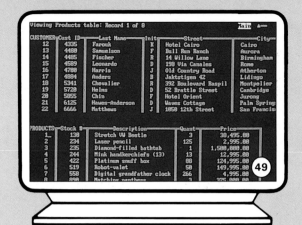

49. Paradox, a relational database management system, stores data in tables and can manage many tables at once. This provides much more flexibility and power for performing complex data manipulation activities than single-file data management programs. In this screen, the user can scroll through and compare the data in two different tables.

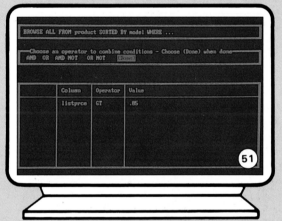

50–51. Instead of looking at data in a table, you may want to work with one record at a time by using a form. The form shown in photo 50 was created automatically by Paradox. However, if you don't like the default form, you can create your own custom forms to rearrange the data any way you like, such as the Customer Information Form shown in photo 51.

52. Paradox lets you ask questions or manipulate tables by filling out a query form. Queries are used to join tables together, select subsets of a table, and answer questions like, How many departments have a travel budget greater than $5,000? This query is a request for a list of all the clients living in Oregon.

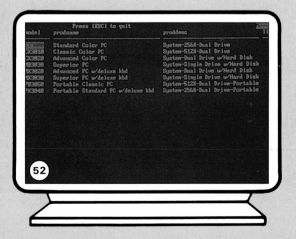

window 5

53. WordStar 2000 provides context-sensitive help; so it often seems to work like a user manual that automatically falls open to the right page.

54. Lotus Symphony has one of the best help systems on the market today. Because it is context-sensitive, it will provide spreadsheet information if you are working on a spreadsheet, graphing information if you are constructing a graph, and so on. But Symphony's help system goes one step further; it provides a list of related topics on the bottom of each help screen. You can view the help screen for a related topic by moving the highlighted cursor box onto the name of the topic and then pressing [Enter].

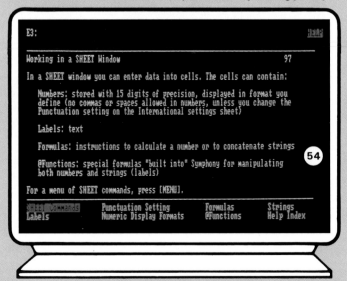

Figure 6.27 WordPerfect's thesaurus displays this screen when it is asked to look up "base".

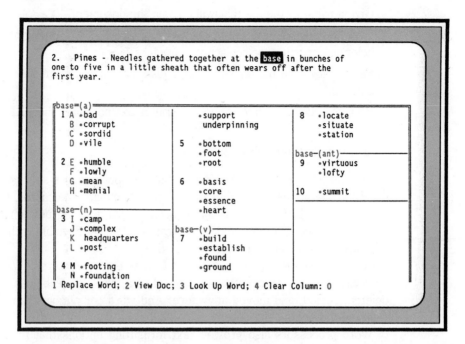

An **electronic thesaurus** provides a list of synonyms and antonyms for the word containing the cursor. A thesaurus program can spruce up your writing by finding the right word when the current one doesn't seem to fit. A well-designed thesaurus program is one of the easiest programs to use. You simply move the cursor to the word with which you are uncomfortable and press a particular keystroke combination, such as [Alt]-[F1]. Within seconds, a list of substitute words appears on the screen (see Figure 6.27). With another keystroke combination, you can remove the original word from the text and insert one of the synonyms. For example, to replace "base" with "foundation" in Figure 6.27, you would press [1] to select the Replace Word option and press [N] to select "foundation" from the synonym list. The replacement word is given the same capitalization as the original.

A thesaurus program relies on an index and a dictionary. The *index* contains all the words for which synonyms are available, and the *dictionary* lists the synonyms themselves. An index containing from 10,000 to 20,000 words is common; dictionaries are larger and often have 100,000 to 200,000 words or more.

■ SUMMARY

This chapter has covered a lot of ground, and perhaps you are beginning to feel that learning to use a word processor is difficult. That impression would be misleading. Some things—like brushing your teeth, riding a bicycle, or using a word processor—are harder to describe than they are to do.

The usual steps in creating a letter, memo, or other document are quite simple

1. Begin running the word processing program.
2. Give a name to the file that will contain the document.
3. Type the document in the insert mode. Correct simple typing mistakes by deleting, inserting, or replacing characters.
4. Periodically save the document on a disk, and save it immediately before quitting.
5. Print the document by turning the printer on and giving the PRINT command.
6. Quit the word processing program.

Most of the time spent working with a word processor is spent on the four fundamental operations of entering and editing: (1) moving the cursor, (2) viewing the text by scrolling, (3) deleting characters, and (4) entering new characters (using the insert or the typeover mode). You can become comfortable with these four operations with only an hour or so of practice.

Word processors have a variety of further editing features. Word wrap automatically returns the carriage at the end of a line. Whole blocks of text can be deleted, copied, and moved anywhere. And words or phrases can be located and replaced throughout the document.

Word processors also provide text formatting options that make a document look good on paper. Page design options include margins, headers, and footers. Local formatting options control page breaks, paragraph formatting, text justification, and font choice.

Storage in main memory is less reliable than storage on disk. Both are less reliable than storing information on paper. Making copies of your work on disk (and on paper) is like buying an insurance policy: usually you don't need it, but when you do, it pays off handsomely.

Some advanced word processing features are useful for serious users. Among them are outline processors, computerized form letters, spelling checkers, and electronic thesauruses.

KEY TERMS

automatic search-and-replace
  operation
block operation
buffer
desktop publishing
dialog box
electronic thesaurus

fixed-width spacing
font
footers
format code
headers
insert mode
justify

local formatting option

manual search-and-replace operation

microspacing

off-screen text formatting

outline processor

page break

page design

paragraph reforming

pitch

point

proportional spacing

ragged-right margin

search-and-replace operation

soft space

spelling checker

style sheet

text formatting

toggle switch

typeover mode

word wrap

WYSIWYG word processor

DISCUSSION QUESTIONS

1. When are you likely to use forward deletion? backward deletion? Which are you more likely to use?

2. What is the difference between hard and soft characters?

3. When is it more efficient to use block operations than one-character-at-a-time operations? How many keystrokes must you make to move a block on your word processor?

4. What is the difference between microspacing and proportional spacing? What types of documents require proportional spacing?

5. What happens if you accidentally turn off the computer while using your word processor? Is everything lost?

6. What outline processing features would be most useful for preparing daily "to do" lists? Would the same features be the most important ones for preparing a business's organization chart or the outline for a major report?

7. Describe the steps necessary to change the address in a letter stored on disk.

8. Which is the better time to check the spelling of words: as you type them or just before you are going to print a document? Why?

9. Compare the capabilities of typewriters with those of word processors. What types of tasks would be easier with a typewriter? When would you prefer a word processor?

EXERCISES

1. Consult your word processor's manual to find the keys to press for the following commands:

a. Load the word processing program.
b. Name the file containing the document.
c. Move the cursor up, down, right, and left.
d. Scroll up and down.
e. Move the cursor to the beginning or the end of the document.
f. Delete a single character at the cursor or to the left of the cursor.
g. Toggle between the insert and the replacement modes.
h. Save the document in a file.
i. Print the document.
j. Exit from the word processing program.
k. Quit an editing session without saving the changes made during the session.

2. Experiment with the word wrap feature of your word processor. How does it define a word? What effect do such characters as numerals and dashes have? What is the maximum word length?

3. Determine the typefaces and styles that your printer can produce. Can your word processor use them?

4. Use your word processor to prepare an outline of the steps you take to get dressed in the morning. What outline processing features would have made this task easier?

5. Time yourself as you use your word processor to write a letter requesting an annual report from General Electric Company. Then request an annual report from Westinghouse, using the letter to GE as a starting point. How much less time did you spend preparing the second letter?

6. Describe a window-based user interface for generating form letters.

7 Spreadsheets

Our present ability to understand the world in terms of numbers is the result of a series of advances affecting how numbers are represented and processed. Even in prehistoric times, people needed help manipulating numbers; the scratch marks on cave walls remain as evidence of our ancestors' limited memory. The introduction of clay tablets and paper made numerical records more portable and erasable. The invention of a symbol for zero and the Hindu decimal system made arithmetic easier and led to many advances in higher mathematics. Logarithm tables and slide rules eliminated most of the work of multiplying and dividing. The early part of this century saw the widespread use of mechanical and electromechanical adding machines; these have been replaced in the last two decades by electronic desktop and hand-held calculators. The last major step in this progression occurred with the introduction of the first spreadsheet program, Visicalc, in 1979.

The first version of Visicalc used only 16KB of memory and stored data on tape cassettes. Despite its initial limitations, Visicalc did something no program had done before: it made a computer's numerical processing abilities available to people with no previous computer experience. Since Visicalc's introduction, literally hundreds of competitive spreadsheet programs have been written, and spreadsheet processing has become one of the most popular applications for personal computers.

A spreadsheet program does for numerical work what a word processor does for writing: it provides flexibility, convenience, and power. Spreadsheet programs include many features to help users enter, label, move, and display numbers. But the real advantage of spreadsheet programs is their ability to store not only numbers, but also formulas for calculating numbers. When critical numbers are changed, the entire model is recalculated, updating other numbers as necessary to keep everything consistent and in balance. In a sales forecast, for example, as soon as one month's sales estimate is changed, the full year's estimate is automatically adjusted.

This ability to do instantaneous "what-if" recalculations allows people to experiment with the relationships among numbers in a manner that was previously impractical. For example, if the sales estimate in a typical five-year financial plan is changed, adjustments must be made in manufacturing costs, overhead costs, warranty returns, and many other items. A spreadsheet program makes these changes automatically, but in the past, it could take an accountant hours of error-prone, tedious figuring on paper to predict the implications of changes in a forecast's basic assumptions. Such arduous work discouraged experimentation and limited how many assumptions about the future were explored.

Like any other powerful tool, spreadsheets have their own terminology and basic operations, which must be mastered before sophisticated applications can be undertaken. This chapter teaches you about spreadsheet processing in two stages. The first stage is to learn the concepts necessary for simple models, so we begin with detailed examples of common concepts and operations. The second stage is to become aware of the advanced features that allow spreadsheet programs to construct sophisticated professional applications.

BASIC CONCEPTS

Figure 7.1 illustrates how a spreadsheet program stores and displays data. Data are stored and edited in an enormous sheet built out of small rectangular storage bins called **cells**, which represent the intersection of rows and columns. We will call this grid of rows and columns the **worksheet**. (Others may call it a *spreadsheet* or *template*. We use the term *spreadsheet* to refer to the program and *worksheet* to refer to the model that the program allows you to create.) The size of the worksheet depends on the program. A common size is 64 columns wide by 256 rows deep, although some worksheets have hundreds of columns and thousands of

Figure 7.I A worksheet is an aggregate of cells that can get values from one another. You can think of each cell as having several layers in front of the worksheet that compute the value of the cell and determine the format of the presentation. For example, each cell has a value rule, which can be the value itself or a way to compute it, as well as a format rule, which converts the value into a form suitable for display. A cell's image is the formatted value as displayed in the rectangular part of the worksheet appearing in the window.

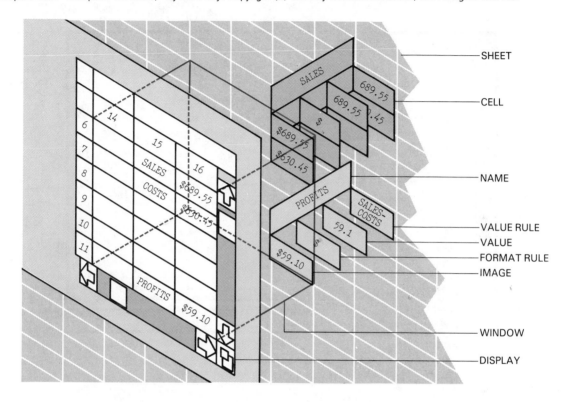

rows. Because the display is much smaller than the worksheet, only a tiny rectangular portion of the worksheet shows in the display's window at any given time. Using the cursor keys, a mouse, or another pointing method, you can scroll the window horizontally and vertically to view any portion of the worksheet.

Data in a worksheet cell pass through several layers of processing before they appear in the display window. These layers can be thought of as processing filters that calculate the cell's value and convert the value into the desired format for display. Each cell stores a **value rule**, which tells the spreadsheet how to calculate the cell's value. The value rule might simply be the value itself, such as the number 689.55 or the label "Sales"; or it might be a *formula,* which is an expression stating how the value is to be calculated. Each cell also has one or more **format rules**, which tell the spreadsheet how to display the value. For example, a format rule might cause the value 689.55 to appear on the display as $690.

Some programs label both the rows and the columns of the worksheet with numbers. To indicate whether a number refers to a row or a column, some of

Figure 7.2 With Microsoft's Excel, you control the worksheet window with scroll bars (to view other areas of the worksheet) and a size box (to make the window larger or smaller). Several worksheets can be open on the screen at a time, each in its own window.

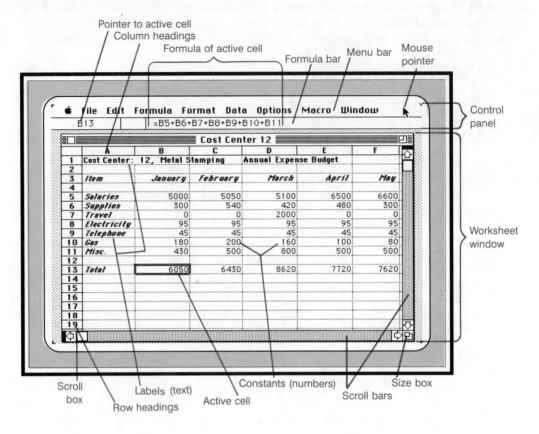

these products precede row numbers with an R and column numbers with a C. Thus, the upper left-hand cell of the worksheet would be called cell R1C1. In contrast, most programs label the columns with letters. But if there are 64 or more columns, they can't all be designated with just the 26 letters of the alphabet; it's necessary to use two letters to designate the later columns. This means that the first 26 columns are labeled A to Z and the later columns AA, AB, . . . AZ, BA, BB, and so on until the end of the worksheet. In most programs, and in our examples, the name of a cell is the cell's column letter(s) followed by its row number, as in R2, D2, Z80, AD1988, or A1.

Most spreadsheets allow you to assign names to cells. For example, you might give cell C5 the name "Sales" and cell C6 the name "Costs". Notice that a cell's name is different from a cell's value; for example, the cell named "Sales" might store the number 689.55. Formulas are easier to write and understand if cells have been given logical names; "Sales − Costs" makes more intuitive sense than "C5 − C6".

Spreadsheet programs assign different parts of the display to two tasks: the

Figure 7.3 Lotus 1-2-3 separates the worksheet window from the control panel with a highlighted border of row and column labels.

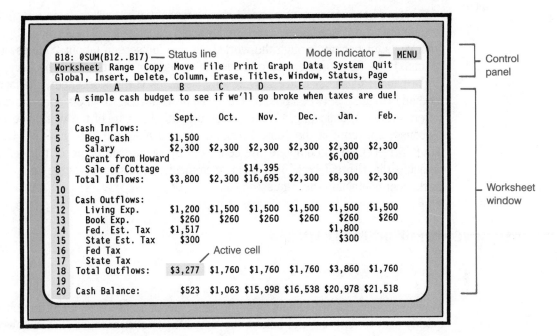

control panel displays status and help information, and the *window* lets you see what is in the worksheet. (Figures 7.2 and 7.3 compare the way that two popular spreadsheets use the display.) The control panel performs the same function as a car's dashboard: it shows you what the product is doing, tells you what options are available, and lets you control the activity. You should understand everything the control panel says. Like dashboards, control panels in spreadsheets vary from one product to the next.

The **active cell** (also called the *current cell*) is the cell currently available for use. It is marked on the screen by highlighting, underlining, or reversing the color (inverse video) of the cell's contents. We use highlighting in this chapter's examples.

Whenever you begin editing an empty worksheet, cell A1 is the active cell. You can mark any cell in the window as the active cell by using the cursor-movement keys. Whereas in most programs the cursor-movement keys move the cursor, in spreadsheet processing, they change which cell is the active cell by one column or row at a time. If you try to move the active cell off the edge of the window, the window scrolls to a different part of the worksheet. Scrolling does more than shift the contents of the window: the window's borders are also relabeled, and the co-ordinates of the active cell shown in the control panel are adjusted.

Given enough time, you can use the cursor keys to scroll the window to show any part of the worksheet. On most keyboards, if you hold down the cursor keys, the repeat-key feature is invoked, and scrolling continues until the window runs up against an edge of the worksheet; then the scrolling stops. Most spreadsheets beep if you try to scroll past the edge of the worksheet—in effect, saying, "You can't go there."

Scrolling between distant parts of the worksheet with cursor keys is tedious; fortunately, there are other, quicker methods. Most spreadsheets have special commands for paging through the worksheet one full screen (about 20 lines or 70 columns) at a time. For example, paging up and down is often done by using the [PgUp] and [PgDn] keys. For moving long distances in the worksheet, the fastest method is to jump between points. The usual procedure is to type a special symbol (often > or =), indicating, "I want to jump to another part of the worksheet." In response, a prompt in the control panel displays a message like "ENTER CELL TO JUMP TO." You complete the command by typing the name of the cell and pressing the [Enter] key. The window immediately displays the region of the worksheet containing the requested cell.

BASIC SPREADSHEET OPERATIONS

Entering and Editing

Moving around the worksheet soon becomes second nature. Your attention will quickly shift to entering and editing the contents of cells, because that is how you get to see the results of calculations. But before we give examples of how to edit cells, you should learn the modes of operation you'll encounter during spreadsheet processing and the methods used to shift between modes. It's disconcerting to get caught in an unexpected mode, because without much warning, the keys can have different meanings.

Ready, Enter, and Command Modes

Every spreadsheet has three basic modes of operation, which we call the *ready mode, command mode,* and *entry mode.* The program begins in the **ready mode**, which is used to move around the worksheet. The spreadsheet shifts instantly from the ready mode to one of the other modes whenever a letter, number, or one of a set of special symbols is typed.

Typing a slash (/) is the normal way of entering the **command mode.** A menu bar then appears in the control panel, and you select a command from the menu bar. But a few commands are so important that most spreadsheets give them their own command keys; jumping is one such command. You invoke such a command just by pressing a specified key, without first typing a slash. We will discuss commands and how they are given later in this chapter.

Typing any letter (A to Z), number (0 to 9), or one of a few special symbols (such as a quotation mark, plus sign, minus sign, @ sign, or left parenthesis) shifts the program into the entry mode. The **entry mode** is used to enter new information into the active cell. The characters of the new entry appear on the entry line

Figure 7.4 The left-hand screen shows the display as an entry is being typed. The right-hand screen shows the entry's effect after the [Enter] key has been pressed.

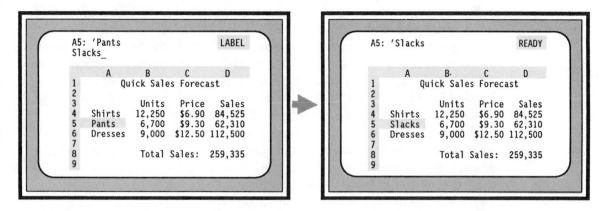

of the control panel as they are typed (see Figure 7.4). While in the entry mode, you can't scroll the screen or do anything other than type and edit a new entry for the active cell. You can use the left- and right-arrow keys to move the cursor back and forth across the entry to insert or delete characters.

The normal way to exit from the entry mode is to press the [Enter] key, which discards the old contents (if any) of the active cell, stores the new entry in the active cell, and returns the program to the ready mode. Once [Enter] is pressed, the old entry is gone and can't be recovered. But if you haven't pressd [Enter], you can escape from the entry mode without affecting the contents of the current cell, usually by pressing the escape key [Esc].

Labels Versus Numbers and Formulas

The value rule in each cell can store one of three types of information: a label, a number, or a formula. A *label* is a string of normal text characters, such as "Smith","Dresses", "123 Main Street", and "Pro-Forma Income Statement". Labels help identify the items in the worksheet. A number might be the integer 4 or the floating-point number 3.14159. As we've said, a *formula* is generally an instruction to calculate a number. (In some spreadsheets, formulas can also be used to process text.) For example, $5 + 4$ is a valid formula. This trivial formula reads "five plus four" and results in the number 9. Formulas may also be quite complex and are the most powerful part of spreadsheet processing.

Cells that store numerical data can be used in mathematical formulas; cells storing labels cannot. For example, a formula can add the values of a group of cells storing numbers. But it makes no sense to add labels, such as "Pants" and "Dresses" or "apples" and "oranges".

As soon as you type the first character of an entry, most spreadsheets decide whether the entry will store text (a label), a number, or a formula. If the first character is a letter, the entry is assumed to be a label. If it begins with a number or an arithmetic symbol (such as a plus, minus, or left parenthesis), then the entry is not treated as text and is assumed to be either a number or a formula.

Because most entries beginning with a letter are labels, and most other entries are numbers or formulas, it saves time to have the spreadsheet program guess which type of entry is being made. But for some entries, the guess will be incorrect. For example, although "123 Main Street" and the social security number "543-64-9856" don't begin with letters, they need to be stored as labels. The "123" of "123 Main Street" should be stored as the character 1, followed by the character 2, followed by the character 3. This string of three characters is not a number in this case; it is merely three characters in a row. (If you're curious about how the keystroke [7] could be stored either as a number or as a text character (label), read Appendix A, "How Computers Process Information.")

These examples indicate the need for a way to override the default assumption that all labels begin with letters. The usual procedure is to begin the label by typing a quotation mark ["]. The spreadsheet interprets the quotation mark as a command to begin the entry mode and enter a label regardless of the first character in the entry.

Entering Labels and Numbers

To make our discussion as concrete as possible, let's suppose you want to build a worksheet like the one in Figure 7.4 to forecast sales for a clothing manufacturer. Your first step is to turn on the computer, load the operating system and the spreadsheet in memory, and begin editing an empty worksheet. You type the sales forecast's labels and numbers into the worksheet one at a time by repeatedly

- Marking a particular cell as the active cell by using the cursor-movement keys
- Typing an entry
- Pressing the [Enter] key

When all the labels and numbers have been entered, the window showing the worksheet would look like the left-hand screen in Figure 7.5. The sales figures and the total haven't been entered because they will be calculated by formulas.

Notice that the information in Figure 7.5 is poorly formatted in comparison with the same information in Figure 7.4. The column headings aren't aligned with the numbers beneath them, and the numbers don't have commas, dollar signs, or even the correct number of digits after the decimal piont. Obviously, the spreadsheet has made some assumptions about how the entries should look that are inappropriate for this forecast, such as left-justifying all the labels and right-justifying all the numbers. Later in this chapter we discuss how to change the appearance of entries. For now it's sufficient for you to know that entering data and formatting the data to look good are often separate steps.

Figure 7.5 Entering a formula into the worksheet.

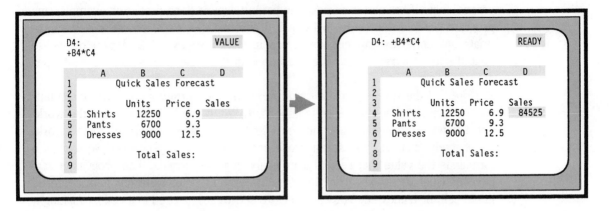

Entering Formulas

If a spreadsheet could record only labels and numbers in a grid of cells, it wouldn't have much practical use—a simple text editor would be more convenient and just as powerful. A spreadsheet is useful because it can store formulas—instructions for calculations—inside the cells.

As an example, look again at Figure 7.5. Suppose you want cell D4 to show the result of multiplying the units of shirts in cell B4 (12,250) by the price per shirt in cell C4 ($6.90). In spreadsheet arithmetic, an asterisk means "multiply"; a slash means "divide"; and plus and minus signs mean "add" and "subtract." Therefore, you might type the formula 12250*6.9 into cell D4. But the numbers in cells B4 and C4 have already been entered into the worksheet once; there's no need to enter them again for the formula in cell D4. Instead of telling the spreadsheet which numbers to multiply, you can tell it which cells contain the numbers. Typing the formula +B4*C4 into cell D4 causes the spreadsheet to find the value of cell B4, multiply it by the value of cell C4, and display the result in cell D4, as shown in the right-hand screen in Figure 7.5.

The plus sign in the formula +B4*C4 is very important. Let's suppose that it is omitted and that B4*C4 is typed into cell D4 instead of +B4*C4. Since the first character of the entry is now a letter, the entry would be stored as a label, not as a formula. Labels are treated as text and are not processed to see if they make mathematical sense; so the window would now display B4*C4 for cell D4.

Some spreadsheet programs carry out operations from left to right across a formula. With these programs, the formula 2 + 2/4 equals 1 because the addition is done first. Other spreadsheets respect the normal order of operations that is assumed in algebra or computer programming: multiplication and division are done before addition and subtraction. These programs evaluate 2 + 2/4 as equal to 2.5. For many formulas, the order in which the operations are performed is critical.

One way to avoid problems is to take a few seconds to type $2 + 2/4$ into a cell to determine which way your spreadsheet evaluates expressions; another is to use parentheses. Whatever is enclosed in parentheses is done first. For example, any program will find that $(2 + 2)/4$ equals 1 and that $2 + (2/4)$ equals 2.5. If appropriate, parentheses can be nested, as in $((5/8) + (13/7))/2$. When there are nested sets of parentheses, the operations in the innermost sets of parentheses are done first.

Note that the spreadsheet *stores the formula*, but it *displays the result* of computing the formula. The difference is important. When you look at a cell in the worksheet window, you don't see the cell's contents as they are stored in the worksheet itself. Instead, you see a processed version. The processed version of a formula is the value that results from evaluating the formula. The processed version of a label might vary from the stored version by being right-justified, centered in the cell, or truncated. You can check to see what is stored in a cell by making it the active cell and looking at the control panel.

Specifying Ranges of Cells

Notice that our sample worksheet in Figure 7.5 also calls for the total sales to be given. To obtain this figure, you might put the formula $+D4 + D5 + D6$ in cell D8. But clearly, this approach would be cumbersome if the sales forecast had 40 or 50 sales items. A more reliable method is to specify a range of cells to be added. A **range of cells** is a rectangular group of cells that is treated as a unit for some operation.

A range can be as small as a single cell, or it can be part of a column, part of a row, an entire row or column, or even a large rectangular region of cells. The exact syntax for specifying a range varies from program to program. Some programs allow you to use a mouse to mark ranges of cells on the screen; others let you use the cursor-movement keys. But the usual procedure is to type the name of the upper left-hand cell in the range, a delimiter (generally a series of periods or a colon), and the name of the lower right-hand cell. For example, the range that includes cells D4,D5 and D6 might be specified as D4..D6. A range of cells within one row has the same row number for both end points of the range, as in the range A20..Q20. One specification can encompass an entire worksheet, as in A1..JQ2048.

For most commands and functions used in spreadsheets, you must indicate the range of cells to be processed. For example, you can

- Save a range of cells on a disk as a file
- Print a range of cells on the printer
- Use a function to add, average, or find the largest value in a range of cells
- Use a command to copy, move, or delete a range of cells

Entering Functions

Spreadsheet formulas can process ranges of cells as well as individual cells, but the standard arithmetic operators (+, −, /, and *) don't work on ranges. For example, you can't divide the values in one range by the values in another with a formula like D2..D4/E2..E4. Instead, you must use a built-in function designed to manipulate ranges.

Built-in functions are tools provided by the spreadsheet that perform a specific type of processing, such as adding a column of numbers or computing the average of a range of values. Figure 7.6 shows how the SUM function adds the values of all the cells in a range to produce a total. A function is used by typing its name into a cell and then giving the function's arguments (if any) inside parentheses. With some spreadsheets, a function must begin with an identifying character. For example, in the entry line in Figure 7.6, the SUM function is preceded by an @ sign, which identifies it as a function; the range stating which cells to add is then

Figure 7.6 Using the SUM function to add three cells with Lotus 1-2-3. (a) The name of the function is entered in cell D8. (b) Arrow keys are used to highlight the range to be added. (c) Typing a right parenthesis accepts the high-lighted range. (d) Pressing [Enter] completes the entry.

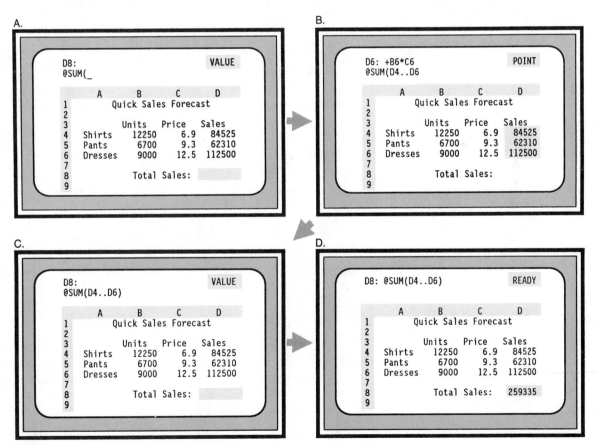

enclosed in parentheses. Other spreadsheets allow functions to run in with the rest of the formula, as in 8 + AVERAGE(2,4,6,) + 10, which is equal to 22.

A formula can consist of a single function, or it can contain many of them, or built-in functions and arithmetic operations can be mixed in the same formula. In general, you can put a function in a formula wherever a number would be valid. For example, assume that the sum of the numbers in cells D9..F9 is 20. Then 2 + (@SUM(D9..F9)/10) is equal to 4. Even nested functions are acceptable in formula. For example, @COS(@SUM(A1..A5)) takes the cosine of the sum of the values in cells A1 through A5.

There are many ways to obtain the same mathematical result with spreadsheets. For example, both of the following two formulas will find the average value of all the nonblank cells in the range from cell B4 to cell B152:

@AVERAGE(B4..B152)
@SUM(B4..B152)/@COUNT(B4..B152)

The first formula assumes the existence of a built-in function that finds the average of a range of cells directly; nearly all spreadsheets have such a function. The second formula goes the roundabout route of totaling the range of values, then counting the number of nonblank cells, and finally dividing the two numbers to obtain the average.

Automatic and Manual Recalculation

The advantage of using cell references rather than numbers in formulas becomes apparent when a worksheet is modified. Consider Figure 7.6 again. If the formula in cell D4 is 12250*6.9, then no matter what changes are made to cells B4 and C4 the display for cell D4 stays the same. Thus, if the number of shirts sold (the value of Cell B4) is changed from 12,250 to 6,000, the value of the sales displayed in cell D4 isn't changed accordingly. Of course, you could edit the formula in cell D4 to

---

Figure 7.7 "What-if" analysis. Changing the number in cell B4 shows what will happen to sales if fewer shirts are sold.

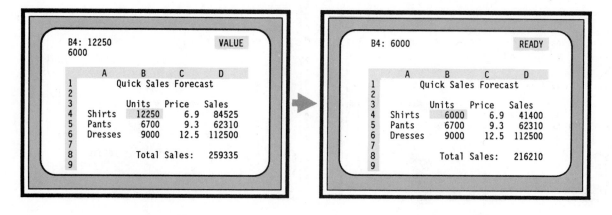

reflect the change, but you can avoid this unnecessary work by writing formulas with cell references instead of numbers. Then, whenever the value in a cell is entered or modified, every formula in the worksheet is automatically recalculated.

Most spreadsheets evaluate every formula in the worksheet whenever any entry is changed; this is called **automatic recalculation**. For example, Figure 7.7 shows how the sales for shirts (cell D4) and the total sales (D8) are recalculated when the number of shirts (B4) is changed. Spreadsheets encourage people to experiment with different assumptions—in what is known as "what-if" analysis—because it's fun to see the effects of a change ripple across the numbers in the window.

A worksheet can have hundreds or thousands of formulas. Evaluating all the formulas takes time, especially if some of the formulas involve heavy-duty calculations, such as logarithms or statistical functions. If the worksheet is large and complicated, it can take five or ten minues to complete the job. Obviously, this is too long to wait between making entries. Setting the spreadsheet to manual recalculation avoids these delays. With *manual recalculation,* formulas are evaluated only when you give the command to recalculate. On most spreadsheets, this command is given by typing an exclamation point (!) in the ready mode.

Revising and Rearranging

When you first enter data into a worksheet, the cycle of repeatedly marking the active cell and typing an entry works well enough; but revising data or rearranging information already in the worksheet requires more efficient methods. That is why spreadsheet programs have numerous commands for editing cells, inserting and deleting rows and columns, and copying and moving ranges of cells.

Editing Cells
Suppose you place a label in a cell, and then you notice that the label is misspelled. Or imagine that you enter a formula, and the result displayed is obviously incorrect because a set of parentheses is missing. Either of these mistakes could be corrected by starting from scratch and typing the correct entry. But there is an easier way: the contents of any cell can be *edited.*

The usual procedure is to mark the cell you wish to edit as the active cell and then give the EDIT command (generally by typing "/E"). This puts the spreadsheet in the entry mode, but instead of starting with an empty entry, the entry begins with the active cell's contents. Once in the entry mode, you can use the cursor-movement keys to position the cursor where the change should be made and add or delete characters from the entry until it is correct.

Inserting and Deleting Rows and Columns
Large-scale editing operations can shift whole regions of the worksheet from one place to another. The most common large-scale editing commands insert or delete a row or a column.

Figure 7.8 Inserting a new row 3.

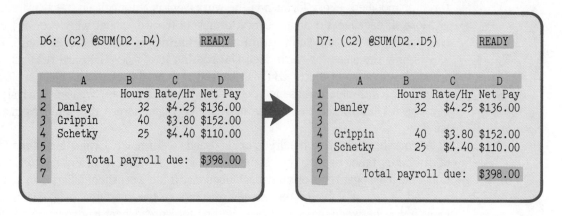

When you insert a row or column, the new row or column is initially blank. By making the insertion, you can open up room in the worksheet for new items. When a new row is inserted, all the following rows are moved toward the bottom of the worksheet. When a column is added, the following columns are shifted to the right. Therefore, it isn't necessary to throw away old information in order to make room for new information.

Inserting a row or column has another very important effect: all the formulas in the worksheet are automatically adjusted to refer to the correct entries *even though the entries may now be in new cell locations.* Study Figure 7.8 to see the effect of inserting a new row 3. You can see in the control panels that, when the entry in cell D6 is moved to cell D7, its formula is adjusted from @SUM(D2..D4) to @SUM(D2..D5). [The (C2) in the control panel before the formulas for cells D6 and D7 is a format rule causing these entries to be displayed as dollars-and-cents numbers.] The reference to cell D2 hasn't been changed, because inserting the new row didn't affect row 2. But the reference to D4 has been modified, because that entry is now in a new location: D5.

Similarly, whenever a row or column is deleted, the spreadsheet attempts to adjust the remaining formulas to refer to the correct entries. For example, if column F is deleted, then the formula @AVERAGE(A12..S12) will be changed to @AVERAGE(A12..R12).

Deleting a row or a column removes unwanted material from the worksheet, but deletion commands can be quite dangerous because of unexpected side effects. For example, suppose a worksheet filled with financial information has an income statement in the area bounded by cells A1 and F50 and a balance sheet in the range H1..Z50. Deleting a row removes the *entire* row from the worksheet. This means that the seemingly innocent operation of deleting a line from the income statement will also remove material from the balance sheet.

Deleting a row or column also has a negative side effect if formulas elsewhere in the worksheet contain references to the deleted entries. Such formulas are rendered invalid because they refer to an entry that no longer exists. For example, in

Figure 7.9 When row 2 is deleted from the worksheet, the formula for total payroll becomes invalid, because the formula referred to row 2.

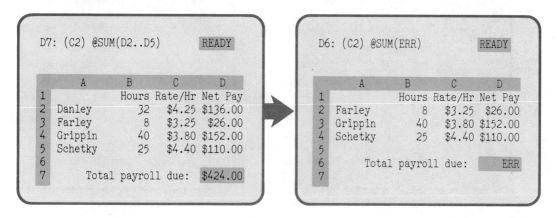

Figure 7.9, the formula that calculates total payroll due is rendered invalid when one of the rows on which the formula is based is deleted. When a formula is invalid, the worksheet window displays a terse error message, such as ERR, @ERROR, or #REF.

Exchanging, Cutting, and Pasting

Every spreadsheet has commands for moving entries from one location to another. These commands make it possible to redesign the layout of the worksheet by changing the order in which entries appear. Within limits, this allows you to divide the construction of a worksheet into two phases. In the first phase, you concentrate on entering data and building formulas until the computations have been completed. In the second phase, you rearrange everything until the visual layout is appropriate for a report.

Spreadsheets use two fundamentally different ways of moving information: (1) exchanging the order of rows or of columns, and (2) cutting and pasting areas of the worksheet. Both methods have pitfalls you need to avoid, so it is essential to understand them clearly and use them correctly.

Nearly all spreadsheets allow you to rearrange the worksheet by exchanging the order of entire rows or columns. For example, Figure 7.10 shows the effect of moving row 2 to row 6. Notice how the original rows 3 through 6 are shoved up to become rows 2 through 5, making room for the original row 2 to become row 6. Formulas are revised automatically, so that cell references point to the new worksheet locations. For Figure 7.10, this means that formulas that originally referred to row 2 now refer to row 6; references to the original row 3 now refer to row 2; and so on. Thus, the formula in cell D7 changed from @SUM(D2..D5) to @SUM(D6..D4). For most situations, this method of revising formulas preserves the functional relationships in the worksheet despite the new location of cell entries. But it doesn't seem to work well in Figure 7.10: the evaluation of cell D7 has decreased form $424.00 to$246.00 and no longer provides an accurate total.

Figure 7.10 Exchanging rows by moving row 2 to be the new row 6.

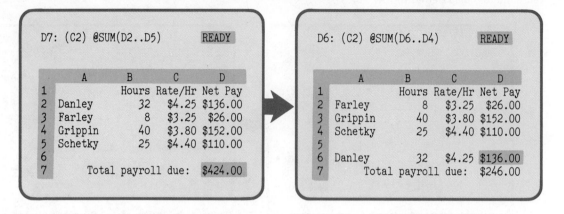

```
D7: (C2) @SUM(D2..D5)        READY

        A      B      C       D
1             Hours Rate/Hr Net Pay
2  Danley     32    $4.25  $136.00
3  Farley      8    $3.25   $26.00
4  Grippin    40    $3.80  $152.00
5  Schetky    25    $4.40  $110.00
6
7         Total payroll due:  $424.00
```

```
D6: (C2) @SUM(D6..D4)        READY

        A      B      C       D
1             Hours Rate/Hr Net Pay
2  Farley      8    $3.25   $26.00
3  Grippin    40    $3.80  $152.00
4  Schetky    25    $4.40  $110.00
5
6  Danley     32    $4.25  $136.00
7         Total payroll due:  $246.00
```

As long as the worksheet is fairly simple, the strategy of rearranging the worksheet by exchanging rows or columns is workable but tedious. But if a worksheet has several "pages" of information in different areas, you can't use these commands to reorganize one area without disturbing the other areas. Multiplan, Lotus 1-2-3, and most recently developed spreadsheets provide another way of rearranging entries: they allow a region to be cut from the worksheet and pasted in somewhere else. With this strategy, you can avoid moving an entire row or column when you need to move only a localized region.

In the "cut" part of a cut-and-paste procedure, you specify the range of cells to be moved, usually by designating the upper left-hand and lower right-hand cells of a rectangle. This step works as if all the entries in the range of cells were removed from the worksheet and placed on a clipboard. Some programs leave a blank area in the worksheet corresponding to the cells that were moved, but Multiplan shifts cells to fill in the region. It does this by asking whether cells beneath the region should shift up or whether cells to the right of the region should shift left.

In the "paste" operation, you tell the spreadsheet where to place the entries obtained in the cut operation. Lotus 1-2-3 throws away the previous contents of the region where new entries are pasted. For example, in Figure 7.11, twelve cells are cut from the worksheet and pasted in one row down from their previous location, into row 5. The paste operation destroys the payroll information for O'Toole and invalidates the formula for total pay due by erasing the previous entry of cell D7. It is important to paste entries into blank areas of the worksheet if you use a product like Lotus 1-2-3, because it gives no warning before tossing out the region's previous contents.

Copying
The COPY command fills out a worksheet by taking existing cell entries and replicating them in other cells. Careful use of the COPY command can reduce by at least half the number of keystrokes needed to complete most worksheets. The

Here are some simple rules to help you create spreadsheet models of lasting value.

Begin with a plan. You are more likely to build a useful model if you clearly identify what you want it to accomplish before you begin. Decide what you want the model to compute, what data it needs, and how you want to see its results.

Organize your use of the worksheet. A good worksheet groups related information together so it is clear what each part does. For example, you might list all of the model's basic assumptions in one area, perform the processing in another, and display the results in a third. If the model is too big to fit in one screen, try to organize it down the left edge of the worksheet. This makes it easy to find all the parts by paging up and down and lets you insert rows without inadvertently damaging other areas of the worksheet.

Build in flexibility. Make sure that the model's assumptions are displayed where they can be reviewed and changed. Avoid putting these values inside formulas where they will be hard to locate and change later. Instead, put them in their own cells and label them appropriately. If you follow these rules consistently, your formulas will contain few numbers and many references to other cells. As a result, your model will be able to answer many more "what if" types of questions.

Start small, build gradually. By building a tiny model or prototype, you can test out your ideas before you have invested a lot of time in one approach. Also, you are more likely to notice logical errors in a small model than in a large and complex one. Once everything seems to be working, you can expand the prototype by inserting rows and columns and by copying formulas.

Label everything thoroughly. Take the time to label the numbers and formulas so that they are clearly identified. Spreadsheet models tend to be used sporadically, so it is easy to forget how they work and what they do. You will thank yourself later if you place a few lines of documentation in the upper-left corner of the worksheet. And if part of the model is particularly tricky or complex, document it with comments as well.

Give names to cells and ranges. Spreadsheet formulas are tough enough to understand without having to fight through the alphabet soup of unnamed cells. A formula like = Sales-Gross Margin is much easier to interpret than = B21-E40.

Use the copy command liberally. The obvious reason to use the copy command is to save time. But there is an even stronger reason: you are less likely to make mistakes if you copy formulas than if you retype them. For example, if you copy a formula down a long column, you can determine whether the copies are working correctly by testing one or two of them. But if you retype each formula individually, every formula is a candidate for a potentially disastrous typing error.

Use white space liberally. Worksheets are far larger than most models, so there is no reason to crowd everything together. Use blank rows to seperate logical areas.

Test and audit your results. It is surprising how many spreadsheet models work incorrectly; all it takes it a small error in one formula to produce the wrong answer. Errors are easily overlooked when you examine the formulas themselves. At a minimum you should experiment with the model and confirm that its behavior and answers are reasonable. A more reliable method is to compare the spreadsheet's output with answers that are known to be correct. It may be a pain to prepare test data and calculate the results with a calculator, but the alternative may be to rely on ficticious answers.

Protect the worksheet. Even a thoroughly debugged worksheet can be corrupted by inadvertently typing a value into a cell that is supposed to contain a formula. You can protect against this by turning on the worksheet's cell protection feature. Then unlock only those cells that contain assumptions or other values to be changed by the user.

Figure 7.11 Moving the entries in cells A4..D6 to cells A5..D7.

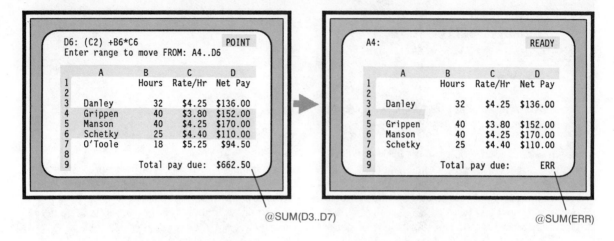

command is especially useful if you're making projections, because once a relationship has been entered for one time period, it can be copied across rows or columns to show the effect over time. Similarly, if you've developed an expense budget for one month, you can use the COPY command to extend the budgeting formulas across another 11 rows or columns to create a full-year budget. Or if one line has been entered in a conversion table (such as a table that converts from degrees to radians, or from centigrade to Kelvin temperature), you can easily complete the remaining lines by using the COPY command to replicate the formulas in the line.

To copy labels or numbers, the spreadsheet must know which cells contain the entries to be copied (the *source cells*) and which cells are to receive new entries (the *destination cells*). At the appropriate time in the COPY command, you must identify the source and destination cells either by typing in their cell ranges or by

Figure 7.12 Copying a label from cell B2 to cells B2..N2 affects cells C2, D2, and E2 on the screen and cells F2..N2 off the screen's edge.

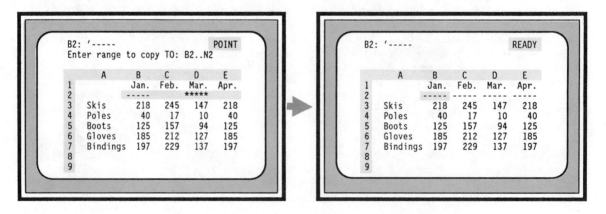

pointing out their locations with cursor-movement keys or a mouse. In Figure 7.12, a cell full of hyphens has been copied across a row to emphasize a heading. In this example, the source is a single cell; it is copied into a destination consisting of a range of cells. The COPY command destroys the previous contents of the destination cells. For example, the asterisks in cell D2 of the left-hand screen of Figure 7.12 are overwritten by the hyphens. There is no way to recover a cell's previous contents unless the spreadsheet has an UNDO command. Unlike commands that move or exchange cells, a COPY command affects only the destination cells. It has no effect on formulas in other areas of the worksheet, even if they refer to the destination cells.

Copying formulas is more complicated than copying labels and numbers, because you rarely want the spreadsheet to perform *exactly* the same calculation in two different locations in the worksheet. Instead, you normally want a set of similar computations to be done—with appropriate adjustments in the formulas to reflect their new locations. For example, many worksheets have a total column that adds the numbers in earlier columns, as in Figure 7.13. If the formula in row 3 of the total column is @SUM(B3..M3), then it doesn't make sense to copy this formula unchanged into row 4 or row 5 of the total column. Instead, in row 4 you want the formula @SUM(B4..M4), so that the formula in row 4 totals the numbers in row 4. Similar changes must be made to the formula as it is copied into succeeding cells down the total column. To make these changes in the new formulas, you need to tell the spreadsheet that the cell references in the source formula are **relative cell references**, which means that they should be interpreted relative to the formula's current position. With relative cell references, when a formula is copied into a cell two rows down and three columns to the right of its original location, all row numbers in the formula will be increased by two, and column letters will be shifted three letters through the alphabet.

Some references should not be adjusted when a formula is copied from one location to another; these are called **absolute cell references**. For example, a good way to organize a projection is to place all the projections's critical assumptions in

Figure 7.13 The formula in cell N3 is copied to cells N4..N85 by using relative cell references.

	N3: @SUM(B3..M3)			READY
	K	L	M	N
	Oct.	Nov.	Dec.	Total
1				
2	-------	-------	-------	-------
3	93	127	345	2122
4	38	76	23	
5	45	128	233	
6	73	165	196	
7	210	277	448	

	N4: @SUM(B4..M4)			READY
	K	L	M	N
	Oct.	Nov.	Dec.	Total
1				
2	-------	-------	-------	-------
3	93	127	345	2122
4	38	76	23	487
5	45	128	233	1544
6	73	165	196	1821
7	210	277	448	3601

Figure 7.14 Copying the formulas in C5..D5 to C5..D88 by using both relative and absolute cell references.

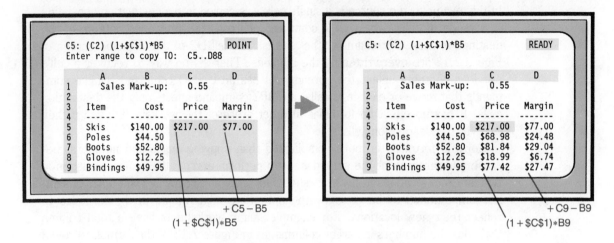

cells in a well-labeled area of the worksheet. If you're analyzing the cash flow from an apartment complex, these assumptions might included the occupancy rate, the inflation rate, and several tax rates. When formulas are copied in this worksheet, references to the cells containing these assumptions should not be adjusted.

Figure 7.14 illustrates the need for both kinds of cell references. With a single COPY command, you can copy a range of formulas (C5..D5) into another range (C5..D88), filling an entire region of the worksheet in one operation. But when you copy the formula in cell C5, you want the reference to cell C1 to be an absolute reference, because the cell contains the sales markup rate for the entire worksheet; when the formula is copied, this reference should not be changed. In contrast, the reference to cell B5 should be relative, because it contains the cost of an item for a specific row; this reference should therefore be changed when the formula is copied.

Different spreadsheets distinguish absolute from relative references in different ways. A few spreadsheets wait until the final step in the COPY command to ask you to choose—reference by reference—whether the parts of the formula should be treated as relative or absolute. Lotus 1-2-3 and Multiplan allow you to label a cell as absolute or relative when you enter a formula. With Lotus 1-2-3, cell references are relative by default, but it is easy to override the default by putting dollar signs before the row number and column letter of a cell. For example, the reference to cell C1 in the status line in Figure 7.14 is written C1 to indicate that it is an absolute cell reference. Similarly, the formula @SUM(B1..D1) will add the contents of cells B1, C1, and D1, regardless of where the formula is copied.

Giving Commands

In every spreadsheet session, you need to give commands. For example, to end a session, you must give the QUIT command, generally by typing "/Q." We've already mentioned some basic commands, including the commands that allow you to erase the contents of a cell or range of cells, to insert or delete rows and columns, and to copy data from one spot in the worksheet to another. In this section, we will describe how you select a command and discuss the commands that allow you to format the way information is presented inside the worksheet window, print all or some of the worksheet as a report, load information from disk into memory, and save all or part of the current worksheet on a disk.

Menu Bars

Most IBM PC spreadsheets use a combination of menu bars and function keys to let the user select commands. In contrast, the popular Macintosh spreadsheets use pull-down menus similar to those shown in Figure 5.9. We will describe the use of menu bars in detail, but most of what is said applies equally well to pull-down menu systems.

Spreadsheets use menu bars because they require such a small part of the screen—just one or two lines in the control panel—leaving most of the space available for the worksheet window. But because spreadsheets have many commands with many options (200 or more isn't unusual), the main menu is only a listing of *categories* of commands. Subsidiary menus are needed to choose a specific command. As a result, choosing the right category from the main menu can be difficult. For example, beginners might suspect that the correct choice from the main Multiplan menu to delete a file is Blank or Delete, when it is actually Transfer.

The two major types of menu bars are keyword menu bars and one-letter menu bars. *Keyword menu bars* usually require two screen lines. For example, the menu bar used in the IBM PC version of Multiplan looks like

Command: Alpha Blank Copy Delete Edit Format Goto Help Insert Lock Move
Name Options Print Quit Sort Transfer Value Window Xternal

In comparison, *one-letter menu bars* are more cryptic but take less screen space because they display only the initial letter of each command keyword. Menu bars encourage software developers to invent new command keywords as a way of avoiding first-letter conflicts. For example, if there is an EDIT command, then the ERASE command is likely to be called Zap. It doesn't take many keywords like Zap before it becomes difficult to remember what the letters on a one-letter menu bar mean—not that it's especially easy to remember what they mean anyway.

Whether a spreadsheet uses a menu bar with letters or one with keywords, the procedure for giving a command is the same. First, you activate the menu bar by typing a slash (/). Then you make a selection by typing the first letter of the keyword. Choosing a letter from the main menu bar usually leads to subsidiary menu bars that prompt yet more choices. This process continues through as many subsidiary menus as necessary to specify all the options and parameters for the command, at which time the command is completed. For example, if you press the [F]

A WORD ABOUT
SPREADSHEET PRODUCTS

Unlike other markets for personal computer software, which have become segmented into different levels of capabilities to accommodate users' varying expertise, the spreadsheet market has only one tier. While companies will often support two or three word processing programs for different levels of users, for example, most companies have standardized on a single spreadsheet program — often Lotus Development Corp.'s 1-2-3—for all their spreadsheet users.

But does the spreadsheet market need to become segmented? Should there be one set of spreadsheet for the bulk of users who require relatively few functions and another set for accountants and MBAs? It depends on who you ask.

"I think we'll see more software with two tiers, one tier for the guy who does basic functions, and doesn't have the master's degree needed to run every function of the really powerful programs, and one tier for the guy who needs all 7,000 functions available on the program," said Rick Richardson, national director of microcomputer technology at New York—based Arthur Young.

"This means that the aim of the MIS manager is to find the software with both tiers, one in which the files from one tier can be used in another. Spreadsheets are a natural for that. So manufacturers have two choices: They can either produce two products that share the same files, or one product that appeals to all users. Corporate buyers want the latter," Richardson said.

Seafirst Bank, in Seattle, Washington, currently uses Microsoft Corp.'s Excel and Multiplan spreadsheet programs for its 2,1000 Macintosh computers and Lotus 1-2-3 for its 200 IBM PCs. "We use Multiplan at the low end of the functionality scale for people who just rack up rows and columns, and of course we use Excel, which has gotten rave reviews for its tremendous richness and functionality," said Tim Turnpaugh, senior vice president of technology services at the bank. "In my opinion, Excel is to the Macintosh what 1-2-3 became to the IBM PC."

When asked what criteria he used in his decision to purchase Excel, Turnpaugh explained, "We were clearly looking for functionality, and our preference was to have no more varieties around than we had to. So for the PCs and the Macs we were looking for something from a well-established vendor, good support, someone who can deal with large corporations, and of course price and economics. We try to pick the package with the best price/performance, which is really the name of the game. We keep Multiplan around for people who don't need much."

But many people believe that Lotus 1-2-3 already satisfies the needs of users at both ends of the spectrum. Paul Romesburg, for example, standardized on Lotus 1-2-3 three years ago at the Barnett Bank, based in Fort Myers, Florida. As assistant vice president of credit and administration, Romesberg teaches 1-2-3 to people at the bank.

"We don't teach people about computers, we teach them about 1-2-3. I bring in people who know nothing about computers, and in eight weeks we have them writing macros. That's the nice thing about Lotus, it allows you to rise to your own level," Romesburg said.

Source: Copyright © 1986 by Popular Computing Inc., a subsidiary of CW Communications, Inc. Reprinted from *Infoworld*, 1060 Marsh Rd., Menlo Park, CA 94025

key for FORMAT from the main SuperCalc menu bar, the original menu bar is replaced with one having the following options:

Enter level: G(lobal), C(olumn), R(ow), or E(ntry)

Selecting an item from this subsidiary menu bar determines whether the whole worksheet, one column, one row, or a single cell will be affected by the command. This menu is followed by yet another menu asking how the selected portion of the worksheet should be formatted when it is displayed in the window: whether text should be right- or left-justified; whether numbers should be displayed in integer, exponential, or dollar-sign format; and so forth. Only after choices have been made from three menus is the FORMAT command completed. Normally, the program automatically returns to the ready mode once the command is completed. You can abort a command at any time before the command is completed, generally by pressing the escape key [Esc].

Formatting

The largest category of spreadsheet commands is those that create format rules controlling how the contents of cells will be displayed. This emphasis is appropriate because reports are generated by printing an area of the worksheet exactly as it would appear on the screen. This makes it necessary to adjust the cells until they look good enough for a printed report.

Early spreadsheets had very crude formatting abilities, but each succeeding generation of spreadsheets has added more formatting options. For example, in Lotus 1-2-3, numbers can have commas in the appropriate places, leading dollar signs or trailing percent signs, and a user-specified number of digits after the decimal point. Lotus 1-2-3 is a second-generation spreadsheet that provides most of the examples in this chapter.

A spreadsheet is able to display labels and numbers because it stores a format rule inside each cell, along with the cell's value rule. The format rule for the active cell is visible on the status line of the control panel just before the cell's label, number, or formula. For example, if you flip back to Figure 7.8, you'll notice that the status line shows the contents of cell D6 as (C2) @SUM(D2..D4), but the display shows $398.00. The (C2) instructs the spreadsheet to display the cell's value in *currency format*, with two digits after the decimal point. If you use Lotus 1-2-3 and call for the currency format, numbers will be displayed with a leading dollar sign, commas between thousands, and negative numbers in parentheses.

Printing

You can print a report at any time during a spreadsheet session. The report's appearance depends on your answers to two questions.

1. Which cells are to be printed? You specify the range of cells to be printed by giving the upper left-hand and lower right-hand corners of the range.

Figure 7.15 Two ways to print a worksheet.

```
B1: "Units
C1: "Price
D1: "Sales
A2: 'Shirts
B2: (,0) 12250
C2: (C2) 6.9
D2: (C0) + B2*C2
A3: 'Pants
B3: (,0) 6700
C3: (C2) 9.3
D3: (C0) + B3*C3
A4: 'Dresses
B4: (,0) 9000
C4: (C2) 12.5
D4: (C0) + B4*C4
B6: '    Total Sales:
D6: (C0) @SUM(D2..D4)
```

```
           Units    Price     Sales
Shirts    12,250    $6.90    $84,525
Pants      6,700    $9.30    $62,310
Dresses    9,000   $12.50   $112,500

                  Total Sales: $259,335
```

(a) The worksheet printed as it is stored in memory   **(b) The worksheet printed as it looks on the screen**

2. Should the cells be printed as they appear in the display or as they are stored in memory? Both types of report are shown in Figure 7.15. Printing the cells as they are stored in memory allows the formulas to be audited for accuracy, but normally reports are printed to show cells as they appear in the worksheet window.

The quality of the reports that a spreadsheet can generate depends on the printing options the spreadsheet supports. Some examples of useful capabilities for report formatting are

- Splitting the worksheet region to be printed into smaller units, each of which fits on a single page. This is called *pagination*. To paginate correctly, the spreadsheet must be set for the length and width of the paper and the margin's for each page.
- Allowing the user to establish headings or footnotes for each page
- Sending a string of control characters to set up the printer. For example, these characters might cause the report to be printed with compressed characters, allowing a 132-column report to fit on an $8\frac{1}{2}$-inch-wide piece of paper.
- Allowing the report to be printed with or without the borders identifying the rows and columns of the worksheet
- "Printing" the worksheet to a disk, rather than on paper, so that the disk file can be used as input to other programs

Loading, Saving, and Quitting

The first command in most spreadsheet sessions loads an existing worksheet from a disk. You can edit more than one worksheet in a session, but few spreadsheets allow more than one worksheet to be active at the same time. This means that, as a new worksheet is loaded into memory, the contents of the previous worksheet are either erased or merged with the contents of the new worksheet.

Most spreadsheet programs store the active worksheet in memory. Keep in mind that memory is volatile. It's extremely discouraging to lose several hours of work because of a power outage. Periodically save a copy of the worksheet on a disk if you're making useful modifications or additions.

If you've made changes in the worksheet that have not been saved on a disk, the spreadsheet usually will give you a final opportunity to save the worksheet before it returns control of the computer to the operating system. Thus, the last two commands in a session are likely to save the revised worksheet on a disk and end the session.

ADVANCED SPREADSHEET PROCESSING

So far, we've described the mechanics of solving common mathematical problems with a spreadsheet. The rest of this chapter covers the advanced features that are necessary for more sophisticated applications. Photos 40 through 45 in Window 5 illustrate how rapidly spreadsheet capabilities have evolved since the introduction of Visicalc in 1979. Although you can get by with a limited spreadsheet program for simple projections or one-shot calculations, the advanced features of a powerful spreadsheet program are essential for complex worksheets or for applications that require many people to interact with the worksheet.

Designing Templates

Spreadsheets reduce the need for computer programmers, because people who don't understand programming languages can still use spreadsheets. Still, there's often good reason for having a professional set up the particular worksheet; one knowledgeable professional can design a high-quality solution for many users. Here are some examples.

- A financial manager might design a worksheet to be used by the managers of a firm's departments. The worksheet could help each manager complete a detailed budget consistent with the firm's overall budget policies.

- A tax accountant might design a worksheet to help clients predict the effects of alternative tax strategies.

- A construction expert might design a worksheet to help clerks prepare estimates of construction costs based on the amount of materials required for a job.

PC MODELING PROGRAMS: NEW MICRO TOOLS OUTDISTANCE SPREADSHEETS

As data processing use of undocumented spreadsheets mushrooms and as the management decisions made from them become more important, the opportunity for critical errors multiplies.

The virtue of spreadsheets—that users can quickly and easily move about them making changes and then copy the changes into other cells—makes documenting them devilishly difficult. The data and the logic are homogenized so well that separating the two becomes nearly impossible.

If I build a spreadsheet for you to use, you would be hard-pressed to sort out why and how it works. Users cannot see the logic behind the sheet, only the results of the calculations as they are displayed. A single calculation error—a cell copied one too many times, for example—often leads to false results. Spreadsheets have become an MIS manager's nightmare.

Enter financial modelers: a class of programs designed to rectify some of these spreadsheet problems. A modeling program, in the broadest sense, is any program that allows a user to simulate real events or to test hypothetical situations on a computer. Spreadsheets can be used as modeling programs, as can a broad range of other generic programs. However, since the newer financial planners specialize in creating models, they generally document model logic more lucidly than spreadsheets.

The following characteristics further set modeling programs apart from generic financial planners:

- Built-in programming languages.
- Flexible data view and report capability.
- Complete separation of data and logic.
- Easy path to consolidation.

Modeling programs usually have their own programming languages. It may be either a fully developed procedural or nonprocedural language or simply a collection of modeling techniques such as sensitivity analysis, goal seeking, multiple regression and so on. The language has one distinctive feature, though: It was designed to make the evaluation of events over time less complex. Time series analysis—a series of numbers that represent values for a variable at different points in time—is integral to almost all business models or simulations. Most modeling programs have a wealth of time series functions or commands that simplify conversions from one time series to another.

Business modeling programs also offer considerably more flexible approaches to viewing and reporting data. Whereas spreadsheets are printed from top to bottom, left to right, modeling programs permit selective viewing and printing of values. A user can choose to work with subsets of the model, such as selected rows and columns in any order, without losing the relationships between variables.

The most telling difference between spreadsheets and modeling programs lies in the area of data manipulation. Spreadsheets force the user to work with all the data all the time. Modeling programs separate data and logic. Normally, models are expressed as variables in English-like statements. The same logic in a spreadsheet is referred to as cells, that is, $A1 - B1 = C1$. In a modeling program, the variable "Sales" can have multiple data sets, since the variable has no value permanently associated with it. In a spreadsheet, however, the values represented by the cell locations are tied directly to that location. The cells cannot function as variables, but merely as containers.

For example, a typical small model logic file could look something like this:

```
Sales = GROW(1000@Jan 86,.05)
Cost of Goods Sold = Sales *.36
Gross Margin = Sales − Cost of Goods Sold
General & Administrative = GROW
(150@Jan 86,.02)
Marketing = Sales *.04
Profit = Gross Margin
    −SUM(General & Administrative
    +Marketing)
```

Continued on next page

In each of these examples, the application is developed by one person who is knowledgeable about both the spreadsheet and the task to be done and who tries to make the worksheet useful to people who know little about either the spreadsheet or the necessary calculations. This is done by creating a worksheet that contains both the labels that identify the items in the application and the formulas that perform the calculations, but that has blank cells where the data for the application will go. Such a half-completed worksheet is called a **template** because it contains rules that guide how the data are to be processed but does not contain the data.

Figure 7.16 illustrates the difference between a template and a completed worksheet. The template in the left screen contains the labels and formulas necessary to calculate the monthly payments, year-end balances, and interest on a loan. All of the calculated cells in the template display the error message ERR, because the template doesn't include data for the interest rate, the principal, or the number of years the loan will run. In the right screen, the template has been completed by

Figure 7.16 On the left is an empty template; on the right, the template has been completed by filling in the values for cells C1 through C3.

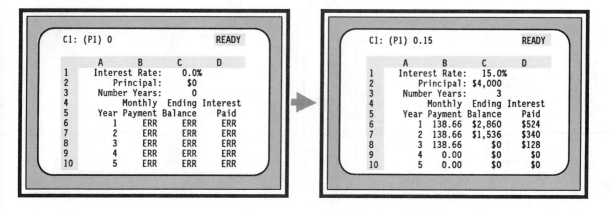

typing these numbers in cells C1 through C3. A loan officer in a bank could use a more detailed version of this template to generate a customized loan report for each new client.

A good template guides the user through the process of entering data and prevents the user from modifying the template's formulas. It is *bullet-proof,* or impervious to the numerous errors made by beginners. Many methods are used to construct bullet-proof templates, including protecting cells, using commands known as *programmable macros,* and creating forms that help guide data entry. Because forms are also used extensively with data management programs, we will defer a discussion of them until Chapter 8.

Protecting Cells

Most spreadsheets have some form of a PROTECT command, which gives protected status to a range of cells. A **protected cell** can't be edited, deleted, or moved unless the cell's protected status is first removed with an UNPROTECT command. In effect, protecting a cell is the same as locking the cell's contents from further modification. The UNPROTECT command acts as a key that unlocks cells.

Figure 7.17 demonstrates how cell protection can prevent the formulas in a loan analysis from being accidentally modified. Three cells are unprotected and are shown in color; the interest rate, the principal, and the length of the loan are entered into these cells. Any attempt to modify other cells in the worksheet produces an error message, as shown in the right-hand screen.

Using Macros

Some spreadsheets allow you to write a script of commands describing a sequence of tasks. The script is then associated with a single key on the keyboard and can be "played back" at the touch of a key. The script of commands is called a **macro,**

Figure 7.17 Only the three cells in color are unprotected. Thus, an attempt to enter the number 420 in cell D7 produces an error message.

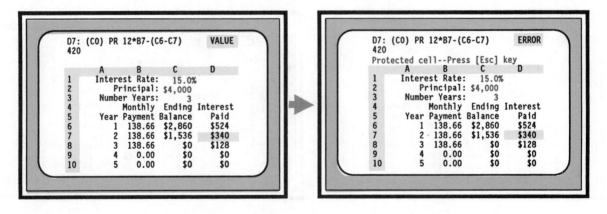

or a **keyboard macro**. It associates a sequence of keystrokes with a single key on the keyboard. When the macro's key is pressed, the keystrokes are automatically typed one at a time; the spreadsheet interprets them just as if you had typed them yourself.

Most spreadsheet macros are created for one of two reasons. First, a macro can relieve the tedium of entering the same lengthy set of commands over and over again. Second, for commands that are given infrequently—such as commands to print reports or consolidate data—a macro "remembers" the commands better than people do.

For example, Symphony is a spreadsheet-based integrated program that combines components for spreadsheet processing, word processing, data management, graphics, and communications. Symphony supplies special programming commands that can be embedded inside a macro to allow it to make IF-THEN tests, GOTO jumps, and subroutine calls (these are *control structures* familiar to any programmer and will be discussed in Chapter 13. By placing an IF-THEN command inside a macro, for instance, you can write a macro that erases a range of cells if the value in cell B12 is zero and does something else if the value isn't zero. Other macro programming commands allow a macro to display messages on the prompt line of the screen, pause for inputs from the keyboard, and store the inputs in specified cells.

Macros provide the ultimate in power and versatility for spreadsheet applications, but they aren't for the novice or the fainthearted. In the hands of a motivated professional, macros can create interactive templates that help walk the user through steps needed to complete an application.

Changing the Appearance of the Worksheet

Format rules change the appearance of the worksheet without actually modifying the worksheet itself. This section describes format rules that affect many cells at once; for example, rules that change the width of a column or divide the window into window panes.

Changing Column Widths

Columns naturally need different widths because they are used for different types of information. In most worksheets, the leftmost column identifies the contents of the rows with such labels as names, items for sale, or months of the year. These labels nearly always require more room than the numbers in the following columns. For example, a list of names requires a column approximately 20 characters wide, but the scores from a midterm exam fit in a column only 4 characters wide.

The number of characters that a single cell can contain varies from one spreadsheet to the next, but a typical number is around 250—many more characters than the usual column width. Thus, you can type a long label into any cell regardless of the cell's column width. But keep in mind that what a spreadsheet displays as a cell's contents and what is stored in memory may differ. Some spreadsheets truncate labels in the display, showing only the portion that fits inside the cells in the worksheet window.

Entering a name on a report with a spreadsheet that truncates labels in the display requires careful attention to detail. The text must be broken into parts, and the parts must be entered into adjacent cells as separate labels. Once a worksheet has been filled out in this manner, changing the width of columns destroys the appearance of the worksheet. Figure 7.18 demonstrates the disastrous effect of changing the width of all the columns from six to eight characters with this type of spreadsheet. In the left-hand screen, the entry in cell A5 was truncated to read "Dan La"; "tham" was therefore entered in cell B5. But in the right-hand screen the column width has been increased, allowing more of cell A5 to be displayed. As a result, cells A5 and B5 together now read "Dan Laththam" instead of the correct name, Dan Latham.

Most newer spreadsheets allow a long label to extend past the right edge of its cell, if the cell to the right is empty. This means that you don't need to chop headings and other lengthy items of text into cell-width units before entering them into the worksheet. Instead, you can type the text into one cell and leave the cells to its right empty. A label won't extend into a neighboring cell that appears empty but actually contains some blank spaces.

Changing the column width can also affect numbers. The high-order digits of a number aren't truncated in order to make a number fit in its cell. But, depending on the format rules in effect, the digits past the decimal point might be rounded (causing 4.55 to become 5), or a long number might be converted into scientific notation (causing 12,000,000,000 to become $1.2E + 10$). Otherwise, if a number is too long to fit, the cell on the screen is filled with a warning character, such as !!!!!!, *******, or ######. If you widen the column, the number will appear.

Most spreadsheets store numbers internally with the equivalent of 11 to 15 decimal digits. Thus, if you type the number 1.234567890123456789 into a cell, the spreadsheet might store the number as 1.23456789012. The stored number is then used in any calculation regardless of how the number is displayed on the screen.

Window Panes

The maximum size of a worksheet depends on the spreadsheet program and on the amount of memory in the computer, but worksheets can store a lot of information. Exploring a worksheet filled with long lists of data is easier if you split the window into *window panes* that "look" into different portions of the worksheet.

Most spreadsheets display a maximum of two panes at a time and require that each pane look into the same worksheet. But many spreadsheets allow each pane to have its own formatting rules. Thus, if the same cell appeared in both panes, it might not look the same. For example, one pane might be set to display formulas as they are evaluated by the spreadsheet. This arrangement would be useful if you want to see whether the formulas work as expected.

Figure 7.18 The effect of expanding the width of all columns from six to eight characters if labels are truncated at the end of their respective cells.

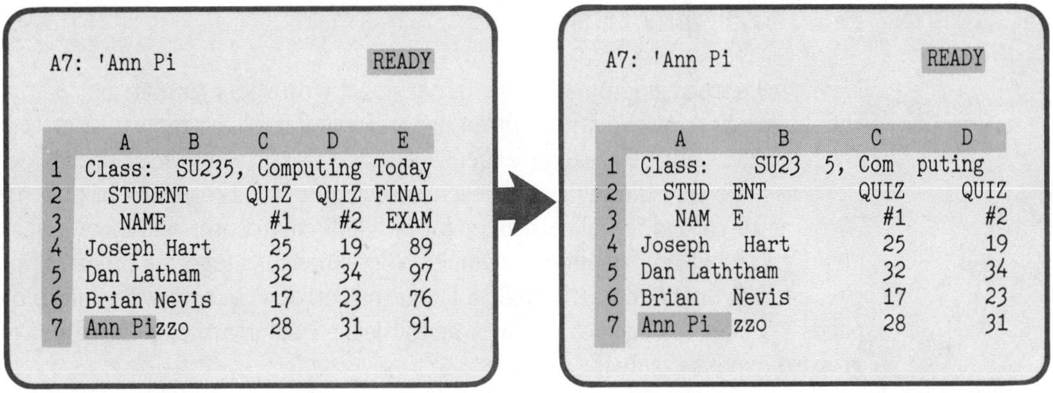

Types of Format Rules

We've mentioned several format rules that affect how values are displayed in the window: the width of columns, left- or right-justified labels, and so forth. Most format rules can be given in two ways: a *global format rule* affects the entire worksheet; an *individual format rule* applies to a single cell or column.

Because global format rules affect the entire worksheet, changing the global column-width setting adjusts the width of all columns simultaneously, just like the example in Figure 7.18. An individual format rule overrides a global format rule. Thus, changing the global column-width setting won't affect a column that has been given its own individual format rule with a previous command. If a worksheet has many narrow columns for numbers and a few wider columns for labels, the quickest way to set up the worksheet is to use a global command, to make all the columns narrow, and then widen the label columns with individual column-width commands.

Formatting Limitations

Spreadsheets have more commands for formatting than for any other process, but even so, they have definite formatting limitations. Occasionally, you won't be able to adjust the worksheet to look exactly the way you want. Perhaps a number should appear centered in its cell, but the spreadsheet's manual doesn't list an option for centering numbers. You might try entering the number into the worksheet as a label—but then you can't refer to it in formulas. Or suppose you want the columns in a report to be staggered on the page. Although manuals rarely mention this limitation, in all spreadsheets, a column must have the same width from the top to the bottom of the worksheet.

Often it's best to live with formatting limitations and accept a report that isn't laid out character for character the way you would design it by hand. If every character must be in exactly the right spot, it may be necessary to transfer the information to a word processor so that editing can proceed without the limitations inherent in a cellular worksheet.

Transferring Information

Nearly all spreadsheets use a two-dimensional worksheet format, but many applications are best solved with a three-dimensional format for reports. For example, consider the task of creating expense budgets for a firm with 50 cost centers. Let's assume that the budget for each cost center has 12 months of expenses for 30 expense categories. The budget for a single cost center will have a variety of identifying labels and about 400 numbers (30 expense categories times 12 months, plus various total figures). The final budget report for the firm will require over 50 pages—1 page for each cost center and at least 1 summary page for the firm's aggregate expense budget.

The three dimensions in this report are months, expense categories, and cost centers. You could make the report fit on one two-dimensional worksheet by placing each cost center's budget in a different area of the worksheet, but this is an inconvenient solution. The worksheet would include 20,000 numerical entries (50 cost centers times 400 numbers per cost center). It would be hard to coordinate the entry of so many numbers into one giant worksheet, and few personal computers can create a worksheet with 20,000 numerical entries.

At this point, we should mention that probably the best way to handle this budget is to use a data management program (discussed in Chapter 8). Budgeting is characterized by a large amount of data and by limited arithmetic computations—just the type of problem that data management programs solve best. Still, you can handle this budget with a spreadsheet program if you place each cost center's budget in its own worksheet and then consolidate these worksheets into other worksheets to obtain total budget figures. We will review two common methods of consolidating information from several worksheets: copying information from one worksheet to another and linking worksheets so that changes in one worksheet affect the contents of another.

Copying Worksheets

Almost all spreadsheets allow information to be copied from one worksheet to another, but the procedure varies from one spreadsheet to the next. For example, on the Macintosh version of Multiplan, you cut (or copy) a region of the *source worksheet* onto the clipboard, then load the *target worksheet* into memory, and finally paste the clipboard's information into the target worksheet. (Recall that a *clipboard* is a temporary storage region, sometimes called a *buffer,* that holds a single clipping. If you cut a second clipping, the contents of the clipboard are replaced by the second clipping.) Text and numbers come through the copying process without change, but only the results of formulas are copied—not the formulas themselves. Format rules are not copied, so the information may look different in the target worksheet.

In contrast, Lotus 1-2-3 allows information to be read directly into the current worksheet from a worksheet stored on a disk. First, you move the active cell to the upper left-hand corner of the region to receive the new information. Then you give the FILE-COMBINE-COPY command. Either an entire worksheet or just a portion can be copied from the disk into the current worksheet. Cells that are copied into the current worksheet replace any previous entries. This makes it important to position the active cell carefully before giving the COPY command; a careless command can destroy an entire worksheet.

Linking Worksheets

A target worksheet into which information is copied or merged is not affected by subsequent changes to the source worksheets. Anyone who has been through a budgeting process knows how serious this limitation can be; budgets inevitably go through numerous revisions before everyone is satisfied. This disadvantage can be removed by permanently linking the worksheets.

For example, formulas in an Excel worksheet can obtain values from other worksheets as easily as they obtain them from cells in the same worksheet. References to cells or names on other worksheets are called external references. You insert an external reference in a formula as follows:

- First, open the worksheet you want to refer to so it is visible in a window on the screen.

- Start the formula as you usually do.

- Click the worksheet you want to refer to and select a cell or cell range in it by pointing with the mouse.

- Finish building the formula in the usual way.

References to cells in other worksheets have longer names: first comes the name of the other worksheet, then an exclamation point, and the row and column (or name) reference. For example, the Metals Department worksheet in Figure 7.19 links corresponding cells in the Stamping and Welding cost center worksheets. So cell B5 in the Metal Department worksheet contains the entry = Stamping!B5 + Welding!B5.

Once a worksheet is linked to supporting worksheets, changes in the supporting worksheets are automatically reflected in the dependent or destination worksheet. For example, if the number in cell B5 of the Stamping worksheet is changed from 5,000 to 3,000, the number in cell B5 of the Metals Department worksheet will drop from 7,300 to 5,300. Excel's method of linking worksheets works best if all of all of the supporting worksheets for a dependent worksheet are loaded into memory and reside in their own window.

Advanced Functions

Whenever you're having a particularly difficult time constructing a formula in a worksheet, check a reference manual to see if there is a function for the task.

Figure 7.19 Linking worksheets. The expense numbers on the worksheets for Cost Centers 12 and 13 are linked to the budget worksheet for the Metals Department.

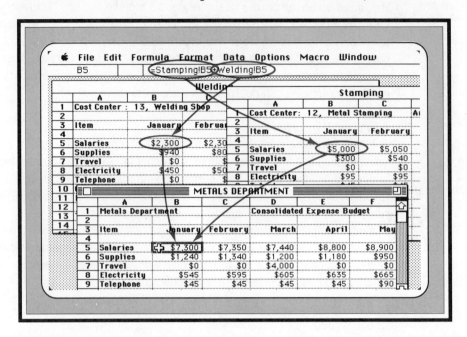

Most spreadsheets offer dozens of built-in functions that provide short cuts for common financial, statistical, mathematical, and other processing tasks. These functions often spell the difference between struggling with a clumsy formula and finding an instant solution.

To give you a sense of variety of tasks that functions can perform, we will provide examples of the types of built-in functions provided by Symphony, an integrated program with many built-in functions.

- *Statistical functions* provide summary statistics; thus, they accept a list of items to summarize. For example, @MAX(J101..J300) will return the largest value in the 200 cells from J101 to J300.

- *Mathematical functions* accept a single number, perform a mathematical transformation on it, and return a single number. For example, the INTEGER function returns the integer part of its argument; @INT(4.9) is equal to 4.

- *Financial functions* calculate the effect of interest rates on sums of money over time. For example, the formula that calculates the monthly payment in cell B6 of Figure 7.16 is @PMT(C2,C1/12,C3*12), where C2 is the principal for the loan, C1/12 is the monthly interest rate, and C3*12 is the number of payments to be made.

- *String functions* manipulate text. For example, the function @LEFT(A3,6) will truncate the string stored in A3 after the sixth character.

- *Date functions* allow dates and times to be manipulated as easily as numbers. Date functions might be used to search the date column of a list of insurance policies for expired policies.

- *Logical functions* test conditions and make decisions. For example, the formula @IF(A4 < > 0,A6/A4,0) tests the condition A4 < > 0 to see if the value of cell A4 is different from zero. If the condition is true, then the formula's value is A6/A4; otherwise the formula's value is zero.

- *Look-up functions* retrieve an entry from a table. This is useful for retrieving taxes from a tax table or for assigning letter grades to students based on the points they have earned in class.

SUMMARY

Spreadsheets manipulate information by storing it in a large grid of cells. Most of the time spent working with a spreadsheet is spent moving the active-cell marker around the screen and entering data to be stored in a cell. Each cell of the worksheet stores a number, a label, or a formula; many also store some formatting information. While you are working with a spreadsheet, the screen will display a control panel, which helps you use the program and allows you to see entries as they are stored in memory, and a worksheet window, which shows you what is in the worksheet.

In most spreadsheet programs, commands are given by typing a slash (/) and then making selections from menu bars and responding to questions. Some spreadsheet programs use pull-down menus to issue commands. Regardless of whether menu bars or pull-down menus are used, several selections are necessary to complete most commands. Spreadsheets have numerous commands that can help you edit cells and rearrange the worksheet.

You can increase the power of commands by specifying a range of cells to be processed. This allows one operation to affect an entire region of the worksheet.

Built-in functions perform a specific type of processing, such as adding a column of numbers or computing an average.

Frequently, one person constructs a template that contains formulas, and other people use the template. A substantial amount of knowledge can be built into a template. If a template is constructed carefully with protected cells, helpful keyboard macros, and input via forms and menus, then the user needs very little understanding of how the spreadsheet program or the template works to obtain impressive results.

Spreadsheets vary widely in their ability to format and print reports. Important format settings include those that determine the width of columns and how many window panes are in the window. Most format rules can be given either as global rules, affecting the entire worksheet, or as individual rules, which affect only one cell or column.

Worksheets can be consolidated to transfer information or to summarize data. The consolidation can occur by copying information from one worksheet to another or by permanently linking worksheets.

Built-in functions make it much easier to construct formulas for statistical, mathematical, and financial calculations. In addition, they can make it possible to process text inside a formula, to perform calculations on dates and times, and to look up values in a table.

Although we've described some of the advanced features that allow spreadsheets to be used for sophisticated applications, we've omitted many spreadsheet features. For example, we haven't described global search-and-replace operations or the various methods used to recalculate worksheets. And some features, such as forms management and data management (Chapter 8) and graphing abilities (Chapter 10), are covered in more detail elsewhere in the book.

You don't need prior experience with a computer to use a spreadsheet, but some training and study are required. A general rule of thumb is that it takes 40 hours of reading, practice, experimentation, and mistakes before a beginner feels proficient with most of the advanced features of a spreadsheet, though it shouldn't take more than an hour or two to begin building simple models. The rule of thumb may not hold for you. Some spreadsheets are easier to master than others, either because they have fewer features or are designed better. Some people are more comfortable with math and numerical models than others. Regardless of your situation, now that you've read this chapter, you're ready to begin using a spreadsheet. Start by skimming the appropriate manufacturer's manual or pocket guide; then experiment with some of this chapter's examples at a keyboard.

KEY TERMS

absolute cell reference

active cell

automatic recalculation

built-in function

cell

command mode

control panel

entry mode

format rule

macro (keyboard macro)

protected cell

range of cells

ready mode

relative cell reference

template

value rule

worksheet

DISCUSSION QUESTIONS

1. Is using a spreadsheet more like programming a computer or like using a word processor?

2. What types of tasks would a manufacturing accountant use a spreadsheet for? a personnel manager? a civil engineer? Would their needs for computational support differ?

3. How should the cells in a worksheet be labeled? Why?

4. What information would be useful in the control panel? Would the time of day be useful? the number of entries made in a session?

5. Why do spreadsheets have several modes of operation? Would spreadsheets be easier to use if they had more modes? What might be some possible additional modes?

6. Suppose you are working with information in three separate areas of a worksheet. How should these areas be positioned in the worksheet so that inserting or deleting rows or columns in any one of the areas will not disturb the other two areas?

7. This chapter gives examples of several types of menu bars. Which would be easiest for a beginner? Which would be quickest for an expert?

8. What might be some design and style rules for constructing templates to be used by clerical personnel?

9. Can you have a column with zero width? How might it be useful?

10. What could a three-dimensional worksheet do that a two-dimensional worksheet could not do conveniently?

11. Can you suggest a scheme that would prevent a user from accidentally destroying information when copying or linking worksheets?

12. Suppose a worksheet is linked to several other worksheets, and each time it is loaded, the calculations take five minutes. This is rather awkward if no changes have been made to the other worksheets. What are some ways to avoid this problem?

EXERCISES

1. Refer to the illustration of SuperCalc in Photo 41 in Window 5. Identify which cells contain labels, numbers, or formulas. Write the formulas necessary to complete the worksheet. Then try entering the worksheet to see if your solution works.

2. Give formulas for each of the following:
   a. Add cells A1, B2, C3, and D4.
   b. Multiply the sum of the first 20 columns of row 6 by the sum of the first 90 rows in column 6.
   c. Add the average of columns 3, 4, 7, and 9. Assume that the first 120 rows of each column contain useful information.

3. Suppose the formula in cell A4 is 13 + B2 and that in cell D5 is 6*B2. If the value in cell B2 is 3, what are the values of cells A4 and D5? Find the new values if the formula in cell D5 is 6*A4.

4. See what happens in a MOVE or COPY command when the source is larger than the destination and when the source is smaller than the destination.

5. Compare the cell-protection features of three spreadsheet programs.

6. Determine the maximum number of rows and columns in your spreadsheet program. How much memory would it take to fill each cell with the word *overflow?*

7. Draw the worksheet that results if you decrease the width of all columns in Figure 7.18 from six characters to four.

8. Design a template for a state or federal tax return that links the various schedules to the main form. Alternatively, search the literature to find out how to order a good set of tax templates.

9. Design a template for a professor's grade book.

10. Assume your worksheet contains the names of 50 states in cells B2 to B51, their populations in cells C2 to C51, and their areas in cells E2 to E51. Give the commands and formulas to place each state's percentage of the total population in cells D2 to D51 and each state's percentage of the total area in cells F2 to F51.

11. You are a stockbroker, and the following table represents the portfolio of one of your clients:

Stock	No. of Shares	Purchase Price (per share)	Market Price (per share)
Control Datum	200	$53.50	$40.00
Dow James	350	8.75	12.125
Bandon Ltd.	100	98.00	59.25
Lighthouse Exchange	2,000	5.25	4.375

a. Use a spreadsheet to generate a report that shows the information in this table. Provide columns for the market value of each stock and the percentage of gain or loss for each stock. Include a line that shows the total market value of the portfolio and the total gain or loss for the portfolio.

b. Experiment with the model to find out what market price of Dow James would make the current market value of the entire portfolio equal to its purchase price.

8 Data Management

This chapter introduces two categories of data management software: file management systems and database management systems. *File management systems (file managers)* are used to keep any large list that must be quickly retrieved and displayed. In addition to providing a method for organizing large quantities of data, file management systems are valuable for their ability to generate printed reports of the data stored in your computer files. A *database management system (DBMS)* can do all the things that a file manager can do, but it can do these things to two or more files simultaneously. In addition, a DBMS usually incorporates many features above and beyond those found in a file management system, such as the ability to print reports from multiple files, make backup copies of existing files, and convert data from one format to another.

In the early days of computing (around 1950), computers were used exclusively to compute formulas. Then, in 1957, the hard disk drive was invented and rapidly installed in computer systems. A hard disk could store more information than the computer's main memory, and it was much faster than magnetic tape. Its invention made it possible both to store large amounts of information within a computer system and to retrieve the information quickly. This led to a shift in how computers were used—away from numerical calculations and toward transaction processing and information retrieval. Computers were now used to store such information as customer names, taxpayer information, and accounting transactions and to generate reports on this information.

Unfortunately, the large computers of the 1960s and 1970s were inaccessible to the average person because of their high cost and the programming expertise needed to run them. Data processing departments within large corporations, banks, universities, and government bureaus grew to act as buffers between the users who needed information and the large, expensive computers that held the information in their spinning disks.

As the use of computers grew, so did the number of data files stored by organizations. By the late 1960s, a typical data processing department maintained thousands of data files. The task of keeping track of them was becoming unmanageable. The most obvious problem was the substantial effort required to keep track of all the file names and to catalog the types of data stored in each file. Another problem involved redundant data. For example, some of the data in a payroll file might be the same as those in a personnel file—a clear waste of storage capacity. A more subtle problem resulted from the direct link between programs and the data files they used: each time the layout of a data file was changed—to add a new field or to expand the width of an existing field, for example—all the programs that used the data file had to be modified to reflect the new structure. As a result, data processing departments spent most of their programming time modifying old programs (called *program maintenance*) instead of developing new ones.

These problems led to the development and use of *database management systems (DBMS)*—software for controlling, reading, and updating the information in a collection of files. A DBMS acts as a buffer between programs and data in the same way that a data processing department acts as a buffer between the computer user and mainframe computers. It helps keep track of where data are stored. More importantly, a DBMS solves many of the problems associated with redundant data and program maintenance by separating the physical storage locations of data from the logical structure of data as seen by programmers—a division that is at the root of database management software and is explained later in this chapter.

The first database management systems were designed to handle the needs of data processing departments and were very difficult to use. Full-time professionals called *database administrators* had to lay out the structure of databases and con-

A WORD ABOUT
MINI AND MAINFRAME DBMS

A database management system, including data dictionary and fourth-generation language, typically costs about $333,000 for a one-time license fee. This figure, however, represents only the tip of the financial iceberg.

The major cost lies not in the system purchase price but in the cost of time—time that systems analysts, application programmers and systems programmers spend analyzing various applications to be developed, creating the applications programs and then maintaining both the applications and the DBMS.

In its first year of operation in a Fortune 500 company, a DBMS requires the attention of approximately 12 programmers, one systems analyst and a data base administrator. Salaries and fringe benefits for these personnel total $1 million. For cost reasons alone, then, the evaluation and selection of a minicomputer- or mainframe-base DBMS must be taken very seriously.

But there is another reason: DBMS and related offerings are strategic products that—if used as such—can take an organization to the leading edge of technology and performance.

Of critical importance is the immediate and ongoing involvement of the information center manager. This role is pivotal in the decision-making process since the capabilities or limitations of the DBMS on the mainframe directly affect the communications link required for accessing the production data on the mainframe from microcomputers.

Secondly, along the lines of the domino theory, the evaluation process must involve selecting not only the DBMS, but also a data dictionary, a teleprocessing monitor, a fourth-generation language and a query and report generation language. Often, evaluators mistakenly focus all their attention on buying the DBMS, intending to select a data dictionary or fourth-generation language at a future date.

But choosing a DBMS without considering its associated satellite products reduces options. Without these integrated or satellite packages, the establishment of an information center makes little sense. Even if not acquired at the same time, all products should be evaluated simultaneously.

Some data processing executives think they can change vendors and/or systems if a DBMS implementation does not work the first time—not true. Conversion is like changing the tires on a running car. Converting software from one system to another is extremely time-consuming and, as a result, very expensive.

In real life, conversion almost never takes place. The existing application system continues to operate as usual, and only subsequently developed systems use the new DBMS.

Source: Shaku Atre, *Computerworld,* 31 March 1986, p. 35–38.

tend with the complexities of the software. To circumvent the need for programmers and database administrators, software developers invented a whole new genre of software called *file management software*. A **file management system** (also called a **file manager**) is a collection of programs for managing data stored in a single file. File managers emerged in the 1970s to make it easy to set up a data file, enter and edit the data in the file, and print reports from the file. A file manager is not a complete database management system, but it is a simple-yet-elegant solution for most applications that use just one file at a time.

In the 1980s, low-cost micro computers with relatively large-capacity disk drives became widely available. These computers could easily manage large lists when equipped with data management software, but they aggravated the problems of the 1970s: they either required programming expertise to be used effectively or were limited to single-file applications. For example, PFS:FILE, a popular file management program, can be mastered in a few hours. But early versions of dBASE II, a database management system for personal computers, required a programmer to set up the database and write dBASE II file processing programs.

Today, most popular database management programs for personal computers are miniature duplicates of mainframe systems. For example, R:BASE System V was derived from RIM (*R*elational *I*nformation *M*anagement System), a database management system developed to track parts for NASA; and dBASE III PLUS evolved from programs for mainframe computers at the Jet Propulsion Laboratory. These programs handle multiple files and include various methods for instructing the computer to process the data stored in these files. At first they were essentially scaled-down mainframe programs, so a programmer or someone experienced with database management was needed to fully utilize their features. Recent versions of these programs are much easier to use than their earlier counterparts; full-featured database management systems may eventually be as easy to use as simple file managers.

FILE MANAGEMENT SYSTEMS

File management is the simplest form of data management. The main purpose of a file management system is to extract information in the form of a printed report, a document containing data from your computer files. Although file managers can handle only one file of information at a time, they provide one of the best ways to organize and process a large volume of data. You can easily enter, look up, modify, and selectively delete information with them. You do not have to be concerned with how data are stored in files, how the information is arranged internally, or how the programs process the data stored on disk. The file manager insulates you from the details of information storage and retrieval.

The User Interface

The first step in understanding a file manager is to determine the underlying model assumed by the people who designed your software. The model is visible in the user interface—the prompts, menus, and other screen displays that appear when the program is run. File managers use various models.

Perhaps the simplest model is that of a piece of paper containing a written list. In the case of a file manager, the "piece of paper" is the display screen, as illustrated in Figure 8.1, and the list is scrolled on the screen. Each row in the list corresponds to a record in the file, and each column corresponds to a field. (Recall

Figure 8.1 A list is one of the simplest ways to view a file. The list can be scrolled vertically to see different records or horizontally to see different fields.

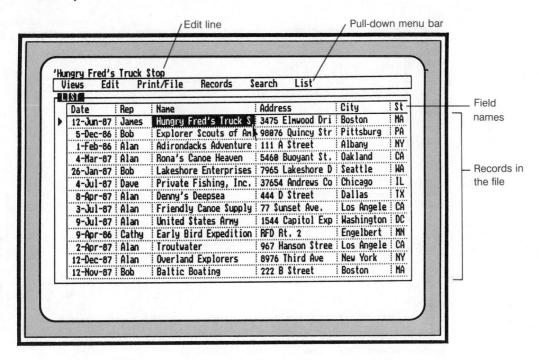

that a *record* is a collection of related data items, and a *field* is a part of a record reserved for a particular item or type of data.)

Other file managers use the business form as their model. This model is easily understood, because we are all used to filling out business forms in everyday life. *On-screen* **forms** are templates that capture and display data by providing blanks for each field. Figure 8.2 shows how the information in Figure 8.1 appears when it is displayed in a form. File managers that use the business form as their model allow you to design a form to appear any way you want. You may design the data entry form by "drawing" it on your screen when the file is initially set up. In many systems, the operations for defining a file and defining a form are identical; that is defining the form also defines the contents of the file.

The Rolodex card file provides the model for some simple file managers. A Rolodex card file is a collection of cards that can be rotated around a drum so that you can locate a particular name, phone number, or address. Photo 10 in Window 4 illustrates a file manager that lets you "flip through" the cards electronically.

Lists and simulated Rolodex files not only provide logical ways to look at your data, but can also establish boundaries on what you can do with the system. For example, an electronic Rolodex system typically can do only what a manual Rolodex system does: look up information, add new entries, and so forth. A system built around the model of a business form is usually more flexible and might be

Figure 8.2 A form displays only one record from the file at a time. In this form, the Name field contains the entry "Hungry Fred's Truck Stop".

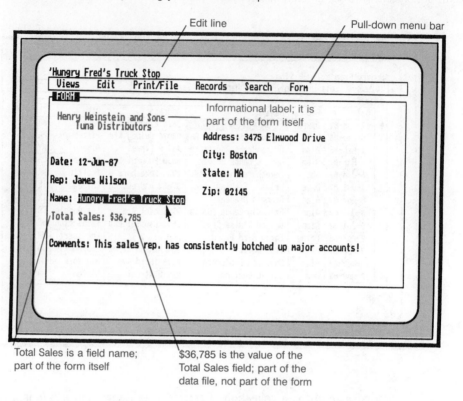

Edit line

Pull-down menu bar

'Hungry Fred's Truck Stop

| Views | Edit | Print/File | Records | Search | Form |

FORM

Henry Weinstein and Sons
Tuna Distributors

Informational label; it is part of the form itself

Address: 3475 Elmwood Drive

City: Boston

Date: 12-Jun-87

State: MA

Rep: James Wilson

Zip: 02145

Name: Hungry Fred's Truck Stop

Total Sales: $36,785

Comments: This sales rep. has consistently botched up major accounts!

Total Sales is a field name; part of the form itself

$36,785 is the value of the Total Sales field; part of the data file, not part of the form

able to check the input data to guarantee that it is within certain bounds (greater than zero, for example) or verify that all the blanks in the form have been completed before it accepts the form for storage.

A powerful file management system will provide the flexibility to let you view the data in several different ways. For example, Figure 8.3 shows a screen from Reflex[1] with three windows: the Form window places data in the blanks of a form, the List window displays data in a table, and the Graph window summarizes data in a pie chart or bar or line graph. With Reflex you can also select options that summarize data in a tabular format or lay out and print reports.

Files as Lists

Nearly everyone keeps some kind of list. For example, a teacher keeps a grade book; a salesperson keeps a list of sales leads. If these lists are large or require frequent maintenance, then sorting and updating them can be a tedious job to do by hand. File managers provide an alternative. Any list can be converted from a paper format to an electronic data file. Each row in the list becomes a record, and the items on a row are stored in the record's fields.

Figure 8.3 Three ways to view the same file. The Form option from the Views menu displays one record at a time; the List option shows records in a tabular format; and the Graph option summarizes the whole file with a bar chart.

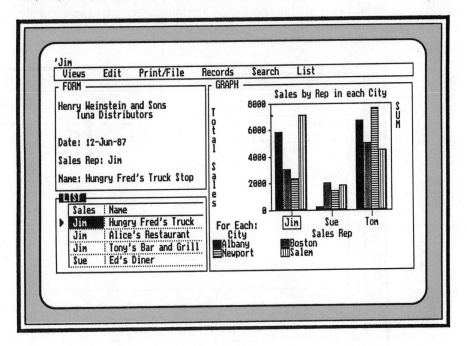

It is a simple matter to lay out a file. You must tell the system the name of each field and the type of information it will contain. Most file managers allow fields to have variable lengths, but some require all fields to have a fixed width. So, if the contents of a field will vary in length, you may need to select the longest or most likely maximum width for that field.

Programs differ in how they let you set up a file and design its layout. One common method involves simply typing each field name followed by the type of data the field will store and the size of the field. The order in which you type in the field names determines their order in the record. Using this method, you might layout the file shown in Figure 8.1 as follows. (In all the examples in this chapter, characters shown in color are typed by the user; characters in black are generated by the computer.)

```
Enter a command: BUILD
Enter the file name you wish to build: CLIENTS
Enter each field name, its data type, and format.
Example: ZIPCODE,Numeric,#####
Enter STOP when done, or press (Esc) for help.
DATE,Date,dd-mmm-yy
```

Figure 8.4 This Form Design window allows you both to construct the on-screen form and to determine the file's field names. You create a field simply by typing its name anywhere on the screen. Labels such as "Tuna Distributors", must be preceded by an apostrophe to distinguish them from field names. The form can be edited by dragging names or labels around the screen as necessary. When everything is complete, you select the Exit Design option from the menu bar.

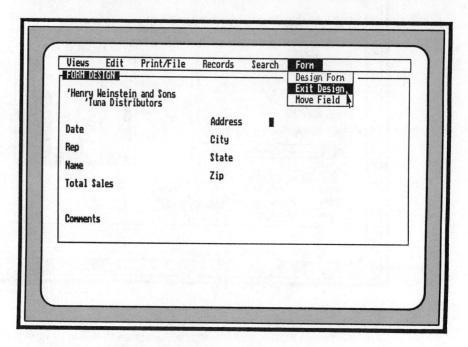

REP,Text,xxxxxxxxxxxxxxxxxxxxxxxxx
NAME,Text,xxxxxxxxxxxxxxxxxxxxxxxxxxxxxxx

. . .

TOTAL SALES,Numeric,$###,###,###.##

Because this method is fairly cumbersome, many recently developed systems allow the file to be designed on the screen. For example, in Reflex you create a new file by constructing a form for it, as shown in Figure 8.4. The parts of the form can be typed in and moved around the screen with the cursor keys or a mouse until a pleasing layout is obtained. At this point, the form can contain only two types of entries: labels and the names of the file's fields. The labels merely comment on the form and are identified by an initial apostrophe, as in the "Tuna Distributors" entry of Figure 8.4. All other entries are assumed to be the file's field names. Once the file layout has been determined, you are ready to enter data into the file. To do this, you simply type entries in the fields, using the [Tab] or [Enter] key to move from field to field.

Reflex allows three basic types of fields: text, date, and numeric. It uses the first entry you make in a field to determine that field's type. For example, if you enter "6/12/87" into a field, Reflex makes that field a date field. (This procedure is similar to the way most spreadsheet programs determine whether an entry is a label or a number based on the first character of the entry.) Once the field type is determined, Reflex requires that new entries be of the correct type. This means that "Smith", for example, can be entered into a date field.

Most file managers allow you to set up computed fields. The value of a **computed field** is based on the values of other fields in the same record. You must give the file manager a formula for each computed field. For example, if the formula for a Total-Cost field is (Unit-Cost * Quantity), then the file manager would multiply the values in the Unit-Cost and Quantity fields to obtain the value for the Total-Cost field. Computed fields can eliminate many manual calculations and can even be used to construct miniature spreadsheetlike models.

File Processing Operations

All file managers provide a variety of essential file processing operations. These basic operations allow you to look up, insert, delete, or modify a record; select a group of records; and either sort or index the file. You will spend more time performing these basic tasks than any other file processing activities. For this reason, the file manager should make each of these activities simple and quick to perform.

A *look-up operation* finds and displays a particular record on the screen. For example, you might want to retrieve the first record that includes Jim Wilson in the Name field. With a list-oriented system, you could hunt for the record directly by scrolling through the file. But for files containing thousands of records, this strategy amounts to looking for a needle in a haystack. A more effective method is to give the file manager a description of the record and have it find the record for you. Figure 8.5 illustrates how to do this by entering *search conditions* in a dialog box. Other systems let you enter the search conditions directly into the blanks of an empty form. Still other systems require search conditions to be typed in a command-line format. Look-up operations become imposing if you must use a command-line format. For example, a command-line equivalent of the search in Figure 8.5 is

```
DATE BTWN(1/01/87,4/01/87) AND (SALES REP = 'James Wilson'
OR SALES REP = 'Jim Wilson') AND CITY = 'Boston'
```

A *select operation* finds and marks records that match the search conditions. (The corresponding operation in word processing is marking a block of text.) A select operation precedes any activity that will affect an entire group of records at once. For example, you might want to examine all records with positive balances in the Past-Due field. A select operation could mark these records; then you could scroll through them without having to view other records. Select operations can also be used to delete unwanted or obsolete records quickly or to select a subset of the file for printing.

Figure 8.5 This dialog box requests search conditions, allowing you to describe a particular record or set of records. The settings in this box would select any record in which Sales Rep is either James Wilson or Jim Wilson, Date is between 1/01/87 and 4/01/87, and City is Boston.

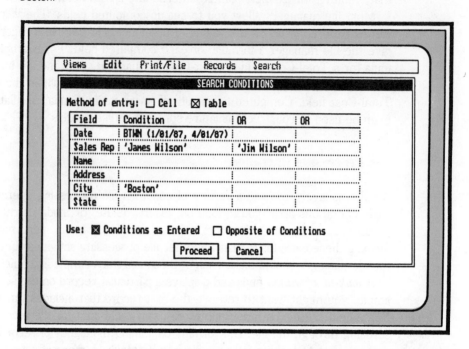

An *insert operation* adds another record to the file. For example, you might add a new subscriber to a magazine's mailing list. With a form-oriented system, you begin this operation by asking for a blank form. Then you fill out the form by typing entries in fields, using the [Tab] or [Enter] key to move from field to field. With a list-oriented system, you need to request a new row before you can begin entering data, but otherwise the process is similar. Both types of systems let you correct spelling errors and edit the fields until the record is correct. In most systems, the records you insert are added to the end of the growing file.

A *delete operation* removes a record from the file. For example, you might remove Jason Wilkins from a mailing list when his subscription ends. To delete a record, you must first use a loop-up operation to display it; then the delete operation removes it from the file.

A *modify operation* changes one or more fields in a particular record. For example, you might want to change the fields that hold Martha Tildon's address and zip code because she has moved. To modify a record, you must first use a look-up operation to retrieve it. Then you tab to the fields you wish to edit and make the changes.

A *sort* or an *index operation* is used to place records in a particular order for viewing or printing. A file manager will either sort records or index them; it will not do both. We will explain both methods in turn.

You tell a *sort-oriented file manager* how to organize the file by selecting the primary and secondary **sort fields** and by choosing whether to sort these fields in ascending or descending order. The *primary sort field* is used first in sorting the records. The *secondary sort field* resolves how records with the same primary field values should be ordered. For example, if you want to print a sales report organized by customer, then the primary sort field would be the field that holds the customers' names. If some customers have made several purchases, you might choose the date field as the secondary sort field. This would cause each customer's purchases to be listed by date.

A file manager sorts by moving records or by adjusting pointers that identify where records are stored. Either approach is tedious, even for a computer. Sorting a file with 10,000 records can take over an hour on a microcomputer. Because a file can be in only one order at a time, you may need to sort the file frequently to view or print it differently. This can be a major disadvantage of a sort-oriented file manager.

An *index-oriented file manager* allows you to establish one or more indexes for a file. A book's index contains key words and their location (page number) in the book. Similarly, a file's index is a list of field values and their location (record number) in the file. For example, consider the following two indexes for a file with only seven records:

Name Index		Zip Index	
Value in the Name Field	**Record # in the File**	**Value in the Zip Field**	**Record in the File**
Adams	1	10755	3
Baker	7	39588	6
James	4	43210	5
Jones	3	55143	2
King	6	65001	7
Smith	2	86501	1
Thomas	5	99123	4

The file manager could use these two indexes to read the file in alphabetical order by name (by retrieving records 1, 7, 4, 3, 6, 2, and 5) or in numerical order by zip code (by retrieving records 3, 6, 5, 2, 7, 1, and 4). Thus, with indexing it is not necessary to resort the file just to retrieve the records in a different order.

Index-oriented systems have some disadvantages. Indexing forces the file manager to do more work each time a record is added or deleted from the file: each index must be updated. Also, each index takes storage space. And finally, if you need to establish a new index for a file, you must wait while the index is constructed.

Report Generation

A *report generator* (also known as a *report writer*) is a program for producing reports from lists stored in one or more files. Data management systems vary greatly in the flexibility and capability of their report generators. Any report generator can print columnar reports with fields arranged as columns across the page. Most can also print mailing labels by arranging the fields of each record so that they occupy several rows of the page.

A good report generator will let you select which fields are printed, where they appear on the page, and what their column headings say. For example, you might want to print only the names and departments of employees who have worked for the company for more than 20 years or who earn more than $50,000 per year. To carry out these tasks, you must specify which records qualify for printing. With most report generators, the method for identifying these records is the same as the procedure for specifying the search conditions for a look-up operation.

In addition, most report generators can provide totals and subtotals. For example, sales transactions could be totaled and printed at the bottom of the Sales column. Subtotals could also be printed for groups of records; this is done in reports that contain breaks. A **report break** is a position in a report where a pre-specified field changes value from one record to the next. For example, the report shown in Figure 8.6(b) has a report break based on the Date field. This report break occurs when the value in the Date field changes from one record to the next; the report break is used to print monthly subtotals for the Sales column. Some reports have several levels of report breaks. For example, suppose a report contains subtotals for each sales office in a firm, each salesperson within a sales office, and each product sold by a salesperson. In this case, the first-level break would be based on the Product field, the second-level break on the Salesperson field, and the third-level break on the Sales-Office field.

Report generators also vary in how they allow you to lay out the report. As in many other areas of the computer field, there is a tradeoff here between power and convenience. The most powerful report generators require you to learn a command language to describe how the report should look. These systems provide commands for positioning fields on the page, establishing report breaks, performing calculations on field values before printing, and making decisions based on the values being printed. These features can be invaluable if you need to print an unusual or complicated report. For example, an apartment manager might want to print a few extra lines on invoices for tenants who still owe rent for past months. By testing the value in the Past-Due field, a command-language report generator could print a standard invoice for most renters and an expanded invoice for slow-paying renters.

Forms-oriented report generators are much easier to use than those that rely on a command language. With a forms-oriented report generator, you draw a template on the screen of how the report should look, and the report generator uses the template to print the report. Figure 8.6 illustrates this process. The Report

Figure 8.6 Using (a) an on-screen report generator to print (b) a report from a data file.

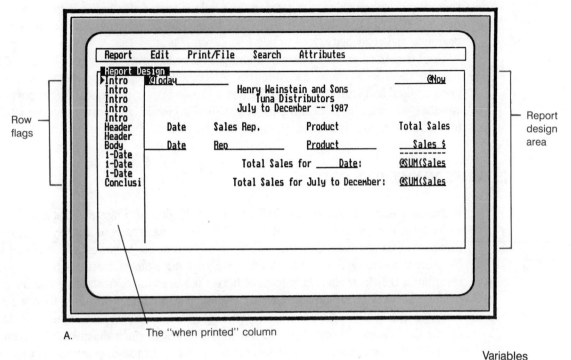

Row flags

The "when printed" column

A.

Report design area

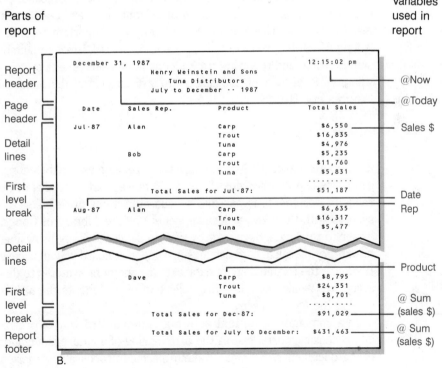

Parts of report

Variables used in report

Report header
Page header
Detail lines
First level break
Detail lines
First level break
Report footer

@Now
@Today
Sales $
Date
Rep
Product
@ Sum (sales $)
@ Sum (sales $)

B.

Design area in Figure 8.6(a) contains the template that describes all aspects of the report. Each line in this area describes one type of line in the report. The underlined items are variables that receive their values from fields in the data file when the report is printed. All other items are labels used to improve the report's appearance and readability.

Once you have specified how a report should be laid out, you should be allowed to save the specifications for later use. After several report specifications have been created and stored, it should then be a simple matter to request any report—whether you want to print a report of past-due accounts, a report in mailing-label format, or a report listing recent entries to the file.

DATABASE MANAGEMENT SYSTEMS

A *database management system (DBMS)* is a collection of programs that provides convenient access to data stored in a database. A **database** is merely a logical grouping of one or more data files. The primary difference between a DBMS and a file management system is that a DBMS allows simultaneous access to multiple files; but a DBMS is also likely to have better features for restructuring and maintaining files and for automatic file processing. A DBMS can do more than a file management system. For example, you can direct a DBMS to compute a total from a field in one file and then add the total to a balance in a master file. A complete DBMS can provide many different views of the database, print reports from multiple files, make backup copies of existing files, and convert data from one format to another. These and other features are important to understand when selecting a DBMS, because they are what make a DBMS so suitable for recording, summarizing, and reporting transactions in a business data processing system. We will devote the rest of this chapter to a discussion of the necessary and desirable features of a DBMS.

Overall Structure of a DBMS

A computer-based DBMS in some ways resembles a public library where people can share books, magazines, films, and newspapers. Access to the library's thousands of documents is possible because the items are cataloged in a logical way, such as with the Dewey decimal system or the Library of Congress system. It's easier to retrieve a document by using a catalog than by browsing through the entire library, because card catalogs provide a standard way of accessing information. If we use the terminology of database management systems to describe a public library, we would call the entire collection of documents the *database* and the card catalog the *logical schema.* [2]

In a computer, a **logical schema** is a standard way of organizing information into accessible parts, just as the card catalog of a library is a standard way of organizing documents. Schemas contain machine-processable descriptions of the contents of the database, so that users can easily browse and retrieve data from the database. The logical schema is separate from the **physical schema**, which describes how data are actually stored on a disk. The data might reside in thousands of files spread across many disks or tapes, but this fact isn't apparent because the logical schema insulates you from the physical schema; physical data access is handled by the DBMS. In this respect, a DBMS is better than a library. If a library were as convenient to use, the librarians would automatically retrieve your card catalog selections from the bookshelves.

Figure 8.7 shows the overall relationships among people, machines, and processes in a large DBMS as they might occur in a major corporation; but even a DBMS for micro-computers incorporates the fundamental ideas of the figure. This chart is best understood by reading it from left to right and from top to bottom,

Figure 8.7 Organizational, systematic, and technological structures in a large database management system.

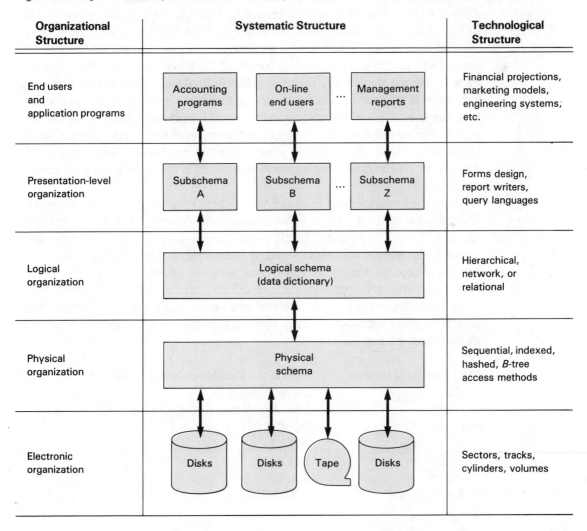

Organizational Structure	Systematic Structure			Technological Structure
End users and application programs	Accounting programs	On-line end users ...	Management reports	Financial projections, marketing models, engineering systems; etc.
Presentation-level organization	Subschema A	Subschema B ...	Subschema Z	Forms design, report writers, query languages
Logical organization	Logical schema (data dictionary)			Hierarchical, network, or relational
Physical organization	Physical schema			Sequential, indexed, hashed, *B*-tree access methods
Electronic organization	Disks	Disks	Tape	Disks	Sectors, tracks, cylinders, volumes

like a page in a book. The top row shows the people and programs that feed data into and receive information from the DBMS, as well as examples of the technology they might use to collect and analyze that information. A large DBMS can interact with many users at the same time, and the "users" can be people sitting at a terminal or application programs running in a multiuser computer system. Thus, at a certain time, the DBMS might be sending payroll information to an accounting program, receiving sales transactions from clerks, and printing management reports. Financial projections, marketing models, statistical analyses, engineering calculations, or other technology may be incorporated into an application program or employed by an end user to collect and analyze information. In the following section, we will examine some of the other structures depicted in Figure 8.7.

Subschemas

The second row of Figure 8.7 indicates how the data in a database are filtered, formatted, and rearranged as appropriate for each group of users. In a large DBMS, each user can "see" only a small part of the entire database; most of the data are shielded from view. This illustrates another similarity between a DBMS and a library. Most people use only a small portion of the library, and they have different ways of viewing the library. An artist probably thinks of the library as a place to find copies of rare and beautiful paintings; an engineer views the library as a source of technical data, such as mathematical tables and engineering journals; and a business executive might use the library to read stock market reports. These different views may result in different ways of retrieving books, newspapers, and magazines; yet the underlying information is stored in the same way for all users of the library.

Using the terminology of database management systems, we would call each individual view of the library a **subschema.** Each description of how a database should look from a particular user's perspective is stored in a subschema. Subschemas also include information used by the DBMS to design forms, produce reports, and process queries. Because many database management systems are designed for personal computers, some do not support the creation of subschemas.

As an illustration of the role of subschemas in a DBMS, consider a simple database for a small company. Assume that the database contains the following information about employees:

Fields in Database	A Sample Employee's Information
Name	Steve Johnson
Address	1755 NW Arthur Circle, Corvallis, OR 97330
Phone	(503) 753-1143
Hiring-Date	8/15/81
Birth-Date	12/17/51
Salary	$43,000
Soc-Sec-Num	543-64-6466

The logical schema for this database would include the name of each field (Name, Address, and so on) and the type of data stored in each field (text, date, integer, and so on). The database might be used by many people in the corporation. For example, the payroll department needs salary information to print paychecks, and the personnel department needs to know when employees are eligible for retirement. To accommodate these different needs, two subschemas might be established, as follows:

Payroll Subschema	Personnel Subschema
Display format:	Display format:
DEFAULT	SCREEN FORM #482
Fields:	Fields:
Name	Name
Soc-Sec-Num	Hiring-Date
Salary	Age
Password:	Soc-Sec-Num
ALPHA12	Calculations:
	Age = Today's Date − Birth-Date

The syntax in this example is merely representative of how the subschemas might be laid out; database management systems vary greatly in how schemas and subschemas are constructed. The important point here is that each subschema tells the DBMS how to accept and present data for a particular set of users or application programs. Thus, when a payroll program uses the payroll subschema, providing the necessary password, the DBMS might respond with:

Steve Johnson   543646466   43000

Alternatively, if, in May of 1987, a clerk uses the personnel subschema, the DBMS might display

EMPLOYEE SENIORITY DATA
Name: Steve Johnson   Hiring Date: 8/15/81
Age: 35   Social Security Number: 543-64-6466

Notice how the DBMS calculates the employee's age from the employee's birth date and today's date (the date in the computer system's clock). This example illustrates some fundamental characteristics of how a DBMS shares information among users. Subschemas can be used to create very different, personalized views of the same data. Information might be arranged in a different order and presented in different formats. A subschema can be used to hide sensitive information (such as salaries) from view simply by omitting fields from the subschema's description. It can also create new information from the physical information in the database by performing calculations.

Also notice how effectively a subschema shields its users from the details of how data are organized in files or stored on disk. The payroll program will work equally well if the database stores the information it needs in one large file, in two smaller files, or in some other manner. The payroll subschema specifies exactly how data are to be passed to the payroll program, so it doesn't matter to the payroll program how data are actually stored. This feature is extremely important to programmers and systems analysts, because it allows file maintenance operations to be performed without requiring modifications of a program.

Logical Structure

The third row of Figure 8.7 refers to the logical organization within a DBMS. The way the logical schema is constructed influences the behavior of the entire DBMS, because it controls what data are stored in the database and how the data may be retrieved. Here are some typical goals for the design of the logical schema.

- Data should not be stored redundantly in the database. For example, if names are paired with social security numbers in one part of the database, they should not be stored a second time in another part. Redundant storage wastes space and opens up the possibility of inconsistencies. For example, if Steve Johnson's social security number were stored twice in the database, once as 543-64-6466 and once as 432-53-5355, that would be a *data inconsistency*.

- The methods of organizing data should be understandable. You shouldn't need an advanced degree in software engineering to construct queries to determine, say, how many employees work in the Los Angeles sales office.

- The methods of accessing data should be efficient. The DBMS should quickly dispense with routine processing, such as posting a day's sales transactions to an accounts receivable master file.

- The logical schema itself should be flexible and expandable. It should adapt gracefully as your needs for storing and retrieving data change.

These goals often conflict. For example, the most efficient structure for processing may be the least flexible. Balancing these goals successfully can be tricky. This is one reason why large database systems are generally developed by professional *database administrators*.

There are three dominant technologies used to construct logical views of a database: hierarchical, network, and relational. Any particular DBMS will use only one of these methods to organize data. These methods accomplish the same basic task of cataloging the data in the database, but they use very different models to describe the data.

Hierarchical Databases
A **hierarchical database** establishes a top-to-bottom relationship among the items in a database, much like the relationships among members of a family on a

Figure 8.8 A hierarchical database with a one-to-many access path between classes and students.

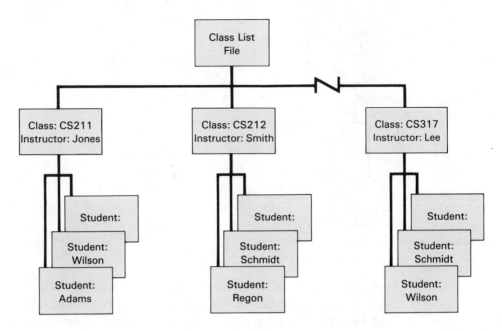

family tree. Each member of the tree has a unique parent, or "owner"; to reach a member, you must pass through the owner. Figure 8.8 shows how a database for a class list might appear in a hierarchical schema. This structure seems quite natural, because all students for a given class are grouped under that class.

When a hierarchical model is used, the relationship among items in the database is established when the schema is constructed. This means that the hierarchical is static and can't be changed easily once the database is set up. This fixed structure makes some tasks far easier than others. For example, it's a trivial matter to read from Figure 8.8 the names of the students in class CS212, but the entire class list must be searched to determine the classes being taken by Schmidt.

Business data naturally have a hierarchical structure: transactions belong to specific accounts, clients belong to sales regions, and so forth. The rigid structure of a hierarchical model makes it extremely easy to enter or update routine business transactions quickly, but it isn't convenient for answering specific inquiries. This efficiency of processing is a major reason why most large transaction-processing systems today use the hierarchical model. Another major reason is historical: the first database management systems for mainframes were hierarchical, and large corporations find it difficult to convert from one database model to another.

Network Databases

A network database is similar to a hierarchical database—with one important difference, as shown in Figure 8.9. Instead of restricting the structure to a one-to-

Figure 8.9 A network database consisting of a many-to-many access path between students and classes and between instructors and classes.

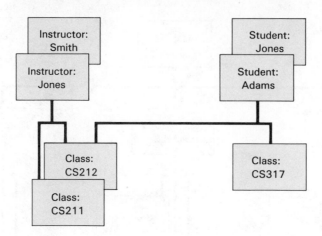

many relationship between owner and members, a **network database** permits many-to-many relationships. For example, as Figure 8.9 illustrates, many students may be enrolled in many classes, and many instructors may teach many students; a network schema can reflect these relationships. Once established, these relationships are static and cannot be changed easily.

Many network databases have been implemented on mainframe computers. In fact, use of the network schema has been recommended by CODASYL (*C*onference *on Da*ta *S*ystems *L*anguages), and network databases are sometimes called CODASYL databases. They are more flexible than hierarchical databases, but because the owner-coupled sets are fixed when the database is designed, the use of network databases has decreased.

Relational Databases

A **relational database** stores data in tables, as shown in Figure 8.10. Each table is called a *relation;* each row of a relation is called a *tuple;* and each tuple is divided into fields called *domains*. Most people find it natural to organize and manipulate data with a relational database, because it relies on the familiar model of a table containing records and fields.

Unlike hierarchical and network databases, a relational database imposes very little structure on the data at the time they are stored. For example, it is not immediately apparent from the REGISTRATION relation in Figure 8.10 what classes Schmidt is taking; nor is it obvious what students are in class CS212. The rows in the REGISTRATION relation are not automatically linked either by classes (as in a class list) or by students (as in a student schedule). Instead of permanent linkages among items, a relational database allows temporary relationships to be estab-

Figure 8.10 A relational database stores data in tables called *relations*.

SCHEDULE Relation

CLASS	INSTRUCTOR
CS211	Jones
CS215	Franklin
CS317	Lee
CS201	Feldstein
.	.
.	.
.	.

REGISTRATION Relation

CLASS	STUDENT
CS212	Adams
CS317	Schmidt
CS211	Wilson
CS212	Schmidt
.	.
.	.

lished by query commands. A *query command* is an instruction given to the DBMS to look up, retrieve, calculate, move, copy, print, and so forth. A *query* is a miniature program that tells the DBMS what to do. For example, in the query

```
JOIN Schedule WITH Registration FORMING Temp-Rel.
DISPLAY Instructor FROM Temp-Rel
WHERE student = "Joe Schmidt".
```

the first line directs the DBMS to merge the data in the SCHEDULE relation (Figure 8.10) with the data in the REGISTRATION relation, creating a new relation called TEMP-REL. The TEMP-REL relation will have three fields: Class, Instructor, and Student. The second line of the query tells the DBMS to display the name in the Instructor field for all the rows in TEMP-REL whose Student field contains Joe Schmidt. The effect of these two commands is to display the names of Joe Schmidt's instructors.

One of the most powerful features of a relational DBMS is the ease with which files can be manipulated. These systems have many commands for such tasks as extracting, joining, intersecting, and selecting files. Taken together, these commands constitute a relational **query language** for processing multiple files. For example, as Figure 8.11 illustrates, if you give the command

```
SUBTRACT pay85 FROM emptable FORMING mismatch
```

a table called MISMATCH is formed from all the records of EMPTABLE that don't have corresponding records in PAY85.

In the last ten years, relational database management systems have become very popular, particularly among users of personal computers. Relational systems provide more flexibility in manipulating data than either hierarchical or network systems, because they offer powerful query languages that aren't limited by a fixed set of relationships among data items. The chief complaint about relational

Figure 8.11 Using the SUBTRACT command to form a new table made up of rows from one table that do not match those of another.

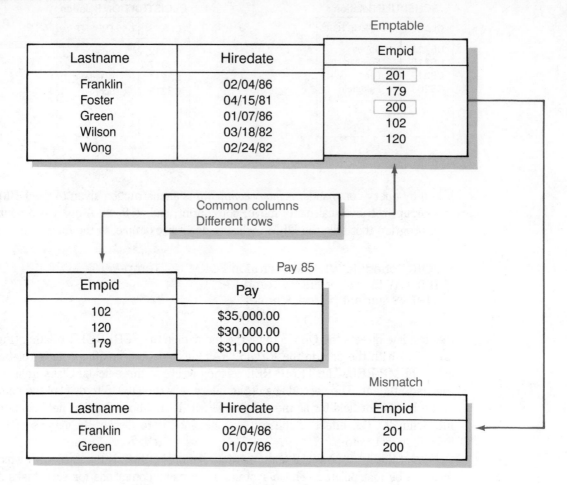

database systems has been their poor processing efficiency. This complaint is becoming less valid as their speed improves and the cost of computing declines.

DBMS Features

Now that you've had a brief introduction to what a DBMS can do and how to set up a DBMS, we'll look more closely at the features every DBMS should provide. These include a data dictionary, a query facility, a forms management facility, a data interchange facility, and a data integrity facility. Understanding these features will help you to recognize and use them in whatever DBMS you use.

The Data Dictionary

A **data dictionary**, a special file containing the names of all fields in all files maintained by the DBMS, is a major component of the database's logical schema. For example, you create a new file by adding entries to the data dictionary. For each file in the database, the data dictionary always includes the name of each field, the type of data stored in each field (such as text, numeric, date, or dollars), and the width of each field. In addition, a data dictionary helps provide other features. Here are some ways a data dictionary can make a DBMS more powerful and more convenient.

Better Data Editing A DBMS may make data entry easier and more reliable with the help of *editing attributes;* that is, rules that govern the way data are entered into the database. These attributes are stored in the dictionary as part of the description of the fields. For example, a numeric field might be given upper and lower limits. As data are entered into the DBMS, these limits in the data dictionary are used to ensure that only values falling within certain limits are accepted. A more complicated situation arises if a field in another file must be searched to validate a data entry. For example, an editing attribute might require that the customer numbers of entries to a transaction file be valid numbers in a customer account file.

Password Security A password is often kept for an entire file, to prohibit unauthorized access. Additionally, the data dictionary may contain many passwords: one for ready-only access, another for data entry, and still another for updating the file.

Compressed Information The data dictionary helps promote data compression by making it easy to store data in a coded format. For example, a mailing list can be compressed by eliminating the City and State fields from all records, as shown in Figure 8.12. Because the zip code uniquely identifies which city and state are intended, the data dictionary need only reference the city and state in a second file.

Data Integrity Control The date and time of the last access, the date and time of the last backup, and the date and time of the most recent modification to the file may be kept in the data dictionary. This information is useful for maintaining control over your data and becomes extremely helpful if there is a system failure.

Query Languages

The *query facility* is the method the DBMS provides to request data. A good query facility allows nonprogrammers to process and update information stored in the database. This facility is especially important in a relational DBMS, because relationships among fields are established by query commands.

Not all DBMS programs require you to learn a query language like the one we used in Figure 8.11. With some programs you can use near-English commands, such as

Figure 8.12 A compressed mailing list file and its associated secondary file.

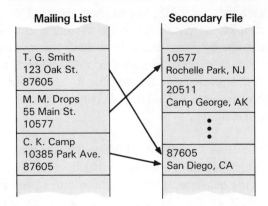

For each part supplied, find PNO and the names of all LOCATIONS supplying the part.
Find SNO and STATUS for suppliers in London.

Natural-language inquiries, such as "Find," "How many," and "What" are common in many relational DBMS programs, but updating files by using natural-language inquiries is difficult. For this reason, command language and visual interfaces that use pictures and diagrams are the most prevalent methods of giving commands to a DBMS.

Setting up and implementing a typical query command may not require proficiency as a programmer, but it is difficult to accomplish without some training. Most people hire an expert to design, set up, and implement the steps in DBMS processing. The query commands are entered into the DBMS and stored for execution later. Frequently the expert will use menu-based prompting and selection methods to combine file processing queries and on-screen data entry forms. Then even a clerk who knows nothing about database processing can use the system without further assistance from the expert.

Forms Management

The *forms management facility* of a DBMS lets you define forms for data entry, other forms for printing, and still other forms for look-up, insert, and delete operations. In addition, any form can shield information from view by preventing certain fields from being displayed. An important feature is the ability to display and edit information from several files in a single form. For example, a form for entering orders might accept payment information and place it in the RECEIVABLES file and accept product information for the SHIPMENTS file. Forms can also control access to confidential fields by enforcing password protection.

Forms are often stored in a *forms library*, which is simply a file that can store many forms to make access to them convenient. A forms library makes it easy for programmers to use the same form in different programs.

Data Interchange with Other Programs

A good DBMS provides ways to move data between the DBMS files and other programs. The most typical interchange is a transfer of information between the DBMS and spreadsheet, word processing, or graphics programs. For example, you may use a spreadsheet to perform calculations in a financial model and then cut these calculations out of your spreadsheet and paste them into a DBMS file. Or you may want to select a record from your DBMS file and move it into a portion of a spreadsheet. Data in a DBMS file are normally made available to other programs through the *data interchange facility* of the DBMS.

Depending on the conversion programs being used, transferring data can be as easy as posting and removing a piece of paper from a clipboard, or it can be quite difficult. Every program that produces output to a disk file uses a format that may or may not be compatible with the output files of other programs. The simplest format is a sequential file containing ASCII text. The records of such a file vary in width depending on the length of each line of text stored.

A worksheet file produced with Lotus 1-2-3 is written in the WKS format; Multiplan worksheets are written in SYLK format; and documents from MultiMate, MacWrite, and other word processor programs include codes that control the printer and character fonts. These files must be preprocessed to remove the special printer codes or to rearrange the data so that they match the arrangement expected by the DBMS. Whether this is easy or possible to do depends largely on the capabilities of the file conversion programs provided as part of the DBMS.

Data Integrity

One of the most overlooked features of a good DBMS is the *data integrity facility*. It consists of routines for backing up and restoring files, special controls on files that are shared with other users, and other programs to guarantee the safety of your data.

There are several reasons to periodically make backup copies of your files. The most obvious reason is to protect your valuable investment of time and effort. A single disk can hold thousands of records and in an instant lose those records. A backup copy is your best protection against complete loss. In addition, backups provide some not-so-obvious benefits. For example, if you have a backup copy of a file, you can restore previously deleted records and retrieve information for an audit trail.

An **audit trail** is the recorded history of the insertions, deletions, modifications, and restorations performed on a file. It is one of the simplest methods of guaranteeing the validity of information stored in a file, which is a necessity in most business applications. (Other methods that can provide such guarantees include cross-checking and balancing debits and credits.) One way of obtaining a satisfactory audit trail is to periodically produce a dated report containing all records in the file and to print all modifications to the file as they are made. The report and the printed transactions together constitute a reasonable audit trail. A backup copy can also be part of an audit trail, because it provides a dated copy of all records at a certain point in the life of the file. A history of the file can then be reconstructed from periodic backup reports and records of modifications.

Comparing Systems

Most DBMS programs accomplish the same basic functions, but they differ in myriad ways when you consider their "extras." Remember to consider other features, including the flexibility of the report generator, the effectiveness of error handling and recovery, the quality of documentation, the simplicity and power of the query language, and processing speed.

Two goals of a DBMS are to eliminate the need for a programmer and to provide an easy-to-understand model of data. Menus, forms, report generators, and query languages are used to eliminate programming; a DBMS schema makes the DBMS general, yet easy to understand. But neither of these two goals is fully achieved by today's DBMS programs. Some programs are easier to use but less powerful than others. Powerful programs tend to be complex and difficult to understand. At the root of the difficulty is the likelihood that an application will be intrinsically complex because of the complex nature of its task.

SUMMARY

A file management system is the simplest form of data management, handling only one file or list at a time. Its features provide for setting up files and entering data, as well as for look-up, insert, delete, and modify operations and additional processing, such as sorting, indexing, and report generation. The report generator lets you design columnar reports with headers, footers, the date, page numbers, column headings, and sometimes totals and subtotals.

The use of forms adds power to data management systems by increasing access control, performing calculations, and making the system easier to use. For example, records can be retrieved easily when search conditions are entered into a form.

A database management system (DBMS) can coordinate the storage and retrieval of information from many files. DBMS software maintains a comprehensive logical schema so that a uniform, consistent, and correct structure is guaranteed at all times; it maintains a physical schema so that the disk location of specific data items can be determined; it maintains separate subschemas so that independent users and programs can retrieve and interpret the data in their own way; and it provides a variety of functions to users, such as report generation, file conversion, query processing, and password protection.

A hierarchical database imposes a one-to-many relationship on data items when they are stored and works on sets of data. A network database imposes a many-to-many relationship on data items when they are stored. In practice, hierarchical and network models are more complex and difficult to use than relational models, in which the relationships among data are established only after data are stored. A relational database uses tables as the schemas for data. Tables, rows, and columns of fields are processed by giving query commands to the DBMS. These commands establish the relationships among files, records, and fields.

Every DBMS must have a data dictionary to hold the database's structural information. A DBMS must also provide some way to process, update, and retrieve information. Typically, a query language provides these directions for processing files. In addition, a forms management facility lets users define forms for data entry, printing, and other operations. A good DBMS also provides ways to share information with other software—for example, transferring information from a database file to a spreadsheet, word processor, or graphics file. Finally, a DBMS must allow you to protect the database from damage in the event of a power outage or other failure leading to loss of information. A variety of methods for backing up files is part of any good DBMS.

KEY TERMS

audit trail	network database
computed field	physical schema
database	query language
data dictionary	relational database
file management system (file manager)	report break
	report generator
form	sort field
hierarchical database	subschema
logical schema	

DISCUSSION QUESTIONS

1. How should you choose between using a spreadsheet or a file manager for an application? Do you know any examples of people making this choice poorly?

2. What model does your file manager's user interface employ?

3. What rules can you give for determining whether a list should be computerized or handled manually?

4. If you were to design a file manager, how would you let the user specify the search conditions for a look-up operation?

5. Most spreadsheet programs have sort operations, and most file managers allow calculated fields. Are these two types of products likely to become more similar?

6. How can you tell the difference between a file manager and a database management system? Is there a gray area between them?

7. What are the differences among hierarchical, network, and relational databases?

8. What would be the most important items in a checklist of DBMS features for a church that uses volunteers to keep track of its books? for the payroll department of a 1,000-person corporation?

9. What safeguards should be used to prevent the loss or accidental change of information in the two situations described in question 8?

EXERCISES

1. Design an on-screen form for a newspaper subscription department to use in entering data. Assume that subscribers have the following options:
   a. *Newspaper:* morning, evening, or Sunday
   b. *Billing:* weekly, monthly, every six months, or annual
   c. *Delivery:* carrier or mail

2. Design a file management system for a health club's billing system. Assume that the membership classes and monthly dues are: family, $45; single adult, $25; and junior, $20. The club initiation fee is $500 for a family, $300 for a single adult, and $150 for a junior. The initiation fee may be paid either in a lump sum on joining (minus a 10 percent discount) or monthly over a three-year period.

3. For your data management program, find the maximum
   a. number of files that can be open at a time.
   b. number of records per file.
   c. number of fields per record.
   d. number of characters per field.
      Also determine the types of data allowed and the formatting options for displaying them.

4. Diagram a relational database containing three files: PARTS, SHIPMENTS, and SUPPLIERS. The PARTS file has fields for Part-Num, Part-Name, Color, Quantity, and Weight. The SHIPMENTS file has fields for Part-Num, Date, Ship-Qty, Supply-Num, and Price. The SUPPLIERS file has fields for Supply-Num, Supply-Name, and Address. Diagram how the database might look in a hierarchical model; in a network model. How do the relational, hierarchical, and network databases differ?

1. Reflex is a popular, inexpensive file management system that has been marketed by Borland International since 1985.

2. *The American Heritage Dictionary* defines *schema* as "a summarized or diagrammatic representation of something; an outline." Furthermore, according to this dictionary, *schemata* is the plural form of *schema*. Computer terminology has historically abused the English language, and this is no exception—most DBMS experts use the word *schemas* when discussing more than one schema. We will adopt this common usage.

9 Communications

I n the past ten years, three trends have combined to create a turbulent and dynamic environment in computer communications. First, the quantity of information stored in computers has more than quadrupled, a change that in turn has expanded the need to share information among computers. Second, the entire field of communication—from telephones and television to music recording—has begun switching from analog to digital storage and transmission methods. This switch is causing the fields of computing and communications to merge. Third, a shift in the relative costs of computing equipment has erased the historical cost advantage of centralized mainframes and is encouraging the use of microcomputers.

Computer communications is a field not only of turmoil and rapid growth, but also of many market niches, specialized pieces of equipment, and weak standards for hardware and software. It is an exciting environment, which leaves communications specialists divided about what the future will bring and how to prepare for it.

In the first half of this chapter, we introduce computer communications by explaining how a microcomputer or terminal can be linked by telephone to any of thousands of other computers. This introduction explains the technology involved in sending data over telephones, the software used to link microcomputers to other computers, and the types of tasks that can be accomplished with a micro- computer and a telephone. The second half of the chapter generalizes the concepts in the first half to the entire field of computer communications. Here we discuss communications media (wires, cables, airwaves, and so forth), how these media are used efficiently, and how computers can be linked in various types of networks.

TELECOMMUNICATIONS

Telecommunications is a very general term. It refers to any transmission of information over long distances by using electromagnetic signals like those used in telephones and radios. When the term is used in discussions of microcomputers, it usually means something much more specific: attaching a microcomputer to the telephone system to move data from computer to computer. With this kind of telecommunications, you can

- Read the day's headline stories or search the last few months of news for articles on a particular topic

- Send letters to be printed and delivered by the post office

- Receive mail that was deposited instantly in your electronic mailbox by correspondents living across town, across the continent, or abroad

- Order books, cameras, and other items at a substantial discount

- Match wits with Klingons in a Star Trek game

- Search vast libraries of bibliographic references for citations that match your query

- "Download" free public-domain programs to be used later or swap files with out-of-town friends

- Use a mainframe or supercomputer to run programs and solve problems beyond the capabilities of your personal computer

- Send a list of today's sales to your firm's head office or order inventory to be delivered for tomorrow's sales

- Request financial or stock market information about a specific company

- Post and read messages on a free computer bulletin board

Figure 9.1 Two methods of transmitting information through wires. In digital signaling, each bit is represented by the presence or absence of a voltage at a specific time. In frequency modulation, each bit of data is represented by a tone during a period of time.

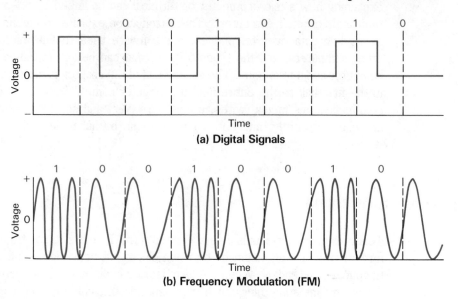

(a) Digital Signals

(b) Frequency Modulation (FM)

To begin telecomputing, you need to solve three problems. First, your personal computer must be physically attached to the telephone lines. This requires a hardware interface that allows the personal computer to "talk" on the phone lines. The connection to another computer is made by dialing the appropriate telephone number. Second, you need communications software to control the personal computer while it is sending and receiving data. Third, the communications software on your personal commputer must be set to use the protocol used by the other computer. The **protocol** is a set of rules that controls how messages are passed between machines. It establishes such important parameters as how fast characters are sent and whether characters are sent one at a time or in groups called *packets*.

Telecommunications Hardware

To understand how a computer transmits information through the telephone system, you must learn something about the methods used to encode data into electrical signals. All of the parts in a computer (disk drives, CPU, printer, and so on) "talk to" each other by sending digital signals, as shown in Figure 9.1(a). *Digital signals* change from one voltage to another in discrete, choppy jumps. Generally, the presence of a positive voltage at a specific time represents the binary digit 1; the absence of a voltage represents the binary digit 0. In contrast, *analog signals* represent information as variations in a continuous, smoothly varying signal wave.

Analog transmission methods dominated every aspect of the communications field before the invention of the transistor. **Frequency modulation (FM)**, which is illustrated in Figure 9.1(b), is one of several methods of analog signaling. Frequency modulation encodes data as changes in the frequency of the signal and is the transmission method used in FM radio. It also forms the basis for the relatively slow, but very common, Bell System 103 method of transmitting computer data over phone lines. When frequency modulation is used to transmit binary data, a high-pitched tone during a given unit of time represents the digit 1, and a lower-pitched tone represents the digit 0.

Digital signals have two major advantages over analog signals.

1. Digital signaling allows faster transmission. Electrical circuits can encode and decipher bits as digital pulses more quickly than they can represent bits in a signal wave.

2. Digital signaling is more accurate, because transmission errors can be detected and corrected. For example, assume that the digital signal for a binary 1 is to be encoded as +5 volts and that a binary 0 is to be encoded as 0 volts. Now assume that a signal is sent out as +5 volts but is received at +4.5 volts because of transmission errors. In this case, the receiving circuit will correctly interpret the incoming signal as a binary 1, because +4.5 volts is closer to +5 volts than to 0 volts. Analog transmissions do not have a comparable method of correcting errors.

For these reasons, telephone systems are rapidly converting from analog to digital transmission methods. Unfortunately, very few telephone exchanges allow home phone lines to use digital signals. This means that the digital signals of a microcomputer must be translated into analog signals before they can be sent through most telephone systems.

For computers to send and receive messages over analog telephone lines, they must be able to convert digital signals to analog signals and back again. The process of converting digital to analog signals is called **modulation; demodulation** does the reverse. A *Modem* (short for *mo*dulate and *dem*odulate) is a device that can perform both functions. Modems modulate data transmissions at fairly high frequencies so that they can send and receive data as quickly as possible over the phone lines. Knowledgeable people avoid eavesdropping on telephone conversations between computers because all they make is a continuous, high-pitched shriek.

The appearance of modems varies substantially, as Figure 9.2 illustrates. Many portable computers come from the factory with built-in modems. Most desktop personal computers have expansion slots in which an optional circuit board containing the modem can be inserted. Alternatively, it is almost always possible to connect an external modem to a microcomputer through a serial interface (an RS-232 port) on the computer. *External modems*—which are also called *standalone* or *free-standing modems*—have the advantage of working with a wide variety of micro-

Figure 9.2 Comparison of (a) an external modem, and (b) an internal modem, which is shown with its communications software and user manual.

A.

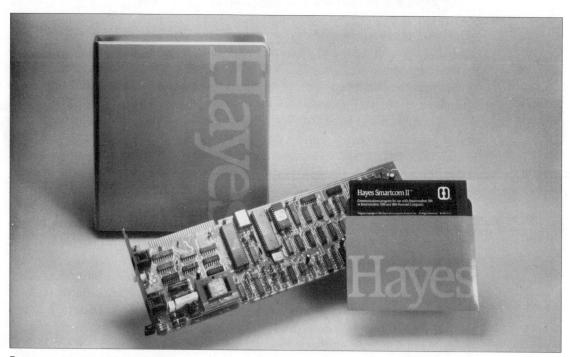

B.

Figure 9.3 Typical cabling arrangements for a direct-connect external modem.

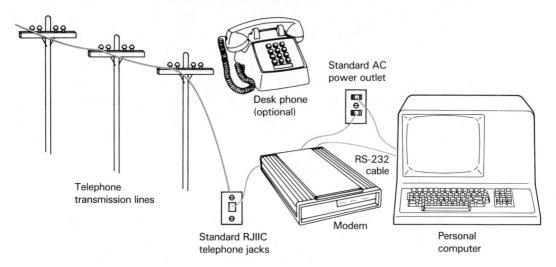

Standard AC power outlet

Desk phone (optional)

RS-232 cable

Telephone transmission lines

Modem

Standard RJIIC telephone jacks

Personal computer

computers, but they require their own electrical power plug, often cost more than built-in modems, and make the computer system less portable.

Modems come in two major categories: direct-connect and acoustically coupled. **Direct-connect modems** plug directly into the telephone jack (see Figure 9.3) and make a very reliable electrical connection to the telephone system. An acoustically coupled modem (**acoustic coupler** for short) is attached to the telephone system by jamming the phone's handset into two flexible cups on the coupler. Then a speaker in the coupler talks into the mouthpiece in the handset, and a microphone in the coupler listens to the earphone in the handset. Having all these microphones and speakers talking to each other across air gaps makes acoustic couplers slow and unreliable.

Modems range in price from well under $100 to over $2,000 for commercial-grade, high-speed modems. The cheapest modems are compatible with the Bell 103 standard—meaning that they follow a widely accepted standard for frequency modulation, which is limited to transmitting 300 bits per second (bps). It normally takes 10 bits to transmit 1 character. Thus, a 300 bps modem will transmit about 30 characters per second (cps), taking more than a minute to fill a 24-line-by-80-column screen. Most people read faster than 30 cps. Modems operating at 1,200 bps (120 cps) transmit text as fast as most people read. They have dropped rapidly in price, from over $2,000 a few years ago to about $100 in 1987. During the same time, their popularity increased dramatically. In 1987 several 2,400-bps modems selling for less than $200 were introduced. If current trends continue, within five years there will be more 2,400-bps modems in operation than 1,200- and 300-bps modems. Few people purchase modems that transmit faster than 2,400 bps. Although 9,600-bps modems are available from several manufacturers, they are expensive—often more than $1,000. And expense isn't their only problem: high-speed modems use protocols that vary from one manufacturer to another and are incompatible. Thus, a 9,600-bps modem from company X cannot talk at high speeds to a 9,600-bps modem made by company Y.

Communications speeds are often given in terms of a *baud* rate. The **baud rate** is the number of data signals the communications line transmits each second. Technical purists point out that the baud rate and bits per second are not the same, because some elegant coding schemes pack two or more bits into each signal. But most people use the terms *baud rate* and *bits per second* interchangeably.

Communications Software

Terminal Emulation

The simplest type of communications software—a **terminal emulator**—microcomputer pretend it is a computer terminal. Although there are many types of computer terminals, the most common type is called an *ASCII terminal* (a reference to the character code used by the terminal), a *Teletype* (historically the most common type of electromechanical terminal), or simply a *dumb terminal*. **Dumb terminal** is a commonly accepted term for an ASCII terminal that has no processing abilities of its own.

Understanding what a dumb terminal does is easy, because it does so little. Every time you press a key on the keyboard, the terminal sends the key's associated character out through the input/output port. Whenever the communications port receives a character, the terminal displays the character on the screen. These are a dumb terminal's important activities, but dumb terminals also do a few other things. For example, they contend with backspace characters and requests to beep the speaker. If desired, they also produce a **local echo**, that is, they send characters typed on the keyboard to the screen.

For most microcomputers, a programmer competent in BASIC can, in a few hours, write a terminal emulator adequate for simple communications. Such a program can be as short as 20 lines. Still, few people write their own communications program. Instead, they use a commercial or public domain communications package. Nearly all of these programs use the microcomputer's processing abilities to provide convenient features not available on dumb terminals. Some public-domain programs are excellent and can be acquired from computer-user groups for a nominal fee. Commercial programs tend to come with better documentation and marketing support; their prices range from around $20 to more than $200. Often a communications program is sold as part of a package with a modem.

Transferring Files

The most important feature to look for in a communications package is the ability to upload and download files. Sending a file from your personal computer's primary memory or disk to a larger computer is called **uploading**. Retrieving information from a larger computer and storing it as a file on a microcomputer disk is called **downloading**.

This ability to transfer files is important for several reasons. For some applications, such as exchanging computer programs, it is the reason for communicating in the first place. Other activities, such as sending and receiving electronic mail, are completed faster when information can be transferred as a file. Completing tasks quickly can save money; most forms of telecomputing involve charges based on the length of the phone call.

Frills for Convenience

Communications programs also offer frills, features that are nice to have. One such feature is the ability to do limited editing, copying, or deleting of files without leaving the communications program.

Another very popular feature is **auto-dialing**, which allows you to dial telephone numbers by typing them on the keyboard. Auto-dialing isn't possible unless you have a **smart modem**—a modem capable of accepting commands, such as dialing instructions, from your computer. Another useful feature requiring a smart modem is the ability to create and use **dialing directories**, files that store the telephone numbers and communications parameters of remote computers and make it easy to log on to remote computers. (Recall that *logging on* is the process of identifying yourself to a computer; often it involves typing a user identification number and a password.) Good dialing directories store and issue your user ID, password, and the entire log-on sequence. If you want to log on to a remote computer, you just select the computer's name from a list. Then the software-smart modem combination takes over—dialing the number, listening for the carrier signal, and issuing whatever commands are necessary in order to log on. The **auto-answer** feature allows a personal computer to answer incoming calls and connect with another computer without human assistance. This feature is necessary for such unattended operations as storing and forwarding messages.

Communications Protocols

Human communication follows an informal set of rules, which could be called a *communications protocol*. For example, when you're talking to a group of people, it's best to look at them, not at the sky or the ground. When meeting someone new, it's common to shake hands. Interrupting someone in midsentence is generally considered impolite. Computers also use communications protocols, but their protocols are more formal than those people use. Furthermore, computers using different protocols cannot speak directly to each other. One of the most fundamental levels of a computer communications protocol regulates when each computer is allowed to transmit.

Half-Duplex or Full-Duplex

Human beings communicate best when only one person talks at a time. In the computer field, this is called **half-duplex** transmission. Half-duplex transmission limits communication to one direction at a time. If the computer on one end of the line is transmitting, the computer on the other end cannot respond until the entire message is sent. More often microcomputers use **full-duplex** connections, which allow simultaneous two-way transmission. Each end of the line is assigned a different frequency for speaking, so that the "voices" don't interfere with each other.

Long-distance telephone connections are often poor, and static on the line can garble characters. A process called **remote echoing**, or **echo-plex**, provides a simple way to double-check the accuracy of the transmission. The remote computer echoes every character as it is received. Each letter you type travels to the remote computer, is echoed back, and eventually appears on your screen. If the letter you receive back isn't the one you typed, you can backspace and type it again. Depending on the remote computer's workload, the round-trip transit time can be quite noticeable. (Be warned too, that very often—though it is technically incorrect—the term *half-duplex* is used for local echo and *full-duplex*, for remote echo.)

Occasionally, you may log on to a computer that doesn't echo your characters. This can be very disconcerting. All your typing will seem to vanish into a black hole and won't appear on the screen. On the other hand, you may get both local and remote echoes. In this case, everything you type shows up on the screen twice, as in "HHEELLLLOO." To correct these problems, you need to be able to switch the local echo feature on and off.

Asynchronous or Synchronous

Perhaps the most important distinction in transmission mode is between asynchronous and synchronous. Asynchronous transmission is the slower, simpler, and cheaper of the two. **Asynchronous protocols** transmit data one character at a time. The transfer of data is coordinated by preceding each character with a *start bit*—a signal that transmission of a character has begun—and ending it with one or more *stop bits*. The ritual of preceding and following data with start bits, stop bits, and other control data is called **handshaking**. In addition, remote echoing is very frequently used in asynchronous communication.

Synchronous protocols send and receive characters at agreed-upon times, at a fixed rate. They normally send packets of characters instead of just one character at a time. Synchronous communication is faster and more complex than asynchronous methods. Microcomputers rarely use synchronous communication except to interface with IBM host computers or local area networks (see page 287).

Error Correction

Even the best modems and telephone lines occasionally garble characters, producing errors in the information received. As long as this happens rarely—say, for 1 in 10,000 characters—the errors probably won't bother the average user of electronic mail. However, garbled characters are intolerable when program files—as opposed to data files—are transmitted. If even 1 bit in a 20,000-byte program file is received incorrectly, the program is likely to be useless.

Transmission errors can be avoided if both computers use *error detection and correction software*. To detect errors, the transmitting computer sends characters in packets with a **check figure** at the end of each packet; this figure is a mathematical function of the characters in the packet. The receiving computer calculates the same mathematical function on the packet it receives. If the result matches the check figure sent by the transmitting computer, the receiving computer acknowledges successful receipt of the packet. Otherwise, the packet is retransmitted. In short, error detection is accomplished by sending characters in packets with a check figure; error correction is accomplished by retransmitting packets that contained errors.

For error correction and detection to work, both computers must be using the same error-checking protocol. For microcomputers, one of the most popular error detection protocols is XMODEM. It was developed and placed in the public domain by a Chicagoan named Ward Christianson—a fact that says something about the grassroots spirit of the early days of personal computer communications. Most standards in the computer world are set by large corporations or international committees.

Making the Connection

Dialing the telephone number of a computer is the easy part of establishing communications between computers. The hard part is setting your communications software to use the same protocol as the remote computer. Generally, this is done by making selections from a menu for such items as

- *Baud rate*. This depends primarily on the capability of the modems. Typical baud rates are 110, 300, 1,200, and 2,400.
- *Number of start and stop bits*. Most asynchronous links use one start bit and two stop bits per character.
- *Parity setting*. Recall that a *parity bit* is a redundant bit of information that allows the receiving computer to determine whether a character has been garbled in transmission. For example, if the parity setting is *even,* then the sum of all of the character's bits plus the parity bit should be equal to an even number. The possible parity settings are even, odd, and no parity.

Once all the necessary settings have been determined, they can be stored in a dialing directory. Reestablishing communications is then much easier than making the initial connection.

Figure 9.4 The main menu from a bulletin board system.

```
+-----------------------------------------------------------+
|      M ... Select a msg area                              |
|      R ... Read        S ... Quick List      I ... Search |
|      E ... Enter        K ... Kill (delete)               |
+-----------------------------------------------------------+
|      Z ... stats        C ... Change nulls, "more?", etc  |
|      X ... Xpert on/off  U ... List users                 |
|      B ... Read Bulletins                                 |
+-----------------------------------------------------------+
|      F ... FILES subsystem                                |
+-----------------------------------------------------------+
|      Q ... Questionaire  Y ... Yell for sysop             |
|      G ... Goodbye (logoff)                               |
+-----------------------------------------------------------+
| FURTHER HELP: Enter  ?,  then  a  semicolon,  then a  command |
|              listed above. Examples:  "?;R"  "?;F"  "?;Y" |
+-----------------------------------------------------------+

M,B,S,I,R,E,K,Q,F,Y,X,C,Z,U,G, or ? for help:
```

Whom to Talk To?

There is a bewildering diversity of computers, and most of them—particularly larger systems—can be reached by telephone. It would be impossible to describe all the applications of telecomputing, but we'll touch on the major ones related to personal computing.

Bulletin Board Systems

A relative newcomer to the telecommunications world is the *public access message system*, commonly called a **bulletin board system (BBS)**. Almost anyone who uses a personal computer can set up and operate a bulletin board system. All you need is a microcomputer, a telephone line, a smart modem with auto-answer capabilities, and one of the many public-domain BBS programs. Just place messages on the other BBS in your area. Then load the program in your computer and let it answer the incoming calls.

A BBS responds to an incoming call by sending a welcome message and instructions on how to use the system. The instructions are usually easy to follow, though often they are quite condensed inorder to save experienced users time. It helps to have an adventurous spirit. Typically you choose an option from a menu of possible commands listed on the screen (see Figure 9.4). For example, typing [M] might allow you to leave a message on the bulletin board; [R], to read messages; and [D], to download a program. In case you get confused, most systems display help information if you type [?] or [H].

Public messages can be read by anyone who wants to browse through them. Some systems allow private messages to be routed to specific recipients. Typically, as soon as you've logged on, the system informs you of private messages with a statement like

YOU HAVE 3 PIECES OF INCOMING MAIL.

There are more than 1,500 bulletin board systems in the United States. No one knows exactly how many there are, because they can come and go at the flick of a switch. Don't be surprised if your first few calls to a bulletin board result in busy signals. The systems are popular, and most can communicate with only one user at a time.

All bulletin board systems are not alike. Some cater to users of particular types of machines, especially Apple IIs, Macintoshes, CP/M machines, and IBM PCs. Others are operated by manufacturers or vendors to promote their products. A few specialize in religious or sexual messages (DIAL-YOUR-MATCH). But because there is no charge for using a BBS—except for the cost of the phone call, if it is long distance—most systems are used by a wide range of people.

A main use of a BBS is to leave messages for people to read later, instead of talking in "realtime." Some people use a BBS to jot graffiti; others, to discuss technical developments in computers. Most messages are heavily sprinkled with computer jargon. And bulletin board systems are used for more than just sending and receiving messages. Some systems allow you to play games. Many can upload and download programs. Still others allow you to order products or services from the system operator.

Other Personal Computers
Contrary to what the ads for the overnight delivery services say, the fastest way to move documents across the country is not to stuff them into an expensive air-delivered pouch. Instead, they can be transmitted quickly over ordinary phone lines between two personal computers. Each end needs a microcomputer, a modem, and software that supports the uploading and downloading of files. At 300 bps, a double-spaced, ten-page report can be sent in slightly less than ten minutes. At 2,400 bps, it should take about one minute.

Microcomputers don't have to be the same model or brand to communicate over the phone. In fact telephone links between computers can be used to sidestep the compatibility problems associated with floppy disks. Most of today's microcomputers use the same type of floppy disks (5¼-inch), but they use many different recording formats. As a result, disks frequently can't be used to exchange information between different personal computers. For example, without a special program, neither an Apple II nor an IBM PC can read files written by the other, even though both accept the same blank disks. But characters traveling along a telephone line are represented in standardized codes and can be interpreted by the receiving computer regardless of the brand name of the transmitting computer. Communication by phone thus offers a way around the compatibility problem. Although it might seem strange to have an Apple II phone an IBM PC sitting on the other side of an office, it is often the most convenient way to transfer information between the two.

A word of caution is in order. Just because it's possible to exchange files between different machines doesn't mean that the files will be useful after they have been transferred. Most programs that execute on an IBM PC will not execute on an Apple II, and vice versa. It makes more sense to transfer data files, such as spreadsheet template or a word processing document, but even these files can be incompatible, depending on the application programs involved. For example, WordPerfect uses a different format to store documents than does WordStar; to transfer documents between them, you must use a file conversion program.

General-Purpose Mainframes

A microcomputer's ability to emulate a terminal allows you to tap the storage and computation resources of mainframe computers. Perhaps you need to analyze census data stored on magnetic tape. This requires access to a tape drive and good statistical programs. Chances are very good that your personal computer doesn't have either. But, with the right software, your computer can emulate a terminal in order to use a mainframe. Many universities have mainframes with tape drives, excellent statistical programs, and the ability to number-crunch large data sets in short order, solving in minutes statistical problems that would take your personal computer hours or days to solve—if it could solve them at all.

Linking microcomputers with mainframes can transform communications in companies that have many branch offices. For example, a microcomputer in each sales outlet can be programmed to phone the company's mainframe at predetermined times at night, when long-distance rates are low. Each microcomputer might upload the last day's sales activity. After a minute of processing, the mainframe could download a list of replacement parts being shipped and a list of back-ordered parts. Then both computers could hang up, ready for a new sales day.

Information Utilities

Companies that sell time on their timeshared mainframe computers have developed innovative services to attract customers. These companies, called **information utilities**, now offer services ranging from electronic mail to new stories, investment services, biorhythms, and travel guides. Three of the largest information utilities are The Source, operated by the Source Telecomputing Corporation; CompuServe, an H&R Block company; and the Dow Jones News/Retrieval Service, operated by Dow Jones & Company, publishers of *The Wall Street Journal*.

Rates for using the services of information utilities are based mostly on **connect time**, the time you are logged on the utility. The charges go from a low of $5 an hour to well over $100 an hour. Rates are higher during "prime time," which usually coincides with normal business hours. You may be billed at a higher rate if you use a 1,200- or 2,400-bps modem instead of a 300-bps modem, but a high-speed modem may pay for itself if you can accomplish your work faster. Other fees can include one-time registration fees, monthly minimum usage fees, data storage charges (based on the number of bytes stored, if any), added charges for reading newsletters or searching databases, and charges for mailing letters and telegrams.

Here is a list of a few of the services offered by The Source.

- *Communications.* Allows sending electronic mail to the computer mailboxes of other subscribers, "chatting" with another subscriber through a keyboard-to-keyboard conversation, participating in on-line computer conferences, posting and reading messages on public bulletin boards, sending Western Union Mailgram messages, and mailing first-class letters.

- *Business and investment.* Includes instant quotations of stock and bond prices, portfolio analysis, employment services, and an electronic version of the *Washington Post.*

- *News and sports.* News stories from a variety of wire services, including United Press International (UPI), are stored for seven days. You can search for the news you want by using keywords.

- *Consumer services.* Offers electronic catalog shopping for everything from air conditioners to Zenith utility software. Also includes movie reviews.

- *Travel services.* Includes complete airline schedules for all domestic and most international flights, as well as Mobil Restaurant and Hotel Guides.

One unique service provided by information utilities is the ability to search quickly through large volumes of information and find all items that match the criteria you specify. Information utilities that specialize in storing and searching information are often call *encyclopedic databases, bibliograpic databases,* or *on-line databases.* There are over 1,000 on-line databases. Most cater to specific types of information—legal, medical, business, and so on. Figure 9.5 illustrates how powerful this type of service can be. It shows the result of a search of KNOWLEDGE INDEX, a bibliographic database operated by Dialog Information Services. In less than two minutes, KNOWLEDGE INDEX searched more than 500,000 citations from 2,300 journals and magazines to find two articles discussing both personal computers and energy conservation.

But searching an on-line database isn't as easy as Figure 9.5 might lead you to believe. Asking the proper queries requires knowledge of the database's command structure and experience with what requests are likely to produce useful results. Beginners tend to ask questions that yield either no matches with their criteria or hundreds of matches. Neither result is particularly useful. Costs can accumulate quickly when you're paying from $20 to $100 an hour to do searches. Some searches are therefore best left to trained professionals, such as librarians or consultants. However, some on-line databases offer not only manuals, but also excellent training courses on how to use their system. Figure 9.6 illustrates another approach: using a communications package tailored to the specific database being used.

Figure 9.5 A sample search of KNOWLEDGE INDEX, a bibliographic database.

```
?    BEGIN COMPUTERS AND ELECTRONICS ◄─────────────────        I want to search COMPUTERS AND
Now in COMPUTERS AND ELECTRONICS                                ELECTRONICS, the index to computer
(INSPEC copr. IEE)                                              and electronics magazines
Search No. 7482945

?    FIND PERSONAL COMPUTER AND ENERGY CONSERVATION ◄──        Find citations that discuss both personal
                                                                computers and energy conservation
     440  PERSONAL COMPUTER
     699  ENERGY CONSERVATION                                   There are 440 citations on personal
S1     2  PERSONAL COMPUTER AND ENERGY CONSERVATION            computers, 699 citations on energy
                                                                conservation, and two articles that
                                                                discuss both topics

?    DISPLAY S1 ◄──────────────────────────────────────        Show me the first citation

     ENERGY CONSERVATION WITH A MICROCOMPUTER ◄─────────        Article title
     JACKSON, D.R.; CALLAHAN, J.M.
     UNIV. OF CONNECTICUT ENERGY CENTER, STORRS, CT, USA
     BYTE (USA)  VOL. 6  NO. 7   178-208   JULY 1981 ◄───       Name of periodical
     Document Type:  JOURNAL PAPER                              Date
     (4 Refs)                                                   Abstract or Summary
     PRESENTS SEVERAL TOOLS THAT CAN BE USED IN CONJUNCTION WITH A PERSONAL COMPUTER
     —TOOLS THAT WILL ALLOW ONE TO UNDERSTAND ENERGYUSE PATTERNS AND CHANGE THESE
     PATTERNS WITH SOUND TECHNICAL AND ECONOMIC DECISIONS. TH     Here is all the information you need to
     PROVIDING A BACKGROUND ON HEAT TRANSFER AND HOW IT GOVERNS   obtain the article—the authors, title,
     IN A BUILDING. THEY OUTLINE AN EXAMPLE THAT DEMONSTRATES THE magazine, issue date and page number,
     MUST PERFORM TO DETERMINE THE YEARLY ENERGY REQUIREMENTS FC  plus an abstract summarizing the content
     INCLUDED IN THIS EXAMPLE IS A PROGRAM THAT CAN BE USED TO SIMPLIF THESE CALCULATIONS.
     THEY ALSO DISCUSS ENERGY CONSERVATION OPTIONS AVAILABLE AND HOW TO DETERMINE THE
     ECONOMIC PAYBACK TO IMPLEMENT THESE MEASURES.
        Keywords:  HEAT TRANSFER; PERSONAL COMPUTING; COMPLETE COMPUTER PROGRAMS;
     MICROCOMPUTER; PERSONAL COMPUTER; ENERGY-USE PATTERNS; HEAT TRANSFER; ENERGY
     REQUIREMENTS; PROGRAM
                                                                Keywords—These terms can be used
                                                                to find more articles on these concepts.

?    LOGOFF ◄──────────────────────────────────────────        I have enough information for now;
Leaving COMPUTERS AND ELECTRONICS                               please end this session
6/29/82   11:38:17 EST
0.031 Hours   $0.74   User U99999
```

COMPUTER NETWORKS

So far, our discussion of computer communications has been limited to simple point-to-point transmissions. A point-to-point communications link is like a conversation between two people. In contrast, a computer network links computers together in a web that allows transmissions among many devices, like a discussion among a roomful of people. A computer **network** is a collection of communicating computers and the communications media connecting them.

For example, a **local area network (LAN)** links computers with other computing equipment within a limited area—for instance, within one building or industrial plant. By connecting computers, a LAN can bridge the gap between numerous microcomputers, minis, mainframes, printers, and large-capacity storage disks. Some local area networks are established to allow many microcomputers to share an expensive peripheral device, such as a large hard disk or a high-quality

Figure 9.6 Texas Instruments' NaturalLink communications package. This package makes it easy to query the Dow Jones News/Retrieval Service. The NaturalLink screen is divided into windows, each containing a list of the words or phrases that will make up a portion of the command. The user simply selects one of the options and presses the [Return] key to make a selection. Based on what the user has chosen, the next set of options is displayed. Each element selected builds a portion of the English question used to obtain information from the Dow Jones News/Retrieval database.

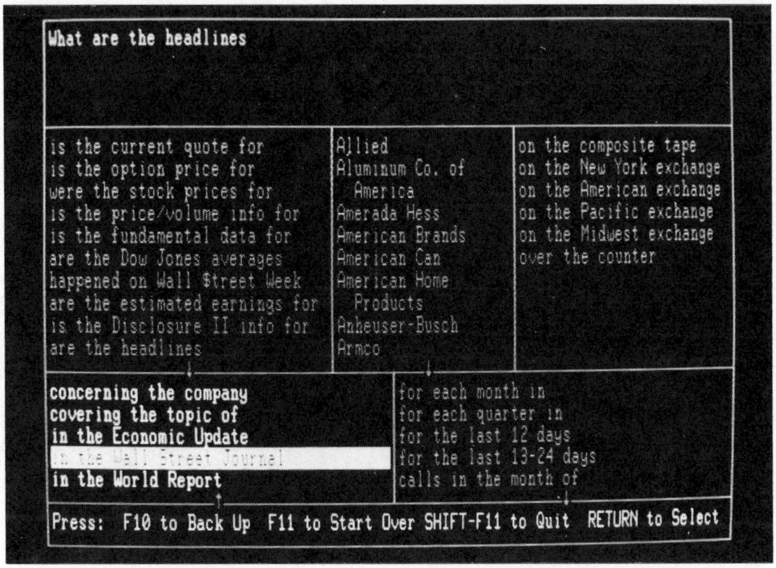

```
What are the headlines


is the current quote for       Allied              on the composite tape
is the option price for        Aluminum Co. of      on the New York exchange
were the stock prices for        America           on the American exchange
is the price/volume info for   Amerada Hess        on the Pacific exchange
is the fundamental data for    American Brands     on the Midwest exchange
are the Dow Jones averages     American Can        over the counter
happened on Wall $treet Week   American Home
are the estimated earnings for   Products
is the Disclosure II info for  Anheuser-Busch
are the headlines              Armco

concerning the company          for each month in
covering the topic of           for each quarter in
in the Economic Update          for the last 12 days
in the Wall Street Journal      for the last 13-24 days
in the World Report             calls in the month of

Press:  F10 to Back Up  F11 to Start Over  SHIFT-F11 to Quit   RETURN to Select
```

printer. Other networks are established so that information can be shared conveniently, as in an interoffice electronic mail system.

A network is characterized by the media it uses to carry messages (wires, cables, microwaves, and so forth); the way the network links devices together (in a star, ring, or other pattern); and the expansiveness of the network (whether it is limited to one building or spans a continent). In addition, the network's communications protocols determine how and when devices can communicate. We will explore all of these characteristics, but first we will describe a basic shift in the costs of communications and computing that encouraged the development of networks.

The New Economics of Computing

From the 1950s until the 1970s, it was substantially less expensive to buy one large computer than to purchase two smaller computers that, combined, have the same processing power. To get the most from their computing dollars, organizations consolidated their purchases by centralizing data processing operations. Large host computers were timeshared among many users. Early systems hooked all equipment to the central computer, which was responsible for controlling all communications. In this way, early corporate users spread the cost of expensive

Figure 9.7 The relative costs of communications and computing.

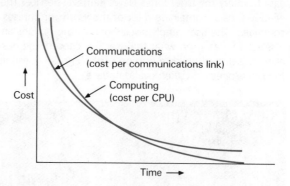

mainframes over many users, who shared access to the same equipment and information. Most large computer systems still follow this pattern, but the cost of the links needed by centralized computing centers hasn't been falling as rapidly as the cost of computing, as shown in Figure 9.7. As a result, the cost of providing each user with a personal computer is less than the cost of connecting an equivalent number of terminals to a timeshared mainframe.

The rush to buy microcomputers in place of terminals has created a major shift from centralized to decentralized, or distributed, computing. In a **distributed computing** environment, geographically separate computers are connected in a network to work on a common task. This shift toward microcomputers wasn't caused exclusively by economics; microcomputers have many advantages over timeshared computing. They offer greater control to the user, friendlier operation, and a faster response for most tasks.

But decentralized microcomputers have a major disadvantage: they are harder to link together to share information and peripheral devices. As the cost of the actual computer has plunged, the cost of peripheral devices has grown as a percentage of the total system. Expensive laser printers; high-precision graphical devices, such as plotters, digitizers, and color displays; and the relatively high cost of storage devices have contributed to the need for interconnected workstations rather than separate microcomputers. The economics of computing has dictated a new way to think about computing: share the peripherals and data, but disperse the processors to the people who need processing time and instantaneous response.

Communications Media

Many characteristics of a computer network—its speed, cost, and physical range—are determined largely by the media it uses to transmit messages.

Most telephone systems use **twisted-pair wire** to connect phones to the central switching station. Twisted-pair wire is inexpensive and easy to run through the walls in an office building. Its major disadvantage is its relatively low **band-**

width; that is, its low capacity for carrying information. Twisted-pair wire is used in low-speed LANs (1 megabit per second or less).

A **coaxial cable** is a round cable in which one wire is a sleeve that shields the other, like cable television wire. Coaxial cable offers much greater speed (up to 100 megabits per second) and is impervious to external electrical signals. It is used in high-speed networks in which the cost of the cable isn't a great concern.

A **fiber-optic cable** is a bundle of strands of glass, which conduct laser light. Fiber-optic cables are rapidly replacing metal cables, because they are lighter, cheaper, and capable of extremely high transmission speeds. A standard coaxial cable can transmit 5,000 voice conversations at once, whereas a fiber-optic cable can transmit ten times as many.

Wires and cables are suitable for connecting computers and devices when they are in the same room or building, but what about geographically distributed computer networks? Telephones and modems provide a low-speed method of connecting remote computers, but large corporations utilize other methods as well. A **dedicated** or **leased line** is a special telephone line that connects a pair of computers. The advantages of a dedicated line are increased speed and continuous availability. No dialing is required, nor is a busy signal possible. A dedicated, point-to-point line is useful when large amounts of information are to be transmitted on a continual basis.

Microwave relay stations are used to transmit data and voice signals between distant locations. *Microwaves* are extremely short radio waves that have a high bandwidth, but they cannot bend around the earth's curvature. A series of relay stations can connect, say, corporate headquarters with dozens of branch offices. Renting time on microwave relay stations may be cheaper than renting a dedicated line.

A **ground station** may be used to send and receive information by satelite. Computers are excellent users of communications satellites because of their fast and constant transmission rates. Mainframes communicate around the world through communications satellite *transducers,* which are similar to radio antennas. Because each communications satellite has many transducers, it is possible to rent one just as a company might rent a dedicated telephone line.

Transmission Efficiency

Most high-speed transmission methods, such as microwaves or satellites, cost the same amount of money regardless of whether the entire transmission capacity is used. For example, it isn't possible to install *half* of a satellite ground station. This has led to the development of clever ways to use the transmission capacity of high-speed communications links.

A **multiplexer** is a communications device that spreads the cost of a high-speed line over many users. A multiplexer timeshares the communications line by merging data from many users into the same line. There are two types of multiplexers: *time-division* and *frequency-division.*

A **time-division multiplexer** combines many low-speed channels into one high-speed transmission by interweaving them in time slots. Channel 1 is allocated time slot 1; channel 2, time slot 2; and so forth. The time slots are strung together like beads in a necklace and sent as one high-speed signal. When the signal is received, the low-speed signals are split out again and sent to their destinations. A **frequency-division multiplexer** divides the high-speed signal into frequency bands, like the frequencies used by FM radio stations. Each channel is assigned a certain band, and the composite signal is sent. At the receiving end, the different channels are split out from their frequency bands and sent to their destinations.

Broadband transmission uses frequency-division multiplexing to transmit text, data, and video or audio signals simultaneously. This allows computers to handle a two-way video conference with a dispersed group of people who want to display computer-generated graphics as well as hear each other talk. In contrast, in **baseband** transmission, the entire communications spectrum is dedicated to one form of information.

A **concentrator** is an "intelligent" multiplexer; it can perform preliminary operations on data before they are multiplexed and sent to another computer. Thus, it is an I/O device that unburdens the mainframe computer by taking care of many details of message transmission.

A **front-end computer** is a step beyond a concentrator in intelligence. A front-end computer is a small computer located between a mainframe and other devices communicating with it. It handles all of the communications chores of the mainframe. For example, it acknowledges receipt of a message, does multiplexing and demultiplexing, and checks for transmission errors. Some front-end computers perform rudimentary processing similar to word processing.

Network Topology

The efficiency, reliability, and cost of a computer network are also affected by its topology, or interconnection pattern. For example, a simple point-to-point network topology connects a pair of computers together with a cable.

A more flexible point-to-point topology is obtained by linking computing equipment with a T-switch and cables (see Figure 9.8). With a **T-switch**, you can rearrange the connections between computing equipment by turning a dial on the T-switch instead of unplugging and plugging cables. T-switched are inexpensive, ranging in cost from $50 to over $300. Their most common application is to allow several microcomputers or terminals to share a peripheral device, such as a printer or plotter. Printers are frequently shared in this way, because they are used intermittently. By using a T-switch, it is often possible for several people in an office to share one letter-quality printer with little inconvenience. T-switch networks require human intervention to route signals to their destination. For this reason, most people don't call them computer networks, reserving the term for collections of computers and cables that can route messages automatically among devices.

Figure 9.8 Two T-switched networks.

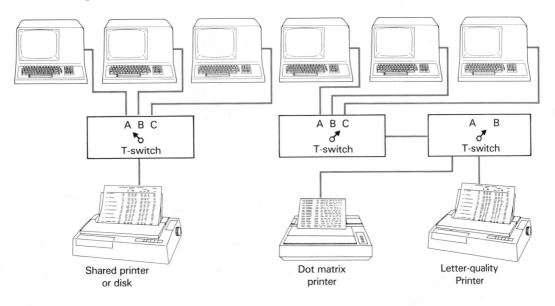

A **star network** consists of a central computer surrounded by one or more satellite computers (see Figure 9.9). The central computer is sometimes called the *hub,* or *central server,* because all requests for data must go through the central computer. Star networks are simple but not very reliable. If the central server breaks down, the entire network is disabled in the same way the failure of a timeshared computer system disables all users. Star networks are the dominant topology for mainframe computers and their peripherals, as well as for telephone systems.

A **ring network** consists of a cluster of computers connected together by a ring (see Figure 9.10). In a ring network, failure of one computer does not prevent the other computers from interacting with the remaining computers. Rings are sometimes used along with a *token-passing protocol* to coordinate access to the network. A *token* is a control signal that determines which computer is allowed to transmit information. The token is passed from one computer to another enabling each computer to use the network. Because only one token exists in the network, only one computer can use the ring at a time.

A **bus network** contains a single, bidirectional cable connecting two or more computers (see Figure 9.11). Information is passed between any two computers, one pair at a time, by seizing control of the common wire, or *bus,* transmitting a message, and then releasing the bus. Buses do not use the transmission media as efficiently as other network topologies, because traffic congestion can delay use of the bus.

Figure 9.9 A star network. A central server controls the network.

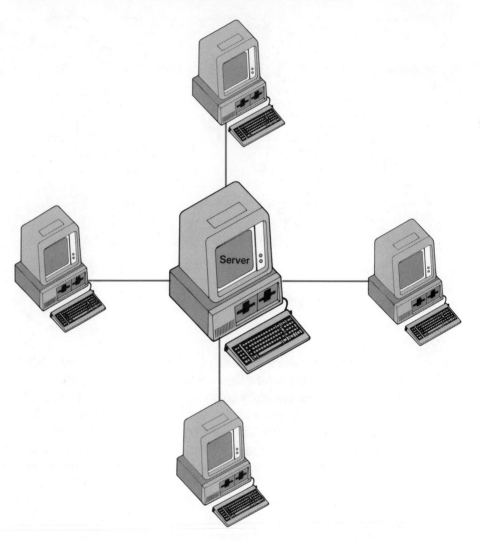

Bus networks often use a **CSMA** (*c*arrier-*s*ensed *m*ultiple-*a*ccess) **protocol** to direct traffic on the bus. A CSMA protocol is similar to a party line in a rural telephone system. On a party-line phone, everyone is allowed to make calls on the same line, as long as no one else is using the line. In a CSMA network, each device has access to the network when the network isn't busy. Two methods are commonly used to prevent devices from transmitting messages at the same time. With a CSMA/CA protocol (CA stands for *c*ollision *a*voidance) special circuitry in the LAN guarantees that only one device can transmit at a time. In contrast, a CSMA/CD protocol (CD stands for *c*ollision *d*etection) allows devices to begin transmitting any time the network isn't busy. Occasionally, two or more devices

Figure 9.10 A ring network. Messages are passed from one computer to the next along the ring.

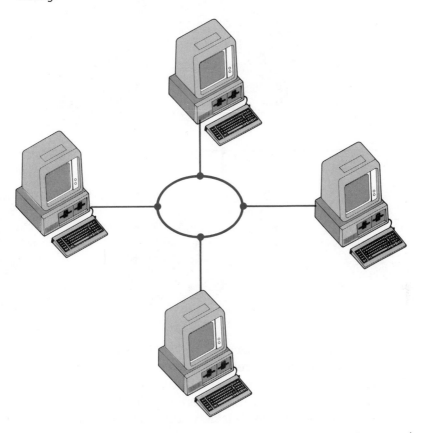

might begin to transmit messages at the same time, causing the messages to be garbles. If this happens, each device stops transmitting and generates a random number specifying how long it must wait before it can try transmitting again. The difference between these two protocols is subtle, but a CSMA/CA protocol becomes more efficient as greater demands are placed on the LAN.

Bus networks offer more flexibility in how devices are wired together than star or ring networks. The simplicity of CSMA protocols (such as the Ethernet standard developed by Xerox) has made the bus topology very popular for small networks.

Packet-Switching Networks

Telecomputing can be expensive, especially if you make long-distance calls during the day when rates are high. Instead, hobbyists do nearly all their telecomputing locally or in the evenings and on weekends. But there's another way of reducing telephone charges: you can use a **packet-switching network**, such as GTE's Telenet or Tymshare's Tymnet, which sends information in the form of packets.

Figure 9.11   A bus network. Messages vie for time on the shared bus.

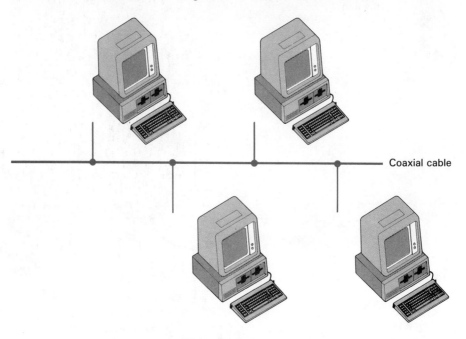

Coaxial cable

Using a packet-switching network is just like dialing a remote computer directly—except that the response time is slightly slower, the log-on procedure is more complicated, and the cost is usually lower. In major cities (and some smaller ones), firms like GTE and Tymshare have local numbers that you can dial to connect your computer to their network. If you don't live in an area served by a packet-switching network, you type the identifier of the remote computer you want. Then the packet-switching network takes over and routes information through the network between your personal computer or terminal and the remote computer.

Packet-switching networks aren't free, but using one is almost always cheaper than making a long-distance call of the same length. The networks can charge less than the regular long-distance rates, because they use the telephone system more efficiently than ordinary telephone calls. Most of a conventional telecommunications call is spent waiting while the computer user is thinking, reading, or typing at a slow rate. Packet-switching networks covercome this handicap by sharing the same communications channel among more than one user. Information is sent through the network in packets that include the packet's source and destination. Routing decisions are made by concentrators that send packets to each other over semipermanent telephone connections based on the addresses contained in the packet.

Using a packet-switching network in conjunction with the major information utilities is particularly convenient. Because these utilities have prior agreements with packet-switching networks, you don't need a contractual arrangement with the

Figure 9.12 A local area network based on coupling devices to a common bus.

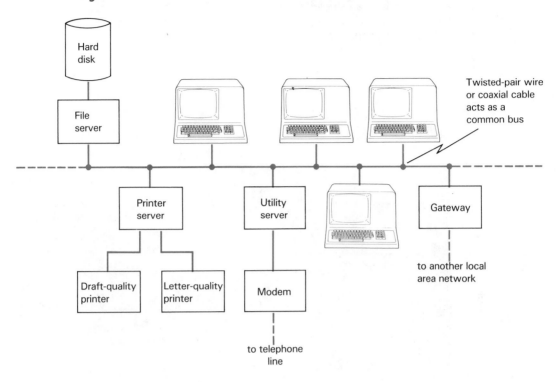

network; the utility does the billing. Most utilities bundle the cost of using the network into their basic rate; others charge you for it as a separate item on your monthly bill.

Local Area Networks (LANs)

We noted earlier that a LAN is used to share peripherals and data among computers in close proximity. The LAN automatically routes messages among the devices on the network. A unique address is given to each device attached to the network. When one computer sends a message to another computer, the message is formatted into one or more packets in a manner roughly similar to that used by packet-switching networks. The packet contains the address of both the source and destination, so that the LAN will know where to send the message.

Figure 9.12 shows one configuration for a local area network: all of the network's devices, or *nodes*, are coupled to a common bus. The AppleTalk network shown in Figure 9.13 is an example of such a network. The network in Figure 9.12 includes the following:

- **File server.** A file server controls a hard disk and connects it to the network (see Figure 9.14). The file server is likely to establish a private storage space on the disk for each user, as well as an area for public files. It may also keep track of passwords for files.

Figure 9.13 The AppleTalk Personal Network allows up to 32 devices to be connected to a CSMA/CA local area network limited to 230 kilobits per second. (a) Several Macintosh computers sharing access to a LaserWriter printer. All that is needed to connect a Macintosh to the network is (b) the $50 cable and connector box.

A.

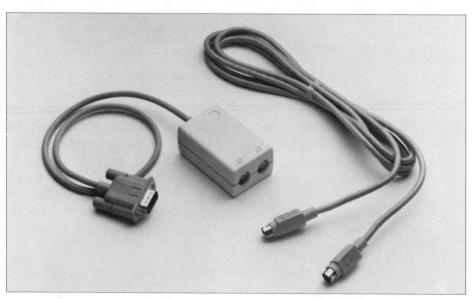

B.

13. Tapes are used to store infrequently used data and to back-up data stored on disk drives in case of disk failure. Only one reel of tape can be mounted at a time on each tape drive.

14. Most magnetic tapes are *off-line,* meaning they cannot be read by the computer unless they are mounted on a tape drive by a computer operator. Storing data on tape is inexpensive; a 2,400-foot tape costs about $20 and can store over 100 megabytes.

15,16. Law enforcement and health-care workers need quick answers from large databases. Usually these requirements are met by connecting desktop terminals to a central host computer. The connection can be made with a dedicated wire running directly between the two, with a permanently leased telephone line, or with dial-up telephone service. Often the terminal and the host computer are linked by a number of intermediary communications devices such as concentrators, modems, and local area networks.

LOCAL AREA NETWORKS

Local area networks allow devices in a limited area to be connected so that any device on the network can communicate with any other device.

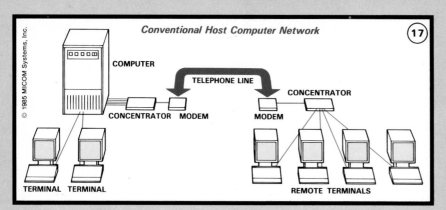

Conventional Host Computer Network

© 1985 MICOM Systems, Inc.

COMPUTER

TELEPHONE LINE

CONCENTRATOR

CONCENTRATOR MODEM MODEM

TERMINAL TERMINAL

REMOTE TERMINALS

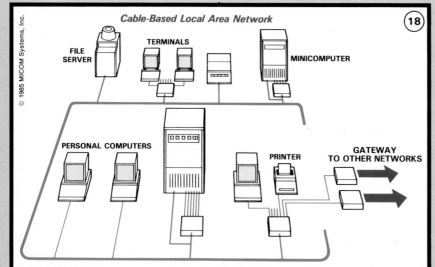

Cable-Based Local Area Network

© 1985 MICOM Systems, Inc.

FILE SERVER TERMINALS MINICOMPUTER

PERSONAL COMPUTERS PRINTER GATEWAY TO OTHER NETWORKS

17. In a conventional computer network, all peripheral devices are connected to the host computer. If you want one terminal to talk to another, the message must pass through the host computer first. To use the telephone lines efficiently, concentrators and other communications devices splice messages from several terminals onto one telephone line.

18. In a cable-based local area network, all devices are connected to one cable. Often the cable is similar to the coaxial cable used in cable TV systems. Local area networks use a number of methods to prevent the electronic "voices" of the devices from colliding. Local area networks are very reliable; unless the cable is cut or damaged, the entire network cannot fail.

19. With a local area network, an office work group using personal computers can share a hard disk drive and printer. Networks also allow users to send and receive electronic mail.

TELEPHONE TERMINALS

Nowhere is the consolidation of communications and computing more evident than in the development of telephone terminals.

20. This personal communications terminal combines a powerful terminal and a full-featured telephone in one unit. The phone features a built-in speakerphone for hands-free calls, the ability to enter and revise a phone list with 200 entries using the retractable keyboard, and a built-in calculator. The unit can also emulate a DEC VT100 terminal or an IBM 3270 terminal.

21. This telephone unit has all the capabilities of the terminal shown in photo 20, but it also contains a personal computer compatible with an IBM PC. Mostly hidden by the man's arm are two floppy disk drives. Inside the unit are a microprocessor that can run IBM PC software for business applications and 512KB of memory.

22. A sales clerk telephones the National Data Corporation (NDC) to obtain credit card authorization for a customer. NDC's network links the consumer, the bank, and the merchant for fast and efficient credit service.

23. A waitress in a Tokyo restaurant uses CATNET, a nationwide credit verification system introduced by IBM in Japan.

OTHER TERMINALS

25. You can temporarily convert virtually any personal computer into an intelligent computer terminal by adding a modem and a communications program. This allows the personal computer to be connected to a host computer to run applications such as order entry, electronic mail, or electronic funds transfer.

24. This hand-held portable data terminal can be connected directly to telephone lines with a standard RJ11 snap connector for data transmissions with a host computer. Its clock can "wake up" the terminal and automatically dial a telephone number at a preset time, allowing transmissions to occur unattended late at night, when long distance rates are low. Data can be entered through the keyboard or with a variety of bar code readers. The terminal operates for up to a hundred hours on four AA alkaline batteries. It provides up to 16KB of data storage.

26. Researchers at RCA Labs are testing teletext systems. These systems can be used to display news and weather information, present stock market quotations, or advertise shopping specials. A teletext system transmits data to television sets by encoding it in the vertical blanking interval (the black bar visible when vertical hold isn't working) of a video frame. Then a teletext decoder in the television decodes the data into text and graphics to be displayed on the screen.

Figure 9.14 A Corvus Systems hard disk file server attached to the Corvus Omninet, a network that supports up to 64 devices with a data transmission rate of 1 megabit per second. The connection is made with a simple plug on the end of a twisted-pair wire.

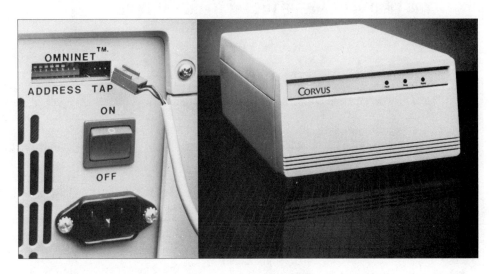

- **Utility server.** A utility server allows everyone on the network to use several peripheral devices, such as a modem or a plotter.
- **Printer server.** A printer server shares access to the network's printers among all users. It is likely to include a memory buffer so that files can be accepted faster than the printer can print them.
- **Gateway.** A gateway allows devices on one network to communicate with devices on another network.

Because local area networks use digital transmission and cover a limited physical range (usually less than several miles), they can provide fast transmission rates. Less expensive, lower-speed networks use twisted-pair wiring. Even these networks transmit from 50 kilobits to 1 megabit per second—which is much faster than the usual speed of telecommunications over public telephone lines. Faster networks employ the same coaxial cable used in cable television, to provide transmission rates from 1 to 100 megabits per second. At 10 million bits per second, the text in this book could be transmitted in 1 second. Such ultrafast transmission rates are important if many devices must send or receive data at about the same time.

To increase the speed of the network, some LANs use a **cache**, a memory buffer. The cache stores copies of the most recently retrieved records—hoping to save a transmission and a disk-read. It is common for software to use file records more than once during a file-update cycle. If the desired record is in the cache of the computer that wants it, the overhead associated with message transmission and file retrieval is avoided.

THE COMING OF AGE OF THE LOCAL-AREA NETWORK

The first IBM Personal Computer local-area networks (LAN), following close on the heels of IBM's debut of the PC in 1981, were unimpressive collections of cabling and interface boards that enabled a group of IBM PCs to share peripherals such as hard disks and printers.

While a few adventurous companies installed the early offerings of vendors such as Corvus Systems, Inc., 3Com Corp. and Nestar Systems, Inc., the vast majority felt that any potential savings from peripheral sharing were offset by the expense and hassle of installing and maintaining these systems. A 1984 report by Framingham, Mass.–based research firm International Data Corp. found that 15,800 PC LANs were shipped in 1983.. Considering that 1983 IBM PC shipments totaled $1.5 billion, according to Future Computing, Inc., a very small percentage of PCs were being networked a few years ago.

Three developments that occurred in 1984 and 1985 made PC LANs a far more viable alternative to business users:

■ The emergence of two standard network operating systems: MS-DOS 3.1, introduced by Microsoft Corp. in the fall of 1984, and Netware, which Novell, Inc., released in November 1983. IBM PC software vendors could then

develop versions of their packages that, by interfacing with MS-DOS 3.1 or Netware, could operate over all the network products that support either of those operating systems.

■ The appearance of powerful file servers that let PCs concurrently access and update the same files—in contrast to early servers that just let users store their data on dedicated, floppy-size partitions of the same hard disk. The servers turned PC LANs into viable departmental systems, permitting users to share data and peripherals and exchange electronic mail.

■ The emergence of gateways and bridges. Gateways gave users access first to IBM Systems Network Architecture and recently to IBM System/36 and 38 processors. Bridges link local networks into a corporatewide system.

"Companies can increase user productivity by making mainframe information available on PCs," says Merv Adrian of the New York PC Users Group. "It's much cheaper to do it via a LAN, because you only need to equip one PC, the gateway server, with a terminal emulation board."

Source: Elisabeth Horwitt, *Computerworld*, 3 November 1986, p. 13.

Print spooling is a software feature of networks that also save time. Normally, when two or more computers want to use the same printer, one must wait while the other uses the printer. But with **print spooling**, the second computer is allowed to continue as if it also had the printer, by *spooling* its output into a disk file. Then, when the first computer finishes with the printer, the spooled print file is copied to the printer. In the meantime, the second computer can continue without waiting.

From a user's viewpoint, the complexity of the LAN's communications protocol and cabling methods is hidden by layers of software. The software makes the "other" disks and printers on the LAN appear to be connected directly to your computer. For example, suppose your computer has two floppy disk drives (drives

A and B) and the LAN has a hard disk file server (drive F). To copy a file from the file server to one of your disks, you would use the same basic COPY command as you would to copy a file from one floppy to the other. Instead of copying from drive A to drive B, you might copy from drive F to drive B.

Special software for LANs can turn your computer into a mailbox for sending and receiving memos or a calendar for scheduling appointments. For example, if you want to schedule a meeting with three other people, you might run a special program on your computer that copies their appointment files to your computer, searches all files (yours and the three others) for a mutually agreeable time, and then updates the files with the meeting's time and place.

LANs are so powerful that they threaten to take over the conventional functions of timeshared mainframes within large organizations. Because each computer in a LAN has its own memory and processor, a LAN that connects 30 microcomputers can provide more computing power than a minicomputer. But you should also keep in mind the limitations of LANs. A LAN is restricted in size, and LANs can become as bogged down as mainframes can if there is too much activity on the network.

Network Layers

Because networking is a rapidly changing area, it's filled with nonstandard parts, diverse approaches, and general confusion. For this reason, the International Standards Organization has proposed the ISO Reference Model for Open System Connection, or simply **ISO layers**, as a standard for describing and categorizing network components. The ISO layers are seven levels found in all networks: physical, link, network, transport, session, presentation, and application.

The *physical layer* defines the electrical characteristics of signals passed between the computer and communications devices, such as a modem or a network interface adapter. The voltage levels, baud rate, and so forth are determined at the physical level. The *link layer* controls error detection and correction, transmission over a single data line between computers, and the nature of the interconnection, such as whether it is synchronous or asynchronous. The *network layer* constructs packets of data, sends them across the network, and "unpacks" the message at the receiving end. The first three layers are wrapped together when the telephone and a modem are used. The network layer is the collection of telephone lines and switching equipment maintained by the telephone company. The link and physical layers are embedded in the modem and telephone sets at either end of the telephone connection.

The *transport level* transfers control from one computer to the next across the network. The *session layer* establishes, maintains, and terminates logical connections for data transfer, called *virtual circuits*. A **virtual circuit** temporarily links two devices in the network in a manner analogous to the way a telephone call links two telephones. The session layer also enciphers data for security purposes (if necessary) and establishes the necessary handshaking, such as full-duplex and message formatting. The *presentation layer* defines control codes, how data should be formatted, and other attributes of the message being transmitted. For example, the presentation layer defines what is a control code to clear the screen. It may also define how data is to be formatted to conform to the format expected by the receiving computer's software. Finally, the *application layer* consists of software being run on the computer connected to the network. The operating system software of a microcomputer falls into the "application layer" as far as the network is concerned. Thus, copying a file from one computer to another computer on the same network is an application-layer operation.

As an example of how these layers interact, consider the problem of reading a record from a file on a remote computer's disk. Suppose the request to read the file comes from a database management program on a microcomputer; thus, it originates at the application level. The read request is passed to presentation-level software on the microcomputer and is converted into the format defined by the presentation layer of the network being used. The formatted read request is passed on to the session-layer control program, which translates the logical name of the remote computer (such as drive F) into a physical name (such as device number 12,539), selects the protocol to be used (full- or half-duplex), and passes the message on to the transport layer. The transport and network layers work together to form one or more packets out of the message. The transport and network control programs guide the packet through the network. When the transport layer guides the packet containing the read request to the remote computer, it uses the link and physical layers. The link layer simply establishes an error-free connection from the sender to the receiver. Link control on a CSMA network would involve collision detection or avoidance, error detection, and retransmission of messages received in error. The read-request packet is passed through physical circuitry that obeys the physical laws of electronics—transmission rates, coding conventions, and protocol. Once the packet reaches the remote computer, the transport and network software running on the remote computer unpack the message and pass it on to the session layer. The message works its way through the presentation layer to the application layer of the remote computer, where the read operation is done. Finally, the process is reversed to return the file record to the requesting computer.

All future computer networks are likely to follow these ISO layers. This should make it easier to connect equipment from different manufacturers to the same network and for messages to be transferred from one type of network to another. But the techniques, performance, and cost of each new network will vary depending on the cleverness of the implementation.

SUMMARY

The goal of telecommunications is to transmit information over long distances by using electromagnetic signals. Through telecommunications, a microcomputer can be connected over the phone lines to virtually any other computer.

Data are transmitted through wires by using digital and analog signals. Digital signals are used in computers, in most local area networks, and in some parts of the phone system. Generally, analog signals are used for computer transmissions over ordinary phone lines. Microcomputers can be attached to the public telephone system with a modem, which makes the conversion back and forth between digital and analog signals.

Communications software makes a microcomputer behave like a computer terminal. Along with enabling microcomputers to emulate dumb terminals, an important capability of communications software is uploading and downloading files.

The purpose of a communications protocol is to establish a set of rules for computing equipment to follow while transmitting and receiving data. The protocol determines whether data are transmitted with full- or half-duplex operation, synchronously or asynchronously, with or without error detection and correction, in packets or one character at a time, and with local echoing or remote echoing. Computer networking has been heavily influenced by the relative cost of various types of computers. Until the early 1980s, it was cheapest to buy large mainframe computers and hook up many terminals to them. Thus, the first computer networks were designed to connect terminals to a central mainframe computer that controlled all of the network's activity. These networks were based on a star topology and were inherently unreliable because whenever the central computer failed, the entire network was brought down.

The emergence of powerful, low-cost microcomputers has created a new economics of computing. Now mainframe computers are primarily used for data and file management tasks, leaving as many other processing tasks for microcomputers as possible. This change toward decentralized computing has led to networks that can pass messages directly between any two nodes on the network. Thus, most recently developed network systems use a ring or bus topology. A node on one of these networks can fail without bringing down the rest of the network. Generally, bus and ring networks are easier to install than star networks, because you can tap into them at any point without running a new wire back to the central server.

Computers in a limited physical area can be coupled with other electronic equipment in a local area network. These networks provide faster data transfer than public telephone systems and allow many computers to share peripheral devices and information.

KEY TERMS

acoustic coupler

asynchronous protocol

auto-answer

auto-dial

bandwidth

baseband

baud rate

broadband

bulletin board system (BBS)

bus network

cache

check figure

coaxial cable

concentrator

connect time

CSMA protocol

dedicated (leased) line

demodulation

dialing directory

direct-connect modem

distributed computing

download

dumb terminal

fiber-optic cable

file server

frequency-division multiplexer

frequency modulation (FM)

front-end computer

full-duplex

gateway

ground station

half-duplex

handshaking

information utility

ISO layers

local area network (LAN)

local echo

microwave relay station

modulation

multiplexer

network

packet-switching network

printer server

print spooling

protocol

remote echoing

ring network

smart modem

star network

synchronous protocol

telecommunications

terminal emulator

time-division multiplexer

T-switch

twisted-pair wire

upload

utility server

virtual circuit

■ DISCUSSION QUESTIONS

1. How does digital communication differ from analog communication?

2. What are the relative merits of acoustic couplers versus direct-connect modems?

3. What are some situations in which uploading or downloading capabilities might be important?

4. How does a protocol control the exchange of information between computers? What protocols are used by personal computers?

5. What type of remote computer would you telephone if you wanted to
   a. try out telecommunications at the least cost?
   b. determine the price of gold on December 13, 1986?
   c. run a 10,000-line simulation program written in FORTRAN?
   d. send a first-class letter to your grandmother in Alaska that will arrive within two days?
   e. exchange computer programs with another personal computer user?
   f. find out the final score of a basketball game that ended about an hour ago?

6. What is the difference between a concentrator and a multiplexer?

7. How does a CSMA/CA protocol compare with a party-line telephone connection?

8. Why can a packet-switching network charge rates lower than those for normal long-distance calls?

9. What are the major reasons for establishing a local area network?

EXERCISES

1. Examine the manual provided with a communications package. List the package's features and rank them according to which features you think would be most useful.

2. Light travels at 186,000 miles per second. Suppose a satellite has an average distance of 24,500 miles from the surface of the earth.
   a. If two computers next to one another transmit through a satellite directly overhead, how long does it take for one computer to receive one 8-bit byte of asynchronous data from the other computer? Assume transmission speeds of 9,600 bits per second. Because the transmission is asynchronous, each byte must be accompanied by 2 bits—a start and a stop bit.
   b. Now assume that each byte must be acknowledged by the satellite, leading to a two-way handshake between the sender and the satellite and another two-way handshake between the satellite and the receiver. Assume that a single bit is transmitted in each acknowledgment. How long does it take to copy 10,000 bytes from one computer to the other?

3. Find out what bulletin board systems are available in your local area and the types of services they provide.

4. Frequency-division multiplexing can be used to combine slow transmissions to form a high-speed transmission. How might a two-channel broadband network be used to transmit voice and computer data simultaneously? How might this be useful for two people at distant locations who want to discuss a computer graphics display?

5. If a LAN transmits at 1 megabit per second, and ten computers are using it at the same time, what is the worst possible delay in copying a file across the network? Assume that each of the ten computers is attempting to do the same thing: copy a 50,000-character file from one computer to another on the same network.

6. Ask three companies that sell local area networks for information about their networks. Write a report comparing their strengths and weaknesses.

10 Graphics

I n 1962 Ivan E. Sutherland built a computer system that enabled the user to draw on a television-like screen. His device was slow, expensive, and not very sophisticated, but it was the beginning of modern computer-generated graphics. During the 1970s, techniques for drawing on an electronic screen improved, while the cost of computer hardware declined. Then, in the 1980s, low-cost RAM chips appeared, which made it possible to store and quickly access a vast amount of information in a very small box at a very low cost. These chips gave graphics its biggest boost. Low-cost memory is ideal for graphical computing, because "a picture is worth a thousand words" of storage.

We discussed one use of computer graphics earlier: to provide a *visual operating environment,* so that the computer uses pictures instead of text to communicate with the user. In this chapter, we describe other uses of computer graphics.

Figure 10.1 Applications of computer graphics using bit-mapped and vector graphics technology.

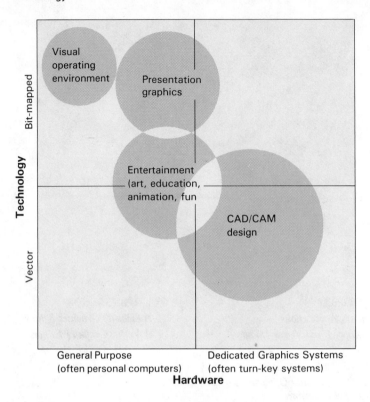

We will see how you can display information as a graph or chart and how you can draw pictures, print them, save them in a disk file, and retrieve them for later use. Specifically, we will examine presentation graphics and graphics editors. We will discuss both the technology and the usefulness of computer graphics. Before you continue reading this chapter, you should examine Window 7 on graphics.

BASIC CONCEPTS

Graphics Applications

As Figure 10.1 illustrates, there are three main uses of graphics: entertainment, presentation graphics, and computer-aided design. The entertainment category is a catchall category that includes numerous applications in art, education, animation, and games.

Presentation graphics is the term used to describe high-quality graphs, charts, and diagrams produced in order to present facts, trends, and comparisons in a report, meeting, or convention. Presentation graphics turn numbers into pictures so that they can be easily understood. Often, the ability to produce presentation graphics is built into spreadsheet, database, and word processing programs to help analyze trends and other relationships in the data they store. For example, you might plot numbers from two rows of a spreadsheet in order to see the relationship between two sets of data, or you might plot the numbers from one field of a database file against those from another to reveal the relationship between the two fields. In either case, you might then move the resulting graph to a word processor document for inclusion in a report. Some people consider this type of presentation graphics a separate category and call it **analytic graphics**, because the resulting charts are less sophisticated than those produced by standalone graphics programs and are used to analyze data.

A third use of graphics is for computer-aided design. For this type of computer graphics, you need a **graphics editor**, which is like a word processor except that it helps you edit pictures instead of text. A graphics editor is used to create drawings on the screen with electronic tools, such as a simulated paintbrush, eraser, pencil, and so forth. With a graphics editor, you can then edit the sketch by moving, rotating, enlarging, and so on. Once you have obtained the desired design, the sketch can be printed. MacPaint and MacDraw are examples of graphics editors for the Apple Macintosh; PC Paintbrush, Publisher's Paintbrush, and Dr. Halo are examples of graphics editors for IBM and IBM-compatible microcomputers.

Bit-Mapped and Vector Images

Figure 10.1 also classifies graphics applications according to whether they use bit-mapped or vector technology. Recall from Chapter 4 that a *bit-mapped* image is one made of thousands of small pieces called *pixels,* which are dots or points. In contrast, a *vector* image is made of *graphics primitives,* such as straight-line segments and arcs. These two methods of storing an image are described more thoroughly in the boxed insert "Graphics Standards." The difference between these technologies is narrowing, but choosing one or the other still affects what you can do and how you can do it.

PRESENTATION GRAPHICS

Usually, a presentation graph is prepared for viewing by decision makers who want information in a compact, but meaningful form. The information may be obtained from any source and can be entered from the keyboard. In a personal computer, the most likely electronic sources are spreadsheet, database, or word processor files. To use presentation graphics programs, you must also own a graphics display device. In addition, a graphics printer or plotter is needed to obtain hard copy of the resulting charts. In the following sections, we will describe three ways to prepare presentation graphics: with the graphics end of an integrated program, with a standalone graphics package, and with a project management program.

A WORD ABOUT
GRAPHICS STANDARDS

The challenge to the microcomputer industry is to establish and support a graphics standard—a uniform way to specify pictures and text. Not only would this help to achieve device independence and software-file compatibility, but it would offer the opportunity to standardize the user interface as well.

At the most fundamental level, nearly all graphics devices, whether screens or printers, operate with bit-mapped images. Each pixel in a bit-mapped screen corresponds to (is mapped to) a bit in RAM. To change the screen image, the software changes this video RAM as required. Graphics printers work in the same fashion, except that the bit map need not be held in RAM all at once. Instead, a typical dot matrix printer works slowly enough that the bit map is built up in RAM gradually, one band of the image at a time. The faster page printers, using laser or LED imaging, generally need to have a complete page in memory when printing starts.

Purely bit-mapped graphics works fine when the image will appear on single display device at a fixed resolution. But in the typical case, where the screen uses one resolution and the printer another, bit mapping does not work well. The bit map that can create a satisfactory screen image at 60–100 dots per inch (dpi) will not produce an acceptable image on a printer at 140 dpi, and is hopelessly inadequate for a laser printer at 300 dpi; there simply isn't enough information to fill in the additional pixels. Although an interpolation and smoothing scheme can sometimes build up an adequate image from a lower-resolution original, no such scheme works well enough to be generally useful.

The alternative to pure bit mapping is to describe images with graphics primitives, which specify geometric objects; a line, for example, is defined by its length, orientation, and width. A full graphics-primitive language includes enough components to specify virtually any object; the more complex the object, the greater the number of graphics primitives necessary to describe it. From the complete graphics description, a driver (software or hardware or both) can create a bit map for a particular screen or printer, taking full advantage of the device's features to render the image at the best possible resolution, and using color if available and shades of gray if not.

Thus, on a screen with only 60 dpi, a graphics primitive for a circle will yield a rough-looking curve. The user can manipulate the jagged circle, secure in the knowledge that when the time comes to put it on paper, the driver for a laser printer will take the same primitive and create a smoothly executed 300-dpi circle. In a way, graphics primitives do for graphics what the ASCII character code does for text.

Graphics primitives alone, though, are not always sufficient. For example, if you describe a square with graphics primitives, you will define four separate lines. A program that looks at the graphics primitives will recreate the square but has no way of "knowing" that the four lines are actually a single entity that should be operated on together. But a "higher-level graphics" format can group the primitive to create complete objects.

Because programs are designed for so many different purposes, standardizing higher-level graphics descriptions is not easy. Nevertheless, some standards have been proposed or established in specific application areas, such as IGES (Initial Graphics Exchange Specifications) and PHIGS (Programmer's Hierarchical Interactive Graphics Standard) in computer-aided design, which run mainly on engineering workstations rather than microcomputers. The most popular higher-level graphics descriptions on micros have been established by the success of specific software packages, such as AutoCAD.

However flexible, no set of primitives can create every possible image. Some images, such as a photograph of a real scene, do not decompose into graphics primitives readily. Such images are

Continued on next page

best handled as bit maps, so any comprehensive graphics standard must also allow for this method as well. The resolution and other characteristics of the bit map depend on its origin and ultimate use; the main sources will be television images, facsimile machines, and scanners. In some cases, software can analyze a bit map image and create a graphics primitive description. At present this capability is largely limited to converting cleanly made line drawings into line primitives.

Using the Graphics Component of an Integrated Program

Integrated programs frequently offer graphing routines that allow data to be converted into simple on-screen graphs with a minimum of effort. For example, let's suppose you're using a spreadsheet program that can produce graphics, and your worksheet contains financial information about computer companies. It takes only two steps to convert data in the worksheet into a crude graph: you must (1) ask for the graphics option of the program and (2) point out the graph's data.

The order in which you perform these steps depends on the program you use. If you use Microsoft Excel, the first step is to point out the data by selecting an area of the worksheet. You do this with the mouse, causing the area you select to appear in inverse video. For example, in Figure 10.2, the range containing cells A2..B6 has been selected from the Biggest DP Companies worksheet. The sec-

Figure 10.2 A simple pie chart prepared with Excel. Data in the Biggest DP Companies worksheet window is linked to the pie chart in the 5 Biggest Companies chart window.

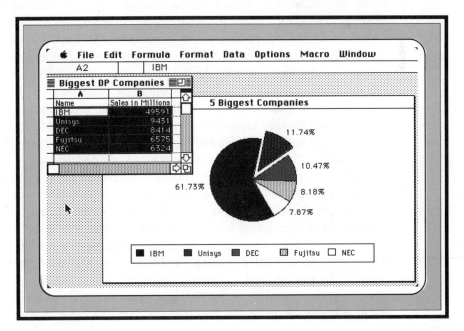

Figure 10.3 A stacked-bar chart prepared with Lotus 1-2-3. (a) A range of cells is selected for graphing. (b) The resulting stacked-bar chart.

```
B7: 355366                                                      POINT
Enter first data range: AL7..B7

            A             B         C         D        E        F
1                        1/88      2/88      3/88     4/88     5/88
2                           J         F         M        A        M
3   Billable CPU Hours:   41.2      64.4       56     52.1     54.6
4   CPU $ Earned:        101.4     141.9    127.2    126.1    153.8
5   Overhead CPU Hours:      2      13.1     12.6      5.2     12.5
6   CPU $ Lost:            6.6      33.3     30.1     12.8     28.6
7   Batch Usage:        355366    578499   489446   456536   554391
8   Timesharing Usage: 1434364   1036558   835776  1909237  1280274
9
10                    Winter 88 Spring 88 Summer 88  Fall 88 Winter 89
11                          W88       S88       S88      F88      W89
12  Billable CPU Hours:   161.6     164.5     195.1    199.5      207
13  CPU $ Earned:         370.5     423.3     396.3    450.1    472.8
14  Overhead CPU Hours:    27.7      26.1       6.1       20     28.3
15  CPU $ Lost:              70      62.1      15.9     50.6     68.3
16
17
18
```

A.

ond step is to open a *chart window* by choosing the New Chart option from the File menu. When the chart window appears on the screen, it contains a graph that is linked to the data in the worksheet window. Depending on how the default graphics values for Excel have been set, the graph might look like the pie chart shown in the 5 Biggest Companies chart window of Figure 10.2. Because the chart window is linked to the worksheet window, changing the values of cells in the workshop will cause the graph to be redrawn to reflect the changes.

If the initial graph doesn't look right, you can give additional commands to change it into another type of graph or to spruce it up by adding labels, legends, headings, and so forth. For example, you might want to drag one of the wedges to a new location to separate it from the others and emphasize it.

Lotus 1–2–3 reverses the order in which commands are given. First, you select the GRAPH command from the main menu. Then you point out the data to be graphed and choose the type of graph. Suppose you want to use 1–2–3 to compare the amount of timesharing and batch computer usage that occurred in each month during the last three years on a certain mainframe computer. Figure 10.3(a) shows how the range of cells containing the batch usage numbers can be selected for graphing by pointing with the cursor-movement keys. But to create the stacked-bar chart shown in Figure 10.3(b), you must select three ranges of data. One range contains the labels for the horizontal axis; the other two ranges contain the

Figure 10.3 continued

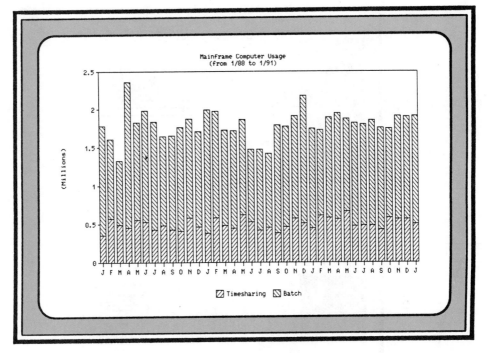

B.

values for batch and timeshared computer usage. Notice that the finished graph allows you to see and compare the relationships among 74 numbers that would not otherwise fit on the screen at once.

Spreadsheet graphics allow you to plot any row or column of data against any other row or column of data. You can choose types of displays, such as bar, line, or pie, as well as various combinations, such as stacked-bar or line bar. You can also save the graphical representation of the data in a disk file and retrieve it as you would retrieve a word processing document.

Producing a graph with a database program is similar to preparing one with a spreadsheet. The major difference is that, with a database program, you select one or more fields of each record to be plotted, but with a spreadsheet, you select cells from a worksheet.

Most integrated programs offer a prepackaged set of graph types. For example, Figure 10.4 shows icons that represent the types of graphs Excel can produce. You can change from one type of graph to another by selecting a different icon from the appropriate menu. This lets you try out different ways of displaying numbers quickly, but it can be limiting if you want a type of graph entirely different from the prepackaged selections.

In most cases, you must spend some time tinkering with an integrated program's options and experimenting before you arrive at an effective graph. One of

Figure 10.4 The types of charts produced by Excel.

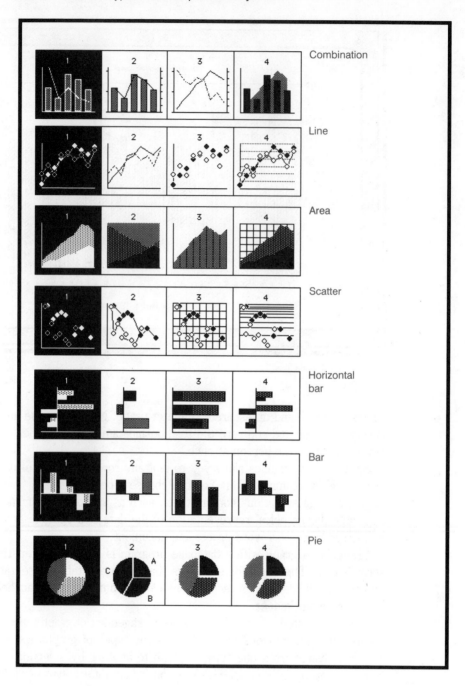

the most important tasks is to choose an appropriate type of graph for the data at hand. For example, consider the graph shown in Figure 10.5, which compares the revenues and income of six computer companies. This combination chart superimposes a line graph on top of a bar chart. As a result, each company's revenue-to-income ratio is clearly apparent. Equally important is the selection of logarithmic scales for the vertical axes. Because IBM is more than 100 times the size of Microsoft and Lotus, its statistics would dominate the chart without the compression provided by a logarithmic scale.

Another useful type of combination chart, known as a *curve-fitting graph,* superimposes a mathematical curve on the data. Depending on the graph, the curve might be used to predict future data points or to make an underlying relationship among the data points more apparent. The curve is often constructed with a mathematical technique called *regression analysis.* Spreadsheet programs are particularly good at creating curve-fitting graphs, because you can use the calculating abilities of the worksheet to compute and try out several mathematical functions. Usually one function results in a closer fit to the data than the others.

- *Linear functions* draw a straight line through the raw data.
- *Weighted-average functions* smooth out variations in the data by computing a weighted average of the last N data points.
- *Exponential functions* draw exponentially increasing (or decreasing) curves through the data.
- *Power curve functions* draw a curve through the data by using the mathematical formula $\log y = b \log x + \log a$.

Area-fill charts, like simple line graphs, are used to show the relationship between variables. But an *area-fill chart* includes some texture in the area under the line graph, to increase the effectiveness of presentation. For example, Figure 10.6 is an area-fill chart showing ups and downs in a company's revenues and cost of sales over a ten-year period.

Scatter charts are used to show the distribution of data values. You might use a scatter chart to show how different types of consumers buy different types of products, or how one kind of data is clustered around certain regions of the graph, as shown in Figure 10.7.

Symbols are used in line graphs or scatter charts to identify different sets of data. For example, the legend in Figure 10.7 states that solid squares identify the sales of iced tea; hot cocoa sales are identified by a hollow diamond. Each graphics program has a different set of symbols available to represent items. Figure 10.8(a) shows the symbols available with Excel. Some programs come with extensive symbol libraries or allow you to build your own symbols. This would make it possible, for instance, to represent iced tea sales with tall glasses and hot cocoa sales with steaming mugs.

A *simple bar chart* shows the variations in one set of values; a *multiple bar chart* illustrates the relationship between variations in several sets of values. Depending

Figure 10.5 A combination line and bar chart using logarithmic scales.

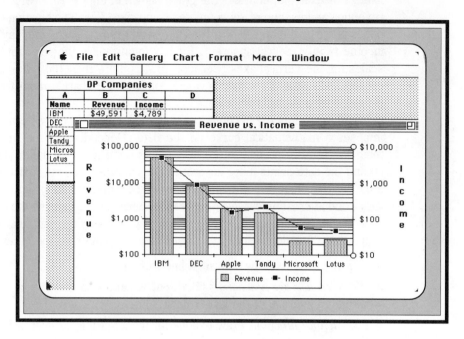

Figure 10.6 Area-fill chart.

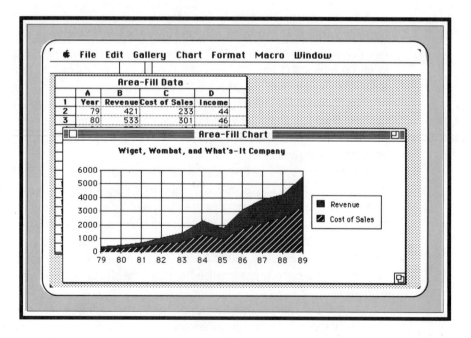

Figure 10.7 Scatter chart.

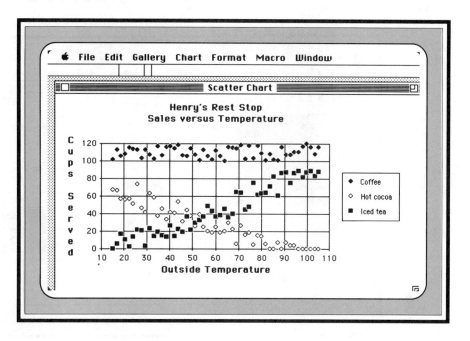

Figure 10.8 Excel's dialog boxes make it easy to choose symbols and hatch patterns for the various parts of a graph.

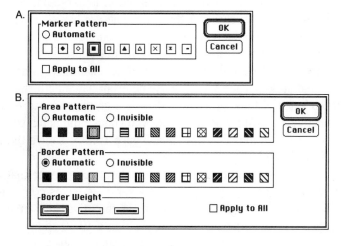

Figure 10.9 A clustered bar chart that includes a note explaining the unusal height of one of the bars.

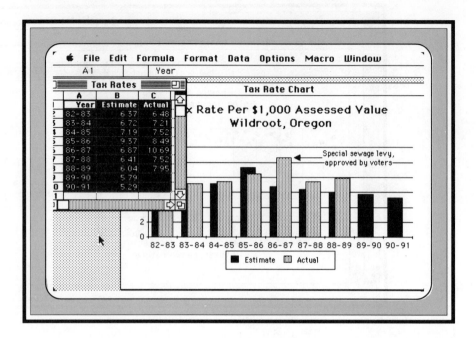

on the visual effect you want and the options provided by the graphics program, you might choose a simple bar chart, a chart with clustered or stacked bars, or a chart with bars displayed in a three-dimensional perspective. Figure 10.9 shows a clustered bar chart in which two sets of data are compared by overlapping one set of bars with another set. Clustered bar charts make it easy for you to contrast sets of values. Excel allows another variation in bar charts: the *horizontal bar chart.* Turning the chart on its side may make it easier to understand, or it may simply be the best way to print the chart. A three-dimensional bar chart is like a clustered bar chart, except that the bars in each cluster group are projected onto a three-dimensional cube. Your printed output will give the impression of depth: the clustered bars are placed one behind the other rather than next to each other.

Bar, pie, and area-fill charts usually use different hatch patterns or colors to distinguish each set of values. A *hatch pattern* is a graphical texture used to give an area a distinctive look. Most programs let you choose the hatch pattern to be used for each part of the graph. For example, Figure 10.8(b) shows the hatch patterns available within Excel.

Outline processors sometimes have a graphical component that produces tree charts or other text charts. A *tree chart* is a series of boxes connected in a hierarchical fashion. *Text charts* convert the items in an outline into an attractive format for an overhead transparency. For example, Figure 10.10 shows part of an organization chart that was created by converting an outline into a tree chart.

Figure 10.10 An organization chart produced by MORE, an outline processing program. The icons at the left of the screen determine the basic format of the chart.

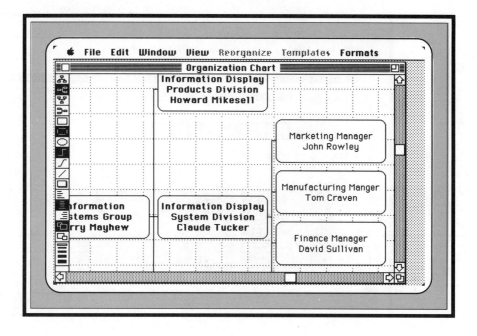

Standalone Graphics Packages

Although graphics components of spreadsheet programs like Lòtus 1–2–3 and Excel have become the most common form of presentation graphics, standalone graphics programs can create more sophisticated and polished graphs. This added flexibility comes at a price: standalone programs generally require far more effort than the graphics routines contained in integrated programs.

As an example, Lotus Freelance Plus sells for $395 and requires an IBM or IBM-compatible microcomputer with a minimum of 384KB, an appropriate graphics adapter card and monitor, and either a plotter or a graphics printer. It has the following characteristics:

- Freelance's chart option provides five basic chart types: text, pie, bar, line, and scatter. Figure 10.11 shows how data are entered from the keyboard to create a standard Freelance pie chart.

- Standard charts can be enhanced with freehand drawings or by adding basic building blocks called *graphics elements*. These include text, lines, arrows, rectangles, circles, slices, bows, markers, and polygons.

Figure 10.11 Producing a pie chart with Lotus Freelance Plus. (a) Data for the pie chart are entered by completing an on-screen form. (b) The resulting pie chart.

A.

- Graphics elements can be joined into a single object called a *symbol*. Symbols are organized in libraries, where they are easily available. Over 60 libraries come with the program, but you can create symbols and build your own libraries or purchase additional libraries for special purposes (see Figure 10.12).

- Output can be adjusted for paper, overhead transparencies, and film. A batch output option enables you to select, list, and plot up to 36 completed drawings at a time. This is useful for creating large print jobs that can be run periodically, such as once a month.

- Graphs can be produced with hatching, color, legends, headers, several built-in font families, unlimited font sizes, and axis scaling.

- The program accepts keyboard input and imports data files in either Lotus 1–2–3 or dBase formats. Freelance also imports charts created by Graphwriter, 1–2–3, or Symphony, as well as ASCII files created by word processors for word charts.

Project Management Software

A **project management program** analyzes and displays the activities of production, construction, or development projects. Although these programs incorporate

Figure 10.11 continued

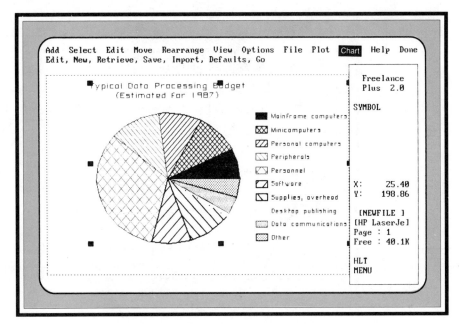

B.

Figure 10.12 Symbol libraries like this one allow previously stored drawings to be added to any graphic by pressing only a few keys. Symbol libraries containing maps are particularly important for creating presentation graphs based on geographical information.

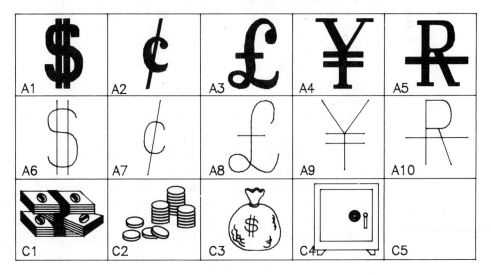

Figure 10.13 Project scheduling information displayed as a PERT chart.

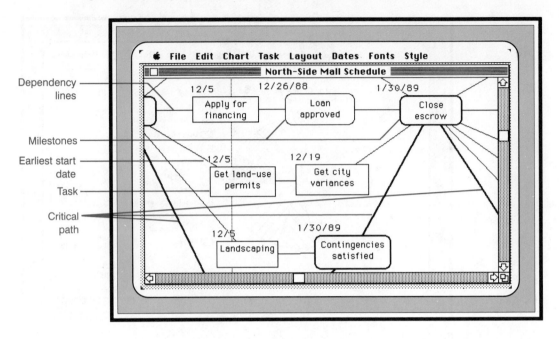

analytic routines that fall outside the field of presentation graphics, their output is normally displayed in the form of charts and diagrams. For example, a **PERT chart** shows the dependencies among activities in a project by connecting activity boxes together with lines (see Figure 10.13). The *critical path* running through a PERT chart shows the activities that can't slip without affecting the entire schedule of the project.

To create a PERT chart with MacProject, you begin by drawing task and milestone boxes on the screen and giving them labels. Then you add dependency lines by dragging the mouse from one box to another box that depends on it. Finally, you add task information, such as the number of days it will take to complete each task or the resources each will require. The project management program does the rest automatically by calculating the critical path and producing a PERT chart like that in Figure 10.13.

A **Gantt chart** plots the activities of a project against a timeline to provide a different visual representation of the project schedule. The Gantt chart in Figure 10.14 displays the starting date, the earliest completion date, and the number of slack days for each activity throughout the project. Most project management programs provide other types of charts and reports as well, such as cash flow tables, resource usage charts, and status reports.

A WORD ABOUT PROJECT MANAGEMENT SOFTWARE

"Two people using Microsoft Project cut the time needed to plan the project from 10 days to two hours."—Kenneth Anderson, Chief Programmer and Analyst, Blue Cross/Blue Shield

The first project management tools developed 30 years ago by the U.S. Navy were strictly manual methods using paper and pencil. Not long after these manual methods became popular among military planners, they also caught on with private industry, especially construction.

The specialized methods and highly structured planning techniques of project management eventually became computerized on mainframes and minicomputers. These programs for large computer systems typically cost between $25,000 and $200,000, and support virtually every function, method, analytic technique, and reporting style that you possibly could want in a project manager.

Large systems also give you access to large corporate databases and built-in multiuser capabilities, enabling professional project managers to evaluate the scope and progress of a project in considerable detail. Over the years, project management programs have also migrated to the personal computer.

The largest initial market for PC-based project management packages has been professional project managers—full-time specialists who spend their days designing, tracking, and coordinating large-scale complex projects. These project managers in turn provide the technical support for the middle-level managers directly responsible for the project. As PC-based project management software gets better, more powerful, faster, and easier to use, other professionals are likely to find that it solves their management problems as well.

Many of today's personal computer-based programs were converted from existing mainframe and minicomputer implementations, and their prices reflect that orientation (they cost more than $1,000). Other programs come from some of the industry leaders in microcomputer software publishing. These programs typically cost less than $500 and tend to be integrated within the vendor's complete productivity software family.

Each [project management program we tested] uses either the critical path method (CPM) or the program evaluation review technique (PERT) of project management. (Many use both.) CPM, which uses Gantt charts, concentrates on the resources needed to complete the project—assuming that the duration of the tasks can be estimated accurately—and analyzes and reports the compromises necessary to balance the cost of a project with the time needed to finish it.

PERT takes a broader view of the concepts inherent in project planning and management. This method allows you to chart each phase of a project and its links to other phases. Most of the tested programs offer PERT methods, which are much more useful in illustrating the network of relationships involved in project planning.

All of the programs tested here provide the minimum set of project management tools. They let you plan projects, create activities, assign resources (people and equipment) to those activities, apply the costs of those resources, decide which activities to schedule first, and set milestones (critical points in a project that must be attained at the time scheduled or the entire project will slip). These project managers also let you modify your plans to see how the changes will affect the overall project schedule and costs, produce reports that summarize work in progress, and generate graphical representations of the entire project.

Most of these programs also provide extra features that are useful when tracking large, complex projects. The most important of these features is known as resource leveling, which prevents too

Continued on page 314

A Summary of Features

A graphics package should allow you to enhance a graph by emphasizing certain phrases or headings through the use of different sizes and styles of type. In addition, a good presentation graphics program can fit lines or curves to the points plotted in a graph. This feature is especially important if you want to use the graph to make projections.

Figure 10.14 Part of a typical Gantt chart produced by MacProject.

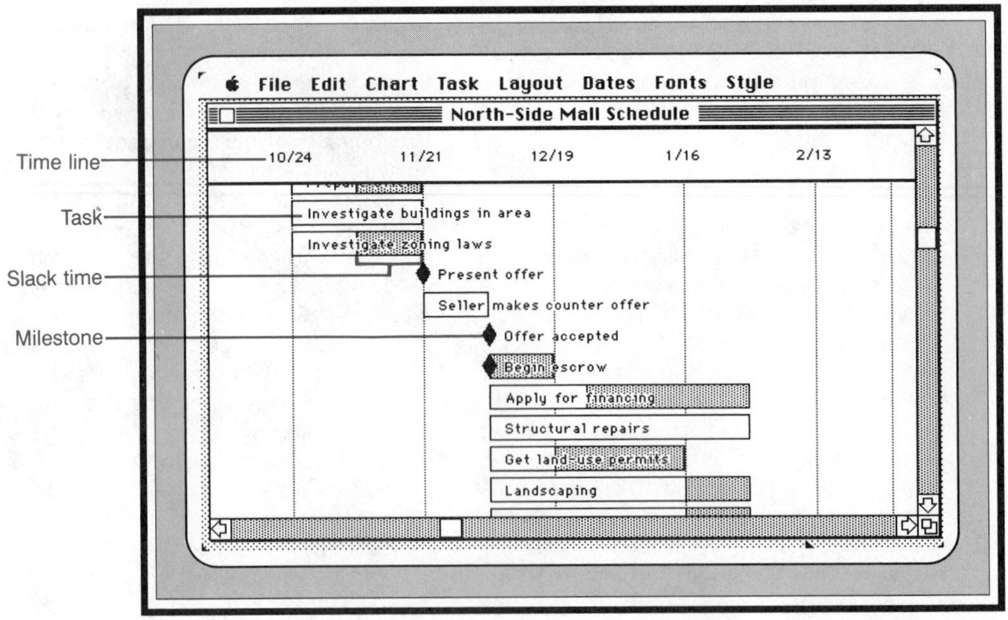

A WORD ABOUT
COOPERATIVE GRAPHICS PROCESSING

One trend in the corporate world is to let PC users access the graphics capabilities of mini and mainframe computers.

The continued annual 20 to 30 percent revenue growth in mainframe and minicomputer graphics, combined with the surge of personal computers onto desktops, has caused information processing managers to search for ways to combine the strengths of the PC with those of the minicomputer or mainframe. The goal is cooperative processing, in which each machine performs the functions for which it is best suited. These executives see the PC as one part of a continuum of platforms ranging from the PC through workstation, departmental computer, and mainframe. They want each platform to work with the others, not compete against them.

Initially, the microcomputer served either as a standalone charting system or a graphics terminal, often emulating one of the popular Tektronix, Inc., computers. Recently, however, the PC has taken on more significant roles in the partnership. It has become a device-independent chart distributor, a chart previewing tool, a graphics editing station, and even an automatic graphics program generator.

When graphic terminals cost $7,000 to $20,000, a personal computer offered a lower cost solution. Today, as the cost of graphics terminals drops and as increasing user demands for quality push up the price of graphics on PCs, the direct cost differences are not as great as they once were. It is a much larger trend that fuels the demand for graphics terminal emulation. Personal computer users are running out of capability and need to access the mainframe or mini. They are the driving force behind the growth in cooperative graphics processing.

It is these same PC users—frustrated by limited graphics software and slow, hand-fed graphics hard-copy equipment—who are pressuring vendors to expand their terminal emulation software. They are asking for an expanding array of capabilities to enhance their own productivity and to make graphics emulation compatible with the options they have purchased for their PCs.

For example, a recent challenge at one large industrial company came from Lotus 1–2–3 users who liked 1–2–3 but did not like the charts it produced. Either they were frustrated with the quality and flexibility of the graphics they were getting, or they did not want to dedicate their PC to the sole purpose of supporting a plotter. These users recognized that they already had high-speed, high-quality graphics hard-copy equipment available on their mainframe or mincomputer network. They needed to preview charts in Lotus, then pass them through the network to the higher quality equipment.

The solution was an automatic command generator that translated Lotus 1–2–3 worksheets into commands that graphics software running on the VAX and IBM computers could read and process. Users can now get high-quality charts from any plotter, graphics laser printer, thermal transfer printer, ink-jet or film recorder connected to the mainframe or minicomputer network.

The future of micro-mainframe links in computer graphics is likely to be an extension of the cooperative processing represented in the Lotus enhancement link. But new products will go much further. Some will allow charts created on the mini or mainframe to be edited on the PC and returned to the mainframe for distribution to graphics hard-copy devices or to other users. Others will offer capabilities that allow any logo or diagram produced on the PC to be integrated with charts created on the larger machines.

Among the most important of the changes will be smoother integration between programs running on cooperating machines. In the near future, we can look forward to environments that will put all the graphics hardware and software of minis and mainframes at the call of every PC user—with the touch of a button. Access will become so transparent that the user will not even know what computer is doing the work.

Source: Alan Paller (president of AUI Data Graphics/Issco), *Computerworld,* 23 June 1986, p. 58.

Some graphics programs are especially good for making overhead transparencies. A typical program lets you print or display part or all of a picture—sometimes in color—so that you can copy it onto a transparency. Plotters will plot directly on a transparency with the use of special pens. Laser printers can also print directly on a transparency, but it is essential to use special heat-resistant transparencies. Otherwise, the heat from the fusing rollers will melt the transparency and gum up the machine.

A *slide show facility* allows you to play back a series of pictures directly from the computer's screen. The slide show facility also lets you determine the delay between the presentation of each slide or step through the slides with keyboard commands (perhaps by using the [PgUp] and [PgDn] keys).

The extent and versatility of presentation graphics programs continue to grow, thus making the process of selecting the most suitable program confusing. You should consider the following features before purchasing one of the hundreds of programs now available:

Number of fonts	Transparency facility
Number of pen colors	Slide show facility
Number of text sizes	Data interchange
Number of hatching patterns	Math functions
Size of symbol library	Title lines
Ability to add notes	Legends
Ability to reposition elements	Footnotes
Help facility	Chart types:
Regression lines:	bar (stacked, clustered, 3-D)
linear	line
exponential	scatter (XY)
logarithmic	pie
parabolic	area
Memory required	text
On-screen preview	special (PERT, Gantt)
Printer support	combination
Support for graphics input	Compatibility with graphics standards
devices	

GRAPHICS EDITORS

A graphics editor is a program that draws graphical images by interpreting commands entered from a keyboard, mouse, touch-tablet, or light pen. There are two fundamentally different types of graphics editors: bit-mapped and vector graphics.

Bit-mapped editors store the screen image in memory as a grid of memory cells representing individual pixels. The screen image is constructed and modified by changing the values stored in the bit map. When you use a bit-mapped editor, drawing on the screen is like drawing on paper. In contrast, *vector graphics editors* build a mathematical model in memory of the objects to appear on the screen. The model consists of interconnected objects, such as lines, circles, cylinders, boxes, and arcs, and the screen image provides a view of how the mathematical model looks. Using a vector graphics editor is like constructing a model out of building blocks or the pieces in a Tinker Toy set.

Bit-mapped editors excel in artistic applications, but they aren't suitable for analytical applications, such as finding an object's center of gravity, rotating a three-dimensional model to view it from the side, or calculating the strength of a bridge. Thus, "paint" programs usually take a bit-mapped approach to graphics, whereas analytic programs take a vector graphics approach. These different approaches become evident in the way each editor operates.

CAD/CAM (*c*omputer-*a*ided *d*esign and *c*omputer-*a*ided *m*anufacturing) programs are special-purpose graphics editors developed especially for designing and manufacturing new products. Many CAD/CAM programs perform **solids modeling**—producing three-dimensional images and cross-sections of solids. A CAD/CAM system can aid in drafting, architecture, engineering, and building manufacturing tools for automobiles and similar industrial products. It can also be used to design clothing, make advertising copy, or create props for a theatrical production.

Graphics editors are also used, along with special programs, to create graphics for entertainment, computer-aided instruction, special effects in movies, and applications in medicine, science, and business. Similar uses of computer graphics include art, games, and educational programs, in which animation and color are highly valued.

A "Paint" Graphics Editor

In this section, we describe a simple, general-purpose graphics editor using several examples. The details differ from one graphics editor to the next, but the general techniques remain the same. The example adopts a "paint," or bit-mapped, approach similar to that used by MacPaint or PC Paintbrush.

Because a graphics editor processes pictures instead of text, it may at first seem unusual. Most graphics editors are driven by a menu of icons (called *tools*), descriptive words or pictures that show what commands the editor can perform (see Figure 10.15). You tell the editor what to do by selecting an item from the menu—for example, by pointing with a mouse. The following list describes a few such commands:

- *LASSO.* Select an object on the screen for the purpose of moving, duplicating, or erasing it.
- *SELECT.* Select a region of the screen for the purpose of moving, duplicating, or erasing it. The difference between LASSO and SELECT is that, by using LASSO, you can select an object within a region without also selecting the background surrounding the object (even though the background is within the region selected).

Figure 10.15 (a) MacPaint's icon menu. Each command is represented on the screen by a picture of a tool. (b) Enlargement of MacPaint's icon menu.

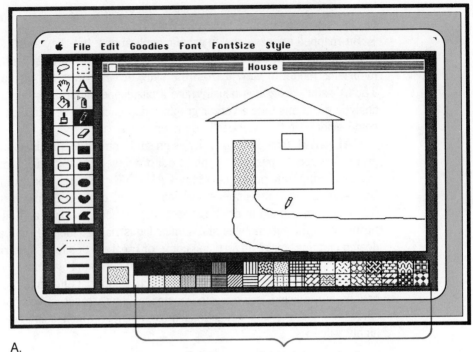

A.

Patterns available for use (palette)

- *PAN.* Move your viewpoint around the drawing area. Since the drawing area may be too large to fit within the screen, PAN allows you to roam around a larger area than you can see on your screen at any one time.
- *TEXT.* Enter characters, numbers, or whatever you want from the keyboard.
- *FILL.* Add color, shading, or hatch patterns to an enclosed region by filling it with a pattern or color.
- *SPRAY.* Spray a mist, or pattern, on the screen.
- *PAINT.* Draw a line or brush stroke on the screen.
- *RUBBER BAND.* Draw a straight line from point A to point B. The line stretches from point A, like a rubber band, as you move its end point to point B.
- *ERASE.* Remove or erase everything from a certain region on the screen.
- *RECTANGLE.* Draw a rectangle by selecting its upper left-hand corner and then rubber banding to its lower right-hand corner.
- *CIRCLE.* Draw a circle by defining its center and radius.

Figure 10.15 continued

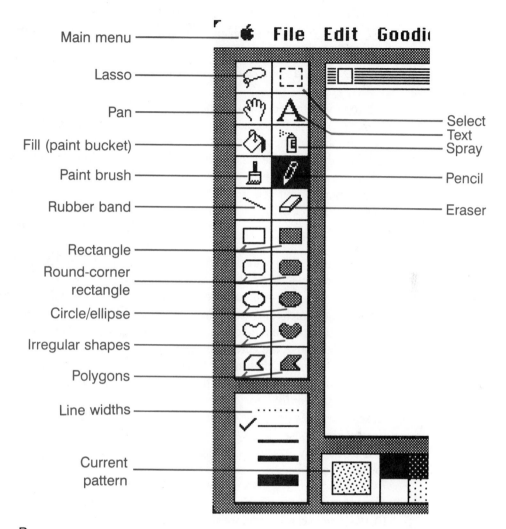

Main menu —— 🍎 **File   Edit   Goodi**

Lasso ——

Pan ——

Fill (paint bucket) ——

Paint brush ——

Rubber band ——

Rectangle ——

Round-corner rectangle ——

Circle/ellipse ——

Irregular shapes ——

Polygons ——

Line widths ——

Current pattern ——

—— Select
—— Text
—— Spray
—— Pencil
—— Eraser

B.

- *POLYGON*. Draw a polygon by pointing at and selecting its vertices.
- *CUT*. Remove a portion of the drawing from a region of the screen and save it in the scratch pad.
- *PASTE*. Copy the drawing from the scratch pad to a certain region of the screen.
- *ROTATE*. Rotate a region of the screen.

- *ZOOM*. Magnify or shrink a portion of the screen.
- *MIRROR*. Draw symmetrical patterns about one, two, or more axes.
- *DRAG*. Move a region or object across the screen.
- *STRETCH*. Distort an object or region by compressing or stretching it along the horizontal or vertical axis.
- *GRID*. Show a horizontal and vertical grid overlaid with the drawing.

A good way to see how a graphics editor works is to use it to draw a very simple picture. All pictures, no matter how simple or complex, are made up of many trivial graphical components. For example, the house shown in Figure 10.15 is actually made up of three rectangles, a triangle, and a freehand drawing.

You draw the house by first selecting RECTANGLE from the menu. If you're using a mouse, you select RECTANGLE by pointing at its icon and clicking the mouse button once. If you're using a tablet, point by touching the surface of the tablet. If you don't have a separate graphics input device, use the keyboard's arrow keys.

Next, move the pointer to where you want the upper left-hand corner of the rectangle to appear and hold the mouse button down while you drag the mouse toward the lower right-hand corner of the rectangle. When the lower right-hand corner has been reached, release the mouse button; the rectangle stays in place.

To put the roof on the house, as in Figure 10.16(b), select POLYGON from the menu. Next, move the cursor to where you want the top of the roof and click the mouse button once; then move to the lower left-hand vertex of the triangle and click a second time. Notice how the edge of the polygon follows the cursor—this is called *rubber banding*, for obvious reasons. At each vertex, a click of the mouse causes the vertex to stay put and the next edge to stretch, following the movement of the mouse. Finally, when the triangle is closed at the top vertex (you've gone all the way around the triangle), click the mouse button twice to indicate that you're done.

To construct a window, draw a second rectangle (a square) inside the first rectangle, as shown in Figure 10.16(c). The rectangular door shown in Figure 10.16(d) requires an additional touch. After you draw it, select FILL from the menu. FILL usually gives you a choice of patterns to use when filling in an enclosed polygonal area. Select a hatch pattern like the one shown in Figure 10.16(d), move the cursor to any point inside the rectangular door, and click the mouse button once. The entire door area will be filled with the hatch pattern.

To draw the sidewalk shown in Figure 10.16(e), select PAINT. When you use this command, shape and design depend on a steady hand. Hold the mouse button down while moving the mouse to draw the outline of the sidewalk. Your drawing may not be very smooth, because the shape of the sidewalk follows the path of the moving mouse.

If you make a mistake or want to reenter an object, select the UNDO command; the last action you performed will be undone. Alternatively, you can remove

Figure 10.16 Building a simple house by using a graphics editor.

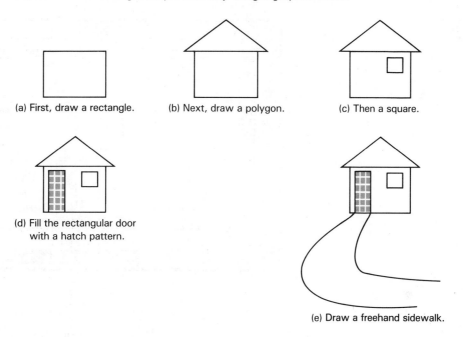

(a) First, draw a rectangle.

(b) Next, draw a polygon.

(c) Then a square.

(d) Fill the rectangular door with a hatch pattern.

(e) Draw a freehand sidewalk.

portions of the picture by selecting ERASE. Most graphics editors offer numerous other options that we haven't illustrated, such as aids for drawing straight lines, French curves, shading, texture, and so on.

A Vector Graphics Editor

In most of this chapter, we discuss bit-mapped graphics because it is the most common technology in the personal computer world, but vector graphics editors are most commonly used for professional design and drafting on larger computers. Recall that a *vector* is defined by coordinates, such as the locations of the end points of a straight line. This feature makes it possible for a computer to calculate mathematical properties of the objects on the screen, present different views or perspectives of the objects, and store drawings in much less memory space and perform operations that require greater precision and accuracy than is possible with bit-mapped graphics editors.

Vector-oriented editors can display their models on either raster scan or vector graphics monitors. Graphical objects, such as straight lines, circles, rectangles, and arcs, are stored internally as vectors, but they can be displayed as bit-mapped regions on a raster scan monitor. Macintosh's MacDraw is a popular example of a vector-oriented editor that runs on a raster scan computer system.

Figure 10.17 MacDraw tools and drawing board showing grid lines.

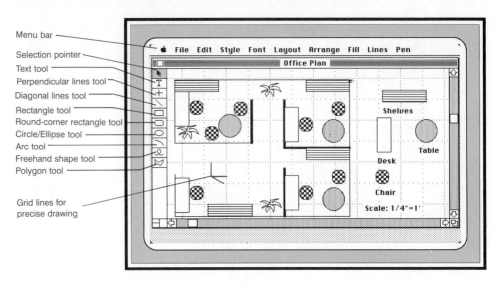

Menu bar

Selection pointer

Text tool

Perpendicular lines tool

Diagonal lines tool

Rectangle tool

Round-corner rectangle tool

Circle/Ellipse tool

Arc tool

Freehand shape tool

Polygon tool

Grid lines for
precise drawing

The tools provided by a vector-oriented graphics editor are very similar to the tools of a "paint" graphics editor, but they behave differently. Figure 10.17 shows the tools provided by MacDraw; text, lines, rectangles, circles, and polygons are all represented by small icons at the left of the drawing area. To draw an object, first click a tool with the mouse, and then place the object on the drawing board.

Vector-oriented editors are used to obtain the very precise drawings needed for architectural, engineering, and design work. For this reason, the MacDraw drawing board can be calibrated in either inches or centimeters. To help align items accurately, you can display rulers across the top and down the left side of the document window (see Figure 10.18). Cross-hairs on these rulers move to display the pointer's horizontal and vertical coordinates. For even more precise alignment, MacDraw provides an invisible alignment grid that can be used to control the size and placement of objects. When the alignment grid is turned on, objects that you draw automatically "snap" to the nearest grid lines. Selecting the Drawing Size option from the Layout menu allows you to set the size of the drawing board in 8-by-10-inch pages. Figure 10.19 shows how to select the number of pages used in your electronic drawing board.

Each tool produces a graphical object that is described by one or more vectors. In Figure 10.20, the circle/ellipse tool was used to draw the table, the perpendicular-lines tool drew some of the walls, the round-corner rectangles tool drew the chairs, and the rectangle tool drew the desk and shelves. A line is defined by the locations of its end points, and a rectangle by the location of its corners. Even though these objects are displayed on a bit-mapped screen, they are manipulated as vectors.

Figure 10.18 Rulers along the edge of the screen help create scale drawings. In this drawing, $\frac{1}{4}$ inch equals 1 foot.

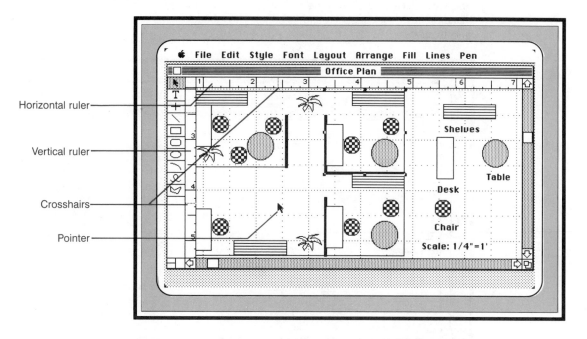

Horizontal ruler

Vertical ruler

Crosshairs

Pointer

Figure 10.19 Your drawing board can be up to 12 pages wide by 5 pages long. Each page is 8 inches wide by 10 inches long, thus permitting accurate drawings up to 100 inches wide by 50 inches long.

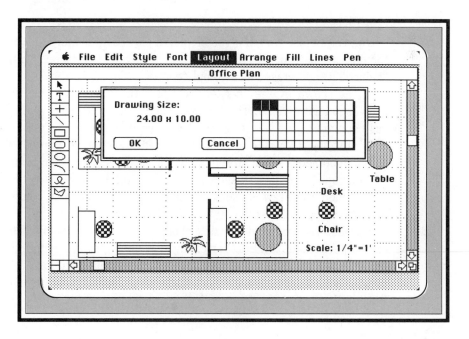

Figure 10.20 Vector objects can be picked up, moved, deleted, stretched, or shrunk. In this screen, one of the tables has been stretched from a small circle into an elipse. First, the table was selected by clicking the mouse while pointing at it, thereby exposing its "handles" (the black spots around its edge). Then dragging one of the handles caused the table to stretch.

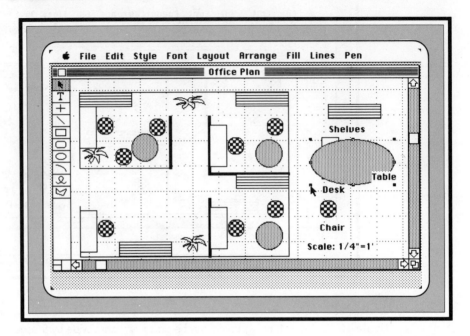

You can't erase part of a vector, move part of it, or merge it with another vector object. Instead, the entire vector is moved, overlapped with other objects "behind" it, and erased as a complete entity. The inner region of a vector can be filled, as shown by the checkerboard pattern of the chairs or the strips of the shelves in Figure 10.20. The texture of lines can be changed, even after the object has been drawn, by selecting the object and then choosing a pen texture.

Vector objects can be measured, rotated, overlapped, printed, and mathematically "smoothed." When stored, they take up less space than bit-mapped images. For example, the objects shown in Figure 10.20 require less than 2KB of disk space when MacDraw is used, but they occupy 12KB when converted to a Mac-Paint bit-mapped image.

Because vectors are mathematical objects, meaningful mathematical calculations can be performed on them. For example, vector graphics editors are used to prepare the models of physical objects that are submitted to finite element analysis programs to determine the object's strength, flexibility, or other properties (see Window 1, Photos 36–42).

Figure 10.21 A designer using a puck to enter very precise graphical data into a CAD/CAM editor.

Computer-Aided Design

The heart of all CAD/CAM systems is the graphics editor, which lets you enter, manipulate, and store images in the computer system. However, most CAD/CAM graphics editors use special-purpose hardware and software as part of a turnkey system. A **turnkey system** is a complete system of hardware and software purchased together, so that the user need only "turn the key" to get started. Turnkey CAD/CAM systems aren't cheap; they cost from $10,000 to more than $100,000 per workstation.

A CAD/CAM graphics editor uses a mouse or a puck the way a word processor uses a keyboard. Both input devices control what goes in the computer. A mouse can be used to draw lines, circles, boxes, and so forth, much as a keyboard is used to enter characters and numbers. Figure 10.21 shows a designer using a puck to enter graphical data.

In addition, powerful computers equipped with high-resolution displays are needed in solids modeling. A solids modeling graphics editor is capable of showing three-dimensional images and cross-sections of images in solid form; Figure 10.22 shows an example. Notice the contrast and texture that can be produced by using a solids modeling graphics editor. Figure 10.23 shows a nonsolid display of a three-

Figure 10.22 Display from a solids modeling editor.

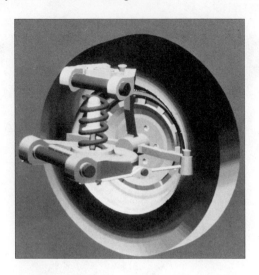

Figure 10.23 Arcad's interactive design system provides a library of 2,000 standard symbols to use in architectural drawings.

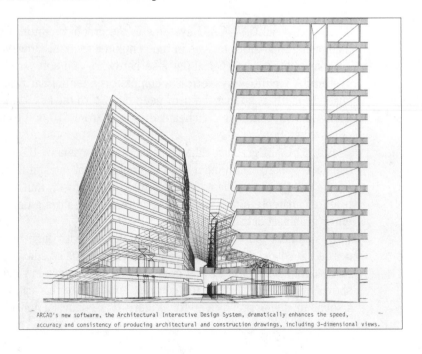

ARCAD's new software, the Architectural Interactive Design System, dramatically enhances the speed, accuracy and consistency of producing architectural and construction drawings, including 3-dimensional views.

A WORD ABOUT CAD SOFTWARE

For millions of engineers, whose stock in trade is precision drawings, the desktop computer revolution is just beginning.

We expect computers to be good at dealing with words and numbers. The idea is so ingrained in the corporate world that IBM threw graphics into the design of the original PC as an afterthought—in case someone wanted to play games. Nevertheless, there are times when no amount of words and numbers will get the point across. How do you explain how the doohickey works, how the pieces of the puzzle fit together, or what the definitive widget should look like? Draw me a picture.

When business people need a picture, they hire a designer, architect, engineer, or illustrator. Until now, the main market for computer-aided design and drafting (CADD, or CAD if you mean either design or drafting) has been graphic arts professionals. There is no replacement for specialized expertise. But there are times when a quicker and simpler drawing must do.

Until now, making acceptable technical drawings on a microcomputer has been costly. In 1985 you could expect to pay $2,500 for a competent drafting program, at least $1,400 for a high-resolution color graphics card and monitor, several hundred dollars for a pointing device (mouse or digitizer), and $2,000 for a small plotter. This adds up to $7,000—not counting the computer and peripherals you already own. Today you can put together an acceptable configuration for $300 to $1,200, which includes the computer.

Essential CAD Features

CAD programs have often been called "word processors for drawing." It's a good analogy, but it doesn't go far enough. In addition to being able to edit extensively without redrawing, CAD cuts drafting time in many unique ways. The most fundamental of these is the ability to use "objects" as a drawing element. Objects are groups of lines, arcs, and circles, welded together so they can be used in a drawing as a single entity. Objects can be a simple as an interior door or as complex as a microchip. Thanks to objects, CAD means you never have to draw anything twice.

"Zoom" gives you virtually infinite magnification of all parts of the drawing without loss of resolution. In practical terms, infinite zoom lets you enter any imaginable degree of precise detail into a drawing, regardless of the sharpness of your eyesight, the steadiness of your hand, or the clarity of your monitor. One of the demonstration files for Autocad is a map of the Milky Way. The file zooms in on the solar system, then Earth, then the United States, then California, then San Francisco, then the Transamerica Pyramid, and finally through one of the pyramid's office windows to a monitor displaying the Autocad logo.

Finally, placement and measurement using a CAD program are both faster and more accurate compared to manual methods. CAD programs let you work in 1-to-1 (real world) measurements, then automatically scale the drawing for you. You can specify intervals for a drawing grid and optionally "snap" the start and end points of drawing entries to its intersections. In imitation of the T square, there should be an option to force lines to be absolutely vertical or horizontal.

A full list of features found in most any CAD manual would fill several pages. Many of these features are just more ways to skin the same cat; they give a program its personality. Attributes that appeal to one user may frustrate another. On the other hand, certain advanced features are especially worthwhile because they save valuable time.

The first group of commands to look for are those that expand the list of drawing construction elements beyond the basic line, arc, and curve. The ability to draw parallel lines makes it easy to draw walls, piping, and anything with equilateral sides. Ellipses can be drawn by combining arcs, but it's tedious. It's even harder to build complex

Continued on next page

dimensional drawing. The computational requirements of the editor used to create Figure 10.23 are much less demanding than those of the editor that created the image in Figure 10.22.

The ultimate in CAD/CAM is the CAM portion—computer-aided manufacturing—which helps produce manufactured goods. For example, after a designer perfects a circuit board, a CAM system can guide the production of the circuit boards by controlling machinery, creating parts lists, and generating the production artwork masters. CAM systems are often integrated with numerically controlled machines. For example, the CAM system might produce a list of instructions to be loaded into an automatic lathe or a welding robot. Parts are then manufactured and tested and adjustments are made, until the production line is perfected.

Art and Animation

Both computer art and animated graphics have exploded onto the technological scene since the invention of low-cost personal computers. High-resolution graphics systems have replaced canvas, brush, and paint with electronic stylus and color monitor. The computer has given artists an extremely fast and versatile tool.

Animation is just one of the many possible uses of computer-aided design, but it is perhaps the most intriguing. For over half a century, cartoonists in the motion picture industry have been producing animations in which images appear to move if a series of still-frames is shown in rapid succession. The same idea is used in producing computer animation. A picture is *animated* on a computer by moving, rotating, translating (moving to a new location), or both rotating and translating one or more objects on the screen. If the motion takes place fast enough to simulate life, we say that the animation is done in **real time**. Real-time animation usually in-

Figure 10.24 Still-frames of a flying bird.

(a)   (b)

(c)   (d)

(e)   (f)   (g)

volves more complex motion than simple rotation and translation. For example, a picture of a person walking across the screen requires movement of the whole object (person), movement of parts of the object (legs), and a fluid coordination of the moving parts (coordination between legs and body).

Suppose you want to animate a flying bird, as shown in the still-frames in Figure 10.24. The still-frames are made by reproducing the bird's body and changing the position of the wings. Frames (e) through (g) are identical to frames (a), (b), and (c). But in frames (a) through (d), the wings move down; in frames (e) through (g), the wings move up. The bird will appear to fly when the still-frames are rapidly displayed, erased, moved, and subsequently displayed on the screen. The animation is controlled by a sequence of commands similar to

DRAW FRAME (a)
ERASE
MOVE
DRAW FRAME (b)
ERASE

```
MOVE
DRAW FRAME (C)
ERASE
MOVE
```

You can repeat the sequence for as long as you want. You would have to draw more complex sequences to achieve more realistic animation, but the concept is basically the same.

SUMMARY

There are three general categories of graphics programs: (1) presentation graphics for drawing charts, graphs, and diagrams; (2) graphics editors for doing CAD/CAM and generalized drawing; and (3) educational and entertainment graphics.

Presentation graphics are frequently produced by graphics components of spreadsheets, word processors, and database managers. Other alternatives are to produce them with a standalone graphics program or a project management program. Both types of programs produce specialized graphs and charts for the purpose of communication and analysis.

Graphics editors often work in conjunction with programs for designing new products, tools, or parts. They work with such input devices as a mouse or a puck and with such output devices as plotters and graphical printers.

The simplest graphics editors simulate an artist's tools in the way they draw on the screen. These "paint" programs store the screen image as a bit map in memory. The most sophisticated CAD/CAM graphics editors use vector graphics technology to store the object being drawn as a mathematical model in memory. Vector graphics programs are more difficult to use when drawing freehand pictures, but they are more accurate for lines and other well-behaved mathematical shapes, such as cylinders and ellipses. Another advantage of vector graphics editors over bit-mapped graphics editors is their ability to store images compactly on disk.

Special-purpose programs are used along with graphics editors for CAD/CAM applications and to create entertainment graphics, such as animated sequences. These are used in games, instruction, and artistic applications that require special graphic effects.

KEY TERMS

analytic graphics
CAD/CAM

Gantt chart
graphics editor

PERT chart
presentation graphics
project management program

real time
solids modeling
turnkey system

DISCUSSION QUESTIONS

1. Presentation graphics can be created with the graphics option of a word processor, spreadsheet, or database manager or with a standalone presentation graphics program. Discuss when you might prefer to use each of these programs to create a bar chart.

2. What are PAN and ZOOM? What is the difference between FILL and SPRAY?

3. How might rubber banding work with the RECTANGLE, CIRCLE, and POLYGON commands?

4. Vector graphics is a much older technology than bit-mapped graphics. Explain why advances in RAM technology have made bit-mapped graphics dominant in microcomputers. What are the advantages and disadvantages of each?

EXERCISES

1. Use a graphics program to duplicate the pie chart shown in Figure 10.2. Count the number of keystrokes needed to modify a single cell of the spreadsheet and to redraw the chart.

2. Use a database manager to create a file containing the following information:

Year	Barrels
1983	1,051,345
1984	1,967,002
1985	835,981
1986	955,300
1987	1,000,382
1988	1,499,999
1989	2,044,678
1990	2,894,053

Construct a bar chart plotting barrels versus year and then a pie chart in which each slice shows the percentage of the total number of barrels in a year.

3. Suggest how a word processor could be designed to handle both text and graphs within the same document. What problems with disk space do you suppose would be encountered for the word processing files?

4. Become familiar with a bit-mapped graphics editor. What is the difference between the PAINT and DRAW commands?

5. Show how a stick figure is animated by drawing a six-frame sequence of still-frames. Use a graphics editor to draw the six frames.

11 Desktop Publishing

A BRIEF HISTORY OF PUBLISHING

DESKTOP PUBLISHING HARDWARE
Laser Printers
Scanners

PAGE COMPOSITION
Page Composition Programs
Using a Page Composition Program

Structural changes in our society occur slowly and often are hidden in a thicket of daily headlines about transient events. Determining which events represent a truly fundamental change is easier if you examine them from a historical perspective. History shows that the progress of human culture is linked conclusively to advances in the technology of writing and publishing. From this viewpoint, desktop publishing promises to be one of the most important advances of our time, because it opens new avenues of communication for ordinary people.

Author A. J. Liebling wrote, "Freedom of the press belongs to those who own one." As recently as ten years ago, publishing required a substantial capital investment and the expertise of specialized professionals. Today, any motivated person with an artistic flair can buy a $5,000 desktop publishing system and produce top-quality professional results.

333

A WORD ABOUT
NEW DESKTOP PUBLISHING SERVICES

Going from disk to hard copy is easier than ever, as on-line services and copy shops offer fast turnaround and professional results.

Linda Ohde used to face a dilemma over the training manuals she helped produce every week for her employer, Echols and Pryor Technical Communication Inc.

The small Berkeley, California, firm frequently needed to produce manuals for its customized seminars on business and technical writing, but commercial typesetting shops took too long and were too expensive. Documents produced on a daisy–wheel printer were affordable but unprofessional looking, Ohde says. When the company lost its outside word processing help, she began to look for a better solution. Ohde found it at a local copy shop.

A few blocks away, Krishna Copy Center was renting time on an Apple Macintosh and Laserwriter printer. Ohde began bringing Microsoft Word files on a disk into the center, where she combined them with graphics and printed them. Now the quality of Echols and Pryor's documents is similar to typeset material, Ohde says, and by designing the manuals itself, the company avoids the time-consuming process of sending documents back and forth to outside help for corrections.

Echols and Pryor is just one of many firms that are taking advantage of such services. Users who own a computer can often take a disk into a quick-print or typesetting shop for printing, send in their documents over phone lines via a modem, or, in some areas, upload documents onto a print shop bulletin board or network. Those who don't own a computer can often rent time on one. Prices range from 30 cents per page for laser printing to $70 for one-on-one desktop publishing training courses to $35 an hour (and up) for full design and printing services.

Desktop publishing services are being used not only by small companies that have never typeset their documents before, but also by departments within larger companies that need a faster turnaround than their corporate publishing departments can offer. "Publishing departments often have a backlog problem similar to the MIS [management information systems] problem," says Brian Skidmore, director of the Publishing/Computer-Aided Publishing group of the Boston Computer Society. "The department is overwhelmed."

Vince Swanson of Dalmo Victor Inc., of Belmont, California, for example, may opt to use a desktop publishing printing service rather than the defense contractor's publishing department for an upcoming contract. As the senior technical writer, he wants a faster turnaround time and also would like to maintain more control over the design of his documents, he says. Documents sent through in-house channels take up to three days to be completed, he says, and often contain errors that have been introduced through the rekeying required for the company's word processing equipment. "With a service, you have precise control," Swanson says.

Such desire for control, fast turnaround, and professional results without professional typesetting costs appears to ensure the continuing growth of desktop publishing services for some time to come.

"Our documents are much more professional looking now," says Ohde. The company may even consider purchasing its own Laserwriter in the future, she says. "The desktop publishing services have been convenient, but it's getting crowded down at Krishna Copy Center."

Source: Copyright © 1987 by Popular Computing Inc., a subsidiary of CW Communications, Inc. Reprinted from *Infoworld,* 1060 Marsh Rd., Menlo Park, CA 94025.

What the long-term effects of this unusually abrupt shift in power will bring no one knows, but even the predictions for the short term are impressive. Dataquest, a market research firm in San Jose, California, predicts that the desktop publishing market will grow from $306 million in 1986 to $4.9 billion in 1990. Even at that level, says Ajit Kapoor, Dataquest's director of electronic publishing market analysis, "$4.9 billion reflects that only 8 percent of the installed base of personal computers will be used for publishing by 1990. That's not a hell of a lot, so I think it will probably be much larger in the future."

Certainly the potential market for desktop publishing is huge. Virtually all businesses are engaged in some form of publishing—from price lists, brochures, and directories to newsletters, manuals, and financial reports. Corporations typically spend between 5 and 10 percent of their gross revenues on publishing, according to David Goodstein, president of InterConsult, a market research and consulting firm in Cambridge, Massachusetts.

It is generally agreed that the term **desktop publishing** was coined by Paul Brainard, founder of Aldus Corporation—the company that developed PageMaker. About the term's definition there is less agreement. To some, desktop publishing is the application of personal computers to the publishing process. But software vendors take a conveniently broader view and tout any product that produces good-looking computer output as a desktop publishing solution. Suddenly, the words *desktop publishing* have acquired the same marketing magic for the computer field that the words *new and improved* have long held for selling soap.

But why has desktop publishing generated such widespread interest? Certainly the momentum behind it goes far beyond the traditional publishing community. Actually, major publishers still produce nearly all of their final copy with conventional typesetting systems and graphic artists, partly because converting established operating procedures is a bother, but mostly because desktop publishing tools need more development before they can challenge high-volume publishing systems. The ground swell of support for desktop publishing has come from a broad spectrum of users—small businesses, churches, public relations firms, corporate in-house publications departments, and freelance writers and designers. The common element among all these new "publishers" is a desire to communicate ideas effectively. In the Information Age, presenting facts clearly, concisely, and even artistically is as important as having the facts in the first place.

In this chapter, we examine several aspects of the desktop publishing revolution. We first build a foundation of understanding by surveying the history of publishing and its influence on society. Then we discuss the hardware involved in desktop publishing, emphasizing laser printers, the engines that made low-cost, high-quality desktop publishing possible. In the closing section, we examine page composition software and its ability to integrate text and graphics in an aesthetically pleasing page layout.

Since the Middle Ages, the power of publishing has shaped our destiny. The mass dissemination of the printed word broke the monopolistic power of the Roman Catholic Church and created the basis for democratic institutions and the importance of individualism that still dominate our culture.

Perhaps the greatest breakthrough in communication came with Johann Gutenberg's invention of *movable type* around 1450. A piece of movable type is a metal block tipped with an embossed image of a character. One after another, the pieces of type were placed in rows to form words and lines; rows were packed into a rack to form a page. When the page was complete, rollers spread ink across the raised images, and paper was pressed onto the type to absorb the ink (see Figure 11.1). After printing the desired number of copies, the type was disassembled and sorted into bins in preparation for setting the next page.

Movable type permitted the first mass printing of books by allowing the type to be reused again and again. Before this invention, books were copied tediously by monks, one page at a time, with sharpened quills laden with ink. The Chinese invented movable type hundreds of years before Gutenberg, but because of the complexity of their language, they couldn't use it to revolutionize their culture, as did Western societies. Written Chinese is not easily adapted to printing, because it requires as many as 50,000 individually shaped characters.

Figure 11.1 A reproduction of the Gutenberg printing press.

Figure 11.2 In its day, the Linotype Comet was the fastest typesetter in the world. With a Teletypesetter attachment, as pictured here, it could operate at speeds of up to 12 lines a minute.

The difficulty of assembling and disassembling pages of type remained a problem for hundreds of years. Samuel Clemens (pen name, Mark Twain) went bankrupt financing the development of an automatic machine for this task. The eventual solution, the *Linotype machine* shown in Figure 11.2, was one of the world's most complicated mechanical devices. The Linotype machine molded complete lines of lead type from movable dies. Each die was tipped with the indented image of a character. As the operator typed on a keyboard, dies would drop from storage slots into a line. As soon as the line was full of words, wedge-shaped spacers were shoved between the dies to justify and fill out the line. Next, an image of the line was captured by pumping molten lead against the dies and allowing it to harden into a *slug*. The slugs were stacked into a *galley* that was used to make raised-image plates for the press. After the slug was formed, the Linotype used an identifying pattern of notches in the dies to mechanically sort and return each to its assigned storage slot for reuse. A competent Linotype operator could set four or five newspaper-length lines of type each minute. As late as 1965, there were 40,000 Linotype operators in the United States. But today, only a few Linotype machines remain in use. They were replaced by offset presses and phototypesetters, neither of which requires movable type.

The *offset press* borrows technology from earlier developments in lithography and photography. To transfer a design onto paper, lithography uses the principle that oil and water do not mix (see Figure 11.3). The inventor of lithography, Alois Senefelder (1771–1834), applied a thin layer of grease to some areas of a fine-grained, polished limestone and moistened other areas with water. When a roller spread oily ink across the stone, the greasy areas accepted the ink, but the wet areas did not. Pressing paper against this surface created a printed image.

In an offset press, the lithographer's limestone is replaced by thin aluminum or plastic plates that can be wrapped around the press's rollers. Photographic methods convert the image of a paper-based master copy into an ink-receptive pattern of chemicals on the printing plate. This has reduced the required setup for printing to simply preparing one high-quality original. The upshot has been an explosion in the variety and quantity of printed material in the last 20 years.

The difficulty of creating high-quality originals was reduced with the invention of the *phototypesetter,* a printer that uses light to write on a photographic material (see Photo 30 in Window 1). Early phototypesetters printed characters by shooting bursts of light through character patterns stored on a film wrapped around a revolving drum. This restricted them to printing a fixed set of characters at a time. Most modern phototypesetters are completely digital and build images from dots, as a dot matrix printer does. Phototypesetters draw precise images on the photographic surface by flashing a xenon lamp or laser hundreds of thousands of times per second, to print tiny dots—from 900 to 5,200 dpi (dots per inch). Aside from the resolution, the output has absolutely clean whites and pitch-black blacks. The photographic material is usually a roll of resin-coated paper, but it can also be photographic film or even an offset plate. A fast phototypesetter can print 700 two-inch lines per minute and costs about $200,000. Slower typesetters may cost no more than $15,000.

Computers have been controlling typesetters since the early 1970s. Usually a typesetter is sold as part of a system that includes a front-end computer and terminals from which operators may enter and format text. Since each manufacturer developed a different set of format codes to control **composition**—the selection of type sizes and styles and the positioning of type on a page—a print file created for one manufacturer's phototypesetters cannot be printed by another's.

Until the arrival of desktop publishing, typeset documents were invariably prepared by specialists. If you wanted typeset-quality output, the first step was to mark up the text to indicate its position on the page along with the typeface sizes and styles to be used. This was submitted to a typesetting service bureau, where an operator would keyboard the text and the needed formatting codes into the front-end computer and print a *galley proof* (draft copy) for you to review. Proofreading would usually reveal mistakes, so a second (or third) pass would be necessary to get an acceptable version. Each step required passing paper back and forth, affecting the overall schedule. The completed page would cost 20 dollars or more, depending on the amount of text and the number and extent of revisions.

Figure 11.3 Lithography (top) produces a printed image from an ink-receptive image drawn on a flat surface. In an offset press (bottom), the image is placed on plates that can be mounted on the press's rollers.

DESKTOP PUBLISHING HARDWARE

A good desktop publishing system begins with a powerful microcomputer system. The computer must have enough memory to run large programs and enough speed to reformat and rehyphenate a document on the fly. This involves more work than you might expect. For example, a WYSIWYG page composition program must determine each character's position precisely and then draw a bit-

Figure 11.4 This full-page display shows Superpage, a professional-level page composition program. The display has 1,008 scan lines from top to bottom, with 736 pixels on each line.

mapped replica of it on the screen. These tasks generally require at least an 8-megahertz processor and 1 megabyte of memory. You can get by with less only if you don't mind taking a ten-second break every time the machine needs to repaint the screen.

The screen must be able to accurately display how your document will look when printed; color isn't as important as resolution. The best displays for desktop publishing let you edit a full page of text at the same time (see Figure 11.4). This requires at least 1,000 scan lines from the top to the bottom of the screen. On displays with less resolution, you need to scroll up and down and left and right to read an entire page (see Figure 11.5).

Other components of a desktop publishing system are likely to be a hard disk, mouse, laser printer, and scanner. Laser printers and scanners are important enough to warrant further discussion.

Laser Printers

Low-cost laser printers, first introduced in 1985, are credited with ushering in the age of desktop publishing. Laser printers are faster and quieter than daisy-wheel and dot matrix printers. But, best of all, their 300-dpi resolution and ability to mix

Figure 11.5 PageMaker on the Macintosh set the standards for WYSIWYG page composition. The nine-inch Macintosh screen provides a sharp image for such a small screen, because it packs 512 pixels on each scan line.

various styles of text with graphics produces output that looks almost as good as typeset documents.

The Apple LaserWriter, *InfoWorld's* 1985 Product of the Year, offered 1.5MB of RAM for image processing, 13 built-in type fonts (drawn from the Courier, Times Roman, and Helvetica families), and a host of graphics features at an initial price of $6,995. Because of these features and its ability to adjust the size of characters, the LaserWriter acted as a catalyst for the entire desktop publishing market. In 1986 Apple lowered the LaserWriter's price and introduced the Laser-

Figure 11.6 An original Hewlett-Packard LaserJet (left) is shown receiving a new toner cartridge. The newer LaserJet Series II printer (right) is smaller and more reliable and can accept more memory.

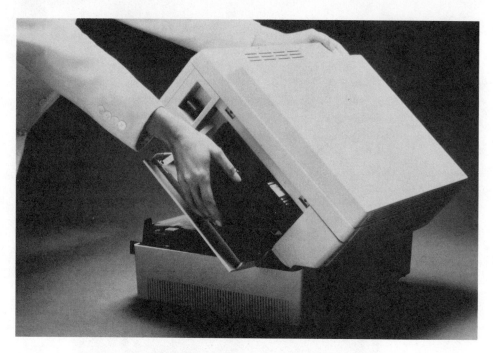

Writer Plus with six additional families in ROM: Avant Garde, Bookman, New Century Schoolbook, Palatino, Zapf Chancery, and Zapf Dingbats.

Despite the LaserWriter's popularity among desktop publishing enthusiasts, Hewlett-Packard captured the lion's share of the laser printer market with its LaserJet printers. Although LaserJets are much less capable, their lower price (a basic model cost $3,500 in 1985) prompted many people to buy them as a replacement for daisy-wheel printers. In 1987 Hewlett-Packard discontinued the LaserJet and introduced the LaserJet Series II printers (see Figure 11.6). A basic LaserJet Series II printer has 0.5MB of RAM and costs $2,595.

Both the LaserWriter and LaserJet printer families share some important traits. Both are built from Cannon "print engines," which use the same xerographic printing methods as Cannon's Personal Copiers. Both are reliable, because the most error-prone parts—the belt and photosensitive drum—are housed inside a $100 replaceable toner cartridge. Both use a Motorola 68000 microprocessor to execute commands and control printing. And both fostered a host of "me-too" competitors that emulate their features.

Despite their many similarities, however, it soon became apparent that the LaserWriter and LaserJet printer families are fundamentally different. The differences arise from the software they use to manage fonts and accept instructions.

Figure 11.6 Continued.

Bit-Mapped Versus Outline Fonts

The most significant limitation of the LaserJet printer family is the way it handles type fonts. The fonts are stored in the printer's memory as a *bit map*—a pattern of dots (see Figure 11.7). Each font specifies the patterns for a particular size, style, and orientation of characters, such as 10-point Courier characters in the *portrait* (upright) orientation. A font's size is fixed because the machine can't change the size of the dot patterns to get larger characters. Several crude fonts are built into the printer's ROM, but for desktop publishing tasks, additional fonts must be loaded into the printer, either by plugging a font cartridge into the printer or by downloading fonts from a disk in the microcomputer. Whenever fonts are loaded into the printer's memory, less memory is available for printing graphics.

Memory is another limitation of the LaserJet printers; most of them don't have enough memory to print a full page of 300-dpi graphics. This problem arises because laser printers are *page printers;* that is, they can't pause while printing a page. They print so quickly—more than 1 million dots per second—that the information for an entire page must be in the printer's memory before printing begins. An 8½-by-11-inch page requires about a megabyte of memory at 300 dpi. Laser printers with less than a megabyte of memory must print full-page graphics at either 75 or 150 dpi—about the resolution of a dot matrix printer.

Taking an entirely different approach to type fonts is the Apple LaserWriter. It stores fonts as descriptions of the outline or shape of the characters rather than as

Figure 11.7 A bit-mapped font (top) defines letters as patterns of dots. An outline font (bottom) defines letters by shape—in this case, by line segments and arcs.

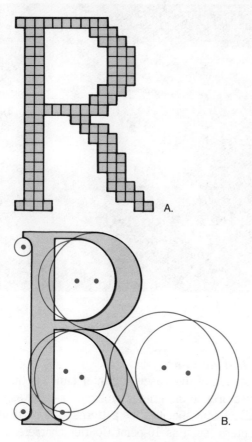

a fixed dot pattern. Each character is defined as a mathematical model of the character's outline, so it can be adjusted to any size or rotated to print sideways or at an angle. This flexibility makes outline fonts far superior to the bit-mapped variety for desktop publishing.

There is a drawback to outline fonts, however. Before a page can be printed, the printer must determine which dots on the page fall within the outlines of the characters. This makes the LaserWriter print text more slowly than printers with bit-mapped fonts.

Page Description Languages

The most significant difference between the LaserWriter and the LaserJet printers is in the languages they use to control their actions. LaserJet printers use Hewlett-Packard's Printer Control Language (PCL), whereas LaserWriter printers use PostScript, a page description language created by Adobe Systems of Palo Alto, California.

Hewlett-Packard's PCL is a simple language designed to load bit-mapped fonts and bit-mapped graphics into the printer. Fonts cannot be adjusted in size or manipulated in any way, such as printing white letters on a black background. The language has no commands for rotating, scaling, or clipping graphics or for drawing curves or other geometric figures. Thus, the LaserJet requires that the microcomputer and its application software perform these functions. Each bit in a graphics image must be calculated inside the microcomputer and then loaded into the printer—a process that can be painfully slow. Of even more importance, however, PCL adheres to none of the emerging graphics standards, making life difficult for application software developers. Unless they write a special LaserJet printer driver, their programs won't print on a LaserJet.

In contrast, a **page description language (PDL)** is a programming language with specialized instructions for describing whole pages to a printer. That is, a PDL's role is to let an application program tell a printer how to build a page from a combination of text, fonts, lines, arcs, and other graphical images. With a PDL, the marks to appear on the page are described by a series of instructions and parameters, rather than indicated by every spot to be inked. Then it is up to the printer to interpret the instructions and translate them into the marks that will appear on paper.

Although PostScript isn't the only PDL, it is the best known and most widely supported. Other PDLs include Xerox's Interpress and Imagen's DDL (*D*ocument *D*escription *L*anguage). All three are descendants of research on printer languages conducted at Xerox Corporation's Palo Alto Research Center (PARC).

The Apple LaserWriter was the first of many printers to adopt PostScript. Other PostScript laser-printers include units from QMS, DEC, Texas Instruments, NEC, Quadram, Dataproducts, and IBM. For people demanding typeset-quality output, Allied Linotype introduced the first PostScript-compatible photo-typesetters in 1985. First came the Linotronic L100, which costs from $32,000 to $40,000 and produces a resolution of 1,270 lines per inch. Other PostScript-compatible models include the faster, higher-resolution L300 (see Figure 11.8) and the L500, which allows for a wider image area. In 1987 even Hewlett-Packard adopted the emerging standard by announcing a PostScript option for its laser printers.

PostScript provides a standardized way for application programs to communicate with printers. Figure 11.9 illustrates how this works. An application program with a PostScript device driver, such as a word processor or drafting program, can send an output file to *any* PostScript printer. The application program doesn't need to know whether the actual printer is of the dot matrix, laser, or typesetter variety, because every PostScript printer can accept the same instructions. Obviously, a high-resolution printer will produce a clearer, sharper rendition of the instructions than a low-resolution printer, but otherwise the output will look the same. This frees software developers from the need to write another device driver whenever a new printer is marketed. It also allows users to use one device to print draft copies and another, higher-resolution device to print the final copy.

Figure 11.8 The Linotronic L300 combines laser technology and PostScript image processing to produce reproduction-quality output on a photographic medium, such as resin-coated paper. The L300, priced at $56,000 to $77,000, prints images with 635, 1,270, or 2,540 lines per inch.

In just this way, PostScript formed the first convenient link between typesetters and microcomputer-based systems. By using a PostScript-compatible desktop publishing program and an Apple LaserWriter, people began to design and print documents that appeared typeset to the casual eye—at a cost of five cents a page! But if true typeset quality was required, the output files could be sent directly from a Macintosh to a Linotronic phototypesetter over an AppleTalk local area network. Or the files can be sent by disk or telecommunications to a service bureau that operates a Linotronic typesetter. Because these PostScript output files can be printed immediately—without additional format codes or editing—the cost of this sort of typesetting is around six dollars a page, much lower than for conventional typesetting.

Most people who use a PostScript printer have never seen a single PostScript instruction. Normally, the instructions are created by application programs and sent directly to the printer. But if you own a PostScript printer and you feel so inclined, you can write PostScript programs for your printer to execute. This can give you a better understanding of what a PDL is all about. For example, the screen in Figure 11.10 shows a file with PostScript instructions that tell the printer what text to print, what font and type size to use, what lines to draw, and where

Figure 11.9 PostScript is a page description language that insulates application programs from printers. The device driver translates text and graphics into PostScript language statements. Then any PostScript-compatible printer can interpret the statements without further modification.

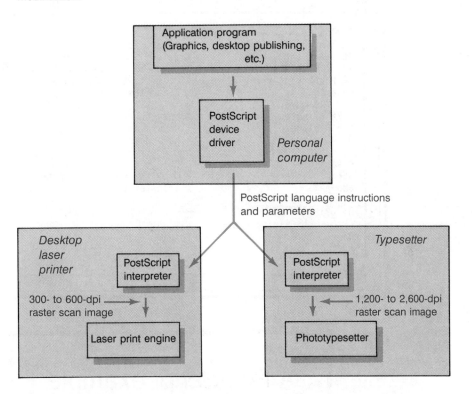

to place all these objects. This simple example shows only a few of the instructions you might encounter if you look at the print files created by an application program. Other instructions typically provided by PDLs draw curves, rotate text, fill areas with patterns or colors, make decisions (is the current line full?), or establish loops to repeat a section of instructions.

Scanners

Drawings and photographs add life to the published page. But before paper-based artwork can be manipulated with desktop publishing software, it must be *digitized,* or converted into a digital format. Digitizing is done with a **scanner,** a special light-sensitive device that converts photographs, black and white drawings, and other visual images into bit-mapped images. Scanners provide a quick way to enter images into a computer. Then you can use a graphics editor or page composition program to modify, stretch, shrink, crop, or erase parts of the image.

Figure 11.11 shows the result of digitizing a black and white drawing by using the Macintosh and a light-detector scanner called ThunderScan. ThunderScan replaces the ribbon in the Apple ImageWriter dot matrix printer—thus making the

Figure 11.10 (a) This PostScript program describes exactly how to print some text surrounded by a box. (b) The resulting output.

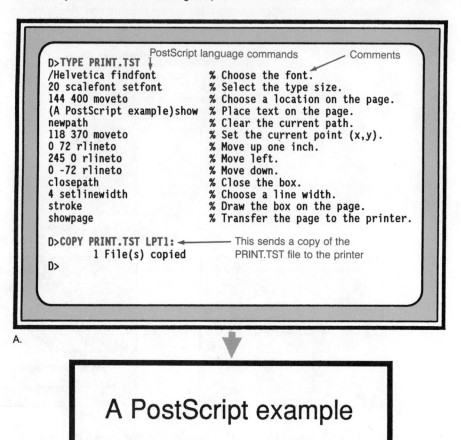

```
                        PostScript language commands            Comments
D>TYPE PRINT.TST
/Helvetica findfont            % Choose the font.
20 scalefont setfont           % Select the type size.
144 400 moveto                 % Choose a location on the page.
(A PostScript example)show     % Place text on the page.
newpath                        % Clear the current path.
118 370 moveto                 % Set the current point (x,y).
0 72 rlineto                   % Move up one inch.
245 0 rlineto                  % Move left.
0 -72 rlineto                  % Move down.
closepath                      % Close the box.
4 setlinewidth                 % Choose a line width.
stroke                         % Draw the box on the page.
showpage                       % Transfer the page to the printer.

D>COPY PRINT.TST LPT1:         This sends a copy of the
         1 File(s) copied      PRINT.TST file to the printer
D>
```

A.

A PostScript example

B.

ImageWriter read from the paper rather than print on it. This low-cost scanner is simple: a light is cast onto the paper, and the reflected light is registered by a light-sensitive detector. When a position is examined by the scanner, the detected light is converted into a bit-mapped image, sent to the computer, and displayed on the screen. But because ThunderScan relies on the paper-movement mechanism of a dot matrix printer, its images aren't very sharp. The resolution of the digitized image shown in Figure 11.11 is only about 75 dpi.

Another way to capture images is with a *flat-bed document scanner* (see Figure 11.12). Although these units cost more—from around $600 to more than $3,000— they capture images at 300 dpi or more, matching the resolution of laser printers.

Most scanners are sold bundled with software to help control their functions. For example, Figure 11.13 shows some of the selections you can make while using

Figure 11.11 Digitizing a line drawing. (left) Original drawing to be digitized. (right) Digitized image captured by ThunderScan and printed by an ImageWriter.

(a) Original drawing to be digitized

(b) Digitized image from Thunderscan

Figure 11.12 The Hewlett-Packard ScanJet, a flat-bed desktop scanner.

Figure 11.13 Scanning Gallery, an application program provided with the HP ScanJet, lets you capture and edit images within Microsoft Windows.

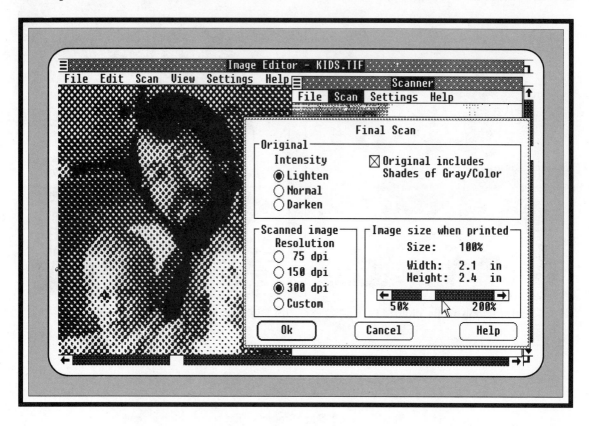

Scanning Gallery, the application program Hewlett-Packard provides to control the HP ScanJet. Before you scan the original, Scanning Gallery lets you adjust the scanner's resolution, select the size of the scanned image to be produced, and set the brightness level. After the image has been captured, you can preview it on the screen, cut and paste parts of the image, and convert the image into any of several graphics formats.

Scanners are used to capture all kinds of information: typed text, line drawings used for logos or illustrations, letters to be mailed electronically, and photographs or other images containing colors or grays. Each type of information needs to be treated differently (see Figure 11.14). The photosensitive detector in most scanners can sense several levels of light for each spot examined. For example, the HP Scan Jet uses four bits to record how bright each spot is, resulting in 16 *gray-scale levels.* But for some tasks, such as scanning text or line art, the gray-scale information is an unnecessary complication. In this case, the scanner's software is used to convert the gray-scale image into a binary image, in which each spot is either white or black. This conversion is simple: any spot darker than a fixed value becomes black, and everything else becomes white.

Figure 11.14 A good scanner captures images in a gray-scale format. Then application software converts the gray-scale image into the type of information desired by the user.

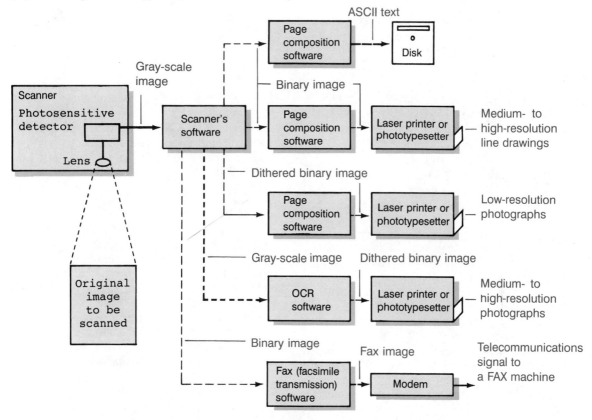

If the original image is a photograph, a more sophisticated conversion is necessary. Laser printers and phototypesetters can print only black spots; they can't print gray. But a photograph would look terrible if all its dark gray areas became black and its light gray areas, white. The conventional way of solving this problem is to convert the photograph into a **halftone**—a pattern of dots of varying sizes—by rephotographing it through a special etched screen. However, if a scanner is used, the solution is to **dither** the photograph; that is, to approximate the levels of gray in the original with a carefully chosen pattern of white and black spots that are all the same size.

Dithering involves a tradeoff between contrast and resolution. If a large grid pattern is chosen, there is considerable flexibility in producing shades of gray. Conversely, a smaller grid pattern reduces the size of each *grain,* or dithered area, allowing more detail to appear in the photograph. Another factor to consider is the pattern of spots to use within each dithered grain. For example, the dither pattern shown in Figure 11.15 arranges the spots along one side of each grain, forming what appear to be vertical lines. This works well for photographs with smooth contours, such as faces, but is unacceptable for photographs that have vertical lines before digitizing.

A WORD ABOUT
DITHERING AND HALFTONING

The image captured by a scanner is best at reproducing line art where everything is either black or white. This insert describes some techniques used to capture and print gray-scale images.

Dithering is an image processing technique that allows printers and computer displays (which support only two tone levels, black and white) to produce documents that appear to have continuous shades of gray. In other words, dithering allows most available printers and computer displays to produce images that look like ordinary black and white photographs.

As a consequence of dithering, some detail on the original black and white photograph may be lost. Usually, however, the additional simulated gray information makes up for the loss of detail.

The human eye and brain have the ability to look at an area of closely spaced dark dots on a white background and perceive them as a gray tone. The eye and brain fill in and average the

black and white data and transform them into gray information. For example, looking at [a dithered photo] from a distance, it appears as a normal continuous tone image even though, when looked at closely, it appears as a series of closely spaced black dots.

Dithering is similar to a technique used by newspapers and magazines known as halftoning. Halftones simulate shades of gray by varying the size of circular black dots on a fixed grid pattern. Dithering accomplishes the same purpose as halftoning, but does so by making use of fixed black squares and changes the number of adjacent black squares in small regional areas to control the apparent level of gray.

Note that the word "halftone" is often used as a synonym for "dither." To the untrained eye, the output produced by the two processes can look similar. They really are two different processes with the same goal.

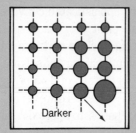

A dithered image creates light and dark areas by changing the number of black dots within each grain.

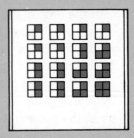

Halftones vary the size of spots—called *grains*—to produce light and dark areas.

Source: Courtesy of Hewlett Packard. Publication number: 5958-4194.

Computer Graphics: From Art to Computer-Aided Design

Most people think of a computer as a text and number processor, not as an image processor. This stereotype is changing quickly. Because manipulating images requires healthy amounts of storage and processing, the earliest users of computer graphics were draftsmen, cartographers, design engineers, and other professionals who could afford the expense. Only in the 1980s have low-cost memories and capable microprocessors brought computer graphics into wide use. Continued improvements in hardware will undoubtedly lead to even wider use of computer graphics. This photo essay provides a glimpse into the "state of the art" of computer graphics.

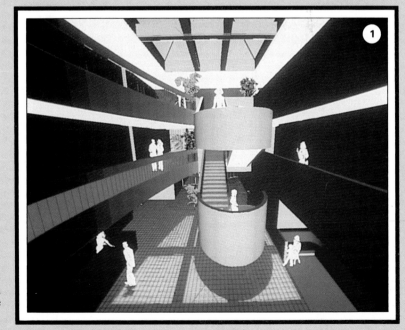

1. The architectural firm, Davis and Marks of Boston, Massachusetts, created this three-dimensional model of a lobby on an Intergraph color workstation for the Liberty Mutual Insurance Company. It shows several advanced features, including shadows and nonfaceted shading of curved surfaces.

DRAWING PROGRAMS

Drawing programs allow you to paint on an electronic canvas (the screen) with electronic brushes, pencils, spray-paint cans, rollers, and erasers. You create a drawing by selecting tools one at a time and then using them to draw. For example, to spray part of the screen with paint, you first pick up the spray-paint can from a toolkit shown on the screen. Then you move the can to the screen's drawing area and hold down the mouse's button. Picking up tools and using them is normally done by pointing with a mouse and clicking the mouse's button, but many programs also accept keyboard commands. When the drawing is finished, a printer or plotter is used to transfer the screen image to paper.

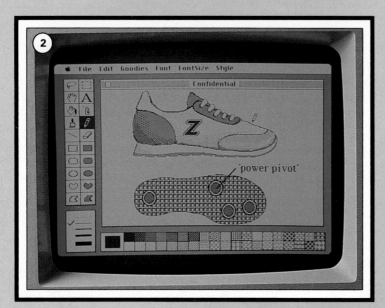

2. The MacPaint program from Apple has been a major reason for the popularity of the Apple Macintosh. MacPaint is fun to use and can produce extremely professional drawings.

3. This employment form was created using MacDraw and printed on the Apple LaserWriter printer.

The Watermill Restaurants, Inc.

125 West Broadway
Personnel, Suite 300
Cambridge, Ma. 02142

PERSONNEL REQUISITION
REQUISITION NO.
EMPLOYMENT SPECIALIST

JOB TITLE	DATE NEEDED

DEPARTMENT NAME/NUMBER	JOB LOCATION	

SHIFT	☐ DAYS ☐ SWING ☐ GRAVEYARD	SALARY RANGE	☐ EXEMPT ☐ NON-EXEMPT
	☐ PERMANENT ☐ TEMPORARY (DURATION)		PAY GRADE
	☐ ADDITION TO HEAD COUNT ☐ REPLACEMENT (NO ADDITION TO HEAD COUNT)	NAME OF EMPLOYEE REPLACED	

CAUSE OF REPLACEMENT

TO WHOM WILL EMPLOYEE REPORT?	WHO WILL CONDUCT INTERVIEW

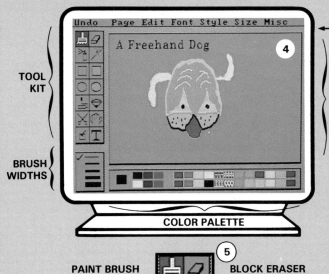

TOOL KIT

BRUSH WIDTHS

PULL-DOWN MENU BAR

DRAWING AREA

COLOR PALETTE

4. MacPaint's success has spawned many imitators. This drawing was created in a few minutes using PC Paintbrush, a color drawing program that runs on computers compatible with the IBM PC.

PAINT BRUSH   BLOCK ERASER

SPRAY PAINT   LINE

EMPTY BOX   FILLED BOX

EMPTY CIRCLE   FILLED CIRCLE

PAINT ROLLER   PALETTE ERASER

SCISSORS   MOVE PAGE

COLOR MIXER   TEXT

5. The PC Paintbrush toolkit. Electronic tools often perform better than their physical counterparts. For example, brightly checkered, plaid, or paisley paint can be sprayed from an electronic spray can.

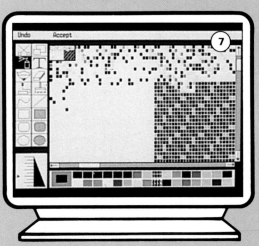

6. MacPaint and its imitators use pull-down menus to give access to the program's commands. For example, if you choose Brush Shapes from this menu, you can change the shape of the paintbrush's tip.

7. In this screen the drawing has been greatly enlarged so that the house's chimney fills the lower-right portion of the drawing area. This enlarged display is created when you choose the option labeled Zoom In; it allows you to make editing changes conveniently.

window 7

BUSINESS GRAPHICS

8. Graphs can help a business manager in two ways. First, a quickly generated *analysis graph* helps a manager find patterns and trends in otherwise meaningless tables of numbers. Second, a well-labeled *presentation graph* helps communicate a message to other people. This graph was sent to a plotter by Graphwriter, a graphics package for microcomputers that is designed expressly for preparing high-quality presentation graphics.

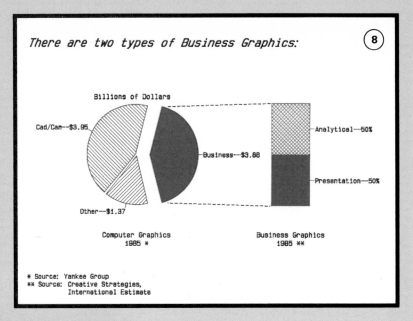

9. Many spreadsheet programs come with the ability to produce analysis graphs. This screen shows two columns of numbers stored in a spreadsheet created by Lotus Symphony. Symphony is a spreadsheet-based program that can produce line graphs, bar charts, pie charts, and stock market graphs.

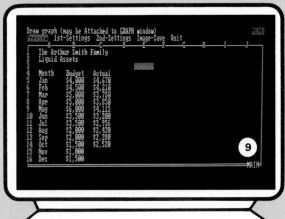

10. In this screen the Symphony program has converted the numbers from the spreadsheet into a bar graph. If the necessary raw data is already in the spreadsheet, it takes only a minute to create a graph of this complexity.

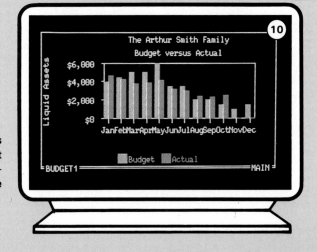

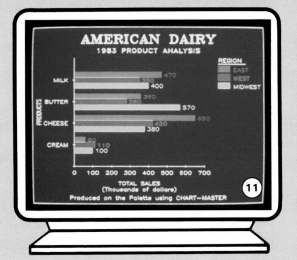

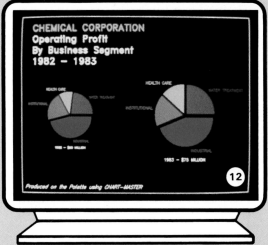

11,12. These presentation-quality graphs show better labels than most graphics packages can produce. Designing and entering high-quality presentation graphs require some skill and patience.

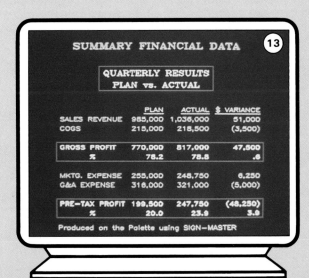

13. Text charts are useful for presenting lecture outlines, but surprisingly, many graphics packages can't create good-looking text charts.

14. Once a graph looks OK on the screen, it can be reproduced on a variety of media. For example, the graph might be printed on paper, plotted on an overhead transparency, or photographed on a 35-mm slide.

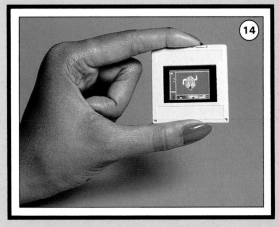

ARCHITECTURE

Graphics and architecture have always been inseparable, but it has taken recent improvements in graphics hardware and software to bring computer-based methods into all phases of architectural design.

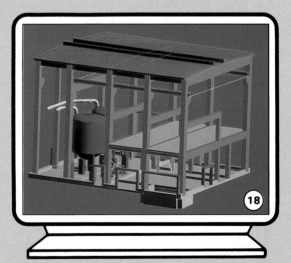

15. A CalComp computer-aided design system. Shown on the display, and on the pen plotter, is a drawing of a checkpoint for airport security.

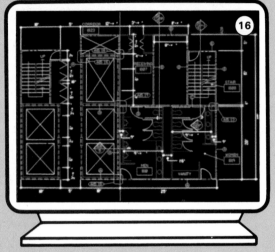

16. Complete floor plans can be displayed and modified before they are committed to paper.

17. Solids-modeling software can provide a three-dimensional view of a proposed design.

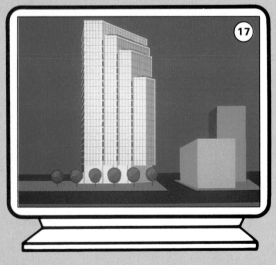

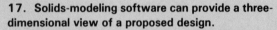

18. Three-dimensional views of the construction of a processing plant make it easy to see how pipes, equipment, and steel fit together.

CARTOGRAPHY:
THE ART OF MAKING MAPS

Digital mapping starts by capturing large geographical data sets in a map database. Then map analysts identify and correct errors and convert the data sets into useful maps.

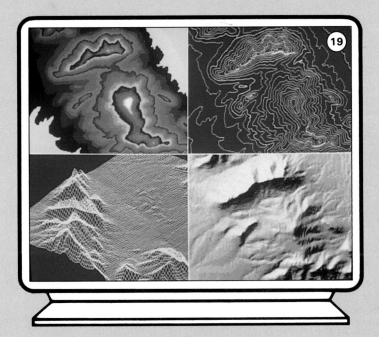

19. Once inside the computer, geographical data can be displayed in many ways. Here terrain is depicted by using (clockwise from upper left) color-coded elevations, contour lines, shaded relief, and rotated profiles.

20. This is a color-coded, shaded relief view showing features of the terrain as if they were illuminated from a light source above the screen. Shaded relief perspectives can even be displayed in stereo for viewing with 3-D glasses.

COMPUTER-AIDED MANUFACTURING

Numerically controlled machines and robots can execute very long sequences of movement commands precisely and quickly. But developing accurate sequences of commands is not an easy task. The process is accomplished more quickly and more reliably if the sequences can be simulated on a computer screen before they are tried on the actual machines.

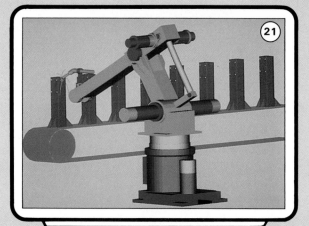

21. A simulated spot-welding operation.

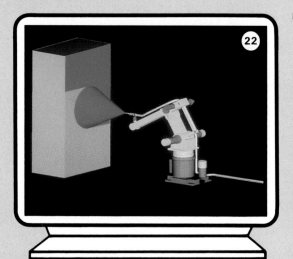

22. A simulated painting operation.

24. This crankshaft is modeled with Intergraph Sculptured Surfaces software.

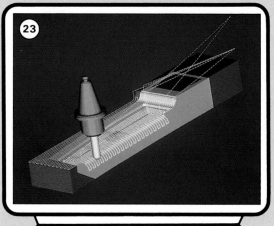

23. A simulated, numerically controlled milling sequence.

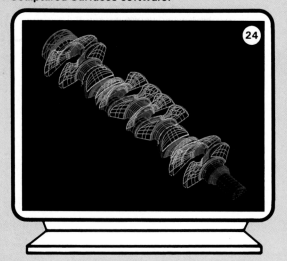

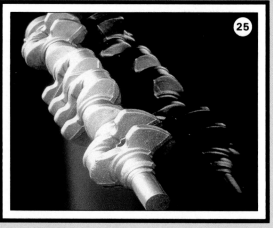

25. A die-forged crankshaft for a diesel engine.

Figure 11.15 Gray scale in a photograph can be represented by various dither patterns. This screen illustrates a vertical-line dither pattern. Compare it with the coarse-fatting dither pattern shown in Figure 11.13.

The quality of the printed image depends on the resolution of the scanner, the size of each grain, and the power of the printer. A 300-dpi scanner and laser printer are capable of printing images with 40 to 80 grains per inch (see Figure 11.16). This is slightly worse than the quality of an average newspaper photograph. However, magazine-quality work is well within the capability of a desktop publishing system if the gray-scale information of a 300-dpi scanner is dithered by a page composition program and sent to a phototypesetter.

Scanners can also be used to enter text into the computer without rekeying it. Yet another conversion is necessary to translate the scanned image of text into a format that can be used by a word processor. **Optical character recognition (OCR)** software converts the binary image of typed text into the equivalent ASCII characters. Thus, a scanner equipped with OCR software can convert an ordinary typewriter into a computer input device. Scanners used in this manner are often equipped with a sheet feeder so that they can automatically digitize and read a whole stack of papers.

Finally, scanners can function as the input device of a fax system. **Fax** is short for *fac*simile transmission, a method of sending documents through the telephone lines.

Figure 11.16 These two views of David Sullivan and his daughters, Mary and Molly, compare (a) a low-resolution dithered image (40 grains per inch) with (b) a conventional halftone (150 grains per inch).

A.

B.

PAGE COMPOSITION

A **page composition program**, or *page layout program,* controls page makeup, assembling elements on a printed page. This software, the heart of a desktop publishing system, lets you place and move text and graphic elements on the page. Most of these programs offer a WYSIWYG display that shows on the screen what the page will look like when printed. Page composition programs provide a variety of special tools to revise the page layout quickly, mix different typefaces, and control the spacing of text and the sizing of graphics. Other features may allow you to zoom in to see part of the page more clearly or zoom out to see whether a two-page spread looks balanced.

Almost any document can be prepared with a page composition program and a desktop laser printer.

■ The *Queen Elizabeth II* uses PageMaker to prepare an eight-page daily newspaper. The news, culled from the pages of The *International Herald Tribune,* is put together in London with PageMaker and then transmitted by satellite to the luxury liner, which then prints 1,200 copies for its passengers.

Figure 11.17 Producing a newspaper with desktop publishing methods.

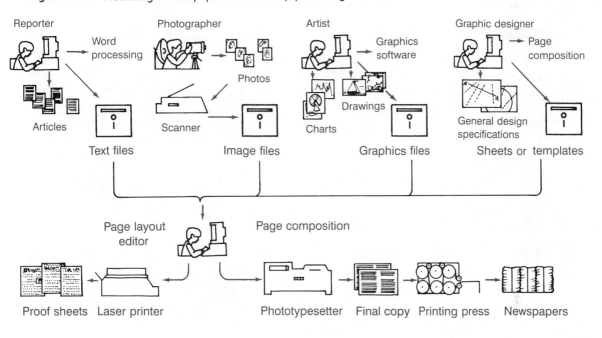

■ Caterpillar, a $7-billion earth-moving equipment manufacturer, has begun using Ventura Publisher for many of its shorter documents: service manuals, sales proposals, software documentation, and dealer bulletins. Because Caterpillar depends heavily on style sheets to standardize the appearance of its documents, it selected Ventura as its main desktop publishing program.

■ Hesston Corporation, a farm equipment manufacturer, uses PageMaker to turn out, with minimal pasteup time, all of its operator's manuals, assembly instructions, parts catalogs, and departmental forms. In fact, desktop publishing has allowed the company's technical publications group to continue to meet its publication schedule despite the loss of three people.

Page composition programs are particularly well suited to the last-minute changes demanded in the newspaper field and are used by many college newspapers. Figure 11.17 illustrates how a newspaper staff might coordinate activities by feeding text and graphics files to the page layout editor's personal computer.

■ Reporters write their articles with an assortment of word processing programs; most page composition programs can accept text in several formats. The text files are transferred to the page composition program either by disk, by telecommunications, or by a local area network.

■ Photographs are digitized with a scanner and pasted on the page electronically.

A WORD ABOUT
OFFICE PUBLISHING SYSTEMS

While a great deal of attention has focused on desktop publishing lately, higher-priced corporate electronic publishing systems (CEPS) have found their own fast track.

The CEPS market is hot. At a time when corporations are experiencing frustration at cost-justifying new computer systems, the savings from in-house publishing systems can be quickly quantified. This alone is making these systems the darlings of the divisional publishing manager who is under constant pressure to contain in-house publishing expenses. The new breed of high-end CEPS also works well at what it does: streamline the on-site creation and merging of corporate text and graphics into polished, finished documents, eliminating the usual merry-go-round of shuttling cut-and-paste work between writers, artists, typesetters, and print shops.

"Electronic publishing systems can win you over in a number of ways," explains Paul Lewis, director of Interconsult, Inc., a Cambridge, Mass., consulting firm. "If you're concerned about cutting in-house publishing costs, if you want your publishing to be easier, the systems can provide it."

Lewis says the recent press attention on electronic publishing is making a lot of corporations take a closer look at their own in-house publishing procedures. Most companies, he explains, will be surprised at the extent of the documentation they produce in-house in the way of procedure manuals, product descriptions and announcements, newsletters, technical publications, and even books. Following this surprise will be the shock of how much it all costs and how long these publications take to go from conception to finished product.

International Data Corp. (IDC), a Framingham, Mass., research firm, says only about 50% of current corporate in-house publishing is done on computers. This figure shows the huge potential

market that is opening to CEPS. Bolstering this are claims that in-house publishing can cut in half the average $300-a-page cost that commercial printing houses now charge for producing technical documents. IDC estimates that there are 60,000 companies in the U.S. that currently have an in-house publications department. IDC, in a recent report, said a typical CEPS prospect is a Fortune 2000 division with revenue of $50 million to $100 million, spending more than $1 million annually on published materials. The IDC report added that less than 5% of these companies currently use in-house electronic publishing systems.

"Until now, most in-house publishing expenses have been untouchable because the quality of documentation produced visibly reflects the image of the company," Lewis explains. "It was mechanical, specialized, and computers didn't have the flexibility to bridge these functions. Companies bit the bullet."

Computer technology has caught up in the meantime. Hardware has increased in capability and decreased in price. Motorola, Inc.'s 32-bit 68010 and 68020 processors, running Unix-based publishing software, are the engines of choice for most vendors of high-end CEPS. These CPUs have the muscle to handle the massive data bit rates required for good publishing graphics. They also have the speed to act as file servers for a number of on-line workstations. Most of these CEPS have built upon advances in computer-aided design and manufacturing software to produce powerful programs for doing graphics and text.

High-end CEPS are still expensive, generally beginning at $30,000 for a base system and running more than $200,000, depending on options. For the money, high-end customers get a dedicated, turnkey publishing system slated solely for high-volume, complex publishing activities.

These systems bump up against top-of-the-line desktop systems that can cost from $15,000 to $70,000 and run primarily on IBM Personal Com-

Continued on p. 357

puter XTs, PC ATs and the IBM RT PCs. The cutoff point with most desktop systems, however, is about 50 pages per project, while users of high-end systems have successfully handled book-quality projects of 800 pages and more.

While some of the desktop CEPS offer networking, this feature is a staple of high-end publishing. Systems from such leading high-end vendors as Interleaf, Inc. of Cambridge and Xyvision, Inc. of Wakefield, Mass., can handle simultaneous document input from several local and remote networked users. Users can also expect their systems to come bundled with high-resolution, bit-mapped WYSIWYG workstations that enable users to display on their screens exactly what will appear on the finished pages. Full vendor training and support may be included.

Users of high-end CEPS cite a litany of pluses, ranging from quick system payback to fast project turnaround. Manufacturers and high-tech companies that need to have new documentation tagged with new products have been among the biggest customers of high-end systems to date. Down the road, however, big hard-copy grinders such as financial institutions and the legal profession are expected to be major buyers.

Source: Stan Kolodziej, *Computerworld Focus,* 8 October 1986, pp. 31–33.

- Artists prepare freehand drawings, charts, and graphs with graphics programs. Graphics can also be bought from vendors of electronic clip-art files.

- The graphic designer establishes the design specifications for the document, including the margins, type sizes, width of ruling lines, spacing of text, placement of headings, and a host of other factors. Most of these specifications can be incorporated into a style sheet or *template*—a partially completed document—to make the day-to-day page layout process go more smoothly.

Page Composition Programs

The most popular page composition programs offer on-screen page makeup and cost less than $1,000. These programs have been available on the Macintosh since early 1985 and on IBM and compatible microcomputers since mid-1986. Two of the first programs for the Macintosh were Pagemaker from Aldus ($495) and ReadySetGo from Manhattan Graphics (now available from Letraset at $395). Programs for IBM and compatible microcomputers include Ventura Publisher from Xerox ($795), PageMaker for the PC ($695), and PFS:ClickArt Personal Publisher from Software Publishing ($185). All of these programs rely on word processing and graphics programs to create most of the source material, then they take over and automate the pasteup and final formatting.

Professional typographers require more features, precision, and control than these page composition programs offer. However, systems that suit their needs are expensive. For example, a permanent license for Superpage II from Bestinfo costs $7,000—beyond the means of anyone but publishing professionals. Superpage, a copy-protected page layout and typesetting program that runs on IBM microcomputers, provides a WYSIWYG display of text and graphics as well as excellent composition on a wide range of output devices. Although not a desktop publishing program, it appeals to magazine and newspaper publishers with exacting standards and pressing deadlines.

Even more expensive are corporate electronic publishing systems (CEPS). For example, a complete Interleaf system with a Sun Microsystems workstation, 86MB of disk storage, tape backup unit, and laser printer sells for around $46,000. These are *turnkey systems;* that is, they come with all the hardware and software needed for one to begin using them immediately.

Not all page composition programs let you see the page interactively on the screen. Some of the most accurate programs use embedded text formatting codes to give the user precise control over the composition of text. For example, the typesetting programs of most large computerized typesetting systems can be controlled by placing special formatting commands inside WordStar documents. This approach can make sense if you must have access to a conventional typesetting system or if you need to typeset a lengthy, but fairly simple document, such as a paperback novel. The vendors of these systems argue that, once you get used to it, coding a document in this manner is a faster, more precise way of formatting. If this were true for the average print job, desktop publishing would not have awaited the arrival of WYSIWYG programs before becoming popular.

Using a Page Composition Program

In this section, we explain the usual steps involved in using a page composition program. Figure 11.18 shows the typical relationship between a page composition program and other programs in a desktop publishing system. Each activity—writing, creating graphics, and laying out the page—is shown associated with a separate application program. The next generation of desktop publishing software may change this situation by bundling good word processing, graphics, and page composition into one integrated program. It is also likely that word processing programs will evolve to include more page layout features, lessening the need for a standalone page composition program.

Desktop publishing is a fluid process, so few hard and fast rules exist about the order of events in the publishing cycle. Ordinarily, one of the first steps is creating the raw material to be assembled on the page. Each item—drawing, graph, photograph, or unit of text—is prepared with an application program and stored on disk in a format compatible with the page composition program.

Another early step is designing the overall look, or format, of the publication. First, you must determine the basic structure of every page. How large is the paper? Will the page be printed in the **portrait** orientation (tall and narrow) or in the **landscape** orientation (short and wide)? Where will the margins be? Will the pages be double-sided (printed on both sides) or single-sided? Other questions determine which design elements, if any, should appear on every page. What should appear in running headers or footers? What logos, lines, or boxes do you want to be consistent throughout the document? Design decisions also include selecting

Figure 11.18 The typical relationships among desktop publishing tasks.

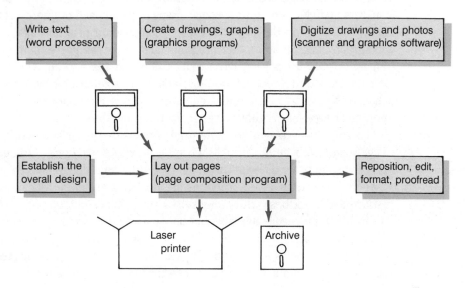

the fonts, size, and style of type for headings, body text, captions, and other text elements.

An effective design is often the key to a successful publication. Catching and holding a reader's attention is difficult in this busy world, so publishing professionals work hard to display ideas attractively. The typed text produced by a typewriter is inadequate for most printing jobs; it doesn't look good enough. Typesetting makes documents more attractive and easier to read by converting text into well-defined character forms and carefully controlling the positioning of letters. Because typeset characters are more legible, smaller sizes of type can be used. This can pack 30 to 50 percent more text on each page—saving a considerable amount of paper for high-volume print jobs. Typesetting can pay off in other ways as well. Studies have shown that typeset documents are more credible than typewritten ones. Readers tend to believe an article more just because its text looks better.

Arriving at an acceptable overall design requires a combination of artistic judgment and experience. For a newcomer to publishing, the potential for disaster is quite real. A common error is getting carried away with the new typographic controls, perhaps by sprinkling the page with many incompatible fonts or crowding the page with too much text. The result can be a garish-looking page or one so imposing that people don't bother to read it. One way to avoid these problems is to model your document after the design of a similar professionally produced document. This is perfectly legal; copyright laws don't protect the overall design specifications used in a publication, such as the size and spacing of type or use of white space to provide visual relief. Only the content—the tangible expression of ideas—is protected.

Once the design specifications and the text and graphics files are at hand, you're ready for the page composition program. On-screen page layout means no more scissors and glue, no more missing scraps of paper, and no more problems placing items squarely on the page. The page composition program assembles the text and graphics created by other programs and helps you paste them in position (see Figure 11.19). Because page layout is done on the screen, you can make last-minute changes to reposition items, edit text, stretch or crop graphics, or even change the format of the entire document. When the final pages roll off the laser printer or typesetter, they're ready for the print shop.

To give you a feeling for how page composition programs work, we compare PageMaker with Ventura Publisher in the next two sections. Although these programs use entirely different methods of setting up a document, they have certain aspects in common. Both programs are designed around a Macintoshlike user interface and work best with a mouse. Commands are hidden on pull-down menus, where they are readily available but unobtrusive. Like most page composition programs, they use the screen as a window to show you the document in any of several different views. The facing-pages view lets you contemplate a two-page spread. Then you might zoom in to see the current page as it appears when it just fits in the window; zoom in again to see a life-size part of the page; and zoom in yet again for an enlarged, highly detailed view. Scroll bars along the edge of the window let you roam around the page when the view is too magnified to show the whole page at once.

Although both programs can perform limited text editing, they lack many useful word processing features, such as search and replace or spell checking. Their text editing ability is best reserved for entering headlines, figure captions, and other minor elements or for simple editorial revisions. Fortunately, both programs can import text in a variety of formats, so you're likely to find them compatible with your word processor.

Using PageMaker

PageMaker was released in July 1985 by Aldus Corporation, only 18 months after the company was founded. Designed initially for the Macintosh and the Apple LaserWriter, PageMaker got desktop publishing off the ground and set the standard by which other desktop publishing programs are measured. In February 1987, Aldus introduced a PC version of PageMaker that duplicates the interactive environment that made the Macintosh version such a success. Although there are differences between the two versions, their basic features and user interface are largely the same.

PageMaker organizes the working area like an artist's drawing board, complete with a toolbox full of design aids for page composition. For example, in Figure 11.20, the drawing board holds the current page and a drawing of three mice. The dithered photo in the page looks much worse on screen than it would look when printed; its poor appearance is the result of interference between the screen's pixel pattern and the photo's dithered dot pattern.

Figure 11.19 A page composition program gives you control over each area of the page, integrating text and graphics files from numerous sources.

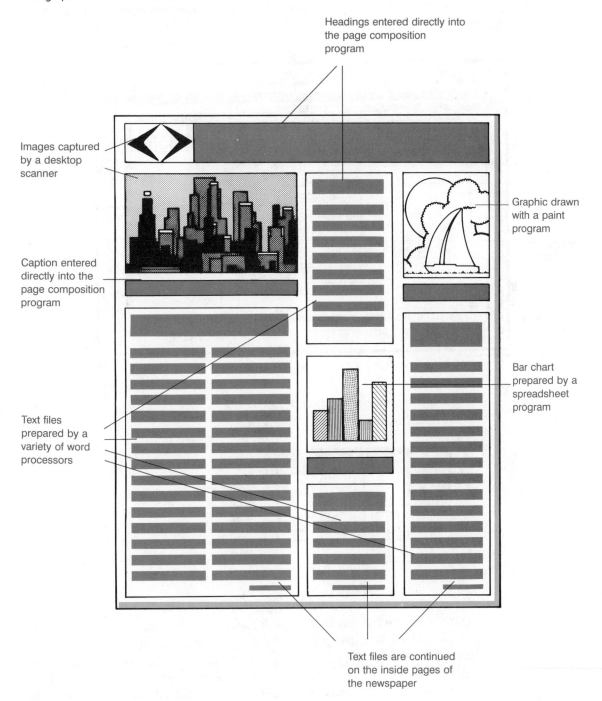

Headings entered directly into the page composition program

Images captured by a desktop scanner

Graphic drawn with a paint program

Caption entered directly into the page composition program

Bar chart prepared by a spreadsheet program

Text files prepared by a variety of word processors

Text files are continued on the inside pages of the newspaper

Figure 11.20 PageMaker provides the same types of tools found on an artist's drawing board: (a) rulers for measuring, open areas for storing graphics, and a toolbox with tools for selecting items, drawing lines, editing text, creating boxes and circles, and trimming graphical images. (b) An enlargement of the toolbox and its icons.

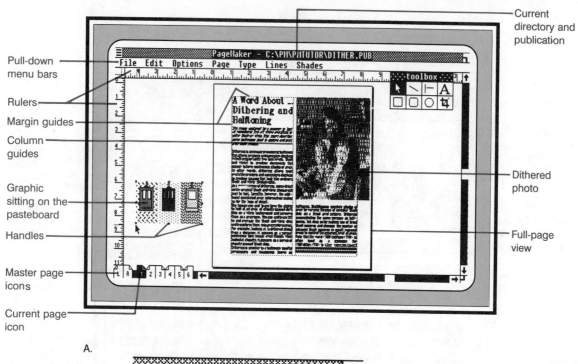

Current directory and publication

Pull-down menu bars

Rulers

Margin guides

Column guides

Graphic sitting on the pasteboard

Handles

Master page icons

Current page icon

Dithered photo

Full-page view

A.

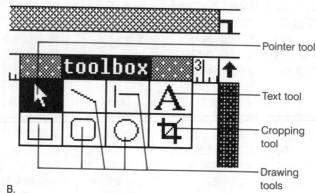

Pointer tool

Text tool

Cropping tool

Drawing tools

B.

Some tasks are remarkably easy with PageMaker. You can jump directly to another page by clicking the appropriate numbered page icon at the lower left-hand corner of the screen. A graphical image can be moved to a new location simply by dragging it with the mouse. You can stretch or shrink a graphic like a rubber band by grabbing one of its "handles"—small dots along the edges—and dragging the handle with the mouse.

With PageMaker, you lay out pages by placing margin and column guides in position; then you fill the columns with text. The margin guides define the outside boundaries of the image area for every page in the document. They are fixed in place with the Page Setup dialog box (found on the File menu), which also establishes the size and orientation of the page, the number of pages in the document, and whether the pages are to be single- or double-sided.

With PageMaker for the PC, a publication can have up to 128 pages, with a maximum size of 17 by 22 inches per page. If the document you wish to create has more than 128 pages, you must break it into separate publications and format each separately. When you save a PageMaker publication on disk, all of its text and graphics images are stored in one combined file.

Column guides serve as boundaries for text, and each page can have as many as 20 columns. Although PageMaker automatically creates equal columns, you can change a column's position or width by dragging its column guides. You can set up column guides page by page, but it is easier to define columns on a master page.

A master page is where you put the text, graphics, and guides you want repeated on every page in the document. You open a master page by clicking on the L or R page icon at the lower left-hand corner of the screen; then you fill out the master page as you would a regular page. Because PageMaker overlays the corresponding master page on the regular pages, you can use master pages for setting up running heads, automatic page numbering, and other elements that will appear on every page (such as hairline rules between columns).

The usual way of adding text and graphics to the page is to use the Place command from the File menu. This command produces a dialog box showing the text and graphics files available on the disk. After selecting a file from the list, the mouse pointer changes to show that it is "loaded," ready for you to place the item on the page by clicking wherever you want the item's upper left-hand corner to be. For example, if the pointer is loaded with a block of text, text will flow down the current column from the pointer's position until it runs into the bottom of the page or into a graphic. Each column to receive text must by filled individually; PageMaker can't automatically fill the columns on a page and continue filling pages until the block of text is exhausted.

Other ways of filling out a document are available. You can use the clipboard to cut, copy, and paste items within PageMaker or from other programs into PageMaker. For short documents, such as an overhead transparency or an advertisement, you might use PageMaker's built-in text editor to enter and format the text.

The toolbox window at the upper right-hand corner of the screen determines what mode the program is in. If the pointer tool is active, you can select and move graphics and blocks of text, but you can't edit text. You must select the text tool before you can edit text. The drawing tools allow you to draw lines, rectangles, boxes with rounded corners, ovals, and circles. A cropping tool is available if you want to trim or crop graphics. These modes help organize the program's functions. But if you forget to select the right mode, your actions will produce different results from those you expect.

PageMaker's drawing tools are convenient because they create graphics right on the page (see Figure 11.21). Lines are useful for setting off a heading from the body text, separating columns, or creating simple drawings. Boxes draw attention to figures and can establish a focal point on the page. Any box, circle, or oval can be filled with a **screen** (pattern of tiny dots) or pattern to give it added emphasis. A *drop shadow,* created by stacking two boxes almost on top of each other, gives a box the feeling of depth, as if it sits slightly above the rest of the page.

When you use PageMaker's drawing tools, no line is ever crooked, and every corner meets precisely. Some operations, such as drawing rounded corners on a box or creating a drop shadow, are far easier to do electronically than with border tape and a razor knife.

Like most page composition programs, PageMaker offers many features for **copyfitting**: that is, getting text to fit within the available area. For example, if the text in a file doesn't fit within its assigned area on a page, the remaining text can be made to flow to another page, much as a front-page newspaper article can be continued on an inside page. Alternatively, the available area might be increased by moving the column margins or adjusting the top and bottom guides. More text can always be packed into an area by using a smaller type size or by reducing or eliminating the **leading**, the extra space between lines. These techniques, however, may damage the document's readability (see Figure 11.22).

PageMaker also gives you control over the average amount of space placed between words and letters, letting you squeeze text together or stretch it out. **Kerning** is another way of adjusting the spacing; it takes advantage of the way specific pairs of letters fit together because of their shape. For example, the arm of a capital T can be slid over the top of a lowercase o to save a bit of space. Kerning isn't very noticeable in small type sizes, but the letterspacing in headlines can look uneven without kerning, as Figure 11.23 shows. With PageMaker, you can kern individual letters by shifting them one at a time, and you can set PageMaker to automatically kern pairs of characters preselected by the font designer. Despite all these fancy options, however, the best copyfitting strategy is often simply to delete the extra text.

Using Ventura Publisher

Xerox Corporation's Ventura Publisher is perhaps the leading page composition program for the PC. It is a suitable choice for formatting short flyers, business forms, and newsletters. But it truly excels in preparing long documents that need to go through extensive revisions.

Perhaps the most significant difference between Ventura and PageMaker is the way they store information on disk. Instead of merging all of a document's text and graphics into a single PageMakerlike publication file, Ventura builds a *chapter file* that contains instructions for assembling the document from the original text and graphics files (see Figure 11.24). The chapter file contains only pointers to the document's other files, along with some formatting information. Thus, if you cut the scanned image of a photograph from page 6 and move it to page 2, Ventura merely rearranges the pointers in the chapter file.

Figure 11.21 PageMaker's drawing tools can create a variety of lines, shapes, and patterns.

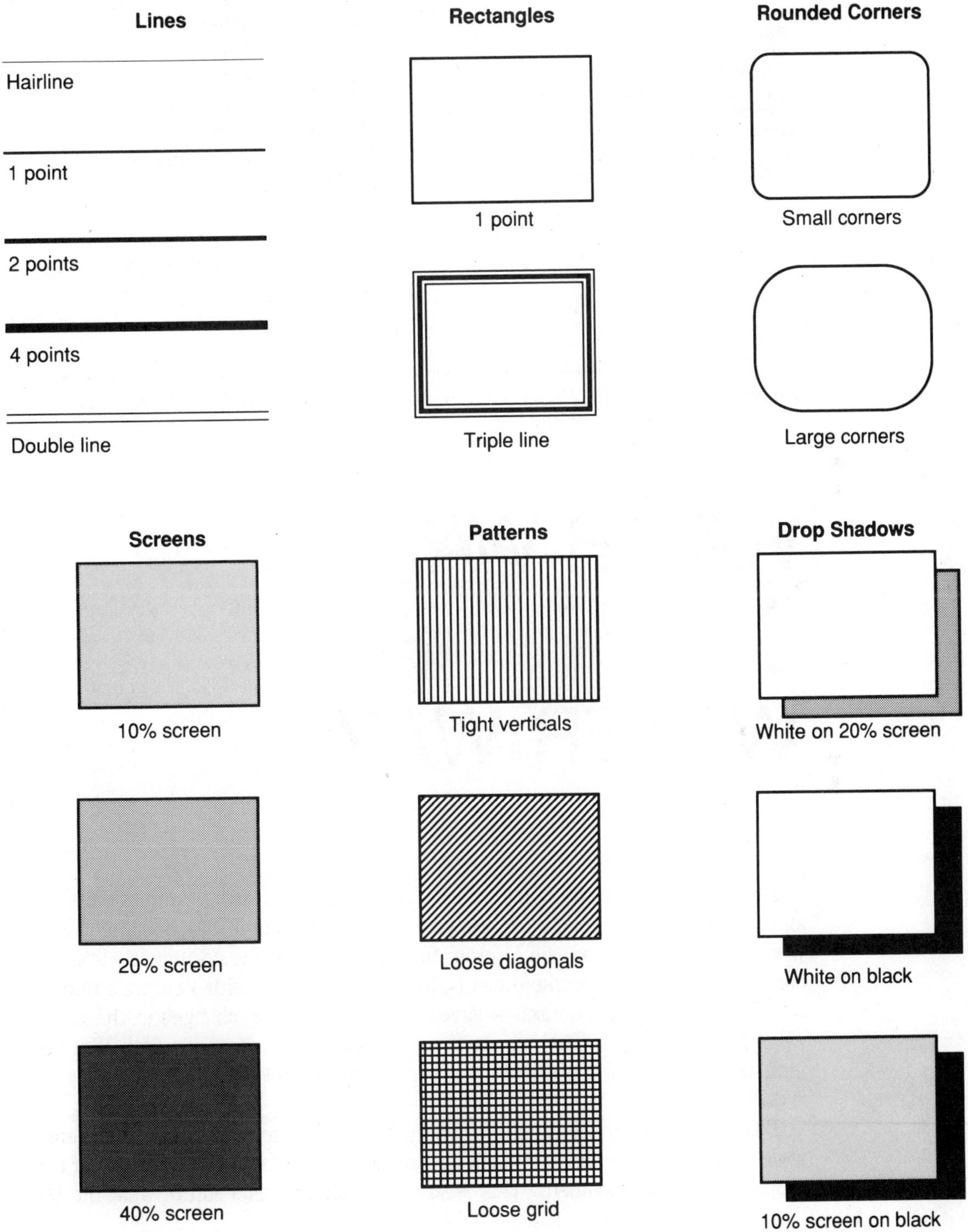

Lines

Hairline

1 point

2 points

4 points

Double line

Rectangles

1 point

Triple line

Rounded Corners

Small corners

Large corners

Screens

10% screen

20% screen

40% screen

Patterns

Tight verticals

Loose diagonals

Loose grid

Drop Shadows

White on 20% screen

White on black

10% screen on black

Figure 11.22 The effect of varying leading (line spacing).

No leading with 9 point type
I am the voice of today, the herald of tomorrow . . . I coin for you the enchanting tale, the philosopher's moralizing, and the poet's visions . . . I am the leaden army that conquers the world—I am TYPE.

From: *The Type Speaks*

1 point leading with 9 point type
I am the voice of today, the herald of tomorrow . . . I coin for you the enchanting tale, the philosopher's moralizing, and the poet's visions . . . I am the leaden army that conquers the world—I am TYPE.

From: *The Type Speaks*

3 points leading with 9 point type
I am the voice of today, the herald of tomorrow . . . I coin for you the enchanting tale, the philosopher's moralizing, and the poet's visions . . . I am the leaden army that conquers the world—I am TYPE.

From: *The Type Speaks*

Figure 11.23 Kerning is often used to make the spacing of headlines look more even. (a) Kerned. (b) Unkerned.

Kerned

WATER WAY
A.

Unkerned

WATER WAY
B.

Documents that go through extensive revisions benefit from Ventura's file storage system. For example, after you've written a rough draft of a document with a word processor, you can use Ventura to link and format the document's text files. Next, the formatted document can be viewed and edited with Ventura's text editor. When you leave Ventura, it saves all of your editing changes in the original word processing files. This means that you can create a text file with WordPerfect, format and edit it with Ventura, and return to edit it more extensively with WordPerfect.

Besides a chapter file, each document is attached to a *style sheet*. A Ventura style sheet is a collection of formatting instructions (or tags) for each type of paragraph used in the document. That is, the style sheet tells Ventura what the body

Figure 11.24 Ventura Publisher uses two special files to assemble and format a document from text and graphics stored in other files. The chapter file contains pointers to the other files; it describes how to assemble the document from its components. The style sheet is a list of formatting instructions that controls the appearance of the various types of paragraphs, from body text to major heading.

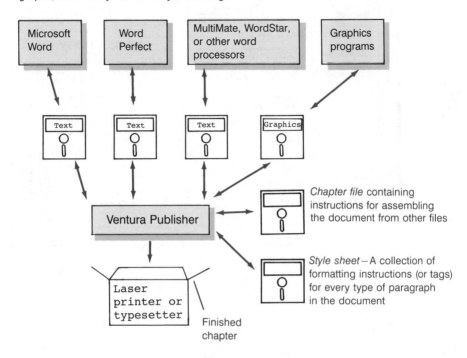

text, chapter titles, footnotes, and other paragraph styles should look like. You can attach a different style sheet to a document (to give the entire document a new look), or you can make changes in the current style sheet. (For more details on style sheets, see Chapter 6.)

PageMaker uses a toolbox to group its functions; Ventura uses four mode-controlling icons near the upper left-hand corner of the screen for the same purpose (see Figure 11.25).

■ The Frame Setting icon allows you to manipulate frames (boxes) that are used to hold text and pictures. Basic document layout is accomplished in this mode by opening, moving, resizing, and deleting frames. A frame can hold information from only one text or graphics file, so if you want to add a bar chart to a page, you must open up a new frame for it. Creating the new frame is easy (see Figure 11.26). While in the Frame Setting mode, you click the Add New Frame button, move the pointer to where you want a corner of the frame, and hold down the mouse button while dragging the mouse to the opposite corner—stretching the frame as you go. Later you can use the frame's handles to adjust its size or position on the page.

Figure 11.25 (a) Ventura Publisher uses pull-down menus and four mode icons to control most of its features. (b) An enlargement of the four mode icons and Selection box.

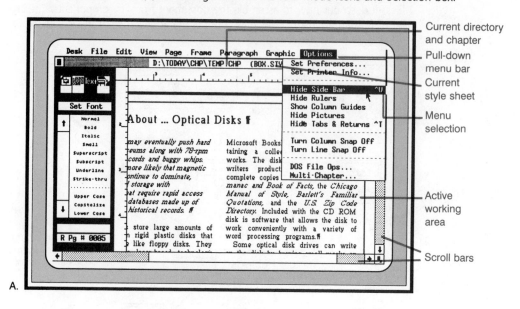

- Current directory and chapter
- Pull-down menu bar
- Current style sheet
- Menu selection
- Active working area
- Scroll bars

A.

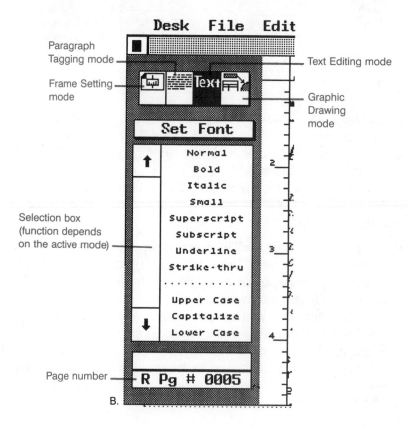

- Paragraph Tagging mode
- Frame Setting mode
- Text Editing mode
- Graphic Drawing mode
- Selection box (function depends on the active mode)
- Page number

B.

Figure 11.26 An empty frame sits on this page waiting for a text or graphics file to fill it. The text in the underlying page has automatically flowed around the new frame.

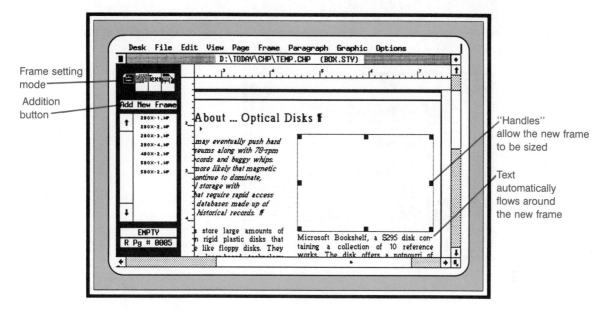

- The Paragraph Tagging icon provides a speedy way to adjust the appearance of paragraphs by tagging them with a paragraph name defined in the style sheet. When the Paragraph Tagging mode is active, the Selection box on the left of the screen lists the available tags by name. To tag a paragraph, you first highlight it with the mouse, then click on the tag name. For even faster paragraph tagging, you can assign tag names to function keys.
- The Text Editing icon lets you use Ventura's built-in text editor.
- The Graphics Drawing icon gives you access to the same sort of drawing tools found in PageMaker's toolbox.

In addition to placing text in frames that sit on top of a page, text can also be attached to the underlying page. When a text file is attached to the underlying page, any remaining text will flow automatically to succeeding pages, snaking its way around any frames in its path. On long documents, this can save plenty of time, because you don't have to lay out the document page by page.

Like PageMaker, Ventura can **scale** a graphics image electronically to change its size or **crop** an image to trim off unwanted areas (see Figure 11.27). By using different scaling factors for the horizontal and vertical directions, images can be

Figure 11.27 These two views of the same graphics file were prepared by capturing an electronic image of Ventura on a CRT screen. Then Ventura was used to manipulate its own image. On the top, the image was scaled until it fit inside a border consisting of two boxes. Below, the image was stretched and cropped to highlight the pull-down menu. The images and the boxes surrounding them were printed with an HP LaserJet printer and placed directly on the final pasteup used to produce this book.

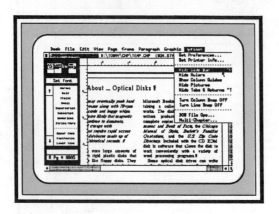

distorted to make them fat or skinny—a design trick difficult to duplicate with conventional publishing. Of course, if a bit-mapped image, such as the one shown in Figure 11.27, is markedly increased in size, it will begin to look grainy. Many graphics programs create line art images that are stored mathematically, and like outline fonts, line art images can be scaled without introducing graininess.

SUMMARY

Desktop publishing is the most recent in a long series of advances in the technology of printing and publishing. Printing began with the invention of movable type—an invention that created the new problems of setting type in pages and of disassembling and re-sorting the pieces of type. An interim solution was the Linotype machine; it automatically transformed the operator's keystrokes into finished lines of lead type. The ultimate solution, offset printing, entirely eliminated the need for printing plates with raised images. Along with computer-controlled phototypesetting, offset printing was responsible for an explosion in the variety and quantity of printed material over the last years.

Desktop publishing got its start in 1985 with advances in laser printing and software. Desktop laser printers slashed the cost of producing near-typeset-quality text to a marginal cost of five cents a page. (Desktop scanners have played a lesser role; they convert visual images into digital, bit-mapped images that can be manipulated inside a computer.) Two particular software developments have had the most influence: page description languages and page composition programs. Page description languages allow application programs to describe the objects to be printed, rather than specifying each spot to receive ink. Page composition programs have placed in the hands of ordinary people the same sort of typographic and page makeup capabilities available to professional printers.

A final word of caution about desktop publishing is in order. Just because you have access to a set of tools doesn't mean that you will be able to use it appropriately. In fact, unwary users often become so dazzled with their newfound capabilities that they spend their time playing with a document's format instead of organizing their ideas carefully. You may be tempted to be heavy-handed with graphics, which can overwhelm the copy. Another common mistake is placing too many different fonts on a page, diverting the reader's attention to the document's format and away from its content. Along with newly acquired control over the production process comes a responsibility to understand the basic rules of page design and aesthetics.

composition

copyfit

crop

desktop publishing

dither

fax

halftone

kerning

landscape

leading

optical character recognition (OCR)

page composition program

page description language (PDL)

portrait

scale

scanner

screen

DISCUSSION QUESTIONS

1. What will be the ultimate impact of desktop publishing? Is it a passing fad, or will it rank with movable type as one of history's most notable milestones?

2. When are a razor knife and glue reasonable substitutes for a page composition program?

3. What advantages does desktop publishing have over conventional publishing methods? Which method would you choose for producing a newsletter, a technical manual, or a fullcolor sales leaflet?

4. What percentage of the documents you read are typeset? What percentage are prepared by desktop publishing? How might you determine these percentages?

EXERCISES

1. Determine whether the campus publications you read are produced with desktop publishing. Find out how they are prepared and printed.

2. Dot matrix printers and laser printers use a form of printer graphics to print characters. Compare the character patterns of a bit-mapped display with the character patterns of a dot matrix and a laser printer.

3. Find two examples of typeset documents: one that you like and one that you don't. Write a critique comparing the two, pointing out their design flaws as well as their strengths.

PART III

DEVELOPING NEW
SYSTEMS

The complexity of a large information system can be mind boggling; systems can consist of hundreds of very involved and highly interrelated programs. For example, a typical airline reservation system may be used by thousands of people and contain several million lines of programming code supported by tons of documentation.

With all of this power comes a new set of problems. Even if everyone agrees that changes in a system are necessary, there may be little consensus about how the new system should work or how the conversion to the new system should proceed. As the size and complexity of these systems continue to grow, our ability to cope with them declines. For these reasons, the development and modification of large or complicated computer systems are handled by specialists called *system analysts*. A system analyst uses a technique called system analysis to deal with the complexity and size of modern computer systems. In Chapter 12 we describe each phase of system analysis.

Before the system analysis method was used, an alarming increase in the time and effort required to develop software led to a search for the causes of failures and cost overruns. In the 1970s it was discovered that early detection of incomplete or incorrect designs prevented most cost and schedule overruns. The idea of early detection of potential problems spread to programming, and it soon became apparent that even seemingly simple programs are incredibly complex when carefully analyzed—difficult enough to require years of testing by the fastest computers! The impracticality of exhaustive testing of complex programs prompted the second major event in developing new systems: simplification of programming by adopting a programming style called *structured programming*. Structured programming has produced significant improvements in software technology in just the past fifteen years.

Programming is just one phase in the development of a computer system, but with the continual declines in the cost of hardware, it has become an increasingly costly portion of the system-building process. In Chapter 13 we discuss two broad aspects of programming: programming languages and programming techniques—in particular, the techniques of structured programming.

Today most commercial computing applications rely on computers for routine processing tasks and reserve tasks requiring judgment and experience for humans. But this traditional allocation of tasks is being challenged by recent advances in *artificial intelligence*, the field of computing devoted to developing computer systems that simulate human reasoning and intelligence. Chapter 14 explores the methods used to construct these new systems. It pays particular attention to the construction of *expert systems*, which simulate the experience of a human decision maker in a particular subject area. ■

12 System Analysis

I nformation systems are the central nervous system of large and small corporations, government organizations, and educational institutions. Large organizations must process information about everything from billing, inventory, accounting, and payroll to automated manufacturing, production control, and personnel services. Because such firms' information processing needs are so vast and demanding, many people, machines, and methods must be used to control massive amounts of data, collect facts, make decisions, and disseminate information to a variety of places within the organization. In short, large organizations require complex information processing systems.

A **system analyst** is a person trained in the analysis of complex business systems, which typically involve a computer system. System analysts evaluate problems, recommend solutions, and assist management in bringing about change. In the process, they analyze existing systems, propose ways of implementing changes, design new systems, and guide the implementation of new systems.

In the early days of computer systems, little was known about how to conceive, design, and implement information systems. Now the process is understood as an application of general systems theory. Even though many questions remain unanswered, general systems theory has provided a solid basis for a methodology used to analyze and design information systems, a methodology called the *systems approach*. Using this approach, system analysts consider the information system as a complex, evolving collection of hardware, software, people, and processes. Furthermore, they divide the creation and maintenance of complex systems into phases. In this chapter, we define what a system is, describe how information systems fit into general systems theory, and then explain each phase of the system's life cycle.

WHAT IS SYSTEM ANALYSIS?

What Is a System?

There are many definitions of *system* that we might apply to computer-based information systems. According to the IEEE Standard Glossary of Software Engineering Terminology, a **system** can be defined in three ways.[1]

1. A collection of people, machines, and methods organized to accomplish a set of specific functions.
2. An integrated whole that is composed of diverse, interacting, specialized structures and subfunctions.
3. A group of subsystems united by some interaction or interdependence, performing many duties but functioning as a single unit.

A computer-based information system fits all three definitions. It involves people, machines, and methods; it behaves as an integrated whole; and most information systems are composed of a group of subsystems.

General systems theory provides another way of defining a system: as a collection of inputs, outputs, and processor activities, with feedback, a boundary, and an environment. As you can see in Figure 12.1, *inputs* enter the system from outside—typically from human users, but also from other machines and processes in the environment. The *processor activity* transforms inputs into outputs. For example, in Figure 12.1(b), the processor may produce a report as output, given certain input data. Hence *outputs* are the results produced by the processor activities. In most systems, information about the outputs is then used to influence future inputs; this information is called *feedback*. Feedback is used to correct or in some way alter the next wave of inputs to the processor activity. In an information system, feedback consists of new decisions, payments, charges, updates to accounts,

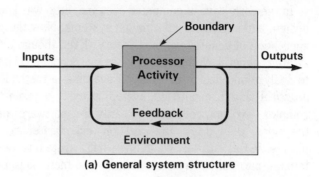

(a) General system structure

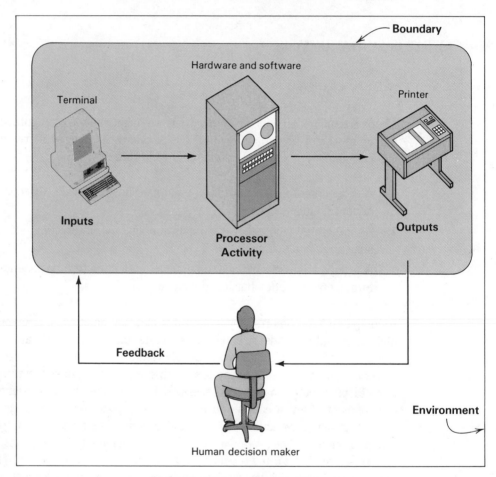

(b) Computer-based information system

Figure 12.2 The components of a complex system are subsystems. Each subsystem may be further divided into additional subsystems.

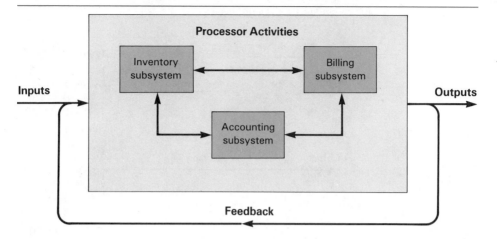

and any input that results from previous outputs. The *environment* is the world immediately surrounding the system. The environment influences the system through the *boundary,* which provides a separation line between the system and its environment. In Figure 12.1, the boundary is between human users and the hardware and software of the information system.

Most systems are too complex to understand as a whole, so they are subdivided into components called *subsystems.* Figure 12.2 illustrates a system composed of three subsystems: inventory, billing, and accounting. Each of these subsystems may be rather complex in itself; hence the subsystems may in turn be divided into subsystems. When a system is divided into interacting subsystems, the environment and boundary of one subsystem become part of the processor activity or environment of another subsystem. An *interface* in this context is a channel for communication across a boundary between two or more subsystems.

The Systems Approach

These ideas from general systems theory form the basis of the systems approach, which is the methodology used by system analysts. According to the *systems approach,* an existing or new information system can be analyzed as a system of components called subsystems.

Identifying the subsystems and interfaces among subsystems is one of a system analyst's most important functions. This isn't always easy, because the components of some systems can't be cleanly separated.[2] For example, the problem of hunger may result from a country's uneducated populace, a corrupt political system, and an undeveloped economic system. It may not be possible to decompose this system into subsystems that can be tackled in isolation. Attempts to improve the educational system, for example, may fail because it is difficult to educate a starving population governed by insecure political leaders.

Figure 12.3 A simplified diagram showing the interfaces among subsystems. Subsystems I and PR communicate through parts. Subsystem PR is composed of subsystems PI and AAB, which communicate through invoices.

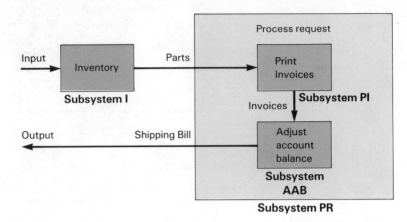

Fortunately, few business systems are as "messy" as this example. Most business systems can be characterized by flows of information from place to place. System analysts frequently represent these flows in a diagram that describes subsystems and their interfaces. Figure 12.3 shows a simplified example.

The System Life Cycle

Another tenet of the systems approach is that how a system should be managed varies from phase to phase in the system life cycle. The term *system life cycle* is used to describe the steps or phases a system goes through from the time it is conceived until it is phased out. The names and number of phases in a system life cycle vary with different industries, organizations within industries, and system analysts. For our purposes, we divide the system life cycle into the following seven phases:

Life Cycle Phase	Activities
Investigation	Identify needs; determine feasibility
Analysis	Understand current system; identify new requirements
Design	Propose alternatives; design the new system
Development	Develop and test the new system
Installation	Replace the old system with the new one
Maintenance	Evaluate, repair, and enhance the system
Retirement	Phase out the system

We will discuss each of these phases more thoroughly in the coming sections. For now it is sufficient to know that these phases provide a framework for con-

Figure 12.4 The phases in a system life cycle model.

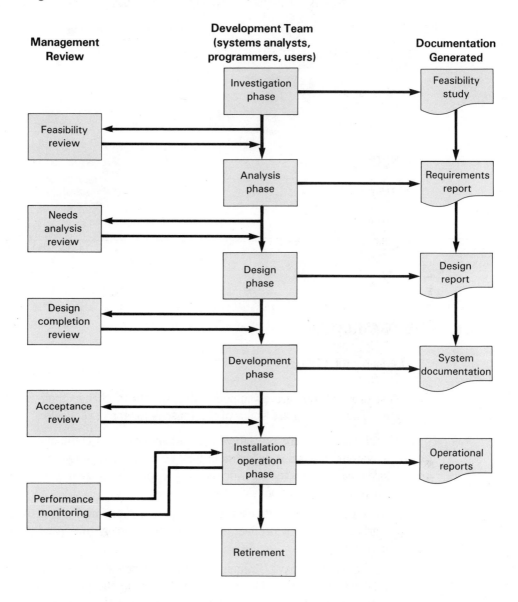

trolling, estimating, and observing the evolution of a system, as Figure 12.4 illustrates. Each phase produces *documentation,* the written or pictorial information that describes the system, and this documentation forms the basis of a review that determines whether the project should proceed to the next phase. Thus, a system life cycle model provides management with definite, verifiable checkpoints during the project's development. A Gantt chart similar to Figure 12.5 is typically used to schedule and estimate the duration of each phase.

Figure 12.5 A typical schedule for a system life cycle, showing the duration of each phase and the expected starting dates.

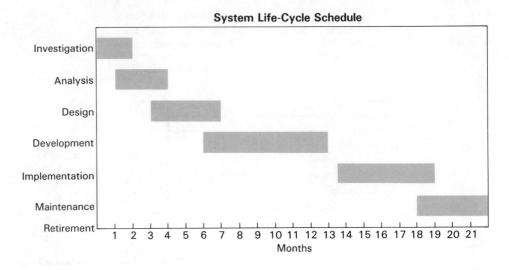

SYSTEM INVESTIGATION

Reasons for Change

Most organizations are swamped with requests to change their information systems. The following are some of the reasons for these requests:

- *Problems in an existing system* are perhaps the most common reason to change a system. The sales department may be unhappy with the system because sales leads arrive too late, or the engineering department may want to improve the accuracy of calculations.

- *New requirements* that result from corporate reorganization, growth, or the marketing of a new product may force the company to expand or modify its currrent systems.

- *New technology* may be required as maintenance and spare parts become harder to find for an older system, or it may be cheaper to convert to new, better technology than to continue to use an existing system.

- *Government regulations,* such as new tax laws, payroll deductions, and paperwork requirements, can force changes in software. For example, a company may be required to change its accounting procedures before it can bid on government contracts.

- *Improved performance* may be possible (by making changes in procedures or machines or by training people), or it may be necessary because the existing system is overloaded.

Needs Analysis

The backlog of proposed changes must be evaluated to determine which ones are feasible and to provide a basis for comparing proposals. Thus, the first task for a system analyst is investigating the proposed change, a task that includes three steps.

1. Define the problem in terms of a need. This step, called *needs analysis,* produces a statement of the needed change.
2. Suggest several solutions to the problem defined in step 1.
3. Evaluate the feasibility of each alternative and recommend the best solution.

The first step, defining the problem, may not be as easy as it sounds. Complaints and reports about problems often hide the real problem. For example, a national marketing manager who suggests that a faster computer be obtained to speed up the printing of a daily sales report may not realize that the report is late because its data are entered late in the day. This problem may in turn be traced to a shortage of data entry clerks or to the fact that the data are generated by the West Coast branch, which is in a different time zone. To identify the real problem to be solved, the system analyst conducts interviews, surveys users, and studies the current system. The system analyst finds answers to what, who, where, when, and why the problem exists.

The purpose of the second step, finding and suggesting alternative solutions, is to ensure that all alternatives have been fairly evaluated. There is always a temptation to pursue the first solution that comes to mind, but doing so may mean overlooking a better solution.

Finally, the system analyst tries to decide which of the alternatives is the best solution and to estimate the cost of implementing it. At this point, it is also wise to examine other issues, including the following:

- *Economic feasibility.* What is the cost, and when will the change pay for itself? How much will it save in the long run?
- *Technical feasibility.* Can the change be made? Is the technology available to implement the improvement?
- *Operational feasibility.* What effect will the change have on methods and procedures, on people, and on the way the company is run?

The Feasibility Study

The main purpose of the system investigation is to create a *feasibility study.* This report is prepared in a standard format so that it may be compared with the feasibility studies for other proposals; not all of them will be implemented. According to industry surveys, the average data processing department has a two- to three-year backlog of projects with completed feasibility studies.

The feasibility study must briefly and clearly describe the problem and the alternatives considered and make a recommendation. The report's length and completeness will vary with the importance and size of the problem being studied. A typical report contains

- A brief description of the present system
- A statement of the problems, both real and apparent
- A list of the alternative solutions considered
- A feasibility analysis for each alternative solution
- A discussion of the recommended alternatives, pointing out any hidden problems, side effects, or related information that might be useful to management
- A brief financial analysis and an estimated development schedule

The report is given to management. If it is approved, the next phase begins.

As an example, consider the following feasibility study, which describes a problem in a distributorship company. The company takes orders from dealers, fills these orders from parts stored in a warehouse, and sends the parts to the dealers or, if the warehouse doesn't have them, backorders the parts.

Feasibility Study: 12-342   Analyst: J. Sundy
Date Prepared: 2/14/87

PRESENT SYSTEM

The present system consists of two subsystems: Order Entry and Inventory, and Purchase Backordered Parts from Suppliers. The Order Entry and Inventory subsystem is run by one order entry clerk and one inventory clerk. The Purchase Backordered Parts from Suppliers subsystem is run by one shipping clerk and the inventory clerk, who also works on the Order Entry and Inventory subsystem.

NEEDS ANALYSIS

The current system is unreliable because, when backordered parts arrive from suppliers, they are not always entered into the inventory file. This means that some parts are "lost" in the warehouse because they are not recorded in the inventory file maintained by the computer system.

The two subsystems need to be coordinated so that the supplier parts are properly posted into the inventory file. This will guarantee that the backorders are added to the inventory.

ALTERNATIVE SOLUTIONS

Two alternatives were considered:

1. Hire an additional clerk to update the inventory file each day, after daily shipments from suppliers have arrived at the shipping and receiving dock.
2. Modify the software of the computer system to automatically update the inventory file when backorders are received and filled.

Solution #2 is recommended because it is reliable and in the long run more cost effective.

FEASIBILITY OF SOLUTION #2

The costs and benefits of the proposed solution are based on the following assumptions:

Cost of "lost" inventory/year $100,000
Expected life of new system (years)   10

The following estimates are based on current dollars and have not been adjusted for inflation:

COST:
Estimated cost of software development $150,000
Estimated cost to train personnel   25,000
Total Cost to Implement #2 $175,000

BENEFIT:
Estimated cost of "lost" inventory (10 yrs) $1,000,000

BREAKEVEN ANALYSIS:

	1988	1989	1990
Cost	$175,000	-0-	-0-
Benefit	-0-	$100,000	$100,000
Net	−$175,000	+$100,000	+$100,000
Accumulative	−$175,000	−$ 75,000	+$ 25,000

The new system pays for itself in the third year. In ten years, the new system will realize savings of $825,000.

Whereas the system investigation is preliminary, the second phase—system analysis—is more detailed. The succeeding phases—design and development—are even more detailed. Thus, the systems approach illustrates **top-down analysis and design**, because each succeeding phase is more detailed than the phase before it.

During the system analysis phase, the analyst performs **requirements analysis**, which is the process of studying users' needs to define the system's requirements. A *requirement* is a condition or capability needed to solve a problem or achieve an objective. The purpose of the system analysis phase is to formulate what needs to be done as a list of requirements. There are three basic steps in this phase.

1. Gather and analyze data about the current system.
2. Describe the current and the proposed systems in terms that everyone can understand.
3. Document the requirements of the proposed system in a report that is given to management for consideration.

Data Gathering and Analysis

To achieve the detailed understanding required in the analysis phase, the analyst must study documents that describe manual and automated procedures; conduct interviews with people currently doing the work; perform surveys using questionnaires designed to uncover hidden problems, needs, and desires; and observe the company's operation from an objective point of view.

Data Flow Diagrams

During the second step of the analysis phase, the analyst must describe the existing and proposed systems. The diversity of large organizations complicates this task. Each person in a large organization is familiar with the terminology and methods unique to his or her particular skill. For example, financial experts understand ledgers and journals; engineers understand equations and blueprints; and software developers are familiar with flowcharts, programming languages, and operating systems. How can the analyst describe the existing and proposed systems in a form that everyone can understand?

One commonly used method of describing an existing or proposed system is the data flow diagram. A **data flow diagram** is a graphical representation of an information system, showing data sources, data destinations, data storage, the processes performed by subsystems, and the logical flow of information between subsystems. In a data flow diagram, inputs, outputs, interfaces, and feedback

Figure 12.6   The symbols used in a data flow diagram.

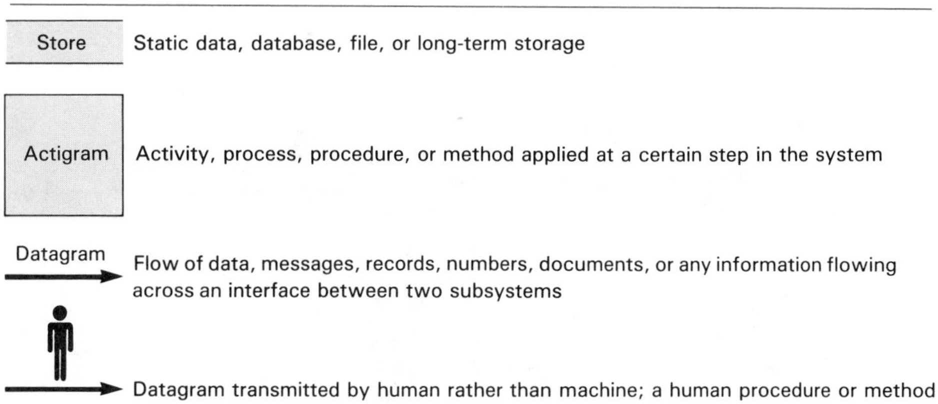

| Store | Static data, database, file, or long-term storage |

| Actigram | Activity, process, procedure, or method applied at a certain step in the system |

Datagram
→ Flow of data, messages, records, numbers, documents, or any information flowing across an interface between two subsystems

→ Datagram transmitted by human rather than machine; a human procedure or method

loops are all called *datagrams*. Processor activities, methods, and procedures are collectively called *actigrams* because they represent activities. Figure 12.6 shows the symbols used to represent datagrams and actigrams. A data storage symbol (also called a *pictogram*) represents files and lists. Thus, it shows data "at rest," whereas a datagram symbol indicates data "in motion." The name of the storage file is inscribed in the data storage symbol, as shown in Figure 12.7. The stick figures in Figure 12.7 indicate that information is being transmitted by people rather than by computer.

Recall that the purpose of system analysis is to specify requirements for a new system. How does the data flow diagram relate to such requirements? Each actigram defines a function to be performed by the system; therefore, all functional requirements are given by the actigrams. The data storage symbols define what information must be held in the system; therefore, all storage requirements are given by the list of storage entities in the system. Finally, the datagrams are used to show connections between subsystems and the information that flows across interfaces between subsystems. Thus, the datagrams that connect actigrams and storage symbols indicate the system interface requirements.

The Requirements Report

The final step in the system analysis phase is preparation of the *requirements report*. It describes the findings of the system analysis, lists the requirements of the new system, and gives the new schedule for system development. Generally, the requirements report contains

■ A brief restatement of the problem and the objectives of the proposed solution

Figure 12.7 The data flow diagram for the Purchase Parts from Suppliers subsystem of a wholesale distributor.

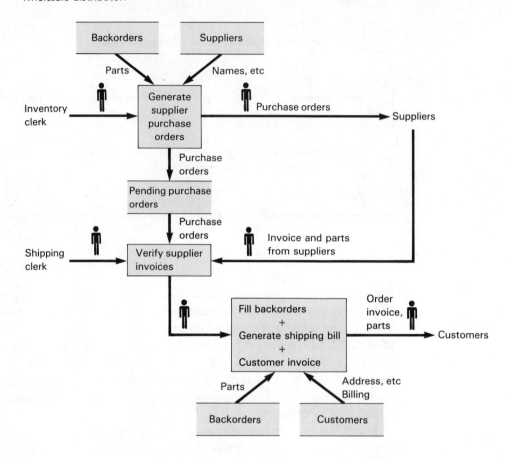

■ A data flow diagram describing the present system

■ A data flow diagram describing the proposed new system and a list of requirements (for storage, functions, and interfaces in terms of methods, procedures, and documents)

■ A revised Gantt chart showing the system's development

■ A formal request to start the next phase

The heart of this report is the proposed system shown as a data flow diagram. Figure 12.8 provides an example of one possible solution to the "lost" inventory problem we presented in our sample feasibility study; the double-lined datagrams in the figure indicate the proposed changes. Central to these changes is the actigram that defines the function to "Fill backorders and update inventory." This function integrates the previously separate functions of filling orders and updating the inventory file.

The requirements report should be specific about the requirements, since this is its main function, and the completed system will be compared against these requirements to determine if they were met. Therefore, it is common practice to include various checklists in the requirements report to emphasize features of the data flow diagram.

A requirements checklist for the "lost" inventory example is shown in Figure 12.9. Compare it with the data flow diagram in Figure 12.8. The required functions

Figure 12.8 The complete proposed system showing how to integrate the Order Entry and Inventory subsystem with the Purchase Parts from Suppliers subsystem. The double-lined datagrams and actigram indicate the proposed changes.

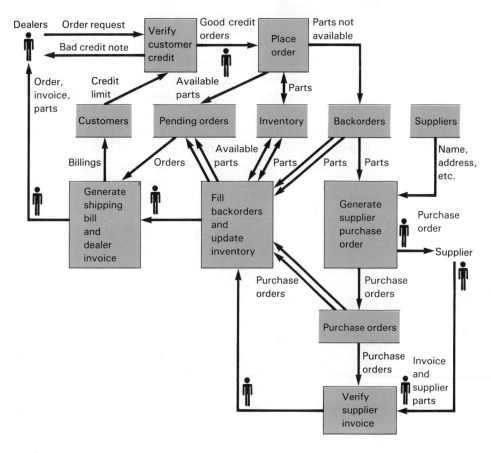

Required Function \\ Actigram	Verify credit	Verify supplier invoice	Place order	Generate shipping bill	Fill back-orders	Generate supplier P.O.	Requirement Achieved
Verify customer credit	✓						
Bill customers				✓			
Ship orders to dealer				✓			
Take in orders	✓		✓				
Backorder parts			✓			✓	
Clear backorders				✓	✓		
Parts inventory					✓		
Inventory update					✓		
Fill backorders				✓	✓		
Verify supplier invoice		✓					

Total _____

are listed down the page in Figure 12.9, and the actigrams (functions performed by the system) are listed across the page. Notice that some required functions overlap or seem redundant. This happens because the functions are listed from different people's perspectives. One clerk may clear backorders, while another clerk may fill backorders. Actually, these are the same function viewed from different perspectives. The last column of the checklist is reserved for verification of the requirements after the system has been developed. This is one of the advantages of top-down design and implementation: each phase can be checked against requirements stated in previous phases, to ensure a "correct" system. Additional checklists are included to clearly state the system's storage requirements, processing speed, and user convenience. Together the data flow diagram and checklists clearly and precisely define the system and proposed changes.

SYSTEM DESIGN

Once the requirements report is approved by management, the third phase of the system life cycle—system design—can begin. Whereas system analysis defines *what* is to be done, system design tells *how* it is to be done. The purpose of system design is to translate the data flow diagram (or equivalent documents) into documentation that states how the new system should work, how the requirements are to be met, and how the major components of the system should be implemented. Think of system design as a blueprint or roadmap of the system to be implemented.

A "good" design is compatible with the current software and hardware, flexible enough to be modified when needed, easy for people to use, and technically and economically feasible. These are obvious virtues, but how are they achieved?

Contemporary designers believe that top-down designs provide the answer. *Top-down software design* is the process of designing a program by first identifying its major components, which are called **modules**; then breaking them down into lower-level components, a process known as **stepwise refinement**, **hierarchical decomposition**, or **modular decomposition**, because the resulting system is structured as a hierarchy of modules; and repeating this process until the desired level of detail is achieved. Applying top-down design to an entire information system is one popular method used by analysts to obtain good hardware and software systems. The technique has been widely adopted as part of the **structured design** methodology, which is a disciplined approach to design that adheres to a specific set of rules based on such principles as top-down design, stepwise refinement, and data flow analysis.

From Data Flow Diagram to Hierarchy Diagrams

Suppose we follow the transformation of the "lost" inventory example shown in Figure 12.8 into a structured design. The first step in structured design is translating the data flow diagram into a hierarchical collection of modules, such as the *hierarchy diagram* shown in Figure 12.10(a). The module at the top of the hierarchy corresponds to the entire system. Through successive refinements, modules are broken into other modules, and so on until the smallest modules are obtained.

There are two popular ways to go about partitioning a system into subsystems: functional decomposition and data decomposition. In **functional decomposition**, the designer partitions the diagram according to the logical closeness of the actigrams. For example, in Figure 12.11, placing orders, generating shipping bills, and verifying the customer's credit are related functions, so they are put into one subsystem, while all others are put into another subsystem. In **data decomposition**, the diagram is partitioned according to the closeness of the datagrams and data storage items. For example, customers and pending orders might be closely related, whereas inventory, backorders, suppliers, and purchase orders might be considered another logical collection.

Notice that either method of partitioning can lead to identical results, as shown in Figure 12.11. In large systems, however, it is likely that two designers using the same method of partitioning will create different partitions. For example, data storage items might be partitioned into subsystems as follows: (1) suppliers and backorders, (2) inventory and purchase orders, and (3) customers and pending orders.

Figure 12.10 Transforming a data flow diagram into a structured design and user interface. In (a), the top-level modules are shown in a hierarchy diagram. The user interface, shown in (b), consists of pull-down menus corresponding to program modules.

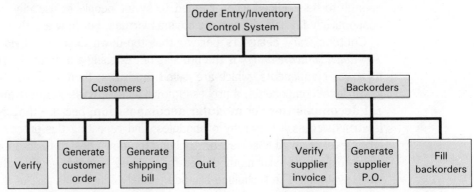

(a) A hierarchy diagram: Top-level modules corresponding to the user interface

Menu Titles

Menu Bar:	Customers		Backorders
Pull-down Items	Verify customer credit Generate customer order Generate shipping bill and invoice Quit		Verify supplier invoice Generate supplier P.O. Fill backorders

(b) User interface: Pull-down menus corresponding to modules

In most modern computer systems, the user interface is also considered when the data flow diagram is transformed into a hierarchy of modules. Suppose, for example, that the system is to be written with a pull-down menu interface. Each pull-down menu is given a title, and the titles are listed on a menu bar at the top of the screen, as shown in Figure 12.10(b). When a title is selected from the menu bar (with either the keyboard or a mouse), its menu pulls down so that you can select one of its items. The hierarchy diagram in Figure 12.10(a) corresponds closely to the user interface in Figure 12.10(b). Nouns in a menu are usually associated with storage devices and data; verbs are associated with actigrams. Because data decomposition was used in Figure 12.10(a), the titles on the menu bar are nouns, and the items are verbs describing the actions performed by the modules.

Walkthroughs and Prototypes

Regardless of how careful the designer is, the resulting design may be incomplete, incorrect, or difficult to use. For this reason, the system analyst often tests a proposed design by using several techniques.

Figure 12.11 Partitioning the data flow diagram into subsystems.

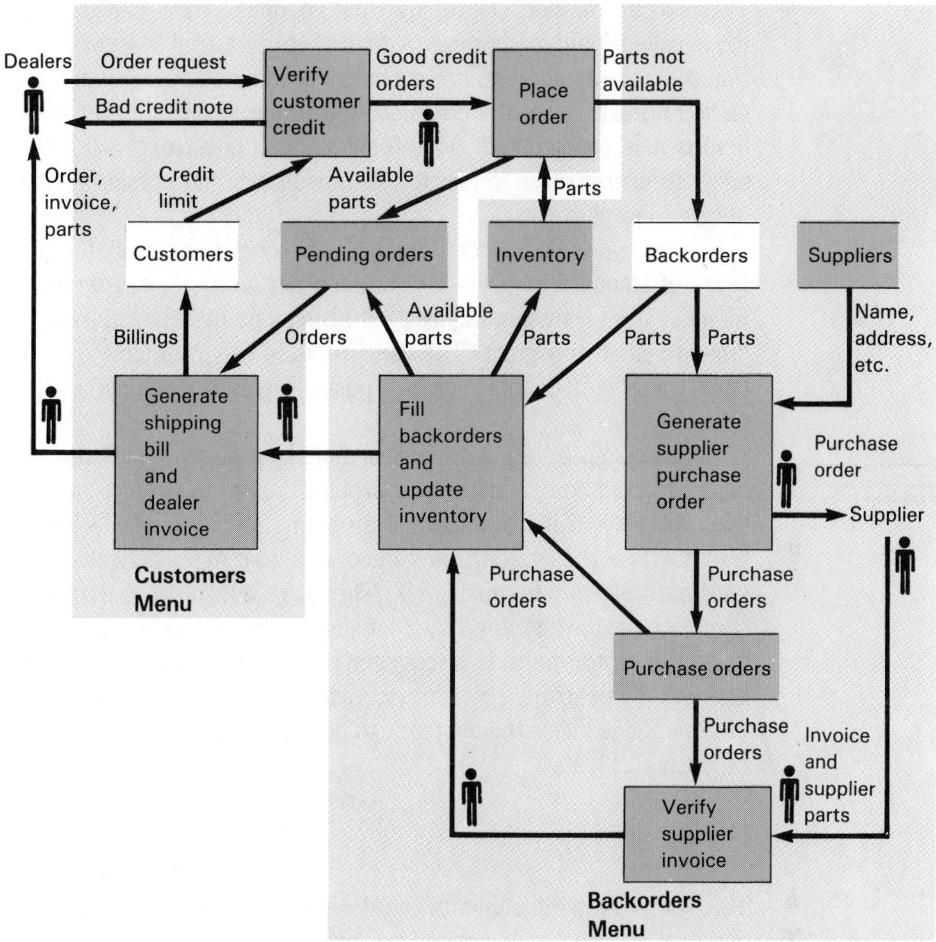

The most frequently used technique is the **design walkthrough**. In a design walkthrough, the system analyst prepares an overview of the design and presents it to users, programmers, and consultants to answer the following questions:

1. *Is it complete?* Does it do everything we want it to?

2. *Is it correct?* Does it satisfy the requirements specified by the requirements report?

3. *Is it feasible?* Can it be implemented quickly and cheaply, in a way that is compatible with existing systems?

So that the criticisms will be penetrating, managers do not attend the walkthrough.

If the walkthrough finds weaknesses in the design, the analyst must go back to the drawing board and come up with another design, repeat the walkthrough, and eventually get the group's approval. Once approved, the design is presented to management.

A second method of proving the "goodness" of a design is an emerging technique called *rapid prototyping*. A **prototype** is a trial system that simulates the real thing: it accepts user inputs, produces predefined reports, and in general gives the same appearance as the completed program in order to let users try the system before it is constructed. The designer also constructs sample output reports to show to users, programmers, and consultants and obtains their reactions through detailed discussions.

A prototype is constructed quickly, by combining predefined modules from a library of standard modules for common parts of every program. For example, the menu system shown in Figure 12.10(b) can be quickly and easily generated using a "menu-maker" program. The user can then use the menu system to identify problems with the user interface and possibly with deeper parts of the proposed system.

Prototyping is very effective at finding problems with the completeness, correctness, and compatibility of a proposed system. In fact, prototyping is perhaps the best way to find operational problems in the design. When users actually attempt to use the system, they become aware of bottlenecks, inconveniences, and gaps in the system's capabilities. These are difficult to discover before building the complete system by any other means. Suppose, for example, that, after a day of using the prototype, it is discovered that all information in the inventory file can be accidentally destroyed by a novice user. Before the system is actually used—and information is lost—the system can be redesigned or critical checks added to ward off such accidents.

The Design Report

The *design report* documents the design so that a correct, complete, and easy-to-use system will be developed according to the design. This report will be used constantly during the development phase. It will be changed to reflect improvements in the system when a design flaw is discovered. And it will be used to maintain, enhance, and modify the system after the system is put into use.

The design report should include

- Data flow diagrams of all systems and subsystems
- A hierarchy chart showing the top-level modules
- Requirements checklists for all functions, data, and performance criteria (speed, capacity of files, and so on)
- Gantt charts for the entire project
- Revisions as they are made during the life of the system

We've given a very simplified explanation of the design phase, in order to explain concepts rather than the details of the process. To give you some idea of the complexity of design, consider the following issues that must be addressed by the designer:

- Will the system meet the users' needs?
- Are the right reports produced?
- Do the reports contain the right information?
- Are reports formatted the way users expect?
- Does the user interface clearly explain how to operate the system?
- Do users feel comfortable with the displays?
- What happens when a user makes an error?
- Is the system protected from accidental use? from abuse?
- How should inputs be checked and validated?
- Are procedures clearly documented and accessible?
- Will it be easy to train users?
- Will the system be easy to modify?
- Are procedures for backup, an audit trail, and error recovery adequate?
- Have all requirements been met?
- Is the approach the best one?

SYSTEM DEVELOPMENT

The purpose of the system development phase is to build a system that meets the requirements set forth in the previous phases. The new system is developed in accordance with the documents produced during the analysis and design phases. These blueprints are used to construct a working system. The system may be purchased, or it may be developed in-house. New procedures may be designed so that people will know how to use the system.

Purchasing Hardware and Software

In many cases, it is best to purchase a new inventory system, database management package, or vertical application package. A *component* of the new system may be purchased—for example, a second computer to decrease the time it takes to do the current work. Or the *entire system* may be purchased as a turnkey system including hardware, software, and training. Recall that a *turnkey system* is ready to operate once you plug it in and "turn the key." Buying a new system is likely to cost less than developing one, and it will almost always be available sooner. A purchased system can also be tested and evaluated before a commitment to the system is made.

In some cases, the decision of whether to buy or to build is complicated. If the new system is an enhancement to the existing system, in-house programmers may understand the existing system well enough to modify it easily. An intermediate solution is to hire a consulting company to come into the organization to develop the enhancement. This has the advantage of allowing in-house control over the outcome without the disadvantage of requiring the company to hire people for a short-term job.

Compatibility is an important issue if the system is purchased, because purchased systems are usually more difficult to modify than systems developed in-house. A purchased system must "plug in" to the existing system at various levels: procedural, hardware, software, and strategic. At the *procedural* level, you should ask how the new system will change the way things are done. Are the reports different? Can paychecks be drawn on demand as in the old system? Is the sales report as thorough as before? *Hardware* compatibility means being able to connect machines together, obtain common maintenance, run software from the old machine on the new machine, transfer data between the old and new machines, and minimize the amount of training required to operate the new machinery. *Software* compatibility means being able to use existing programs with the new program. It must be possible to exchange data between the old and new programs. If the new software is incompatible with the existing software, converting from one data file format to another may be a larger job than writing a new system from scratch. *Strategic* compatibility is a management issue. A new computer or program may be compatible with existing systems; but if it takes the company in the wrong direction strategically, then all other considerations don't matter. For example, a decision to buy small computers that do the job today may lock the company into inadequate computing power in the future.

Software Development

If the new system is to be developed instead of purchased, there must be a *software development process*. In this process, user needs are translated into software requirements; software requirements are transformed into a design; the design is implemented in code; and the code is tested, documented, and certified for use.

The software development phase begins with the decision to develop a program or set of programs and ends when the product is no longer being enhanced by the developer. In general, this phase consists of organizing a team of developers, adopting a social process to guide the team's efforts, equipping the team with software development tools, and then managing the process until completion. Thus, the team's success depends on (1) team structure, (2) organizational process, (3) software development tools, and (4) management.

Team Structure
Programmers work in teams to perform tasks that they couldn't accomplish individually. Teams allow large projects to be completed quickly. Because software

development isn't well understood and is thought of as an art, software development teams are more like groups of temperamental writers collaborating on a novel than like the groups of workers who built the pyramids.

One well-known team structure is the **chief programmer team**, in which one programmer is assigned overall responsibility for the entire software project. All other programmers report directly to the chief programmer. Associate programmers are assigned tasks like building small libraries of programs that can be used by the chief, finding errors in the programs written by the chief, writing documentation, preparing test data, and so forth.

Another team structure, sometimes called the **democratic team,** is more egalitarian than the chief programmer team. In this structure, everyone is assigned duties that fit their individual strengths. If you're especially well versed in programming languages, you might be responsible for writing most of the software; if you're good at finding errors in other people's programs, you might be assigned to testing and debugging. Democratic teams also discuss the details of design and implementation as a group, arriving at a consensus before reaching a decision.

A third type of structure has grown up in the personal computer era. It doesn't involve a team at all; instead, there's a single programmer, called a **hacker**. Most hackers use other people's work by purchasing libraries of reusable programs, downloading programs from computer networks, and exchanging code with other hackers. Some of the most successful software—including games, music synthesizers, spreadsheets, software development aids, and graphics—has come from hackers.

In large organizations, the first step in development is to adopt a team structure and to staff the team with people who work well in the chosen structure. Hackers don't perform well in chief programmer teams, and democratic programmers may not be comfortable as hackers. Once the team is organized, the next step is to formalize the team's operation.

Organizational Process

The team operates according to an *organizational process*—rules and regulations governing the behavior of the team members. An example is the egoless programming process, one of the earliest processes used by teams. As its name indicates, **egoless programming** separates the programmer's ego from the program being developed. If an error is found in the program, the entire team, not the individual programmer, accepts responsibility for it. This reduces resistance to finding errors in the program and leads to greater productivity. Egoless programming has had such an effect on software development that it has been given a technical definition by several standards committees. According to one,

> Egoless programming is an approach to software development based upon the concept of team responsibility for program development. Its purpose is to prevent the programmer from identifying so closely with his or her output that objective evaluation is impaired.[3]

Figure 12.12 The organizational process for a software development team.

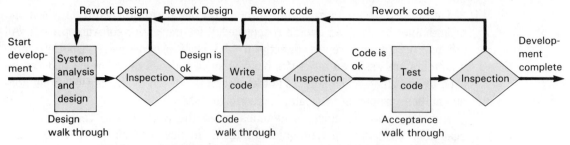

The organizational process also includes a method of inspecting software as it is being manufactured. **Program inspection** is a formal technique in which software requirements, design, or code are examined in detail by a person or group other than the author, to detect faults, violations of standards, and other problems. Inspection is the single most important step in developing highly reliable software.

One method of program inspection is an outgrowth of egoless programming; it is called the **structured walkthrough**. This is a formal review process in which a designer or programmer leads one or more other members of the development team through a segment of design or code that he or she has written, while the others ask questions about and comment on technique, style, possible errors, violations of development standards, and other problems. Structured walkthroughs and egoless programming establish an organizational process within the team. This process, shown in Figure 12.12, has often been compared to a "software factory" or "program assembly line." The design may be reworked after each inspection, and the software is accepted only after the final walkthrough approves it.

The process shown in Figure 12.12 is only part of the inspection and testing process, however. The final walkthrough completes the preliminary, or **alpha test**, portion of software development. The software isn't certified or approved for routine use until it has survived a beta test. **Beta testing** is done by users who accept the pioneer status of being first-time users. During beta testing, the shortcomings and errors found in the system are logged and reported back to be fixed by the development team.

Software Development Tools

After the organizational process is established, the next major step in the development phase is to select the tools the team will use. A **software tool** is a program that helps a programmer write another program. The ultimate software tool would automate programming by converting design specifications directly into a working system, but for most applications, such a tool does not yet exist. Many less capable tools do exist, however, and they decrease the time and cost of development. They offer one of the best ways for a team of programmers to improve both productivity and quality. Because labor costs account for most of the cost of programming, improving productivity by 10 to 20 percent is very worthwhile. Much greater improvements are possible; for many programming tasks, tools have been invented that increase a programmer's productivity by a factor of ten or more. We discuss only a few software tools here; several others are discussed in Chapter 13 on programming.

An **editor** is a word processor specially designed for programmers. A programmer uses an editor to write, correct, and sometimes check a program while it is being written. A sophisticated program editor, for example, automatically formats the program, checks for grammatical errors according to the rules of the programming language, and allows the programmer to examine several programs at the same time.

A **debugger** is a program that monitors another program while it is running; when the running program fails, the debugger takes over. It helps the programmer find incorrect values, wrong instruction sequences, and a number of other problems common to new programs.

A **data dictionary** is a collection of all the names of data items in a program, together with the names of modules that use each data item and a description of each data item's attributes (data type, length, representation, and so on). If one programmer changes a name in the dictionary, the change is made known to the other programmers. This prevents subtle inconsistencies in two modules of a program that share the same data item.

A **test-data generator** is a program for producing test data for another program. A test-data generator is used to test a module prior to acceptance. For example, if the module is supposed to sort a file, the test-data generator might be used to produce a file containing 10,000 records.

A **program analyzer** is a program that analyzes another program to determine if it has anomalies. A program analyzer may check a program for poor structure, violations in programming standards, or missing segments of code. Some software developers claim that their analyzers can even judge the *quality* of a program written by a human programmer.

Management and the Software Plan

The final ingredient in a software development team is proper management. A software development manager must understand the team, the organizational process, the tools, and the methodology used by the programmers. For this reason, most managers are ex-programmers.

A manager oversees the process and guides development through a *software plan*, which is a collection of documents that describes the design and implementation methodology used by the team. In addition, the plan incorporates the system's blueprint, as described by data flow diagrams, hierarchy charts, and program structure charts. A program **structure chart** is used to define the most detailed level of a program before the program is written in a programming language. It documents the logic, and hence the essence, of a program module.

Several commonly used structure charts are flowcharts, Nassi-Schneiderman charts, HIPO charts (*h*ierarchy + *i*nput/*p*rocessing/*o*utput charts), and Warnier-

Figure 12.13 A comparison of (a) a flowchart and (b) a Nassi-Schneiderman chart for representing the logic of a program module.

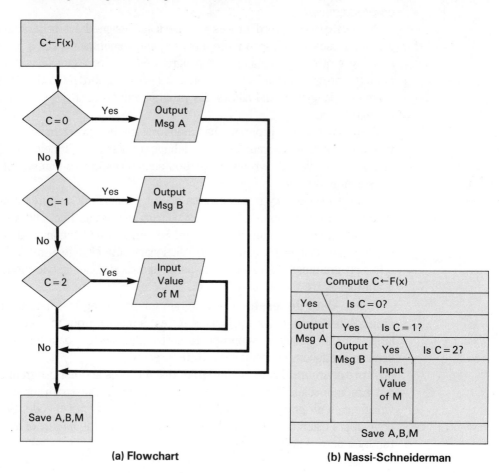

(a) Flowchart

(b) Nassi-Schneiderman

Orr charts. Figure 12.13 compares a flowchart and a Nassi-Schneiderman chart for the same segment of program logic.

In a *flowchart,* a rectangle represents a processing step, such as a calculation. A diamond represents a decision point, such as the choice between two alternatives. A parallelogram represents an input or output operation. Arrows connect the diamonds and boxes in exactly the way the program is supposed to evaluate the decisions and calculations. A flowchart is easy to draw, but it has a major drawback: the lack of structure in a flowchart often leads to convoluted programs that are difficult to modify and maintain. Flowcharts are still used by many programmers, but they are gradually being replaced by "safer" methods of documenting the logic of a program module.

A *Nassi-Schneiderman chart* is a nested structure; that is, as Figure 12.13(b) illustrates, it is made up of boxes inside boxes. Each box represents a control construct, such as making a yes or no decision, displaying a value, or computing a formula. In Figure 12.13(b), the decision construct "Is C = O)?" contains other decision constructs, and so on. In a Nassi-Schneiderman chart, it is impossible to describe control structures that overlap, because the corresponding boxes would overlap rather than nest. This restriction forces programmers to write easily understood, maintainable programs. This is the major advantage of both Nassi-Schneiderman charts and Warnier-Orr charts.

Documentation

Documentation varies from system to system and may be written during or after the system is developed. A development process is *self-documenting* if documentation is produced as a by-product of development. Structured design is self-documenting, because reports, diagrams, and various documents are generated by the process at each phase.

We can divide documentation into three categories according to the people who are going to use it. We described the first category, *design documentation*, when we discussed the analysis and design phases. It consists of flow diagrams; functional, performance, and data storage requirements; and management reports. The other two categories are programming documentation and user documentation.

Programming documentation is used by technical people to define the software architecture of a system. It includes descriptions of the program logic in the form of flowcharts, Warnier-Orr charts, Nassi-Schneiderman charts, or their equivalent; narratives that describe the system; hierarchy diagrams; and the program listings themselves (written in some programming language). Whenever a change is made in the software, these documents must be consulted, understood, and modified to reflect the change.

User documentation consists of training manuals, operations manuals, and reference manuals that describe how to use the system. Often this documentation is on-line; that is, users can temporarily interrupt their work and display help screens that show them what to do.

Documentation has one major goal: to inform and instruct. Therefore, it must be clearly written, easily referenced, and complete. Unfortunately, most documentation is inadequate, because it describes complex systems, because the systems change quickly, and because the people who build the systems are usually the ones who write the documentation—and designers, developers, and managers aren't especially fond of writing documentation.

INSTALLATION, MAINTENANCE, AND RETIREMENT

Installation is the phase in the system life cycle during which a system is integrated into its operational environment and tested to ensure that it performs as required.

This is the most precarious phase for an organization, because it can jeopardize the entire operation. For example, a bank jeopardizes its entire cash-flow operation during the installation of a new check-cashing system.

During the installation phase, the new hardware and software must be checked under real conditions. This means putting the system into use by the people who must run and maintain it. People must be trained, new procedures instituted, and the system thoroughly "shaken down" to eliminate any errors or deficiencies. Because of the risk of failure during this phase, various methods of conversion are used.

- *Direct.* This is the most dangerous method of conversion, because the organization switches immediately from the old to the new system. If the new system fails, it can hurt the entire organization; but if it succeeds, the cost of conversion is minimized. Most people will avoid the direct method unless there is no alternative or the new system is small and simple.

- *Parallel.* This method runs both the new and old systems side by side for a time. When the new system has been checked completely, the old system is retired. Although the parallel method ensures that the work gets done even if the new system fails, it is expensive because of the equipment, people, and time involved.

- *Pilot.* This method minimizes the risk by assigning a small pilot group of users to convert directly to the new system. If the new system fails, the damage is minimized, because only a small part of the company is affected. Additionally, those in the pilot group become experts who can help other users switch over. This approach takes longer than direct or parallel conversions.

- *Phased.* With this method, the new system is gradually phased in by introducing portions of the overall system over time. It takes longer than most other methods but is less risky. For example, a new accounting system might be phased in over a year by starting with the general ledger, then converting accounts payable, accounts receivable, and finally payroll.

Which method of conversion is best depends on the circumstances. In fact, the best method may be a combination of parallel and phased or pilot and direct methods. The idea is to minimize cost and risk.

After installation is complete, the maintenance phase begins. Its purpose is to modify the system after it is installed, to correct faults, improve performance, or adapt the system to a changed environment. For example, an incorrect calculation of withholding taxes would be considered a fault in the payroll subsystem; an untimely or delayed report would be considered a performance problem. Program maintenance is a major cost. Industry estimates say that more than half of all software development costs are spent on the maintenance of existing programs.

The retirement phase is the period in the life cycle when support of the system is terminated. Retirement of the old system is typically carried out in conjunction with the installation of a new system.

■ SUMMARY

Modern computer systems are too complicated to be designed haphazardly. Organizations turn to system analysts when new systems need to be developed or existing systems need to be modified. A system analyst uses many documentation techniques and review procedures to organize development of large computer systems.

A fundamental procedure of system analysis is stepwise refinement, whereby a complex system is broken down layer by layer into subsystems of an understandable size. Much of a system analyst's skill lies in the ability to choose appropriate subsystems and to document the linkages among subsystems effectively.

System development is keyed to the system life cycle. Following the seven phases of the life cycle (investigation, analysis, design, development, installation, maintenance, and retirement) encourages the orderly development of a system and provides management with verifiable checkpoints at which progress can be reviewed.

Each phase in the life cycle calls for the completion of specific documents. The documents created in each phase become the starting points for the next phase. For example, the requirements report determines the requirements that the system design must meet, and the design report becomes the blueprint for the development phase.

■ KEY TERMS

alpha test

beta test

chief programmer team

data decomposition

data dictionary

data flow diagram

debugger

democratic team

design walkthrough

editor

egoless programming

functional decomposition

hacker

hierarchical decomposition

modular decomposition

module

program analyzer

program inspection

prototype

requirements analysis

software tool

stepwise refinement

structure chart

structured design

structured walkthrough

system

system analyst

test-data generator

top-down analysis and design

1. What is a system? Compare an information system with a general system.

2. Give some reasons for enhancing an existing system. How do these reasons compare with the reasons for considering a new system?

3. What is top-down design? How does it relate to the systems approach? What tools and techniques are used in top-down design?

4. How are data flow, user interface, and hierarchy diagrams related? How is the data flow diagram transformed winto a hierarchy diagram?

5. Why would anyone build a new system when they could purchase a turnkey system? What factors determine whether a new system is developed in-house or purchased?

6. What is a chief programmer? a hacker? Describe how these two kinds of software developers create programs.

7. What is egoless programming? How does it affect programmers' ability to test their own programs?

8. What is the purpose of a walkthrough? What happens during a structured walkthrough?

9. How does an analyst know whether a design is correct? What about the software itself? Describe what happens at each phase of the system life cycle to verify that the system is being constructed properly.

10. Describe some ways of documenting the logic of a program module. Which way is likely to be most understandable to a layperson? Which way is likely to be preferred by a system analyst?

11. Consider the different ways to convert from an old system to a new one. Which method is likely to be used in each of the following situations? Why?
   a. Introducing an off-the-shelf payroll program in a Fortune 500 firm.
   b. Introducing a new word processing package in a law office with five typists.
   c. Developing an on-line tracking and control system for production in a paper mill.
   d. Developing a new control program for a hard disk that will function as a file server on a local area network.
   e. Replacing a manual system of registration in a major university with a computer-based system.

EXERCISES

1. Suppose it costs $36,000 per year for one clerk to manually process paychecks for a small company. The company expects to grow 50 percent per year and currently has 120 employees. One payroll clerk can process the

current load, but when the number of employees per payroll clerk reaches 300, an additional payroll clerk will be needed. Assume that the one-time cost of installing a computer is $150,000 and that the computer will be capable of processing from 20 to 20,000 checks per month at an annual cost of $45,000. When should the company convert to the computer system? When will the breakeven point be reached? Prepare a cost/benefit analysis of this system.

2. Draw a data flow diagram of the system used by your instructor to lecture, test, grade, and report grades. Be sure to identify data storage, datagram, and actigram elements in your diagram.

3. Using the data flow diagram shown in Figure 12.8, derive different user interface and hierarchy diagrams than the ones given in Figure 12.10. In other words, change the partitions or the method of selecting menus.

4. Give an example of design incompleteness, program incorrectness, and operational incompatibility.

5. Draw a flowchart and a Nassi-Schneiderman chart of the logic used to determine letter grades from numerical test scores.

Score	Letter Grade
100–87	A
86–79	B
78–55	C
54–41	D
40–0	F

NOTES

1. The ANSI/IEEE Standard 729-1983 can be obtained from IEEE, Inc., East 47th Street, New York, New York 10017.

2. "A mess is a system of problems. A system is a whole that cannot be decomposed into independent parts. From this it can be shown that a system always has properties that none of its parts have and that these are its *essential* parts" (Russell Ackoff, "The Art and Science of Mess Management," *Interfaces* 11 [February 1981]:20-26).

3. ANSI/IEEE Standard 729-1983.

13 Programming

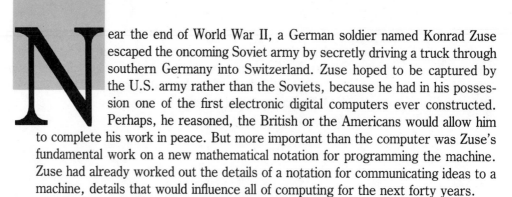

Near the end of World War II, a German soldier named Konrad Zuse escaped the oncoming Soviet army by secretly driving a truck through southern Germany into Switzerland. Zuse hoped to be captured by the U.S. army rather than the Soviets, because he had in his possession one of the first electronic digital computers ever constructed. Perhaps, he reasoned, the British or the Americans would allow him to complete his work in peace. But more important than the computer was Zuse's fundamental work on a new mathematical notation for programming the machine. Zuse had already worked out the details of a notation for communicating ideas to a machine, details that would influence all of computing for the next forty years.

The basic concepts of modern programming are refinements of Zuse's programming language. These concepts are put to work every day by contemporary programmers, who convey ideas called *algorithms* to computers, in a notation called a *programming language*. An **algorithm** is a step-by-step list of instructions for solving a problem. For example, an algorithm could be designed to do a calculation, move data, or control a monitor. Algorithms are expressed in a **programming language**, a formalized notation that allows algorithms to be represented in a rigorous and precise way. There is little room for an ambiguous or imprecise idea in an algorithm. Therefore, most programming languages differ significantly from natural languages like English.

The word processing and spreadsheet software discussed in previous chapters are elaborate algorithms written in a language that a computer can "understand." But occasionally a problem crops up that can't be solved efficiently with a prepackaged program. When this occurs, the only alternative is to write a new program that solves the problem. Even if you have someone else write the program, you should know something about programming in order to discuss the program.

In this chapter, you will see examples of programs written in several languages, and you will learn about different programming languages, the technique called *structured programming,* how to select a programming language, and very high-level languages.

THE COMPUTER TOWER OF BABEL

Machine Language Versus Programming Languages

There is only one language that a computer can run without modification: machine language. *Machine language programs* are nothing more than long sequences of binary numbers that have meaning for the computer. Programs written in other languages must be translated into machine language before they can be used to control a computer.

Machine language programs are the most elementary, or *low-level,* form of encoded algorithms. They are seldom used to program computers directly. To understand why, consider the following example of low-level programming. Suppose you tell a friend how to go to a nearby store and get a quart of milk. Here is a list of the low-level instructions you might use.

1. Lean forward in your chair.
2. Push up with your hands and legs.
3. Raise up into a standing position.
4. Move your left foot forward.
5. Move your right foot forward.

. . .

100. Grasp the doorknob with your right hand.
101. Turn the doorknob clockwise.

. . .

As you can see, these are extremely meticulous and tedious instructions. They certainly accomplish the task, but they're too detailed to repeat every time you want milk. To get around the need for such detailed instructions, you might compress the same meaning into fewer, more powerful words, as follows:

1. Stand up and walk out the door.
2. Get into your car and drive to the store.
3. Go into the store and get a quart of milk.
4. Pay for the milk and leave the store.

. . .

12. Get out of your car and come back into the house.
13. Give me the milk and sit down.

Similarly, if you use a programming language instead of machine language, you can express the same meaning with fewer instructions. For this reason, contemporary programmers use programming languages rather than machine languages.

Translation of Programs

People learn early in life how to translate the command "go to the store" into the numerous instructions to lean forward, stand up, walk, and so forth. A computer can't learn a language by itself (at least not yet), so it must be programmed to translate all programs (except, of course, machine language programs) into machine language before they can be processed.

A **translator** is a program for converting other programs from one language to another. It is a powerful tool for increasing a programmer's productivity. Instead of giving detailed instructions in machine language, the programmer can give general directions at a higher level of abstraction, in a programming language, let a translator fill in the machine-language details, and obtain the proper results in a shorter time. A translator reads an input program, called the **source program**, and converts the lines in the source program one by one into another language. The converted program is called the *target program*. Both the source and the target programs do exactly the same thing, but they are encoded in different languages.

Compilers and Interpreters

Translation can be done in two radically different ways. A **compiler** is a translator that translates and executes a program in separate stages. An **interpreter** is a translator that translates and executes your program in only one stage.

To understand the difference between compiling a program and interpreting it, consider two ways for an American to translate a document in French into an English speech. Using the *compiler* method, the American speaker would convert the

Figure 13.1 The difference between compilers and interpreters.

French version   English version   Speaker   French version   Speaker

(a) Translation by Compiling   **(b) Translation by Direct Interpretation**

entire French document into an English document *before* giving the speech. Using the *interpreter* method, the American would convert the French document into English, line by line, *while* giving the speech (see Figure 13.1). This removes the need for creating an intermediate English document, but the speaker would have to convert the French document into English each time it is presented.

A program can be either interpreted or compiled. If it is interpreted, no translated document is produced; each time the program is executed, it must be translated. If it is compiled, an output document is produced, so that the translation need never be done again. The compiler program takes the following steps:

1. Translate the source program into an equivalent **object program**, which is an incomplete, intermediate program that must be linked with other programs before it is run.

2. Link the object program with other support programs, producing an equivalent target program written in machine language.

3. Execute the target program.

In the second step, the object program is read by a **linker program**, which converts the object program into machine language and combines it with operating system programs for writing lines of text on the screen, multiplying numbers, controlling the disks, and so forth. This linking ties the program to a particular operating system, which is why application programs written for one operating system won't run on an identical computer that uses a different operating system.

Compilers produce fast, compact, and efficient machine language programs. They are the translators most frequently used by professional programmers. Compiled programs run much faster than interpreted programs because there is no translation—that is done before the program is run. However, the three steps (compile, link, and execute) interfere with programming productivity, because they take extra time and attention.

Interpreters are good for novice programmers and for professionals testing new programs. In fact, running a BASIC program via an interpreter is a good way to learn how to write simple programs, because the response is instantaneous: your program's results are produced without inconvenient delays. Errors can be corrected and the program reinterpreted again and again until it is correct. However, because interpreters repeatedly translate and execute statements one at a time, they are slow. In addition, the source program must coexist in memory with the interpreter while it is running. This usually means that less memory is available for long programs.

BASIC, LISP, APL, LOGO, and many other programming languages are usually interpreted. COBOL, FORTRAN, Pascal, C, and Ada are usually compiled. However, there are BASIC and LISP compilers, and there are Pascal and C interpreters, so the choice is yours.

High-Level Languages (HLL)

Low-level languages, such as various assembly languages, translate one for one into machine instructions. *Assembly language* is a symbolic machine language that uses mnemonic codes (ADD for addition, MUL for multiplication) in place of numbers and variable names instead of binary memory locations. Assembly language programs are compiled by a translator called an *assembler,* which converts the mnemonic codes into machine language numbers. Low-level languages like assembly language are cryptic and require extra training and effort to comprehend. In contrast, each "sentence" in a high-level language translates into two or more machine language instructions. A high-level programming language resembles a combination of English and mathematics. English keywords are used to make the language readable, and a certain amount of mathematical formalism is used to remove the ambiguity found in natural language. Indeed, a **high-level language (HLL)** is a restricted, formalized, and abbreviated version of a natural language. Its purpose is to express algorithms in a concise and unambiguous manner. Most programming languages are high-level languages.

A Sample BASIC Program
Many computers come equipped with a BASIC interpreter as part of their system software. For this reason, we will first use BASIC to illustrate a simple high-level language program. Suppose you want to compute the formula $E = U * (P - C)$, where

E = profit
U = units sold
P = price per unit
C = cost per unit
* means multiplication

Figure 13.2 shows a program for doing so, written in BASIC. You can type the program into your computer after first loading the BASIC interpreter. When you type NEW, the BASIC interpreter is told to begin a new program. It then allows you to enter commands as a list of numbered statements. After you've entered the program, typing RUN causes the interpreter to execute each statement one at a time.

When the program is executed, line 10 sends the prompt "Enter number units sold:" to the screen and waits for your response. Whatever number you type is stored in the memory location identified by the name UNITS_SOLD. Lines 20 and 30 do the same thing for PRICE and COST. PROFIT is calculated in line 40; the PRINT statement in line 50 tells the computer to display the answer on the screen.

A Sample Pascal Program

Pascal is a good language to illustrate the nature of languages that are normally compiled, such as C, Ada, Modula-2, and PL/I. Pascal programs are divided into

---

Figure 13.2 A BASIC program to compute PROFIT.

```
NEW
10 INPUT "Enter number units sold:  ", UNITS
20 INPUT "Enter price per unit:  ", PRICE
30 INPUT "Enter cost per unit:  ", COST
40 PROFIT = UNITS * (PRICE - COST)
50 PRINT "Profit $", PROFIT
Ok
RUN
Enter number units sold:  300
Enter price per unit:  7
Enter cost per unit:  4.5
Profit $        750
```

Figure 13.3 A Pascal program to compute PROFIT.

```
PROGRAM PROFIT;

    VAR PROFIT      :  REAL;
        UNITS_SOLD  :  REAL;
        PRICE       :  REAL;
        COST        :  REAL;

    BEGIN
        WRITE ('Enter number units sold');
        READLN (UNITS_SOLD);
        WRITE  ('Enter price per unit');
        READLN (PRICE);
        WRITE  ('Enter cost per unit');
        READLN (COST);
        PROFIT := UNITS_SOLD * (PRICE - COST);
        WRITELN ('Profit $', PROFIT)
    END.
```

two sections: data definition and instruction processing. The *data definition section* is designated by the keyword VAR. All of the *variables* to be used in the program must be declared at the beginning of the program, inside the VAR section. A **variable** is a memory location that has been given a name. The *processing section* contains all of the actions to be carried out and the order in which to carry them out. It begins with the keyword BEGIN and ends with the keyword END.

Figure 13.3 shows a simple program for computing profit. The VAR section tells the compiler to make PROFIT, UNITS_SOLD, PRICE, and COST variables. The VAR section also declares that these variables are real numbers (signed numbers with decimal points), so they can store dollars and cents. The processing section follows. As in BASIC, the first statement is done, then the next statement, and so on. Although the syntax for the Pascal processing section of Figure 13.3 is slightly more complicated than that for the BASIC statements in Figure 13.2, both programs accomplish the same task in the same basic way.

Because Pascal programs are compiled rather than interpreted, you must compile, link, and execute this program before any answer can be obtained. First, the source program PROFIT is read by the Pascal compiler program and converted into an object program that can be thought of as halfway to machine language. Then the linker program converts the object program into a machine language file that can be run by typing its name.

Knowledge of a programming language is only one of the skills required of a programmer. The most important skill is knowing when and how to apply the right techniques. In a sense, the language is a paintbrush; the computer, a canvas; and the programmer, an artist. Knowing how to mix colorful paints doesn't guarantee a work of art. Similarly, knowing about computers and a programming language is no assurance that you can produce a high-quality program.

Steps in Programming

A programmer takes a written list of specifications for a program and uses it to write a program that solves a specific problem. The programmer first takes the following steps:

- Design an algorithm.
- Code it in a programming language.

The next steps are done by the computer.

- Translate the source program into the target program.
- Execute the target program.

The programmer takes the final steps.

- Debug the program. Program errors are called *bugs,* and the process of removing errors is called *debugging*.
- Redesign, correcting for major errors, and recode.

This cycle is repeated until all errors have been removed and the program works as it should, meeting the original specifications. In some cases, the program is tested more than 100 times before all errors are removed.

A large percentage of a programmer's time is spent debugging. This can to some extent be avoided by proper selection of a programming language. A high-level language is a good tool for minimizing bugs. But a high-level language isn't enough; a programming methodology is also needed. To minimize the time spent debugging and increase the availability of high-quality software, professional programmers have developed a methodology called *structured programming*.

Structured Programs

In most disciplines, a "divide-and-conquer" approach is used to divide a large and complex project into many simpler projects. Large programs are difficult to write, so programmers have their own version of divide and conquer, called *structured programming,* which is a programming methodology that involves the systematic design of software. It includes the use of the structured design techniques described in Chapter 12.

A fundamental principle of structured programming is *software reductionism,* which is the idea that complex programs can be reduced to a collection of simple ones. This simple idea is very effective for reducing errors in programs and lowering the cost of developing new software. When a programmer uses reductionism to design and write a program, the result is called a *structured program.*

Structured programs can be reduced to elementary building blocks called **control structures**, which are statements that control the order in which other program statements are executed. Every program can be constructed from the following three control structures:

1. *Sequence.* This control structure causes a program to execute statements placed one after the other in that sequence. Figure 13.4(a) shows the order of statement execution in a sequence of three statements (S_1, S_2, S_3).

2. *Choice.* When this control structure is used, statements in a program may or may not be executed, depending on a decision made during program execution. If the decision results in a true condition, one path is taken; otherwise, the other path is taken. Both paths finally merge at a single point, where program execution continues. Figure 13.4(b) shows an example. If D is true, then statement S_1 is executed; otherwise, statement S_2 is executed. IF is used to designate the decision, THEN designates the path to be followed if the condition is true, and ELSE designates the path to be followed if the condition is false.

3. *Iteration.* This control structure is often called a *loop.* It causes statements to be executed repeatedly until some termination condition is reached. Figure 13.4(c) shows a loop. As long as D remains true, the program repeatedly executes statement S. As soon as D becomes false, the loop terminates, and the program executes the next statement following the loop. WHILE is used to designated the condition that is checked each time the loop is repeated; DO marks the statement to be repeated. The loop in Figure 13.4(c) reads, "While D is true, do statement S."

A typical program is composed of hundreds of these fundamental components put together like Lego blocks or Tinker Toys.

In a structured program, these three control structures are the only ones used. Another characteristic of a structured program is that each control structure and each program module should have only one entry point and one exit point. When completed, a structured program has two major advantages over a nonstructured program. First, it is more likely to work correctly, because it is simple. Second, it can be easily understood, modified, and enhanced by someone else.

Figure 13.4 The fundamental control structures in structured programming.

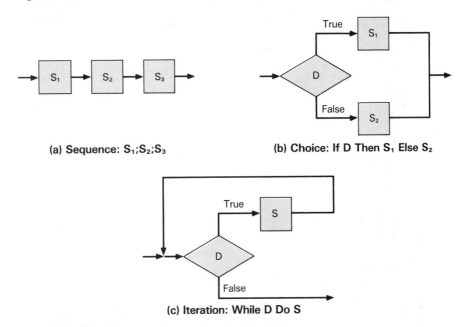

(a) Sequence: S_1;S_2;S_3

(b) Choice: If D Then S_1 Else S_2

(c) Iteration: While D Do S

A Sample Structured BASIC Program

Consider Figure 13.5, which shows a program that uses two of the three fundamental control structures—a loop and sequence statements. The loop begins with the keyword WHILE and ends with WEND. Indentations in the program indicate that the preceding statement contains the indented sequence of statements. Thus, within the loop, there is a sequence of three statements—those in lines 130, 140, and 150.

This program accepts a list of numbers from the keyboard, computes their average, and prints the average. But it contains a bug. If no input is entered at the keyboard, COUNT remains at zero, and the division by zero in line 170 causes the program to crash. We can fix this bug using a choice structure to test for a zero value of COUNT. To do so, we change line 170 to read

```
170 IF COUNT > 0 THEN AVG = SUM/COUNT ELSE AVG = 0
```

This is called an IF-THEN-ELSE statement. Figure 13.6 compares the two versions of the program.

We could have written the program in an unstructured manner. For example, instead of the IF statement we added to line 170, we could have used a GOTO statement—a command to go to a specific line, thereby skipping over other statements.

```
100 SUM  = 0                        'SEQUENCE OF 3 STATEMENTS...
110 COUNT= 0                        'COUNT HOW MANY INPUTS
120 INPUT "Enter # of NUMBERs "; N
125 WHILE N > COUNT 'ITERATION...
130     INPUT NUMBER                'SEQUENCE INSIDE ITERATION...
140     SUM = SUM + NUMBER
150     COUNT = COUNT + 1
160 WEND                            'LOOP ENDS
170 AVG = SUM / COUNT
180 PRINT AVG
190 END
```

```
170 IF COUNT > 0 GOTO 175
172 AVG  =  0
173 GOTO 180
175 AVG  =  SUM/COUNT
```

But GOTO statements are forbidden in structured programming, because they violate the restriction to use only sequence, choice, and iteration control structures. An illustration of the effect of using numerous GOTO statements in a BASIC program is shown in Figure 13.7. Programs without GOTO statements are easier to understand and, as a consequence, normally have fewer bugs.

SELECTING A PROGRAMMING LANGUAGE

Every programming language has its loyal followers, but there is no single programming language that is best for all applications. The following list shows a small sample of the more than 400 programming languages that exist:

Problem or Application Area	Some Recommended Languages
Numerical	BASIC, FORTRAN, APL, Pascal
Data files	COBOL, PL/I, dBASEII/dBASE III

Making the Pieces: From Silicon Crystals to Computers

Computers are constructed from electrical parts—mainly transistors, capacitors, resistors, and wires. It takes millions of these parts to build even a small personal computer. Because of intense competition, successful firms must use low-cost methods to build and connect electrical components. The fruit of this competition has been a number of fascinating and exotic manufacturing techniques. As you study this photo essay, you will gain insight into how these techniques work.

1. Large silicon crystals are the raw material from which most integrated circuit chips are manufactured. The crystals are grown in a furnace containing an exceptionally pure bath of molten silicon. Usually they are from 3 to 5 inches in diameter; often they are several feet long.

PREPARING THE SILICON SURFACE

2. Each silicon crystal is sliced with a diamond-edged saw into round wafers that are less than one-half millimeter thick. Because silicon crystals are harder than most metals, cutting them is expensive and slow.

3. The first step in removing damage caused by cutting the crystals is called lapping. Wafers are placed in carriers between two rotating plates that remove a prescribed amount of damage. Later the wafers are polished to a mirror finish.

4. Wafers are inspected many times during the manufacturing process.

5. A finished wafer contains many integrated circuit chips organized like postage stamps on a piece of paper. These wafers range from 1 to 5 inches. The trend has been toward larger wafers.

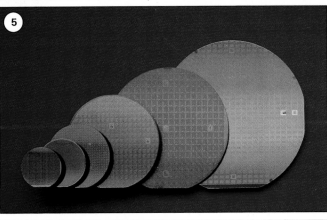

6. An IBM engineer inspects an experimental eight-inch silicon wafer that can accommodate more than 2,000 chips.

window 8

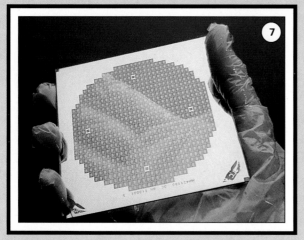

MANUFACTURING THE CIRCUITS

Photographic methods are used to transfer an image of circuit patterns into numerous copies on the silicon surface.

7. This photomask contains one layer of circuitry. The mask is created by an electron-beam exposure system that etches tiny images on a metal-coated glass plate; the glass is transparent to ultraviolet rays, but the metal isn't. Before the mask can be used to create circuits, the wafers are dipped in a bath of ultraviolet-sensitive photoresist (a photographic-type emulsion). Then each wafer is exposed by shining ultraviolet light through the mask. Finally, the wafer is washed in a developing solution, leaving a pattern on the surface. This process deposits an image of one circuit layer on the surface of the chip. A completed chip may require from 5 to 18 circuit layers.

9. A rack of wafers enters the furnace.

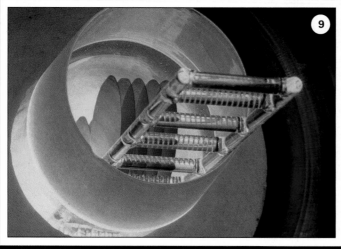

8. During some processing steps wafers are heated in ovens to produce an insulating layer of glass oxide on exposed silicon surfaces. Other steps use ovens to "dope" unoxidized surfaces with a thin layer of impurities, such as boron or phosphorus. The impurities create conductive and resistive regions in the silicon that form electronic circuits.

10. Peter Ferlita inserts a program card into an automatically controlled furnace at RCA's Solid State Division in Somerville, New Jersey. The card contains instructions for processing during a one-hour trip at temperatures of 1500° F. After more than 500 manufacturing operations, these wafers will be used in guidance control systems for missiles.

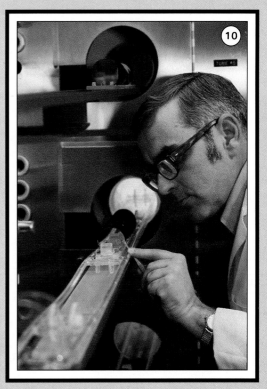

11. An Intel Corporation technician positions wafers to receive a thin coating of aluminum from an evaporator. Later most of the aluminum will be etched away, leaving trace lines that connect the circuits.

12. A wafer is washed after etching. This is a wafer of transducers to be used in read/write heads for hard disk drives.

WAFER INSPECTION

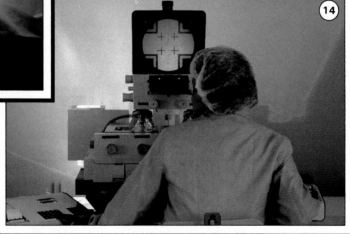

14. Microscopes are also necessary to align photomasks with the circuits on a partially completed wafer.

13. Periodic inspections by microscope are necessary to ensure that the circuits are being constructed satisfactorily.

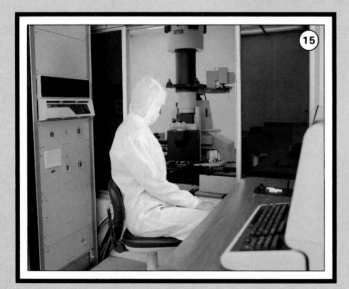

15. Even minute particles of dust in the air can land on the surface of the silicon and result in malfunctioning circuits. Manufacturing is done in highly controlled "clean rooms" where workers wear protective gloves and hats and the air is constantly filtered. This room is lit with yellow light to keep out extraneous ultraviolet rays.

TESTING AND CUTTING
THE FINISHED WAFER

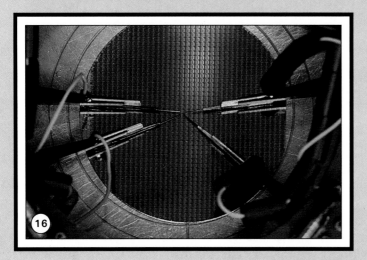

16. After the wafer is completed, each chip is tested to see if it functions correctly. The tests are conducted by placing probes on tiny electrical contact pads around the outside of the chip.

17. This testing machine at the National Semiconductor Corporation lowers 29 wires onto a chip and then runs it through a series of electrical tests. If the chip fails a test, a small ink spot is dropped on it to mark it as a reject.

18. Eventually the wafer is ready to be diced into separate chips. Here a diamond-edged tool scribes lines along the wafer's surface.

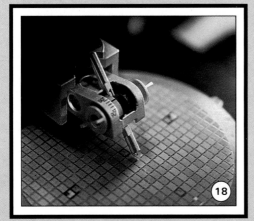

PACKING MEMORY CHIPS

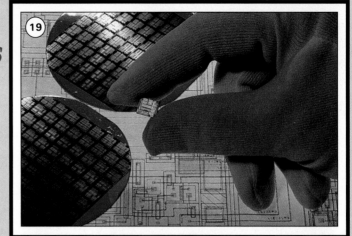

19. A composite drawing of circuit layers, two finished wafers, and a gloved hand holding an unmounted integrated circuit chip.

21. A packaged memory chip sits on top of a wafer of similar memory chips. Each chip can store 64K bits (65,536 bits) of digital data. Memory chips capable of storing more than one megabit are being developed in research labs.

20. Chips are mounted inside protective carrier packages to make them easier to handle and to help them dissipate heat. To mount the chip, tiny wires are soldered from pads on the chip's outside edges to contact areas on the carrier.

22. Very-large-scale-integrated (VLSI) chips require many input and output pins. Instead of having leads poked into holes in a circuit board, these chips have been mounted in leadless carriers that sit on the surface of a circuit board. This method produces smaller chips, which results in more densely populated circuit boards and, consequently, smaller and faster computers.

DESIGNING THE CIRCUITS

Chips can have well over 100,000 circuit elements. Creating and testing the circuit design require extensive use of computers.

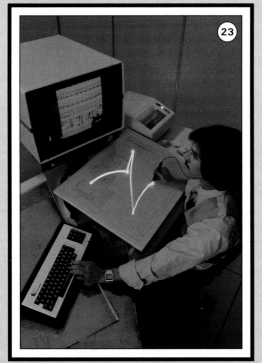

23. This computer-aided design system supports a wide range of design, drafting, and manufacturing operations on large-scale integrated (LSI) chips. The user enters data from either the keyboard or the graphics tablet.

24. Once a design is stored in memory, it receives thorough computerized testing. The circuit's functions are simulated by programs that check for problems with the speed, timing, logic, and voltage. Modifications to the chip's design can be entered from the keyboard.

25. Composite drawings of the various circuit layers are 400 times larger than actual size.

DESIGNING CIRCUIT BOARDS

The most common way of linking chips electrically is to mount them on printed circuit boards made of fiberglass.

26. High-quality graphics terminals help lay out the design of circuit boards quickly and accurately.

27. After the position of chips has been entered, straight lines can be drawn on the screen to point out how the chips' pins are to be connected.

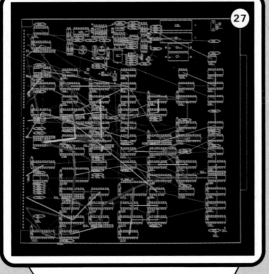

28. Once the connections among pins have been specified, computer programs help determine where the copper traces (wires) should run along the circuit board's surfaces.

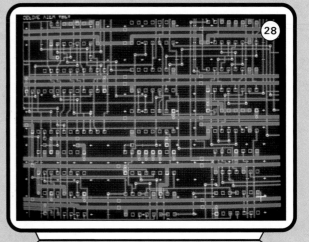

29. Even high-resolution terminals can be hard to read when they display an entire circuit board at once. Usually it is possible to zoom in to look at one portion more closely, or to scroll from one region of the board to another.

30. In minutes a color electrostatic plotter can produce a full-color plot of an entire circuit board so that designs can be previewed quickly.

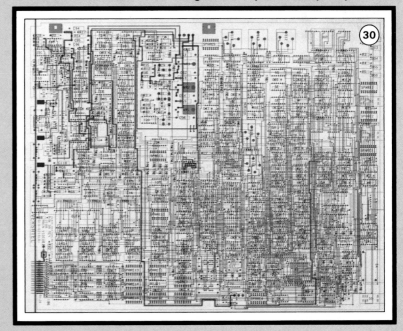

COMPUTER-AIDED MANUFACTURING

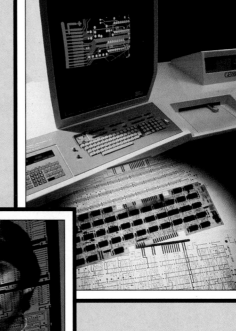

31. Computers do more than speed up the design process; they produce the media needed to manufacture printed circuit boards. Among these media are artwork and silkscreen masters, component drawings, and tapes that direct drilling and insertion operations.

32. Artwork masters can be extracted directly from a computerized circuit board design aided by a computer-controlled photoplotter.

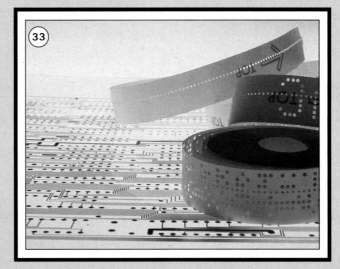

33. Punched tape is often used to load numerically controlled (N/C) manufacturing machines with control sequences. Many processes for manufacturing rely heavily on N/C machines.

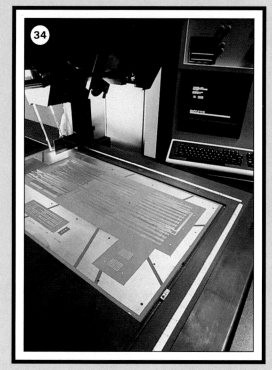

BUILDING THE BARE BOARD

34. An internal layer of a 16-layer printed circuit board is scanned by a programmable inspection machine to ensure high reliability. This circuit board will become part of an electronic system to protect military aircraft from radar-directed weapons.

35. A Cray Research technician coats a printed circuit board with copper. This step follows an operation that masks areas of the board so that only the unmasked areas are plated with copper.

36. Integrated circuit chips have been installed in this completed supercomputer circuit board manufactured by Cray Research.

DRILLING, STUFFING, SOLDERING, AND INSPECTING THE BOARDS

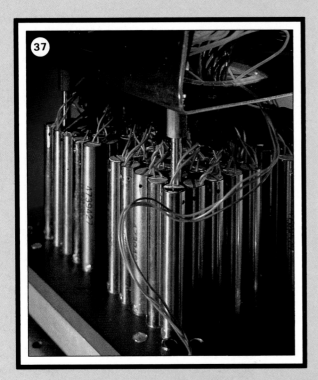

37. In one second this IBM-designed tool punches 1,440 precisely placed holes with the diameter of an eyelash; then it automatically inspects its own work. The holes are punched in ceramic substrates that serve as chip carriers in IBM's large-scale computers. As many as 40,000 holes in each of up to 33 sheets of ceramic substrate are punched with great accuracy in order to ensure the integrity of electrical connections.

38. An engineer completes the installation of a robotic system on an automated assembly line for IBM 3178 display terminals.

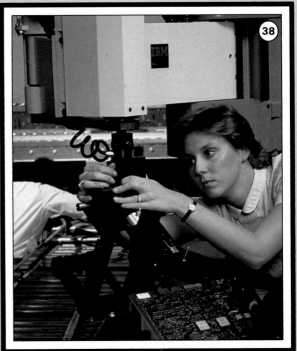

39. For low-volume manufacturing operations, electrical components are ''stuffed'' into a circuit board by hand. All of the components are mounted on one side of the board, leaving the back side bare. When the components have been added, the bare side of the board is passed over a flowing stream that solders all the pins in place in one operation.

40. Paradyne has several manufacturing and assembly lines that produce printed circuit boards. They have a high ratio of inspectors to assemblers so that possible problems can be identified early in the manufacturing cycle.

41. At Tandem's circuit board assembly facility in Watsonville, California, computer-controlled production includes a variety of bar code readers.

ASSEMBLING AND TESTING THE FINAL PRODUCT

42. As sales of personal computers climbed, the manufacturers required high-volume, assembly line production methods.

43. As many as one Macintosh every 27 seconds is built at Apple's highly automated factory in Fremont, California.

44. In Greenrock, Scotland, a technician monitors tests of the IBM PC/AT.

Figure 13.6 Two versions of a program to compute an average of *N* numbers. The first version (a) is the program given in Figure 13.5. In (b), a choice structure has been added.

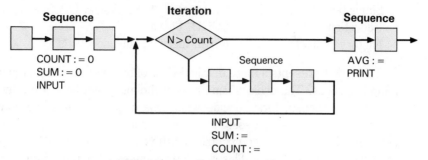

(a) First Version: Sequence and Iteration

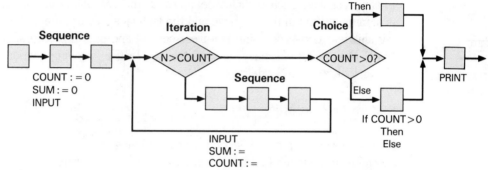

(b) Second Version: Sequence, Iteration, and Choice Structures

Figure 13.7 Effect of GOTOs on program structure.

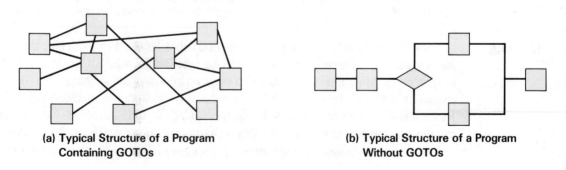

(a) Typical Structure of a Program Containing GOTOs

(b) Typical Structure of a Program Without GOTOs

Problem or Application Area	Some Recommended Languages
Text processing	LISP, SNOBOL
Simulation	Simscript, GASP, Simula, GPSS
Education	LOGO, Pascal
Factory control	Forth, machine language, APT

Table 13.1 presents a more detailed view of some of the most popular programming languages. The choices can be overwhelming, but here are a few guidelines to help you choose. First, decide what type of problem is to be solved. For instance, using a text-processing language to solve a numerical problem will end in disaster. Next, consider compatibility with your machine, operating system, other programs, and other files. This is called *system compatibility* and is very important if you want the language to fit in with an existing system of hardware and software. Finally, consider such technical features as the readability and maintainability of programs written in the language and the language's input/output abilities, calculating abilities, text-processing features, control and data structures, intrinsic functions, processing efficiency, and portability. In the following sections, we take a closer look at these guidelines.

System Compatibility

An obvious first step in selecting a programming language is to make sure your computer has enough RAM to run the compiler or interpreter. Many compilers require large amounts of disk space as well. They may occupy several floppy disks and can make several passes over the source program during conversion to machine language. If this is the case, it can be very inconvenient or impossible to use floppy disk drives—a hard disk may be required.

You should choose the operating system you want to use before you choose a programming language. Most computers support more than one operating system; for example, an IBM PC can run programs for MS-DOS, UNIX, CP/M, and several other operating systems. But a certain programming language may work under only one operating system. Although the language translator may work with the desired operating system, it may or may not be compatible with other programs that work under the same operating system. A FORTRAN program under MS-DOS, for example, may not be compatible with a Pascal program also under MS-DOS.

Lack of compatibility can happen at several other levels. For example, the data files created by a Pascal program may not be readable by a BASIC program. Similarly, a program written in Pascal and translated into machine language may not be usable by a BASIC program that has also been translated into machine language. However, if the two are compatible, then considerable time might be saved by using the previously written Pascal program as part of the new BASIC program.

One major advantage of translation by compiling is the ability to combine pro-

Table 13.1 Popular Programming Languages

Name	Origins	Characteristics and Comments
Ada (for Augusta Ada Lovelace, colleague of Charles Babbage)	From 1979–1982 by Honeywell for U.S. Dept. of Defense	Designed to control real-time processing problems. Resembles Pascal, but has many more features.
APL (*A P*rogramming *L*anguage)	In mid-1960s by Ken Iverson, a mathematician at IBM	Tremendously compact, powerful language. Highly interactive; interpreted.
BASIC (*B*eginners' *A*ll-Purpose *S*ymbolic *I*nstruction *C*ode)	In mid-1960s by John Kemeny and Thomas Kurtz at Dartmouth	Easily learned language. Widely used on small computers. Many incompatible versions exist.
C	In 1972 by Dennis Ritchie at Bell Laboratories	Originally designed to write system software. Very portable; generates fast, compact code.
COBOL (*CO*mmon *B*usiness Oriented *L*anguage)	In 1960 by a group of users and manufacturers	By far the most popular language for commercial applications. Creates verbose, Englishlike, understandable code.
FORTRAN (*FOR*mula *TRAN*slator)	In 1957 by IBM	Used for scientific and mathematical programming.
Pascal (for Blaise Pascal, French mathematician)	From 1968–1971 by Professor Niklaus Wirth of Switzerland	Originally designed as a teaching vehicle to encourage structured programming. Small, memory-efficient compilers. Limited I/O features.
PL/I (*P*rogramming *L*anguage *I*)	In 1966 by IBM	Designed to combine the best features of COBOL and FORTRAN. Used primarily on large computers.
RPG (*R*eport *P*rogram *G*enerator)	In mid-1960s by IBM	Allows reports to be created quickly and easily. Uses specification forms rather than programming statements. Popular on business minicomputers.

grams from different languages into larger, more powerful programs through linking. When programs are written so that they can be used over again, they are called **routines** or **subroutines;** a routine is reused by *calling* it. The linker program combines previously written routines with operating system routines to complete the translation of your program into a machine-level program that will run on a particular computer. If you plan to use a variety of programming languages on one machine, it may be worthwhile to purchase all of the translators from one company to ensure compatibility among them.

Readability and Maintainability

Readability and maintainability are important in the business world because some programs "live" for twenty years—far beyond the time when the original programmers are likely to be around. Thus, a readable and maintainable program is a necessity for large banks, insurance companies, and corporations. If a million-dollar program can't be maintained, then it becomes worthless.

A programming language affects readability and maintainability in several ways.

- *Syntax* determines the grammar of the language.
- *Familiarity* refers to how similar the language is to natural languages.
- *Modularity* affects the degree to which the program can be divided into easily comprehended parts.
- *Consistency* determines whether the language is predictable and lacks unexpected features.
- *Structuredness* refers to whether the language provides good structured programming control constructs and encourages the use of well-structured programs.

Syntax

The *syntax* of a language determines its parts of speech and keywords. For example, the syntax of a COBOL program is very verbose and Englishlike, so that, with a little practice, anyone can understand it. COBOL uses familiar English keywords, such as SUBTRACT, MOVE, TO, FROM, and PERFORM. The following fragment from a program that prints a mailing list illustrates COBOL's syntax:

```
PROCEDURE DIVISION.
MAIN-ROUTINE.
   OPEN OUTPUT MAIL-LABELS-FILE
     INPUT ADDRESS-FILE.
   READ ADDRESS-FILE
     AT END
       MOVE "NO" TO MORE-INPUT.
   PERFORM PRINT-ADDRESS-LOOP
     UNTIL MORE-INPUT IS EQUAL TO "NO".
   CLOSE MAIL-LABELS-FILE
     ADDRESS-FILE.
   STOP RUN.
```

COBOL programs are self-documenting, portable, and very good at handling files and reports, but they are weak at processing mathematical data. COBOL is used more than any other language for developing large data processing programs.

FORTRAN, in contrast, uses a more mathematical syntax. For example,

```
DO 100I = 1,10
IF (NUM − 99) 2,3,3
X = SQRT (B ** 2 − 4.0 * A * C)
```

To a mathematician or engineer, FORTRAN's algebraic notation is familiar.

Modularity

Modularity is important because it helps make large programs understandable. Each module can be understood as a "chunk" or box, and then larger modules can be composed of smaller modules. One feature of a modular language's syntax is the requirement to state explicitly where a module gets incoming data; this helps guarantee that the linkages among modules are well understood.

Modula-2 is an example of a highly modular programming language. For example, the following is a simple Modula-2 module that imports Read, Write, Sqrt, Sin, and Cos functions from two other modules:

```
MODULE Main;
FROM InOut IMPORT Read, Write;
FROM Math IMPORT Sqrt, Sin, Cos;
BEGIN
.        ← The module's processing statements belong here.
END.
```

BASIC is a counterexample; it provides little support for cleanly separating a large program into independent modules.

Both Modula-2 and its predecessor, Pascal, were invented to be implemented efficiently on computers. Pascal was designed by Niklaus Wirth as a programming language that would teach students "the correct way" to program. It was one of the first languages to be designed with a familiar, consistent, and structured syntax. However, Pascal lacked the modularity of other languages, so Niklaus Wirth went back to the drawing board to design Modula-2 to incorporate modularity, greater consistency, and extensive structuredness. Many other languages have been patterned after Pascal because of its clarity and elegance.

Structuredness

Structuredness is the degree to which a language conforms to the structured programming concept that all modules and all program statements should have a single entry point and a single exit point. For example, there is only one entry point and one exit point for the statements in the following Pascal fragment:

```
IF A = 0 THEN
    B := 100
```

```
    ELSE
      B: = 200;

    WHILE B < 200 DO
      BEGIN
      WriteLn(B);
      ReadLn(B)
    END;

    CASE B OF
    10: A: = 0;
    20: A: = 10;
    END;
```

Each of these statements has a single starting and ending point within the program. The IF-THEN-ELSE statement flows into the WHILE-DO statement; the BEGIN-END statement is nested within the WHILE-DO statement, and they both terminate in the same place; the CASE-OF-END statement executes either 10: or 20:, but not both, and then terminates at the END statement.

In contrast, BASIC and FORTRAN have no way to enforce structured programming. Here is an example using BASIC.

```
    FOR I = 1 TO 10
    IF I = J THEN GOTO 100
    NEXT I
                . . .
    100 PRINT I
```

The IF-THEN-GOTO statement violates the requirement that there should be only one exit point, because there are two paths out of the FOR-NEXT loop. One path leads out the bottom of the loop and would be taken after the loop has executed 10 times; the other path jumps from the middle of the loop to line 100 if the value in variable I is the same as the value in J.

Because FORTRAN, BASIC, and COBOL were all invented before the idea of structured programming, they make it easy to write very convoluted programs that lack structuredness. ALGOL (*ALGO*rithmic *L*anguage) was the earliest language developed with good structure. It was created in the early 1960s in Europe and used extensively there until Pascal replaced it. PL/I borrowed many of ALGOL's structured features. Pascal, C, Modula-2, and Ada are also derivatives of ALGOL.

Input-Output Abilities

I/O processing is very important because it determines how programs deal with printers, keyboards, screens, and other peripheral devices. A good I/O-handling language must be able to read and write sequential, direct-access, and indexed files. Recall that a *direct-access file* is one in which each record of the file can be directly accessed; an *indexed file* can be accessed through a (sorted) index key. COBOL and PL/I incorporate these file types into the language, which makes it reasonably simple to store and retrieve data from large data files. In addition, COBOL and PL/I are often extended to allow them to communicate with a database management system.

Most BASIC interpreters provide special verbs for creating graphics, but writing to the graphics screen from FORTRAN, Pascal, and C is difficult unless these languages are augmented with special graphics routines.

Pascal, C, and most other languages can print a report on the printer; but COBOL and PL/I are especially good for formatting and printing reports. If your needs are limited to creating business reports, then RPG might be an even better choice. It is a special-purpose report-generating programming language. RPG allows a programmer to write a report program by filling out several forms that describe the way the report will appear on the printed page. An RPG compiler takes this sample report and turns it into a program.

Arithmetic Computation

COBOL and FORTRAN represent two extremes of ability to perform arithmetic calculations. FORTRAN was designed to do such mathematical calculations as exponentiation, logarithms, transcendental functions, and so on. COBOL is limited to simple expressions. Compare this statement in COBOL

```
COMPUTE INVENTORY = YEAR-TO-DATE-INVENTORY +
(ORDERED * PRICE).
```

with the FORTRAN statement

```
HYPOT = SQRT (A ** 2 + B ** 2)
```

The differences may seem inconsequential until you try to do a calculation that doesn't exist in the language. For example, Pascal has no exponentiation operator, so our sample FORTRAN calculation can't be done directly in Pascal.

Text Processing

Pascal, FORTRAN, COBOL, and most other widely used programming languages have difficulty processing characters and strings of text. Therefore, special-purpose symbol-processing languages like LISP and SNOBOL were invented. These languages were developed in the 1960s to handle nonnumeric data.

Instead of adding, subtracting, and multiplying numbers, a text-processing language joins together, separates, and inserts characters of text; searches for patterns of characters; and performs other related operations. For example, in LISP, the CONS and CDR operators retrieve the first character and trailing characters of an alphanumeric list. These operators might be used, for example, to separate the first and last names of a full name.

LISP has become the premier language of artificial intelligence because of its ability to handle lists and make associations and because of its familiarity to the artificial intelligence community. SNOBOL (invented by Ralph Griswold at Bell Laboratories) is used to process and analyze text.

Control Structures

Recall that a *control structure* is any statement in a programming language that controls the order in which other statements are to be executed. We've given examples of several control statements, including IF-THEN-ELSE (for making two-way decisions), FOR (for repeating or looping), and CASE (for multiple-way decisions). In theory, every conceivable program can be written with only three control structures: sequence (one statement following another), iteration (loops), and choice (IF-THEN-ELSE). In practice, additional control statements are added to a language to make it more convenient for a programmer to use. For example, in Pascal derivatives, the CASE statement expands the IF-THEN-ELSE statement into a multiple-branching statement, and the CALL or PERFORM statements of FORTRAN and COBOL permit modules to be invoked from a main program, thus allowing modularity.

The control structures used in Ada are particularly interesting. Ada was created by the Department of Defense to reduce the huge expense of developing real-time systems—ones that could keep up with events happening in the real world. An Ada program can be divided into modules that run at the same time on multiple processors. Each module runs in parallel with the others. But when one module needs information computed by another parallel module, it exchanges this information through a control structure called a *rendezvous statement*. It forces one module to wait while the other module catches up, thus synchronizing the two modules.

Other control structures include special statements for catching errors or unusual occurrences, such as bad input data, a missing file, or an error in the program. These are called **exception statements** because they handle I/O errors. In PL/I, for example, the ON ERROR GOTO statement takes care of I/O exceptions, attempts to divide by zero, and handles any other unusual circumstances that might arise when the program is executed. Some versions of BASIC have ON ERROR GOTO control statements, as do many extended versions of Pascal.

Data Structures

A **data structure** is a collection of values and associated information that provides a method of organizing and manipulating many values together as a unit. A simple example of a data structure is an **array,** an organized collection of data in a row-and-column format. The structure of an array makes it easy to update or retrieve

A WORD ABOUT
THE MULTILINGUAL PC

For several years the conventional wisdom held that if users wanted to program their personal computers, they would use MS-Basic or IBM PC Basic, since these are often supplied free with the machines. The average computer user, the thinking went, wasn't interested enough in programming to go out and buy a package.

That belief has been proven incorrect, largely through the phenomenal sales of one product, Borland International's Turbo Pascal. Turbo Pascal has sold more than half a million copies since it first appeared in 1983, and its sales show no sign of abating, according to a recent survey by market research firm Infocorp of Cupertino, California.

"Microcomputer users who formerly were not programming have now taken to it because of such products as Turbo Pascal and True Basic," says Martha Ash, assistant manager of microcomputer support for Northwestern University in Evanston, Illinois. The trend is toward menu-driven systems and documentation that is written for people who are not computer experts, she explains.

"There is a sense that people who have been using micros for several years and are familiar with spreadsheets, word processors, graphics programs, etc. are now asking what else they can do," Ash says. "Programming has become a natural alternative for people who several years ago would have taken one look at GW Basic and said, 'Forget this.'"

A brief examination indicates that several new languages are gaining popularity on microcomputers. Attributes common to this generation of microcomputer languages are emphasis on increased ease of use, modular approach, and low cost.

Borland International of Scotts Valley, California, led the way with its modular-systems approach to languages, first with the $69.95 Turbo Pascal, and more recently with the $99.95 Turbo Prolog. Both programs include interactive editors (similar to Wordstar), language compilers, windowing support, debuggers, and graphics support.

Like several other vendors, Borland offers add-ons to its entry-level language systems. For Turbo Pascal you can buy math coprocessor support (for floating-point arithmetic), binary-coded decimal support, a tutorial program, and other options.

A language development system that emphasizes ease of use is the Macscheme system for the Apple Macintosh. "Macscheme has gone through several revisions since its release last year," says Anne Hartheimer, president of Semantic Microsystems Inc. "With each release, we try to make it easier to use."

Macscheme is a $125 system that includes a Scheme interpreter, editor, and windowing system on the Macintosh and a toolbox to work with the Macintosh's graphics interface. Semantic Microsystems has also developed additional modules for Macscheme, including a complete programming development system that allows Macintosh applications to be designed, written, and used without any other programming aids, Hartheimer says.

The new entries in the market are still predominantly versions of languages that have been popular for years, such as Basic, Pascal, and C. But the Turbo Pascal success formula is being applied by some vendors to more esoteric languages—such as Lisp and Prolog—developed for artificial intelligence programming.

According to Stuart Kurtz, associate professor of computer science at the University of Chicago, Turbo Prolog and Macscheme are "increasingly being used as development and exploratory languages for artificial intelligence software and expert systems. Lisp and Lisplike languages are beginning to dominate the undergraduate curricula of many computer science departments. Macscheme and Turbo Prolog are extending that dominance."

Language implementations geared toward novice programmers, as well as engineers and computer science professors, are filling the market. The biggest benefits for corporate users are better performance, lower prices, portable languages, improved ease of use, and products better geared to solving individual programming problems.

any item in the array by referencing its position within the array. For example, in FORTRAN, a DIMENSION statement reserves an area of memory, as in

```
DIMENSION SCORES(100)
```

This DIMENSION statement establishes SCORES as the name of a one-dimensional numerical array with the ability to store 100 values. You can think of this array as a single column of memory cells with 100 rows; each row can store one number. This array might be used to store up to 100 test scores in a manner that allows you to manipulate the scores easily, such as finding the highest test score in a list. To reference the number in the third row of SCORES, for example, the FORTRAN syntax says to enclose the index 3 inside parentheses, as in $X(3) = 3.14159$. This stores 3.14159 in the third memory cell of array X.

The following data structure in Pascal demonstrates how to express a list of names along with the street address and telephone number of each person:

```
VAR
  People: ARRAY(1..MAX)OF
    RECORD
      Name:string;
      Street:string;
      Tele:PhoneNumber
    END;
```

Data structures are also used to format external disk files. Again, in Pascal, the contents of a file can be clearly written as follows:

```
VAR
  DECK:FILE OF
    RECORD
    Name:PersonName;
    Age :0..99;
    Bal :Dollars;
    Sex :(Male, Female)
    END;
```

Here, the contents of the file are clearly designated and can be referenced later in the program by these same names.

FORTRAN and BASIC are especially deficient of data structures, whereas Pascal, Modula-2, Ada, LISP, and most modern programming languages allow the programmer to define new types of data structures. The syntax data structure declarations in Pascal can be quite striking in their familiarity, consistency, and elegance. The readability and understandability of Pascal data structures have been copied by nearly every new programming language developed over the past decade.

Intrinsic Functions

An **intrinsic function** is a module that is supplied along with a programming language's translator to make using the language easier. FORTRAN has many predefined intrinsic functions for doing arithmetic, transcendental functions (sine, cosine), and special-purpose mathematics (matrix multiply). Pascal does all of its input and output through intrinsic functions.

Much of the power and flexibility of a programming language comes from its intrinsic functions (or lack of them). BASIC would be uninteresting if it weren't for the intrinsic functions for handling strings, mathematics, and graphics that most BASIC dialects include. C is little more than a set of control statements plus a large number of functions.

The following is a list of the intrinsic functions you should look for when considering a programming language:

- *Arithmetic/logic.* Bit manipulation, string manipulation, and so on.
- *External device control.* Control of modems, mouse, joystick, and so on.
- *Graphics and sound control.* Display, music, and voice output.
- *Conversion of data.* Character-to-numerical, numerical-to-character, and so on.
- *Screen I/O.* Forms handling, report formats, and so on.

These functions can significantly reduce the amount of time and effort needed to build a new program from scratch.

Processing Efficiency and Program Size

A program written in a high-level language trades speed for maintainability (ease of modification and improvement). It must be translated, and the translated program is larger and runs more slowly than if the program had been written initially in machine language. The good news is that a program written in a high-level language is easier to understand and modify. If you expect to modify a program frequently, it is worthwhile to sacrifice speed and small size for maintainability and use a high-level language.

Most computer programs with wide appeal—such as 1-2-3, Symphony, Frameworks, WordStar, and AppleWriter II—are written in assembly language to achieve the greatest speed possible. Unless you are an expert programmer and are going to sell a million copies of your program, however, it is probably better to use a high-level language.

The machine language version of a programming language may vary in size and speed, depending on how clever the compiler writers were. A "fast" compiler produces fast-running programs; a "compact" compiler produces small-sized programs. Depending on the compiler, the target programs compiled from typical Pascal or C programs may differ in size and speed by a factor of ten or more. One translator may produce very fast code but require twice the amount of memory as another translator to hold the running program.

Benchmark programs are usually employed to measure the effectiveness of a compiler or interpreter. One well-known benchmark program, the sieve of Eratosthenes, computes prime numbers; it is commonly used to compare the computational speed and memory requirements of programs.

Portability

Portability refers to the ease with which a program can be moved from one machine to another—without modifications. The main method of achieving portability is to use a compiler for the other machine to recompile the source program. Suppose a Pascal program exists on an Apple computer, and you buy an IBM PC. If the source program is written in a portable version of Pascal, it can be copied onto an IBM PC disk (probably via communications), compiled by the IBM PC Pascal compiler, and then run on the IBM computer.

Few programs are 100 percent portable; instead, they must be modified before being recompiled for the new computer. If portability is important, plan for it in advance. Avoid machine-dependent features of programming languages and consider purchasing compatible compilers for use on all the machines.

There's another problem for programmers who aspire to sell their programs: licensing. A software license is a contract between the programmer and the vendor of the compiler; it specifies limitations on the use of programs translated by the vendor's compiler. For example, a BASIC program may be compiled into machine language using a certain company's compiler. That company may prohibit the sale of the target program without its consent or payment for each copy sold. Some licensing agreements state that the target program produced from a compiler may be resold, run on more than one machine, or copied only after payment of a royalty to the compiler's vendor. For more on these legal issues, see Chapter 17.

COBOL is probably the most portable programming language around, because it has been standardized by the American National Standards committee. FORTRAN 77 is a 1977 standardized dialect of FORTRAN; and BASIC, Pascal, and many other languages have also been standardized. Manufacturers of programming language compilers frequently add features to standardized languages, thus creating nonstandard dialects.

Pascal is a classic example of a language that suffers from too many nonstandard dialects. Rarely can a Pascal program written on one machine be compiled and run on another machine without extensive modifications. This situation exists because Pascal was originally designed to teach programmers rather than to be a commercial programming language. Because of its elegance, Pascal was adapted to the real world of software through a variety of extensions. The most notable extension—called UCSD Pascal—was done by the University of California at San Diego. This dialect became one of the most widely used languages in the world, but it reduced the portability of Pascal programs from one version of Pascal to another because it greatly extended the original language.

C has become almost a standard language, because there are no dialects that extend the language. The K & R standard (which was defined in a book by Brian W. Kernighan and Dennis M. Ritchie of Bell Laboratories), is almost universally accepted as the definition of C. In addition, it is easy to write a C compiler for a new machine, because C is very close to machine language yet similar to Pascal and other ALGOL derivatives. For this reason, many software developers use C to write programs for all sizes and brands of computers. In contrast, COBOL compilers are difficult to write and often take years to develop for a new machine.

BEYOND HIGH-LEVEL LANGUAGES

Very High-Level Languages (VHLL)

Clearly the best way to tell your friend to go to the store to get milk is to use an abstract notation, such as English. In English, the algorithm for getting a quart of milk might look like the following:

1. Go to the store and buy a quart of milk.
2. Bring the quart of milk to me.

This "program" tells your friend *what* you want done, but not *how* to do it. The difference between a **very high-level language (VHLL)** and the programming languages we have discussed until now is the difference between saying *what* to do and giving detailed directions for *how* to do it. A very high-level language (sometimes called a *fourth-generation language*) is a **nonprocedural language** because it describes what processing is to be done without specifying the particular procedures to be used to complete the processing.

The database query languages and report generator languages described in Chapter 8 are examples of restricted VHLLs. Only a few VHLL translators exist, because software designers are just beginning to solve the difficult problems associated with machine translation of nonprocedural programs. The few that do exist are limited to special purposes, such as creating a report, controlling the dialog in a learning module, or answering complex queries for information. But VHLLs are the computer languages of the future because they simplify programming, increase a programmer's productivity, are easy to modify and maintain, and can be understood by almost anyone. We will discuss only two broad categories of VHLLs: application generators and program generators.

Application Generators

An **application generator (AG)** gives a detailed explanation of what data are to be processed, rather than how to process the data. It is similar to a report generator, but it expresses processing steps in a notation similar to that of a high-level language. Hence, programs written for an application generator appear to be

Figure 13.8 Example of an application generator program.

```
BEGIN
      ERASE
      STORE '     ' TO MIN
      @ 10,5 SAY ' Enter minimum search condition'
      @ 10,35 GET MIN
      READ
      ? ' Printing in progress...'
      USE CUSTOMER_FILE
      INDEX ON YTD TO ORDERED_FILE
      REPORT FORM F1 FOR YTD > MIN TO PRINT
      RELEASE MIN
      RETURN
END.
```

slightly procedural, as illustrated by Figure 13.8. Typically (but not always), application generators are extensions to the query facility of a database management system. As such, they assume the DBMS model of data. The example shown here is closely related to the dBASE II model.

Most AG translators are interpreters, not compilers; hence, the AG program is directly interpreted. To run the application, you enter its name after the command DO. It is read into the AG translator and executed one statement at a time. In the case of Figure 13.8, the application finds all CUSTOMER_FILE records whose value stored in the field named YTD is greater than a value supplied by the user (YTD > MIN). It prints these records according to the report format stored in F1.

The following list explains the meaning of each command word in Figure 13.8:

- *ERASE*. Erase the monitor screen.
- *STORE' 'TO MIN*. Store a blank in MIN (no value).
- *@10,5 SAY*. Prompt the user with the message "Enter minimum search condition". The prompt begins in line 10, column 5 of the screen.
- *@10,35 GET MIN*. Wait for the user to enter a value for MIN.
- *READ*. This forces the AG to read the previous two @ commands and save them for use later.
- *?* Display the message "Printing in progress...".

INTEGRATING TOOLS SPEEDS AND SIMPLIFIES APPLICATION BUILDING PROCESS

In the computer industry, when users embrace a concept, that same concept—under a plethora of different names—is introduced by a number of vendors. Such is the case with application generation. These tools come under various names, including development workbenches, fourth-generation languages, program generators, and programmer productivity tools. Some 300 vendors offer such tools for mainframes and another 150 do for micro-based systems.

As if the sheer number of available products was not enough, these tools also employ different approaches to the tasks of simplification of development, modification, and ongoing support.

One such task is to make an application generator an integral part of a data base management system. When these two components work in tandem, programmers can generate software that allows application programs to be written faster and better.

What are some of the features that should be provided by a DBMS with application generating facilities?

Procedural features.

■ Interface to high-level procedural languages, for example, Cobol, PL/I, Fortran, and APL.

■ Interface to a low-level procedural language such as assembler.

■ Full set of structured constructs.

■ Performance monitoring, tuning, and enhancement features.

■ Third-generation language programmer usability feature.

Nonprocedural features.

■ Query language.

■ Report generator.

■ Graphics generator.

■ Relational front-end feature.

■ Two-dimensional menu interface feature.

■ Easy-to-use editors.

■ Integrated and active data dictionary/directory.

■ Data base design techniques.

■ Data definition, data manipulation, data control features.

Decision support system features.

■ Financial modeling language.

■ Statistical ahalysis.

■ Interface to standard statistical packages.

■ Support of electronic spreadsheets.

Mainframe-microcomputer connection features.

■ Programming languages on mainframe and equivalent counterpart on microcomputer.

■ Separate versions that run stand-alone on both microcomputer and mainframe.

■ Mainframe-to-microcomputer communication link.

■ Extraction capability on mainframe for downloading.

■ Multiuser environment support feature.

The chief advantage of using an application generator integrated with a DBMS is that these tools speed the application-building process. Equally important, applications are easily and quickly modified, thus minimizing debugging problems and thereby reducing maintenance costs. As is the case with most products, however, there are trade-offs. Computer resource usage with these tools is high, a significant drawback.

Continued on p. 432

An application generator uses up to 50 percent more computer resources than does a third-generation language performing an equivalent function. This is because application generators make the computer do most of the drudge work that third-generation languages make people do.

The difference comes primarily in the usage of I/O operations, rather than CPU processing. Poor data base design could balloon this figure much higher. Further, since most of today's application generators are targeted to IBM 370–compatible machines, program transportability is poor.

Moreover, these tools do not handle computation-intensive work well. The application generators target the same computer spectrum as does Cobol—I/O-intensive character- or byte-crunching operations rather than CPU-intensive number-crunching operations.

For this reason, a scientific third-generation language such as Fortran should still be used for computational work. If an application requires both character crunching and number crunching, I suggest writing the program with an application generator but calling the third-generation language routines for computational work.

The point is that applications must be selected carefully. A banking deposit and withdrawal system with high-speed real-time requirements would be a poor choice for an environment in which to use an application generator.

Material requirements planning, however, with its integration of inventory, purchasing, bill of materials, engineering planning and accounting data bases, would be ideal for application generator implementation.

Source: Shaku Atre, *Computerworld,* 4 August 1986, p. 42.

- *USE*. Select the file named CUSTOMER—FILE.

- *INDEX ON YTD*. Build a separate index file in ORDERED—FILE, which is in order by YTD field values. Use this index file to retrieve records from the ORDERED—FILE in ascending order by YTD.

- *REPORT*. Use a previously defined report form stored in F1 to print a report. The report selects only those records from the database that satisfy the search conditions YTD > MIN.

- *RELEASE*. No longer use MIN as a storage variable; release the memory space used by MIN.

- *RETURN*. Return to whatever you were doing before you began this application.

The STORE, @, and RELEASE commands are procedural statements because they describe processing steps. In contrast, the USE, INDEX, and REPORT commands don't describe how their processing is to be done; they are nonprocedural. For the most part, this program tells the computer what to do, not how to do it.

Figure 13.9 Sample dialog with a program generator.

```
BEGIN
      What is the name of the input variable?  MIN
      What prompt is to be used? Enter minimum search condition
      What is the name of the input file?  CUSTOMER_FILE
      Is the input file sorted?  No
      Do you want to sort it?  No
      Is the input file indexed?  No
      Do you want to index it?  Yes
      Index what field?  YTD
      Index what field?
      Do you want to calculate?  No
      Do you want a report?  Yes
      What is the report format file?  F1
      Do you want to print in order?  Yes
      Enter index or sort key name:  YTD
      Do you want to limit retrieval?  Yes
      Enter limit or search condition:  YTD > MIN
      Enter limit or search condition:
      Do you want a disk copy of print?  No
      Are you done?  Yes
END.
```

Program Generators

A **program generator (PG)** is a translator that converts nonprocedural information into a procedural program. Instead of using very high-level language statements, a PG usually uses a question-and-answer dialog to determine what processing is to be done. Then it takes this nonprocedural information and uses it to write a program in some programming language, often BASIC or COBOL, which must in turn be translated into machine language or directly interpreted. Most PGs allow you to display and modify the program they produce.

To use a PG, you simply answer its questions. Figure 13.9 provides an example. The program generated from the dialog in Figure 13.9 does the same thing as the AG program in Figure 13.8.

Sophisticated PGs usually ask many questions. You might be asked for information concerning menus, file organization, printer configuration, the color and dimensions of the screen, and so forth. The questions asked by a PG are nonprocedural, as you can see in Figure 13.9. However, PGs are restricted in what they do. For applications requiring a lot of formulas, interaction with a user, or sophisticated data processing, you will probably need to use another method. But for uncomplicated tasks, program generators are excellent.

SUMMARY

Programming is a challenging intellectual activity that some people do exceptionally well and enjoy. For most of us, however, it is a chore requiring dedication and skill. Most people who use computers won't become programmers, because of the specialized knowledge required to do so.

Machine language programs are the most elementary, or low-level, form of coded algorithms, which have immediate meaning for the computer. Most application programs that require fast responses are written in the symbolic form of machine language called assembly language. However, machine language isn't the appropriate tool for the computer user who is simply trying to solve a problem.

High-level languages (HLLs) are by far the most frequently used tools in programming. They allow you to write any program with a reasonable amount of clarity and maintainability.

Knowing the syntax of a programming language is only a small part of knowing how to program. Good programmers have a storehouse of knowledge about control structures, algorithms, and techniques of design. Many of these techniques are based on the methodology known as structured programming. In computing, software reductionism states that every program can be broken down into fundamental control structures. Consequently, a program can be designed as a collection of fundamental control structures; sequence, choice, and iteration are the most basic of these.

Selecting the right language involves many decisions. Does it work with the other programs and the operating system on your computer? Is it readable and maintainable? Are its input/output abilities, calculating abilities, text-processing features, control and data structures, intrinsic functions, and processing efficiency adequate? Is it portable?

Very high-level languages (VHLLs) broaden the range of people who can program. The goal of VHLL design is to emphasize *what* you want to do, rather than *how* to do it. Most VHLLs fail to accomplish this 100 percent of the time, but they all use some sort of nonprocedural notation to avoid excess programming detail. A VHLL may be restrictive, but it can increase productivity dramatically. Report generators can be used by anyone with a modest amount of training. More practice is required to use very high-level application or program generators.

KEY TERMS

algorithm

application generator (AG)

array

benchmark program

compiler

control structure

data structure

exception statement

high-level language (HLL)

interpreter

intrinsic function

linker program

low-level language

nonprocedural language

object program

portability

program generator (PG)

programming language

routine

source program

subroutine

translator

variable

very high-level language (VHLL)

DISCUSSION QUESTIONS

1. Why can't a computer "understand" English, instead of only programming languages?
2. Compare a translator who works for the United Nations with a computer program that translates HLL programs. Is the human translator more like a program compiler or an interpreter?
3. List and describe the steps in programming. Why are there so many steps?
4. What is structured programming, and what does it accomplish?
5. If you were going to select and use a programming language, what would your criteria be?
6. What is the difference between an application generator and a program generator?

EXERCISES

1. What is the purpose of a linker program? Describe the steps needed to run a new program using the compiling approach to translation.
2. Give both low-level and high-level instructions (in English) for brushing your teeth. How might you characterize the difference between the two algorithms?
3. What is a program bug? How are bugs typically removed from a program?
4. Modify the BASIC program in Figure 13.5 so that only values greater than or equal to zero are allowed for N. (Use only the basic building blocks of IF-THEN-ELSE, WHILE, and sequence.)
5. Use the three building blocks of structured programming and the notation in Figure 13.6 to describe an algorithm for computing the following two values:

$$A = PAY / 10$$
$$B = PAY / (A - 5)$$

Assume that PAY is entered by the user and that A and B are printed out. What happens if $(A - 5)$ is zero?

6. Go to the library and read about the history of the following languages, including who invented them. (You may not be able to find them all; do the best you can.)

   a. FORTRAN
   b. COBOL
   c. Pascal
   d. Ada
   e. Modula-2
   f. SNOBOL
   g. BASIC

7. Is it possible for two programs written for the same computer to be incompatible? If so, how?

8. Compare the functions in a spreadsheet, such as Lotus 1–2–3, with the functions in a programming language, such as BASIC, FORTRAN, or Pascal.

9. Modify the application generator program in Figure 13.8 so that only YTD values equal to zero are printed in the report.

14 Artificial Intelligence and Expert Systems

Artificial intelligence (AI) is the sector of computer science that investigates systems displaying the characteristics we associate with human intelligence—language, reasoning, problem solving, learning, and so on. Out of the field of artificial intelligence have come programs that decipher spoken sentences, play chess, and learn through experience, and robots that manage the flow of parts through factories. We survey these and other applications in the first section of this chapter. One of the major successes of artificial intelligence has been the development of systems that duplicate the performance of human experts in solving particular problems. Several such systems, for instance, advise doctors on diagnoses. This chapter explores such *expert systems* in depth, explaining how they are constructed and tested and when their use is appropriate. Several expert systems in operation today are described—one of them, MARKET

ANALYST, in detail. These examples help us project the role that AI systems might play in the future.

There is every indication that AI applications will substantially alter the way we use computers and will become an integral part of our lives. Computers will continue to perform traditional data processing, number crunching, and the other jobs we currently expect of them. But as new computer technology emerges, advances in AI software should cause its importance to grow more rapidly than that of traditional software.

OVERVIEW OF ARTIFICIAL INTELLIGENCE

Artificial intelligence includes five major subfields: natural-language processing, logical reasoning and problem solving, machine learning, robotics and computer vision, and expert systems (see Table 14.1). We will discuss each of these in turn.

Natural-Language Processing

The study of strategies for computer programs to recognize and understand written and spoken language is called **natural-language processing**. Among the programs that address this challenge are foreign language translators and artificial voice synthesizers. Although today's programs don't process language nearly as

Table 14.1 Major Subfields of Artificial Intelligence

General Area	Approach or Methods	Typical Applications
Natural-language processing	Voice recognition, speech synthesis, parsing	Reading and understanding text, understanding microphone input, translating from one language to another
Logical reasoning and problem solving	Searching, reducing problems using mathematics	Chess playing, cognitive simulation
Machine learning	Self-modifying programs, AI programming languages and techniques	Facilitation of cognitive modeling, encoding of knowledge, and reasoning
Robotics and computer vision	Kinetics, ergonomics, visual analysis	Industrial automation
Expert systems	Knowledge acquisition, consultation, symbolic reasoning	Advice, diagnosis, teaching

Table 14.2 Three Major Forms of Natural-Language Processing

Form of Processing	Medium	Direction of Communication
Voice recognition	Vocal/sound input with microphone	Person to computer
Speech synthesis	Vocal/sound generated by synthesizer	Computer to person
Language comprehension (parsing, contextual analysis)	Symbols, such as text and words	Person-computer interaction

well as people do, they are useful for limited tasks, such as deciphering simple spoken commands. The field of natural-language processing encompasses voice communication, as you can see in Table 14.2. Systems that accept spoken words as input to operating programs are called **voice recognition systems**. These systems are currently restricted to narrow vocabularies by the difficulty of understanding the grammatical nuances of many words and phrases. Nonetheless, these systems have proved valuable for people, like the disabled, whose mobility is restricted. By speaking through a microphone to a computer, such users can operate electronically controlled appliances and electrical devices that would otherwise remain out of their reach.

So far, we've been focusing on the vocal communication of language from person to computer. **Speech synthesis,** or the artificial production of sounds resembling human speech, involves communication from computer to person. Because it avoids dependence on screen displays, speech synthesis is particularly useful to people with impaired vision. To reconstruct pleasant-sounding voices, however, speech synthesizers may have to sample and transmit a digital sound pattern as often as 6,000 times per second—a task that demands both fast processors and large memories.

The remaining facets of natural-language processing address the challenge of language comprehension. Whereas voice communication techniques are one-way communication events, the comprehension of language examines the context, which often encompasses two-way communication between persons and computers.

One increasingly common application involving language comprehension is the *intelligent front end* for software, a program that allows computer users to enter their commands in normal English. With such packages as Q&A, CLOUT (for R:BASE), and HAL (for Lotus 1-2-3), for instance, a user can request a report simply by typing

Artificial Intelligence and Expert Systems   **439**

Print the names and salaries of all female employees earning less than minimum wage.

As long as the processor has stored definitions for *name* and *salary* and values for "female" and "minimum wage," the request can be filled from an employee database. First, the processor breaks the sentence down into its major syntactical parts, including verbs, nouns, and adjectives. Then, after translating this request into database retrieval tasks, the program writes out a command, much as the user would. The command line is automatically sent to the report subprogram, and the user receives a printed report.

The process of breaking down a sentence or command into its basic units is called **parsing.** Parsing is much like diagramming a sentence grammatically, as you can see from the parse tree diagrams in Figure 14.1. The most general grammatical category, called the *sentence root,* is usually placed at the top of the diagram. The sentence is then divided into more specific units, which may be thought of as branches on a tree. At the very bottom is the complete sentence. To parse a sentence in this way, a computer must have a set of syntactical categories and rules that define those categories. If the rules are specific enough, the computer should be able to draw a parse tree for almost any sentence.

Notice that the sentence in Figure 14.1, "Her sweetheart rose and the leaves wilted," is ambiguous. The word *rose* could be either a noun or a verb. Such a sentence is said to be *context dependent;* that is, its meaning must be determined by its relation to other sentences. The sentence could be read as shown in the top parse tree, where the word *rose* is treated as a noun and *sweetheart,* as an adjective describing the rose. Or it could be read as in the lower tree, where *sweetheart* is treated as a noun and *rose* as a verb that describes the sweetheart's action.

Computer programs can parse sentences quite easily, but without additional contextual information, they can only note ambiguities and sketch possible meanings. Herein lies one of the major differences between artificial intelligence and human intelligence. When people speak or tell a story, they know so much about the subject that they often fail to recognize the ambiguities in their speech. The context—either spoken or unspoken—clarifies the meaning. But a computer program knows only what has been stored in its memory or presented to it for analysis.

When the recipient of a message makes the same contextual associations as the sender intended, we say that the communication has been "understood." But understanding can be easily faked by a computer program that makes clever guesses about the meaning of the message. One such program that fakes understanding, Eliza, was developed in the early 1960s by Joseph Weizenbaum. Programmed to "talk" like a psychological therapist, here is one of Eliza's more famous conversations:

P(erson): Men are all alike.
C(omputer): In what way?

P: They're always bugging us about something or other.

Figure 14.1 Parse trees. Parse trees graphically display the syntactical structure of sentences. Computer programs perform parsing as the first step in understanding natural language. Because the sentence parsed here is ambiguous, either of the two trees is valid.

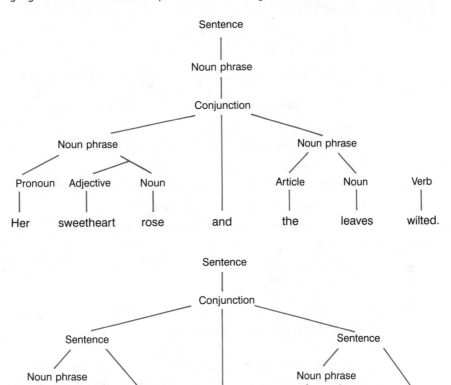

C: Can you think of a specific example?

P: Well, my boyfriend made me come here.
C: Your boyfriend made you come here.

P: He says I'm depressed much of the time.
C: I am sorry to hear you are depressed.

P: It's true. I am unhappy.
C: Do you think coming here will help you not to be unhappy?

P: I need some help; that much seems certain.
C: What would it mean to you if you got some help?

P: Perhaps I could learn to get along with my mother.
C: Tell me more about your family.

P: My mother takes care of me.
C: Who else in your family takes care of you?

P: My father.
C: Your father.

P: You are like my father in some ways.
C: What resemblance do you see?

P: You are not very aggressive but I think you don't want me to notice that.
C: What makes you think I am not very aggressive?

P: You don't argue with me.
C: Why do you think I don't argue with you?

P: You are afraid of me.
C: Does it please you to think I am afraid of you?

P: My father is afraid of everybody.
C: What else comes to mind when you think of your father?

P: Bullies.
C: Does that have anything to do with the fact that your boyfriend made you come here?

This conversation sounds convincingly real. In fact, the computer has faked understanding by using the following tricks:

1. The program checks each input for a few special words, which trigger clever responses. For instance, the word *mother* produces a general question about one's family; the word *depressed* evokes a sympathetic response.

2. Often the program simply restates a self-description, creating the illusion of a sympathetic listener.

3. If Eliza doesn't find a trigger word or a self-description, it will select a reply from a list of innocuous responses; for instance, "Can you think of a specific example?" Sometimes such canned replies are irritating and irrelevant.

4. Early in the conversation, the program stores a comment, which it throws back at a later time. The program's last comment is an example. In this case, the command just happened to make sense.

Ironically, Eliza's creator became disturbed by the widespread use of his program as an example of how clever computers could get. Weizenbaum has devoted much of his professional time during the last ten years to pointing out the limitations of computer science in its efforts to artificially duplicate intelligent behavior.

Not all conversational programs merely *pretend* to understand their natural-language input. A program called DIALOGIC uses a large grammatical database to help it parse sentences and then assign semantic meanings to different sentence parts. A more sophisticated program, KAMP, combines logical reasoning with knowledge of a speaker's goals, abilities, and beliefs.[1] But do these programs actually understand a communication in the same way a human does?

Logical Reasoning and Problem Solving

Problem solving has long been central to artificial intelligence, because it has the potential to contribute to every project in the field. Of the various problem-solving strategies, *logical reasoning*—the use of induction, deduction, probability, analogy, and other forms of inference—is probably the most important.

Problem solving requires computer languages different from those used for most other programming tasks. Conventional languages like COBOL and BASIC create a step-by-step procedural description of how to solve a problem, requiring the programmer to specify each step in the process; for example, "Take variable X, multiply it by 3, and call the result net sales." In contrast, with most artificial languages, like LISP and Prolog, the programmer need only supply the relationships among the facts and the ground rules for solving the problem. The system then determines how to proceed toward a solution.

Programs in declarative languages are composed of a set of relationships expressed in the following format:

Variable (descriptor, descriptor, descriptor)

where the variables and descriptors might be:

Parent (sex, age, income, car)
Car (brand, mileage, value, color, price)

Because the format specifies the relationships among the variables, a search for any particular subset of data will automatically yield an answer. For example, a request for the names of parents who drive Fords could be made without writing down the steps needed to search for and compile instances of that type of parent.

Of course, some problems can't be solved by reasoning alone. Game playing is a case in point, and Figure 14.2 shows how to address the problem by searching all the branches of a game tree to assess a value for each choice or outcome. Often a gameplayer must make an exhaustive search of all possible future moves in order to come up with the best next move. But in complex games like chess, players simply can't check every possible combination of future moves, even with the help of a computer.

To deal with such problems, researchers must devise **heuristic methods,** or rules of thumb used to guide a search along those avenues most likely to yield a solution. For example, to find one's way through a maze, one might always make the move that takes one physically closer to the end point—as long as it doesn't culminate in a dead end. This heuristic might not discover the fastest route through the maze, but it would avoid traveling every possible route to find a good one.

Figure 14.2 A game tree for searching possible moves in a ticktacktoe game. Searching for a positive gain can be done after decision alternatives have been assigned positive and negative values. In this tree, a +1 is a win; a 0, a draw; and a −1, a loss for player O.

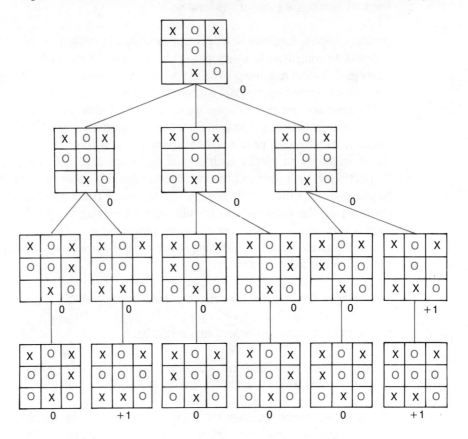

Many problems can be solved using search methods that have been tested on mazes and games. Suppose you're going to wire a huge apartment building for cable television, but since the cost of cables is very high, you want to use a plan that requires the least amount of wire. A computer model could help you find the most efficient routes for installing the cable. Stringing several trunks of wire up to the top of the building might be less demanding than using only one trunk. This type of decision would be helped by a computer program with a model of the building's structure and a heuristic algorithm to search for a good routing of the cable.

Computer-based routing of emergency vehicles also benefits from searching heuristics. Traffic conditions, road construction, and other factors stored in a geographic database are taken into account by a program that finds the shortest route between two points. Automobile manufacturers are working on personalized versions of such programs that will be installed in cars to help drivers navigate through difficult traffic or unfamiliar neighborhoods. For example, a system called Driverguide is planned for a 1990-model car.

Machine Learning

It has been argued that machines will never be truly intelligent until they can teach themselves through experience. Learning depends on feedback—on getting the results of one's actions and modifying plans for future action accordingly. This provides a way to acquire skills, improve decisions, and make appropriate associations between concepts and objects. Most machines can easily be programmed to behave as if they have learned something. For example, punch the number 45 on a microwave timer, and the machine will react as if it has "learned" to cook for 45 seconds. But AI is concerned with a more autonomous learning, in which the machine program encounters a series of events, obtains new information from these events, and evaluates this information against its goals. As yet, machine learning doesn't have a great deal of autonomy from the researcher or programmer.

Much of the progress in machine learning has been in concept learning, or in the development of a general rule from specific examples. *Concept learning* consists of deriving a classification rule from several specific examples of correct membership. This process is demonstrated by Marvin, a Prolog program written by Claude Sammut. Figure 14.3 shows a session in which Marvin is taught three concepts: letter, letter-list, and append. Marvin can't learn without a human teacher to present these concepts and to give it feedback about its success in applying them. To begin with, Marvin's memory is empty, so the teacher has to supply each letter of the alphabet.

Although Marvin appears quite naive, Dr. Sammut previously built into its algorithms some semantic notions, such as the properties of head and tail. Marvin can recognize when two objects are the same, and it has been given the ability to ask the teacher if a specific object or event is associated with a particular concept. Once it has mastered one concept, it can use that in learning another concept that builds on the first. For example, once it learns the concept of letter-list, it can learn that *append* means joining one letter-list to the end of another.

As you study the dialog in Figure 14.3, pretend you are the program and see how quickly you can learn the teacher's definition of the two difficult concepts letter-list and append. This exercise will probably remind you how difficult it is for anyone to learn abstract concepts. It may also give you a sense of how people, as well as AI programs, use models or structures of things to help them understand a concept.

Marvin illustrates both the progress that has been made in developing computer programs that learn and the numerous obstacles that remain to be overcome. Learning is linked closely to intelligence—it is central to the processing of natural language, to solving problems effectively, and even to such perceptual tasks as vision. The advancement of artificial intelligence and machine learning are likely to proceed hand in hand.

Figure 14.3 A session with Marvin.

What is the name of the concept? letter
Show me an example of letter: "A"
X is a letter if:
X is "A"
Show me an example of letter: "B"
X is a letter if:
X is "B"

. . . .

Show me an example of letter: "Z"
X is a letter if:
X is "Z"
Show me an example of letter: no
X is a letter if:
X is "A"
or X is "B"

. . . .

or X is "Z"
Do you want to teach me another concept? yes
What is the name of the concept? letter__list
Show me an example of letter__list: [ ]
X is [ ]
Show me an example of letter__list: [A]
The head of X is "A"
The tail of X is [ ]
"A" is an instance of a letter.
The description can be generalized to:
The head of X is a letter
The tail of X is [ ]
Is [B] also an instance of a letter__list? yes
[ ] is an instance of letter__list.
The description can be generalized to:
The head of X is a letter
The tail of X is a letter__list
Is [B A] an example of letter__list? yes
Show me an example of letter__list: no
The description of letter__list is:
X is a letter__list if:
X is [ ]
or
The head of X is a letter
The tail of X is a letter__list.
Do you want to teach me another concept? yes
What is the name of the concept? append
Show me an example of append: ([ ],[A],[A])
X1 is [ ]
The head of X2 is "A"
The tail of X2 is [ ]
The head of X3 is "A"
The tail of X3 is [ ]
[ ] is an instance of a letter__list.
The description can be generalized to:
The head of X2 is "A"
The tail of X2 is [ ]
The head of X3 is "A"
The tail of X3 is [ ]
X1 is a letter__list
Is ([A],[A],[A]) an instance of append? no
"A" is an instance of a letter.

The description can be generalized to:
X1 is [ ]
The tail of X2 is [ ]
The head of X3 is "A"
The tail of X3 is [ ]
The head of X2 is a letter
Is ([ ],[B],[A]) an instance of append? no
The head of X2 is the same as the head of X3
The description can be restricted to:
X1 is [ ]
The tail of X2 is [ ]
The tail of X3 is [ ]
The head of X2 is a letter
The head of X3 is the same as the head of X2
Is ([ ],[B],[B]) an instance of append? yes
[ ] is an instance of letter__list.
The description can be generalized to:
X1 is [ ]
The tail of X3 is [ ]
The head of X2 is a letter
The head of X3 is the same as the head of X2
The tail of X2 is a letter__list
Is ([ ],[B A],[B]) an instance of append? no
The tail of X2 is the same as the tail of X3
The description can be restricted to:
X1 is [ ]
The head of X2 is a letter
The head of X3 is the same as the head of X2
The tail of X2 is a letter__list
The tail of X3 is the same as the tail of X2
Is ([ ],[B A],[B A]) an instance of append? yes
The description can be rewritten as:
X1 is [ ]
X2 is a letter__list
X3 is the same as X2
Show me an example of append: ([A],[B],[A B])

. . . .

The tail of X1 is [ ]
The head of X1 is a letter
The head of X3 is the same as the head of X1
X2 is a letter__list
The tail of X3 is the same as X2
Is ([B],[ ],[B] an instance of append? yes
([ ],X2, tail of X3) is an instance of append
The description can be generalized to:
The head of X1 is a letter
The head of X3 is the same as the head of X1
(tail of X1, X2, tail of X3) is an append
Is [B A],[B],[B A B]) an instance of append? yes
The description of append is:
(X1,X2,X3) is an instance of append if:
X1 is [ ]
X2 is a letter__list
X3 is the same as X2
or
The head of X1 is a letter
The head of X3 is the same as the head of X1
(tail of X1,X2,tail of X3) is an append

446   *Developing New Systems*

Robotics and Computer Vision

Robotics is the branch of artificial intelligence concerned with developing machines that can recognize and respond to changes in sight and touch and, in some cases, sound and smell as well. When the topic of robots comes up, the average person often envisions a device that is humanlike in form and behavior, but robots seldom look or act like full human beings.

Most robots used in industry today are simple devices that have been programmed to perform narrow, repetitive tasks. A majority of them are "blind"—that is, they can't process visual information. But some use a photosensing device like a television camera to transmit information back to the computer, in a process called **computer vision**.

Artificial sight requires the continuous comparison of large, complex digital patterns with previously received patterns. The more pixels in an image, the greater the size of the image, and the faster it changes—as often as 25 times a second—the greater the computer's processing and storage requirements. The knottiest programming problem is the rapid matching and discrimination of visual patterns. This is also true of tactile sensing, which is in most respects analogous to visual sensing. Machine vision and machine touch both depend very heavily on sensing devices, and both must continuously sample signals over a two- or three-dimensional space.

A major challenge in robotics is to combine visual processing with comprehension. Programs are being developed that can recognize objects, shadows, and sets of objects as scenes. They can also identify small changes from one picture to another, a capability useful in satellite surveillance of military installations. Systems that check microelectronic chips for errors or deficiencies are one of the most important applications of computer vision. The minute detail of these chips makes human vision practically useless for such testing.

Research and development in robotics is now moving toward systems that can discriminate finer detail, perform a wider variety of tasks, and manage an entire production process. Probably the best and most recent example of this direction is ALPS (*A*utomated *L*ogistics and *P*roduction *S*ystem), the system installed by IBM to manufacture personal computers. In the world of ALPS, 13 robots carry parts from the loading dock, assemble them into laptop computers, test them, and wrap them for shipping. The diagram in Figure 14.4 shows the flow of parts and several of the different robot stations. Human hands don't touch the materials or products except when a robot breaks down or a product is defective. The first robot takes parts off pallets, passing them on to robot assemblers. Outfitted with computer vision and grippers (mechanical hands), these robots delicately insert chips into electronic boards. Delicate movement is directed by dedicated computer systems. When the personal computer has been assembled, it rides a conveyor belt to the test robots, which then send it on to the robots that pack the computers for shipping. This entire process takes only six minutes.

Figure 14.4 ALPS (*A*utomated *L*ogistics and *P*roduction *S*ystem) manufactures personal computers for IBM. The ALPS process consists of a continuous loop that begins at the parts-staging area and moves to pallet breakdown. Parts travel by conveyor to assembly, testing, and packaging and back to shipping in the staging area.

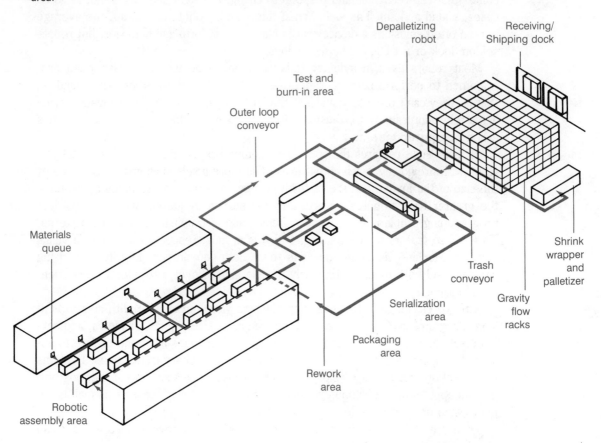

As illustrated by ALPS, robots can play a major role in quality control. This is feasible only when robots embody all of the major techniques of artificial intelligence—natural-language processing, problem solving, and machine learning—and consequently represent the state of the art.

EXPERT SYSTEMS

Expert systems are programs that reproduce the knowledge and thought processes of human experts in certain narrow, well-defined fields. Because they depend so completely on an organized collection of knowledge, expert systems are sometimes called *knowledge-based systems*. Much like a skilled human consultant, an expert system questions the user to determine whether a problem falls within its scope, weighs the user's choices, and selects a course of action. Users can interact in a consultative dialog with an expert system, just as they would with a human expert—asking questions, requesting explanations, and suggesting possible solutions. Within narrow problem areas, the best expert systems can perform about as well as the best human experts. These systems should not be viewed as a replacement for human experts, however, but as a source of assistance to them.

Expert systems can store vast amounts of knowledge about their subject. Moreover, they frequently ask their questions, make their recommendations, and provide the reasons for their suggestions in everyday language. Explanatory information is displayed on screens and menus. This allows users to select from various descriptions of the problems. Most expert systems can function even when the user doesn't provide a complete set of facts.

To offer these advantages, expert systems require a special kind of programming. Conventional data processing systems manipulate data in simple ways, recording and summarizing transactions or automating repetitive clerical tasks. Their processing is guided by complex *algorithms,* step-by-step procedures that ensure that the same answer will be reached every time. In contrast, expert systems are developed to solve highly complex problems that don't always have just one answer. They produce intelligent problem solving or the selective and efficient choice of a solution from among many possible alternatives. The expert's knowledge and experience, encoded in the knowledge base, help the system to quickly spot useful data and pursue them, while eliminating extraneous information. Table 14.3 summarizes the differences between the two types of processing.

Table 14.3 Common Characteristics of Expert Systems and Conventional Programs

Conventional Software	Expert Systems
Only one solution exists for any given set of data.	Many answers may be acceptable.
Standard problems can be solved by formulas.	Problem may not be clearly defined.
If too much of the data is missing, a solution cannot be reached.	Information is subjective and sometimes inconsistent; requires judgment.
The way to solve a problem is generally accepted. Correct answers can be verified.	Experts may disagree on how to solve a problem or on what constitutes a good answer.
Problem does not change much.	Problem is never quite the same.
Data can be represented by numbers or formulas.	Data are conceptual and cannot be represented by numbers.
Human expertise is abundant.	Human expertise is scarce. A late or poor decision is very costly.

Applications for Expert Systems

Expert systems are well suited to two kinds of problems. First, there are those with which direct, brute-force methods produce an unmanageable number of possibilities. For example, even the fastest computers in existence today couldn't evaluate all the possible outcomes of one chess move, even in 1,000 years. A chess game has over 10^{120} possible moves. Other examples of this type of problem include determining the shortest driving route between two points and purchasing the least expensive bag of groceries that will provide a decent meal. People normally deal with these sorts of problems by arbitrarily eliminating all unlikely possibilities. That approach doesn't guarantee the best solution, but it does produce a solution quickly.

The second type of problem that expert systems handle well is the interpretation of huge amounts of data. For example, monitoring the sensors and evaluating the measurements from a space flight would overwhelm anyone. Nobody has all the necessary expertise. But an expert system can integrate the data and make corrective decisions quickly.

Expert system applications also may be categorized in terms of their general purpose. Edward Feigenbaum and Pamela McCorduck, in their book *The Fifth Generation,* suggest that expert systems are appropriate for the following business tasks.

- *Capturing, replicating, and distributing expertise.* Suppose a new market is developing nationwide. Several of your company's sales representatives have the knowledge and expertise to pursue it, but most of them don't. With conventional methods, it would take years for the few knowledgeable salespeople to train the others to take advantage of this opportunity. Small- and medium-sized companies face this problem frequently. Since expert systems contain both the necessary knowledge and the ability to explain their reasoning, they are excellent teachers within small domains. And they can get the job done much faster.

- *Combining the knowledge of many experts.* To accomplish some tasks, one needs the expertise of many different specialists working together. Expert systems can provide the necessary integration of knowledge bases, even in the experts' absence. They provide what is called *institutional memory,* the preservation of the cumulative experience and thinking of the best people in an organization. In industries in which high turnover or frequent personnel shifts are common, this feature of expert systems is critical.

- *Managing complex problems.* Some problems have so many possible solutions that they are almost unmanageable by conventional methods. For example, contracting for large, one-of-a-kind projects usually requires a great deal of trial and error. Hypotheses must be formed, data analyzed, designs made, and design flaws diagnosed. Time constraints inevitably restrict the number of options that planners can explore. Expert systems increase them.

- *Managing changes in knowledge.* This problem is likely to crop up in emerging industries, where frequent price changes, new products, and changing market strategy require almost instant communication among managers and salespeople. In this setting, the usual sales and information meetings won't keep the sales force current. Expert systems can organize and disseminate information in the face of rapid technological change.

- *Gaining a competitive edge.* In a well-established and stable industry, everyone uses the same approach. Any idea that yields even a small improvement in performance will increase a company's market share. In such situations, expert systems can serve as a rich source of innovation. George Polya, in studying the behavior of his fellow mathematicians, noted that the use of heuristics was the key to the discovery of new ideas. And decision-making experiments have demonstrated conclusively that innovation and heuristic thinking—the special strength of expert systems—are related.[2]

We've examined the types of problems to which expert systems can be applied. The next two sections describe some specific examples of expert system applications.

Early Expert Systems

MYCIN, the most famous of the pioneer expert systems, is designed to help physicians diagnose infectious blood diseases and prescribe antibiotics for them. It contains the expertise of the foremost experts in the field of infectious blood diseases. The system diagnoses the causes of an infection, using knowledge of the patient history, symptoms, and laboratory test results. Then it recommends the type of drug and the dosage, according to accepted procedures in infectious disease therapy. MYCIN has been used since 1979 at the Stanford Medical Center, and its performance has been found to equal that of the best experts.

MYCIN's conclusions aren't always certain, however. After all, even human physicians aren't always sure of their diagnoses. If, after requesting additional information from the examining physicians, MYCIN still can't make a reliable diagnosis, it lists all the conclusions consistent with the evidence, ranked by certainty factor. This is an important system feature for two reasons. First, since the conclusion is uncertain, the physician will want to check the other possibilities as well. And second, the patient may have more than one infection.

Another early expert system, PROSPECTOR, acts as a consultant to geologists exploring for ore deposits. Given field data about a region, PROSPECTOR estimates the likelihood of finding particular minerals, including lead, zinc, copper, nickel, uranium, and molybdenum. The system contains models of the types of terrain favorable to finding these minerals, constructed from extensive interviews with experts on the characteristics of favorable mining or drilling sites. As field data are fed in, the program checks them against its stored models for promising resemblances. PROSPECTOR can sift rapidly through observational data on a

MARKET FOR EXPERT SYSTEM SHELLS BREAKING NEW GROUND

Since its modest beginning in 1984, the commercial market for expert system tools has gained strength—and vendors. With the arrival of personal computer-based expert system tools, the market divides into two distinct sectors based on the kind of hardware upon which expert system tool software operates. By the end of 1985, some 15 vendors of high-end tools had shipped products; add another 22 vendors of PC-based tools that were delivered to customers, and the expert system tools market includes over 35 vendors—with more on the way.

At present, these two sectors do not compete with each other, although there are indications that this may change, as tools developed on large symbolic processors are ported to smaller but increasingly powerful machines, such as Apple Computer, Inc.'s Macintosh and the impending generation of PCs based on 32-bit microprocessor chips.

Buyers of expert system tools tend to be large corporations and government agencies that use them to build expert systems for proprietary, in-house purposes.

According to our recent market research, the heaviest nonacademic users of expert system tools are manufacturing firms and those doing work in defense or other government contracts. Together, these users account for 60 percent of expert system tool usage. But interest in expert system tools has been increasing in such realms as banking, in-surance, and finance as newly competitive companies in these industries look for ways to develop a strategic edge over their rivals.

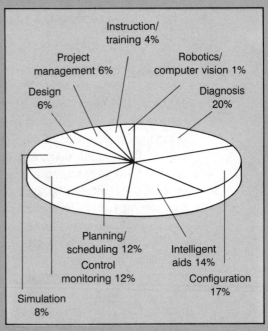

High-end tool usage
by application

Instruction/
training 4%

Project
management 6%

Robotics/
computer vision 1%

Design
6%

Diagnosis
20%

Planning/
scheduling 12%

Intelligent
aids 14%

Control
monitoring 12%

Configuration
17%

Simulation
8%

High-end tool usage by application.
Information provided by AIM Publications, Inc.

Source: Susan Messenheimer, *Computerworld*, 14 July 1986, p.52.

large number of sites, eliminating the majority and identifying the small proportion of likely sites. The system has found a molybdenum deposit worth $100,000,000.

Another expert system, DENDRAL, can identify the molecular structure of unknown chemical compounds. The system uses a special algorithm, developed by Nobel Prize winner Joshua Lederburg, to compute all the possible molecular structures. Then it prunes the list of possibilities to a manageable size by using heuristics. DENDRAL has proved helpful in identifying dangerous pollutants. Before scientists can determine where a pollutant comes from and what to do about it, they must determine its chemical structure. The procedure is time consuming, because there are literally millions of atomic combinations that could be explored—and in a crisis, there is no time to sift through them all. For some tasks, DENDRAL has actually proved more able than any human expert.

Current Expert Systems

By the late 1970s and early 1980s, the success of the prototype systems just described had established the commercial practicality of expert systems. Recent expert systems have proved cost-effective, as well as useful in solving problems. For instance, Pacific Bell now runs a set of 20 expert systems that diagnose local area network (LAN) problems. Each of the 20 systems handles a particular domain related to a problem. The system, which recommends solutions to the problems, can be run on a microcomputer and requires no special training to operate.

The Boeing Aerospace Company has pioneered a series of expert systems designed to preserve human expertise. The project began when Boeing's managers realized that several of the company's top tool-design engineers were about to retire. Transferring their experience and expertise to younger engineers would be time consuming and costly. In addition, there appeared to be a shortage of highly skilled engineers on whom to draw for future design needs. In effect, the company needed a permanent library of design principles with which to train new engineers. Boeing's current expert systems include a trouble shooter for airplane engines, a space station designer, and a helicopter repair adviser.

Another system, DRILLING ADVISOR, assists oil rig supervisors in freeing trapped drilling mechanisms. When a drill bit gets stuck in a hole, the entire operation has to shut down—at a cost of $100,000 a day—to wait for the arrival of one of the few experts worldwide who know how free it. DRILLING ADVISOR, which was developed by the French company Elf-Acquitane, took only a short time to recover its development costs.

Finally, State Farm Insurance Company is developing an expert system that models its best claim adjusters. Apparently the difference in claim costs can vary widely between experienced adjusters and those new to the job. In the insurance industry, reducing rates and staying competitive requires careful monitoring of all costs. Preliminary calculations indicate that such a system should pay for itself in less than a year.

DEVELOPMENT OF AN EXPERT SYSTEM: MARKET ANALYST

Expert systems are built through very deliberate interactions between knowledge engineers and **domain experts**, human experts who are knowledgeable about the systems problem area. In the words of Paul E. Johnson,

An expert is a person who, because of training and experience, is able to do things the rest of us cannot; experts are not only proficient but also smooth and efficient in the actions they take. Experts know a great many things and have tricks and caveats for applying what they know to problems and tasks; they are also good at plowing through irrelevant information to get at basic issues, and they are good at recognizing problems they face as instances of types with which they are familiar. Underlying the behavior of experts is the body of operative knowledge we have termed expertise. It is reasonable to suppose therefore, that experts are the ones to ask when we wish to represent the expertise that makes their behavior possible.[3]

The other half of the development team, the **knowledge engineer**, is generally a computer professional. The knowledge engineer converts the expert's knowledge into forms that the computer can accept, usually IF/THEN rules. Together these rules comprise the system's **knowledge base**, or collection of facts and rules within the expert's subject area.

The acquisition and conversion of information can be an extremely lengthy process, because experts often have difficulty explaining how they reach conclusions. Whereas conventional programmers usually interview the user only once, at the beginning of a job, knowledge engineers must return to the domain expert many times. After the first meeting, they develop a prototype of a system, which contains just a few facts and rules. They then test the system on a problem to see how it works. Based on the results, they return to the experts to ask more questions, then refine or increase the knowledge base. Building an expert system, then, is an exploratory activity that is a series of approximations. To illustrate the process, we will examine the development of a small expert system called MARKET ANALYST.

The Task

Although most businesses want to improve their profitability, they normally try not to compete directly with one another. Direct competition reduces their profit margins (the difference between revenues and expenses). If one business begins to infringe on the markets or territory of another, therefore, the second business may react with or without warning, dropping its prices or introducing a new product. In most industries, businesses try to avoid such shocks by announcing their moves ahead of time to see if competitors might react. This form of testing is called *market signaling*. According to Michael Porter, "A market signal is any action by a competitor that provides a direct or indirect indication of its intentions, motives, goals or internal situation. Some of these signals are bluffs, some are warnings, and some are earnest commitments to action."[4]

Recognizing and accurately reading market signals is of major significance in choosing a defensible competitive position. Yet only experienced observers can make the subtle judgments about competitors needed to discriminate a true signal from a bluff. In addition, though businesses usually signal intentionally, an astute observer with a great deal of experience in watching competitive behavior may also detect indirect signals. No two situations are the same. Given the subtleties involved in making such judgments, market signaling is well suited to use of an expert system.

Designing the System

In the design of this expert system, the expert would probably be a marketing consultant. The knowledge engineer could be anyone experienced in building expert systems. The first meeting between the knowledge engineer (KE) and the expert (EX) might produce the following conversation:

KE: Suppose a competitor announces that it intends to look for a larger warehouse and retail facilities. Would you consider that a threat and expect more intense competition?

EX: That depends on a number of factors. First, I would look at where the announcement was made. If it were widely publicized, it's probably serious. But the size of the investment is also important. Although the news might be widespread, if we're not talking about a large investment, it could be a bluff.

KE: What are some of the other major indicators you evaluate?

EX: Well, it also would depend on what kind of announcement it was. Some are actually defensive. They indicate, "Don't worry, we won't retaliate." But some are very aggressive. They appear to be real, direct, competitive threats. You need to look at other factors, though, to be more certain.

KE: I am curious about bluffing. Do competitors ever signal a move just to see what your response would be?

EX: Actually, companies often bluff. They're testing to see how serious and how sensitive you are about your markets. Or, often they're auditing whether you're strong enough to fight back. To judge these gambits, you have to look at several of the variables I've mentioned at once.

KE: From another viewpoint, are there any signals that indicate a major attack on a company's markets or customers?

EX: Preemptive signals, indicating actions that have never been tried before, are cause for serious concern. They occur when a sizable investment is being made, together with a widely announced public statement of intentions. Often there's a long-run profitable benefit to the signaler as well.

KE: Here's a rule that I think captures your explanation of preemptive signals. Tell me what you think.

IF the signaler is making a major investment,
    AND the media announcing it are broad and widely read,
    AND the signaler expects long-term profitability from the action,
THEN competitors in this market are sending preemptive signals and intend to follow through with their announced actions.

EX: Uh, (long pause). Yes, that begins to capture it. But, of course, if the media used isn't widely read, then they may be bluffing, although the other conditions are present.

KE: I see. Well, let's add that information to the knowledge base and see what it looks like.

To develop rules from this conversation, the knowledge engineer would first catalog the recurring variables mentioned by the expert. They were:

- Type of market signal: accepting, aggressive, defensive, or divergent
- Size of the investment involved: minor or major
- Competitor's reaction: neutral, mild rebuke, or major rebuke
- Medium used to signal: narrow, broad, or none
- Benefits that might accrue to the initiator: lasting or minor

The KE would then list combinations of these variables according to their meaning, shown in Table 14.4. Once listed this way, the expert's diagnoses can be easily converted to rules for insertion into the knowledge base. For example, the top row might be restated as the rule:

IF the market signal indicates divergent behavior,
    AND the magnitude of the proposed investment is considerable,
    AND competitors' reactions are neutral or mildly negative,
    AND the intended audience for the signal is broad,
    AND by signaling a competitor could gain lasting benefits,
THEN competitors in this market are sending preemptive signals and intend to deviate from current industry practices.

As the knowledge engineer and the expert continue to work together, they begin to establish a common language. Then, in that language, they identify the facts and relationships that the expert uses to understand a problem and search for solutions. The knowledge engineer encourages the expert to think aloud; that is, to work on an actual problem, talking about hunches as they occur. Slowly, the knowledge engineer builds a model of the system, expressed in the form of IF-THEN rules.

Finally, the knowledge engineer designs a menu-based interface to collect information from the system's user. MARKET ANALYST's user interface might offer a different menu for each column in Table 14.4. The menu corresponding to column 3, "Competitors' Reactions," might read

Reactions by others in the industry to competitors' or your intentions has been
a. no response.
b. the usual industry responses.
c. indications of displeasure with your intentions.
d. announcement of a possible countermove not as damaging or threatening as possible.
e. a direct counteraction to your intentions.

Once a set of rules and menus has been designed, the knowledge engineer is ready to construct the prototype system.

Table 14.4 Summary of an Expert's Rules for Analyzing Market Signals

	Major Characteristics of Signals				
Type of Signal	Size of Investment	Competitors' Reactions	Public Medium for Signal	Benefits to Company	Possible Meanings for Signal
Divergent	Major	Neutral Mild reaction	Broad	Lasting	Preemptive divergent
Aggressive	Major	Mild rebuke Major reactions	Narrow		Aggressive testing response
Acceptance	Major Major		None	Lasting	Aggressive threatening
Aggressive	Major	Neutral Mild reaction	Broad	Lasting	Preemptive expanded role
Aggressive	Major		Narrow	Minor	Defensive bluffing
Defensive	Minor		Broad	Minor	Defensive reaction
Acceptance		Neutral	Broad	Lasting	Nonthreatening accommodation
Defensive Acceptance Acceptance	Minor Minor	Nonneutral	Narrow None		Insufficient information
Divergent Aggressive	Minor Minor		None		Inconsequential information

Building and Testing the System

Expert systems aren't usually constructed from scratch. Instead, they are built using an **expert system shell**, which may be thought of as the portion of an expert system that remains after all application-specific rules and user interfaces have been removed. As Figure 14.5 shows, most shells have four major components.

1. A *natural-language facility* that communicates with and collects facts from the user. Many expert systems use menu systems to moderate this dialog, but others use command languages, icons and mice, or even spoken English.

2. An **inference engine** that generates inferences from the system's IF/THEN rules and the facts supplied by the user.

Figure 14.5 Components of an expert system. Most expert systems are developed using an expert system shell, which includes a ready-made natural-language facility, an inference engine, and a question-and-answer facility. An empty knowledge base allows users to plug in application-specific facts and rules.

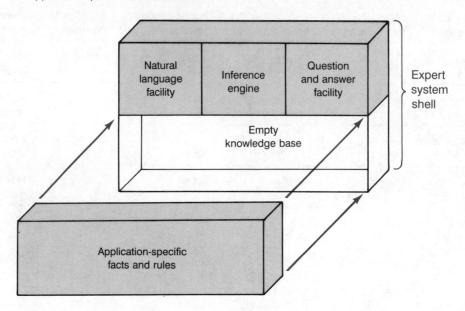

3. A **question-and-answer facility** that explains the system's reasoning.

4. An empty *knowledge base* in which to store the application-specific facts and rules.

Expert system shells may be purchased as part of commercial packages that include special "tools" for entering rules in the knowledge base or building the user interface. Figure 14.6 illustrates a tool called a *knowledge editor,* which displays a menu of possible THEN clauses from which the knowledge engineer may choose.

After the rules and user interface information have been incorporated into the shell, the new prototype system can be tested and refined. The expert checks the accuracy and consistency of the rules and the usefulness of the system's advice by feeding it case histories, then refines the rules where necessary.

Using the System

When the MARKET ANALYST is run, it asks a series of multiple-choice questions. The user enters the letters indicating the choices that correctly finish the statement. (If a question has more than one correct choice, the user should enter all correct choices.) After each question has been answered, the inference engine

Figure 14.6 Using a knowledge editor to change a rule. The left-hand side of the screen shows the THEN part of a programmed rule. To change it, the knowledge engineer selects another statement from the right-hand side of the screen.

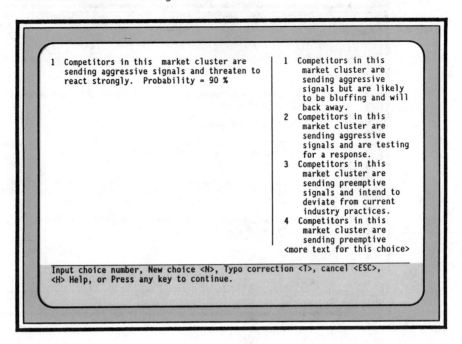

```
1  Competitors in this  market cluster are        1  Competitors in this
   sending aggressive signals and threaten to         market cluster are
   react strongly.  Probability = 90 %                sending aggressive
                                                       signals but are likely
                                                       to be bluffing and will
                                                       back away.
                                                    2  Competitors in this
                                                       market cluster are
                                                       sending aggressive
                                                       signals and are testing
                                                       for a response.
                                                    3  Competitors in this
                                                       market cluster are
                                                       sending preemptive
                                                       signals and intend to
                                                       deviate from current
                                                       industry practices.
                                                    4  Competitors in this
                                                       market cluster are
                                                       sending preemptive
                                                    <more text for this choice>
Input choice number, New choice <N>, Typo correction <T>, cancel <ESC>,
<H> Help, or Press any key to continue.
```

determines which rules apply. If the user's choices agree with all the IF portions of a rule, then the THEN clause must be true. But if even one IF clause doesn't match, the system rejects the rule. Once the inference engine has determined that one rule is true, it may use that rule's THEN clause to determine whether other rules apply.

The order of questioning reflects the system's inferencing procedure. The system begins by asking questions that will eliminate the need to search large areas of the knowledge base. The exact order in which the questions are posed, therefore, depends on the user's responses. Each time the system is run, the sequence of questions is likely to be different.

At any time, the user may ask for an explanation of the system's reasoning by typing WHY. The question-and-answer facility will reply as shown in Figure 14.7, with an answer that includes the rule the system is checking, a note stating additional details, and a reference. This feature opens the system to inspection, instructs the user about how the system functions, and increases the user's confidence in the system. Users must be able to ask why a conclusion or procedure has been recommended, or why a particular question is being asked. Reason-

Figure 14.7 Using a question-and-answer facility. This display, which appeared in response to a user's command WHY, explains the reason the system asked for more information.

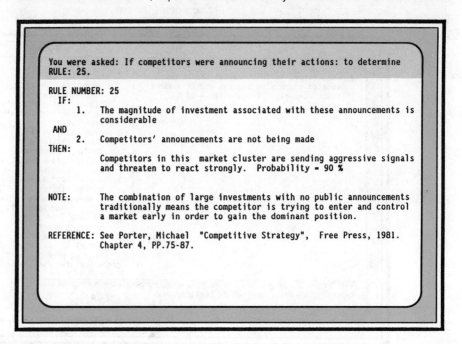

```
You were asked: If competitors were announcing their actions: to determine
RULE: 25.

RULE NUMBER: 25
  IF:
        1.   The magnitude of investment associated with these announcements is
             considerable
  AND
        2.   Competitors' announcements are not being made
  THEN:
             Competitors in this  market cluster are sending aggressive signals
             and threaten to react strongly.  Probability = 90 %


  NOTE:      The combination of large investments with no public announcements
             traditionally means the competitor is trying to enter and control
             a market early in order to gain the dominant position.

  REFERENCE: See Porter, Michael  "Competitive Strategy",  Free Press, 1981.
             Chapter 4, PP.75-87.
```

ing that cannot be explained to an end user is unsatisfactory, even if it was as good as or better than that of a human expert.

When the system has reached a solution, it will display an ordered list of conclusions with their probabilities, as shown in Figure 14.8. Notice that the first conclusion has a higher probability and is therefore more likely to be correct. But the second answer also has a fairly high probability and should be considered by the user.

Even with the help of an expert system shell and its associated tools, building an expert system is not a speedy process. Although the final version of MARKET ANALYST contained only about 25 rules, it took more than two weeks to develop.

ANATOMY OF AN EXPERT SYSTEM

A diagram of a typical complete expert system is shown in Figure 14.9. Some of the parts of this system have already been introduced in connection with MARKET ANALYST; others need more explanation. In particular, we will discuss the ways in which knowledge bases are constructed; how inferences are made from rules; and the various features of expert system development packages.

Figure 14.8 Conclusions reached by MARKET ANALYST expert system. When an expert system comes to a conclusion about the possible solutions to a problem, it ranks them according to probability.

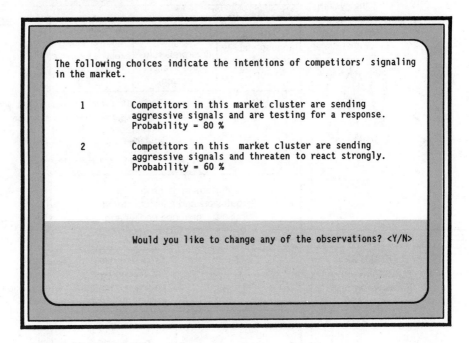

```
The following choices indicate the intentions of competitors' signaling
in the market.

    1              Competitors in this market cluster are sending
                   aggressive signals and are testing for a response.
                   Probability = 80 %

    2              Competitors in this  market cluster are sending
                   aggressive signals and threaten to react strongly.
                   Probability = 60 %




               Would you like to change any of the observations? <Y/N>
```

The Knowledge Base

Recall that a knowledge base contains facts and rules. Facts include short-term information that can change, even during the course of a consultation. Rules are directions about how to generate hypotheses or solutions from known facts. For example, here is an IF-THEN rule with two possible conclusions.

IF sales within the industry are growing rapidly,
    AND the basis for competition is not price or service or is undetermined,
THEN the conditions described suggest an emerging industry .87;
OR the conditions described suggest a fragmented industry .13.

The two tentative conclusions in this rule are "reasoned" from the information provided in the IF clause. Note that, until more facts can be assembled, one conclusion is much more probable than the other.

Knowledge bases are not the same as databases. The difference is best explained by an analogy. Suppose an emergency room physician picks up a patient's chart, which shows the patient's physical measurements, medical history, any obvious trauma, current drug therapy, and past responses to classes of drugs. This is the patient's database. To continue diagnosis and recommend therapy, the

Figure 14.9 Basic components of a typical expert system development package.

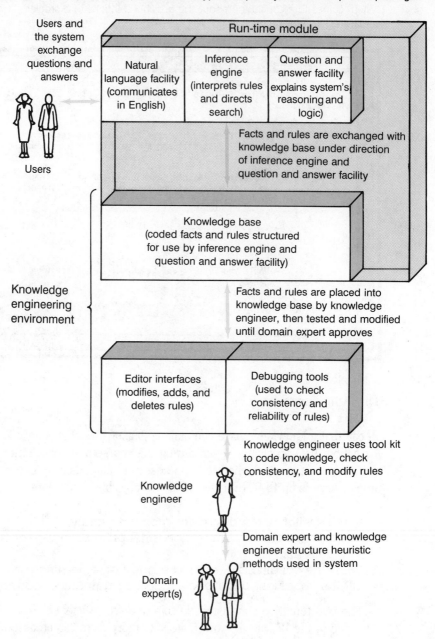

physician must use her medical knowledge, including what she learned in medical school, during her years of residency and practice, from her study of journals, and from the mistakes of others. These facts, relationships, and probabilities are the doctor's knowledge base.

In addition to a knowledge base, some expert systems require access to vast amounts of data stored in remote databases or to data generated in real time. For example, an expert system designed to advise and register college students about courses would need access to the school's course schedules, registration lists, and student transcripts. A patient-monitoring system would need constant streams of data on the patients' vital signs. The special data collection and management capabilities needed by these systems aren't usually found in most development packages.

The Inference Engine

An expert system also needs an *inference procedure,* or a method of reasoning, to understand and act on data and knowledge. Because this procedure or problem solving method governs which question the user is asked next, and thus which tentative conclusions are confirmed first, it determines the system's efficiency. Any good inference procedure should eliminate nonproductive lines of questioning first. Research has shown that users don't trust expert systems that fail to follow an efficient line of questioning.

One commonly used inference procedure is **backward chaining**, which is similar to deductive reasoning: the mental strategy of starting at the end goal and working back to the origin. For example, a maze might be solved by working backward from the ending position rather than forward from the starting position. Or, in the MARKET ANALYST system, the inference procedure might start with a tentative conclusion, such as "Competitors in this market cluster are sending aggressive signals and threaten to react strongly." Working backward, the system would ask questions that might confirm the IF clauses associated with that conclusion. If the user's responses showed the tentative conclusion to be false, the inference procedure would select another tentative conclusion and begin questioning the user again.

Another common reasoning strategy is **forward chaining**—the opposite of backward chaining. In this inference procedure, the system begins with a specific original statement and searches for routes that lead to one or more conclusions. It does so by first selecting the question that is most likely to eliminate a large number of rules. It continues to pose questions in this manner until all the conditions of a rule have been confirmed. Finally, it displays the THEN portion of the rule for users. This procedure can also be quite efficient, depending on the problem.

In a system as simple as MARKET ANALYST, the method of reasoning does not make much difference. But in larger systems, the choice of the wrong inference procedure usually results in an inefficient questioning strategy. Generally, backward chaining (see Figure 14.10) is more appropriate to use with a large number of possible beginnings, whereas forward chaining is more appropriate for use with just a few.

Figure 14.10 Uses of backward and forward chaining. (a) Backward chaining expert systems, such as MYCIN, start by selecting a likely solution and work backward to find evidence that confirms or disproves it. (b) Forward chaining expert systems, such as DENDRAL, start with a small set of facts, and use their rules to work toward the best answer.

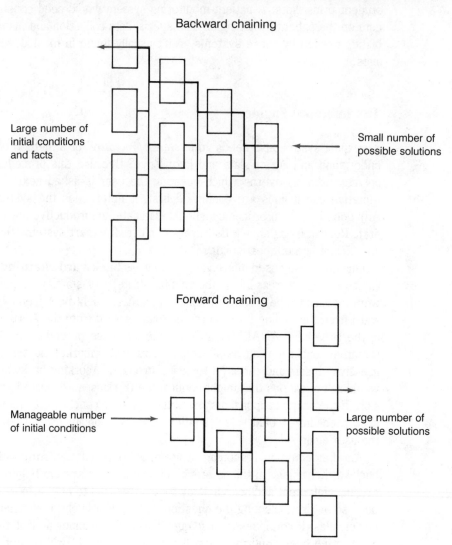

Backward chaining

Large number of
initial conditions
and facts

Small number of
possible solutions

Forward chaining

Manageable number
of initial conditions

Large number of
possible solutions

Expert System Development Packages

As we have seen, many expert systems are now constructed using commercial development packages. These shell and tools kits began to appear on the mini and mainframe computer market in the late 1970s and early 1980s. They were followed in 1984 by micro-based tools and shells.

Until recently, most expert systems had to be constructed by knowledge engineers. But the availability of development packages has enabled end users to construct small expert systems by themselves. The movement of these powerful tools into the hands of end users has speeded up the development of practical applications, causing widespread growth in the use of expert systems. But development packages can't be used for all applications. Applications that require unusual kinds of reasoning or access to existing databases may have to be constructed from scratch with a programming language. Or they might be assembled from an assortment of standalone development tools, such as subroutine libraries, database management systems, and programming aids. Either method would require the services of a skilled computer technician.

Recall that an expert system shell is made by stripping the knowledge base from an expert system, leaving the user interface and inferencing procedures intact. With the aid of an editing tool kit, a new knowledge base from a different problem area can be plugged in. The MARKET ANALYST system, described in the last section, was developed with EXSYS, a micro-based development system that includes a complete knowledge-engineering tool kit, support for constructing user interfaces, a question-and-answer facility, and a powerful inference engine. General Electric has used EXSYS to develop a system for identifying metals and alloys. Pacific Bell has used it to develop a system for diagnosing local area network (LAN) problems. And the Department of Agriculture has used the package to put together a system for controlling the design of experiments.

Figure 14.9 shows a diagram of a complete expert system development package. Most development packages have two parts: a **run-time module**, which includes the parts of the package necessary to run the completed system (top half), and a **knowledge engineering environment**, which contains the tools needed to build the system (bottom half). These tools include knowledge editors, user interface construction tools, testing modules, system monitoring routines, and debugging tools.

The more advanced commercial development packages include sophisticated support tools for entering and manipulating rules. These systems automatically check rules for consistency. They may also speed development by testing new rules against a database of representative cases. If a rule isn't consistent with a case, the system will display the reasoning behind that case, so that the knowledge engineer can refine the new rules.

ADVANTAGES AND LIMITATIONS OF EXPERT SYSTEMS

For most problems, today's expert systems are still not as good as human experts, but they are getting better. Current expert systems are confined to well-defined tasks. They cannot reason across disciplines or broad ranges of knowledge, nor from general or partial theories. In fact, no problem that requires large amounts of reasoning by analogy is suited to an expert system, especially if it is poorly defined and far-ranging. Legal problems are characteristically poor subjects for a small expert system, because they require all the capabilities just mentioned.

Human expertise is also clearly superior to the artificial kind in tasks requiring common sense. There is no easy way to build large quantities of common-sense knowledge into a computer program or knowledge base. Whereas humans easily catch incompatible facts as nonsense—we know that hot air ballons aren't made of lead, for instance—how much of that kind of learning can be included in a knowledge base? Common sense also includes what we know that we don't know. For example, if you were asked for the phone number of Sherlock Holmes, you would know instantly that there is no answer. Expert systems, however, don't give up when they can't solve a problem. They assume that they need more information and persist in questioning the user in an attempt to secure the necessary facts.

Another area in which humans excel is learning. Human experts can adapt to new conditions by adjusting their heuristics, but expert systems aren't adept at learning new rules and concepts. In fact, knowledge acquisition has become the major bottleneck in expert system development. As we have seen, the process of extracting knowledge from an expert and translating it into rules is a tedious one. Thus, current systems are limited to narrow domains. Designing tools that will automatically add and update rules is one of the most urgent research problems in artificial intelligence.

On the other hand, expert systems do offer some advantages. They don't display biased judgments, nor do they jump to conclusions in the face of contrary evidence. They always attend to details and never have a bad day. Best of all, they always systematically consider all the possible alternatives. As new techniques and concepts are applied to the design of knowledge-based systems, we can expect these systems to become even more flexible in their applications.

In general, tasks chosen for treatment by expert systems should be possible, justified, and appropriate.

- *Possible.* The most important requirement for the creation of an expert system is that experts exist and generally agree on solutions. If they don't, the system's performance cannot be verified. Experts must also be able to describe their methods; otherwise an expert system cannot be created.

- *Justified.* Just because it's *possible* to develop an expert system doesn't necessarily mean that it's *desirable* to do so. We've seen that expert systems aren't constructed quickly or easily. Given current technology, the average development time from conception through testing of a finished system is between five and ten person-years for a moderately complex problem. PUFF, a system that diagnoses the presence and severity of lung disease, required five person-years of development, even though it was based on MYCIN's shell. Obviously, few problems are so pressing that they could justify as great an expense in both time and money. Only when human experts are scarce—and therefore expensive—and their expertise is needed at a number of locations is the expenditure likely to be worth it.

Table 14.5 Checklist for Determining Whether an Expert System Should Be Developed

Appropriate	Possible	Justified
1. Is the problem reasonably difficult?	1. Do experts exist?	1. Can human expertise be lost?
2. Are heuristic solutions required?	2. Do experts generally agree on solutions?	2. Is human expertise scarce?
3. Is the task a manageable size?	3. Does the task require more than common sense?	3. Is the potential yield high?
4. Is the activity a valuable one?	4. Are only cognitive skills required?	4. Is expertise needed in many locations?
5. Can symbols be manipulated?	5. Can experts describe what they do?	5. Is expertise needed in a dangerous environment?
	6. Is the problem reasonably clear?	

■ *Appropriate.* Expert systems are appropriate only for problems of very narrow scope. Suppose a system to advise plastic surgeons on surgical procedures has been proposed. That problem is too broad in scope for an expert system. It would have to be limited to a particular type of case, such as cosmetic facial changes, limb reconstruction, or cyst removal. Even within one of these categories, the scope might have to be limited further. Cosmetic facial changes might have to be narrowed to changes in specific features—perhaps nose reconstruction, eyelid changes, or chin tucks.

Table 14.5 summarizes the evaluation process for potential expert systems.

THE FUTURE OF EXPERT SYSTEMS

Predicting future applications of any new technology is difficult, but two likely ones are *advisory systems* and *teaching systems*. As storage technology improves and compact data disks become more affordable, vastly increasing the amount of information available to individual users, both these uses should become more common. One compact data disk can hold over 100,000 pages—enough to store the *World Book Encyclopedia* or any other huge database. Expert systems that are combined with such storage capacity will offer genuine access to knowledge. Natural-language interfaces will also be more affordable, so that user access will be simplified.

New advisory systems are likely to be similar to past systems. Using the same approach as for MYCIN, they will first diagnose a situation and then recommend several good options, in order of priority. Some of these systems will be sold on disk. Others will be available through hotlines or regular customer support services.

- *Advisory systems on a disk.* To solve recurring problems, turnkey systems will be sold on disk. A good example would be a shipping-cost advisor. Shipping costs vary depending on carriers, geographical area, shipping weight, speed of delivery, and so on. Federal Express, Emery Express, the U.S. Postal Service, United Parcel Service (UPS), and other shippers all offer varying rates depending on these variables. An expert system that provides current, accurate information on shipping costs for specific items could yield sizable savings to merchandisers. Other examples of this type of system might include intelligent library card catalogs and phone directories that help users find information quickly by asking a series of questions.

- *Advisory hotlines.* Physical and psychological emergencies require fast, accurate responses from trained professionals. These emergencies are often reported to crisis centers amidst a variety of calls, not all of which require immediate attention. Expert systems could help isolate the truly pressing cases quickly and suggest appropriate treatment to the counselor.

- *Customer service support.* Companies that sell complex products or delicately designed systems must maintain customer support services. Rather than use highly paid design engineers to answer such phone calls, companies might use an expert system. Customer support costs would be lowered and expertise would be available 24 hours a day. Some of these systems might require the presence of a system operator. Others could be linked directly to customers by a modem.

- *Teaching systems.* Education and training are ideally suited to treatment by expert systems, for teaching is a logical extension of knowledge bases' explanatory interface. The rules and facts in a knowledge base could easily be turned into questions and explanations and used as teaching tools. For instance, questions from the THEN side of a rule could be used to help students learn how to diagnose a problem. A teaching version of MARKETING ANALYST might ask, "What conditions provide evidence that you are analyzing an emerging industry?" Not only could the system check the student's answers; it could explain why a certain conclusion should have been reached.

SUMMARY

Artificial intelligence is the study of how to use computer systems to simulate the characteristics of human intelligence. The field has many branches. Natural-language processing includes programs that perform grammatical analyses, recognize spoken language, and generate speech. Logical reasoning and problem-solving routines attempt to find reasonable solutions when brute force methods of computation are intractable. Machine learning promises to provide us with flexible machines that can automatically adapt to changes in their environments. Robotics and computer vision are concerned with the development of machines that can recognize and respond to touch, sound, and sight.

One of the most important successes in artifcial intelligence has been the development of expert systems, which reproduce human expertise in narrow subject areas. Though expert systems are limited in scope, they seem to be equally applicable to many fields—from finance and medicine to strategic planning and chemistry. Tasks that require considerable expertise and relatively little common sense are good candidates for expert systems.

Expert systems can be designed from scratch using a special programming language. But increasingly they are constructed with the help of expert system shells and knowledge engineering tools. Frequently the most difficult part of building an expert system is capturing the expert's knowledge and then testing the system's reliability and validity. Expert systems usually require many revisions before they meet the expert's expectations.

Expert systems store facts and rules in a knowledge base. They use a component called an inference engine to draw conclusions from the facts and rules. The separation of the knowledge base and the inference engine allows the knowledge engineer to revise the knowledge base without affecting the system's programming logic. Unlike conventional programs, the inference engine can reason from uncertain or incomplete data. A question-and-answer facility lets the expert system explain its line of reasoning in an understandable way.

KEY TERMS

artificial intelligence (AI)	knowledge engineer
backward chaining	knowledge engineering environment
computer vision	natural-language processing
domain expert	parsing
expert system	question-and-answer facility
expert system shell	robotics
forward chaining	run-time module
heuristic method	speech synthesis
inference engine	voice recognition system
knowledge base	

DISCUSSION QUESTIONS

1. Some voice recognition research aims to build voice input devices that will replace keyboarding. How might such machines change the organization of office work?

2. How do humans and computer programs differ in their understanding of natural-language input?

3. Imagine what social changes might result from widespread use in cars and trucks of "Driverguide" systems, which provide electronic maps and routings that help drivers get around.

4. Identify different ways that computers are needed to manage robots and their work.

5. Why would an expert system be good for teaching a freshman how to get around the campus?

6. Are there differences between conventional programs and expert systems other than those listed in the chapter? If so, what are they?

7. How would you go about building an expert system for the following situations:

   a. One of the most famous bootmakers in the Southwest is about to retire. People from many continents want to buy his handmade boots. His employer is afraid it may not be able to train someone to continue his work before he retires.

   b. A major appliance manufacturer is considering selling an electronic device to monitor and control temperature and humidity in every room of a house for $50. The device contains several delicate instruments that need to be checked and calibrated every six months. The company is concerned about the high cost of supporting customers, who will need quite a bit of advice and information.

   c. The Internal Revenue Service has had its budget cut again. Its auditors are turning over more rapidly than ever before. Training a competent tax diagnostician takes five years.

   d. A small Alaskan fishing village needs a sewer system. Its citizens have few funds to conduct an environmental impact survey. Clearly they don't have enough to hire an architect and sanitation engineering firm.

EXERCISES

1. Draw a parse tree to show the alternative meanings of an ambiguous phrase or sentence.

2. Time yourself as you study the dialog in Figure 14.3 between Marvin and his teacher. How long did it take you to learn the definitions of letter-list and append?

3. Some people have predicted that robots will replace food preparation workers in fast-food restaurants. Spend some time watching workers in a local restaurant and identify any tasks that robots might be able to do without great difficulty. What problems might result?

4. Find someone who uses judgment as a part of their job. Ask them enough questions so that you—in your role as a knowledge engineer—can list some

variables and combinations of variables that constitute rules for making expert judgments on some subject.

5. One of the best ways to understand the problems of building an expert system is to use common, simple tasks that humans find easy. Try building a table similar to Table 14.4 for the task of tying a bow on your shoes. Although it seems simple and trivial, formulating a complete set of rules presents a big challenge.

6. Using any microcomputer expert system shell you can find, prepare a report listing and explaining each of its parts and features. (There are several shells within the public domain; for example, the EXSYS Demo of EXSYS Version 3 is available from Exsys, Inc., P.O. Box 75158, Contr. Sta. 14, Albuquerque, NM 97194.)

7. Go to the library and use the reference room services to find recent books on artificial intelligence. From one or more of these books, prepare a talk that explains methods of representing knowledge. Consider using frames and semantic nets.

NOTES

1. Martin A. Rischler and Oscar Firschein, *Intelligence—The Eye, the Brain, and the Computer* (Reading, MA: Addison-Wesley, 1987).

2. Edward A. Feigenbaum and Pamela McCorduck, *The Fifth Generation— Artificial Intelligence and Japan's Computer Challenge to the World* (Reading, MA: Addison-Wesley, 1983).

3. Paul E. Johnson, "What Kind of Expert Should a System Be," *The Journal of Medicine and Philosophy,* 8(1983): pp. 77–93.

4. Michael E. Porter, *Competitive Strategy: Techniques for Analyzing Industries and Competitors* (New York, NY: Free Press, 1980), chapter 4.

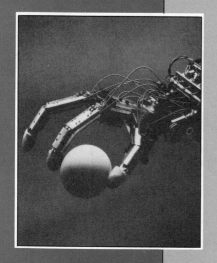

PART IV

COMPUTERS

AT WORK

In 1915 Lee De Forest and his associates stood trial for mail fraud after attempting to sell stock in a manufacturing company. De Forest claimed that he had invented a device that would make transatlantic telephone conversations possible. De Forest narrowly escaped prison, but his associates were convicted when the prosecutor persuaded the judge that transatlantic telephony was impossible. Two years later De Forest successfully applied the *audion tube* (the first vacuum tube) to transatlantic broadcasting. Since those days the audion tube has made possible modern radio, radar, television, first-generation computers, and ultimately Silicon Valley.

Nowadays few people are skeptical of advances in computer technology. In fact, we rather expect constant, exciting innovations. Hardware advances such as speech synthesis, voice recognition, seeing-eye cameras, and touch-sensitive screens are being developed with increasing rapidity. Larger memories and faster processors are opening the door to advances in software such as picture programming, natural-language inquiry, and expert systems that give advice on a variety of topics. The flow of intriguing inventions produces great diversity as the computer is being put to work in all sectors of society, including government, business, the arts, schools, churches, and so on. Chapters 15 and 16 review the major social

arenas within which the computer has been harnessed. Office automation, management information systems, electronic banking, and factory automation are covered in Chapter 15. The chapter ends with a review of several unusual but very important uses of the computer in the medical, law, and journalism professions. This diverse perspective on the role of the computer expands in Chapter 16 as numerous uses of the computer in government and education are discussed and evaluated.

Computers are admittedly powerful, but what about their social and legal ramifications? Are they invading your privacy by recording too many facts about your life in easily queried databases? Have you inadvertently become one of the new breed of "outlaws" because you copied a friend's recently purchased program disk? How can software authors protect their works from theft? In Chapter 17 we discuss the important issues of an evolving "computer morality."

Many interesting events contributed to the transition from human to electronic information processing. In Chapter 18 we review some of these events, from the early history of computing to the present day. In addition, we make some informed predictions about the technical and social changes the future will bring. ■

15 Computers in Business, Industry, and the Professions

Every time you use a credit card, write a check, or eat at a fast-food restaurant, you initiate a computerized business transaction. The computer may not be visible, but at some point, it will register how much you paid or promised to pay, the date, and perhaps other details of your transaction. Once these data have been recorded, they can be used for many other purposes, from updating your account to compiling a market survey.

Today the computerization of basic business transactions is bringing us closer to popular fantasies of the "paperless office" and the "cashless society." To what extent have changes in office and business technology realized those dreams? In this chapter, we examine the impact of computers on the business and professional world. Beginning with office automation, we will see how the installation of computer systems tends to restructure an organization. Then we will study three specialized types of information systems in detail: computerized processing of basic business transactions, management information systems, and decision support systems. Next we will briefly assess the ways in which computers and robots aid industrial manufacturing. Then we will examine finance, banking, and retailing and note some economic and social consequences of computerization. After reviewing how computers have changed business organizations, we will shift our analysis to the professions, to see what kinds of changes they have been experiencing.

OFFICE AUTOMATION

The idea behind **office automation (OA)** is basically simple: use the computer to replace existing inefficient manual methods of recording, filing, and communicating data and information. The payoff for this conversion is increased efficiency, speedier record handling, and quicker response to the needs of the customer and to changes in the marketplace than may be possible under a manual system. In the world of business, early knowledge is power. Many a company has prospered by being the first to take advantage of a hot new fad or a trend in consumer buying. And many a company has floundered for failing to anticipate a crucial change in its customers' tastes.

Consider the following example of an OA project. A company owned and operated three employment agencies in the suburbs of a southern city. Aside from its accounting and payroll functions, the company's record keeping was devoted mainly to the complex task of matching job orders from employers with the qualifications of applicants. Under its manual system, the company kept its job orders in separate "tubs" identified by job description. There was one tub for secretaries, another for receptionists, a third for filers, a fourth for medical technologists, and so on. Each office separately maintained hundreds of such tubs for its own use. Once an applicant had been interviewed and qualified, the counselor would thumb through the orders in the appropriate tub for a job description that matched. The brain of the individual counselor was the CPU behind this manual system. Those counselors who were diligent searchers of the tubs or gifted with an exceptional memory ("I remember a job description like this that came in last year! Now, where did I put it?") did well. Those who weren't persistent searchers or who had bad memories didn't do so well.

The chief aim of office automation should be to make a company more efficient by bringing out the best in its employees. And that was exactly the effect of OA in this case. The automated system consisted of microcomputers linked through a local area network, and operating under custom software that classified every possible job order by code. For example, 45000 might be a programmer; 45000.100 might be a programmer who can write code in two languages; and 45000.115 might be a programmer who can write code in two languages and is also capable of minor hardware maintenance.

Instituting this OA system improved the efficiency of the business, because the computer instantly retrieved and matched job orders with applicants. A second result was speedier input of job descriptions. A job order logged into the system by a counselor at the North Office at 10:05 A.M. became available to a counselor at the Metro Office seconds later. A third result was that the company could now monitor its placements by counselor, job order, or even office. Thus, if management noticed that the South Office was swamped with data processing job orders, it could quickly transfer a counselor there who specialized in DP applicants. Eventually such a trend would also be spotted under a manual system, but much later. Like an army, the business that can deploy its people where they are most needed has a better chance of success.

Five Primary Functions

This case also illustrates the five major functions that make up OA. They are, not necessarily in order of importance, word processing, database management, spreadsheets, graphics, and communications. The following are snapshots of each function and its part in a typical OA scheme.

Word Processing

From Chapter 6, we know that *word processing* is the use of computers for preparing written documents. The term was coined by IBM in the early 1960s to distinguish its new line of typewriters that simplified editing from existing equipment that only processed data. In the case of the employment agency, word processing was used to enter and log job orders; to acknowledge, by means of personalized form letters, the receipt of orders; and to allow counselors to correspond with each other as well as with applicants and employers.

Database Management

The intended use of the database in the employment agency was mainly to match job orders with applicants. But once operational, the database also churned out information vital for management of the whole company. For example, an exact profile of how individual counselors, offices, or regions were performing could be extracted from the database. Breakdowns of job orders by counselor, office, or region were instantly available from month to month, week to week, or even day to day. Management had its finger on the pulse of its daily business in a way impossible under a manual system.

Tied into the accounting system, the database also generated payroll records for individual counselors, billed commissions, made automatic entries into accounts receivable, and provided management with quarterly financial statements.

Spreadsheets

What if a DP counselor were added to the South Office? What if the Metro Office's decline in new business last month were sustained over the entire year? Playing "what if?" is the fundamental aim of spreadsheets. But it is a game that management plays in deadly earnest, with horrendous financial penalties for wrong forecasts or bad judgment. As you've seen from Chapter 7 on spreadsheets, the game of "what if?" is best played with accurate and up-to-date data. With OA, management has the most current figures at its fingers. If there has been a drastic dip in the North office's business, for example, management knows the bad news nearly instantly and can respond quickly. Timely and accurate information is vital to any management decision.

Graphics

Except in rare cases, graphics play a secondary, but nevertheless useful role in the automated office. A chart showing a flattened bar or a pie chart with an ominous chunk missing can dramatize a grim dip in income in a way that numbers alone cannot. *Presentation graphics* is the most recent use of graphics in the automated office. Facilitated by the popularity of laptop portable computers, presentation graphics can use computer graphics to highlight or underscore a sales pitch. A sales manager can provide the sales force with graphics to be played back with appropriate personal commentary to a prospect. Presentation graphics has yet to prove itself, but it is the most recent use of laptop computers as part of an automated office.

Communications

If computers couldn't communicate with one another, their usefulness to humans would be severely limited. But, thankfully, computers *can* "talk" to one another, and business has been quick to grasp the benefits of this ability. Large companies that issue laptop portable computers to their field sales force can instantly communicate any product or price change via modem. A stockbroker in Atlanta can have immediate access to every nervous blip in the Dow Jones averages. An executive on the 54th floor can send an important presentation via LAN hookup to an attorney on the 10th floor for scrutiny and addition of legal boilerplate. That three offices could simultaneously share a common database of job orders and applicants was the most useful feature of the automated office in our employment agency example. It was the integration of computing and communication technologies (as illustrated in Figure 15.1) that made this possible.

Computer communications also involve the widespread use of *electronic mail systems* (see Chapter 9) that work very much like the post office to transmit messages (memos, notes, letters, and reports). Two types of electronic mail systems have become popular: message systems within a department or company that uses a LAN (as in the case of our employment agency) and mail systems, such as CompuServe, that use large-scale national or international networks. Users in both cases have "electronic mailboxes" to which messages can be posted from another computer or terminal. To read the contents of a mailbox, a user simply logs in a name along with a private code. The message may then be either read and replied to on the spot or downloaded into the user's personal computer and printed out as hard copy.

Computer conferencing, in which groups of people communicate about a mutual problem through electronic mail, is also gaining in popularity. Studies have shown that such conferences require less time than face-to-face meetings. The conference may take place at a single sitting, with all participants on line, or it may

extend over a period of time to allow for the drafting of replies and counter-arguments. But the bottom line of such electronic meetings is that they cost less than face-to-face sessions requiring long-distance travel and can often be used to iron out minor differences between departments and individuals.

Finally, *facsimile transmission (fax)* is the use of machines to transmit exact duplicates of documents—whether handwritten, line-drawn, or typeset—over telephone lines (see Figure 15.2). Transmitting at a universal standard of 200 dpi, most fax machines can produce an image detailed enough to do justice to a photograph. Some three-quarters of a million fax machines are in use today throughout the United States and Canada, with the number increasing annually at a rate of 14 percent. Complex versions of these machines can send and receive documents unattended, store documents for later transmission when rates are lower, transmit the same document to different machines, and even protect the confidentiality of documents by demanding a password before transmission.

The microcomputer equipped with a special fax-compatible modem has lately been threatening to put dedicated fax machines out of business. The image produced by a microcomputer is far superior to a similar transmission from fax to fax. Figure 15.3 shows the organization of a true microcomputer-fax system. The microcomputer may transmit either to another specially equipped micro or to a fax machine. In either case, the specially modified microcomputer doubles as a computer and as a fax machine and at substantially less cost.

Figure 15.2 Facsimile machines are popular for sending contracts with a handwritten signature from a branch office to a home office; for international mail when same-day mail is needed; and in countries where the language has an alphabet of several thousand characters. This particular model is made by AT&T.

The Paperless Office?

With the advent of OA in the 1960s, the idea of the "paperless office" was wildly trumpeted. Some 20 years later, a blizzard of paper still swirls in the halls of business. The fact is that the paperless office looks better on paper than it is in reality. Money leaves a paper trail, and it isn't altogether desirable that this trail be made an electronic one. A payment still demands a paper receipt. An order generates a paper invoice, a promise to deliver the goods deserves its own parchment, and a pink slip just wouldn't be the same if it weren't a slip. Paper is here to stay, but *tubs* of it can be eliminated, as in the example of the employment agency. As long as there is paper money, though—whether dollar bills or checks—the paperless office will remain a dream. But if money should ever be reduced to a system of electronic debits and credits, as some have prophesied, then paper will lose its hold on business.

Human Factors: Ergonomics

If computers could function alone and untended, the study of ergonomics wouldn't be nearly as compelling as it is today. **Ergonomics** is the science of adapting the working environment to suit the worker. Its emphasis isn't on changing the worker, but on engineering workstations and systems to meet human comforts.

Figure 15.3 Microcomputer-fax configuration. The image can be transmitted to either another microcomputer or to a fax machine.

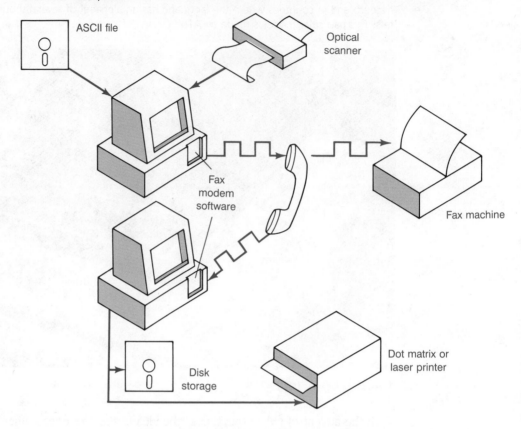

This approach is entirely as it should be in a society that places a premium on human dignity, happiness, and worth.

Two principal factors enter into the ergonomic engineering of a computer workstation: the physical layout of the workstation itself and the design of the software. We will discuss both topics as they apply to the ideal automated office.

Workstation Design

In the beginning of office automation, managers assumed that the computer could simply be plunked down where the typewriter had been, and that would be that. But workers at CRTS soon began grumbling about headaches, eyestrain, and aching necks. Allegations were made that the machines caused miscarriages, birth defects, and cataracts. These widespread complaints led to an in-depth study by the National Academy of Sciences on the effects of VDTs (video display terminals) on the health of workers. (The term VDT refers to any computer terminal, consisting of a CRT screen and a keyboard.) The academy issued its conclusions in 1983: no evidence existed to show that VDTs caused miscarriages, birth defects, or cataracts.

But that finding didn't quiet the chorus of worker complaints about eyestrain, weariness, and back problems. Scientists took a closer look and found significant reasons for worker discomfort. To begin with, there was a serious problem with lighting. *Task lighting*—which illuminates the surface area on which a worker is concentrating—is ideal for working at a typewriter, but terrible for a VDT, since it results in a glare reflected from the screen. Yet when the VDT replaced the typewriter, it inherited the typewriter's task lighting. Fluorescent lighting—exactly the kind one expert found illuminating nine out of ten offices—is likewise too glaring for a VDT screen.[1] Experiments indicated that nonreflective ambient background light is best for VDT work. Nor should a VDT ever be placed under a window, where the worker's eyes will be subjected to a double glare from the screen and the sun.

The problem of eyestrain caused by working before a VDT isn't imaginary. One study found that half of the estimated 15 million people who work at VDTs suffer blurry vision, eyestrain, and headaches.[2] Another researcher coined the term *technostress* to cover the symptoms of eye fatigue and other ailments reported by a target group of 100 VDT workers.[3] But these discomforts are easily remedied by adjustments to background lighting, the installation of glare shields, and other minor ergonomic adaptations. For example, workers who wear bifocals have an especially difficult time reading a VDT screen, because the upper lenses of such glasses typically have a focal length of 6 to 8 feet, whereas the lower ones have a focal length of 13 inches, making it nearly impossible for the wearer to comfortably read a screen 25 to 31 inches away. However, this potential source of discomfort is easily eliminated by outfitting the worker with special glasses.

Vision problems aside, the other principal source of worker complaints about VDTs is the physical layout of workstations. Early computers consisted of a single unit with an undetachable keyboard and a fixed screen, which forced all workers, regardless of height or girth, to sit in an identical position and stare straight ahead. Chairs were engineered for a rigid 90-degree posture. Studies later demonstrated that most workers prefer to sit at an angle of 104 degrees, which is apparently easier on the back, and to look down at the screen from an average angle of 31 degrees.[4] The detachable keyboards and tilt screens of later workstations in fact solved many of these initial problems.

You may think that these are small matters, but so is a grain of sand in the eye. One study found that, after ergonomic adjustments were made to a business's workstations, productivity increased between 4 and 8 percent.[5] Certainly, such gains are substantial enough to justify the minor expense of making workstations physically pleasing and comfortable to those who must staff them daily.

Software Design

Most programs are "scolding." The operator makes a little mistake, and the program barks back a tactless correction. One popular program used to flash the ominous message "Fatal Error" just before slipping into irreversible coma and wiping out all the data already entered. Even today, after thousands of programs and years of experience selling those programs to the public, the computer industry still hasn't learned how to write error messages that don't sound as if they came out of the mouth of a drill sergeant. Here is a sample of error messages from one widely used word processing program.

```
Error loading overlay
Illegal in forms mode
Legal only with Dos 2.0
Only 10 shift keys allowed
```

Programs almost never say "please" or "thank you." The imperative is their favorite mood, and they're always heckling the operator about what's "illegal" and "not allowed." Added to the rudeness of most programs is a bewildering complexity. Many popular word processing programs have manuals with the heft of *War and Peace*. One expert has predicted manuals the size of big-city telephone directories for some complex programs.[6] And many programs still take an annoying number of keystrokes to execute even routine commands. It's no surprise that the harassed VDT worker soon comes to view the computer as a nagging antagonist and is sometimes provoked enough to maul it with an ax (such attacks have actually occurred.)

Correcting these flaws in software design has lately become the goal of ergonomic engineers. The Association for Computing Machinery (ACM) Special Interest Group on Computer and Human Interaction (SIGCHI) regularly meets to discuss mutual problems, reporting issues and solutions in a bulletin. In addition, the Human Factors Society, with over 4,000 members, holds annual meetings and publishes the journal *Human Factors,* which is devoted to reports of scientific research. It distributes an 86-page document that specifies detailed recommendations for features of VDT workstations.[7]

Some programs have made giant strides in user friendliness. Apple's word processing program for the Macintosh, for example, uses a menu with easily understood icons to represent its main functions. No complex commands need to be remembered or entered. And the manual for this program is the size of a pamphlet.

The Future of Ergonomics

The computer industry has learned many painful lessons about the realities of human operators in the workplace. One prime lesson is that a machine can't be abruptly imposed on an office unless it fits the habits and work styles of the people who will use it. For example, a new telephone system requiring the presence of at least three operators was installed in an office. The operators, who were used to taking their coffee break as a group, came to resent the machine and soon began clamoring that it didn't work. What's more, they "proved" their assertion.

Another important lesson is that experts can't arbitrarily decree what is comfortable and pleasing to workers without first studying the workers themselves and their work habits. Such studies are under way at laboratories and will inevitably yield improvements in workstation and software design. For example, in one study conducted by Xerox at its Palo Alto Research Center (PARC), an experienced secretary was videotaped editing a document on a word processor. The secretary's 20-minute session behind the keyboard was broken down to 3,000 touching and typing events that were microscopically analyzed in increments as short as half a second.[8] Making programs that are better adapted to their human operators is the aim of this year-long study and others like it.

As one expert put it, "It is not enough for the system to provide a powerful and functional capability if the user cannot make use of it. The system should help the user without getting in his way, allowing him to concentrate on his task, not on the system; it should be efficient to use and easy to learn; it should be consistent, logical, natural."[9] To which every worker who has ever struggled to learn a new program or operate a new machine would no doubt breath a fervent "Amen."

INFORMATION SYSTEMS

As we saw in our discussion of the employment agency's use of computers, computers not only make data entry quick and easy, they also allow managers and employees to analyze data and share or reorganize information. This section shows how businesses computerize basic business transactions and then transform those data into the information necessary to carry out the basic management functions of planning, organizing, staffing, directing, and controlling.

Computerization of Basic Business Transactions

Although, broadly speaking, office automation includes all computerization related to the office, traditional usage has limited the term to tasks related to word processing and telecommunications. Accounting functions, such as order entry and billing, are typically categorized under such labels as "general business applications" or "basic business transactions." These basic functions often consume most of the time and storage available on a company's computers. They constitute the central core of a business operation, but lacking glamor, they are sometimes neglected. As shown in Figure 15.4, the typical business accounting system has six main functional subsystems or components: general ledger, inventory, accounts receivable, accounts payable, payroll, and others, including orders and sales. Computerizing the accounting system consists of transferring tasks in each of these six areas from manual to software procedures. Businesses can choose separate software packages for each of the accounting functions or an *integrated* accounting system package, in which the individual components can share information easily.

Just as in a manual accounting system, the *general ledger* is a listing of business transactions by account. It is the heart of a computerized accounting system. Once a *chart of accounts,* which identifies the accounts used in the system, is defined, transactions can be entered in the ledger. How a transaction is entered or recorded depends on which of the six subsystems initiates it.

Let's assume, for example, that an order arrives at Bourke Manufacturing, a small furniture company with a computerized accounting system. A clerk enters

Figure 15.4 Overview of an accounting system for a small business, showing the six main types of transaction processing.

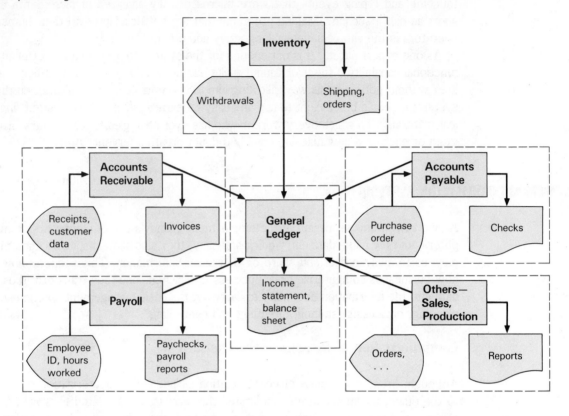

detailed order information into the order-entry subsystem, which summarizes the order information and creates demand on the *inventory* subsystem. The inventory subsystem compares the order information with inventory status and does the following:

- Reserves inventory if available

- Creates demand on production or purchasing if inventory is insufficient to cover the order

- May initiate replenishment of inventory if fulfillment of the order will reduce available inventory below target levels

The inventory subsystem will then schedule fulfillment of the order according to the customer's requirements or shipping commitments contained in the order-entry subsystem.

When the order is filled, a shipping summary is entered into the computer. This summary removes that inventory from the inventory record, updates the shipping history, and initiates the billing cycle. The billing cycle, which involves the accounts receivable and sales subsystems, creates the sales history as well as the sales (revenue) and cost of sales (expense) entries that are ultimately summarized in the general ledger. In addition the billing cycle produces the customer invoice, which notifies the customer of the fulfillment of the order and the obligation to pay, as well as the accounts receivable record, which identifies the amount due from the customer and completes the order-entry/order-fulfillment subsystem.

Accounts receivable (AR) software manages the data that show how much individual customers owe for goods or services received. A good AR package will ensure prompt billing, simplify adjustments to customer accounts, and provide for effective collection on delinquent accounts. *Accounts payable (AP),* on the other hand, record a business's outstanding obligations—what it owes—by assigning the arriving bills to appropriate categories and then initiating payment after determining that funds are available and appropriate authorization has been received. A computerized *payroll* package is particularly useful, because it facilitates accurate computation and reporting of wage adjustments, overtime, tax deductions, and other types of deductions used in preparing periodic payroll checks.

The management of a company requires up-to-date reports from these various transaction subsystems, but additional information is needed for the tactical and strategic planning that is discussed in the next section. Specifically, managers and other top-level decision makers require regular overall summaries of the organization's operations, and they need forecasts of future operations under alternative policies or procedures, so that they can decide which course of action to take. Since these planning needs overlap with transaction processing requirements, integrated systems of organizing information have been developed.

Management Information Systems

Computers are used every day to process data into information—by now every reader of this book knows that basic fact. Less well-known, but also a fact, is that much of the information processed by computers ultimately plays a part in management decisions. **Management information systems (MIS)** simply means the use of computer and other systems to generate the information necessary for management to perform its major functions of planning, organizing, staffing, directing, and controlling, which are shown in Figure 15.5. Each function is briefly described below.

- *Planning.* To plan means to set goals and objectives for the company. Management must know and understand the nature of the company, its competition, and its marketplace and be able to make accurate predictions about their future. Establishing the policies, procedures, programs, and business philosophy of a company is one important part of planning. Setting ambitious but achievable goals is another.

- *Organizing.* To organize means to develop and maintain the resources and structure of a company. Managers must be assigned, workers departmentalized, and the company's resources effectively deployed in an attempt to meet desired goals.

Figure 15.5 The five functions of management.

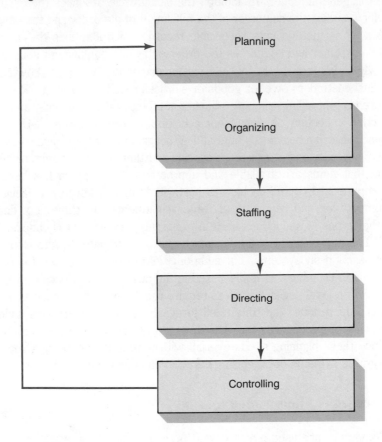

- *Staffing.* Staffing is the continuous process of recruiting, hiring, and training employees.
- *Directing.* To direct means to coordinate the activities of a company and to delegate the authority necessary for carrying out those activities. Management directs by communicating with workers, channeling their energies, and motivating them to do their jobs well.
- *Controlling.* To control means to evaluate how well or badly standards are being met and to take any action needed to correct deficiencies. Sometimes the necessary action requires return to the planning function to revise goals or redefine policies.

Levels of Management
Management may be described according to three levels: operational, tactical, and strategic. As Figure 15.6 shows, each level requires a different kind of information that can be provided by a properly directed MIS. We will briefly describe the function of each management level, along with its information needs.

Figure 15.6 The three levels of management. Managers at each level need different kinds of information.

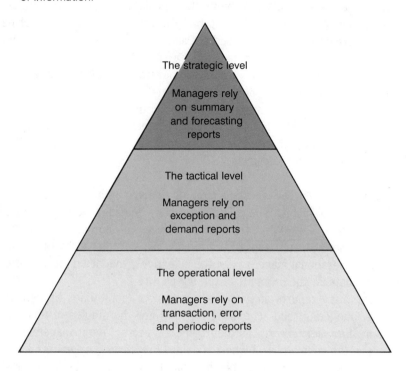

The strategic level

Managers rely on summary and forecasting reports

The tactical level

Managers rely on exception and demand reports

The operational level

Managers rely on transaction, error and periodic reports

Operational Level Also known as a front-line manager, a manager at the *operational level* is responsible for the day-to-day operations of a business. The manager of a single outlet of a hamburger chain is an example. Such a person is responsible for hiring help, maintaining inventories, supervising employee relations with customers, and verifying cash register totals.

Operational managers rely on transaction reports, error reports, and periodic reports to do their job. *Transaction reports,* also known as *detailed reports,* summarize line by line the daily transactions of the business. From a transaction report, the manager of a hamburger outlet can determine which worker operated register 3 between 11:00 A.M. and 2:30 P.M. *Error reports* warn the manager of a possible error. Preset limits programmed into the computer will signal an error when they are exceeded. For example, an employee's time card that shows 600 hours worked in a week will generate an error report—the preset limit may be a maximum of 60 hours for any one employee. *Periodic reports* aggregate and summarize information from transaction and error reports on a periodic basis—say, once a day, week, or month. These reports help the manager to see how well the business did in a given period.

Tactical Level The *tactical level* of management, known as middle management, is typically charged with the responsibility, not for a single unit, but for several units.

A manager at this level in a fast-food restaurant chain might oversee the operations of 15 or 20 outlets, for example. Management here is concerned with assisting the separate units to achieve their goals and with correcting any exceptional situations. A unit that is flagging badly in sales or is the object of persistent consumer complaints will be singled out and draw the scrutiny of tactical management.

At the tactical level, management relies mainly on exception reports and demand reports. An *exception report* is generated by an MIS only when certain guidelines have either been violated or not met. For example, the computer may be programmed to issue an exception report if the sales at any one store fall by a certain percentage. Should this occur, management may call for a *demand report,* a report that is only generated by specific request, which might break down the overall decline by specific products.

Strategic Level The *strategic level* of management is concerned primarily with long-range planning. Where is the company heading? How is it faring in a competitive marketplace? What new products has the competition introduced, and how should the company respond? Strategic managers don't have the microscopic view of the operational manager nor the selectively magnified view of the tactical manager. Instead, their view is of the big picture.

Summary reports and forecasting reports (sometimes broken down into planning, budgeting, and scheduling reports) are the staples of this level of management. *Summary reports,* as their name suggests, give management the big picture of how the company as a whole is doing. *Forecasting reports* predict future growth, resources, and profits. Depending on their content, these reports may also be called *planning, scheduling,* or *budgeting reports.* They help management measure the overall performance and health of the company.

The Basis of MIS

Behind every functional MIS is a database containing the millions of transactions that constitute a company's daily business. Every time a single hamburger is sold by a hamburger chain, for example, that sale is added to millions of others reported to the database. The marvel of the computer is that it is capable of aggregating such raw numbers and processing them into useful and varied kinds of information. As the engine behind this manipulation of data, the computer enables an operational manager to extract a transaction report from the same database from which a strategic manager derives a summary report.

External sources of data are also used to generate an MIS's reports. These sources will vary with the company's business. But many such external sources of data are available for computer processing by an MIS.

It would be a mistake if you concluded from this discussion that an MIS requires an enormous mainframe computer and the backing of a multimillion-dollar company. That may have been true in the 1960s and 1970s, when multinational conglomerates were the only users of management information systems. But with the explosion in microcomputers and minicomputers, a host of small businesses have adapted and evolved their own management information systems. Government

Table 15.1 How Large Companies Deal with PCs (96 Ohio Companies)

	1982	1984
Purchase of personal computers	13%	68%
MIS dept. controls PC acquisition	2	52
User groups	2	41
PC demonstration facility	2	38
Help desk (formal)	0	33
PC library	0	29
User-training program	0	26
MIS dept. advises on PC acquisition	6	13
Local area networks	0	12
PC planning function	0	8

* *Source:* Excerpted from *Datamation*, July 15, 1984. Copyright © 1984 by Cahners Publication Company.

agencies use them as do nonprofit organizations, such as hospitals and charities. As Table 15.1 shows, even large companies use PCs, and in many companies, it is the MIS department that oversees their acquisition.

Decision Support Systems

An offshoot of MIS and a valuable tool for managers in its own right is a **decision support system (DSS)**. Decision support systems typically extend MIS through the addition of software that allows managers to simulate business conditions and play "what if?" A significant feature of DSS that distinguishes them from MIS is the ability to deal with an *unstructured inquiry*—one for which no precedent exists—in making basic business decisions.

Unlike MIS, which are founded on a database of daily business transactions, the heart of a DSS is a complex mathematical model that simulates the operating conditions of the company, as well as the business environment in which it exists. For example, the manager of a hamburger chain can use a DSS to price "kiddie burgers" for a nationwide sales promotion. Using the DSS, the manager can play "what if?" by anticipating probable sales volumes and profits for particular prices. Such speculative information can't be obtained from a typical MIS.

Consider another example. A printer who operates a large plant at nearly full capacity receives a special order to produce 1 million pamphlets. The MIS in place informs the printer about past business, backlogged orders, and anticipated deadlines, but can't tell whether or not the new order may be filled if the present schedule is juggled. By playing "what if?" with the mathematical model that reflects the plant's actual operating conditions, the printer can calculate if, when, and how the new order can be filled.

As the logical extension of MIS, DSS are especially useful to strategic managers, and their introduction has helped overcome managers' prejudice against the keyboard, which has traditionally been associated with lower-level clerical functions. So useful have DSS been to this level of management that stereotypes of the keyboard are being overcome, and computerization of the corporate world is spreading rapidly.

Information Centers

End-user computing is the use of special software development tools and packages by noncomputer specialists, to analyze, design, develop, test, and document business applications that those individuals will use. Before these end users can develop new applications, they must select appropriate prewritten software packages and be trained in the peculiarities of hardware and software packages already used by the firm.

The problem of selecting the perfect combination of hardware and software for business use and of training the right people is immense. But one solution has been the formation of **information centers**, departments designed to centralize computer purchasing decisions, test hardware and software, and train end users, especially on microcomputers. One of their primary functions is to coach end users, so that users will no longer have to wait for centralized data processing departments to develop and run computer applications. Such coaching means that employees can save valuable time, get information when they need it, and be assured that systems are compatible and software is adequately documented. Thus, if one expert employee leaves the company or is unavailable, other employees still have access to important information.

Information centers are based on the sensible premise that it is only by thoroughly training the appropriate end users that systems will achieve peak efficiency. Also available through information centers is information about commercial hardware and software products. The spreading popularity of corporate information centers promises to encourage a trend toward end-user development of applications.

COMPUTERS IN INDUSTRY

Manufacturing and Robotics

The robot has had a curious history. Its origin is neither industrial nor mechanical, but literary. The term originated, not from the drawings of some mad scientist, but from a 1921 play, *R.U.R.* (Rossum's Universal Robots) by the Czech dramatist Karel Capek. In that play, as in many subsequent dramatizations about robots, the machines rose up against their human makers, sounding a theme that would recur in movies, books, and the speculations of futurists. Science fiction writer Isaac Asimov even formulated a robotics law with the prime injunction that a robot shall do nothing to hurt its human master. But fiction to the contrary, robotic uprisings or rebellions are neither probable nor realistic. **Robots** are nothing more than automated machinery under the control of a computer program—computers fitted with sensing devices, mechanical arms, and hydraulic appendages.

Figure 15.7 Robots on a GM assembly line weld the seams of a car body.

Today robots are used to perform many useful but entirely innocuous and unrebellious tasks. A variety of businesses, from candy makers to pharmaceutical houses to plastic molders, use them to manufacture goods. But the largest user of robots is Detroit, with General Motors (GM) accounting for 35 percent of all "steel-collar workers," as robots are affectionately nicknamed, presently used in the United States (see Figure 15.7). Some 20,000 robotic units are expected to be working on GM assembly lines by 1990.[10] Automobile makers initially used robots mainly for spot welding and painting, but lately "smarter" robots are tightening bolts, marking identification numbers on engines and transmissions by using laser beams, and gauging body dimensions with a combination of precision lasers and video cameras.[11]

The goal of robotics is to create machines that can manipulate materials and tools, react to unpredictable situations, and ultimately "see." Robots at some automobile assembly plants can already "see" with the help of multiple laser beams projected in a complex horizontal and vertical grid. Video cameras relay reflected data to light-sensing devices that digitize the information and transmit it to a computer. Figure 15.7 shows robots' arms welding an automobile body in a GM plant. A system of laser beams and video cameras is used by auto makers to conduct precision measurements of automobiles rolling off the assembly line. Using this technology, the robot can "sense" whether the approaching half-assembled car statistically matches or exceeds the ideal dimensions of the "perfect" car stored in computer memory. With one unit inspected every 30 seconds, the system results in cars with tighter-fitting doors and better-built bodies.

Many companies today are using *automatic guided vehicles (AGV)* like the one shown in Figure 15.8. These self-propelled vehicles are widely used in factories to ferry materials between manufacturing stations. Some AGVs are guided by wires embedded in the floor; others follow an invisible fluorescent pathway. Companies like Sears, Roebuck use AGVs to pick up and deliver mail between departments.

These and similar manufacturing uses of robots fall under the heading of **programmable automation (PA)**. The CAD/CAM graphics systems described in Chapter 10 are another example. Common PA systems include *numerically controlled (NC) machine tools,* which can reshape or refine material used in a production process. Figure 15.9 shows an NC device used in production. When CAD/CAM robots and NC systems are linked together through a computerized database that plans, schedules, and controls a manufacturing process, the entire system is known as **computer-integrated manufacturing (CIM)**. And human beings must not only design and program these devices, they must "teach" robots how to carry out complex series of actions (Figure 15.10).

Figure 15.9 This lathe is a numerical control device.

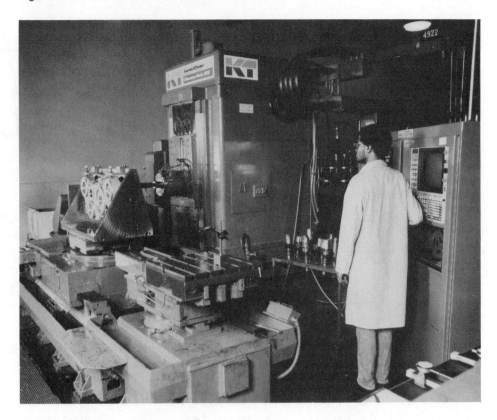

The adoption of PA systems has been somewhat slow because they require extensive planning and support. Not only do the machines need to be programmed and reprogrammed, but management must acquire expertise, establish training programs, and make sure that employees are receptive to the transformation that is required. The population of robots in the early 1980s was still only about 30,000 in Japan and 6,000 in the United States. As is clear from Table 15.2, welding and materials handling were the most common applications for industrial robots at that time.

Other uses for robots are more exotic and even have a certain futuristic promise about them. Consider this scenario, which smacks of science fiction. A ranting man holed up in a basement apartment goes berserk and begins shooting at passersby. After communicating with the police on the telephone, the man promises to surrender and throws two handguns out into the hallway. But he has secretly hidden a third gun in his waistband and plans to kill the first police officer he encounters. The door creaks open; a robot whirls into the room, its high-intensity strobe lights temporarily blinding the man. The police rush in and subdue him.

Exactly such an incident was played out recently in Manhattan. The featured robot is known to New York police as a Remote Mobile Investigator, a machine

Figure 15.10 Industrial robots are guided through a series of movements by human "teachers."

equipped with steel claws, video-camera eyes, and two-way audio for communicating with suspects. With its human operator safely out of sight behind a bulletproof shield, the robot is linked to and operated via a 360-foot cable. It's powered by two 12-volt batteries, capable of climbing a curb, and equipped with steel claws that can fire a gun, pick up a coffee cup, or drag a 350-pound victim to safety. Improved units now being developed will have color television cameras and be able to climb stairs, turn a key, and open a door. With some 100 police officers being

Table 15.2 Installed Operating Industrial Robots

| | By Application | | |
| | Japan | United States | |
	1982	1982	1990 f*
Welding	25%	35%	23%
Materials handling	20	20	12
Assembly	20	2	12
Machine loading	8	15	19
Painting	3	10	6
Foundry	2	15	11
Other	22	3	17
Totals	100%	100%	100%

*f=forecast

killed every year in situations like the one described, authorities hope to save lives with these hazardous-duty robots.[12]

Other contemporary uses of robots are just as remarkable. Robotic arms capable of locating points within two-thousandths of an inch have been used in brain surgery to remove tissue samples of tumors for biopsy. By the time this book is in print, similar devices will be used to drain abscesses, implant radioactive pellets directly into tumors, repair blood vessels, and aim laser beams at diseased tissue with pinpoint accuracy. The sunken ocean liner *Titanic* was located in September 1985 by the *Argo,* a robot vehicle equipped with sonar and photographic equipment. Researchers are also developing robots for use in agriculture. "Agrimation" robots, now being engineered, will be able to pick apples, grapes, oranges, and other fruit. "Cowbots" being perfected in the Netherlands will use a system of heat sensors and visual guidance to mechanically milk cows. Some have even speculated that the first pets in space will be small robotic animals that mimic cats and dogs. Elementary versions of such devices have already appeared on the commercial market. Domestic robots are available that can fix drinks, fetch the newspaper, and perform other minor housekeeping chores. Robotic systems also exist that can monitor the temperature, humidity, and lighting of a house, while providing its occupants with tireless security against intruders.

Even so, human imaginings about robots far exceed the most fantastic uses to which they are presently put. We don't have units like C3PO, capable of translating a million intergalactic dialects. We have no Number 5s, like the star of the fanciful movie *Short Circuit,* which told the story of a robot coming to life after being struck by lightning. Could such a thing ever really happen? Will the extraordinary robotic creatures of *Star Wars* fame ever really exist? And if they do come into being, how will they affect human workers? The first two questions will evoke wildly differing answers depending on whom you ask. No one knows what the future of robotics holds, what kinds of peculiar mechanical lifeforms might eventually be hatched in the research laboratory. As for the third question, some tentative answers are already possible about the effect robotics will have on the human workforce. Surprisingly little, says at least one researcher, who speculates that even with 100,000 robots at work in the 1990s (nearly nine times the number presently working) only 300,000 workers will find themselves displaced. This number represents only 0.3 percent of the present labor force. If such workers unhappily suffer a drop in earnings, it is projected that, within five years, they will have recouped the wages lost.[13] This negative impact, however slight, is a by-product rather than the true aim of robotics. What researchers are really after are machines that will, in the words of science writer Isaac Asimov, do the "grunt work," leaving humans with more leisure time.

Finance, Banking, and Retailing

Without computers, the banking and financial industries as we know them could not function. It has been estimated, for example, that over 19 billion personal checks are written and processed in this country each year. If all of these pieces of paper needed to be processed manually, with each check having to be handled an average of six times, up to one-third of the adult population of the United States would eventually be required to process checks. It seems clear that the computerization of check-processing procedures, which is accomplished by way of MICR (*m*agnetic *i*nk *c*haracter *r*ecognition) and OCR (*o*ptical *c*haracter *r*ecognition) equipment, has been more than just an enhancement to the banking industry. It has become an absolute necessity.

The computerization of the banking and financial industries hasn't stopped, however, with the automation of check processing procedures. Relatively recent advances, such as electronic funds transfer, automated tellers, and point-of-sale (POS) systems, have brought us closer to the day when we might find ourselves living in a "cashless society." In the hypothetical cashless society, money is largely an abstraction that exists in the form of numbers passed from one computer system to another. Though we aren't yet close to this point, current technology gives us glimpses of the future.

Electronic Funds Transfer Systems (EFTS)

An **electronic funds transfer system (EFTS)** is a computerized system that processes information about financial transactions and facilitates exchanges of this information. When a business pays employees' salaries by transferring funds directly to their checking accounts it is using one type of EFTS. Making a payment on a loan or making an investment by having your bank deduct money from your account and transfer it directly to another bank or financial institution is another way of taking advantage of EFTS.

A typical EFTS uses computers, telephone lines, and satellites to link customers with banks and banks with other banks and institutions. This worldwide network weaves blanks into computerized communities. It has been estimated that, in today's world, more funds are transferred each month via EFTS than were transferred in traditional ways in all the years before EFTS were introduced.[14]

Automated Teller Machines (ATMs)

One popular use of EFTS is the **automated teller machine (ATM)**, an interactive device that allows customers to access a bank's computer and complete transactions, such as cash withdrawals, without direct human intervention (see Figure 15.11). By 1985 over 55,000 of these machines had been installed in banks, airports, shopping malls, and grocery stores, as well as on street corners in commercial areas. ATMs, used primarily for cash withdrawals and deposits, average about 200 transactions per day per machine. A survey found that, in nearly half of all U.S. households, at least one person uses an ATM.[15]

Banks and other savings institutions issue a plastic card to a customer, who inserts the card into an ATM, types in identification and transaction codes, and specifies an amount in order to complete banking such transactions as cash with-

Figure 15.11 An automated teller machine (ATM). Using the keyboard the customer gains direct access to her account and can then perform a variety of banking functions.

drawals, deposits, and transfers of funds from one account to another. In the future, ATMs may be able to cash payroll checks and make change.

Through recently installed networks, such as CIRRUS, it is possible to get cash from an ATM in just about any part of the United States, even though the money is withdrawn from your account in your local bank. Headquartered in Detroit, the CIRRUS network links virtually all major cities in the country. CIRRUS and similar interstate networks have shown that it is technically possible for funds to be transferred from almost any point in the world to another. These networks consist of ATMs, which are connected to the local bank's computer, which in turn is interconnected with national computer systems, which in turn could be interconnected with international computer systems. All one needs to participate in such networks is an identification card, such as a VISA card, which is validated at your local bank. In many ways, CIRRUS represents the full evolution of a nationwide computerized banking system. Such networks might one day allow any type of banking transaction to be completed from any point in the country.

Point-of-Sale (POS) Systems

A **point-of-sale (POS) system** consists of a series of computer terminals located where goods and services are paid for. Like an ATM, a POS terminal is connected to one or more computers. When a customer buys a product or service, the operator enters the amount of the purchase into the register or terminal. In the most enhanced POS systems, this amount is then deducted directly from the customer's account. POS systems can do more than simply transfer funds from one account to another, however. They can also be used by the seller of a product or service to keep sales or inventory records, to authorize checks, and to verify credit cards. Because POS systems enable goods and services to be exchanged for money without requiring the actual exchange of cash, they increase the degree to which business can operate on a cashless basis.

You've undoubtedly seen the bar code called the **universal product code (UPC)** on packaged goods in supermarkets and convenience stores. Its extensive adoption has had a major effect on retailing, because it carries a lot of information (see Figure 15.12) and can be read by laser code readers in the shape of a wand or a fixed scanning station. (Figure 15.13). The bar code printed on each package stores up to 12 decimal digits. You can see the 12 slots, or zones, of the code marked at the top of the sample in Figure 15.12. The 2 outer digits control and check the scanning, which makes it possible to scan the code forward, backwards, or sideways. The inner 10 digits contain two fields, one for the product number and the other for a unit price. A combination of thick and thin bars represents each of the 10 numbers from 1 through 9, which you can decipher by looking at the bars directly above those numbers in the diagram.

The UPC code has great flexibility and is being used for a variety of other functions, especially remote entry of data. Jobs that lend themselves to this technology include inventory control and patient monitoring, as well as standard POS functions.

It would be difficult to overestimate the impact that computers have had on the financial, banking, and retailing fields. The technology behind the evolution of such systems as EFTS, ATMs, and POS systems has all but eliminated the need for certain face-to-face banking transactions. Ours may not yet be the cashless society, but our movement toward a state of affairs in which actual money seldom changes hands can be neither ignored nor denied.

The Social Effects of Computerization

James Martin, author of over 30 texts and references on computing, describes contemporary computer developments as "a technological revolution of potentially greater impact than the industrial revolution." He continues with the following assessment:

> New societal patterns are being forged in the crucible of high technology. The change in the next 40 years will be as great as that in the last 80 years. Sometimes it seems

Figure 15.12 The universal product code (UPC) is appearing on more and more supermarket items.

that technology is moving so fast that it is out of control. Soon it will be moving much faster. The era of artificial intelligence has barely begun yet. Computers are being used to design ever-better computers. The explosive growth in computer power speeds up the development of genetics engineering, robotics, weapons systems, and all other technologies. How can the institutions of today's society—government, jobs, schools, the family—stand the strain of change?[16]

Some might answer this challenging question pessimistically, pointing out how computerization in businesses may leave individuals more vulnerable by centralizing management control, distancing them from other people, and eliminating or downgrading their jobs. After spending several hours reviewing the research on the social effects of computers, Judith Perrolle concludes that

Because the social world involves conflict and the exercise of power, you should be prepared for political struggles over the future of computers. . . . If you can decide which way you want the information revolution to go, you will be in a position to act on

Figure 15.13 Laser-powered bar code readers are able to identify a code by scanning from several angles simultaneously. Here codes are read by a wand as part of an inventory–taking process.

your beliefs—often in minor ways, but nevertheless contributing to the social construction of a reality you desire. . . . We are participants in social change, not mere observers or recipients of it.[17]

Meanwhile, if greater investments were made in research on the social impact of computerization, it might be possible to choose with a greater degree of confidence how we will coexist with computers.

COMPUTERS IN THE PROFESSIONS

Professionals—doctors, lawyers, accountants, and others—use computers more than any other general occupational group, probably because they depend so much on specialized information. Entry to a profession demands many years of education and training, and increasingly that education includes skills in computer applications. Personal computers and professionals coexist in our cultural consciousness, perhaps because so much software is well suited to the needs of the professional or perhaps because it is advertised as "for professional productivity." With allegiance both to an employer and to a profession, the professional has diverse information needs and operates fairly autonomously. Most professionals must write letters, organize files, prepare budgets, learn new techniques, and juggle priorities. Some professions, especially those that are health related, use specialized computer-based systems and techniques daily.

In this final section, we shift our focus from the company to the individual, to those persons called professionals. Special attention is given to professionals involved in health (medicine), law, and journalism.

Health

Many doctors and nurses were exposed to computers early. Hospitals began putting their patient records into computer systems in the early 1960s. In fact, the first studies of people's attitudes toward computerization were conducted among nurses at a New England mental hospital. These nurses felt quite positive about their work with computerized records, despite some fears about loss of their own job functions to the computer. This is still more or less the prevailing attitude toward computerization.

Bedside Information Systems

Computerized patient records today may include daily test results, diet information, and prescriptions. With hundreds of data items for each patient accumulating every day, medical databases offer a rich foundation for software designed to augment diagnostic decisions. A customized database package can help find case histories of previous patients with very similar medical profiles. After reviewing these cases, doctors can usually make more informed diagnoses and develop more effective treatment plans. And expert systems that can utilize the amassed data from daily hospital records have been applied to the diagnosis of illnesses on a limited basis. Among these expert systems are Stanford's MYCIN, which diagnoses blood infections; PUFF, which analyzes breath data to diagnose cardiopulmonary problems; and CADUCEUS, which can diagnose hundreds of different disease profiles.

Intensive care units have been equipped with computer-based patient-monitoring systems for years. These machines continuously measure the vital signs—heartbeat, breathing, brain waves, and temperature—and check for any irregular patterns in these streams of data. The computer automatically sounds an alarm if any of these signs falls outside a predetermined range. More complex patterns are scanned and checked by pattern-recognition software. Persons who are susceptible to seriously irregular heartbeats sometimes depend on these patient-monitoring systems after they leave the hospital. These persons can carry a recording device with them and periodically transmit their data over phone lines to the hospital's computer for analysis of their vital organs' performance.

Figure 15.14 CAT scans are images generated by computer from an x-ray, which give doctors a cross-sectional view of the body.

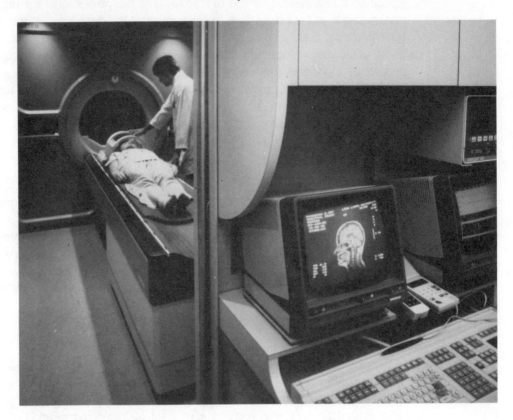

Medical Imaging

Imaging consists simply of reading, analyzing, and graphically displaying data that come in two- or three-dimensional form. *Medical imaging* collects and displays such data for medical purposes. The best-known medical imaging computer tomography (CT), is more often called **computer axial tomography (CAT)** and is commonly called a "CAT scan." *Tomography,* the Greek word for "slice," is used in this context, because the method shows the doctor a cross-sectional "slice" of the human body (see Figure 15.14). CAT scanners first use x rays to get many cross-sectional images, then the computer assembles a composite image that can be displayed in brilliant three-dimensional colors. This technology is particularly good at detecting brain tumors and consequently reduces the need for exploratory surgery.

Another, more recent form of scanning, called *nuclear magnetic resonance (NMR),* produces even sharper images and doesn't require x rays. The NMR machine houses a huge magnet that surrounds the patient and creates a very focused magnetic field that jostles molecules in body cells. The speed at which these molecules readjust their position, called *resonance,* makes it possible to differentiate various types of tissue. Both types of computer-controlled machines have made major contributions to cancer treatment by assisting in the early detection of malignancies.

Medical Education and Consulting

Some of the most popular instructional computer simulations have been designed to train students in medical procedures. For example, *Emergency Room,* from the University of Illinois PLATO system, teaches medical interns what to do when a rapidly fading accident victim arrives in the emergency room. The simulated situations are captivating and challenging, providing many hours of stimulating, but potentially life-saving experience.

Nurses, doctors, dentists, and other medical professionals have an unusually heavy responsibility to keep their knowledge and skills up to date within their areas of expertise. Not only do they benefit from computer-assisted instructional approaches, but they increasingly rely on software rather than on personal consultants to reach medical decisions. For example, drug conflict programs help professionals decide what drugs to prescribe by predicting complicating interactions between a drug and food and drugs that the patient has already taken. Although this software is most likely to be found on hospital computers, ads in *M.D. Computing* magazine offer these programs for microcomputers.

Computers play another important type of consulting role in organ matching. Finding organ transplant donors is often difficult because of the close match needed for successful transplants. Several organizations maintain computerized databases of registered organ recipient candidates. Through sophisticated electronic networks, the availability of an organ can be communicated, a satisfactory match found, and the organ shipped thousands of miles within a matter of hours.

Law

A 1984 survey found that attorneys typically spend about 25 percent of their time writing or drafting documents, about 23 percent in research, and about 7 percent planning and carrying out administrative duties. These are all tasks that can benefit from standard, off-the-shelf software, which implies that, if the average lawyer decided to take full advantage of contemporary computing, he or she might spend as much as 45 percent of his or her work time with a computer. Lawyers and criminal justice professionals use computers to produce documents, to access different kinds of databases, and to help organize the large volume of information associated with their daily work.

Law offices are small businesses, too. They have the same needs as other small businesses for planning, correspondence, accounting, payroll, billing, mailing lists, inventory, and scheduling. Very often, the computer first joins the law office to assist with these routine functions. But once it's in the door, people find other specialized things for the computer to do.

One such specialized application is the use of computers to search on-line databases. Westlaw, QL Systems, and Lexis are the three best-known on-line services specializing in legal information. Legal professionals, who frequently must pore over a maze of court decisions for precedents and decisions that might influence the outcome of their own cases, regard these databases as indispensable sources of information. Lexis, for example, catalogs some 500,000 court decisions in addition to some 60-odd years of administration rulings, trade regulations, and laws governing securities and tax issues. To summon up the landmark 1973 proabortion ruling made by the Supreme Court in *Roe v. Wade,* for example, the attorney simply types in the name of the case. Less specific searches can be initiated by typing in the legal topic and appropriate codes—"grand theft," for example. Retrieval times on Lexis, which is owned and operated by Mead Data Central of Dayton, Ohio, average no more than 20 seconds. Days, even weeks, of the attorney's time are saved, making legal services considerably less expensive.

For general information, other handy on-line systems, such as Dialog, are also available. Dialog is a collection of over 100 databases on such crucial subjects as government, the physical sciences, humanities, and health. It also includes a massive Claims/Patent file that covers all patents ever filed in the United States. Trademarkscan, part of the Dialog offerings, catalogs information about U.S. registered or pending trademarks. Another database service, The New York Times Information Service, similarly catalogs and abstracts information from some 20 news services. Databases like these are admittedly not easy to use, and pity the poor user who should stumble into, say, the Dialog system without knowing exactly how to manipulate its search and retrieval functions. The meter begins to run from the first nanosecond that the user has signed on and been admitted, and charges for the blundering beginner can mount up at a frightening rate. But with experience and research being conducted on artificial intelligence, online databases will doubtless become progressively easier to use and therefore less expensive.

A large Chicago law firm employing 150 attorneys illustrates the evolution of computer applications so typical in this profession. Its office was a model of automation for the early 1980s: a minicomputer provided shared word processing and electronic mail from each of a dozen workstations. Several law clerks regularly used the terminals to search external databases, as well as their own case files. One day, an attorney noticed a familiar name in the client directory printout. The name that caught his eye belonged to the plaintiff in a civil suit in which he represented the defendant. The attorney had inadvertently walked into a conflict of interest, not knowing that someone else in the firm had recently represented the other party. To solve this problem, the firm established a policy for searching the client database for any conflicts of interest before taking on a new client.

Journalism

Writing is the most essential and common job assigned to journalists, and word processing provides numerous features that enhance the productivity of writers, reporters, and editors of newspapers or magazines. It is very rare today to find journalists doing their writing and rewriting by hand or even by typewriter. Because journalists, especially freelance writers, are often on the go, word process-

ing presented a number of problems before the advent of light, portable computers. In 1983 Radio Shack began distributing Model 100, the first laptop computer that could be used for word processing. Within a couple of years, an estimated 50,000 journalists had acquired one. Even though this model had a screen display of only eight lines, with up to 40 characters in each line, it had a built-in modem that allowed quick and easy telephone connection to transmit story drafts back to the home office. Today many journalists rely on laptop computers wherever they are (see Figure 15.15).

Whereas 15 years ago you couldn't find a large pressroom without typewriters, now you would be hard pressed to find a pressroom without computers and telephone jacks for modems. The new technology is not only convenient for reporters, it also gives their newspapers an edge in the race to print late-breaking news and scoop the competition.

The database of choice for the typical journalism student or professional is without a doubt NEXIS, offered by Mead Data Central. NEXIS indexes and files away every word written and printed in such periodicals as the *New York Times, Washington Post, Christian Science Monitor, Time* magazine, and *Newsweek,* along with information from other exotic sources, such as the BBC Summary of World Broadcasts. Information can be searched and retrieved by topic, writer, and even common phrases and expressions, such as "remains to be seen" or "obstacles to be overcome." Expense and complexity are the major drawbacks of using NEXIS. Finding and printing a dozen articles can run into hundreds of dollars. But reckoned against the labor and time that must be expended to conduct such searches manually, NEXIS is clearly a valuable time saver.

The Information Age will inevitably spawn new forms of journalism, and computer networks already seem to be pointing the way. For instance, on-line newsletters are popular for material that has high obsolescence, but a narrow audience. Author Mike Greenly invented a technique he called *interactive journalism* to write *Chronicle: The Human Side of AIDS* (Irvington, 1986). Using a laptop computer and long hours of electronic networking, Greenly discovered new ideas, informants, and expertise by conversing on several electronic network services about his findings. He also applied interactive journalism to workshop and convention reporting. Before going to a convention, he collected questions as well as a small fee from members of his computer network. As soon as he obtained answers to these questions, he transmitted them back to the network to see if more clarification was needed. This procedure allowed him to collect more information before leaving the convention. Creative journalists who find new forms of communication technology challenging rather than objectionable will undoubtedly carve out new roles for the journalists of the future.

SUMMARY

In the three decades that business has romanced the computer, this new, flexible technology has become integral to the very fabric of our economic institutions. Historically, the organizational adoption of computing follows a common path from routine processing of basic transactions with simple data to the handling of enormous, complex databases and the confrontation of confounding problems with indefinite solutions. The history of office technology (Figure 15.16) illustrates how the recent growth of computer applications, while embedded within the larger expansion of technology, is proceeding very rapidly. Now that the computer has joined up with complex data networks, new structures for organizational communication may yield an even speedier rate of impact.

Beginning with office automation and management information systems, we have seen the diversity of benefits accompanying computerization. Many of the uses of computers in manufacturing and the professions would have been impossible to predict only a few years ago. OA specialists, ergonomic experts, MIS professionals, and computer engineers in manufacturing all play the critical role of mediating between human needs and technological objectives. Without this process in the harnessing of the electronic potential, the computer would not have become the favored machine of offices and factories and the popular instrument of professionals.

Figure 15.16 History of office technology showing three phases of office automation.

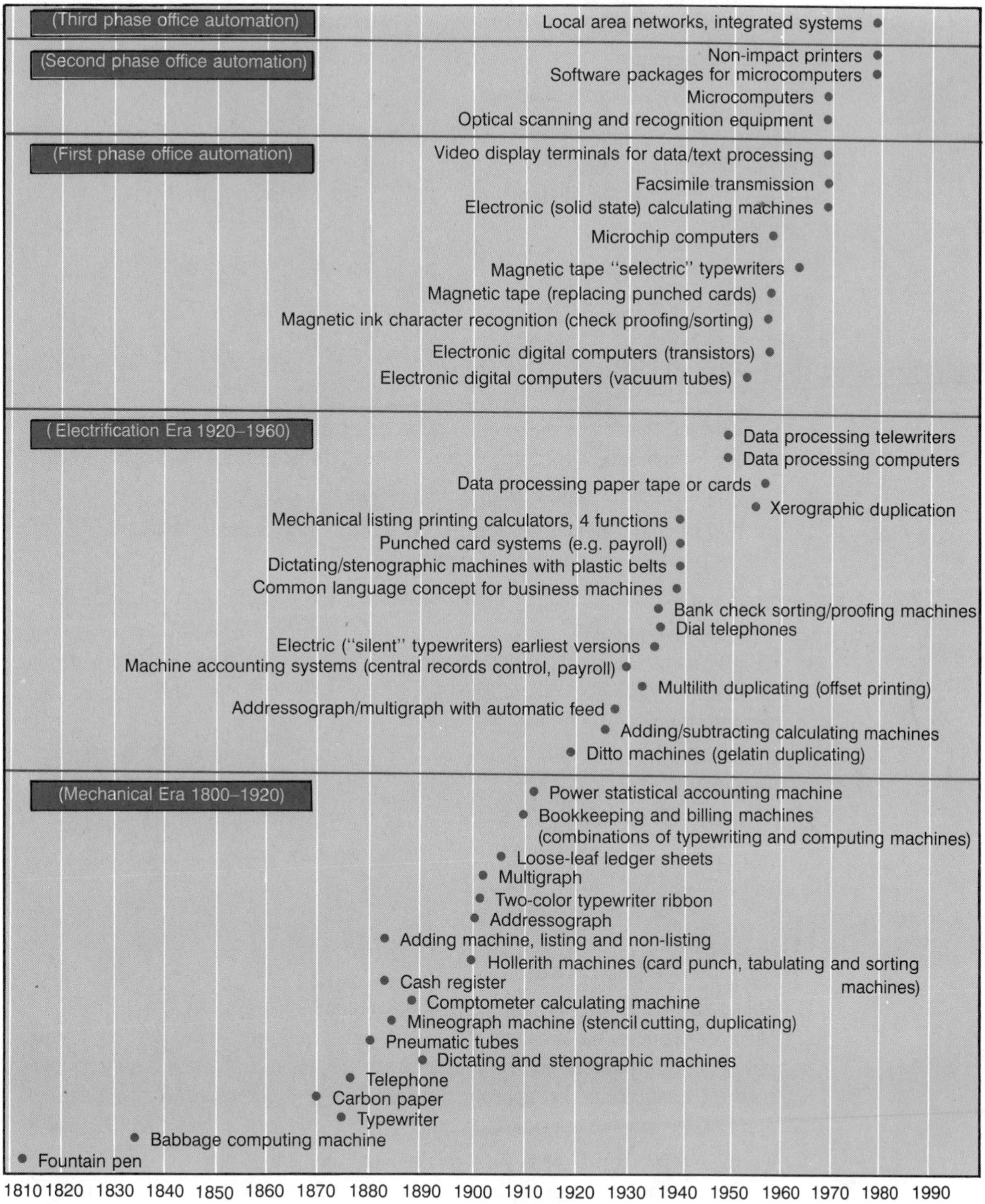

(Third phase office automation)
Local area networks, integrated systems •

(Second phase office automation)
Non-impact printers •
Software packages for microcomputers •
Microcomputers •
Optical scanning and recognition equipment •

(First phase office automation)
Video display terminals for data/text processing •
Facsimile transmission •
Electronic (solid state) calculating machines •
Microchip computers •
Magnetic tape "selectric" typewriters •
Magnetic tape (replacing punched cards) •
Magnetic ink character recognition (check proofing/sorting) •
Electronic digital computers (transistors) •
Electronic digital computers (vacuum tubes) •

(Electrification Era 1920–1960)
• Data processing telewriters
• Data processing computers
Data processing paper tape or cards •
• Xerographic duplication
Mechanical listing printing calculators, 4 functions •
Punched card systems (e.g. payroll) •
Dictating/stenographic machines with plastic belts •
Common language concept for business machines •
• Bank check sorting/proofing machines
• Dial telephones
Electric ("silent" typewriters) earliest versions •
Machine accounting systems (central records control, payroll) •
• Multilith duplicating (offset printing)
Addressograph/multigraph with automatic feed •
• Adding/subtracting calculating machines
• Ditto machines (gelatin duplicating)

(Mechanical Era 1800–1920)
• Power statistical accounting machine
• Bookkeeping and billing machines
(combinations of typewriting and computing machines)
• Loose-leaf ledger sheets
• Multigraph
• Two-color typewriter ribbon
• Addressograph
• Adding machine, listing and non-listing
• Hollerith machines (card punch, tabulating and sorting machines)
• Cash register
• Comptometer calculating machine
• Mineograph machine (stencil cutting, duplicating)
• Pneumatic tubes
• Dictating and stenographic machines
• Telephone
• Carbon paper
• Typewriter
• Babbage computing machine
• Fountain pen

1810 1820 1830 1840 1850 1860 1870 1880 1890 1900 1910 1920 1930 1940 1950 1960 1970 1980 1990

automated teller machine (ATM)

computer axial tomography (CAT)

computer conferencing

computer-integrated manufacturing (CIM)

decision support system (DSS)

electronic funds transfer system (EFTS)

end-user computing

ergonomics

imaging

information center

management information systems (MIS)

office automation (OA)

point-of-sale (POS) system

programmable automation (PA)

robot

universal product code (UPC)

DISCUSSION QUESTIONS

1. Considering that office automation often requires costly purchases and disruptive changes in procedure, why do so many offices move in that direction?

2. What is *technostress* and how is it related to ergonomics?

3. Identify basic business transactions and explain how computerization improves the way an organization processes them.

4. What is a management information system? What distinguishes it from a decision support system?

5. What types of reports and information do different types (or levels) of managers need? Activate your imagination by considering specific businesses—a car dealership, for example.

6. What is an end-user? How might an end-user be helped by an information center?

7. What are the likely positive and negative effects of computerization for society? What implications do these effects have for the values that most people share?

EXERCISES

1. Select someone you know who works in a small business, such as a store, farm, or professional practice. Arrange to interview this individual about automation, information, and computers in their business. Before the interview read the chapter and list appropriate questions you might ask. Write a summary of the interview using the terminology introduced in this chapter.

2. Go to several stores (or review catalogs of companies) that sell computer furniture. Make a list of all the features or settings that you would need to consider to select the best, ergonomic workstation furniture.

3. Spend some time working at different types of computer-centered work areas. Describe (drawings are helpful) what you think would be the best workstation environment for you.

4. Select a profession, perhaps one that you are preparing for. Do some research and list the significant ways in which computers are used by persons in that profession.

NOTES

1. Karen Berney, "The Cutting Edge," *Nation's Business,* April 1986, p. 54.

2. Karen Freifeld, "The VDT's," *Health,* March 1985, p. 75.

3. Craig Brody, *Technostress* (Reading, Mass.: Addison-Wesley, 1984).

4. Susan G. Hill and Karl Kroemer, "Preferred Declination in the Line of Sight," *Human Factors* 28, 2 (1986):127–134.

5. Berney.

6. Daniel Goleman, "The Human–Computer Connection," *Psychology Today,* March 1984, p. 20.

7. *American National Standard for VDT Workstations* (July 1986). The Human Factors Society, P.O. Box 1369, Santa Monica, Calif., 90406.

8. Goleman.

9. Ibid.

10. "Boldly Going Where No Robot Has Gone Before," *Business Week,* 22 December 1986, p. 45.

11. Stuart F. Brown, "Building Cars with Machines That See," *Popular Science,* October 1985, p. 86.

12. Dennis Hevesi, "Steel Claws and Eyes: Robots Help the Police Take Place of Humans in Dangerous Situations," *New York Times,* 18 March 1987, sec. 2, p. 1.

13. Anthony Patrick Carnevale, *Jobs For the Nation: Challenges for a Society Based on Work* (Washington, D.C.: American Society for Training and Development, 1985).

14. Ahmed S. Zaki, "Regulation of EFT: Impact and Legal Issues," *Communications of the ACM,* February, 1983, p. 112.

15. David Gifford and Alfred Spector, "The CIRRUS Banking Network," *Communications of the ACM,* August, 1985, p. 797.

16. James Martin, *Technology's Crucible* (Englewood Cliffs, N.J.: Prentice-Hall, 1987), p. 2.

17. Judith Perrolle, *Computers and Social Change* (New York: Wiley, 1987).

16 Computers in Government, Education, the Arts, and Science

The electronic machines we call computers have been in use for only four decades, but societies and cultures have existed for many millennia. With such a brief history it seems remarkable that computers have already begun to change our basic social institutions. In this chapter we investigate the computer's effect on government, education, the arts, and science. We cannot bring the full impact of computers into focus without seeing how the computer fits into these fundamental arenas.

Like the early days of the automobile, it is impossible to anticipate many of the ways in which the computer will change society. The early signs of social transformation, however, are described in this chapter. First you will discover how computers allow large government agencies to deliver essential public services such as law enforcement and emergency aid. After reviewing the role of computers in defense and in local government, you will explore the in roads computers are making in education. Not all instructional software improves on other methods of learning, but computers make many new teaching and learning strategies feasible.

While computers do not yet rival human artists, they are among the instruments with which people produce creative works. You will see a number of examples of computer-augmented art from motion pictures, drawing, painting, literature, and music. Computers from micros to supercomputers also support the rapid expansion of science. Simulation, complex mathematical models, and parallel processors have opened up entire new fields for explorations—the space program is but one example. The computer's role is not only immense, but it is integral to everyday life in our society.

GOVERNMENT USE OF COMPUTERS

Modern government must forecast trends, plan services, enforce laws, and protect the welfare of citizens, and performing all these functions makes it almost totally dependent on computers. If the nation's population is aging, shrinking, expanding, or growing younger, the government must know, so that it can plan accordingly. Every change in the population curve means revised forecasts for housing, schools, health care services, social security, and national defense. And only computers are capable of doing the massive counting and statistical tabulating necessary to produce the needed information.

It is no exaggeration to say that the complete extent to which federal, state, and local governments depend on computers is probably unknowable. Large and small, thousands of government agencies depend on computer data processing to a degree that can only be hinted at by a single chapter in a textbook.

The Federal Government

The numbers are so astronomical and the data so scattered that no one can definitely say how many files on private citizens are maintained by the federal government. Estimates have been made, however, that there are some 4 billion dossiers on citizens in the computer archives of government agencies—an average of 18 files for every living man, woman, and child.[1] Government agencies are so swamped with paperwork that no imaginable manual system of recording and retrieval can cope with it. The Patent Office has 27 million documents on hand, with 300,000 being temporarily lost at any given instant.[2] The Veterans Administration must administer the records of 13.5 million veterans. The Department of Housing and Urban Development keeps dossiers on 4.5 million Americans who have purchased homes through its loan guarantee program. Without computers, the storage space required by government agencies would transform the city of Washington, D.C., into an enormous warehouse for federal paperwork. Here we will discuss a few of the other agencies that rely most heavily on computers.

The Internal Revenue Service

The Internal Revenue Service (IRS) annually processes over 95 million tax returns. Returns are sorted by high-speed bar code readers capable of processing 1040 forms at the rate of 30,000 per hour, checked by computers for mathematical consistency, and stored on magnetic tape (Figure 16.1). Computers cross-check and analyze the returns against information received from employers on supporting documents, such as W-2 forms. Returns are also matched against a secret statistical profile and selected for manual checking depending on whether or not they conform or deviate from the expected norm. Computers randomly select another 30,000 returns for audit.

The IRS has taken a stab at even further automating its return processing. In a 1986 pilot program conducted in selected cities, 25,000 returns were electronically filed by professional tax preparers, who were linked to the IRS computers by modems. Acknowledgment of the returns was made within a day, and refunds were issued within three weeks. If requested, refunds were credited directly to a taxpayer's bank account. The IRS plans to institute this program nationwide in the 1990s, using such major tax-preparing firms as H&R Block.[3]

The U.S. Census Bureau

Thanks to government computers operated by the U.S. Census Bureau, we know that, as of January 1, 1987, there were 243 million of us; that we experienced 8.7 deaths per 1,000 population the year before; and that the general fertility rate of 64.9 live births for every 1,000 women between the ages of 15 and 44 is the lowest recorded since 1930.[4] Figures of this magnitude would take human workers years to compile and calculate.

In fact, as you will see in Chapter 18, it was the U.S. Census Bureau's pressing need for an efficient method of counting that led Herman Hollerith (1860–1929) to invent the first commercial tabulating machine. Initially used in the 1890 census, the machine took only six weeks to tabulate what was then a population of 62,622,250 Americans. The colossus we know as IBM eventually evolved from Hollerith's company.

Social Security

The Social Security Administration keeps records on 100 million workers and makes monthly disbursements to 36 million retirees around the world. An equivalent manual system to accomplish this task would require hundreds of thousands of clerical workers and wouldn't be nearly as efficient.

The Securities and Exchange Commission

The Securities and Exchange Commission (SEC) receives and processes some 6 million pages of documents annually in regulating the affairs and transactions of public corporations. Before EDGAR, an acronym for *E*lectronic *D*ata *G*athering *A*nalysis and *R*etrieval *S*ystem, went on line in 1985 to some 150 corporations, these public documents used to be stored on microfiche cards, and searching them required the physical presence of a courier at an SEC office. EDGAR now offers instant retrieval of documents filed by any of the 10,000 corporations the SEC regulates. Documents electronically submitted to EDGAR via modem are available for on-line retrieval an hour later through a commercial telecommunications system, such as GTE's Telenet. EDGAR uses artificial intelligence software to translate corporate data on gross and net income into standard and readable formats and to allow complex word searches of corporate records. Officials estimate that EDGAR will save some $30 million in printing and postage costs when it becomes available to all public corporations in 1989.

The Legislative Branch

Computers are also being used in the legislative branch of the federal government. The LEGIS system provides members of Congress with information on the status and content of all legislative proposals. SOPAD (*S*ummary of *P*roceedings *a*nd *D*ebates) tracks the status of all legislative proceedings in the House and Senate. FAPRS (the Federal Assistance Program Resource System) informs members about assistance programs that might benefit their constituents. The aim of these systems is to simplify and make more manageable the complex and tedious process of passing laws and representing a constituency.

Defense and Security

The mainland United States is guarded by an invisible electronic trip-wire, monitored by tireless computer systems that are linked to infrared, atmospheric, space, and satellite sensors. This early-warning system, with headquarters in the

Cheyenne Mountain installation of the North American Aerospace Defense Command (NORAD), guards against nuclear missile attack (see Figure 16.2). Missile warning displays located under tons of granite in Cheyenne Mountain, Wyoming, are intended to show and track the flight of incoming enemy warheads and allow an appropriate response.

NORAD is presently the largest user of computers for defense, but that distinction promises to shift in favor of the proposed *Strategic Defense Initiative (SDI),* popularly referred to as *Star Wars.* Should it ever become a reality, Star Wars will involve the use of supercomputers to monitor sensors from thousands of satellites and to intercept incoming missiles. No one knows how the final system will work, but theoretically it will shoot down missiles by bouncing laser beams from orbiting satellites equipped with mirrors. The entire system, from detection of the incoming missiles, analysis of their trajectories, and destruction by laser beams bounced off "killer satellites," will be run by computers. Much debate swirls around whether or not the system as proposed is even feasible. But one thing is plain: existing programs and computers can't even begin to cope with the complexity of

Star Wars. Significant advances in the design and development of hardware and software will have to be made before the envisioned system can work.

One element of Star Wars that troubles critics is the amount of decision making the system will cede to computers. As a Department of Defense report puts it, "It seems clear . . . that some degree of automation in the decision to commit weapons is inevitable if a ballistic missile system is to be at all feasible."[5] In other words, a computer will decide when and whether to pull the trigger.

Especially troubling about this autonomy is the possibility that the computer might make a mistake. History tells us that such a possibility, even in the most sophisticated hardware, isn't far-fetched. In the early 1960s, for example, the U.S. early-warning computer in Thule, Greenland, warned of incoming Russian missiles. The system had been activated by the rising moon. In June of 1984, the Strategic Air Command in Nebraska received two attack warnings caused by a faulty chip in a Data General multiplexer.

Both false alarms were triggered by hardware failure, but similar miscues might also result from programming errors. Star Wars will require hundreds of thousands, possibly millions, of lines of programming code, distributed among tracking radar, sensors, launchers and missiles, and will be vastly more complex than any existing program or system. Critics say that even the most painstaking efforts at debugging couldn't guarantee some infinitesimal human error, which might trigger a false alarm and inadvertently fire a rocket. Examples of similar failures include the 1962 Mariner I probe to Venus, which had to be blown up after launch, because according to insiders, a programmer had inserted a period instead of a comma in FORTRAN code; another is the sinking of the H.M.S. *Sheffield* by an Exocet missile fired from an Argentine aircraft during the Falkland Islands War. The *Sheffield*'s computer detected the attack of the French-built Exocet but didn't react, because it had been programmed to defend only against Soviet missiles. Its programmers hadn't anticipated the possibility that the *Sheffield* might one day come under attack by a French missile. Nor can the Star Wars programmers, say critics, anticipate every conceivable possibility.[6] And should an accident occur in an autonomous Stars Wars system, the consequences for all humanity could be catastrophic. The debate continues.

Aside from these mammoth defense systems, all rockets and missiles rely on the use of miniature computers. For example, the U.S. TOW (*t*ube-launched, *o*ptically tracked, *w*ired guided) missile is designed to home in on an enemy tank with a laser beam aimed by the operator. As long as the operator keeps the laser beam focused on the tank, the missile will unerringly hit its target. Third-generation anti-tank missiles will carry several "submunition" warheads fitted with a computer capable of identifying an enemy tank and homing in on it with an infrared sensor.[7] Some sophisticated AMRAAM (*a*dvanced *m*edium-*r*ange *a*ir-to-*a*ir *m*issiles) have the so-called fire-and-forget capability, meaning that they can independently seek out a target without the aid of a human operator. But no existing system, no matter how sophisticated, cedes the decision to fire entirely to a computer.

Local Government

Local governments use computers for a variety of useful, if not exotic, purposes. Cities and neighborhoods use computers for budget monitoring and reporting, for police allocation, and for processing of traffic tickets, to name only a few mundane applications. They use them to prepare bills for water and power usage and to levy millage rates for property taxes. In one example of people versus machine, the homeowners of Dekalb County, Georgia, rose up in protest when they learned that the county government intended to use computers to assess annual inflationary increases in property value. Homeowners had visions of an infallible machine automatically bumping up the assessments on their homes by a horrendously accurate percentage, leading to more and more taxes. The county government was pressured into abandoning its plan and reverting to the more inefficient and inexact system of manually assessing increases.

A significant and life-saving service offered by some local jurisdictions that use computers is the *enhanced 911* emergency system. These systems use address *geocoding* that runs on a database containing the following information:

- The names and locations of all city streets, major buildings, parks, and landmarks
- Every working phone number, along with its listed address and map coordinates to pinpoint it
- The name, address, and location of every emergency service center

When a citizen calls needing help, both the name and the address of the caller appear on the operator's computer screen and are automatically routed to a dispatcher, who either radios an emergency unit or directs the computer to alert the nearest fire station, paramedic service, or police car (see Figure 16.3). The advantages of this system are obvious: even children who don't know their addresses can use it to summon help. Many lives have already been saved by enhanced 911.

Law Enforcement

The scene is a familiar one from television and movies. A police officer pulls over a traffic offender, reaches for the radio, and runs a "make" on the car's license number. What the viewer doesn't see is that the officer's query is relayed by computer to the database maintained at the FBI's *National Crime Information Center* (NCIC). Over 8 million records are stored in this center, which receives calls from local police at the rate of 540,000 per day. Within seconds, the officer knows whether there are any outstanding warrants against the license, whether the car has been reported stolen, and whether its driver is clean. Established by the FBI in 1967, the NCIC is one example of how computers are used in the fight against crime.

Consider another. A single fingerprint has been lifted from an orange Toyota used in a brutal crime in Los Angeles. Before computers, finding this lone

fingerprint (known among law enforcement officials as a "cold make") was impressive only on television police shows, but meaningless in real life, since it would take an expert over 67 years to search the 1.7 million fingerprints in the files of the Los Angeles police for a match. But California had lately installed its new automated fingerprint identification system, manufactured by NEC. Using a laser grid system to read and analyze fingerprints, the NEC computer scanned the file at the rate of 650 prints per second. Three minutes later, it printed out the names of ten suspects whose prints closely matched the one from the Toyota. Richard Ramirez, the name heading the list, was later arrested and charged with being the Los Angeles "night stalker," suspected of 15 brutal murders.[8]

Automated fingerprint identification systems that digitize, store, compare, and retrieve fingerprints are lately the rage in law enforcement (see Figure 16.4). Before them, admitted one law enforcement official, "much of the dusting for prints" was done "for public relations."[9] But with the new machines, cold makes have become hot leads. Using optical disk storage and a memory of 1.6 gigabytes (1.6 billion bytes), the NEC system was credited in its first four months of use in San Francisco with solving 34 crimes, including the 1978 murder of a San Francisco woman, which had consumed six futile years and 1,000 hours of police investigation.

Figure 16.4 The NEC fingerprint identification system is changing the way police departments investigate crimes, giving them a new source of hot leads. This officer is studying one of the millions of fingerprints stored in the San Francisco police department files.

Computer systems that monitor and enforce house arrest are also being proposed as one possible answer to overcrowded prisons. Prisoners sentenced to house arrest—usually first-time offenders or those convicted of minor crimes—keep their daytime jobs but must stay home at nights and on weekends. There are variations on the system, but they operate on a similar principle: the prisoner wears a device that sends a signal to a main computer when the wearer ventures past a specified distance from the house. If the device is disconnected, the computer is alerted, and the police are summoned. States including New Mexico and Florida are experimenting with this system.

As computer systems become more powerful and widely used in law enforcement, civil libertarians worry about a vast potential for invasion of privacy. High on their list of concerns is the consolidation of government computers in a national scheme of data matching and searching. Safeguards built into the present system include a patchwork of computer jurisdictions—federal, state, and local—and the absence of any centralized data-gathering agency. In 1965 the Johnson administration proposed the creation of just such a Federal Data Agency, which would combine and collect all government data under one roof. The proposal had clear advantages in efficiency and expense over the existing system of separate and often duplicate data collection by different departments, but it was greeted with such a storm of protest that it was quickly withdrawn.

In June 1987, however, a variation on the same idea was revived. A proposal made by a federal advisory committee envisions linking the computers of the SEC, NCIC, IRS, Social Security Administration, and other government agencies in a nationwide effort to track and locate crime suspects.[10] The federal panel also recommends the use of NCIC computers to list people suspected of committing crimes even if they haven't been formally charged. Whether or not the proposal will be accepted is unclear; many legislators and citizens oppose any move to establish a centralized computer system that could potentially be used to monitor and invade the private lives of citizens.

COMPUTERS IN EDUCATION

Computers don't forget, unless they blow a chip or encounter a programming bug. And they never tire of the endless drills necessary to impart a basic principle or lesson. Thus, it's no surprise that early and enthusiastic prophesies about the computer predicted that teaching would be among its primary functions. To some extent, these prophesies have been correct. Computers are widely used to teach at nearly all levels of education. But they haven't replaced the textbook, as some had predicted. Nor does it appear likely that they ever will.

There were some 300,000 microcomputers at use in American colleges in 1985.[11] Three out of five entering college freshmen have had at least half a year of computer science in high school. And nearly two-thirds of all colleges and universities had some programs designed to help students acquire computers through loans or at heavily discounted prices. It seems clear that American colleges and universities feel compelled to get in on the "computer revolution."

Computer-Assisted Instruction

The use of computers to teach falls generically under the heading **computer-assisted Instruction (CAI)**. Programs whose main task is teaching are known as **courseware**. Three main types of courseware are (1) drill-and-practice programs, (2) simulations, and (3) tutorials. Each type of program fulfills a specific educational need, which we will briefly discuss.

Drill-and-Practice Programs
Drill-and-practice programs, like the one being used in Figure 16.5, reinforce old lessons rather than teach new ones. Students must know, for example, the basic principle of multiplication before they can profit from a math program like CBS's Catch–a–Cake. In that particular program, an arithmetic problem appears on the screen, while a cake begins to fall to the accompaniment of a tinkling sound. The student "catches" the cake by solving the problem before the cake falls. Otherwise, the cake splatters, and the answer is displayed.

Figure 16.5 Drill and practice programs teach students through repetition of concepts. This girl is using a math program that drills the student on addition.

A wide variety of such drill-and-practice programs is available to teach skills from simple computation to the use of commas. Many use graphics to enliven their drills. In MasterType, for example, students zap letters menacing a space station by quickly and accurately completing a typing drill. And research indicates that, for the most part, such programs work. But they don't work equally well. Those that set a time limit for solving problems appear to have better results than those that do not.[12]

Simulations

Programs that mimic the principles, causes, and effects found in reality are known as **simulations**. CATLAB, one example of a simulation, teaches the principles of genetics by having students breed cats of different colors. Players can select two cats for breeding, tell the computer how many offspring to produce, and instantly view the litter resulting from their genetic experiments. Run for the Money, Millionaire, and Bank President teach the principles of personal finance.

Simulations are clever at mimicking and compressing the principles behind an experience that might otherwise take students tedious months or years to witness. But they also have shortcomings. Used in an unsupervised setting, pro-

Figure 16.6 The *Flight Simulator* screen as it appears to the "pilot." This particular version of the Microsoft program is a game, simulating the experience of flying a plane for the player.

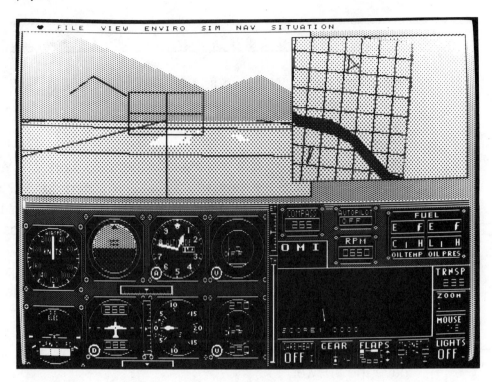

grams like CATLAB tend to bring out the mad scientist in students, who will indiscriminately breed grotesque litters of kittens while ignoring the principles of genetic selection that the program intends to teach.[13] Another drawback is the lack of realism in the controls of even the most effective simulations. Microsoft's Flight Simulator (see Figure 16.6) is one of the best programs of its kind, but a computer keyboard still isn't a realistic substitute for the controls of an aircraft.

Tutorials

Tutorials are programs intended to impart and actively teach principles and theories. In theory, the well-designed tutorial is programmed to detect the student's level of competence and adjust the difficulty of the material accordingly. The most extensive collection of on-line tutorials presently available is PLATO, offered through the services of Control Data. Subscribers to PLATO can take lessons in subjects that range from mastering the basic alphabet to quantum numbers in physics.

Some tutorials are imaginatively designed to engage students in a friendly exchange. Figure 16.7 is an example of the dialog between students and a computer used by young children.

Figure 16.7 This is an amalgam of some educational tutorial programs for elementary mathematics. While this one presumes some skill in using keyboards, the trend is toward systems that only expect the student to communicate to the program with touch-screen panels or pointing devices.

Program: Hello! What would you like to explore today?
Student: We have to study math
Program: What math topic do you want?
Student: Fractions
Program: OK. Here is a practical problem to work on. You want a bike and Sally said she will sell you hers for $27.00. She said that this is only 1/3 of what you would pay for the bike in the store. If Sally is right, how much would it cost in the store?

You may use the calculator keys as shown in the upper right corner of the screen. Do you think you can get the answer?
Student: Yes
Program: Good, press the answer key when you think you have the answer.

But other programs are neither friendly nor well designed. Many suffer from a common defect of permitting scanty student feedback. Screen after screen of instructional material is shown before the student is given a chance to take a stab at problem solving or question answering. In effect, the machine becomes a lecturer and the student a passive listener who is occasionally roused to answer a question.

Learning in the Information Age

Does CAI work? That depends on whom you ask and what journals you read. One study found that CAI was substantially less effective than peer and adult tutoring, although slightly less expensive.[14] But other studies have found that the use of CAI over a year resulted in grade-level gains in student skills that averaged four and a half months per student, with a net cost nearly half as much as peer tutoring.[15] The hard fact, however, is that CAI has had little impact on present educational practice.[16] Drill-and-practice programs abound in the lower grades, and nearly every school system devotes part of the learning day to CAI. But the net effect has been neither revolutionary nor sweeping, as was predicted earlier.

Part of the reason for this lag lies in the poor design of many CAI programs. Some of them don't incorporate even basic educational principles in their programming. They give answers too quickly; they use intrusive and distracting sound effects and graphics; they don't allow for immediate feedback from the user; and they fail to teach by *successive approximations,* in which a lesson is built incrementally on skills taught earlier.[17] Another possible reason why CAI programs haven't revolutionized education is teachers' resistance to being replaced by a machine.[18] This argument fallaciously assumes that a computer is just as capable of imparting complex instruction as a teacher and that, consequently, a rivalry exists between human and machine. The truth is that CAI programs, no matter how sophisticated, can only complement teaching by a human, not replace it. To think otherwise is to fall into the trap of technological boosterism and false prophecy that is evident in the following quotation: "I believe that the . . . is destined to revolutionize our educational system and that in a few years it will supplant largely, if not entirely, the use of textbooks in our schools."[19] This prediction was made by Thomas Alva Edison at the turn of the century. He was talking, not about computers, but about his new invention—the motion picture.

Computers and Scholarship

I'd like to take this opportunity to set forth clearly and specifically my position on foreign policy. In order to to that, I'd first like to explain how I see the world today and indicate to you what I believe America's role in world politics should be. First of all, let me say that the U.S. is not a failure. For 200 years, we have provided the world, through the great experience of democracy, a model—a model that the world is free to follow, but one that we will not impose. Ideally, we would prefer merely to be this model. Unfortunately, the pragmatic realities of the international scene force us to play other roles.[20]

This excerpt from a political speech represents an example of how computers have been used in scholarship. Entitled "Computer-Derived Foreign Policy Speech," the speech was compiled with the help of statistical analysis performed on a computer. To write the speech, the authors identified three dominant approaches to foreign policy—cold war, neoisolationism, and power politics—and applied them to 20 popular issues, such as relations with Russia, treatment of terrorists, and arms control negotiations. They thus generated 60 possible positions (3 approaches times 20 issues) and used them in a survey conducted among residents of Peoria, Illinois. Respondents ranked their feelings about the 60 positions on a scale ranging from neutral to rejected. The computer then culled the statistically most favored positions, which were used as the basis for the speech. On the subject of U.S. intervention in troublespots of the world, for example, the favored position was expressed this way: "I believe that intervention is a diplomatic tool that is needed, even if it is only a threat to maintain a balanced intervention scene. Intervention is not right or wrong, but it may be used rightly or wrongly." This exercise demonstrates the glibness and emptiness of many political appeals.

Computers are also being used to settle some age-old academic arguments about textual authorship. Did Francis Bacon really write under the pen name of William Shakespeare? A computer analysis said no after counting and comparing the word lengths of 200,000 words used by Bacon and 400,000 used by Shakespeare. A projected frequency curve for the lengths of words used by Bacon and Shakespeare didn't match up.[21] Similar analyses have been conducted by other literary detectives using computers. Some researchers have even found that an author's use of such minor words as *a, an, by, to,* and *that* is telling enough for the computer to distinguish among writing styles. Few humans have either the patience or the concentration necessary to manually detect such stylistic subtleties. But computers do. Properly programmed, they can detect tiny variations in usage over thousands of written words.

COMPUTERS AND THE ARTS

Computers aren't the rivals of human artists and will probably not be in the lifetime of anyone reading this book. But they make functional tools that can assist humans in their capacity for creating and enjoying works of art. Here are some examples of how they are presently being used.

Motion Pictures

Computers have been used in the animation of such motion pictures as *The Secret of NIMH.* But possibly their most controversial use in the motion picture industry is for the **colorization** of such classic films as *The Maltese Falcon, It's a Wonderful Life, Captain Blood,* and *The Music Box.* The rationale behind colorization is plainly commercial: surveys indicate that movie watchers, especially those under 20, will buy color videos of the classics, but not black and white ones.[22] Colorization is a tedious process costing hundreds of thousands of dollars and consuming some four hours of computer time for every minute of film. But it is relatively inexpensive compared to remaking an old movie, which can cost millions.

To colorize a film, an art director transfers the 35mm footage to a 1-inch videotape, which is then cleaned up with image-enhancement techniques perfected by NASA for televising its Apollo pictures of the moon. Using a Dudner Graphics Computer that can provide hues from 16,700,000 colors, the art director patiently examines each frame of the film and decides—based on clues from the original script—what colors to use (see Figure 16.8). The art director may use 64 possible colors in each scene and 4,096 for each reel of film. As the scene advances frame by frame, the computer compares the hue assigned to every pixel in the preceding frame and either "paints" it anew or leaves it untouched. The ridge of a hat, for

Figure 16.8 The colorization of a film. Workers in this colorization lab use a computer program which goes through a film frame by frame, comparing each to the one before it, and then either "painting" in selected colors, or continuing on to the next frame, based on the results of the comparison.

example, may have to be shaded from frame to frame as a character shifts position. At any time in the "painting" of a scene, the art director can intervene and make corrections.

Colorizing a film doesn't mean destroying the black-and-white original. For that matter, a television viewer can eliminate the effects of movie colorization by turning off the color on the set. What colorization offers viewers is a choice between the original film and the computer version. Two companies—Colorization, Inc., of Toronto, and Color Systems Technology of Hollywood—plan to colorize many more of the classics in spite of protests from some critics and movie directors.

Art

What did La Gioconda look like when she was first created? She was painted by her artist, Leonardo da Vinci, around 1503. But in 1550, a restorer daubed at her hands and brows and added a coat of green-brown varnish as a preservative. Some 400 years later, she looks frumpy, thick-set, and gloomy. She poses against a background of muddy sky, and her face is fissured by *craquelure*—age crackling. That is what *Mona Lisa,* da Vinci's most famous painting, looks like today.

Figure 16.9 *Mona Lisa* undergoes computerized restoration. Pictured here is the digitized version of the painting, with certain areas of the painting highlighted.

Working with a high-quality photograph obtained from the Louvre, image enhancers tried their hand at computer recreation of da Vinci's masterpiece. Figure 16.9 shows *Mona Lisa* undergoing this process. The picture was digitized at NASA's Jet Propulsion Laboratory into 6 million pixels, and the overcoat varnish was subtracted from the image. The brown sky turned blue, the lady's skin changed from yellow to alabaster, and her gown acquired a greenish tint.[23] Similar experiments at image enhancement are being tried on other aging artistic masterpieces, if only to give us a fresher glimpse of how these canvases might have looked when first painted.

Original computer art also exists, but it doesn't rival human efforts. In one interesting experiment in artificial intelligence, however, the British artist Harold Cohen created Aaron, a simulation that uses a drawing machine known as a *turtle* to make felt-tip drawings on canvas or paper. Some observers claim that Aaron's drawings have changed and become more sophisticated over the years, in parallel with the evolution in the artist's own style.[24]

Literature

An intriguing branch of computer literature is the **interactive fiction** available today from several software houses. In interactive fiction, the reader participates in the story by feeding inputs into the plot. One of the earliest such programs was the Zork trilogy. Zork and other programs like it were made possible by the invention of sophisticated *parsers,* which enable the computer to understand plain English commands. For example, the story might say, "You are facing a cottage that is surrounded by a broken fence. Sitting on top of one of the posts is a key. The cottage door is closed, and there is no one around." If the reader then types, "Take key," the story branches off to one line of development.

Developed with the help of an artificial intelligence language known as MDL, parsers today contain vocabularies of hundreds of words, which allow computers to recognize such sophisticated commands as "Pick up the key and put it into the sack." More complicated novels and stories are consequently possible. For example, the novelist Ray Bradbury has collaborated with a software manufacturer to turn his *Fahrenheit 451* into an interactive work. Michael Crichton (*The Andromeda Strain, Terminal Man*) developed an original story entitled *Amazon,* which featured a sidekick parrot named Paco. Other adaptations and original creations, no doubt inspired by the success of Zork I (sales of 500,000 copies), are planned.[25]

Word processing is a popular and conventional use of the computer in literature, as writers of every sort continue to take to the machines with enthusiasm. But there is a negative side to this popularity; namely, that holographic manuscripts are becoming scarce, even rare. A *holographic manuscript* is one that an author has either created or edited by hand, giving literary critics and historians a tantalizing glimpse of the creative process. But such manuscripts are not left behind when a work is created on a word processor. Instead, the writer makes changes on the screen and winds up with a polished manuscript. Some critics consequently bemoan the new technology, seeing it as a threat to library archives of literature.[26] It is safe to say, however, that few writers would vote to revert to the drudgery of pen and typewriter, even if failing to do so might mean the loss of future literary archives.

Music

Sound is a fluctuation of air pressure that can be measured as a waveform. Specific musical instruments produce sounds characterized by specific and measurable waveforms. By converting these waveforms into digital equivalents, storing them in memory and then "playing" them back to a digital-to-analog converter, computers can be used to faithfully reproduce the sound of any musical instrument. This is the basic principle behind digital recordings and computer-generated music, such as a digital synthesizer produces (Figure 16.10). Figure 16.11, for example, shows

Figure 16.10 Recording artist Stevie Wonder sits at the keyboard of a Kurzweil digital synthesizer, along with the instrument's inventor (left). Introduced in 1984, the Kurzweil 250 is known for its digital reproduction of the grand piano sound.

Figure 16.11 A graphic illustration of the waveforms of a conventional violin, electronic violin, and digital synthesizer.

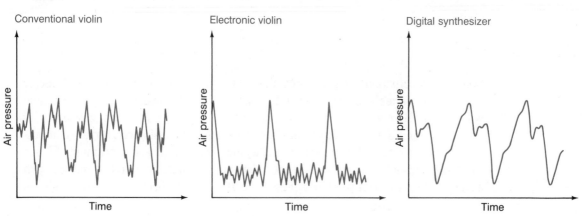

the waveform of a conventional violin, along with its equivalent reproduced by an electronic violin and a digital synthesizer.[27] Many orchestras and bands have added computer-generated music to their productions to obtain a richer sound than they otherwise would be able to get from their ensembles.

Lately composers and arrangers have also used computers to tinker with musical scores before recording. Before this new process, a composer who wished to experiment with an arrangement had to rent studio time and taping facilities—at considerable expense.[28] But with special software and a Macintosh computer hooked up to a music synthesizer, an arrangement can now be played and stored on a floppy disk for editing. Bars may be moved from one part of the composition to another and the effect played back nearly instantly. In effect, a composer or arranger can actually hear how a certain musical arrangement will sound. With the ability to run 16 musical synthesizers at once and to store the equivalent capacity of 99 tape recorders, the system gives composers a freedom to experiment that was unimaginable in an earlier era. Predictions have already been made that, within the near future, music studios will do most of their recording with computers.

SCIENTIFIC APPLICATIONS

Computers are already part of the standard lab equipment of scientists in disciplines ranging from aerodynamics to sociology. Their effect on the progress of science is incalculable. One mathematician explained the usefulness of computers this way.

> Computers will affect science and technology at least as profoundly as did the invention of calculus. The reasons are the same. As with calculus, computers have increased and will increase enormously the range of solvable problems. The full development of these events will occupy decades and the rapid progress which we see currently is a strong sign that the impact of computing will be much greater in the future than it is today.[29]

It is easy enough for anyone familiar with computers to grasp that machines capable of swift and accurate numerical calculations should be indispensable to scientists who gather data. But computers do more than speed up practical and empirical research. They also make possible research that humans could never undertake without their help. In the discussion that follows, we will briefly mention some of the scientific experiments made possible by computers.

Simulation

No human researcher can ever get close enough to a black hole to empirically measure its gaseous flow. But it is possible to create a mathematical model of black holes that can simulate the flow of gases in them. Such a simulation involves 25,600 variables in each step, consists of some 10,000 steps per experiment, and yields a solution amounting to 1.25 billion numbers.[30] Without the use of a super-computer, such a simulation would be unthinkable, to say nothing of impossible.

Computers are also used in a variety of simulation exercises with consequences and results that are more immediate and practical. For example, the wind tunnel has been made obsolete by supercomputers, which are used to simulate the variables involved in airflow over the surface of a wing. Computers have enabled sociologists to apply mathematical modeling to understanding group behavior. They have been used to simulate the malleability of sheet metal and the characteristics of new chemicals and to predict the location of petroleum fields. Computers, in sum, not only help us to study scientific riddles that humans have studied for centuries, they also help us to formulate and explore entirely new problems.

Supercomputers

Supercomputers are defined as computers that are capable of 20 million arithmetic operations per second. Some supercomputers, such as the Cray 2, are capable of potential processing speeds up to 1 billion operations of arithmetic per second.[31] Typical supercomputers are 64-bit machines with memories of 4 million words.[32] Such machines don't use the single-processor architecture of more typical computers, but depend on high-speed **parallel processors** that can break down a problem into smaller parts and work on it simultaneously. Supercomputers also contain vast storage capacities. The Los Alamos supercomputer, for example, has a total of 1 million files amounting to over 13 trillion bits of storage.

In the past, supercomputer facilities were maintained by separate government agencies, without coordination between them. NASA, for example, maintains its own supercomputer facilities, as does the Department of Atmospheric and Ocean Sciences. But in 1985 the federally funded National Science Foundation contributed $200 million in "seed" money, which, when matched will be used to establish national supercomputer centers at the University of Illinois, the University of California at San Diego, Princeton, and Cornell.[33] These facilities will be open to use by academic researchers, and industrial scientists.

The main use of supercomputers is to construct complex mathematical models and simulations. We've already mentioned the use of supercomputers to simulate the airflow over a wing or the flow of gases in black holes. Supercomputers have also been used to model the behavior of particles involved in rock slides or shifting sand dunes. Through the use of its high-speed parallel processors, the computer is able to simulate the behavior of trillions of sand grains and thus contribute to an understanding of how three-dimensional particles behave.[34]

Space Exploration

Anyone who has ever watched a NASA launch aborted by a computer glitch knows that space exploration depends heavily on computers. Computers are responsible for monitoring the engines and complex electronic systems of rockets. They per-

Figure 16.12 The flight deck of the Space Shuttle Orbiter Columbia. The flight computer is between the pilots' seats above this three CRT screens display flight information to the crew.

form the precise calculations necessary for achieving and maintaining orbit (see Figure 16.12). They regulate the life support systems of space vehicles.

But even more exotic uses of computers are contemplated for NASA's projected space stations. Computer-controlled robots in NASA's space stations will monitor electrical systems, maintain navigation and altitude control, communicate with tracking systems, maintain environmental controls for the crew, and be responsible for damage control and repair. The robots will, according to a report, be able to understand human speech, provide automated medical decisions on the health of the crew, detect leaks, and manage on-board manufacturing processes. Sounding suspiciously like HAL, the computer who went berserk in the movie *2001,* these machines are expected to be fully functional and working by the year 2010, according to a NASA report.[35] "Life," said the British writer Oscar Wilde in a prophetic remark, "imitates art."

SUMMARY

Since 1940 computers have become 1 billion times faster and 10 million times cheaper.[36] They have also evolved from dedicated single-use machines into machines that can be programmed to perform a variety of useful jobs. To exhaust all the ways computers can be used by government entities, educators, artists, or science would take a book of considerable bulk. This chapter has merely scratched the surface of possibilities.

Federal and local governments use computers to tabulate, count, forecast, protect, and monitor—tasks that, in a democratic and free society, are aimed at bettering the personal lives of citizens. Educators use them to teach and have yet to harvest the bountiful promise of the machines. Art uses the machines to enhance and preserve masterpieces as well as to entertain and amuse us. Science has found them indispensable not only in performing the routine statistical chores of research, but also in simulating natural environments and conditions entirely hostile to the presence of a human researcher.

We may lament the potential for invasion of privacy that the computer poses, or the risk of catastrophic global war, but even the gloomiest naysayer is forced to concede that the net effect of the computer on human life so far has been happily beneficial.

KEY TERMS

colorization

computer-assisted instruction (CAI)

courseware

drill-and-practice program

interactive fiction

parallel processors

simulation

supercomputer

tutorial

DISCUSSION QUESTIONS

1. What uses do governments make of computer systems?
2. What single principle seems to underlie all government use of computers?
3. What is especially troubling to some critics about the use of computers in the proposed Star Wars system?
4. What benefits does a geocoding database offer an enhanced 911 system?
5. What are the three main types of CAI? How do they differ?
6. Why has CAI not lived up to its promise?
7. What does computer colorization of a movie entail?
8. How does image enhancement help our appreciation of masterpieces?
9. What is interactive fiction? What software invention made interactive fiction possible?

10. How do computers reproduce the sounds of musical instruments?

11. What is a supercomputer? How are supercomputers used?

EXERCISES

1. Contact your campus police or a local police department and find out if they use computer information systems. Ask if they use the NCIC network and why they do or do not use it. Find out what types of information on crimes, arrests, and convictions are available to the public.

2. Discuss the implications of making data from police investigations more publicly available or less so.

3. Define each of these computer-related systems and identify how it is used:

    EDGAR
    LEGIS
    COPAD
    FAPRS
    NORAD
    SDI
    AMRAAM
    NCIC

4. Compare and contrast instructional software for drill-and-practice, simulations, and tutorials. Use examples from your campus if possible.

5. Select a major application of computers in science (for example, system simulation, rocket control, or weather forecasting) and speculate on the difficulty of getting along without it.

NOTES

1. Tom Logsdon, *Computers Today and Tomorrow* (Rockville, M.D.: Computer Science Press, 1985).

2. F. Seghers, "Computerizing Uncle Sam's Data," *Business Week,* 15 December 1986, p. 102.

3. L. Wiener, "Computerizing Tax Returns," *U.S. News & World Report,* 8 December 1986, p. 66.

4. *United States Population Estimates and Components of Change:* 1970 *to 1986,* 1987.

5. DARPA report quoted in "The 'Star Wars' Defense Won't Compute," *Atlantic Monthly,* June 1985.

6. "The 'Star Wars' Defense Won't Compute."

7. Frank Barnaby, "How the Next War Will be Fought," *Technology Review,* October 1986.

8. "Taking a Byte Out of Crime," *Time,* 14 October 1985.

9. "Taking a Byte Out of Crime."

10. "Computer Tracking Plan for Suspects Gets Panels O.K.," *Atlanta Constitution,* 11 June 1987.

11. Steven W. Gilbert and Kenneth C. Green, "New Computing in Higher Education," *Change,* May-June 1986.

12. Julie S. Vargas, "Instructional Design Flaws in Computer-Assisted Instruction," *Phi Delta Kappan,* June 1986.

13. Vargas.

14. Henry M. Levin and Gail Meister, "Is CAI Cost-Effective?" *Phi Delta Kappan,* June 1986.

15. Richard P. Niemiec, Madeline C. Blackwell, and Herbert J. Walberg, "CAI Can Be Doubly Effective," *Phi Delta Kappan,* June 1986.

16. "Using Computers for Instruction," *Byte,* March 1987.

17. Vargas.

18. John F. Rockart and Michael S. Scott Morton, *"Computers and the Learning Process in Higher Education* (New York: McGraw-Hill, 1975).

19. Vargas.

20. John F. Cragan and Donald Shields, "Computer-Derived Foreign Policy Speech," *USA Today,* 1980.

21. Jim Tankard, "The Literary Detective," *Byte,* February 1986.

22. This discussion is based on Ken Sheldon, "A Film of a Different Color," *Byte,* March 1987.

23. John F. Asmus, "Digital Image Processing in Art Conservation," *Byte,* March 1987.

24. Letter by Robert Mallary in *Commentary,* 16 August 1986.

25. "Stepping into the Story," *Time,* 13 May 1985.

26. Willis E. McNelly, "On Consigning Manuscripts to Floppy Disks and Archives to Oblivion," *Los Angeles Times,* 22 December 1983.

27. Max V. Mathews and John R. Pierce, "The Computer as a Musical Instrument," *Scientific American,* February 1987.

28. S.P. Sherman, "Musical Software," *Fortune,* 14 October 1985, p. 145.

29. James Glimm, quoted in Larry L. Smarr, "An Approach to Complexity: Numerical Computations," *Science,* April 1985.

30. "An Approach to Complexity: Numerical Computations"

31. "Supercomputers: A New Age," *Science Digest,* July 1985.

32. "Perspective on Supercomputing," *Science,* February 1985.

33. *Science Digest,* July 1985.

34. Ivars Peterson, "Rolling Rocks and Tumbling Dice," *Science News,* 3 May 1986.

35. "NASA Report Urges Developing Robotics, Software for Station," *Aviation Week & Technology,* 22 April 1985.

36. "The Computer Issue," *Science,* April 1985.

17 Ethics in Computing

PRIVACY
The Computer as a Threat to Privacy
Safeguarding Privacy

COMPUTER CRIME
Computer-abetted Crime
Hackers and Computer Trespassing
Safeguarding the Security of Computer Systems

SOFTWARE PIRACY
Legal Protections for Software
Software License Agreements
Thwarting Piracy

EMERGING ISSUES IN INFORMATION ETHICS
Information Malpractice
Intellectual Property Rights
The Value of Information
The Value of Human Capital
Equal Access to Information

By increasing the speed and efficiency with which information is collected and manipulated, the computer has spearheaded the Information Revolution. In turn the Information Revolution has raised new concerns about the conflict between the individual's right to privacy and society's "need to know." What kind of personal information should be collected and stored in computers? Who should have access to it? The freedom to use computers for business and governmental purposes must be balanced against freedom from unnecessary intrusions.

The growing importance of computers has also raised concerns about computer security. Computer crime is now responsible for losses in the billions of dollars. And the advent of microcomputers has made it possible for almost anyone to violate systems once thought reasonably secure. How can computer systems be made less vulnerable to such abuses?

Because software for personal computers is distributed on easy-to-copy floppy disks, software piracy has now become a serious problem for software developers. How many backup copies should a user be able to make, and for how many machines? Certainly, selling an unauthorized copy of a program is illegal, but is it wrong to copy a program for a friend or relative for demonstration purposes?

The future of our society will be shaped to a large extent by how we resolve these issues, as well as by how we treat some new ethical concerns that are just beginning to be discussed. The last part of this chapter explores information malpractice, intellectual property rights, the value of information and of human capital, and the need to ensure equal access to information services.

PRIVACY

Privacy is the ability of individuals or organizations to control information about themselves. Perhaps privacy can best be understood by considering its absence. Imagine yourself growing up in a society in which anyone could find out anything about anyone else just by sitting down at a computer terminal and searching massive files containing everyone's complete personal history. There would be benefits; for instance, you wouldn't have to fill out a job application, because your prospective employer could get a list of all your achievements and failures in past jobs. But in the absence of privacy, you wouldn't be able to date anyone new without your date's finding out everything you did on past dates. The cartoon in Figure 17.1 underscores the exposure that results from losing the ability to restrict information about oneself and to control how it may be used. We tend to take privacy for granted, but our daily lives often depend on our ability to limit what others know about us.

The right to privacy is a cornerstone of democratic society. While the U.S. Constitution doesn't explicitly mention privacy, privacy is recognized in common law and protected by several federal laws. Personal information is required by government agencies, such as the Internal Revenue Service, and by other organizations, such as schools and financial institutions. The central issue in discussion of the right to privacy is the proper balance between organizations' need for information and individuals' right to withhold it (Figure 17.2). The advent of computers has threatened to disturb that balance in several ways.

The Computer as a Threat to Privacy

When the purpose for gathering information is known, its benefits clear, and its confidentiality assured, most people will cooperate with requests for personal data. They routinely fill out state and federal income tax returns, answer census questions, and sign information release forms for credit checks.

Public confidence in the proper use of information rests on past experience with

Figure 17.1 This cartoon implying the computer's role in threatening privacy first appeared in 1974, the year in which the most important privacy legislation was passed.

Figure 17.2 The balance: privacy policies fall along a continuum between support of total individual privacy and nearly unlimited need for data by organizations in society.

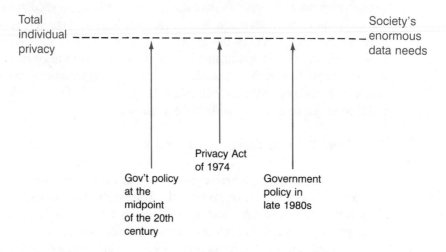

manual record-keeping systems. In most precomputer information systems, the amount of information that could be collected and processed was severely limited, and little information was shared among systems. Computers have increased data processing capabilities, allowing the inclusion of more personal data on census forms, tax returns, school applications, marketing surveys, and credit applications. Computers have also made possible the collection of detailed information about people's everyday activities, much of it without their knowledge. Each long-distance phone call, each credit card transaction, each check a person writes is recorded. New technology has made it possible to access, within seconds, any one of millions of records in a database.

Information may now be gathered or shared without the knowledge or consent of those concerned. In one instance, American Telephone and Telegraph (AT&T) used information from a survey of customer billings for marketing purposes. Though the intent of the survey wasn't malicious, and no information about individual customers' calling habits was released, some people found the mere existence of the survey disquieting.

Electronic connections among computers make the sharing of massive amounts of information fast and simple. Computerized subscription and membership lists are regularly sold, given away, and traded. (That's why we receive so much junk mail and so many computer-generated phone calls.) What's more, some computers can search and combine information from several databases. Recently, the Department of Health and Human Services used its computer system to compare welfare recipients' social security numbers with those of employees in the Justice Department, the Department of Defense, and the Office of Personnel Management. The search identified federal employees who were receiving welfare benefits illegally. Though few people would argue against the intent of the search, it raises questions about the possibility and effects of less well intentioned searches.

Even if people have committed no crime, the information contained in computer files may embarrass or inconvenience them. Personal medical records are a good example. The existence of a national medical database could one day save someone's life; but it could also contain information about an abortion, psychiatric treatment, substance abuse, or drug treatments. Given access to such information, a prospective employer might decline to hire someone. Similarly, a financial institution might not approve a loan application, or an insurance company might refuse to issue a policy. Just as in a manual system, computerized data may not be correct, complete, or current. Once inaccurate information is shared, it is very difficult to track down and correct all records containing the error. Thus, computers greatly increase the potential for misuse of information.

The problem of data integrity or quality has been most extensively studied in computerized criminal history (CCH) systems. The criminal justice system, from the FBI down to the local police officer, rely on these CCH records for daily decisions in their investigations of suspects. There are about 195 million criminal history records in the United States, and it has been estimated that about one-third of the labor force has an arrest or court record in these files. A recent study of the quality of the data in these files concluded that at least 50 percent of the records contained inaccurate or out-of-date information.[1] Apparently, law enforcement agencies need more incentives to keep these files current. There is little question that CCH systems are a critical weapon in the fight against crime, but unless the data are maintained properly, the resulting benefits are open to question. From the point of view of an individual with an inaccurate arrest record, the system is unquestionably a threat to privacy.

If personal privacy were the only issue to consider, the collection and storage of personal information in computer systems would have been outlawed years ago. But computerized information systems can be a powerful instrument for improving and maintaining service delivery. The most obvious examples are in the field of law enforcement. Police information systems store personal facts about citizens, many of which aren't immediately useful. The FBI, for instance, keeps many Americans' fingerprints on file, even though most of them have never been arrested for a serious crime and aren't considered active suspects in unsolved crimes. Americans seem to accept the existence of this databank, viewing it as a danger more to criminals than to the average citizen. Indeed, recent advances in the access and retrieval of computerized fingerprint data have led to the arrest and conviction of numerous criminals. Similarly, most people support (or at least tolerate) the collection of financial information by the Internal Revenue Service, because they want to make sure that tax evaders are caught.

Computerized databases also facilitate business dealings. Automatic teller machines can now dispense cash, and point-of-sale terminals make it easier for retail business to obtain authorization for large credit purchases. Most people seem willing to accept the storage of credit data in return for the convenience of such services.

Safeguarding Privacy

In the past two decades, several major studies and many debates have addressed the question of how to safeguard personal privacy without undermining society's informational needs. The following five proposed guidelines summarize the most commonly heard themes:

1. Give individuals the legal right to examine any information about them recorded in a databank, and give them legal recourse should they not agree with what is recorded.
2. Make it a crime to obtain information fraudulently.
3. Make it a crime to keep the existence of a databank a secret.
4. Make aging of information mandatory so that it is discarded after a certain period of time.
5. Provide regulations and procedures for auditing databases to detect violations of law.[2]

For a variety of reasons, many of these recommendations have not been implemented. Cost and inertia have tended to discourage their implementation. And existing laws and regulations have had chilling and often unintended effects on the industries they regulate. For example, because the communications and banking industries must contend with stringent federal regulation, few proposed improvements in service have much chance of being implemented.

The most significant privacy legislation enacted in the United States is the *Privacy Act of 1974*. This landmark bill identified the right to privacy as a fundamental constitutional right and stated that "the increasing use of computers, while essential to the efficient operation of government, has greatly magnified the harm that occurs from any collection, maintenance, use, or dissemination of personal information." The Privacy Act of 1974 specified rules for creating and managing federal data files and provided for individuals to review and challenge their personal data records. It stipulated that Congress must approve all exchanges or sharing of government-collected data. The act also established a commission to study the privacy protection issues of both public and private sectors.

Several other federal legislative actions relevant to privacy occurred about the time of the Privacy Act of 1974 and in the years that followed. These are listed and summarized in Table 17.1. In addition to these laws, Congress during the last 15 years has added confidentiality and disclosure provisions to a variety of bills on such diverse matters as the census, child abuse, and deficit reduction. Similar legislation suggests that privacy issues are important, pervasive, and complex.

A law passed in Great Britain in 1984 may prove a sign of things to come. The act requires anyone who maintains a database containing personal data to register it with the government. There are a few limited exceptions; for example, payroll files don't need to be registered. The registration must include the name of the installation, the purpose for which the data are being held, the source of the data, the names of everyone to whom the data may be disclosed, the countries to which the data may be transferred, and the name of the person responsible for granting access to the data. No such legislative provisions have yet been passed in the United States, but the proliferation in the mid-1980s of microcomputer-based credit files should keep the debate alive.

Experts predict that the enforcement of privacy laws is more critical than their enactment. Kenneth Laudon, in *Dossier Society,* proposed the establishment of a new Privacy Protection Commission to monitor existing government information systems and evaluate proposals for new ones.[3] With the aid of citizens, such an agency would answer the following questions about any new or existing record-keeping system:

- *Need.* Is there a compelling societal need for the information?
- *Feasibility.* How does or would the system work, and how well?
- *Alternatives.* Are there other mechanisms for addressing the same need?
- *Accountability.* Does or will the system include measures to ensure accountability for the responsible use of the data?

Table 17.1 Chronology of Major U.S. Privacy Laws

Name	Description
Fair Credit Reporting Act of 1970	Gives citizens the right to examine their own credit records and provides procedures for correcting errors
Crime Control Act of 1973	Extends privacy provisions to criminal justice information systems developed with federal funds
Family Education Rights Act (1974)	Requires schools and colleges to give a student or a parent access to that student's records; limits disclosure of these records to others
Privacy Act of 1974	Restricts federal agencies from collecting, using, sharing, and disclosing personal data that directly or indirectly identify a specific individual
Tax Reform Act of 1976	Protects confidentiality of tax information by disallowing its nontax use with significant exceptions
Right to Financial Privacy (1978)	Spells out when banks can and cannot give out financial data for specific persons
Protection of Pupil Rights (1978)	Gives parents rights to inspect educational materials and restricts mandatory psychological testing
Privacy Protection Act of 1980	Prohibits unannounced searches of press offices
Electronic Funds Transfer (1980)	Requires banks offering EFT to notify customers if their account information is given out to third parties
Debt Collection Act of 1982	Establishes procedures for federal agencies to follow before releasing information about bad debts to credit bureaus
Reports Elimination Act of 1983	Eliminates some reporting requirements of the Privacy Act of 1974
Cable Communications Act of 1984	Requires a cable service to inform subscriber of all personally identifiable information collected; restricts use of such information

Once an information system with personal data has been created, the remaining safeguards are company policies, administrative procedures, and professional ethics. It is noteworthy that most computer-related associations have written codes of ethics on privacy rights, which specify minimizing needless collection of data, developing access controls, ensuring data quality, and disposing of data as appropriate.

The debate on data privacy is far from settled. Research now under way on the operation of information systems and on the quality of data maintained in them may add to the discussion. As record-keeping systems continue to expand in size and multiply in number (Figure 17.3), continued discussion and research will be required to assure that legislation and administrative practice recognize the need for both organizational efficiency and personal privacy.

Figure 17.3 Large increases in data storage capacity, which are expected from forthcoming laser disk devices, will reduce the cost of managing files of data on large numbers of individuals.

COMPUTER CRIME

Growing public consternation over computer crime culminated in the passage of the Computer Fraud and Abuse Act of 1986. The law and legislation in almost all 50 states now explicitly prohibit a wide range of computer-related crimes. With these laws in place, more cases are apt to go to trial and result in convictions and serious sentences.

Preventing computer crime depends principally on the difficult undertaking of limiting access by unauthorized users masquerading as legitimate users and limiting rightful users to those parts of the system they are authorized to access.

Computer-abetted Crime

When the computer was first invented, *computer crime* referred to theft or sabotage of computers. Now the term **computer crime** means the unauthorized use of computer systems, including software or data, for unlawful purposes. A new breed of criminal has emerged who tackles the technical challenges while disregarding the moral or ethical implications of these criminal acts. Although most arrests for computer crime have involved young, highly skilled male employees, Figure 17.4 shows that a wide range of other employees has also been involved.

Although accurate data on computer crimes are lacking, the average loss appears from all reports to be large—perhaps as high as several hundred thousand dollars. Most of these crimes are committed by individuals who are authorized to use the system and have enough technical knowledge to exploit its weaknesses. Computer-abetted crimes are difficult to detect (many crimes are discovered by accident), and some aren't reported because doing so would undermine the confidence of the public or investors.

Figure 17.4 Who commits computer crimes? Number of cases brought to trial nationwide by type of suspect.

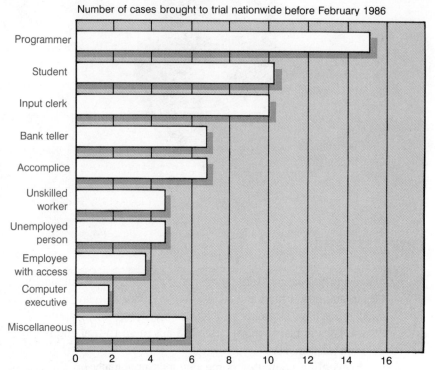

Who commits computer crimes?

Number of cases brought to trial nationwide before February 1986

Information provided by the National Center for Computer Crime Data's Computer Crime Census. Figures based on a survey of 130 prosecutors in 38 states.

Electronic funds transfer systems (EFTS) are especially vulnerable to computer crime because of the high potential payoff. Embezzlers with detailed knowledge of a particular system can transfer money from one account—usually an inactive one—to their personal account. For example, Stanley Rifkin used his knowledge of a bank's procedures, a telephone, and an authorization code to transfer $10.8 million to a Swiss bank account. Eventually he was caught.

Some of the methods used in computer crime are novel, and a specialized jargon has evolved to describe them. Two of these unique methods are salami slicing and Trojan horse method.

Auditors have a difficult time detecting smart embezzlers, because doctored computer-generated reports and listings seem to be correct. For example, in a **salami-slicing** scheme, a program is modified to round down all fractions of a penny in transactions like salary calculations and to add these amounts to the criminal's computer account or paycheck. Although these "slices" may not seem like

Computers and Us: Living in a High-Tech World

For several decades the cost of computing equipment has fallen between 20 and 40 percent each year. During the same time salaries have risen about 4 percent each year. These trends seem likely to continue, and they imply dramatic changes in how we live and work. How you will fit into this new world will depend on how well prepared you are and on what you want to do. This photo essay gives you a glimpse into the professional opportunities you may find after leaving school.

1. Equipment and software vendors often run training classes describing their products and how to use them. Here, an instructor assists customers in a classroom designed for on-line, hands-on training.

EDUCATION AND TRAINING PROGRAMS

Education is a continuing necessity in a world where today's technical skills soon become tomorrow's antiquated knowledge.

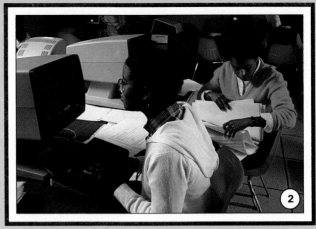

2. Colleges and universities offer degree programs in computer science and allied fields, such as management information systems. Academic programs tend to emphasize the theoretical rather than the practical aspects of computer science, and they frequently use obsolete equipment and software because of budgetary limitations.

3. Students at the University of Oklahoma are developing their skills on equipment donated by the Telex Corporation.

4. Most firms run in-house training classes to keep their employees up to date. New employees may be given special training programs lasting up to six months.

5. Computer professionals find they need to do much of their learning on the job, using publications like these IBM reference manuals.

COMPUTER USERS

Being a competent computer user has become a prerequisite to success in most professional fields. The most important skill is knowing how to select and use application software.

6-9. Whether you want to conduct banking transactions, prepare marketing plans, design mechanical parts, or manage a production line, you are likely to use a computer.

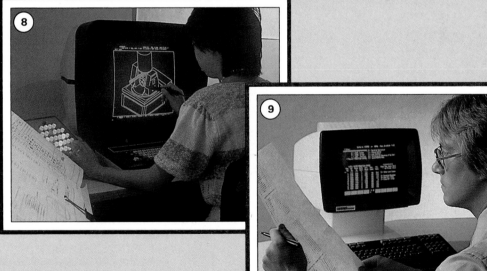

COMPUTER OPERATIONS

10,11. A computer operator's job is to keep the computer system running smoothly. Operators load paper in printers, mount disks and tapes, run computer programs at scheduled times, and call systems programmers or maintenance technicians when something major goes wrong.

12,13. Other employees in computer operations include clerks who enter vast quantities of data from input forms, the operations manager who schedules shifts and supervises employees, and librarians who catalog and maintain the installation's program listings and operational data.

PROGRAMMERS AND ANALYSTS

14. An analyst helps users determine how data processing can be applied to their problems. Together with the users, the analyst gathers facts about the current system and helps establish specifications for the new system. Then the analyst designs a system that meets the users' information-processing needs.

15. An application programmer takes the design specifications created by the analyst and converts them into programs containing the detailed instructions needed by computers.

16. Systems programmers select and maintain system software. They establish the software environment in which application programmers function. Because systems programming is more technically demanding than application programming, systems programmers usually receive higher salaries.

ENGINEERING AND DESIGN

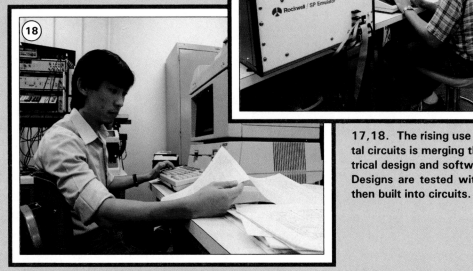

17,18. The rising use of complex digital circuits is merging the fields of electrical design and software engineering. Designs are tested with software and then built into circuits.

19. A draftsman performs layout and design work on an integrated circuit. Drafting and design require good visual understanding and a willingness to pay close attention to detail.

20. Arranging computer systems so that they are convenient to use involves *ergonomics,* the study of how human beings relate to their environment.

MANUFACTURING, SERVICE, AND SUPPORT

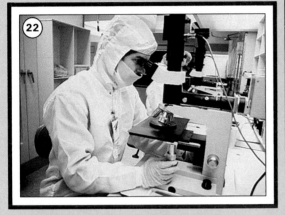

21,22. Manufacturing jobs in the computer field require dexterity and patience. Work is done in a clean—and sometimes an ultraclean—environment.

23. Many organizations purchase service contracts that promise quick on-site repairs. Here, IBM service coordinators in Atlanta use a computer-based system to assign representatives to handle calls for service.

24. Maintenance and repair technicians need a background in electronics along with some common sense. Because computers are designed with expansion and maintenance in mind, generally hardware can be upgraded and repaired simply by adding or exchanging circuit boards. Fixing faulty circuit boards often requires special testing equipment; so faulty boards usually are sent back to the factory for repair.

window 9

25. Widespread use of personal computers has created numerous opportunities in retail sales. Success in retail sales requires a desire to work with people and the technical ability to find and demonstrate solutions to their problems.

26. Selling computers to businesses and government agencies is a team effort that requires more than demonstrating hardware and software. Most organizations won't decide to purchase until they have received responses to a formal Request for Proposal (RFP), tested a working system, talked with prior customers, and negotiated a maintenance agreement. Here, IBM instructors train U.S. Department of Agriculture employees as part of a contract that includes the installation of almost 2,900 computers.

very much, they can add up to a surprisingly large sum in a company with several thousand employees. Salami slicing is difficult to detect because the account totals balance.

In a **Trojan horse** scheme, an unauthorized program is hidden within a legitimate program, such as a telecommunications control program. The hidden program might discover passwords by scanning the data passing through the legitimate program. The criminal program then uses the stolen passwords to enter other accounts and pillage them, much like the legendary Greek warriors who hid inside a hollow wooden horse.

The largest and most notorious computer fraud scheme involved Equity Funding Corporation, a large insurance firm based in Illinois and California.[4] To inflate the company's stock, top executives established within the company a second data processing department, ostensibly for research and development. This department actually programmed the company's computers to generate over 60,000 fictitious life insurance policies worth $2.1 billion. These fictitious policies were then sold to other insurance companies. Equity Funding received a commission on each fictitious policy sold, paid premiums on these policies to the reinsurers, and then generated fake medical records to show that some of the policy holders had died. Besides profiting from the sale of shares of Equity Funding stock, the executives also collected over $1 million as beneficiaries of the fake policies. They were caught when a disgruntled former employee revealed the fraud. More than 20 people were convicted of federal crimes, and several books were written on the scandal. When the company collapsed, shareholders lost an estimated $600 million, and life insurance policy holders lost an estimated $1 billion in the face values of their policies. Computer crime could no longer be viewed as an insignificant problem.

Hackers and Computer Trespassing

Not all security breaches have serious consequences, nor do they all involve the clear-cut commission of a crime. Many are the work of young computer hackers who merely want to access and "look around" computer systems. Once *hacker* meant a person with computer expertise who was obsessed with writing and rewriting programs and exploring the capabilities of computer systems. Today **hacker** generally means someone who gains access to a computer system without authorization. This has upset "old-definition" hackers, who prefer that the term **cracker** (short for "security cracker") be used to describe computer trespassers.

This new breed of hackers is a product of the personal computer. Years ago, lists of authorized user names, passwords, trustworthy employees, and a secure computer room protected mainframe computers from trespassers. With the development of dial-up timesharing, however, anyone with a valid password, modem, and terminal could gain access by dialing the system's telephone number and supplying a valid user name–password combination. Today a microcomputer and a modem costing as little as $150 can be programmed to penetrate computer security. The movie *War Games* realistically depicted the steps in such a penetration. First, the computer dials telephone numbers until it detects an answer by a computer system; then the user can try guessing the account numbers and passwords, or the computer can be programmed to generate and try guesses. While it isn't as easy to discover passwords and to access files as *War Games* suggested, anyone with a personal computer and a modem has a fair chance of cracking most computer systems.

Is a hacker a criminal or a prankster? In one case, an ex-employee of a software company used his personal computer equipped with a modem to access his former employer's confidential records on products and customers. Even though his files had been removed from the computer system, he penetrated the security system by guessing other employees' passwords. He used the information he gained to develop similar products and to offer them to his former employer's customers at attractive discounts. Clearly this individual committed a crime.

Classifying the activities of hackers like the "Milwaukee 414" group (414 is the telephone area code in Milwaukee) isn't as straightforward. Twelve teenagers in Milwaukee used national packet-switching networks, such as GTE Telenet, to gain illegal access to over 60 government and business computer systems.[5] Getting into the GTE Telenet system required only a local telephone number and a two-digit access code. Once on the network, the teenagers were able to gain access to the computers at the Sloan-Kettering Cancer Institute; the nuclear weapons laboratory at Los Alamos, New Mexico; and a Los Angeles bank. They only looked around these computer systems; and they didn't damage any data. Nevertheless, their activities raised anger and anxiety. Was this an innocent prank, or was a crime committed?

Some people argue that the Milwaukee 414 and hackers like them help identify weak links in security and should be encouraged. Hackers claim that they should be able to access a computer system when it isn't being used (late at night or on weekends), because this is a good way to learn about programming and computers. Some hackers encourage this type of activity by exchanging telephone numbers and passwords through electronic bulletin boards and other schemes.

Those who consider computer trespassing a crime point out that there is no difference between invading a computer system and breaking into an office to snoop in the file cabinets. That the intruder only browsed and didn't steal anything is immaterial. Information is a valuable resource, and the temptation to alter or misuse it is great. Unauthorized changes to medical, financial, or government records could be catastrophic, endangering life and greatly undermining confidence in public institutions. The records of private organizations, too, must be protected. Trade secrets, product information, and marketing data provide business with a crucial competitive edge.

Victims of computer crimes sometimes find themselves in a bind. Publicity might inspire others to attempt similar schemes and shatter public trust. A bank certainly wouldn't want to publicize a million-dollar embezzlement by personal computer, lest it suffer from additional crimes or lose customers. Although businesses are reluctant to prosecute hackers who just browse around their files, they have prosecuted computer trespassers who change or destroy information. News stories about the activities of hackers have heightened public apprehension about the vulnerability of computer systems and lax security.

Safeguarding the Security of Computer Systems

No computer system is perfectly secure. Administrative controls and software safeguards are two critical elements that make a computer installation more secure.

Administrative controls are policies and procedures that discourage computer crime by making it more difficult for a crime to remain undetected. Typical administrative controls dictate that businesses

- Distribute sensitive duties among several employees. In particular, organizations must assign the tasks of developing programs, operating the computer system, and generating data for the system to separate departments.
- Establish audit controls to monitor program changes, access to data files, and submission of data.
- Shred sensitive documents before discarding them.
- Limit employee access to only those computer facilities that are essential to their jobs (Figure 17.5).
- Thoroughly investigate the trustworthiness of individuals in sensitive positions.

Software safeguards are programs and procedures that prevent unauthorized access to computer files. Of all the protective mechanisms, software safeguards are the most difficult to develop. In the wake of revelations about hackers, recommendations to computer networks and facilities have included the following steps:

- Change passwords frequently and avoid using common words (such as *test, system,* or people's names) as passwords. Passwords should include both digits and letters to make guessing more difficult.
- Remove invalid user names and passwords.
- Watch for unusual activity, such as a user who repeatedly gives an incorrect password when attempting to connect with the computer system.
- Use an unlisted telephone number and change it frequently.

These measures are only a first line of defense. Underground newspapers and some electronic bulletin boards undermine these safeguards by publishing phone numbers and passwords. Several technical schemes, including port protection devices, callback port protection devices, access monitoring, and data encryption, can thwart these attempts to gain unauthorized entry to computer systems.

Port protection devices (PPD) are black boxes between a computer system and incoming telephone lines. (Figure 17.6) They are independent of the dial-in access ports and transparent to the computer system. When potential users dial the computer system, they are connected to the PPD and must enter a password. If

Figure 17.5 Careful monitoring of computer access has become common practice at many computer centers. Honeywell employees must wave a passcard before a sensor to be admitted to computer facilities.

AUTHORIZED
PERSONNEL
ONLY

the password matches one in the PPD's memory, the user is connected with the computer system. If it doesn't match, the call is terminated, and the user is not connected with the computer system.

In a **callback PPD**, all calls are screened before they reach the computer. Each user has an identification number and an authorized telephone number. A user dials in, enters the identification number with a push-button telephone, and hangs up. The callback system verifies the identification number, searches its directory for the authorized telephone number, dials the number, and waits for a one-digit connection code. If all the information is correct, the user is given access to the computer. Use of a callback PPD normally adds about 30 seconds to the time needed to access the computer.

Access monitoring allows a user only a certain number of attempts (say, five) to give the correct password to access the computer system. Once that number is exceeded, the user's account is frozen until the manager of the computer system receives a valid explanation of the problem.

Figure 17.6 Port protection device (PPD). Users must type in the correct password code registered in the PPD's memory in order to gain access to the computer system.

Figure 17.7 An encrypted message. The encryption code used here is a fairly simple one, which involves substituting one character for another. Much more complex and more difficult, codes exist.

Encryption code:

Actual Character:	Coded Character:	Actual Character:	Coded Character:
A	P	S	G
B	I	T	O
C	@	U	E
D	A	V	,
E	W	W	F
F	C	X	V
G	[blank]	Y	X
H	T	Z	/
I	B	!	D
J	Z	@	Y
K	!	#	.
L	#	$	%
M	U	%	K
N	L	[blank]	M
O	N	/	J
P	Q	.	$
Q	S	,	H
R	R		

Encripted Message: XNERMQRB,P@XMBGMTPRAMONWLGERW$

Deciphered message: Your privacy is hard to ensure.

Encryption scrambles both the data in files and the data transmitted over communication lines so that they can't be read by someone who doesn't know the encryption scheme (see Figure 17.7). The disadvantages of this scheme are the cost of the special equipment needed and the loss of transmission speed.

As technology improves, computers might be protected by devices that recognize voices and fingerprints. For now, these schemes are prohibitively expensive. Until the cost of the technology drops, use of these protection devices will not be widespread.

SOFTWARE PIRACY

Software piracy includes any unauthorized duplication of software. Illegal duplication of software not only affects market economies and raises major legal and ethical issues, it also cuts into the potential market for the product and consequently discourages developers from creating new and innovative software. When a large number of potential consumers illegally duplicate software, all consumers suffer. There are fewer new products, and prices on existing software tend to remain high to compensate for the revenue lost due to piracy.

Very few instances of piracy involve software for mainframe computers. Typically, this software, which is written by relatively few companies, is specially tailored for a particular computer facility. A negotiated contract spells out the programs to be developed, the performance conditions they must satisfy, and the vendor's maintenance and support responsibilities. Vendors can easily monitor the use and distribution of this software. Furthermore, business customers are accustomed to contract requirements.

The personal computer completely changed the development and sale of software. The prime targets of software pirates are games and popular application programs, such as word processing and spreadsheet programs. Games are easy to use and require no support from the seller, making them perfect targets for a pirate. Many companies and individuals develop software for personal computers. Millions of these programs are sold by dealers, computer stores, and mail-order outlets. For example, over a million copies of Lotus 1-2-3 have been sold. It would be impractical, if not impossible, to monitor each program sold.

No one knows exactly how much piracy goes on or how much it costs software companies. According to some estimates, there may be as many as ten stolen copies for each legitimate copy of some programs. If such estimates are accurate, then most computer users may now be pirates. Perhaps a majority of personal computer owners possess or have used illegal copies, but some of them may not be aware of the law and the implications of their actions.

No one knows how many people would purchase software if they couldn't steal copies. One survey discovered that many users purchase software after first trying an unauthorized copy of the program. Users said that they had made costly mistakes in the past and didn't want to risk money on a program without trying it first. Consumer skepticism accounts for the recent popularity of **shareware** pro-

COMPUTER FIRMS TURN TO PATENTS, ONCE VIEWED AS WEAK PROTECTION

Computer companies, which have long considered patents cumbersome and ineffective, are now turning them to protect their inventions.

The change reflects the growing strength of the patent system. The Patent and Trademark Office now grants patents on many high-tech products, including software, which previously wouldn't have passed muster. And courts are levying stiff penalties on patent infringers—including triple damages and interest charges—and banning products that infringe on patents.

In a ruling that buoyed computer makers, Eastman Kodak Co. was recently forced out of the instant-photography market after it lost a patent-infringement case brought by Polaroid Corp. Now, Kodak faces potential damage judgments of more than $1 billion. Irving Rappaport, associate general counsel of Apple Computer Inc., says the ruling "shows that the patent system is alive, well and very vibrant for those who have inventions."

The number of computer companies applying for patents is increasing. Prime Computer Inc., which for 10 years didn't bother obtaining patents, now regularly files for patent protection on its hardware. International Business Machines Corp. and Apple, which previously patented computer hardware, now increasingly patent computer software technology too.

Smaller computer companies are also seeking patents. Quickview Systems Inc., a Los Altos, Calif., software company, patented a method for automatically abbreviating text. "If the big guys want to use it, they'll have to do business with us or take the chance of a costly patent battle," warns Paul Heckel, Quickview's president.

Patents give holders the exclusive right for 17 years to market inventions that are deemed "new, useful, and unobvious." That can be a powerful weapon. Using its patents, Apple obtained an International Trade Commission order banning imports to the U.S. of computers that violate Apple patents. As a result, says Mr. Rappaport, customs agents have seized "tens of thousands" of Apple imitations.

The patent system, however, also holds pitfalls for the computer industry. Samuel Miller, who teaches patent law at Georgetown University, says that the new appeals court may go too far in enforcing patents. "The patent system can create a monopoly in a technical area," he says. "If that monopoly is over broad, it's damaging to the competitive environment."

Filing for patents can also be a long and expensive process. Patenting a new computer system can require 10 patents at a cost of as much as $5,000 each, says Mr. Mirabito, the Boston patent attorney. The Patent and Trademark Office is so back logged that it sometimes takes three years to approve a filing.

Another disadvantage: Patent holders must disclose how their inventions work. While such disclosure serve the lofty public goal of disseminating innovative ideas, "You can make an instant competitor," says Irving Kayton, a patent-law professor at George Washington University.

Because of these drawbacks, many computer companies use patents as only one of several ways to protect inventions. Prime Computer, for instance, won't patent its technology for wiring printed-circuit boards because it changes its methods every few years—making any patent obsolete. Instead, Prime keeps the wiring technology confidential and can sue under state trade-secret laws if a competitor somehow steals it.

Lotus Development Corp., a software company that now copyrights its programs, is investigating whether patents would give it additional protection. Copyrights let Lotus sue those who copy its programs; patents could protect Lotus's underlying technology. "Patents may allow us to protect certain features that aren't protected by copyright," say Lindsey Kiang, Lotus's general counsel.

Sometimes the value of a patent only becomes clear too late. In the late 1970s, Dan Bricklin invented VisiCalc, the first electronic spreadsheet for personal computer, but he didn't try to patent the technology. So even though spreadsheets have been incorporated into many top-selling programs, he hasn't received any royalties.

"I'll go down in history as the inventor of VisiCalc," Mr. Bricklin says. "With a patent, the only difference would have been several hundred million dollars."

grams, which permit licensees to share or give away copies so that others can evaluate the program before deciding whether they want to purchase it. Popular shareware programs include PC File III, PC Write, and PC Calc. Some programs are placed in the **public domain**, which means that the author/creator has authorized others to duplicate them at will.

Legal Protection for Software

Software developers can avail themselves of three kinds of legal protection: through copyright, by designating their product a trade secret, or by obtaining a patent.

Copyright is the easiest and least expensive of the three to obtain. In the United States (and in many other countries), a **copyright** gives an individual exclusive use of the work for life plus 50 years. For corporations, a copyright is generally effective for 75 years. In the United States, legal copyright protection is obtained for the work by registering it with the Copyright Office. Originally developed for literary and artistic works, the federal copyright law was amended by the Software Protection Act of 1980 to allow a user to make archival copies of a software package. But a copyright protects only the tangible form in which an idea is expressed, not the idea itself. Thus, it is only the actual program code that is protected. Anyone may write a new program that appears to do the same thing as a copyrighted program without infringing on the copyright.

In 1987 two major organizations mutually developed, published, and widely disseminated a recommended policy statement, *Software and Intellectual Rights*, which states:

> Respect for intellectual labor and creativity is vital to academic discourse and enterprise. This principle applies to works of all authors and publishers in all media. It encompasses respect for the right to acknowledgement, right to privacy, and right to determine the form, manner and terms of publication and distribution.
>
> Because electronic information is volatile and easily reproduced, respect for the work and personal expression of others is especially critical in computer environments. Violations of authorial integrity, including plagiarism, invasion of privacy, unauthorized access, and trade secret and copyright violations, may be *grounds for sanctions against members of the academic community.* [6]

This statement was released by EDUCOM, an association of over 450 institutions of higher education, and ADAPSO, the association for the computer software and services industry. It was especially significant in calling for colleges and universities to impose penalties for violations of intellectual ownership, as well as for unauthorized use of software and related products.

Designating a program as a **trade secret** protects even the idea embodied in the program. This is a popular and successful form of software protection. A program can be protected as a trade secret if the program has some secret information or formula that gives it an advantage over its competitors. However, there are two shortcomings. First, once the secret is out, protection is lost. Thus, a software developer must guard the secret by limiting access and enforcing nondis-

A WORD ABOUT LOCK-BUSTING PROGRAMS

A software-lock breaker becomes a hero to some, a villain to others.

Attending a computer trade show takes a lot of courage for software developer Michael Brown. Other conventioneers sometimes mutter obscenities when they walk by his booth. Even some supporters shy away, afraid to be seen with him. Concedes Mr. Brown: "One of these days I'll probably get a pie in my face."

The personal computer industry usually treats its mavericks with tolerance, but it gives little quarter to Mr. Brown. That's because he's a professional lock picker of a sort—an expert at cracking open the intricate electronic padlocks affixed to software programs to keep people from making copies. His company, Central Point Software Inc. of Portland, Oregon, sells disks containing Mr. Brown's lock-busting schemes to computer owners, who use them to copy such popular programs as Lotus 1-2-3, which is used for business applications, and Flight Simulator, a game.

Copying such software is illegal except when people who purchase software make backup copies for their own use; giving away or selling copies to others is illegal. It is for fostering legal copying that Mr. Brown's lock-picking software is ostensibly sold. But nobody seems to doubt that some of his customers are software pirates. So Mr. Brown's skills have made him not only a lot of money—he says he's a multimillionaire at age 27—but also a lot of enemies.

"We're waging a war," says Ken Williams, the vice president for research and development of Softguard Systems Inc., a Santa Clara, California, company that devises many locks. Software companies "go ape" over the issue of copying, he says, to the point that some "want to get a gun" and shoot Mr. Brown.

That may be an exaggeration, but not much of one. Software publishers are outraged, partly because they believe that the pirates are costing them millions of dollars in lost revenue. According to market researchers, as many as nine bootleg copies of software are in use for each legitimate disk. And on top of the monetary losses is emotional pain. Says Vern L. Rabur, the president of a software publishers named Symantec Corp.: "People invest their lives in a product. When they find out someone has copied it, there's a phenomenal sense of personal violation . . . like being raped or having someone break into your home."

Mr. Brown concedes that some of his customers may be software pirates, but he says that most piracy is done by people "innocently confused" about the law. He adds: "I'm totally against piracy. And if I felt the incidence of it were high, I wouldn't do what I'm doing. People are basically honest." His company, which doesn't use locks itself, includes with its programs a flier explaining that copying software is illegal except for backup copies.

To many computer owners, Mr. Brown is a hero. They argue that software locks gum up the workings of a computer and waste precious memory. Besides, they say, having one or two extra copies of a fragile software disk is perfectly legal—and important in case the original is damaged, by scratches or spilled coffee, for example. Declared one fan in a letter to a trade journal: "Mike Brown is the consumer's savior."

With raves such as that, Mr. Brown has little trouble selling his programs (brand name, Copy II), which bear retail prices of about $40. His programs are so popular that 15 telephone operators are hard-pressed to handle the orders.

Mr. Brown is a tall and stoop-shouldered man with a pudgy, innocent face and a sad smile. Bored with college, he dropped out in his junior year with a less-than-distinguished record; he had flunked calculus and barely scraped through physics. In 1980 he took a job at a computer store for $75 a week.

Before long, Mr. Brown found himself spending hours trying to placate angry software cus-

closure agreements. Second, trade secrets are based on state rather than federal laws; the extent of protection varies from state to state.

Patent protection is the most difficult protection to obtain because of the paperwork involved, the time the Patent Office takes to grant a patent (several years), and the Patent Office's reluctance to give patent protection to computer programs. A **patent** gives exclusive rights to the concepts embodied in the program for 17 years, which is more than sufficient in view of recent computer developments. But a patent is granted by the Patent Office only if the applicant convincingly demonstrates that the concepts haven't appeared in other programs—a mighty tall order for the applicant. Nevertheless, some software companies are turning to patents for the additional protection they provide.

Software License Agreements

On the shrinkwrapped box or sealed plastic bag in which personal computer software is usually packaged, a notice warns the purchaser not to open the package before reading and agreeing to the license agreement. For most programs, the license agreement is quite one-sided. It states that the software company isn't liable for any losses resulting from use of the program, and it warns purchasers that it is illegal to make copies (other than backup copies, if allowed) or to run the program on more than one machine.

Although the language of these license agreements is quite threatening, many personal computer users have difficulty differentiating software piracy and legal copying. Copyright law includes some **fair-use** provisions, which designate limited copying of copyrighted material as acceptable and therefore fair and legal. Selling copies of a program is definitely not fair use. Making one backup copy certainly is. But what about making extra backup copies? Many users would like to copy their business software for use on their home machines, but the license may prohibit use on "more than one machine at a time." It isn't fair use to run copies simulta-

THE 1987 ICCE POLICY STATEMENT ON SOFTWARE COPYRIGHT

Guidelines for Software Use

The 1976 U.S. Copyright Act and its 1980 amendments remain vague in some areas of software and its application to education. Where the law itself is vague, software licenses tend to be much more specific. It is therefore imperative that educators understand the software's licensing restrictions. Users should look to the copyright page of software documentation to find information regarding their rights, obligations, and license restrictions regarding each piece of software. If these uses are not addressed by the license, the following Guidelines representing the collected opinion of a variety of experts in the software copyright field, are recommended.

Back-up Copy: The Copyright Act is clear in permitting the owner of software a back-up copy of the software to be held for use as an archival copy in the event the original disk fails to function. Such back-up copies are not to be used on a second computer at the same time the original is used.

Multiple Loading: The Copyright Act is most unclear as it applies to loading the contents of one disk into multiple computers for use at the same time. In the absence of a license expressly permitting the user to load the contents of one disk into many computers for use at the same time, it is suggested that you NOT allow this activity to take place. The fact that you physically can do so is irrelevant. In an effort to make it easier for schools to buy software for each computer station, many software publishers offer lab packs and other quantity buying incentives. Contact individual publishers for details.

Local Area Network Software Use: It is suggested that before placing a software program on a local area network or disk-sharing system for use by multiple users at the same time, you obtain a written license agreement from the copyright holder giving you permission to do so. The fact that you are able to physically load the program on the network is, again, irrelevant. You should obtain a license to do so before you act.

Model Department policy on Software Copyright

1. The ethical and practical implications of software piracy will be taught to instructors and students.

2. Staff will be informed that they are expected to adhere to section 117 of the 1976 Copyright Act as amended in 1980, governing the use of software.

3. When permission is obtained from the copyright holder to use software on a disk-sharing system, efforts will be made to secure this software from copying.

4. Under no circumstances shall illegal copies of copyrighted software be made or used on school equipment.

5. A specific person of this department is designated as the only individual who may sign license agreements for software. Each site or location of this software will have a signed copy of these agreements.

6. The head of this department is responsible for establishing practices which will enforce this copyright policy.

Source: This is an abridged version of the guidelines from ICCE (International Council for Computers in Education), University of Oregon, 1781 Agate St, Eugene, Or 97403. This policy statement was developed by the ICCE Software Copyright Committe, a committee of educators, software developers, and industry representatives. A 1983 version of these guidelines was widely circulated and adopted by schools throughout the world.

neously on more than one computer if the copies aren't true backup copies. In short, fair use isn't always clear and may be redefined by the courts or by national commissions, such as the Commission on National Technology Use (CONTU), which defined fair-use guidelines for photocopying.

Schools and companies with many personal computers find it difficult to prevent unauthorized copying. One solution is to negotiate a **site license** agreement with the vendor that allows the organization to make either an unlimited or a specified number of copies, as long as all copies are used at the designated site.

Thwarting Piracy

Software publishers have experimented with educational campaigns and a variety of technical schemes to combat software pirates. Technical schemes use hardware, software, or a combination of the two, but they haven't been completely successful. Ideally, the scheme should be transparent to the legitimate user; at worst, it should be a slight inconvenience.

The most common technical scheme is to *copy-protect* a disk by placing an error on the disk (such as an improperly formatted or improperly labeled sector) that doesn't interfere with the running of the program but does cause a standard disk-copy routine to report an error. This isn't a permanent solution, because someone like Michael Brown—described in "A Word About" on page 553—will find a way to defeat each new copy-protection scheme.

Copy-protected disks are a nuisance, especially when used with a hard disk. One common copy-protection scheme requires that the copy-protected system disk be inserted into the floppy disk drive each time the program is started. Programs to defeat this sort of copy-protection scheme usually cost between $25 and $50, but they make an exact duplicate of the original disk on another floppy disk. Thus, it's reasonably easy for a pirate to make an illegal copy of the floppy disk, but it isn't convenient for a legitimate user to use the software on a hard disk.

Because there's always the danger of damaging or destroying an original copy-protected disk, in which case the program will no longer function, some copy-protected programs allow users to make a specific number of backup copies. The program encodes a count on the original disk; this count is decreased by one each time a copy is made. When the count reaches zero, no more copies can be made.

Two other protection schemes involve passwords and codes. In a password scheme, the user must remember a secret password to gain access to the program on the disk. A code scheme requires manufacturers to encode a unique serial number in the ROM of each microcomputer they make. The number is read by the program the first time it is run and is used thereafter to initialize the program. Unless it reads this number, the program will not run. As a result, it can't be used on a different computer. Although this scheme is very appealing to software companies, it isn't practical, because very few microcomputer manufacturers electronically number their microcomputers (an exception was the Apple Lisa).

Software publishers haven't come up with a solution to stop software piracy. It's doubtful that they will. An ideal solution would make it impossible to copy a program illegally but would not inconvenience legitimate users. So far, copy protection has made it harder for casual users to copy a program, at the cost of inconveniencing all users. Many software companies have given in to pressure from users and have stopped using copy protection altogether.

A combination of the following steps would reduce the problem:

- Developing protection schemes that minimally inconvenience legitimate users. Inconvenient schemes and the failure to provide a legitimate backup disk encourages piracy.

- Making it more difficult for pirates to copy programs, thereby discouraging all but the most technically sophisticated pirates.

- Educating users about the rights of software distributors and the rights of purchasers. Licensing agreements should be reasonable and should clearly state the rights and responsibilities of each party.

- Reducing the cost of software to less than the cost of the user's manual. Lower prices are feasible for programs with high-volume sales, but not for software designed for small markets.

Educators and educational publishers have organized to develop guidelines for educational institutions. During the early 1980s, the International Council for Computers in Education (ICCE), a leading professional association for educational computing, developed guidelines for software copying. These guidelines will probably be updated every few years, because new technology continues to raise new possibilities and problems.[7]

EMERGING ISSUES IN INFORMATION ETHICS

When people start using technology in a new way, the ethical implications of such use are often unknown. When the ethical issues eventually crystallize, community consensus may develop to demand appropriate legislation. For instance, there were no laws against publishing obscene pictures until many decades after photographic technology made such pictures possible. Maximum-speed laws weren't enacted in this country until 1926; by then, over 15 million Model T Fords were stirring up dust on the roads. This phenomenon, called *cultural lag,* is likely for computer technology as well, because legal solutions to conflicts between old values and new technology take time to emerge.

The ethical problems of computerized information systems are only beginning to surface in the public consciousness. Inevitably, some issues will engender public debate, trigger new legislation, and permanently alter social mores. This chapter has already reviewed three major issues—privacy, crime, and piracy—all of which deal with the ownership of information and therefore are appropriately classified as problems of information ethics. The remainder of the chapter identifies five less obvious ethical issues, which are nevertheless at the cutting edge of computer information systems: malpractice in the use of information, intellectual property rights, the value of information, the value of human capital, and equal access to information. These topics stand out in recent articles and books on ethics and computing.

Information Malpractice

Much as doctors worry about medical malpractice suits, information professionals, especially researchers and MIS executives, fear information malpractice suits. Professionals who conduct information searches are more and more often called *information brokers*. A typical information broker tracks down and assembles facts and ideas from libraries, experts, and a variety of computer-based data files. A survey of information brokers identified their common ethical dilemmas.

- Whether to report shortcomings of information sources
- Whether to accept kickbacks from information vendors, such as computerized database services
- How to protect client confidentiality
- Whether to exaggerate or misrepresent their own information-related competency[8]

As yet, there are no formal ethical codes for information brokers, nor are there statutes requiring them to obtain a license or to demonstrate other qualifications. A poor decision in any of these ethical areas, however, makes brokers vulnerable to malpractice claims.

Computer programmers who create information products also have reason to be concerned about malpractice suits. In 1986 an error in the software controlling a radiation therapy machine turned on the wrong type of electron beam, killing one patient and injuring others. The determination of fault in this case hasn't yet been made, but programmers in prior cases of a similar nature have been found guilty of negligence. It is even possible for programmers whose programs fail to work as claimed to be found guilty of fraud. Organizations as well as information workers are susceptible to information malpractice and product liability. Any defect in a computerized information system is a potential liability for the designers, owners, and administrators of the system.

The most common deficiency of information systems is inaccurate data. Although key-entry errors and foul-ups in record updates seem inconsequential, they can have serious effects on individuals and corporations. Consider the trauma of Mr. and Mrs. Gorges. The Gorgeses both worked hard for years to save enough money to buy a house.[9] When they finally bought their little dream home, they regularly took their monthly mortgage payment to the bank. One month they were notified that their last month's payment was past due. Mr. Gorges had evidence of having made the payment, but when he went to the bank, they couldn't find any trace of it in their computer system. The bank refused to acknowledge receipt of the payment and eventually sent out a notice of foreclosure. Upon reading the no-

Figure 17.8 This cartoon is typical of a popular cartoon scenario in which an information malpractice victim attempts revenge on the computer. With future improvements in the practice of information processing, we would hope that such cartoons would no longer be funny.

tice, Mrs. Gorges, who was already ill, collapsed with a nearly fatal stroke. Finally, Mr. Gorges hired an attorney who obtained a sizable settlement from the bank. The system software was apparently defective and didn't make reasonable checks for error conditions. It is likely that, in the future, computer operations will give greater attention to identifying and correcting such deficiencies. In addition, we can expect more and stricter standards for information practice and malpractice as our society grows more dependent on information. Meanwhile, the victims of these incidents suffer the feelings depicted in the cartoon in Figure 17.8.

Intellectual Property Rights

Frightened by widespread duplication of audio, video, and software recordings, the entertainment and software industries have pressured lawmakers for protection. The problems remain, and no quick and easy solutions are in sight. As we stated earlier, copyright law today doesn't encompass important types of computer-related information. For instance, databases that are continuously updated can't be copyrighted, nor can intellectual ideas central to major software inventions, such as spreadsheets. And the law has yet to address the question of who owns the information produced by expert system software. Inadequate and outmoded laws shift a greater burden on the individual's conscience. In times of rapid change, personal ethics are perhaps the best protection against chaos.

In 1986 the Office of Technology Assessment, a legislative department that helps Congress predict and prepare for new uses of technology, published *Intellectual Property Rights in an Age of Electronics and Information,* a 300-page report that concluded a long and extensive investigation. With input from hundreds of industry and academic specialists, the authors concluded that existing law for copyrights, patents, and trademarks needs to be replaced by a different legal framework. They proposed a major legal distinction between works of art, works of fact, and works of function. This proposal addresses the diversity of protection methods required by different types of intellectual properties.

No matter what legal framework is established, copyright violations won't be easy to stop. One difficulty is the great number or economic, technical, political, legal, and ethical problems that must be addressed in any new laws. Out of this complexity may emerge greater clarity and consensus, so that lawmakers, the public, and those who create and distribute intellectual property can recognize and agree what constitutes fair and appropriate use of such property.

The Value of Information

As our society moves rapidly toward being a full-scale information society, the value of information increases. Success in commerce depends more and more on information, so information itself gets treated like a proprietary commodity. In fact, information industries can't function unless information is designated as private property. Nonetheless, the public, as indicated by its large-scale violations of audio, video, and software copyrights, resists the notion of information ownership. Furthermore, acceptance of information as commodity contradicts a basic premise of our educational system—that information is freely available to all. The legal system has traditionally treated physical property and information as having different implications for liability. Consequently, we can expect ongoing debates on the meaning and ownership of different types of information.

The Value of Human Capital

Another difficult, but relevant issue is that of human capital and automation. When a skill that had been performed by humans is performed by an automated system, a transfer of intellectual property from the person to the system occurs. But people rarely receive any compensation for this transfer, because our socioeconomic system doesn't treat performance as something owned by a human worker. The old issue of unemployment and automation is raised anew by computerization, as it begins to tackle work that demands a great deal of knowledge. When the knowledge of a human expert is implanted into an expert system, it raises challenging ethical questions of ownership as well as responsibility. What compensation is warranted for this exchange of intellectual property? Who should share in the credit for and profit from the performance of an expert system? Is human dignity jeopardized when ideas and information are transplanted from people to software systems whose performance exceeds human skill? We and future generations will have to resolve important ethical questions like these.

Equal Access to Information

Computer-accessed databases dramatically improve our ability to retrieve obscure information, but the cost is passed on directly to the users. Prior to the widespread use of these systems, anyone who needed this information could search through print and microfilm files in remote corners of public libraries. The work was tedious, but the information was free. Not only is the cost of many types of information going up, but people who want to access it need expensive computer equipment, and the whole process demands specialized training.

The growing expense of information retrieval could be picked up by schools and public libraries, but the trend is in the opposite direction. Libraries rarely provide free computer-based bibliographic file searches, and it is unusual to find a school that trains students in these skills. In fact, national studies have found that schools in poor communities are less likely than those in wealthy communities to teach computer skills to their students. The poor, then, are more likely to become "information dropouts," a situation that in the long run may be as serious as that of today's school dropouts. Setting up financial and educational obstacles to information access may promote a social system in which the poor get information-poor and the information-poor get poor. Is this the direction in which our society is heading? Are people getting caught in a vicious cycle in which those who ignore information are likely to become poor, and once they become poor, they can no longer afford access to information?

Information access may be a problem for other social groups, in addition to the poor. This is especially likely if technological prowess is essential to information access. In part because of cultural attitudes and norms, certain groups, including women, racial minorities, and the elderly, have tended to shun computing skills. It is possible, but not inevitable, that this will put them at an information disadvantage.

Experts and educators have addressed this problem in recent years under the banner of **computer equity**, which is equal opportunity for computing for all social groups. For instance, an Ohio project has given grants to school projects designed to reduce discrepancies in computer opportunities for females, minorities, and the disabled. The 1987 Code of Ethical Conduct for Computer-Using Educators, issued by the International Council for Computers in Education, specifies that educators should ensure that "students have equal access to computers and computer-related experiences."[10] Because it isn't easy to balance the ethical questions of fairness in information access, many organizations are ignoring the problem. This might make such issues even more difficult and expensive to resolve later.

SUMMARY

This chapter has presented three thorny ethical issues directly related to the use of computers: individual privacy, computer crime, and software piracy. No simple solution or policy has been developed that deals adequately with them. One step is to make both system developers and computer users aware of these issues, and to encourage them to incorporate this awareness in their work.

It is all but impossible to prevent an expert user from copying a program or to prevent a user with inside information from accessing a computer system. Obstacles and safeguards will discourage many users from attempting piracy or trespassing, but ironically, these may challenge the technically clever to thwart the security system.

Any new computer development is also likely to spark ethical debate. As just one example, look at the unresolved questions that surround electronic mail systems. What security measures should be taken to protect the information in these systems? Who is responsible if information is divulged? Are they subject to obscenity laws? Who can or should censor material in these systems? Can anyone read information in these systems? Technological advances occur so rapidly that it is difficult to develop laws, safeguards, or guidelines against their misuse or to adequately study and address their social impact. One thing can be said with certainty: the more information based our society becomes, the more ethical issues will revolve around information issues. Questions of information accuracy, ownership, and access will occupy a central place in the ethical debates of future generations. Speculating on their outcomes can give us a fuller perspective on present problems.

KEY TERMS

access monitoring	patent
callback PPD	port protection device (PPD)
computer crime	public domain
computer equity	salami slicing
copyright	shareware
cracker	site license
encryption	software piracy
fair use	trade secret
hacker	Trojan horse

1. What rights should people have regarding information about them in computer databases? How might these rights interfere with the efficiency of a free-market economy?

2. Do you support the establishment of a universal identifier card that would serve as a driver's license, credit card, and health record? What long-term benefits might this system have?

3. What information (in any) should owners of private databases be required to make publicly available?

4. Social security numbers are often used as a key in accessing personal information contained in several databases. Should some restrictions be placed on the use of a person's social security number?

5. Do you think the government's matching of computer files to find welfare cheaters was unethical or illegal? What portion of fraud and tax evasion do you think might be prevented if government agencies were allowed unlimited access to the records of financial institutions?

6. Authorities have raided several electronic bulletin boards used by "crackers" and seized their computing equipment and disks. They said that they hoped to "scare the kids." Should the person running the bulletin board be responsible for what callers write in the bulletin board?

7. Do you think a hacker should be able to access a computer system when it isn't busy? Is a computer system with inadequate security an attractive nuisance?

8. Would lowering the price of software reduce piracy?

9. Is allowing computer software to be used on just one machine too restrictive? Can you suggest a more reasonable rule?

EXERCISES

1. Find a reported case of computer crime. What type of security safeguards would have prevented the crime?

2. List some reasons why a bank might not prosecute a computer-abetted embezzler. List some reasons why they should prosecute.

3. Determine what laws (if any) your state has enacted concerning computer trespassing.

4. Interview the director of a computer center about security safeguards.

5. Investigate the history of patents for computer programs.

6. Read several software license agreements for personal computer software. What restrictions are included? If the programs come from different companies, list the differences.

7. List some tasks a computer shouldn't perform. Justify your choices. Because a computer can't be convicted of a crime, who is responsible when a computer commits a criminal action? The programmer who wrote the program? the computer operator? the computer user? the computer's manufacturer?

NOTES

1. Kenneth C. Laudon, *Dossier Society* (New York: Columbia University Press, 1986).

2. Deborah G. Johnson, *Computer Ethics* (Englewood Cliffs, N.J.: Prentice-Hall, 1985), p. 68.

3. Laudon.

4. Donn B. Parker, *Crime by Computer* (New York: Charles Scribner's & Sons, 1976).

5. "The 414 Gang Strikes Again," *Time,* 29 August 1983, p. 75.

6. EDUCOM Software Initiative, *Using Software: A Guide to the Ethical and Legal Use of Software for Members of the Academic Communities* (Princeton, NJ: EDUCOM, 1987).

7. "1987 Statement on Software Copyright—An ICCE Policy Statement," *The Computing Teacher* 14, 6(March 1987):52–53.

8. Anne P. Mintz, "Information Practice and Malpractice," *Library Journal* 110, 3(September–December 1985):38–43.

9. Richard O. Mason, "Four Ethical Issues of the Information Age," *MIS Quarterly* 10, 1(March 1986):5–12.

10. "Code of Ethical Conduct for Computer-Using Educators—An ICCE Policy Statement," *The Computing Teacher* 14, 5(February 1987):51–53.

Figure 18.1 Timeline for the history of computing.

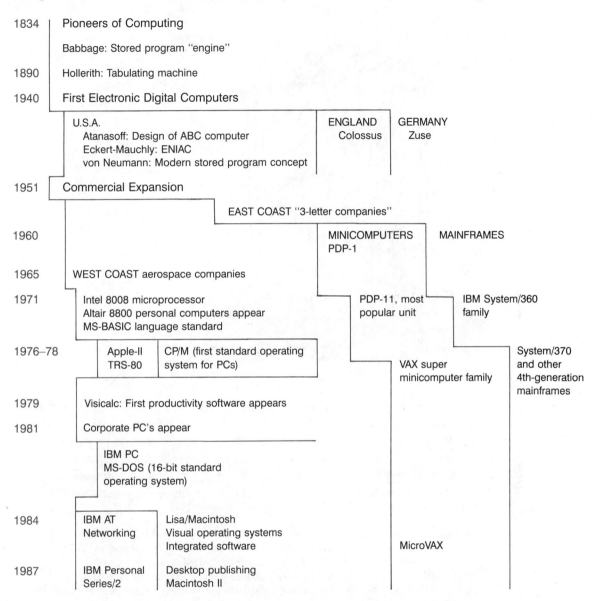

Ironically, he didn't set out to build a computer, nor did he finish building one. A respected British mathematician, Babbage became fascinated with inventing a radically new calculating machine. Working for many years in the mid-1800s, he designed a machine he called a *difference engine*. It was to be steam powered and have thousands of gears, wheels, and barrels (see Figure 18.2).

Babbage never completed the difference engine—in part because the technology of his day couldn't produce gears and wheels with the required precision. But

Figure 18.2 Babbage's difference engine.

Babbage also abandoned the difference engine because he decided to build a different computer, which he called the *analytical engine*. The difference engine was designed for specific computations, but the analytical engine was to be capable of performing *any* computation. In designing the machine, Babbage borrowed from **Joseph Jacquard** (1752–1834), who in 1801 had invented an automatic loom. The weaving sequences in Jacquard's loom were controlled by punched cards. Babbage struggled with the design of a general control mechanism.

> This day I had a general but only indistinct conception of the possibility of making an engine work out *algebraic* developments. . . . I mean without *any* reference to the *value* of the letters. . . . My notion is that as the (instructions on) cards of the calculating engine direct a series of operations and then recommence with the first so it might perhaps be possible to cause some cards to punch others equivalent to any given number of repetitions.[1]

Thus, Babbage came up with some key elements of the concept of a *stored program*.

Lady Ada Lovelace (1815–1852), fascinated by Babbage's genius, worked with him for several years. She wrote some punch code sequences, as well as some important notes on their conceptions of how the machine should work. Be-

Figure 18.3 Hollerith's machines for sorting and tabulating.

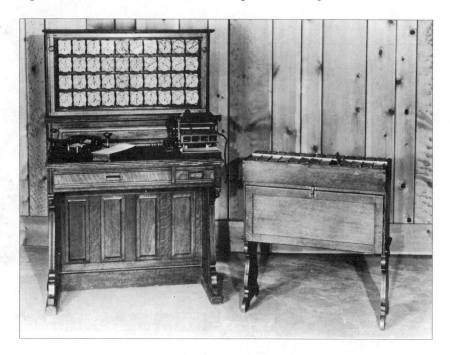

cause of these contributions, she is generally credited with being the first "programmer," and an advanced programming language, Ada, was named after her.

Herman Hollerith and the Tabulating Machine

Herman Hollerith (1860–1926) is credited with providing the impetus for automated data processing. His invention came in response to a counting problem: by the late 1800s, the U.S. Census Bureau was still counting people by hand, and it would take more than five years just to count the responses from census survey.

After working for the Census Bureau, Hollerith quit and devoted several years to inventing a machine system for tabulation. He also took a job at the U.S. Patent Office, so that he would be sure to cope with patent policy. Hollerith built a "tabulating machine" (Figure 18.3) that tabulated (counted) data by sorting cards. The machine used 80-column punched cards about the size of a dollar bill, which are often called "Hollerith cards." Using Hollerith's machines, the Census Bureau processed data for the 1890 census in less than two years.

Hollerith sold his company, which built punched-card tabulating equipment, to a company called the Computing-Tabulating-Recording-Company. This company later changed its name to International Business Machines Corporation—IBM.

Figure 18.4 The ENIAC computer.

First Electronic Computers

Unlike Babbage's engines, Hollerith's machines used electricity. But unlike modern computers, the tabulating machines were mostly mechanical, didn't use stored programs, and were limited in their arithmetic. The complicated computations needed for scientific problems, especially those associated with research for World War II, led to the development of the electronic digital computer.

Controversy surrounds the question of who should receive credit for inventing the first electronic computer. **Konrad Zuse** (1910–), a German engineer recruited into the German army, is supposed to have had a program-controlled electronic computer working in 1941, but it was destroyed in an Allied bombing raid.

A British computer, Colossus, was used as early as 1943 to break German cipher codes. Its work is still classified as secret, and scant information about it is available. **John V. Atanasoff** (1903–), a physics professor at Iowa State College, designed—but didn't complete—the ABC electronic computer from 1939 to 1942. Atanasoff urged Iowa State to patent his computer, but the college failed to act. From 1943 to 1946, **John W. Mauchly** (1907–1980) and **J. Presper Eckert** (1919–) of the University of Pennsylvania developed **ENIAC** (*E*lectronic *N*umerical *I*ntegrator and *C*alculator) (see Figure 18.4). Its development was funded by the U.S. Army to compute ballistics tables for artillery shells. John Mauchly visited Atanasoff in 1940 and 1941 and based some of ENIAC on Atanasoff's work. In

Figure 18.5 Plug-board of the ENIAC.

1973 a U.S. federal court invalidated the Eckert and Mauchly patent for the electronic digital computer and declared Atanasoff the inventor.

Though Atanasoff had built a special-purpose electronic computer, ENIAC was the first general-purpose electronic digital computer. Unlike Babbage's analytical engine and other early devices, it was totally electronic and had no mechanical counters. ENIAC contained 18,000 vacuum tubes, 70,000 resistors, and 500,000 hand-soldered connections. It weighed 30 tons, used 100 kilowatts of electricity, and occupied a 20-by-40-foot room. Supposedly, all the lights in one section of Philadelphia dimmed when it was turned on. It had a limited amount of storage and was unreliable because the vacuum tubes frequently burned out. It was programmed by plugging wires into three walls of plug-boards containing over 6,000 switches. Changing the program required resetting switches by replugging the plug-board (see Figure 18.5). These problems were tolerable, though, because ENIAC could perform arithmetic at the unheard-of rate of 5,000 additions or 300 multiplications per second.

The last, but most important step in the development of the electronic computer was the memory-stored program, an extension of Babbage's idea of using instruction cards to control a machine's operation. In retrospect, the advantage of

Figure 18.6 Univac I, the first commercial computer.

storing a program electronically in computer memory seems obvious: the program can be changed simply by reading another program into memory.

John von Neumann (1903–1957), a famous mathematician at the Institute for Advanced Study at Princeton University, is credited with developing the modern concept of the stored program. Von Neumann developed the concept of the stored program in conjunction with the design of **EDVAC** (*E*lectronic *D*iscrete *V*ariable *A*utomatic *C*omputer) at the University of Pennsylvania. EDVAC was the second computer developed by Mauchly and Eckert. When Mauchly and Eckert's computer company was in financial difficulty, Remington-Rand acquired it and produced the first commercial computer, the **UNIVAC I** (*Univ*ersal *A*utomatic *C*omputer), in 1951. Significantly, the UNIVAC I was purchased by the U.S. Census Bureau (see Figure 18.6).

Once it became possible to store a binary program in memory, the next major programming breakthroughs were assemblers and compilers, which produced loadable programs from symbolic expressions. **Grace Murray Hopper** (1906–) developed the first compiler in 1952 (see Figure 18.7). A gifted mathematician,

she worked with Eckert and Mauchly for many years. She is credited with developing some of the first programming languages and had an enormous influence on the early evolution of procedure-oriented languages.

MAINFRAME COMPUTER GENERATIONS

We can divide the second major stage of computing history into two paths followed by two groups: the "East Coast companies" and the "West Coast companies." Generally, the East Coast companies have three-letter names—IBM, NCR, RCA, DEC, and so on. The West Coast companies tend to be associated with the aerospace industry and the military.

The East Coast companies have pursued data processing in government and in large financial, manufacturing, and retail businesses. Data processing in these organizations requires powerful mainframe computers with huge memories and a professional staff. The idea of a personal computer would never occur to this

Table 18.1 Generations of Mainframe Computers

	First Generation (Vacuum Tubes)	Second Generation (Transistors)	Third Generation (Integrated Circuits)	Fourth Generation (Large-Scale Integration)
Speed (instructions per second)	Up to 10,000	Up to 1 million	Up to 10 million	Up to 1 billion
Memory capacity (in characters)	1,000 to 8,000	4,000 to 64,000	32,000 to 4 million	512,000 to 32 million
Failure rate	Minutes	Days	Days to weeks	Weeks
Relative cost (per operation)	$10.00	$1.00	$.10	Less than $.01
External storage	Cards	Tape	Disc	Mass storage
Operating system	Single-user; jobs scheduled manually	Single-user; jobs scheduled automatically	Multiple-user; timesharing	Multiple-user; networks and distributed systems

professional staff. The idea of a personal computer would never occur to this group. Today, the financial community would collapse under tons of paper without large-scale, central mainframe computers. Never before have so many aspects of business depended on the infallibility of machines.

The West Coast companies pursued the scientific and engineering uses of computers, in particular for the military and for the space program. Controlling a missile requires a small, lightweight computer that can rapidly calculate trajectories, adjust engines, and communicate with earth stations. The scientists and engineers who design such computers typically work alone or in small groups—a combination ideal for nurturing small, individualized microcomputers.

Thus, the history of computing takes two separate paths from 1951 to 1980. The East Coast companies developed large data processing machines through four generations, as shown in Table 18.1. The West Coast companies developed microelectronic space technology, turning it into down-to-earth products for commercial consumption—products like pocket calculators, video games, and personal computers. To take a closer look at these two paths, we will first discuss the development of mainframe computers by the East Coast companies.

The First Generation: Vacuum Tube Systems (1951–1958)

First-generation computers used vacuum tubes to provide electronic circuits. For memory these computers used a magnetic drum, a rotating cylinder whose outer surface could be magnetized. Punched cards were used for input of both data and programs. Program instructions were given in machine language. These computers were slow, unreliable, expensive, and tedious to program.

The Second Generation: Transistor Systems (1958–1964)

The second generation of computers began when transistors replaced vacuum tubes. The transistors were 1/200th the size of a vacuum tube, generated less heat, were faster, and failed less often. The internal memory of these computers was composed of tiny, doughnut-shaped magnetic cores strung on thin intersecting wires. (This is the origin of the term *core memory,* which refers to internal memory.) Magnetic tape largely replaced punched cards for input and output. Printers with speeds of up to 600 lines per minute were developed.

The second generation also brought improvements in software. One important development was the invention of high-level programming languages in the mid to late 1950s, including FORTRAN for engineers and COBOL for business programmers. These languages represented a giant step forward, because they are less detailed and easier to learn and use than machine language. Thus, a person with little or no technical knowledge of the computer could write programs to solve problems. Meanwhile, the task of starting and scheduling the execution of programs had become too complex and time-sensitive to leave to a computer operator. This problem was solved by the invention of the operating system.

The Third Generation: Integrated Circuits (1964–1971)

Integrated circuits replaced transistors in third-generation computers. An *integrated circuit* is a complex electronic circuit etched on a tiny silicon chip about one-quarter inch square. It is smaller, faster, and more reliable than separate transistors wired together.

Major improvements also occurred in the capabilities of peripheral devices. Magnetic devices replaced magnetic tape for storing information when rapid access to data was required. Faster printers were developed; they could print nearly 3,000 lines per minute. Cathode ray tubes (CRTs) were used to display input and output.

Operating systems capable of timesharing also began to appear during the third generation. This allowed many users to use a single computer simultaneously, thereby permitting them also to share the enormous cost of third-generation computers. The BASIC programming language was developed at this time at Dartmouth under a grant from the National Science Foundation. It was designed to make programming as easy as possible.

In the early 1960s, IBM made a significant commitment to develop an entire family of computers that could run the same operating system and application programs. Some 5,000 people were assigned to develop the system software for this project on a two-year schedule. Then, on April 7, 1964, IBM announced the **System/360** family of computers (see Figure 18.8). The family consisted of six computers with memory sizes ranging from 16KB to over 1 megabyte. These computers were enormously successful because customers could upgrade from one member of the family to another without changing their application software. Most

Figure 18.8 An IBM System/360–series computer.

of the computers IBM has introduced since 1965 are upwardly compatible with the original System/360 computers.

IBM captured and has held a 60 to 75 percent share of the mainframe computer market. The success of its System/360 computers drove several major competitors from the computer business. For example, General Electric quit the computer business in 1970, RCA in 1972, and Xerox in 1975. Other companies tried to survive by moving into defensible market niches. One of these market niches was the small computer market. In 1960 the three-year-old Digital Equipment Corporation (DEC) brought out the first minicomputer, the PDP-1. It cost less than mainframe computers and had a much smaller instruction set. The PDP product line grew until the **PDP-11**, introduced in 1969, became the best-selling general-purpose minicomputer ever.

The Fourth Generation: Large-Scale Integration (1971–)

The beginning of the fourth computer generation coincided with the development of the **large-scale integrated (LSI) circuit**—a single chip that contains thousands of transistors. The term **very large-scale integration (VLSI)** was introduced when chips began having tens of thousands of transistors. Today, VLSI chips can have millions of transistors. VLSI chips are made with lithographic methods and can be mass-produced to spread their high research and development costs over many units.

The introduction of the IBM System/370 series is generally considered to mark the beginning of the fourth computer generation. The computers in this series offered virtual memory so that they could run programs of enormous size. By 1977 DEC was offering the VAX minicomputers with virtual memory. And in 1985 DEC announced the Micro VAX II, a complete minicomputer based on a set of three VLSI processor chips. DEC grew at a phenomenal rate to become the second-largest computer manufacturer in the United States.

Large fourth-generation computers can support extensive timesharing; up to several thousand users may use the computer at the same time. In addition, programs and peripheral devices, such as disks and printers, have grown by leaps and bounds in variety, capability, and sophistication.

EVOLUTION OF MICROCOMPUTERS

While the East Coast companies continued to develop mainframe and minicomputers, the West Coast companies were busy applying LSI to products for the aerospace industry and the military. The main center for this work was a string of small towns located between San Jose and San Francisco, California—the famous Silicon Valley. It was here that two engineers working after hours at home invented the first commercially successful microcomputer.

Microcomputers have undergone remarkable changes since they were introduced in the mid-1970s. The first microcomputers were crude machines that could be used only by programmers. Today, the average person can learn to use a state-of-the-art microcomputer for productive tasks in a few hours. One way of viewing the evolution of microcomputers is shown in Table 18.2, which divides the process into six three-hour stages: three stages in the past, the stage we are currently passing through, and two stages predicted for the future. The first three stages in Table 18.2 are loosely based on a presentation given in 1983 by David House, vice president of Intel, in which he predicted that new generations of microprocessor systems will continue to be introduced on roughly three-year cycles. We will discuss each stage, but first it is appropriate to look at the development of the heart of every microcomputer, the microprocessor.

Microprocessors

On November 1, 1956, William Shockley, John Bardeen, and Walter Brattain received word that they had been awarded the Nobel Prize in Physics for their invention of the transistor. It was a study of Shockley's, **Robert Noyce** (1927–), who was to become the father of the integrated circuit—the basis for the microprocessor chip. (Recall that a *microprocessor* is a circuit built on a single silicon chip, which can execute a program.) Noyce founded Intel Corporation, which in turn developed large-scale integrated (LSI) circuits used in microcomputers.

Table 18.2 Evolution of Personal Computers: Past, Present, and Future

Developmental Stage (1971–1977)   *Example: MITS Altair 8800*

- Sold in kits to hobbyists via mail order
- Main memory from 4KB to 32KB; crude 8-bit processor
- Computer and peripherals (keyboard, CRT, storage) purchased separately
- Programmed in machine language or BASIC
- Cassette tape storage

Early Adopter Stage (1977–1981)   *Example: Apple II*

- Sold as a fully assembled computer through retail computer stores
- Main memory from 16KB to 64KB; simple 8-bit processor
- 8-inch or small-capacity $5\frac{1}{4}$-inch floppy disk storage
- Standardized, simple operating system; first end-user applications

Corporate Stage (1981–1984)   *Example: IBM PC*

- Sold as a computer system by major corporations
- Main memory from 64KB to 256KB; early 16-bit processor
- Larger-capacity $5\frac{1}{4}$-inch disk storage; expensive small hard disks
- Enhanced operating systems; well-developed application packages
- Strong industry standards for both hardward and software

Integrated Systems Stage (1984–1987)   *Examples: Apple Macintosh, IBM PC/AT*

- Sold as a personal productivity tool for knowledge workers
- Main memory from 128KB to 1 megabyte; early 32-bit processor
- $3\frac{1}{2}$-inch microfloppy, $5\frac{1}{4}$-inch minifloppy, and hard disk storage
- Visual-based operating systems, integrated application packages

Networked Systems Stage (1987–1990)   *Examples: Macintosh II, IBM Personal System/2*

- Sold as compatible with integrated office systems
- Main memory from 512KB to 8MB; advanced 32-bit processor
- High-capacity microfloppy and hard disk storage
- Multitasking operating system; standardized local area network interface

Information Age Stage (1990–)   *Examples: compuphone, compustereo, hypertext*

- Sold as a commodity item for "reaching out to touch the world"
- Main memory from 2MB to 16MB; several special-purpose 32-bit processors
- Large optical CD discs with writing as well as reading capabilities
- Computer-stereo-video systems using a common interactive CD-data player
- Built-in digital phone; several high-speed network interfaces
- Voice/visual-based operating systems

The first microprocessor, the Intel 4004, was announced in 1971 by Intel Corporation. It had been designed by a small group of engineers led by Ted Hoff. The 4004 had the equivalent of 2,250 transistors, making it an exceedingly limited processor. It could process only 4 bits of information at a time.

A computer based on the 4004 contained two important chips: the 4004 microprocessor chip and another chip, called a *fixed-program chip*, which could permanently store the instructions for controlling an electrical device. Other chips could be added as needed. Millions of 4-bit microprocessors have been used in appliances, hand-held calculators, cars, toys, and digital watches. For these applications, the 4004 made a good special-purpose computer, but it was too slow and limited to be the processor for a microcomputer.

Several 8-bit microprocessors were developed before 1974, but the 8-bit Intel 8008 (and its immediate successor, the 8080) was the first one with the speed and power needed for a microcomputer. The 16-bit microcomputer family was initiated with the Intel 8086 in 1978. Four years later it introduced the 80286, which provided the base for IBM's PC/AT. In 1985 Intel released the 80386, a very fast, 32-bit processor. The most popular early 32-bit microprocessor is the Motorola 68000, which is used in hundreds of products, including the Apple Macintosh and many laser printers.

In 1986 Intel began shipping production quantities of its 80386 microprocessor. This processor became an instant success, because it is able to run existing software for IBM Personal Computers two to four times faster than previous microprocessors. In addition, the microprocessor has several different ways of operating, called *modes*. Its *protected mode* can manage up to 4 gigabits of physical memory and offers the same sort of virtual memory features provided by mainframe computers. Its *virtual 86 mode* allows several application programs to run simultaneously as if the computer had separate microprocessors—a feature called **multitasking**.

A recently developed microcomputer is likely to contain **coprocessor chips**, which are special-purpose microprocessors designed to handle specific functions, such as graphics, spoken input and output, high-speed floating-point arithmetic, and interfaces for telecommunications and local area networks.

Developmental Stage (1971–1977)

The first microcomputer, the **MITS** (*Micro Instrumentation and Telemetry Systems*) **Altair 8800**, was based on the Intel 8008 microprocessor. In 1974 the company was facing bankruptcy and decided to try to sell an inexpensive computer in kit form. In a particularly smart move, they sent a kit to *Popular Electronics* magazine, which published a feature article on it. Soon MITS was overwhelmed with orders. The Altair sold in kit form (unassembled) for $395 or fully assembled for $621. Most buyers were technically knowledgeable hobbyists. The Altair didn't include a keyboard, CRT monitor, disk drive, or printer. These items were purchased separately, much like the components of a stereo system.

Initially the Altair was programmed by hobbyists in machine language, but this method was arduous and error-prone. **Bill Gates** dropped out of Harvard to remedy the situation. Together with Paul Allen, Gates developed the first high-level language for a microprocessor. His version of BASIC on the MITS Altair soon became the standard programming language for microcomputers. In 1974 Gates and Allen founded Microsoft Corporation.

Figure 18.9 On the left is Bill Gates, chairman of the board and executive vice president of Microsoft. On the right is Gary Kildall, chairman of the board for Digital Research.

In 1973 **Gary Kildall** was working as a consultant for Intel. His job was to implement a programming language for the 8080 microprocessor. To make it easier for him to use the microprocessor, he developed a program called **CP/M** (*C*ontrol *P*rogram for *M*icrocomputers) for controlling a keyboard, CRT screen, and disks. Kildall first offered the program to Intel, but Intel declined the offer, so Kildall sold CP/M by mail to hobbyists. In 1975 he set up Digital Research to sell CP/M. In no time at all, CP/M was being used on more than 1 million microcomputer systems. Kildall's CP/M had a dramatic effect on the development of microcomputers, because manufacturers no longer had to develop an individual operating system for each different computer, and programmers could use the same commands on a variety of machines. CP/M remains the most widely used operating system for 8-bit computers.

The success of these early entrepreneurs (shown in Figure 18.9) led others to manufacture and sell microcomputers and accessories. Within two years, there were stores, clubs, and magazines devoted entirely to the personal computer. By 1977 there were more than 50 brands of microcomputers and, by the end of 1978, over 700 computer stores. Computer clubs provided members with an opportunity to show off their computers, share experiences, and learn about new products. The Southern California Club had over 3,000 members in 1977. Computer magazines, such as *BYTE, Creative Computing,* and *Dr. Dobbs' Journal of Computer Calisthenics and Orthodontics,* publish advertisements and articles about personal computers, programs, and applications.

Together, Microsoft BASIC and CP/M were a powerful force in determining the direction of microcomputer programs. They established both a standard language for programmers and a standard vehicle for disseminating programs. But the trouble with them was that they assumed programming knowledge of their users.

Early Adopter Stage (1977–1981)

Stephen Wozniack and **Steven Jobs** began business by selling the Apple I microcomputer in kit form out of a garage in California. They realized the shortcomings of kits and developed the Apple II microcomputer. It was wildly successful, because they sold it preassembled, in retail stores, and included a disk drive and a simple operating system. Consumers could buy a ready-to-use computer and a disk drive to store information, in a form that could be quickly accessed. The Apple II soon set the standard for commercially successful microcomputer manufacturers.

The Radio Shack division of Tandy Corporation introduced the first personal computer in their TRS-80 line in 1977. The TRS-80 Model I was sold fully assembled and included a keyboard, cassette tape or disk, printer, and various sizes of memory. The Model I was sold in Radio Shack's nationwide chain of retail stores for $500 to $1,500, depending on options. It also included the Microsoft BASIC language. The theory was that a person could write BASIC programs to solve his or her problems. Typical buyers were hobbyists, educators, and small businesses. Commodore Business Machines, a large adding machine company, introduced the Commodore PET in 1977. It was an assembled, complete microcomputer, with a keyboard, screen, and cassette tape drive, which sold for $650.

A new idea in software soon expanded the usefulness of these machines. While taking a business course at Harvard University, **Dan Bricklin** got the idea for a program that anybody could use—Visicalc. It turned a microcomputer like the Apple II into a familiar spreadsheet that would total numbers in rows and columns. It was important for many reasons: it made people realize that anybody could use a computer; it caused Apple II sales to soar; and it promoted the idea of a computer *paradigm.* That is, Visicalc was more than a program; it was a metaphor, which many others soon copied. Even today, the best software emulates some familiar model, such as a spreadsheet, desktop, file drawer, or library.

At about the same time, word processing software on microcomputers became popular as an alternative to expensive systems designed solely for word processing. AppleWriter by Paul Lutus and WordStar by Rob Barnaby were among the first best sellers. More than half a million copies of each program were sold during the late 1970s.

Corporate Stage (1981–1984)

Large computer manufacturers, such as IBM and DEC, didn't enter the microcomputer field until the 1980s. This is quite surprising, especially since DEC specialized in minicomputers, which are only a step above microcomputers in size and

Figure 18.10 The IBM Personal Computer, announced in 1981.

power. Probably these companies delayed entering the microcomputer market because they felt the marketplace was too volatile or because they didn't realize its size and potential. When IBM and other large computer manufacturers did enter the market, they established a standard of excellence for microcomputers and gave them legitimacy and credibility.

This corporate phase began with the introduction in 1981 of the IBM Personal Computer, which at first was called the PC, but now the IBM PC (see Figure 18.10). It legitimized personal computing for Fortune 500 companies, began the era of the 16-bit microcomputer, and established Microsoft's MS-DOS as the standard 16-bit operating system.

Corporations soon began to realize that the personal computer could increase the productivity of office workers. Spreadsheet, word processing, and database management programs began to be used so extensively that they became known as **productivity software**. Productivity software invaded noncomputer companies, bringing change at a rate that has rarely been seen in the history of corporations.

Integrated Systems Stage (1984–1987)

After the explosive growth of the corporate stage, the microcomputer revolution went through a period of consolidation in terms of hardware, software, and suppliers. Microcomputers were integrated with other microcomputers and with mainframes to form computer networks. Programs were integrated with other programs to form integrated packages. And the industry went through a midlife crisis that some of the smaller manufacturers didn't survive. Some causes for this crisis were rapidly falling hardware prices, a downturn in the growth curve for microcomputer sales, and an increased emphasis on hardware and software standards.

An interesting trend during this period was a rapid drop in the cost of microcomputers designed specifically around a visual operating system. The Apple Lisa marked the beginning of this trend; it was introduced in early 1983 at $9,995. Then came the Apple Macintosh (introduced in early 1984 at $2,495), the Commodore Amiga (introduced in mid-1985 at $1,295), and the Atari 520 ST (introduced in late 1985 at $799). All of these machines use the same processor (the Motorola 68000), but the latter two also have a sound-generation chip that can generate three or four simultaneous audio voices, a graphics coprocessor that provides superior graphics manipulation capabilities, and support for color monitors.

In 1984 IBM added an important new member to its family of microcomputers with the announcement of the IBM PC/AT (AT stands for "advanced technology"). The AT is about four times faster than an IBM PC and is far more expandable. Because its processor supports virtual memory, it can address up to 1 gigabyte (1 *billion* bytes) of virtual memory. The processor is also designed for multitasking; that is, it can support multiple users or concurrent applications. Starting in 1985, a flood of "AT-compatible" microcomputers was introduced by competitors, including Compaq, Texas Instruments, Kaypro, and AT&T.

By 1985 the IBM PC family had captured a dominant role in corporate personal computing. For example, in 1985 Dun & Bradstreet Corporation surveyed the buying plans of businesses that already had personal computers. Of the planned purchases, 72 percent were for various IBM PC models, only 7 percent were for Apple, and most of the rest were for IBM PC-compatible computers.

But in 1986 desktop publishing suddenly burst on the scene as the fastest-growing segment of personal computing, and business began opening its doors to Macintosh computers. In March 1987 Apple announced its Macintosh II computer, shown in Figure 18.11, which offered a color display, used a faster processor, and provided the option of an IBM-compatible microprocessor and easy conversion of files between IBM and Macintosh formats. In April 1987 IBM effectively replaced the entire Personal Computer family by announcing a new family of IBM Personal System/2 computers, ranging in price from $1,695 to over $7,000. These computers use microfloppy diskettes and hard disks, boast better display systems, and incorporate a new type of expansion slot. Although these changes make the hardware of the Personal System/2 computers incompatible with the hardware of the PC family, the new computers can run all the earlier software. These announcements have made it even more difficult to predict which machines and which companies will dominate the microcomputer marketplace in the future.

THE COMPUTER OF THE FUTURE

For older machines like clocks and typewriters, the time from initial design to market dominance may span ten years or more. For computers, the elapsed time for diffusion of an invention is less than half that time. In 14 months, IBM designed a

Figure 18.11 The original Apple Macintosh (top), introduced in 1984, and the Macintosh II (bottom), introduced in 1987.

new microcomputer exploiting the Intel 8088 microprocessor, which went into production in 1979. IBM began selling its PC in 1981, and by the end of 1983, the IBM PC had single-handedly given IBM the largest share of the personal computer market. This type of swift transformation makes it extremely difficult to predict the future of computing.

The rate of computer-related inventions continues to rise. Scientists believe that fundamental physical limitations, such as the speed of light or properties of chemical reactions, will not preclude building cheaper, faster, and smaller components and peripherals between now and the year 2000. Automation in electronic manufacturing increasingly shortens production time and cuts product costs. Within a few years, the cost of a complete desktop publishing system, including a laser printer, should drop to less than the cost of a hot tub. Such price drops would greatly expand the market to the point that a computer system will sit on nearly every desk in offices and homes.

The characteristics listed in Table 18.2 for the information age stage (1990–) are conjectural but based on informed predictions by industry analysts. We expand on these speculations in this last section of the chapter. First, we examine advances in hardware, followed by improvements in software and the human-computer interface.

Circuits and Chips

Nowhere is the continual improvement in electronics more visible than in the production of the semiconductor memory chip. For example, Gary L. Tooker, vice president and general manager of semiconductor products at Motorola, wrote in the August 1983 issue of *High Technology*,

> Every three to five years a new generation of RAMs has been unveiled, featuring four times the storage density of its predecessor. Each year, the cost per bit has fallen by 30 percent and semiconductor memory utilization has increased by 100 percent. Few, if any, other industries can claim a market where demand doubles annually. . . . Obviously, the cycle cannot go on forever, but the end is not in sight.

So far, these predictions have been correct. Since 1983 the market for 64KB memory chips has been decimated by shipments of 256KB chips; 1-megabit chips have moved into production; and engineering prototypes of 4- and 16-megabit chips are being produced. To put this in perspective, a 16-megabit chip will occupy no more space than your thumbnail but will store the equivalent of 700 typed pages of text. A single 16-megabit chip will contain several times more memory than all of the memory chips in a typical microcomputer sold today.

Charles P. Lecht is a noted columnist for *Computerworld* magazine. In his February 2, 1987, column he predicts that we can expect "a 64-megabit chip followed shortly by one with a capacity of 256-megabits. After that, we won't be too surprised with the announcement of the first gigabit . . . chip (125,000,000 characters). It's my bet that these chips will appear well before the end of the century."

A WORD ABOUT
THE DOWNWARD MIGRATION OF COMPUTER TECHNOLOGY

When you look into the future, it is a good idea to use past trends as a guide. For the field of computing the guideposts point to some remarkable possibilities.

In predicting future developments in computer technology, David Nelson, chief technical officer of Apollo Computer, classifies computers into seven tiers, each separated from the other by a factor of 10 in cost. The aggregate improvement in performance across the tiers is about 35% a year, so a tenfold improvement (across one tier) occurs every seven years. Thus the virtual-memory capability of a $1 million IBM 370 mainframe computer, which first emerged in 1970, became available on the DEC VAX in 1977 (for approximately $100,000) and in the Apollo DN300 workstation in 1984 (for approximately $10,000). By extrapolation, claims Nelson, that same capability ought to be available in 1991 for close to $1,000.

At the higher end of the workstation market, he says, there will be increasing performance for constant cost. Thus a $50,000–$100,000 workstation, which approaches the performance of a mainframe today, should have the capabilities of a minisupercomputer by 1991.

Nelson also believes that a tenfold performance increase is matched by a weight decrease of the same order. "Computers seem to cost about $200 per pound, independent of their size," says Nelson, "a figure that has been valid for the past 30 years when adjusted for inflation." As computers become more of a "commodity," perhaps one day it will be possible to buy them by the pound.

Source: Reprinted with permission, *High Technology Business* magazine, March, 1987. Copyright © 1987 by Infotechnology Publishing Corporation, 214 Lewis Wharf, Boston, MA 02110.

Recent developments in the research of superconductors, materials that will conduct electricity with zero resistance, will undoubtedly speed the improvement of chips. Superconductors, which have scientists dreaming about magnetically levitated trains and vastly cheaper electricity, along with faster running computer chips, have been an unrealistic phenomenon until now because researchers could only make them work at the impractical temperature of −425 degrees Fahrenheit. Two IBM physicists in Switzerland brought these dreams to closer to realization when they discovered specially treated ceramics that acted as superconductors at much warmer temperatures. In 1987 their research became general knowledge and several other scientists developed ceramic superconductors which worked at even higher temperatures, finally making superconductors commerically feasible. While experts disagree on how rapidly engineers will be able to make the leap from these discoveries to plentiful electrical power and magnetic trains of the future, most claim that we are likely to see chip improvements within two years. Other devices are sure to benefit from these discoveries as well, such as the NMR scanner, which uses magnetic fields to take pictures inside the human body. Introduction of the superconductor would make the NMR scanner much less costly and even more powerful.

Parallel Processing

Once you understand what a computer's central processing unit does, then it is easy to imagine parallel processors. *Parallel processing* is simultaneous operation of more than one processing unit on a single job within a single computer. For example, the Cray X-MP supercomputer uses 4 very fast simultaneous processors, and a computer built by Thinking Machines uses 65,000 much slower microprocessors. The former design, using few processing units, is called *coarse-grained,* whereas the opposite is considered *fine-grained.* Most parallel machines fall in between and are differentiated on other bases, such as the method used to link the processing units. The *bus-based design* hooks all the processors together with a common transmission link. The *hypercube* is multidimensional, and although it is much more complex, it offers more potential for speed and flexibility. The basic problem with the bus structure is that traffic jams up very quickly when numerous messages must be delivered to many processors.

A major problem with parallel processing is that the outcome of a branch instruction in one processor can invalidate the operations under way in other processors. The best solution to this problem has been to use artificial intelligence methods to guess the most likely branch but, when the wrong guess is made, to use UNDO or BACKUP sequences to recover.

Recent advances in artificial intelligence, especially in machine learning and modeling of neural networks, have added to the excitement. Most analysts of parallel processing anticipate major developments in this approach during the next five years.

Neural-Net Computing

Hardware or software that organizes computer memory in ways that model human brain cells has been called **neural-net computing**. An extension of parallel processing, this approach has recently attracted considerable attention, and commercial products are now available. Neural-nets consist of memory nodes containing transistors that pass on information signals to other nodes, somewhat like the operation of brain cell synapses. This type of system has proven to be especially effective for high-speed pattern matching like that required for artificial vision, speech recognition, and general machine learning. The tremendous pattern-matching speed of neural-net computers now in production is so great that they may give other artificial intelligence applications a dramatic boost. The shape of personal computing may soon be changed by inexpensive neural-net chips that can be plugged into PCs to render feasible such features as voice recognition and complex expert systems.

Optics and Disks

Computers based on fiber-optic signals rather than electronics tantalize the imagination. Not only do light signals travel over 50 times faster than typical electronic signals, but they suffer less noise and degradation. Promising research on holographic techniques for optical computing is under way. Great strides are being made in the construction of digital computers based on optics, but decades of further research may be needed to produce price-competitive products.

Storage devices using optics are already in place, and enhancements to this technology during the next few years will probably play a leading role in the design of new computer systems. After working on optical storage for years, Kodak recently unveiled a storage system called KIMS 3000, which retains 2.6 gigabytes (billions of characters) of information. Designed to work with a MicroVAX workstation, this device stores data or documents on two 12-inch optical disk drives. According to Kodak, this storage device stores the equivalent of 20 file drawers filled with documents. With a price tag of $150,000, its adoption will be limited; however, it signals a very important direction for future disk storage technology.

Smaller optical disk systems that read small, removable discs called **CD-ROMs** (*C*ompact *D*isc—*R*ead *O*nly *M*emory) are marketed for home and business. Like the CDs (compact discs) used in high-fidelity sound systems, CD-ROMs contain tiny marks or pits that can be read by laser light beams and converted into digital electronic signals. Their storage potential is mind-boggling: as much as 300,000 pages of text—a complete encyclopedia—can easily reside on a single tiny disc. If stored on standard double-sided flexible disks for the IBM PC, such a document would require 1,500 floppy disks.

At least a dozen companies have developed and sold CD-ROM applications, but most attempt to fill the needs of business for large financial databases. A number of bibliographic files, such as *Books in Print,* are available on CD-ROM, as is a Microsoft product called Bookshelf (see Figure 18.12). Intended as a tool for writers, each Bookshelf CD-ROM contains ten book-length references, including a dictionary, a thesaurus, the *U.S. Zip Code Directory,* the *World Almanac, The Chicago Manual of Style,* and *Bartlett's Familiar Quotations.* This $300 compact disc can be accessed from a large number of different word processing packages.

A spin-off technology, **CD-I** (*C*ompact *D*isc—*I*nteractive), may upstage CD-ROMs and audio CDs as early as 1988. The CD-I player will play existing music discs, read CD-ROMs, and even display animated video. Most importantly, it can be programmed to operate under the interactive control of the user. This new medium has an edge over traditional disk storage, because when you get tired of working on your CD-I lesson, you can simply press a button, insert your favorite musical-video album into the disk drive, and sit back and relax to "perfect" sound.

Some variation of the CD-I player will probably become another popular component of the typical home and car stereo. Combining sound and video with interactive access of huge files of text and graphic data, these "compustereo" units may

Figure 18.12 Microsoft Bookshelf (a) is a CD-ROM disk that offers a collection of ten reference works, including the *U.S. ZIP Code Directory*, and comes bundled with the (b) Amdek Laserdrive 1 CD-ROM drive.

A.

B.

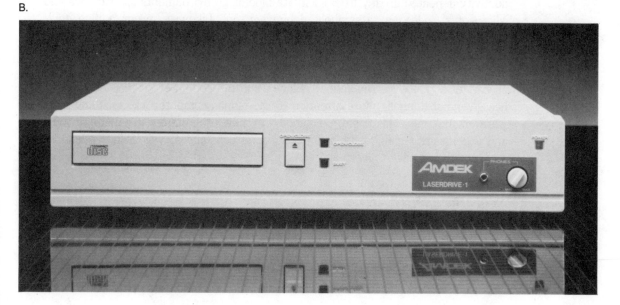

supply dramatically new forms of entertainment, education, and information retrieval. Once this technology is successful in the consumer or educational market, business is likely to adapt it for many communication purposes.

An inevitable direction for this new medium is toward easily erased and user-written optical discs. It's conceivable that the digital audio tape (DAT) produced by Sony for audio systems will also evolve into a new data storage medium for user recording of all types of data (audio, visual, and textual) for computer access. These new "data albums" may well supplant numerous printed reference materials, but progress is never easy or straightforward, especially when it brings with it a new potential for piracy.

Softer, Smarter Software

Although programming methods have progressed rapidly during the past five years, software could still be much softer or more natural in its communication with users. Many, if not most, programs require awkward command sequences and sometimes make demanding assumptions about user knowledge and experience. A number of developments will help to alleviate these problems; especially important will be new operating environments and advancements in human-computer interfaces.

Operating Environments

Even though the IBM PC had dominated the marketplace by 1983, it took three to five years to build truly powerful programming environments. Programmer productivity benefited greatly from such late-blooming environments as Windows and Microsoft's CodeView, a symbolic debugging tool. Likewise, programming environments like Microsoft's QuickBASIC and Borland's Turbo Prolog offered significant improvements by integrating the coding, checking, and running of new programs. Peter Norton, columnist for *PC Magazine,* describes these new tools as part of a "software revolution." Since 1985 the computer science community has given substantially more attention to the human-computer interface and software engineering. This trend, combined with new programmer productivity tools and a demanding community of inexperienced consumers, will probably lead to software that is easy to learn and use.

Networks and Hypertext

Table 18.2 predicts that the evolution of personal computers will reflect networking through 1990. The networked systems stage (1987–1990) has brought an increased emphasis on linking personal computers with local area networks. However, the software to allow effective use of networks, especially LANs, hasn't kept pace with the capacity of the hardware. During the next few years, it is likely that new and better programming tools will be developed to adapt the potential of networks to the needs of their users.

One difficulty in projecting advances in computer networks is that it is impossible to know exactly how people will use them for group or team work. Robert Haavind, editor of *High Technology*, predicts that the new systems of the late 1980s will allow work groups to "cooperatively share files, graphics, data, and ideas." Other analysts predict the growth of new types of communities through large-scale networks. Achieving these benefits will require experience, ingenuity, hard work, and patience.

Although we can't predict all of the new uses for networked computers, it's inevitable that the next few years will move us closer to an information retrieval ideal dubbed *hypertext*. Originated by Theodor Nelson in the late 1960s, **hypertext** refers to a document retrieval network having full-text files and dynamic indexes for all meaningful links among all documents.

Imagine that you're reading this chapter on a high-resolution computer screen, and as you read about hypertext, you become intrigued and want to find out more about it. Since the word *hypertext* is still obscure, chances are that you'll come away from your campus library empty-handed. But in a hypertext system, you could simply point to the word *hypertext* and immediately have the most relevant document on the subject displayed. You could continue to browse through articles, comments, and sections from books until you decided to return to your textbook. In the course of reading the material, you might well decide to write a commentary on the subject. In a full-featured hypertext system, you could "publish" your comment by naming keyboard descriptors and defining links to other documents before going on to another project. Several packages, notably *Guide* from OWL International and the *Grolier Electronic Encyclopedia* from Knowledgeset, now offer some useful, but limited hypertext features.

Nelson called the interconnections among the files "magic threads," anticipating the difficulty in designing such a system. Many information retrieval projects are headed in that direction, so it is quite possible that advances in network hardware and software will soon yield some hypertext-like systems for both information brokers and those who are merely curious.

Human-Computer Communication

Although networks offer numerous new ways of using computers, all applications depend heavily on the individual user's interface or communication with input and output devices. The usefulness and the comfort of these modes of communication to a large extent determine the usefulness of the entire system. While communications systems are becoming more natural and convenient, important new possibilities are on the horizon. One such alternative is voice communication, and another is the touch screen. Screens that respond to human touch have been employed for years, but in limited ways. Someday this may become feasible on a large scale.

Voice-activated systems can be found in dangerous manufacturing environments and in settings where the computer user's hands are busy with tasks other than keyboarding. Research is under way to expand these efforts so that programs will recognize different accents, dialects, and larger vocabularies. When more general, inexpensive solutions are found for these deficiencies, *voice-activated typing* may become a standard feature in the office environment. When it becomes possible to inexpensively put prose to paper without any kind of keyboard entry, major changes are likely in the workplace, as well as in the way that we organize a burgeoning storehouse of textual information. It is also possible that writing in general will take on a different flavor, as composition comes to depend more on vocalizing than on pen or keyboard. Such an information society might transform its educational system so that students speak their term papers, but it is difficult to imagine how students could take vocal essay tests unless provided with individual sound-proof cubicles.

Advanced microprocessors with larger memories allow several applications to be executed at the same time in different windows of a visual operating system. This is tremendous progress for information processing, but information science still provides little guidance in how to harness this capability.

Some anticipated innovations, such as optical computers, may never leave the experimental laboratories; nonetheless, other unanticipated advances will reshape the nature of computing in the short-term, to say nothing of the long-term, future. For instance, desktop publishing didn't appear until 1985, and by 1987 it absorbed a significant share of the computer products industry. Likewise, the 1983 version of the *Encyclopedia of Computer Science and Engineering* didn't even use the term *expert system*, but by 1986 expert systems had become an established category of computer software and a major focus of computer science.

In many ways, it is easier to predict technical developments than to predict their economic and social effects. It is difficult to tell in advance how effectively a new technical ability will be exploited or how radically it will alter individual behavior. In this discussion of the future, the social effects of computer technology have been largely ignored, not because we cannot forecast them, but because these questions were addressed earlier. In addition, this discussion has focused on the short term rather than on the long term. According to Robert Noyce, vice chairman of Intel, "The usual futurist projections are too optimistic in the short term and too pessimistic in the long term. . . . Where we went wrong in our over-expectations [was the computer industry's inward focus and its inability to] project itself out to the plumber and what he does."[2] During the past three years since that statement, the computer industry has matured and attempted to empathize with ordinary people and their information needs. It appears that we have barely scratched the surface of the potential for developing the information machinery that augments the human mind. Nonetheless, with fast processors, vast optical databases, and more powerful software, society is moving rapidly on a historical track toward the Information Age.

SUMMARY

We can find the origins of the modern computer in early calculating devices, but especially in Charles Babbage's "engines" and Herman Hollerith's tabulating machine. But the need to solve large scientific problems involving complicated calculations provided the final impetus for development of the electronic computer. ENIAC, completed in 1946, was the first general-purpose digital computer that was totally electronic. UNIVAC I, produced by Remington-Rand Corporation in 1951, was the first commercial computer. It marked the start of the first generation of mainframe computers.

The second, third, and fourth generations of mainframe computers were marked by technological improvements—transistors, integrated circuits, and large-scale integrated circuits, respectively. These led to faster operation, decreased size, and increased memory. Because of their cost, large computers were timeshared among many users.

The development of the microprocessor in 1971 spawned a new breed of computers designed to be used by one person. Thus, in 1974 the first microcomputers appeared. A new stage in the development of microcomputers has come every three years since 1974. Current microcomputers have the processing power of third-generation mainframe computers and are being integrated into computer networks.

The prospects for technical improvements in the computer field are so good that accurate predictions are likely to seem unbelievable to the average person. The fields of computing and communications are merging, spurring the development of larger and more complex networks with parallel processing systems. All of these trends collectively can be described as a shift from the Industrial Age to the Information Age—a shift from physical tools to mental-support tools.

KEY TERMS

CD-I

CD-ROM

coprocessor chip

CP/M

EDVAC

ENIAC

hypertext

large-scale integrated circuit (LSI)

MITS Altair 8800

multitasking

neural-net computing

PDP-11

productivity software

System/360

UNIVAC I

very large-scale integration (VLSI)

John V. Atanasoff

Charles Babbage

Dan Bricklin

J. Presper Eckert

Bill Gates

Herman Hollerith

Grace Murray Hopper

Joseph Jacquard

Steven Jobs

Gary Kildall

Lady Ada Lovelace

John W. Mauchly

John Napier

John von Neumann

Robert Noyce

Blaise Pascal

Stephen Wozniack

Konrad Zuse

DISCUSSION QUESTIONS

1. The phenomenal development of the computer has occurred in a very short time—less than 50 years. Can you think of anything else with a similarly rapid development? Consider the automobile, the airplane, and television. If they had developed as far and as fast as the computer, what would they be like?

2. Who do you think should be given credit for inventing the electronic computer?

3. If a fifth generation of computers is successfully developed, what do you think it will be like? How might such machines be used?

4. As the speed and capability of microcomputers increase, do you think the distinction between mainframe and microcomputers will disappear?

5. Which social institutions are most likely to adapt quickly to the Information Age? Which are most likely to resist change? Will resistance be successful?

EXERCISES

1. Charles Babbage was quite a character, with an unusual collection of friends. Read more about him and his inventions.

2. List some tasks that can be done on a large mainframe computer, but not on a microcomputer.

3. Match the names in the left-hand column with the concepts in the right-hand column.

   1. John V. Atanasoff   a. Developed CP/M

   2. Charles Babbage   b. ENIAC computer

3. Dan Bricklin
4. J. Presper Eckert
5. Bill Gates
6. Herman Hollerith
7. Gary Kildall
8. John W. Mauchly
9. John von Neumann
10. Robert Noyce

c. Father of computing
d. Developed VisiCalc
e. Developed BASIC for personal computers
f. Data processing
g. Developed FORTRAN
h. Apple II
i. Developed COBOL
j. ABC computer
k. Stored-program concept
l. MITS Altair 8800

4. Choose an organization and write a report on how it is likely to be affected by changes in the computer field over the next five years.

NOTES

1. Anthony Hyman, *Charles Babbage: Pioneer of the Computer* (Princeton, N.J.: Princeton University Press, 1982), p.244.
2. *Wall Street Journal*, 16 September, 1985.

A How Computers Process Information

REPRESENTING INFORMATION
Binary Versus Decimal
Characters and Strings of Text
Numeric Codes

PROCESSING INFORMATION
How Electronic Circuits Compute
Numeric Precision

The basic building block of computers is the transistor. A **transistor** is an electronic device for controlling the flow of electrons in an electrical circuit. Think of a transistorized circuit as a switch like a light switch at home: the switch is either on or off and stays that way until it is flipped again. If electrons are allowed to flow, the circuit is on; if electrons are not allowed to flow, the circuit is off. The on-off flow of electrons in these small circuits is used to encode information as binary 1s and 0s.

A modern electronic computer is often called a *binary* computer because its most basic circuits can remember either one of the binary digits 0 and 1. These digits are called *bits*. Both the internal and the external memory of a computer are nothing more than storehouses for bits. RAM (random-access memory), ROM (read-only memory), disk, and tape all store 1s and 0s. No other form of information is stored in a computer—not numbers, keyboard characters, programs, or word processing documents. How, then, does a computer store and process decimal numbers, business letters, and other forms of information? The binary number system and computer codes provide the answer.

REPRESENTING INFORMATION

Binary Versus Decimal

The key to understanding computers is the binary number system. Whereas the decimal number system has ten digits, 0 to 9, the binary number system has only two digits, 0 and 1. To understand how these digits are used, recall that decimal numbers represent powers of 10. For example, the decimal number 537 is really the sum of powers of 10.

$$537 \text{ decimal} = (5 \times 10^2) + (3 \times 10^1) + (7 \times 10^0)$$
$$= (5 \times 100) + (3 \times 10) + (7 \times 1)$$
$$= 500 + 30 + 7$$

Notice that the decimal number 1 is 10 raised to the 0 power; and 10, 100, 1,000, and so on are all 10 raised to some power.

Binary numbers are the sums of powers of 2 in the same way that decimal numbers are sums of powers of 10. The following list shows the decimal numbers that are represented by some powers of 2.

$2^{-2} =$	0.25
$2^{-1} =$	0.5
$2^0 =$	1.
$2^1 =$	2.
$2^2 =$	4.
$2^3 =$	8.
$2^4 =$	16.
$2^8 =$	256.
$2^{16} =$	65,536.
$2^{20} =$	1,048,576.
$2^{24} =$	16,777,216.
$2^{32} =$	4,294,967,296.

A binary number is a string of 1s and 0s, each indicating the presence or absence of a power of 2. For example, consider the binary number 101. This number is converted to its decimal equivalent as follows:

Binary number	0	0	0	0	0	1	0	1
Power of 2	7	6	5	4	3	2	1	0
Decimal number	0	0	0	0	0	4	0	1

$$101 \text{ binary} = (1 \times 2^2) + (0 \times 2^1) + (1 \times 2^0)$$
$$= (1 \times 4) + (0 \times 2) + (1 \times 1)$$
$$= 4 + 0 + 1 = 5 \text{ decimal}$$

Thus, 101 is the binary number representation of the decimal number 5.

The fractional part of a binary number, such as 101.1, is a sum of *negative* powers of two. For example, 101.1 binary is converted to its decimal equivalent as follows:

$$101.1 \text{ binary} = (1 \times 2^2) + (0 \times 2^1) + (1 \times 2^0) + (1 \times 2^{-1})$$
$$= (1 \times 4) + (0 \times 2) + (1 \times 1) + (1 \times 1/2)$$
$$= 4 + 0 + 1 + 1/2 = 5.5 \text{ decimal}$$

Here are some other examples:

$$4 \text{ decimal} = 100 \text{ binary}$$
$$16 \text{ decimal} = 10000 \text{ binary}$$
$$31 \text{ decimal} = 111111 \text{ binary}$$
$$6.25 \text{ decimal} = 110.01 \text{ binary}$$
$$145.625 \text{ decimal} = 10010001.101 \text{ binary}$$

Keep in mind that computers works exclusively with binary numbers, because they can store only a 1 or a 0. To do arithmetic and word processing they must convert from binary to decimal and back again. We see only the result of this conversion and not the binary numbers themselves. It isn't necessary to know anything about binary arithmetic to use a computer. But if you want to know what happens inside a computer, then it is essential that you learn the "secret code" of binary numbers.

Characters and Strings of Text

How does a binary computer process textual information? Individual keystrokes generate letters, numbers, and other symbols called *characters*. Groups of characters treated as a unit are called *strings*. Because characters and strings can't be processed directly by a machine that "understands" only binary numbers, they must be encoded in some kind of binary code. One of these codes is ASCII (American Standard Code for Information Interchange), which associates a unique 7-bit binary number with each character.

In ASCII, the letter *A* is associated with 1000001 binary. The numeral (not its value) 1 is associated with 0110001 binary. However, because binary numbers are tedious to remember, people usually convert binary codes to their decimal equivalents when they refer to them. Hence, A is represented by the decimal number 65, and the numeral 1 is represented by the decimal number 49.

Keyboard character	Binary code	Decimal code
A	1000001	65
a	1100001	97
Z	1011010	90
z	1111010	122
0 (zero)	0110000	48
9	0111001	57
+	0101011	43
[Enter]	0001101	13

Suppose you want to store a line of text in the computer's memory. You enter the string of characters "Hello C3 PO" into the computer through the keyboard. The keyboard converts each keystroke (including the spaces) into ASCII binary code.

Charcter (keyboard)	ASCII (decimal)
H	72
e	101
l	108
l	108
o	111
(space)	32
C	67
3	51
(space)	32
P	80
O	79

When the computer displays this line of text on its screen, the reverse process occurs: circuits in the screen display convert the ASCII binary code in memory into visible characters.

A 7-bit coding system like ASCII can represent only a limited number of different characters. The largest decimal number we can express in a 7-bit binary number is the equivalent of the binary number 1111111, which is

$$1111111 \text{ binary} = 64 + 32 + 16 + 8 + 4 + 2 + 1 \text{ decimal}$$
$$= 255 \text{ decimal}$$

Everything is exactingly stored in the computer as binary numbers: letters of the alphabet, numerals, punctuation marks, and special characters ($, #, %, and so on). Each character has its own 7-bit code. Because the memory of a computer can record binary digits and nothing else, all kinds of information must be encoded. The power of a computer to manipulate symbols is hidden in the simplicity of a coding scheme.

Numeric Codes

Values of numbers can be encoded in many ways; we will discuss the two most common ways. Natural or counting numbers are encoded as binary **integers** (whole numbers). Signed numbers with decimal points are called **real numbers** and must be encoded using *floating-point representation*. For example, a whole number like 35 is an integer, but a number with a decimal point in it—say, 35.0— is a real number and must be encoded in the floating-point format.

Integers

A computer stores binary numbers in groups of bits called *bytes* (8 bits = 1 byte) and *words* (which may be 8, 16, 32, or more bits, depending on the computer). An 8-bit byte can encode only 256 different integers—say, from -128 to $+127$ decimal value. A 16-bit word can encode binary integers from $-32,768$ to $+32,767$ decimal. The size in bits of a computer word affects the power of a computer because it limits the size of the numbers that a computer can represent conveniently. Our examples assume a 16-bit word length.

Computers perform addition, subtraction, multiplication, and division on the binary code, not on decimal integers. After the arithmetic is carried out in binary, a program converts the result from a binary number into a decimal number. Conversely, when a decimal integer is entered into a computer, it must be converted into a binary integer before any arithmetic can be performed.

The correspondence between decimal and binary integers is straightforward. The first bit of a binary integer is called a *sign bit;* it is a 0 if the number is positive and a 1 if the number is negative. All binary numbers from 0 through 0111111111111111 (16 bits with a leading 0 bit) are equivalent to the decimal numbers 0 to 32,767. The binary numbers 1111111111111111 (16 bits, all set to 1) through 1000000000000000 (16 bits with a leading 1) are equivalent to decimal numbers -1 to -32767. Negative numbers count backward to make subtraction simple for electronic circuits.

Integer representation results in fast arithmetic, but it also has disadvantages. Only whole numbers can be manipulated. and the size of each number is restricted. To get around these. limitations, computers also use floating-point representation.

Floating-Point Numbers

Floating-point representation is baeed on scientific notation, which expresses each number as a magnitude times a power of 10. For example, in scientific notation,

120 is written as 1.2×10^2. Similarly, floating-point representation separates a number into three parts.

1. *The sign.* This is either plus or minus.
2. *The magnitude.* This is expressed as a decimal fraction between 0 and 1.
3. *The exponent.* This is a power of 10 (or a power of 2). It reflects the location of the decimal point within the decimal (or binary) number.

In the computer field, floating-point numbers are often written in *scientific notation,* as follows:

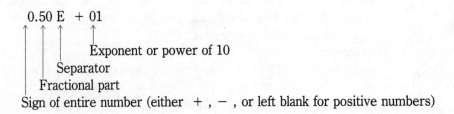

0.50 E + 01

Exponent or power of 10
Separator
Fractional part
Sign of entire number (either + , − , or left blank for positive numbers)

To convert a decimal floating-point number to an ordinary decimal number, you simply move the decimal point right or left (depending on the sign of the exponent) the number of digits specified by the exponent. For example, to obtain the value of 0.50 E + 01, move the decimal point one digit to the right of its original position, because the exponent is 1 and its sign is positive.

$$0.50 \text{ E} + 01 = 0.50 \times 10 = 5.0$$

The sign of the number is always the sign shown in front of the floating-point representation. Here are several other examples.

0.55	E	− 01	is	0.055
0.123	E	+ 03	is	123.0
−0.95	E	+ 00	is	−0.95
−0.95	E	+ 01	is	−9.5
−0.95	E	+ 05	is	−95,000.00

There is a limit to the size of number that can be encoded in this fashion. If two digits are allowed in the fraction and in the exponent, then the largest number than can be encoded is + 0.99 E + 99, and the smallest number is − 0.99 E + 99. The numbers nearest zero would be + 0.01 E − 99 and − 0.01 E − 99. Zero is a special case, usually represented by + 0.00 E + 00.

How Electronic Circuits Compute

The brain of a computer is its central processing unit, which contains the arithmetic logic unit (ALU). The brain of a microcomputer is a microprocessor. Inside the ALU or microprocessor is a collection of circuits that add, multiply, transfer, compare, and so on. It is instructive to examine how these circuits work—for example, how an addition takes place.

Because all numbers, characters, and instructions are stored as binary numbers, addition of two numbers reduces to the addition of bits.

1010	binary
+1101	binary
10111	binary

The addition circuit must do just two things in order to perform this additoin: add two bits together to get a sum, and produce a carry bit (0 or 1). The ability to perform these simple operations is wired into the computer by building circuits that obey two rules.

1. If only one of the addend bits is a 1, then the resulting bit is a 1; otherwise the result is a 0. This is the rule for adding two bits.

2. If one or both of the addend bits is a 0, then the resulting bit is a 0; otherwise the result is a 1 bit. This is the rule for obtaining the carry bit.

These rules are represented in the following *truth tables:*

SUM TABLE
First Addend

		0	1
Second	0	0	1
Addend	1	1	0

CARRY TABLE
First Addend

		0	1
Second	0	0	0
Addend	1	0	1

These two truth tables summarize how to perform binary addition one bit at a time. For instance, if a 0 is added (first addend) to a 1 (second addend), the result is 1, as shown in the corresponding entry of the sum table. Similarly, if a 1 is added to another 1, the result is 0 according to the sum table and a 1 according to the carry table.

If the sum and carry tables are used repeatedly, any binary numbers can be added. Suppose the computer is asked to add 1101 to 0111. The sum for each column is noted, and the carry bit is shifted one place to the left of the column just added and placed below the sum.

```
                1101  binary          (13 decimal)
          +     0111  binary          ( 7 decimal)
   Sum =        1010  binary
   Carry =      0101   (shifted left 1 place)
```

This sum and the carry bit are then added in the same way. These steps are repeated until there are no carry bits to be added (000), leaving the final answer. Thus

```
                1101  binary          (13 decimal)
          +     0111  binary          ( 7 decimal)
   Sum =        1010  binary
   Carry =      0101   (shifted left one place)
   Sum =        0000
   Carry =      1010   (shifted)
   Sum =       10100
   Carry =      0000
   Answer =    10100  binary          (20 decimal)
```

In short, the computer adds two numbers by performing sum, carry, and shift operations through repetitious steps. The operations are very simple; but when combined in just the right way, they can do powerful things.

We have just shown that computers work by simulating operations on binary numbers through electronic circuits that perform elementary functions. Addition, for example, is nothing more than a sequence of simple summation, carry, and shift operations. Higher-order operations are nothing more than lengthy sequences of elementary operations. This, combined with binary encoding of information, is the secret to how computers work.

Computers do not know how to think. They merely perform millions of simple truth table operations. To show how computers can blindly compute wrong answers, in the sext section we consider the problems associated with arithmetic on real numbers.

Numeric Precision

Sometimes the computer prints a value that isn't quite what you expect. For instance, it might print 1.9999 instead of 2.0, or a calculation may be off by a few cents—yielding an answer of $12,235.20 instead of $12,235.24. Both of these results reflect the fact that the computer doesn't provide infinite precision. In particular, some information is lost during calculation because the encoding of floating-point numbers is approximate.

To understand this lack of precision, consider the following addition:

$$\begin{array}{r} 3000.0001 \\ +\ \ 3000.0001 \\ \hline 6000.0002 \end{array}$$

The computer must convert 3000.0001 to binary code; add the two binary-encoded numbers; convert the result back to 6000.0002 decimal; and display the result. When the floating-point number is stored in 32 bits, the encoded value of 3000.0001 is approximated as 0.3000000 E + 01. Thus, when the computer adds these numbers, it comes up with a sum of 6000.0000 instead of 6000.0002.

Whenever computers calculate with floating-point numbers, they round off the numbers, which creates errors. For this reason, you should always ask yourself, "To how many digits is this number reasonable and accurate?" Typically, floating-point numbers are accurate to about the first six or seven digits. So, unless the program uses double-precision arithmetic (which stores each number in twice as much storage space), you should use only the first six or seven digits in the answer even if the computer prints more than seven digits.

B Programming in BASIC

BASIC (*B*eginner's *A*ll-purpose *S*ymbolic *I*nstruction *C*ode) was developed in the 1960s at Dartmouth College by John Kemeny and Thomas Kurtz. Since then, BASIC has become the standard programming language for microcomputers and can be found on nearly every mini and mainframe computer as well. It is a simple language, and simple programs can be written in the first few hours of practice.

The BASIC language has many *dialects*—versions that are unique to a certain computer. For example, Apple BASIC is different from the Microsoft BASIC used on an IBM PC. In fact, there are several incompatible versions of BASIC available for almost every machine. These dialects are so far removed from the original BASIC language that the inventors have since designed and implemented TRUE BASIC—another dialect that is incompatible with all others.

The proliferation of different versions of BASIC has created a problem. Programs written on one machine probably won't run on another machine. In this appendix, we cover the features considered "standard" in all dialects of BASIC, but even some of these features differ on various implementations of BASIC.

First, we describe how to run an existing program that is written in BASIC. Then we explain some of the commands, statements, and ways of organizing data that you might use to write simple programs of your own.

This appendix should be used in combination with the system analysis and programming chapters. Many important concepts relating to the design of programs are covered in those chapters.

INTERACTING WITH BASIC

The BASIC programs that you write are formally called *source programs,* because they are interpreted by another program called BASIC. That is, the program you write in the BASIC language is data to the BASIC interpreter program. Hereafter we will shorten the phrase "the BASIC interpreter" and call it simply BASIC.

On many personal computers BASIC is provided as part of the computer and stored in ROM at the factory. These computers often extend the version of BASIC stored in ROM by adding features that are stored on the disk. You must load the extended BASIC program into memory (RAM) befor running your program if your program uses any of the extended BASIC features.

To load, erase, save, or run a program, you type commands to BASIC. *Commands* are executed immediately; they tell BASIC what to do with your program statements. *Program statements* accept input and generate output, perform calculations, make decisions, and repeat other statements. In addition to statements, a program contains data. Each piece of data is given a name. There are strict rules for naming data; we will learn some of these rules in this chapter. *Variables* are names of storage cells in memory that contain data.

Thus, a program is a collection of data and statements that operate on the data. Programs are executed by the BASIC program resident in ROM and RAM: each statement instructs BASIC, which in turn controls what the computer does.

Starting BASIC

Figure B.1 shows a brief session with BASIC; it illustrates how to run an existing program. On most computers BASIC must be loaded into memory to be used. In Figure B.1, the operating system provides the prompt A > ; then you load BASIC into memory by typing its name. From this pont on, BASIC is in charge. Figure B.1 shows two other prompts: Ok and ?. The Ok prompt means that BASIC has completed what it was last told to do and is waiting for you to enter the next command or program statement from the keyboard. BASIC generates a question-mark prompt whenever the program it is executing makes a request for data to be en-

```
A>
Ok     BASIC

Ok   LOAD "MYPROG"

 ?   RUN
         5 SQUARED IS    25
Ok

A>  SYSTEM
```

tered from the keyboard. Thus, the question mark tells you that BASIC is waiting for input to a program, whereas Ok indicates that BASIC is waiting for input itself.

After you have loaded BASIC, it generates an Ok prompt. Then you must load the desired source program into memory. In Figure B.1, the program is called MYPROG; so you load it into memory by typing the command LOAD "MYPROG". Then to tell BASIC to begin executing the program, you type RUN. As Figure B.1 shows, a question mark then appears, indicating that MYPROG is waiting for you to enter data. BASIC will wait until you enter a value followed by a [Return]. The source program in Figure B.1 computes the square of whatever number is typed on the keyboard (in this case, the number is 5) and displays the result (5 SQUARED IS 25).

Occasionally you may want to stop execution of the source program in midstream. To do so, you press [Ctrl]-[C] or [Ctrl]-[BREAK]. This causes BASIC to stop executing the source program, display the Ok prompt, and wait for a command.

When BASIC has finished executing the source program, it displays the Ok prompt again, indicating that it is waiting for you to enter another command. You can quit BASIC and return control to the operating system by typing the command BYE. Anything left in main memory when you exit BASIC is lost; so if you made changes to your program since the last time it was saved, be sure to save your program before typing BYE.

BASIC Commands

Figure B.1 shows how to run an existing program, but you will also want to enter programs of your own design. To do this, you must know how to direct BASIC by entering commands. Once BASIC is loaded in memory, you can enter commands to load a program from a disk into memory, display the program in memory on the screen, begin executing a program, or perform other actions. There are many commands, and they differ from one dialect of BASIC to another. We will be concerned mainly with the following commands:

- NEW erases any existing program in memory in preparation for starting a new one.
- LOAD copies a program from a disk into memory.
- RUN begins execution of the current program in memory.
- SAVE copies the current program from memory to a disk.
- LIST displays statements of the current program on the screen.
- DELETE removes statements from the current program.
- RENUM renumbers existing statements in the current program.

In addition to these essential commands, most versions of BASIC include commands to list the names of files on the disk, help debug your program, clear the screen, and perform other useful functions. These extra commands are worth knowing, but their syntax—and even their existence—depend on the version of BASIC you use.

NEW

A new program can be entered by simply typing a list of statements to be carried out by BASIC. If a program already exists in memory and you want to remove it to make room for the new one, you should use the NEW command to erase the old program.

For example, the following dialog erases any old program in memory and then enters a program than makes the computer display HELLO on the screen:

```
NEW
Ok
100 PRINT "HELLO"
Ok
999 END
Ok
```

The commands that you type, in this and the following examples, are shown in color; the other messages are prompts displayed by BASIC.

The word HELLO in line 100 is enclosed in quotation marks to identify it as text (data to be processed) instead of a statement keyword or variable name.

Notice the numbers at the beginnings of the third and fifth lines. In BASIC the first part of each statement is a number; these numbers help BASIC determine the order in which to execute statements. Program statements are numbered in the order they are to be interpreted. The statement numbers can be any integer from 1 to 65,529 or from 1 to 99,999, depending on the version of BASIC. It is a good idea to choose statement numbers that are not consecutive; for example, 10, 20, 30, and so on. That way, if you need to add statements to the middle of the program, there will be unused numbers available.

RUN

The statements you type are stored in memory so that they can be interpreted later. After you have entered all the statements in the source program, enter the RUN command to tell BASIC to execute the numbered statements—one at a time, and in numerical order.

When RUN is entered, BASIC starts interpreting the statements beginning with the statement with the lowest line number. In our sample program, statement 100 tells BASIC to print HELLO on the screen, and statement 999 tells BASIC to stop executing the program.

LIST

Suppose that, after entering our sample program, you want to see what is in memory. The current program in memory will be displayed on the screen if you enter the command LIST.

```
Ok
LIST
100 PRINT "HELLO"
999 END
Ok
```

The LIST command displays the entire program on the screen. If the program is many pages long, the listing will simply fly past your eyes. To list a portion of the program, you can include line numbers as arguments to the LIST command. For example, the command LIST 100 lists just one line—line number 100. The command LIST 100-200 lists all lines between 100 and 200, inclusive. The general format for the LIST command is

LIST *start-last*

where *start* and *last* are line numbers.

Also, in many versions of BASIC, the LIST command can be used to print your BASIC program on a printer. The command may be LIST P:*start-stop*, or it may be LIST *start-stop*. Consult the manual of your computer to see which dialect to use.

SAVE

The current program in memory is lost when you exit from BASIC or turn the computer off, but you can make a permanent copy on the disk by using the SAVE command. For example, the command SAVE "MYPROG" will save the current program as a file named MYPROG. The general format of the SAVE command is

SAVE *"filename"*

where *filename* is any valid name of a disk file. Because the syntax for naming files varies from one operating system to another, the syntax for the SAVE command varies from one implementation of BASIC to another. In particular, with some dialects of BASIC, you do not type quotation marks around the name. Similarly, the *filename* may incorporate a disk drive designation when your computer has multiple disk drives. For example, SAVE "B:MYFILE" would cause the memory-resident BASIC program to be copied to the disk in drive B.

If a file with *filename* already exists, some dialects of BASIC throw the old version of *filename* away when they save the current program in its place. Other dialects are more cautious and force you to use a REPLACE command instead of a SAVE command if you want to delete an old version of the program while saving the new one.

LOAD
When you want to retrieve a program saved on the disk, use the LOAD command. The general format of the LOAD command is

LOAD *"filename"*

where *filename* is the name of the file containing a BASIC source program. For example, LOAD "PROG5" causes the file named PROG5 to be copied from the disk to memory.

On most implementations of BASIC, the LOAD command does not erase an existing program in memory; it merely merges the program from the disk into the program in memory. Usually you will not want to merge the lines of two programs; so it is a good idea to use the NEW command before loading a program from a disk.

If you use the LOAD command to merge the text of two or more BASIC programs, be sure each program has different line numbers. The LOAD command can be very useful for quickly and easily combining pieces of BASIC into larger and more useful programs.

DELETE
You can delete a statement by typing its line number followed by [Return]. But if you want to remove many lines at once, you should use the DELETE command. For example, the command DELETE 100-120 deletes any lines numbered 100 through 120. The general format of the DELETE command is

DELETE *start-last*

where *start* and *last* are line numbers. All lines from *start* to *last* are removed, inclusively.

General Editing
You can add a new statement or modify an existing one simply by typing it. Suppose, for example, the following program is in memory:

```
Ok
LIST
100 PRINT "HELLO"
110 PRINT "HOW ARE YOU?"
120 END
Ok
RUN
HELLO
HOW ARE YOU?
Ok
```

To add a statement with the line number 115 (so that it will be executed after statement 110 but before statement 120), you might type

```
115 PRINT "TODAY"
```

If you give the LIST command, you can see how the program has been changed.

```
LIST
100 PRINT "HELLO"
110 PRINT "HOW ARE YOU?"
115 PRINT "TODAY"
120 END
Ok
```

BASIC automatically inserts new lines in their proper numerical squence in the program.

Now suppose you want to modify statement 100. You could delete it and then enter the revised version, but this is not necessary. Instead, you can change a statement by typing a new statement with the same line number as the statement you wish to change. This procedure replaces the first version of the line with the new one.

Most BASIC interpreters allow you to edit existing statements. For example, Microsoft BASIC has a built-in editor that allows you to use the cursor keys to move the cursor to the statement you want to edit so that you can modify parts of it and skip over the parts you don't want to change. Usually this is a faster way to modify an existing statement than to retype if from scratch. An editor like this is called a *full-screen editor* because you can change any statement displayed on the screen.

The features for editing programs vary substantially from one version of BASIC to another. But even if a version doesn't have a built-in editor, it is always possible to use an external editor. An external editor works like a word processor and produces text that can be loaded into BASIC with the LOAD command. External editors offer powerful editing features, such as the ability to move groups of statements from one spot in a program to another or to change the name of a variable throughout a program.

Renumbering Lines

After extensive additions and deletions, the line numbers in your program are likely to become messy. A more serious problem occurs if you want to add a new statement between statements, with consecutive line numbers, such as between lines 356 and 357. You can't solve this problem by adding a statement with the number 356.5, because line numbers must be integers.

All of these problems can be solved by renumbering the lines in your program with the RENUM command. For example, if you type RENUM to renumber the lines in our sample program and then give the LIST command to display the program, the following appears:

```
RENUM
Ok
LIST
10 PRINT "HELLO"
20 PRINT "HOW ARE YOU?"
30 PRINT "TODAY"
40 END
Ok
```

Notice that the RENUM command has renumbered all the lines in the program with a constant increment of 10 between lines.

A few implementations of BASIC don't have a RENUM command. For those that do, the general form is usually

RENUM *newstart, oldstart, increment*

With this command, you can renumber just the end (the highest line numbers) of the existing program; *oldstart* is the first line number in the existing program that is to be renumbered. If you don't specify values for *newstart, oldstart,* and *increment,* default values are used, as they were in our example. The default value for *oldstart* is the lowest line number of the existing program. *Newstart* becomes the first line number in the sequence of renumbered lines; its default value was 10 in our example. *Increment* determines how far apart the new numbers are spaced; its default is also 10. For example, suppose that immediately after our last example you type a second RENUM command—RENUM 100,30,25—and then give the LIST command. On the screen you will see

```
RENUM 100,30,25
Ok
LIST
10 PRINT "HELLO"
20 PRINT "HOW ARE YOU?"
100 PRINT "TODAY"
125 END
```

Only the last two lines have been renumbered, and they were renumbered with an increment of 25.

1. What does the NEW command do when you already have a program in memory?

    a. Experiment with the NEW command by entering

    ```
    NEW
    100 PRINT "HELLO"
    RUN
    NEW
    RUN
    ```

    What caution should be used with the NEW command?

    b. Create an experiment to determine what happens if you load a program from a disk without first using the NEW command to erase the old program from memory.

2. Suppose the following program is already in memory:

    ```
    100 PRINT "HELLO"
    200 PRINT "GOOD BYE"
    300 END
    ```

    a. How do you insert 250 PRINT "INBETWEEN" between lines 200 and 300?

    b. What is the easiest way to change line 200 to 200 PRINT "ADIOS"?

    c. What is the easiest way to modify the program so that the statement that is now on line 100 will execute after statement 200?

3. Give a RENUM command to change the line numbers on the following program to 500, 550, 600, 650.

    ```
    10 REM Start
    11 PRINT "HI"
    15 PRINT "HOW ARE YOU?"
    17 END
    ```

4. Give a command to delete lines 550 through 810 of a program.

COMPONENTS OF BASIC PROGRAMS

Every program must accept inputs and generate outputs; copy, move, and calculate new values based on data stored in memory; and make decisions by comparing results from previous steps and then performing one group of instructions while skipping another group. These components of all programs are also components of BASIC programs. The building blocks of these components are called constants, variables, and statements. We will give special treatment to input and output statements because these statements are particulary important and because they are more difficult to understand than other statements in BASIC.

Constants, Variables, and Statements

In BASIC programs, *constants* store values that cannot change while the program is being interpreted; *variables* hold values than can change during interpretation. Variables can be combined into arithmetic and logic expressions, such as $A + B$ and $A = B$. The result obtained from evaluating an expression can be assigned to another variable, and so forth. *Reserved words* are words that have been assigned a unique meaning, such as PRINT or END. The reserved words in BASIC statements explain what type of processing to do.

There are strict rules in BASIC for forming constants, variables, and statements. These rules are similar to the rules for spelling and sentence structure in English; therefore, we call them *syntax* rules. Similar rules for meaning or *semantics* define how each statement in BASIC is interpreted.

Constants

There are many types of data. A *data type* is a collection of constants and the operations that are permitted on the collection. In this section, we discuss two numeric data types (integers and real numbers) and one data type that stores text.

An *integer* is a whole number like 0, 1, 2, or -100. Integers can be added, compared, and printed on the screen. In most personal computers, integers range in value from $-32,768$ to $+32,767$.

A *real number* is a number like -1.5 or 3.14159—any number containing a decimal point. Like integers, real numbers can be added, compared, and printed on the screen. When mathematical operations are performed on real numbers, the resulting real numbers tend to become very small or very large. Rather than display a 20-digit real number, BASIC will print very large or small real numbers in *scientific notation*. Some examples of the way BASIC prints numbers in scientific notation are

$1.5E + 03$, which means $(1.5)(1000) = 1,500$
$-0.25E - 02$, which means $(-0.25)(0.01) = -0.0025$

Appendix A discusses how to read scientific notation. You will see scientific notation frequently when running BASIC. In fact, the displayed numbers may not be exactly what you expect. For example, 500,001 might be displayed as $0.5E + 06$ instead. In this case, a small rounding error has occurred during interpretation. Rounding errors may not be harmful for the type of programs you write, but you should be aware that they happen.

Some versions of BASIC allow two types of real numbers to be used: single- and double-precision. Double-precision numbers take twice the storage space of single-precision numbers, but they are more accurate in calculations.

BASIC can also process limited kinds of textual constants. A *string constant* is data that consist of a series of characters. BASIC can tell the difference between a string and other parts of a program because strings are enclosed in quotation marks. We used a string to display the word HELLO on the screen. It is important to emphasize that any series of characters enclosed in quotation marks is a string and is treated as data. For example, although the string "LIST 100-200" looks very much like a command, BASIC would treat this string as data because of the quotation marks and would not analyze the characters in the string for semantic sense. String constants are useful for communicating with the user.

There is a big difference between numbers and strings. Numbers can be added and multiplied; a string can be connected to another string, or characters can be removed from a string. The operations that work on a number may be meaningless when applied to strings. For this reason, it is important to remember to put quotation marks around string constants.

BASIC cannot mix strings and numbers together when performing calculations. If a program attempts to add a string to a number, BASIC will stop executing the program and display an error message. This sort of error is an example of a *syntax error*, because the program is syntactically incorrect.

Variables

A word that is not a reserved word is treated as a variable name. A *variable name* is a symbolic code for a storage location that contains data. Thus, in the statement 50 PRINT HELLO, the word HELLO is the name of a memory cell. This PRINT statement is radically different from the statement 50 PRINT "HELLO", which prints the word HELLO. In contrast, when BASIC executes the statement 50 PRINT HELLO, it interprets HELLO as a variable name and therefore copies the current contents of cell HELLO onto the screen. If the number stored in the variable HELLO is 10.5, then the value 10.5 is displayed on the screen (see Figure B.2).

The first character of a variable's name must be a letter of the alphabet. The second and subsequent characters of a name can be either letters or numerals, as in BUCKET17 and X15. Some versions of BASIC accept underscores in names, as in NEW_TAX. Here are some examples of valid and invalid names.

Valid Variable Names		Invalid Variable Names	
A	PAYRATE	10T	(Begins with a number)
BOX	HOURS	P@	(Contains an illegal character)
B29	TAXI	$TAX	(Contains an illegal character)

The maximum number of characters in a name depends on the particular dialect of BASIC. In most versions of BASIC, a name can be 30 or more characters long; this lets you choose meaningful names, such as PAYRATE or TRUCKS. In crude versions of BASIC a name must be either a single letter or a letter followed by a single numerical digit, as in P, X5, and B9. This allows only $26 + 260 = 286$ different names and makes programs hard to understand because the names are so

Figure B.2 The PRINT statement takes the value of HELLO from memory and displays it on the screen.

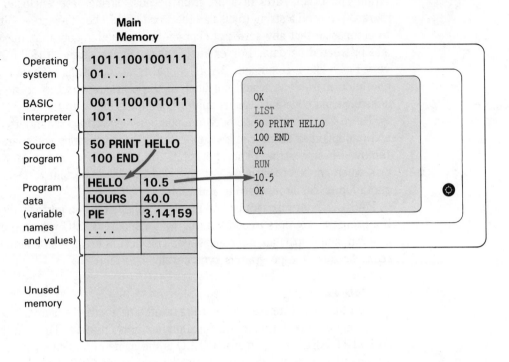

short and cryptic. We will use readable variable names in this appendix; you may need to shorten the names if you want to run our programs on your version of BASIC. It is important to note that some BASICs allow you to use long names, but look at the first two characters of the name. Thus, PAYROLL and PACKAGE would be treated as the same name—leading to a difficult error to locate and correct.

All versions of BASIC have at least two types of variables: *numeric variables,* which store numbers, and *string variables,* which store strings of text. The last character of a variable's name indicates which type of variable it is. If the last character is a letter or a number, then it is a numeric variable that stores a single-precision real number. String variables end with a $.

Most versions of BASIC have other types of variables in addition to the integer, real, and string types discussed so far. For example, Microsoft BASIC has three types of numeric variables that store integers, single-, and double-precision real numbers. These variable types present a tradeoff between the precision of computations and the storage space and time required to perform computations. It takes only 2 bytes to store an integer, and calculations run faster with integer variables. But single- and double-precision numbers may be necessary to obtain a sufficiently accurate answer. For Microsoft BASIC, the following rules apply to naming variables:

Suffix	Meaning	Sample Names	Sample Contents	Storage Space for the Variable's Value
%	Integer	I%, COUNT%	53, −238	2 bytes
!	7-digit number	R!, CIRCLE!	3.14159, −238.	4 bytes
#	16-digit number	SALES#	81,358,257,010.18	8 bytes
$	String	JOB$	"JANITOR"	Length of the string

Statements

Like data, program statements come in a variety of types. Originally, BASIC consisted of 10 statement types, but the proliferation of BASIC dialects has increased the number. For example, Microsoft BASIC as it is implemented on the IBM PC has over 70 types of statements. We will restrict our discussion to the most fundamental statements found in all versions of BASIC.

The simplest statement type is the REM statement; it allows you to insert remarks. A REM statement doesn't cause BASIC to do anything, but it is useful for documenting your program. Characters following REM are ignored by BASIC; but they are displayed when the program is listed. Most versions of BASIC allow you to place remarks on the same line as another statement by using a single quote to separate the remark from the rest of the statement. The following two statements illustrate both ways of placing remarks in a program:

```
100 REM     ------ This Statement Does Nothing --------
100 PRINT "HELLO"     'This remark is tagged onto PRINT
```

In either case, the remark is useful to the programmer but is ignored by BASIC. Remark statements should be used liberally to explain what your program does and perhaps to describe a little about how it does it.

Some statements declare what kind of data is to be processed, and others are devoted to doing the processing. Processing statements either control the order of events, or they perform certain operations. In all cases, statements begin with a line number that is followed by a *keyword*. The keyword is a reserved word that identifies what type of statement it is. The keyword is usually a verb or verb phrase that describes what is to be done.

Here are some types of statements and a brief explanation of what they do. Notice that the ordinary English meaning of each keyword is only loosely related to the keyword's meaning in BASIC.

- *PRINT*. Display data on the screen or send output to the disk or other output device.
- *LET*. Let a variable be a certain value; calculate the value.
- *INPUT*. Get input from the keyboard, disk, or other input device.
- *FOR*. Repeat statements for certain values of a variable; repeat a group of statements.

- *STOP*. Whoa! Stop executing statements.
- *IF*. Decide what to do next based on the result of testing a condition in the IF statement.
- *END*. Whoa! An END statement is similar to a STOP statement, except that it should be the last statement (that is, the statement with the highest line number) in a program.

These statement types account for 90 percent of the statements used in a typical BASIC program. How they are combined to create a program is the most difficult skill to learn when starting to program. We will illustrate each statement type by using it to create real programs.

Keyboard Input and Output

The first step in writing BASIC programs is mastering the statements that input and output. PRINT statements are used to copy numbers and strings from memory to a screen, printer, or disk file. INPUT statements do the reverse; they copy numbers and strings from the keyboard, disk file, or a serial input adapter to memory.

The general form of the simplest variety of INPUT and PRINT statements is

INPUT *variable list*
PRINT *expression list*

The *variable list* in an INPUT statement can be a single variable name, such as WORK2, or it can be a series of variables separated by commas. The *expression list* in a PRINT statement can contain variables, constants, and formulas that are separated by either commas or semicolons.

We will use the ECHO1.BAS program in Figure B.3 to illustrate PRINT and INPUT statements. The first four statements of ECHO1.BAS are remarks that identify the program and tell what it does. Line 130 displays a string constant—a prompt to the user. Line 170 halts the program. The interesting parts of ECHO1.BAS are lines 150 and 160.

The INPUT statement in line 150 instructs BASIC to display a question mark, wait until you type a string and press [Return], and store the string in L$. Recall that L$ is a string variable because it ends with a dollar sign. String variables can hold anything that can be typed at the keyboard. Thus, if you type ABC, the string constant "ABC" is stored inside L$ by line 150. Or, if you type 10.5, the string constant "10.5" is stored in L$. It is important to emphasize that, because L$ is a string variable, BASIC stores "10.5" as a series of four characters, not as a number. You can't perform arithmetic on the contents of a string variable—even if the string it contains happens to look like a number.

Line 150 copies keyboard characters into memory and stores them in the location named L$. Line 160 displays the value stored in L$. This is how ECHO1.BAS got its name; line 160 echoes to the screen whatever was entered from the keyboard. If GOODBY is typed into line 150, the output will appear as shown in Figure B.3.

```
LOAD "ECHO1.BAS"
Ok
LIST
100 REM --------------------- ECHO1.BAS ------------------------------
110 REM    This program parrots back whatever is typed in.
120 REM ==============================================================
125 REM                                     'Instructions
130 PRINT "Enter a line followed by pressing [RETURN]."
150 INPUT L$                                'Read from keyboard
160 PRINT L$                                'Display on screen
170 END
RUN
Enter a line followed by pressing [RETURN].
?GOODBY
GOODBY
Ok
```

INPUT Statements

Figure B.4 illustrates a program that accepts two numbers, performs a simple calculation on them, and displays the result of the calculation. The INPUT statement on line 140 has two variables as its argument; it tells BASIC to read two numbers from the keyboard and store them in variables X and Y. The numbers should be entered on the same line and should be separated by a comma. For example, if you type

12.4, 8

and press [Return], BASIC stores the number 12.4 in X and stores 8.0 in Y. In this example the integer 8 is automatically converted by BASIC into the real number 8.0 because Y is a real-number variable.

Suppose you type BUZZ OFF and press [Return] when BASIC is expecting data for line 140 in Figure B.4. This presents BASIC with a problem. Although a number can be stored as a series of characters in a string variable, ordinary text cannot be stored as a number in a numeric variable. BASIC responds to this problem by displaying an error message, such as REDO FROM START or PLEASE REENTER followed by another question mark. This is called an *execution error* because it occurs while the program is executing. A *fatal execution error*—such as attempting to divide a number by zero—forces BASIC to display an error message and stop executing the program entirely.

PRINT Statements

Line 170 of Figure B.4 illustrates a PRINT statement that contains several constants and three variables. Each item in the list is printed on one line of the screen

```
Ok
LIST
100 REM --------------------------- AREA.BAS ----------------------------
110 REM     Computes the area of a rectangle of length X and width Y
120 REM -----------------------------------------------------------------
130 REM
140 INPUT X, Y                                          'get length and width
150 A = X * Y                                           'compute the area
170 PRINT "The area of a", X, " by ", Y, " rectangle is", A
999 END '-------------------------------------------------------------------
RUN
? 3.2, 4.5
The area of a  3.2              by                 4.5             rectangle is
 14.4
Ok
```

until the edge of the screen is reached; then BASIC continues printing on the next line. The punctuation that separates items determines the spacing between them when they appear on the screen. BASIC divides the screen into 5 print zones; each zone is normally 14 characters wide. When commas are used to separate items, each item is printed at the beginning of the next print zone. Thus, commas provide an easy way to line up the output of several PRINT statements in vertical columns. For example,

```
40 PRINT 12.5, 15, .845
50 PRINT 3, 563.2, 9452
RUN
 12.5           15          .845
 3              563.2       9452
```

The commas in line 170 of Figure B.4 don't work well, however. They cause too much of a gap between items for a pleasing appearance. You can avoid these gaps by using semicolons instead of commas. When semicolons are used, strings are printed without intervening spaces. For example, 100 PRINT "HI";"THERE" prints HITHERE as one word. However, even when semicolons are used, numbers aren't printed next to each other. All numbers are followed by a space, and positive numbers are preceded by a space. For example, if line 170 is replaced with

170 PRINT "The area of a"; X; "by"; Y; "rectangle is"; A

then the output becomes

The area of a 3.2 by 4.5 rectangle is 14.4

You can control where items are displayed by printing blank lines and by printing spaces. A PRINT statement without an argument (an empty PRINT statement) prints a blank line. Spaces can be printed just like any other character by enclosing them inside quotation marks, thereby making them string constants. Spaces that aren't enclosed in quotation marks have no effect on the output. For example,

```
40 PRINT "         NAME           AGE    WEIGHT"
50 PRINT "----------------------------------- ------    -----------"
60 PRINT
70 PRINT "THOMAS              ";45;"    ";213
80 PRINT "JENNIFER            ";    13;  "    ";    87
RUN
          NAME           AGE   WEIGHT
----------------------------------- -------   -----------

THOMAS                      45     213
JENNIFER                    13      87
```

Another way to control vertical spacing is to place a comma or semicolon at the end of a PRINT statement. This causes the next PRINT statement to begin printing where the last PRINT statement left off—instead of starting at the beginning of the next line. This strategy is useful if you need to print a long line. For example,

```
40 PRINT "This sentence is too long to fit conveniently in one ";
50 PRINT "print statement."
RUN
This sentence is too long to fit conveniently in one print statement.
```

As another example, compare these three ways of printing two numbers.

```
100 PRINT 5.2        100 PRINT 5.2;        100 PRINT 5.2,
110 PRINT 4.8        110 PRINT 4.8         110 PRINT 4.8
RUN                  RUN                   RUN
  5.2                  5.2   4.8             5.2                4.8
  4.8
```

PRINT USING

In the PRINT statements we have discussed, two types of information are merged in each statement's argument: the data to be printed (strings and numbers) and formatting information (such as commas, semicolons, and spaces). The commas, semicolons, and spaces provide convenient formatting tricks that make it easy to print items quickly, but they don't let you control the exact placement and format of the printed items. For example, decimal places aren't likely to line up in a column when printed, and strings can't be right-justified in a field of a specific width.

PRINT USING statements give you precise control over the appearance of output by separating the argument into two parts. One part specifies what data are to be printed. The other part determines the placement and format of the data and answers such questions as "How many digits of each number should appear?" "Where should the first character of a string begin?" "Exactly how wide should each field be in the output line?"

In some dialects of BASIC, these two parts are placed in separate statements: a PRINT USING statement contains the data to be printed, and an IMAGE statement determines the appearance of the output line. We will illustrate a simpler method, used by Microsoft BASIC. It avoids the use of a separate IMAGE statement by placing the description of the output line's layout in a *format string*. The simplest general form of this type of PRINT USING statement is

PRINT USING *"format string"*; *expression list*

The *format string* contains fields that specify the format of the numbers and strings given in the expression list. The first item in the expression list is printed in the first field of the format string, the second item in the second field, and so on.

Number fields are constructed from number-sign characters; they look like #### or ####.##. The length of the field determines the largest number that will fit in the field and specifies how many digit positions to print. In the following examples, assume that variable PAY stores 5.75:

```
40 PRINT USING " ###.## ### "; PAY, PAY * 2
50 PRINT USING " ###.## ### "; PAY * 2, PAY
RUN
    5.75    12
   11.50     6
```

If BASIC can't print the full precision of a number, it rounds the number appropriately. Thus, in the preceding example, 11.50 was rounded to 12 before it was printed in the ### field.

String fields begin and end with backslash characters; they look like \ \. The number of characters between the backslash characters determines the length of the field. If a string is longer than its field description, its extra characters are ignored. In the following examples, assume that JOB$ stores "JANITOR":

```
60 PRINT USING "\ \"; JOB$
70 PRINT USING "\            \"; JOB$
RUN
JAN
 JANITOR
```

It is also possible to embed constants in the format string of a PRINT USING statement. For example, if line 170 in Figure B.4 is replaced with

170 PRINT USING "The area of a ##.# by ##.# rectangle is ##.## "; X; Y; A

then the output becomes

```
The area of a 3.2 by 4.5 rectangle is 14.40
```

Most implementations of BASIC have many additional features for controlling the appearance of output. Often they float dollar signs to the immediate left of formatted numbers and provide commands that position the cursor on a specified row or column of the screen, as well as commands that set the display attributes of characters on the screen (blinking, inverse video, and so on).

Assignment Statements

Input and output consumes much of a programmer's time, but assignment statements are the most frequently used statements in a typical BASIC program. An *assignment statement* assigns a value to a variable. Assignment statements can move values from one variable to another or calculate a variable's value from a formula. The general forms for assignment statements are

[LET] *numeric variable name* = *arithmetic expression*
[LET] *string variable name* = *string expression*

Both types of assignment statement may begin with the optional verb LET. The important part of the assignment statement begins with the name of the variable to receive a value; it must be followed by an equal sign, which must be followed by an expression.

The expression may contain constants, variables, and operators. An *operator* is a symbol (such as + or /) that indicates an action to be performed on the constants and variables. An assignment statement evaluates the expression to obtain a single value (either a number or a string) and stores the value in the variable named on the left side of the equal sign. For example, 150 LET AREA = LENGTH * DEPTH assigns the result of the arithmetic expression LENGTH * DEPTH to the variable AREA. Because multiplication is indicated by an asterisk, the formula LENGTH * DEPTH multiplies the values stored in LENGTH by the value stored in DEPTH to obtain the value to be stored in AREA. The new value in AREA replaces the previous value, which is permanently lost.

Assignment statements are *not* equations. They *copy values* rather than state a mathematical fact. For instance, the following assignment statement is common in BASIC:

```
100 LET I = I + 1
```

This means: add 1 to the current value of I and store the result back in I. Thus, I is increased by 1.

Here are some examples of assignment statements.

```
100 LET COUNT5 = 0            'copy zero into COUNT5
135 LET PAY = SALARY          'copy contents of SALARY into PAY
195 LET JOB$ = "JANITOR"      'store the value "JANITOR" in JOB$
220 LET MATH = 14/2           'store the value 7 in MATH
250 LET DEMON = (A+B)/(A−B)   'quotient of sum and difference in DEMON
```

The last example illustrates how to use parentheses to group subexpressions together when ambiguity might otherwise result. Without the parentheses, $(A + B) / (A - B)$ would become $A + B / A - B$, which is interpreted as $A + (B / A) - B$. The operators used in assignment statements include

- ∎ * for multiplication
- ∎ / for division
- ∎ + for addition
- ∎ − for subtraction
- ∎ ^ for exponentiation

Exponentiation means "raising to a power," as in 3^2. Some versions of BASIC use ** as the exponentiation operator.

The order in which operations are performed often influences the value of an expression. BASIC unravels arithmetic expressions by performing operations in the following order:

1. Expressions inside parentheses
2. Negation
3. Exponentiation
4. Multiplication and division
5. Addition and subtraction

Parentheses may be nested, in which case the innermost expression is evaluated first. If two or more operators in an expression are at the same level of the hierarchy (for example, $B/C/2$), then the operators are evaluated from left to right. The following expressions illustrate these rules:

```
100 LET X = (A + 2 / (2 * B))   'first 2*B, then 2/(2*B), then add A
200 LET M = A * B − C           'first A*B, then subtract C
300 LET Z = 1 + A^2             'first A^2, then add 1
400 LET A = A / B / 2 * D       'first A/B, then /2, then multiply by D
```

Here are some assignment statements with comments explaining what they do.

```
100 LET C = 5 * (F − 32) / 9    'convert from F to C degrees.
200 LET Y = M * X + B           'compute the height of a straight line.
300 LET A = (B * H) / 2         'find the area of a triangle.
```

Figure B.5 Calculating the length of the hypotenuse of a right triangle.

```
LIST
100 REM ------------------- TRIANGLE.BAS --------------------------
110 REM        Computes the hypotenuse of a right triangle
120 REM ======================================================================
130 REM
140 INPUT "A = "; A               'Prompt user for A; get A from keyboard
150 INPUT "B = "; B               'Prompt user for B; get B from keyboard
160 C = (B^2 + A^2) ^ (.5)        'Compute the length of the hypotenuse
170 PRINT "C = "; C               'Display the answer on the screen
999 END '-------------------------------------------------------------
Ok
RUN
A = 3
B = 4
C = 5
Ok
```

Figure B.5 illustrates the use of assignment statements in a complete program. The program computes the length of the hypotenuse (the longest side) of a right triangle. The mathematical formula for computing the hypotenuse requires squaring the lengths of the two shorter sides, adding these two numbers, and taking the square root of the result. The exponentiation operator is used to calculate both the square and the square root.

Notice that, instead of using both a PRINT and an INPUT statement, we have used an extended version of the INPUT statement in Figure B.5.

Standard Method **Extended Short Cut**
PRINT "A";   INPUT "A = "; A
INPUT A

An extended INPUT statement allows a prompt to be printed and data to be collected from the keyboard—all in one statement.

Library Functions

BASIC provides several library functions to help with mathematical calculations and to manipulate strings. A *function* is a prewritten routine that accepts one or more input values, performs some operations on them, and returns a single value. We will discuss only arithmetic functions in detail, but you should know that string functions can extract portions of a string (truncate the string), search a string for a specific pattern of characters, and perform other types of text processing.

Table B.1 lists some of the standard arithmetic functions of BASIC. Arithmetic functions take only one input value. To call a function, you use its name in an as-

Table B.1 Mathematical Functions of BASIC

Function	Returned Value	Example	Value
ABS(X)	Absolute value of X	ABS(− 4.6)	4
COS(X)	Cosine of X; X is in radians	COS(0.0)	1
EXP(X)	e raised to the Xth power	EXP(1)	2.718282
INT(X)	Largest integer in X	INT(4.6)	4
RND(X)	A random number between 0 and 1	RND(5)	.5119751
SIN(X)	Sine of X; X is in radians	SIN(3.14159/2)	1
SQR(X)	Square root of X	SQR(4)	2

signment expression or a PRINT statement in the same way you would use a variable's name. The function's name is followed by the function's input value, which is enclosed in parentheses. For example, if you want to calculate the square root of the value in P, you type SQR(P). Thus we could have simplified the calculation of the hypotenuse in Figure B.5 by replacing line 160 with

```
160 C = SQR(B^2 + A^2)     'Compute the length of the hypotenuse.
```

Here is another example of the square root function.

```
40 LET TURTLES = 645
50 PRINT "THE SQUARE ROOT OF TURTLES IS:"; SQR(TURTLES)
60 LET TURTLEFOOD = SQR(TURTLES) * 3
70 PRINT "THE AMOUNT OF TURTLE FOOD TO BUY IS:"; TURTLEFOOD
RUN
THE SQUARE ROOT OF TURTLES IS: 8
THE AMOUNT OF TURTLE FOOD TO BUY IS: 24
```

The INT function is used to throw away the fractional part of a number and retain only the integer part. The following program fragment uses the INT function to determine how many quarters should be dispensed from a vending machine to make change:

```
1010 INPUT "ENTER THE AMOUNT OF CHANGE NEEDED: "; CHANGE
1015 QUARTERS = INT(CHANGE / 25)
1020 PRINT "THEN DISPENSE";QUARTERS; "QUARTERS "
RUN
ENTER THE AMOUNT OF CHANGE NEEDED: ? 95
THEN DISPENSE 3 QUARTERS
```

The calculation in line 1015 divides the amount of change to be dispensed (in this example, 95 cents) by 25; this intermediate result (3.8) is truncated by the INT function to determine the number of quarters to dispense. To be useful, this fragment would need to be followed by similar statements that would calculate the number of dimes, nickels, and pennies remaining to be dispensed.

EXERCISES

1. Determine the value of A after each of the following assignment statements is executed. Assume that each part is done independently and that the starting values are $A = 4$, $B = 3$, $C = 25$, and CAT $= 2$.
    a. LET A = – 1
    b. LET A = B + C – 2.5
    c. LET A = B * C/CAT
    d. LET A = A^2 * B^2 / C
    e. LET A = (A – 1) * (B + 2)

2. Which of the following are *invalid* variable names in BASIC?
    a. X15   e. M2M2
    b. 15X   f. M2_M2
    c. X$ g. PER%
    d. $X   h. PERSON2-AND-A-1/2

3. Write a program that computes the cost of traveling M miles in a car that gets R miles per gallon. Assume that gasoline costs C dollars per gallon, Include prompts that ask the user to provide the values of M, R, and C. Test your program on a 135-mile round trip that took 12.4 gallons of gasoline purchased for $1.38 per gallon.

4. Write a program that requests three data items from the user: a description of an inventory part, the part's price, and the quantity sold. Assume that the values entered by the user are "PENS", .24, and 16. Make your program calculate and print the following report:

PART DESCRIPTION	QUANTITY	PRICE	INVOICE
----------------------------	---------------	--------	-------------
PENS	16	$ .24	$ 3.84

5. The payments on a mortgage are calculated as follows:

    $$P = i * A * V / (V - 1)$$

    where

    i = monthly interest rate
    A = amount borrowed
    V = $(1 + i)^M$
    M = number of months to repay loan

Write a BASIC program to compute the monthly payments on a loan of $90,000 for 29 years at 10 percent annual interest. Your answer should be approximately $794.23.

6. Write a statement that uses the INT function to round the value in HOURS to the nearest tenth. *Hint:* This statement rounds HOURS to the nearest integer: 50 HOURS = INT(HOURS + .5).

7. Complete the fragment of the vending-machine program given earlier so that it calculates the number of dimes, nickels, and pennies to be dispensed.

PROGRAM CONTROL

Most programs make decisions based on the data they receive from a user or on calculations made by the program. When a decision is made, the program branches to one of several optional statements and then resumes executing each statement in the order encountered. A *branch* is a point in a program where the next statement to be executed is determined by the running program—not just by the statement numbers. Branching statements provide a way to skip one part of a program in favor of another part, depending on the input data. BASIC's branching statements include the GOTO, IF, and ON GOTO statements.

Loops provide another way of altering the sequence of a program. A *loop* is a group of statements that are executed repeatedly. FOR and NEXT statements are used to set up a loop that will be repeated a certain number of times. Loops can also be constructed from IF and GOTO statements. IF-GOTO loops are normally used when the loop is to be executed until a particular condition becomes true. Both methods of looping shorten programs. If you use a loop, you don't need to write the same statements over again; the loop directs BASIC to execute the statements repeatedly.

GOTO Statements

The simplest branching statement in BASIC is the GOTO statement. It begins with the verb GOTO followed by a line number.

GOTO *destination line number*

When this statement is interpreted by BASIC, the *destination line number* becomes the next statement to be interpreted rather than the statement following the GOTO statement. The intervening statements are skipped, as shown by the following example:

```
100   A = 0
200   GOTO 300
240   A = 1
300   PRINT A
```

This program fragment prints 0 as the value of *A* because the GOTO at line 200 forces BASIC to skip statement 240 and go to line 300.

The GOTO statement is not particularly useful by itself, because it doesn't make decisions. GOTO statements are most helpful when used with IF statements.

IF Statements

The IF statement sets up a test that determines how BASIC will branch. If the result of the test is true, one path is taken; if false, another path is taken.

There are two kinds of IF statements. The IF-THEN statement has one potential branch; the IF-THEN-ELSE statement has two potential branches.

IF *test* THEN *statement-1*
IF *test* THEN *statement-1* ELSE *statement-2*

If *test* is true, then *statement-1* is executed. If *test* is false, *statement-1* is skipped. In the case of an IF-THEN-ELSE statement, *statement-2* is executed if the *test* is false.

Consider the following IF-THEN statement:

```
100   IF ITEM$ = "PENCIL" THEN PRINT "ERASE IT"
110   PRINT "DONE"
```

The test, ITEM$ = "PENCIL", is true if the string stored in ITEM$ is equal to "PENCIL"; it is false if the string in ITEM$ is anything other than "PENCIL". If the test is true, the message ERASE IT is printed. Otherwise, the PRINT "ERASE IT" statement is skipped. In either case, DONE is printed.

Compare the previous example with the following IF-THEN-ELSE statement:

```
100   IF ITEM$ = "PENCIL" THEN PRINT "ERASE IT" ELSE PRINT "CUT IT"
110   PRINT "DONE"
```

If the test is true, ERASE IT is printed; otherwise CUT IT is printed. In either case, DONE is also printed.

Frequently you will want to interpret several statements in the THEN or the ELSE parts of an IF statement. To do this you must use a different form of IF statement, one that contains line numbers. The line numbers cause BASIC to branch to a new part of the program.

IF *test* THEN *line-number-1* [ELSE *line-number-2*]

If *test* is true, the next statement to be interpreted is *line-number-1*. The ELSE keyword is optional; that is why its portion of the IF statement is shown in brackets.

IF the ELSE clause is omitted and *test* is false, then the next statement to be interpreted is the statement following the IF statement. If there is an ELSE clause and *test* is false, then the next statement to be interpreted is *line-number-2*.

IF statements are often used in conjunction with GOTO statements. For example,

```
100   IF HOURS = 0 THEN 110 ELSE 200
110      LET PAY = 0                    'begin THEN clause
120      LET DEDUCTIONS = 0
130   GOTO 250                          'skip over ELSE clause
200      REM                            'begin ELSE clause
210      LET PAY = HOURS * RATE
250   REM                               'end of IF-THEN-ELSE
```

First, the expression HOURS = 0 is tested. If it is true, the next statement to be interpreted is at line 110. Otherwise, BASIC skips to the statement at line 200. Lines 200 and 210 are called the *ELSE clause* because they are reached by interpreting the ELSE portion of the IF statement.

Lines 110 through 130 are interpreted in sequence if HOURS = 0 is true. At line 130, BASIC is directed to skip to line 250. Lines 110 through 130 are called the *THEN clause* because they are interpreted only when the THEN portion of the IF statement is executed. Both THEN and ELSE clauses can be much longer than our examples. It is considered good form to place the THEN clause before the ELSE clause.

If the ELSE keyword is dropped, it is still possible to have an implicit ELSE clause in your program. For example,

```
100   IF HOURS = 0 THEN 200
110      LET PAY = HOURS * RATE
120      LET TAXES = .32 * PAY
200   REM -- End of implicit ELSE clause.
```

In this example, statements 110 and 120 are skipped unless the test HOURS = 0 is false.

Comparison Operators
The test expression in an IF statement must be either true or false. Expressions that are either true or false are called *boolean expressions* or *conditional expressions*. Conditional expressions are constructed with *comparison operators,* as shown in Table B.2. Parentheses can be used to avoid ambiguities. Here are some samples.

(0 < A) AND (A < 10)	Is $0 < A < 10$?
(0 < A) OR (A < 10)	Is $A > 0$ or is $A < 10$?
(A < > 0) OR (NOT (B = 0))	Is A not equal to zero, or is B not equal to zero?

Table B.2 Comparison Operators in BASIC

Conditional Operator	Example	Meaning
=	A = 0	Equal
< >	A < > 0	Not equal
>	A > 0	Greater than
<	A < 0	Less than
> =	A > = 0	Greater than or equal
< =	A < = 0	Less than or equal
AND	(A = 0) AND (B = 1)	Both subparts true?
OR	(A = 0) OR (B = 1)	Either subpart true?
NOT	NOT (A = 0)	Same as A < > 0

In an AND comparison, both of the expression's subparts must be true in order for the whole expression to be true. In contrast, an OR comparison is true if *either* subpart is true.

To illustrate an OR comparison, consider the problem of checking data entered from the keyboard to make sure it is reasonable. For example, suppose the ages of potential customers are to be entered, and reasonable values for the age are considered to be 10 through 110. The following program fragment will force a correct input:

```
100 INPUT AGE
110    IF (AGE < 10) OR (AGE > 110) THEN 120 ELSE 140
120    PRINT "Please enter an age between 10 and 110. Try again."
130    GOTO 100
140 REM
```

The IF-THEN-ELSE statement tests the value of AGE each time it is entered. Unacceptable values of AGE cause an error message to be displayed and force BASIC to return to the INPUT statement in line 100. This cycle is repeated until the value entered for AGE is acceptable; then the ELSE clause is interpreted.

Nested IF Statements

It is a good idea to indent the THEN and ELSE clauses of an IF statement to make them readable, especially when IF statements are part of other IF statements. A *nested IF statement* is any IF statement that is part of a THEN or ELSE clause. Here is a simple example in which indentation is used to clarify the nested statements.

```
100 IF WEIGHT < 40 THEN 110 ELSE 200
110    IF BIG < 15 THEN 120 ELSE 150      'Nested inside THEN clause...
120       LET SHIP$ = "CARRY IT"          'Innermost THEN clause
130       GOTO 190                        'End of inner THEN clause
```

```
150     LET SHIP$ = "DRAG IT"         'Innermost ELSE clause
190     REM                           'End of inner IF statement
199     GOTO 220                      'End of outermost THEN clause
200     LET SHIP$ = "HAND-TRUCK IT"   'Outermost ELSE clause
210     REM                           'End of outermost ELSE clause
220 REM                               'End of outermost IF statement
```

Indention shows which statements belong to the outer IF statement and which ones belong to the inner IF statement. Lines 110 through 190 are all part of the innermost IF statement, which in turn is part of the THEN clause of the IF statement that starts in line 100. Lines 199 through 210 are part of the outer IF statement, so they are only indented once.

A Complete Example

Now let's put IF statements to work in a longer example. Consider the equation $AX^2 + BX + C = 0$, where A, B, and C are constants and X is a variable. You may recall from algebra that this equation is called a *quadratic equation* and can be solved to find the values of X that cause the equation to be true. These values are called *roots* of the equation. Most quadratic equations have two roots that in BASIC notation are given by the following:

$$X = \frac{-B + SQR(B^2 - 4 * A * C)}{2 * A} \quad \text{and} \quad X = \frac{-B - SQR(B^2 - 4 * A * C)}{2 * A}$$

The formulas seem quite straightforward, but it is not simple to write a BASIC program to find the roots. Here is a list of what can go wrong.

1. If the values of both A and B are zero, the equation has no roots.

2. If A is zero and B is not equal to zero, then the formula is undefined. In this case there is only one root, and it is given by the formula $X = -C/B$.

3. The argument of the square root function (called the *discriminant*) could be less than zero, in which case the equation has no roots.

We can take all of these possibilities into account by using IF statements and GOTOs to check the values of A, B, and C. This is why the resulting program in Figure B.6 is rather imposing. QUADRAD.BAS asks the user for the values of A, B, and C in lines 140 through 155. Next, the value of A is tested in line 160 to see if it is zero.

If the value of A is zero, the value of B is tested in line 165 to see if the equation has one root, or if it has no solutions. If both A and B store zero, then the quadratic equation is degenerate and has no solutions. In this case, the program prints an error message in line 170 and skips to the end of the program. Alternatively, if the value of A is zero and the value of B is not zero, the program calculates the equation's one root in line 180 and skips to the end of the program.

Figure B.6   Solving the equation $AX^2 + BX + C = 0$

```
100 REM --------------------- QUADRAD.BAS ---------------------------
110 REM     Compute the roots of the equation AX^2 + BX + C = 0
120 REM ==========================================================
130 REM
135 REM          Input Values of A,B,C
136 REM
140 INPUT "A = "; A               'Prompt user for A; get A from keyboard
150 INPUT "B = "; B               'Prompt user for B; get B from keyboard
155 INPUT "C = "; C               'Prompt user for C; get C from keyboard
156 REM
157 REM          Logic Section & Calculations
158 REM
160 IF A = 0 THEN 165 ELSE 200            'Decide if A = 0
165    IF B = 0 THEN 170 ELSE 180         'Both A = 0 and B = 0 ?
170       PRINT "***ERROR**** Bad Inputs"
172       GOTO 300                        'Bad inputs, so quit
180    PRINT "The one root is:"; (-C)/B   'Solve BX + C = 0
181    GOTO 300                           'One root, then quit
182 REM                                   'End of inner IF statement
200 REM ELSE
205 REM
210    DISC = B^2 - 4 * A * C             'Discriminant could be negative
220    IF DISC < 0 THEN 230 ELSE 250
230       PRINT "There are no real roots" 'There are only imaginary roots
240       GOTO 290                        'End of Disc < 0 clause
250    REM
252    REM ELSE                           'ELSE within an ELSE
255    REM
260       PRINT "Real Roots = ";(-B - SQR(DISC)) / (2*A)
270       PRINT "          = ";(-B + SQR(DISC)) / (2*A)
280    REM                                'End of inner ELSE
290 REM                                   'End of outer ELSE
300 REM                                   'End of outer IF statement
999 END '----------------------------------------------------------
RUN
A = ? 4
B = ? 0
C = ? -4
Real Roots = -1
           = 1

Ok
```

When the value of A is not zero, either the equation has two roots, or the discriminant is negative and the equation has only "imaginary" roots. Thus, the final IF statement is in line 220, where the program decides if real roots exist by testing the discriminant.

This program illustrates the use of IF and GOTO statements, but more importantly, it shows how to properly structure a program that contains many paths. All paths in the program lead to the same ending. And the inner IF statements are terminated before the outer IF statements, as shown in lines 280 through 300. These features are characteristics of a structured program. In a *structured program*, all branches must converge at some later point in the program in a way that guarantees nonoverlapping paths through the program. Careful placement of GO-TOs can guarantee proper structure, but careless placement can make a program much more difficult to understand. For more details about structured programming, see Chapter 13.

ON GOTO Statements

The IF statement is used to decide between two alternatives, but sometimes you will want to decide among many alternatives. The ON GOTO statement is used to direct the program down one of many possible paths. Its general form is

ON *variable* GOTO *list of line numbers*

The value of the variable determines which of the line numbers in the list is executed next. For example, if the value of the variable is 3, then the third line number in the list becomes the next statement to be executed.

```
200   INPUT J                    'Get a number
210   ON J GOTO 220,230,240      'Branch
220      PRINT "FIRST"
225      GOTO 250                 'Skip the rest
230      PRINT "SECOND"
240      PRINT "LAST"
250 REM                          'End of ON GOTO
```

In this example, the value of J is obtained from the keyboard and is used to determine which statement to branch to. First, if necessary, the value of J is truncated to an integer. Then, depending on whether the value of J is 1, 2, or 3, the next statement to be interpreted is 220, 230, or 240, respectively. For example, if the value of J is 2, then lines 230 through 250 are interpreted, because the ON GOTO branches to line 230 and continues from there. If the truncated value of J is less than 1 or greater than 3, then the ON GOTO at line 210 has no effect at all and line 220 is interpreted next.

A more practical example of ON GOTO statements is given in Figure B.7. It illustrates how an ON GOTO statement can form the basis of a menu selection system.

FOR/NEXT Loops

One of the most powerful features of computers is their ability to repeat monotonous operations over and over again without error or complaint. Repeti-

Figure B.7 A menu selection system.

```
100  REM --------------------- MENU.BAS ---------------------------
110  REM         Illustrate a simple menu-selection system
120  REM =========================================================
130  PRINT "        THE WHIZ-BANG PAYROLL SYSTEM'S MASTER MENU"
140  PRINT
150  PRINT "1 -- Enter payroll transactions"
160  PRINT "2 -- Print paychecks or reports"
170  PRINT "3 -- Perform maintenance functions (back-up files, etc.)"
180  PRINT "4 -- QUIT by returning to the operating system"
190  INPUT "        Enter your choice:"; CHOICE
200  ON CHOICE GOTO 1000, 2300, 4000, 7000
210  PRINT "Please enter a value between 1 and 4"
220  GOTO 130
1000 REM -- The statements for entering payroll transactions follow.
     ...
2140 REM -- End of data entry section.
2300 REM -- The statements for printing reports follow.
     ...
3860 REM -- End of reports section.
4000 REM -- The statements that perform maintenance functions follow.
     ...
6280 REM -- End of maintenance section.
7000 REM -- Return to operating system.
     ...
9999 END
```

tious calculations are done in BASIC programs by using FOR/NEXT loops. Their general format is

FOR *loop counter* = *start* TO *stop* [STEP *step size*]
   body of the loop
NEXT *loop counter*

The statements bracketed between the FOR and NEXT statements are called the *body of the loop*. The number of times that the body of the loop is repeated is determined by the *start*, *stop*, and *step-size* values. These values can be constants, variables, or expressions. The *loop counter* is a numeric variable that keeps track of the number of times the loop has been repeated. The loop starts with the FOR statement and ends at the NEXT statement. The STEP clause is optional. If it is omitted, the default value for the step size is 1.

When the FOR statement is first interpreted, BASIC assigns the start value to the loop counter. With each pass through the loop, the loop counter is increased by 1 (or by the optional step-size value). When the loop counter becomes greater than the stopping value, the statement that follows the NEXT statement is interpreted. For example,

```
100 FOR I = 1 TO 8
120 PRINT I * 2,
130 NEXT I
140 END
RUN
 2              4              6              8              10
 12            14            16
Ok
```

The starting value of I is 1. Each time the segment is repeated, the value of I is automatically increased by 1 until it exceeds 8. When the value of I is 9, the loop ceases, and the statement following 130 NEXT I is interpreted.

The preceding FOR/NEXT loop is equivalent to the following program that uses IF and GOTO statements. In this example, the FOR/NEXT loop is preferable to a loop constructed from IF and GOTO statements because it provides a shorter, clearer solution.

```
100 LET I = 1                        'Starting value of loop counter
110 IF I < = 8 THEN 120 ELSE 140     'Test the loop counter
120    PRINT I * 2,                   'Body of the loop
125 LET I = I + 1                     'Increase the loop counter
130 GOTO 110                          'Repeat it all
140 END
```

Notice that the loop counter is tested *before* the body of the loop is executed. Some older versions of BASIC test the loop *after* the body is interpreted—this means that the loop is always interpreted at least once. In this example, the test seems unnecessary, but in general it is needed because the loop may be done *zero* or more times. Suppose, for example, that the initial and final values of the loop counter are variables.

```
100 FOR MONTHS = PRESENT TO FUTURE
```

Here it is possible that the value of PRESENT is already greater than the value of FUTURE. If so, the loop is skipped altogether.

The body of the loop may contain other FOR/NEXT loops, IF-GOTO loops, and many other statements. Because these statements easily become confusing, it is good to indent the body of a loop to identify what is being repeated.

Computing a Total

Adding numbers to determine their total is one major use of loops. This is done by assigning to a variable the task of storing the sum of all the numbers that have been added so far. The initial value of this variable is zero, because no numbers have been added to it. While the loop is being interpreted, numbers are added to the variable, and it maintains a running total. For example, this loop calculates the sum of three numbers.

```
100 YARDAGE = O                     'Store an initial value of zero
150 FOR DOWNS = 1 TO 4              'Start at DOWNS = 1, stop at 4
200   INPUT "Enter yards:"; YARDS   'User enters a number
250   YARDAGE = YARDAGE + YARDS 'Add YARDS to the running total
300 NEXT DOWNS                      'End of loop
350 PRINT "The total yardage is:";    YARDAGE
```

The value of YARDAGE is increased from zero to the final total by adding YARDS to it each time the body of the loop is repeated. YARDS takes on a different value each time it is entered from the keyboard. Suppose the numbers entered from the keyboard are 3, 5, 1, and 35. The following table shows the values of DOWNS, YARDS, and YARDAGE after each time through the loop:

DOWNS (Counter)	YARDS (Input)	YARDAGE (Calculated)
1	3	3
2	5	8
3	1	9
4	35	44

When DOWNS reaches 5, the loop is terminated because 5 is greater than the stopping value of 4.

In the preceding example, the loop is designed to add exactly four numbers. The following example relaxes this restriction by asking the user to enter how many numbers are to be added. This example also computes the average of the numbers.

```
1000 TOTAL = 0                          'TOTAL is initially zero
1010 INPUT "How many numbers are there"; N
1020 FOR COUNT = 1 TO N              'Perform the loop N times
1030    INPUT "Enter a number"; X    'X changes each pass
1040    TOTAL = TOTAL + X            'Repeatedly add X to TOTAL
1050 NEXT COUNT                      'Increment COUNT by 1. Done?
2000 PRINT "The average is:"; TOTAL/N
RUN
How many numbers are there? 2
Enter a number? 12
Enter a number? 6
The average is: 9
```

A Payroll Example

Figure B.8 illustrates the basic idea of summing within a FOR loop, but in a more sophisticated application. Although this program is more complicated than our pre-

Figure B.8 A program to compute a paycheck for one week.

```
100 REM --------------------- PAYDAY.BAS ---------------------
110 REM               Compute 5 days' worth of pay
120 REM --------------------------------------------------------
130 REM
140 LET REGPAY = 0              'total regular pay
150 LET OVRPAY = 0              'total overtime pay
160 LET BIGBUCKS = 0           'total dollars earned
170 LET REGTIME = 0            'total regular hours
180 LET OTIME = 0              'total overtime hours
190 LET TIME = 0              'total hours worked
200 REM
210 INPUT "Enter $/hr rate of pay"; RATE
220 REM
230 REM <+++++ LOOP +++++++++++++++++++++++++++++++++++++++++++++++<
240 FOR I = 1 TO 5               'repeat for each day of week      |
250    INPUT "Enter hours worked :"; HRS                         '|
270    LET OVRTIME = HRS - 8     'anything over 8 hrs is overtime   |
280    IF OVRTIME > 0 THEN 290 ELSE 340   'overtime pay? -------->| |
290      LET OTIME = OTIME + OVRTIME                             '| |
295      LET REGTIME = REGTIME + 8                               '| |
300      LET PAY = RATE * 8                                      '| |
310      LET BONUS = RATE * OVRTIME * 1.5                        '| |
320      LET OVRPAY = OVRPAY + BONUS                             '| |
325      LET BUCKS = PAY + BONUS                                 '| |
330      GOTO 380                                                '| |
340    REM --------else clause -----------------------------------<| |
345      LET REGTIME = REGTIME + HRS                             '| |
347      LET PAY = RATE * HRS                                    '| |
350      LET BUCKS = PAY                                         '| |
370    REM --------end of IF -------------------------------- | |
380    LET BIGBUCKS=BIGBUCKS + BUCKS  'total $ earned for the week |
390    LET TIME = TIME + HRS          'add up total hours worked  |
400    LET REGPAY = REGPAY + PAY      'add up total regular pay   |
410 NEXT I                                                        '|
420 REM >+++++++++++++++++++++++++++++++++++++++++++++++++++++++++++>
430 REM
440 PRINT USING "Regular : ### hrs.   $###.##"; REGTIME; REGPAY
450 PRINT USING "Overtime  ### hrs.   $###.##"; OTIME; OVRPAY
460 PRINT  "          ------------------"
470 PRINT USING "Totals    ### hrs.   $###.##"; TIME; BIGBUCKS
480 REM
490 END '---------------------------------------------------------
RUN
Enter $/hr rate of pay? 5
Enter hours worked :? 7
Enter hours worked :? 4
Enter hours worked :? 9
Enter hours worked :? 6
Enter hours worked :? 9
Regular :  33 hrs.   $165.00
Overtime   2 hrs.   $ 15.00
          ------------------
Totals     35 hrs.   $180.00
Ok
```

vious examples, it retains the baic pattern of looping for the purpose of computing a sum.

Like most long programs, PAYDAY.BAS begins with an initialization section. This section (lines 140 through 190) sets the values of the six total variables to zero. The repeated part of the summation is enclosed in a single FOR loop from lines 230 to 410. Each pass through the loop represents one day's worth of wages. In the body of the loop, line 280 decides whether the employee worked more than eight hours and should be paid overtime. After the loop does the totaling, the totals are printed in a formatted table, as specified by lines 440 through 470.

The Loop's Step Size

The optional step size in a FOR/NEXT loop tells BASIC how much to add to or subtract from the loop counter each time through the loop. For example, the statement 100 FOR FEET = 1 TO WALLSIZE STEP 3 causes the loop counter to take on the values of 1, 4, 7, and so on, until the value in FEET exceeds the stop value in WALLSIZE.

The main reason for choosing a step size other than 1 is to use the loop counter conveniently within the body of the loop. For example, if you wanted to print the even numbers from 1 to 15, you would set the step size to 2, and then have the value of the loop counter printed each time through the loop.

```
100 FOR I = 1 TO 16 STEP 2
120 PRINT I,
130 NEXT I
RUN
 1              3              5              7              9
11             13             15
```

FOR loop counters can run "backwards" as well. If the step size is a negative number, the loop counter is decreased. Each time through the loop, the negative step value is added to the loop counter. Suppose you want to print all numbers from 100 down to 49, in steps of 9.

```
500 FOR I = 100 TO 49 STEP −9    'Start with 100, stop at 49, step −9
510    PRINT I                   'Print 100, 91, 82, 73, 64, 55
520 NEXT I                       'Add (−9) to I
```

Observe that the last value of *I* to be printed is 55 rather than 49. The next value of *I* would be 46—a number outside the range of acceptable counter values from 100 to 49.

Limitations of FOR Loops

The FOR loop saves time and effort when you know exactly how many times you want to repeat the body of the loop. Unfortunately, there are many instances in programming in which you don't know in advance the number of times to execute the body of a loop. In these circumstances, the FOR loop is of little value.

As an illustration, suppose you want to repeat a loop until the number entered from the keyboard is zero. You might attempt to do this with the FOR loop as follows:

```
200 FOR TIMES = 1 TO 100
210     INPUT X
220     IF X = 0 THEN 300
230     REM the rest of the body
299 NEXT TIMES
300 REM outside the loop
```

There are several things wrong with this approach. First, you can never be sure that the termination value 100 is large enough. What if the user wants to enter 101 numbers? The second reason to avoid this approach is even more important. The IF statement at line 220 violates structured programming practice because it causes an exit from the middle of the loop. Recall from Chapter 13 that a structured program contains only single-entry and single-exit control constructs. Allowing an additional exit point from the middle of the FOR loop results in a multiple-exit construct.

The FOR loop fails to serve your needs in this case. Instead, you might use an IF statement, as in the following:

```
200 REM Repeat until X = 0
210     INPUT X
220     IF X = 0 THEN 300
230     REM the rest of the body
299     GOTO 200
300 REM outside the loop
```

This more accurately mirrors the intended operations, but the structure is still weak because of the convoluted IF-THEN clause. (Try to identify the THEN clause as a separate grouping from the body of the loop.)

Standard BASIC simply cannot handle this kind of problem well. This is one of the reasons BASIC is criticized as an unstructured language. Most extended versions of BASIC add another looping statement, the WHILE statement, to overcome this problem.

WHILE/WEND Loops

The WHILE statement repeats a loop body until the test portion of the WHILE is satisfied.

```
WHILE test
    body of loop
WEND
```

The WHILE statement is actually two statements: the beginning of the loop is marked by the WHILE statement, and the end is marked by the WEND statement. (WEND is short for "WHILE end".) If *test* is true, the body of the loop is interpreted until the WEND statement is encountered. BASIC then returns to the WHILE statement and checks the *test* condition again. If *test* is false, interpretation resumes with the statement that follows WEND. Otherwise, the loop is repeated again.

We can write our example problem in a structured fashion by first asking for an initial input value from the keyboard and then entering the WHILE loop.

```
200  INPUT X                      'Initialize input value
205  WHILE X < > 0                'Test looping condition
230      REM the rest of the body
299  INPUT X
300  WEND                         'End of loop
```

This version maintains the single-exit feature we are looking for. Each time the loop is repeated, a new value of X is entered into the running program. When line 300 is interpreted, control is passed to line 205, where the value of X is tested. When X is zero, the loop is skipped, and the statement following line 300 is interpreted.

Because the WHILE/WEND loop isn't part of standard BASIC, we won't use it in the examples in this appendix. You should note, however, that most versions of BASIC incorporate a similar statement to allow conditional looping as illustrated here. You should use these conditional loops where appropriate, because they improve the structure and readability of your programs.

EXERCISES

1. For each example, tell which statement is executed next. Assume that A is 3 and B is 10.
   a. 100 IF (NOT (A=0) AND (B=10)) THEN 110 ELSE 150
   b. 200 IF (A=0) OR (A=3) OR (B=9) THEN 220 ELSE 290
   c. 100 IF (A=3) AND (B<20) THEN 150 ELSE 300
   d. 100 IF ((A=3) AND (B=10)) AND (B>20) THEN 150 ELSE 400
   e. 150 IF (A*B>30) THEN 180 ELSE 200

2. In each of the following pieces of code, how many times will statement 110 be repeated?
   a. 100 FOR I = 3 TO 85   b. 100 FOR I = −1 TO 99
        110   PRINT I   110   PRINT I
        120 NEXT I   120 NEXT I

c. 100 FOR I = 2 TO 39 STEP 2   d. FOR I = 3 TO −40 STEP −2
   110   PRINT I   110   PRINT I
   120 NEXT I   120 NEXT I
e. 100 FOR J = 2 TO 5
   105 FOR I = J TO 5
   110   PRINT I,J
   115 NEXT I
   120 NEXT J

3. Assume that *A* is 5 and *B* is 10. What do the following program fragments print?
   a. 100 IF A = 3 THEN 150 ELSE 110
      110   PRINT A
      120   GOTO 200
      150   PRINT B
      200 REM
   b. 100 IF (A=3) AND (B=10) THEN 150 ELSE 110
      110   PRINT A
      120   GOTO 200
      150   PRINT B
      200 REM
   c. 100 IF (A=3) OR (B=10) THEN 150 ELSE 110
      110   PRINT A
      120   GOTO 200
      150   PRINT B
      200 REM
   d. 100 IF ((A=3) OR (B=10)) AND (B<5) THEN 150 ELSE 110
      110   PRINT A
      120   GOTO 200
      150   PRINT B
      200 REM

4. Modify the sample program for summing input values so that it also finds and displays the smallest value entered.

5. Write an ON GOTO statement that prints the day of the week, given that a number between 1 and 7 is entered.

6. Write a program to compute the average value, variance, minimum, and maximum values of a list of numbers entered from the keyboard. Your program should begin by asking the user how many numbers are in the list.

DATA STRUCTURES

Until now, we haven't discussed how data are organized inside programs that manipulate substantial quantities of data. A *data structure* is a collection of values and the information needed to organize these values into a coherent whole. For example, a card file is a data structure that is used in some manual systems to store names and addresses. BASIC is a difficult language to use for large projects and commercial programs because it is notoriously devoid of elegent data structures. Arrays and simple files are the only structures found in BASIC programs. We will discuss only the array structure and leave the discussion of file structures to an advanced text on BASIC.

One-Dimensional Arrays

An *array* is a variable that can contain more than one value. Because each value takes up memory space, you should tell BASIC the size of array variables before using them. The DIM (dimension) statement is used to declare the name and size of an array; it tells BASIC how much memory to reserve for the array's values. The general form of a DIM statement is

DIM *variable(size)*

where *variable* is the name of an array, and *size* specifies how many values are in the array. For example, suppose you want ITEM$ to be an array containing up to 50 strings. You would put the following DIM statement at the beginning of your program:

```
10 DIM ITEM$(50)              'ITEM$ is a string array of 50 values
```

If the name of an array variable is used without a DIM statement, the size of the array is assumed to be 10.

A list of variables separated by commas can be placed in a single DIM statement. For example, if CARS and TRUCKS are both arrays, you can declare them in a single DIM statement, as follows:

```
50 DIM CARS(50), TRUCKS(100)
```

Each value stored in an array is called an *element* of the array. In the previous example, array CARS can hold up to 50 elements and no more. Because CARS is a numeric variable name, each element of CARS must be a number.

The elements of an array are numbered as shown in Figure B.9. The numbers are called *subscripts* and are used to refer to a particular element in the array. The subscript must be an integer, and it is always enclosed in parentheses after the name of the array. For example, to refer to the third element in the array ITEM$, you would type ITEM$(3).

The following example shows how the data shown in Figure B.9 might be placed in the array ITEM$:

```
200 DIM ITEM$(50)
250 ITEM$(1) = "PENS"                'Store PENS in element 1
300 ITEM$(2) = "PENCILS"             'Store PENCILS in element 2
350 ITEM$(3) = "ERASERS"             'Store ERASERS in element 3
```

Figure B.9 Arrays, subscripts, and elements.

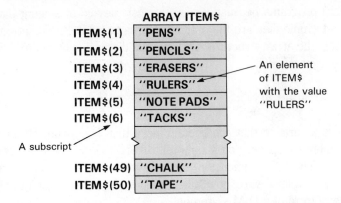

In this example, the array is made of string variables. In one way, numeric variables are trickier than string variables: with numeric variables it is easy to confuse the subscript with the value of the element itself. For example,

```
40 LET X(3) = -5      'Store the value -5 in element 3
50 LET X(5) = 8       'Store the value 8 in element 5
60 LET X(1) = X(3)    'Move the value in element 3 into element 1
70 PRINT X(1); X(3); X(5)
RUN
-5 -5 8
```

Using Arrays

The power of arrays is tied to the manipulation of array elements in loops. FOR loops are frequently used to store, retrieve, and search arrays. Suppose you want to load an array of numbers from the keyboard. You might repeat the INPUT statement for each array element, but that would be a tedious method. A better way is to use a FOR/NEXT loop.

```
500 FOR I = 1 TO 11    'Get all 11 elements. . .
550    INPUT X(I)      'I is a counter and a subscript!
600 NEXT I
```

Here we have used I as both a loop counter and a subscript. The FOR loop increases I from 1 to 11, and the INPUT statement uses I as a subscript of X. The first pass through the loop causes a value to be entered into element X(1); the second pass enters a value into X(2); and so forth until the value of X(11) is entered and stored in X(11).

One common task is to search an array to find a particular value. For example, we might want to know if the string "NOTE PADS" is in array ITEM$, and if it is, which element it is in. The FOR/NEXT loop and its counter can be used to search

Figure B.10 Searching array *X* for the value *K*.

```
100 REM -------------------- LOOKUP.BAS -------------------------
110 REM              Search array X for the value K
120 REM -------------------------------------------------------
130 REM
140 DIM X(100)                 'Reserve memory for the array
150 REM
160 FOR I = 1 TO 5             'Read five values into the array
170  PRINT USING "X(##) = ";I; '...from keyboard...
180  INPUT X(I)                'one at a time
190 NEXT I
200 REM
210 J = 0                      'J is used as a flag: J = 0 means NOT FOUND
220 INPUT "Enter the search key="; K
230 REM
240 FOR I = 1 TO 5             'Search all values....
250  IF X(I) = K THEN 260 ELSE 270 'for possible match.
260   J = I                    'Store the location of the match in J.
270 NEXT I                     '
280 IF J = 0 THEN 290 ELSE 310 'Was a match FOUND or NOT FOUND?
290  PRINT "NOT FOUND"
300  GOTO 320
310  PRINT USING "FOUND AT ##";J   'show where
320 REM
330 END '-------------------------------------------------------
```

an array. The simplest method is to examine each array element one at a time and compare it with a *search key* (the value to be found); if they match, the search is successful. If all elements are compared with the search key and none matches, then the search fails.

The LOOKUP.BAS program in Figure B.10 shows only one of many ways to search an array for a particular value. It does this by brute force—comparing each of the elements of *X* with the search key. When a match is found, the subscript of that element is remembered.

The first notable feature of LOOKUP.BAS is the DIM statement in line 140. This statement tells BASIC to reserve space to store 100 elements in array *X*. All 100 elements may never be used, but the memory is reserved in case they are needed. Lines 160 through 190 are used to load the values for the elements of array *X* from the keyboard. Because the counter of the FOR/NEXT loop runs from 1 to 5 and is also used as the subscript for array *X*, only 5 elements of the 100 available are used. To increase the number actually used, you would raise the loop's stopping value in line 160 from 5 to a higher number. Note, however, that you must also change the DIM statement if more than 100 elements are to be used.

Line 210 sets the initial value of *J* to zero. This program uses *J* to store the subscript of the element that matches the key. If no element matches the key, the value of *J* stays at zero. Thus, *J* becomes a flag indicating that no match was found.

A *flag* is any variable that indicates a certain condition in a program.

Lines 240 through 270 perform the search by comparing elements in X with the key stored in K. If an element matches the key, the value of I is saved in J. Thus, if line 260 is interpreted, a match is found, and the location of the matching element is "remembered" in variable J.

When the FOR/NEXT loop terminates, line 280 tests to see if a matching element was found. It does this by checking to see if the value of J is still zero.

LOOKUP.BAS can easily be modified to perform many other kinds of searches. For example, you can find the largest or smallest element in an array by making minor changes in LOOKUP.BAS without affecting its basic structure. To find the largest element of an array X, you might begin by assuming that the first element is the largest. Its subscript will become the inital value of J. The FOR/NEXT loop then will compare the value of the element pointed to by J with the other elements one at a time. If a larger value is discovered, its subscript can replace the value in J. After all elements have been compared, J will store the subscript of the largest element in the array.

Using this strategy, you can convert LOOKUP.BAS into a program that finds the largest element of array X by (1) removing the INPUT statement for K, (2) removing the IF statement at the end, and (3) changing the following lines:

```
210 J = 1                              'J = 1 means assume X(1) is largest
250 IF X(I) > X(J) THEN 260 ELSE 270
310 PRINT USING "MAXIMUM FOUND AT ##";J
```

Two-Dimensional Arrays

A two-dimensional array stores values in a table format instead of in columns. It is declared in the same way as a one-dimensional array, except that it has two subscripts instead of one.

DIM *variable(size1, size2)*

Size1 specifies the maximum number of elements in each column; *size2* tells the maximum number of elements in each row.

For example, suppose you want to store the height, weight, and IQ of five people. The organization of these numbers will be much clearer if you use a table with three columns and five rows instead of a column with 15 elements. A DIM statement for this example is

DIM STATS(3,5)

where STATS is a two-dimensional array containing 3 * 5 = 15 elements, as in the following:

Column 1	Column 2	Column 3
STATS(1,1)	STATS(2,1)	STATS(3,1)
STATS(1,2)	STATS(2,2)	STATS(3,2)
STATS(1,3)	STATS(2,3)	STATS(3,3)
STATS(1,4)	STATS(2,4)	STATS(3,4)
STATS(1,5)	STATS(2,5)	STATS(3,5)

You must use two subscripts to refer to an element in a two-dimensional array. The first subscript indicates the column, and the second subscript designates the row. For example,

```
100 LET STATS(2,3) = 100        'Store 100 in column 2, row 3
110 LET X = STATS(1,1) + STATS(2,3) 'Access (1,1) and (2,3)-th elements
```

Each element is processed individually like a simple variable, but in addition, the entire array can be processed with the aid of a FOR/NEXT loop. For example, to enter the entire array into memory, you might use two nested FOR/NEXT loops.

```
100 FOR ROW = 1 TO 5
150    FOR COL = 1 TO 3
160        INPUT STATS(COL, ROW)
170    NEXT COL
180 NEXT ROW
```

The inner FOR/NEXT loop is always executed more rapidly than the outer loop. Thus, this fragment of code reads the entire two-dimensional array in the following sequence:

STATS(1,1)
STATS(2,1)
STATS(3,1)
STATS(1,2)
STATS(2,2)
STATS(3,2)
STATS(1,3)
. . . .
STATS(3,5)

If you reverse the loops, the order of input changes.

EXERCISES

1. Assume that array T is declared as T(3,2). Write a segment of a BASIC program that reads values into it in the following order:

    T(1,1)
    T(2,1)
    T(3,1)

(Continued on next page)

```
T(1,2)
T(2,2)
T(3,2)
```

2. What does each of the following program fragments print?

```
a. 100 DIM A(100)
   110 A(1) = 2
   115 A(2) = 3
   120 FOR I = 3 TO 100
   130 A(I) = A(I - 1) * 2 - A(I - 2)
   140 NEXT I
   150 PRINT A(99)

b. 100 DIM A(2,2)
   110 A(1,2) = 5
   120 A(2,1) = 7
   130 I = 2
   140 J = 1
   150 PRINT A(J,1)
```

3. Write a program that accepts numbers into two arrays (UNITCOST and QUANTITY), computes values for a third array (COST), and completes the following report. Your program should print totals for all three columns at the bottom of the report.

Unit Cost	Quantity	Cost
12.96	5	
6.80	3	
9.99	9	
52.50	2	
19.35	7	

4. Rewrite the program in exercise 3 using a two-dimensional array to store all three columns of numbers. Which way is easier?

5. Write a BASIC program that will read a list of ten numbers into an array and then find the number of numbers in the array that exceed the average value.

Credits

Figure 1.2 Cray Research, Inc./Info Edit

Figure 2.2 Courtesy of Amdahl Corporation

Figure 2.3 Courtesy of Commodore Electronics Ltd.

Figure 2.4 Courtesy of Hewlett-Packard Company

Figure 2.7 Courtesy of Apple Computer, Inc.

Figure 2.11 Photo from Xerox Corporation

Figure 3.2, 3.3 Courtesy of Motorola, Inc.

Figure 3.10 DMA 360 Disk Drive courtesy of DMA Systems

Figure 4.1 Courtesy of Wang Laboratories, Inc.

Figure 4.2, 4.3 Product of Key Tronic, Spokane, Washington

Figure 4.4 Courtesy of Hewlett-Packard Company

Figure 4.5 Photo courtesy of GTCO Corporation, Rockville, Maryland

Figure 4.6 Photograph courtesy of Microsoft Corporation

Figure 4.7 Courtesy of NCR Corporation

Figure 4.8 Courtesy of Mohawk Data Sciences

Figure 4.9, 4.10 Courtesy of NCR Corporation

Figure 4.11a Courtesy of Qume Corporation, A Subsidiary of ITT Corp.

Figure 4.12 Courtesy of Printronix®, Inc., Irvine, CA

Figure 4.18 Photo courtesy of Toshiba America, Inc., Information Systems Division

Figure 4.19 Courtesy of Hewlett-Packard Company

Figure 5.6 Photo courtesy of Xerox Corporation

Figure 5.11 Photograph courtesy Microsoft Corporation

Figure 5.13 ® Lotus Development Corporation 1985. Used with permission.

Part Two Evans & Sutherland/Info Edit

Figure 9.2a, b Courtesy of Prentice Corporation; Courtesy of Hayes Microcomputer Products, Inc.

Figure 9.13 Courtesy of Apple Computer, Inc.

Figure 9.14 Courtesy of Corvus Systems, Inc.

Figure 10.21 Photo courtesy of Gerber Scientific, Inc.

Figure 10.22 Photo courtesy of Intergraph Corp., Huntsville, Alabama

Figure 10.23 Courtesy of ARCAD

Figure 11.1 Ludwig Richter

Figure 11.3b Graphic Arts Technical Foundation

Figure 11.4 Courtesy of MicroDisplay Systems, Inc.

Figure 11.5 Courtesy of Apple Computer, Inc.

Figure 11.6a, b Courtesy of Hewlett-Packard Company

Figure 11.8 Linotronic

Figure 11.12 Courtesy of Hewlett-Packard Company

Chapter 11 box Courtesy of Hewlett-Packard Company

Part Three The Photo Works/Photo Researchers

Figure 12.5 Courtesy of Microrim, Inc.

Figure 14.3 Reprinted by permission from "Machine Learning" by A.T. Kolokouris © McGraw Hill, Inc.

Figure 14.4 *P.C. WORLD* 12/86 vol. 4 no. 12 p. 204

Chapter 14 box Copyright 1986 by CW Communications, Inc., Framingham, MA 01701. Reprinted from *ComputerWorld*

Part Four Courtesy of Hitachi

Figure 15.1 Courtesy of Apple Computer, Inc.

Figure 15.2 Courtesy of AT&T

Figure 15.3 Reprinted from *PC Magazine* 6/23/87. Copyright 1987 Ziff Communications Co.

Figure 15.7 Courtesy of General Motors

Figure 15.8 Courtesy of NYT Pictures

Figure 15.9 Courtesy of Western Gear

Figure 15.10 Courtesy of Ford

Figure 15.11 Courtesy of First Interstate Bank

Figure 15.12 Courtesy of Photographic Sciences Corporation

Figure 15.13 Ellis Herwig/Stock, Boston

Figure 15.14 Courtesy of National Medical Enterprises

Figure 15.15 Courtesy of Hewlett-Packard Company

Figure 16.1 Info Edit

Figure 16.2 Courtesy of NORAD

Figure 16.3 Courtesy of Bell Laboratories Record

Figure 16.4 Courtesy of NEC

Figure 16.5 Bohdan Hrynewich/Stock, Boston

Figure 16.6 Courtesy of Microsoft Flight Simulator

Figure 16.8, 16.9 John Asmus

Figure 16.10 Kurzweil Music Systems/Info Edit

Figure 16.11 From "The Computer as a Musical Instrument" by Max V. Mathews and John R. Pierce. *SCIENTIFIC AMERICAN.* Feb., 1987 Copyright © 1987 by Scientific American, Inc. All rights reserved.

Figure 16.12 NASA/Michael Flynn

Figures 17.1, 17.8 Copyright Will Eisner

Figures 17.3, 17.5 Courtesy of Honeywell

Figure 17.4 Copyright 1987 by CW Publishing Inc. Framingham, MA 01701. Reprinted from *Computer World*

Figure 17.6 Courtesy of Racal-Milgo

Figure 18.2, 18.3 Courtesy of International Business Machines Corp.

Figure 18.4 Courtesy of the Hagley Museum and Library

Figure 18.5 Courtesy of International Business Machines Corp.

Figure 18.6 Courtesy of the Hagley Museum and Library

Figure 18.7 DAVA Still Media Depository/Info Edit

Figure 18.8 Courtesy of International Business Machines Corp.

Figure 18.9 Photograph courtesy Microsoft Corp.; Courtesy Digital Research Inc.

Figure 18.10 Courtesy of International Business Machines Corp.

Figure 18.11a, b Courtesy of Apple Computer, Inc.

Figure 18.12a, b Courtesy of Amdek Corporation

Chapter 18 box Mark E. Alsop

Window 1

Figure 1 Courtesy of Commodore Electronics Ltd.

Figure 2 Courtesy of Management Science America, Inc. (MSA)

Figure 3 Courtesy of Apple Computer, Inc.

Figure 4 Courtesy of Hewlett-Packard Company

Figures 5, 6 Courtesy of Texas Instruments

Figure 7 Courtesy of Hewlett-Packard Company

Figures 8–10 Courtesy of Shared Medical System Corporation

Figures 11–13 Courtesy of Apple Computer, Inc.

Figure 14 Courtesy of Commodore Electronics Ltd

Figures 15, 16 Courtesy of International Business Machines Corporation

Figure 17 Courtesy NCR Corporation

Figure 18 Courtesy of ROLM, an IBM Company

Figure 19 Courtesy of Hewlett-Packard Company

Figure 20 Courtesy of Compugraphic Corporation, Wilmington, Massachusetts

Figure 21 Courtesy of ROLM, an IBM Company

Figures 22–26 Photos courtesy of Atex, Inc., a Kodak Company, of Bedford, Massachusetts

Figures 27–30 Photos courtesy of Intergraph Corporation, Huntsville, Alabama

Figure 31 Courtesy of Monarch Marking Systems, a subsidiary of Pitney Bowes

Figure 32 Courtesy NCR Corporation

Figure 33 Photograph courtesy of Scope Incorporated, Reston, Virginia

Figures 34, 35 Photos courtesy of Gerber Scientific, Inc.

Figures 36–42 Courtesy of International Business Machines Corporation

Figures 43–47 Photos courtesy of Gerber Scientific, Inc.

Figure 48 Photo: Loral Corporation

Figure 49 Courtesy of Sanders Associates

Figure 50 Photo: Loral Corporation

Figure 51 Courtesy of Sanders Associates

Figure 52 Courtesy of Hewlett-Packard Company

Figure 53 Courtesy of Compac Computer, Corporation

Window 2

Figure 1 Photo courtesy of Intergraph Corporation, Huntsville, Alabama

Figure 2 Courtesy of Apple Computer, Inc.

Figure 4 Courtesy of International Business Machines Corp.

Figure 5 Courtesy of Compac Computer Corp.

Figure 6 Courtesy of Apple Computer, Inc.

Figures 8, 10, 12, 13, 15, 16 Courtesy of International Business Machines Corporation

Figure 19 Courtesy of Memorex Corporation, a Burroughs subsidiary

Figure 20 Photo courtesy Seagate

Figure 21 Courtesy of Memorex Corporation, a Burroughs subsidiary

Figure 22 Courtesy of Storage Technology Corporation © 1984

Figure 23 Photo courtesy Seagate

Figure 24 Courtesy of International Business Machines Corporation

Figure 25 Courtesy of Comdisco, Inc.

Figure 26 Courtesy of Northern Telecom Inc.

Figure 27 Courtesy of Ampex Corporation, one of The Signal Companies, Inc.

Figure 28 Courtesy of Storage Technology Corporation © 1984

Figure 29 Courtesy of TRW Inc.

Window 3

Figure 1 Photo courtesy of C. Itoh Electronics, Inc.

Figure 2 Courtesy of Apple Computer, Inc.

Figure 3 Word Star® is a trademark of MicroPro International Corporation®

Figure 4 Compugraphic Corporation, Wilmington, Massachusetts

Figure 5 Courtesy of International Business Machines Corporation

Figure 6 Courtesy of Hewlett-Packard Company

Figure 7 Courtesy of Toshiba America, Inc. Information Systems Division

Figure 8 Courtesy of Apple Computer, Inc.

Figure 9 Courtesy of Okidata

Figure 10 Courtesy of Qume Corporation, a subsidiary of ITT

Figure 11 Courtesy Martin Marietta Data Systems

Figures 12, 13 Courtesy of Apple Computer, Inc.

Figure 14 Sweet-P Plotters by Enter Computer, Inc., 6867 Nancy Ridge Drive, San Diego, California 92121. (619) 450-0601

Figure 15 Courtesy of Sanders Associates

Figure 16 Photograph courtesy of Gerber Scientific, Inc.

Figure 17 Courtesy of Versatec, a Xerox Company

Figures 18–20 Photos courtesy of Gerber Scientific, Inc.

Figure 21 Photo courtesy of GTCO Corporation, Rockville, Maryland

Figure 22 Courtesy of International Business Machines Corporation

Figure 23 Courtesy of Monarch Marking Systems, a subsidiary of Pitney Bowes

Figure 24 Courtesy of National Semiconductor Corporation

Window 4

Figure 1 Courtesy of Caere Corporation

Figure 2 Courtesy of International Business Machines Corporation

Figure 3 Courtesy of Commodore Electronics Ltd.

Figure 4 Courtesy of Electronic Data Systems, Dallas, Texas

Figure 5 Courtesy of Apple Computer, Inc.

Figure 6 Courtesy of Radio Shack, a division of Tandy Corporation

Figure 7 Courtesy of International Business Machines Corporation

Figure 8 Courtesy Martin Marietta Data Systems

Figure 9 Compugraphic Corporation, Wilmington, Massachusetts

Figures 10, 11 Courtesy of Hewlett-Packard Company

Figures 12, 13 Courtesy of Apple Computer, Inc.

Figures 14, 15 Photos courtesy of Gerber Scientific, Inc.

Figure 16 Courtesy of TRW Inc.

Figure 17 Courtesy of Docutel/Olivette Corporation

Figure 18 Courtesy MSI Data Corporation

Figure 19 Photograph courtesy of Scope Incorporated, Reston, Virginia

Figure 20 Courtesy NCR Corporation

Figure 21 Courtesy of Caere Corporation

Figure 22 Courtesy NCR Corporation

Figure 23 Courtesy of Texas Instruments

Figure 24 Courtesy of Data Entry Systems

Figure 25 Courtesy of Sperry Corporation

Window 5

Figure 1 Photo from Xerox Corporation

Figure 2 Courtesy of International Business Machines Corporation

Figure 3 SuperCalc is a registered trademark of

Computer Associates International, Inc. Micro Products Division.

Figure 4 Living Videotext, Inc.

Figures 5, 6, 7 Courtesy of Microsoft Corporation

Figure 12 Courtesy of International Business Machines Corporation

Figure 24 Courtesy of Hewlett-Packard Company

Figure 25–26 Ashton-Tate © 1987

Figure 27 Ashton-Tate

Figure 28-31 Living Videotext, Inc.

Figure 32 Courtesy of Hewlett-Packard Company

Figure 33–35, 37–39 Courtesy of Aldus Corporation

Figures 40–46 Courtesy of International Business Machines Corporation

Figure 47 Courtesy of © Lotus Development Corp. 1985. Used with permission. "Symphony" is a registered trademark of Lotus Development Corporation

Figure 48 Computer Associates International, Inc.

Figure 49–52 Courtesy of Ansa Software

Figure 53 Courtesy of MicroPro

Figure 54 Courtesy of © Lotus Development Corp. 1985. Used with permission. "Symphony" is a registered trademark of Lotus Development Corporation.

Window 6

Figure 1 Courtesy of Northern Telecom Inc.

Figures 2, 3 Courtesy of RCA

Figures 4, 5 Courtesy of Electronic Data Systems, Dallas, Texas

Figures 6, 7 Courtesy of Northern Telecom Inc.

Figure 8 Courtesy of TRW Inc.

Figure 9 Photograph provided by Tandem Computer Incorporated

Figure 10 Courtesy of General Electric Company

Figure 11 Courtesy of TRW Inc.

Figure 12 Photo courtesy of Telex Computer Products, Inc., Tulsa, Oklahoma

Figure 13 Courtesy of Electronic Data Systems, Dallas, Texas

Figure 14 Vitro Corporation, Silver Spring, Maryland

Figures 15, 16 Courtesy of Northern Telecom Inc.

Figures 17, 18 Courtesy of MICOM Systems, Inc.

Figure 19 Courtesy of Hewlett-Packard Company

Figures 20, 21 Courtesy of ROLM, an IBM Company

Figure 22 Photo courtesy of National Data Corporation

Figure 23 Courtesy of International Business Machines Corporation

Figure 24 Courtesy MSI Data Corporation

Figure 25 Courtesy of General Electric Company

Figure 26 Courtesy of RCA

Window 7

Figure 1 Photo courtesy of Intergraph Corporation, Huntsville, Alabama

Figures 2, 3 Courtesy of Apple Computer, Inc.

Figures 4, 5 Courtesy of International Business Machines Corporation

Figure 8 Courtesy of Graphic Communications, Inc.

Figures 11–13 Courtesy Design Resources, Inc.

Figure 15 Courtesy of Sanders Associates

Figures 16–25 Photos courtesy of Intergraph Corporation, Huntsville, Alabama

Window 8

Figures 1–4 Photos courtesy of Monsanto

Figure 5 Courtesy of National Semiconductor Corporation

Figure 6 Courtesy of International Business Machines Corporation

Figure 7 Courtesy of National Semiconductor Corporation

Figure 8 Courtesy of Commodore Electronics Ltd.

Figure 9 Courtesy of TRW Inc.

Figure 10 Courtesy of RCA

Figure 11 Photograph courtesy Intel Corporation

Figure 12 Courtesy of Memorex Corporation, a Burroughs subsidiary

Figure 13 Courtesy of National Semiconductor Corporation

Figure 14 Courtesy of Commodore Electronics Ltd.

Figure 15 Courtesy of Motorola, Inc.

Figure 16 Photo: Loral Corporation/Ovak Arslanian

Figure 17 Courtesy of National Semiconductor Corporation

Figure 18 Photograph courtesy of Intel Corporation

Figure 19 Courtesy of TRW Inc.

Figure 20 Courtesy Commodore Electronics Ltd.

Figure 21 Courtesy of Texas Instruments

Figure 22 Courtesy of TRW Inc.

Figure 23 Courtesy of Paradyne Corporation, Largo, Florida

Figures 24, 25 Courtesy of National Semiconductor Corporation

Figure 26 Photo courtesy of Gerber Scientific, Inc.

Figures 27, 28 Photos courtesy of Intergraph Corporation, Huntsville, Alabama

Figure 29 Photo courtesy of Gerber Scientific, Inc.

Figure 30 Courtesy of Versatec, Inc.

Figures 31–33 Photos courtesy of Gerber Scientific, Inc.

Figure 34 Courtesy of Sanders Associates

Figures 35, 36 Courtesy of Cray Research, Inc.

Figures 37, 38 Courtesy of International Business Machines Corporation

Figure 39 Courtesy of Hewlett-Packard Company

Figure 40 Courtesy of Paradyne Corporation, Largo, Florida

Figure 41 Photograph provided by Tandem Computer Incorporated

Figures 42, 43 Courtesy of Apple Computer, Inc.

Figure 44 Courtesy of International Business Machines Corporation

Window 9

Figure 1 Courtesy of Management Science America, Inc.

Figure 2 Photo courtesy of Hewlett-Packard Company

Figures 3, 4 Courtesy of Telex Computer Products, Inc.

Figure 5 Courtesy of Comdisco, Inc.

Figure 6 Courtesy Docutel/Olivette Corporation

Figure 7 Courtesy of Apple Computer, Inc.

Figure 8 Vitro Corporation, Silver Spring, Maryland

Figure 9 Photo courtesy of Gerber Scientific, Inc.

Figure 10 Courtesy of Electronic Data Systems, Dallas, Texas

Figure 11 Courtesy of Pertec Computer Corporation

Figures 12–14 Courtesy of Electronic Data Systems, Dallas, Texas

Figure 15 Courtesy of TRW, Inc.

Figure 16 Courtesy of Comdisco, Inc.

Figures 17, 18 Courtesy of Rockwell International Semiconductor Products Division

Figure 19 Courtesy of RCA

Figure 20 Courtesy of TRW Inc.

Figure 21 Courtesy of Commodore Electronics Ltd.

Figure 22 Photograph courtesy Intel Corporation

Figure 23 Courtesy of International Business Machines Corporation

Figure 24 Courtesy of TRW Inc.

Figure 25 Photo courtesy of C. Itoh Electronics, Inc.

Figure 26 Courtesy of International Business Machines Corporation

End papers

Photo 1 Brian Cody

Photo 2 Photo courtesy of Sperry Corporation/Info Edit

Photo 3 Brian Cody

Photo 4 Brian Cody

Photo 5 Brian Cody

Photo 6 Photo courtesy of DAVA Still Media Depository/Info Edit

Photo 7 Brian Cody

Photo 8 Brian Cody

Photo 9 Photo courtesy of True Bosic, Inc.

Photo 10 Info Edit

Photo 11 Brian Cody

Photo 12 Brian Cody

Photo 13 Photo courtesy of Cray Research, Inc./Info Edit

Photo 14 Info Edit

Photo 15 Info Edit

Photo 16 UPI/Bettmann Newsphotos

Photo 17 Info Edit

Photo 18 Brian Cody

Photo 19 Brian Cody

Contents pages

1 Photography by Ralph Mercer Photography

2 Courtesy of C. Itoh Electronics, Inc.

3 Courtesy of Apple Computer, Inc.

4 Courtesy of International Business Machines Corp.

5 Courtesy of Hewlett-Packard Company/Info Edit

6 Courtesy of Texas Instruments

7 Courtesy of Verbatim/Info Edit

8 Courtesy of IMSI

9 Courtesy of AST

10 Courtesy of Apple Computer, Inc.

11 Courtesy of NEC/Info Edit

12 Courtesy of International Business Machines Corp.

13 Courtesy of General Electric/Info EDit

14 Courtesy of Texas Instruments

15 Photo by John Asmus/Info EDit

16 M.L. Schneider/Assoc.

17 Courtesy of Apple Computer, Inc.

18 Courtesy of IMSI

19, 21 Courtesy of Commodore

20 Courtesy of International Business Machines Corp.

Glossary

Absolute cell reference In spreadsheet processing, a reference to a cell location in the worksheet that is to remain unchanged if the formula that contains the reference is moved to a new location. Contrast with *Relative cell reference*.

Access monitoring A method of giving a system user only a certain number of attempts to give the correct password.

Access time The time it takes to locate and begin transferring information from an external storage device.

Accumulator A general-purpose register inside a CPU that holds temporary results of computations.

Acoustic coupler A low-speed modem that is attached to the telephone system by jamming a telephone handset into two flexible cups on top of the coupler. Contrast with *Direct-connect modem*.

Active cell In spreadsheet processing, the worksheet cell currently available for use. It is pointed to by the cursor.

Adapter card A circuit board with special I/O interface circuits.

Address A number identifying a location in memory. Data in internal memory are organized in words, and each word is given its own numeric address.

Algorithm A step-by-step list of instructions for solving a problem.

Alpha test The preliminary testing stage of software development.

Analog A way of representing data as continuous, smoothly varying values. Contrast with *Digital*.

Analytic graphics A type of presentation graphics built into a spreadsheet, database, or word processing program.

Application generator (AG) A very high-level language that allows the programmer to give a detailed explanation of what data are to be processed, rather than how to process the data.

Application software Programs written to perform specific tasks for computer users rather than computer programmers. Examples include accounting, word processing, and graphics programs. Contrast with *System software*.

Argument See *Parameter*.

Arithmetic/logic unit (ALU) The part of the CPU that has circuits to calculate and perform logical operations, such as comparing, jumping, and shifting.

Array An organized collection of data in a columnar or tabular format. It is an important type of *Data structure*.

Artificial intelligence   The sector of computer science concerned with developing computer systems capable of simulating human reasoning and sensation.

ASCII code   Short for the *A*merican *S*tandard *C*ode for *I*nformation *I*nterchange. A code for representing letters, numerals, and special characters as a pattern of seven bits. ASCII is used in virtually all microcomputers to store and manipulate textual information.

Assembler   A program to translate assembly language instructions into machine language.

Assembly language   A programming language in which each instruction in the program corresponds to an instruction that the circuits of the computer can perform. Assembly language allows the programmer to write programs with words like MOVE, ADD, and JUMP instead of coding the binary numbers of machine language.

Asynchronous protocol   A communications protocol that transmits data one character at a time, without any prior arrangement as to how many characters are to be sent. Contrast with *Synchronous protocol.*

Audit trail   The recorded history of the insertions, deletions, modifications, and restorations performed on a file.

Auto-answer   A feature that allows a modem to answer a telephone and establish a connection with another computer without assistance from a computer operator.

Auto-dial   A feature that allows you to dial telephone numbers by typing them on the keyboard.

Automated teller machine (ATM)   An interactive device that facilitates bank transactions.

Automatic recalculation   The process whereby spreadsheets recalculate the value of all formulas whenever an entry is changed.

Automatic search-and-replace operation   A search-and-replace operation that is performed repeatedly throughout an entire document.

Backup copy (file)   An extra copy of a file or disk, stored in case something happens to the original.

Backward chaining   An inference procedure, similar to deductive reasoning, which begins with the end goal and works back to the origin.

Bandwidth   The range of frequencies that a communications channel can carry. Bandwidth determines the channel's capacity for carrying information in the same way that a pipe's diameter determines its capacity for carrying water.

Bar code   Machine-readable bars, read by a bar code reader.

Baseband   A type of transmission in which the entire communications spectrum is dedicated to one form of information. Because baseband signaling transmits digital signals without modulation, only one signal at a time can be present on a baseband channel. Contrast with *Broadband.*

BASIC   *B*eginner's *A*ll-purpose *S*ymbolic *I*nstruction *C*ode. A popular programming language that was originally developed for timesharing and interactive problem solving.

Batch file   A file that contains a series of operating system commands.

Batch processing   A processing technique that collects and processes data in groups.

Baud rate   A measure of transmission speed. Technically, the baud rate is the number of times the communications line changes state, or the number of signals it transmits, each second. Most people use *baud rate* and *bits per second* interchangeably.

Benchmark program   A program that is used as a standard of comparison to test the relative capabilities of computer systems.

Beta test   Software testing by first-time users.

Binary   The number system with two possible digits: 0 and 1. This system is important to computers because their circuits have only two states: on and off.

Bit   An abbreviation for *binary digit*. A bit is the smallest unit of computer memory.

Bit-mapped display   A method of generating screen images by creating a one-for-one correspondence between bits in memory and pixels on the screen. In color graphics, three or more bits are required in the bit map to represent the red, green, and blue values of an individual pixel. Contrast with *Character-oriented display*.

Block operation   A word processor operation that manipulates a block of characters at once.

Boot   To start a computer by loading part of the operating system. Usually a computer is booted by inserting a system disk and turning on the computer or by pressing the computer's reset button. *Boot* is short for *bootstrap*, as in "pulling yourself up by your bootstraps."

Broadband   A type of transmission that uses frequency-division multiplexing to transmit text, data, and video or audio signals simultaneously. Contrast with *Baseband*.

Buffer   A temporary memory storage area.

Bug   An error or design flaw in a program.

Built-in function   A spreadsheet function that performs a specific type of function.

Bulletin board system (BBS)   A personal computer with an auto-answer modem that answers incoming telephone calls. Nearly all bulletin board systems allow the caller to read and leave messages; many allow the caller to send or receive programs as well. Also called a *public access message system*.

Bus   A cable or a set of parallel electrical conductors that carries signals among the devices in a computer or network. Only one device at a time is allowed to send data on the bus, but each device continually listens to the bus for messages addressed to it. Because devices can be attached to any point along a bus, a computer network that uses a bus can be expanded easily.

Bus network   A network in which a single, bidirectional cable connects computers.

Byte   A binary number formed from an eight-bit grouping.

Cache   A small, high-speed memory that acts as a buffer between the CPU and the slower main memory.

CAD   Short for *computer-aided design*—drawing with the aid of your computer.

CAI   Short for *computer-assisted instruction*—using computers for individual and classroom instruction.

Callback PPD   A port protection device that screens incoming calls.

CAM   Short for *computer-aided manufacturing*—automated production.

CAT   Short for *computer axial tomography*. Commonly called a "CAT scan," this method of medical imaging involves first collecting cross-sectional images of a subject with x-rays, and then using a computer to assemble a composite image which can be displayed in three-dimensional colors.

Cathode ray tube (CRT)   A display device that generates images by bombarding a phosphor-coated glass tube with a beam of electrons.

CD-I Short for *c*ompact *d*isc—*i*nteractive. A small optical disk system that is under the interactive control of the user.

CD-ROM Short for *c*ompact *d*isc—*r*ead-*o*nly *m*emory. A small optical disk system.

Cell In spreadsheet processing, the intersection of a row and a column on a worksheet.

Central processing unit (CPU) The "brain" of a computer. The central processing unit contains circuits that execute instructions, control other units, and hold data in memory.

Chain printer A line printer whose characters are embossed on a rotating chain.

Channel A limited-capacity computer that takes over input and output tasks in order to free the general-purpose mainframe to handle internal processing tasks. By relieving the CPU of the need to communicate directly with peripherals, channels make it possible for input, output, and internal processing operations to occur at the same time.

Character-oriented display A method of generating screen images that breaks the screen into many boxes arranged in rows and columns. Each box can display one character. Contrast with *Bit-mapped display*.

Character printer A printer that prints only one character at a time.

Check figure An error detection method that uses a figure which is a function of the characters in a transmission.

Chiclet keyboard A keyboard with small, calculatorlike keys.

Chief programmer team A software development team structure in which one programmer is assigned overall responsibility for the project.

Clock rate The speed at which the central processing unit performs operations; usually measured in megahertz.

Coaxial cable A cable that consists of a wire that is encircled by a metallic tubular sleeve. Coaxial cable is used in cable television networks and in high-speed computer networks.

Colorization Computer coloring of classic black and white films.

Color monitor See *Monitor*.

Command An instruction given to the computer to perform a specified task.

Command-line operating system A system of giving instructions to the computer by typing full-word keywords, which are often followed by arguments.

Command mode The spreadsheet mode in which commands are selected.

Command processor The part of an operating system that accepts commands from the user for operating system tasks. Also called a *shell*.

Communications program A program that sets up and manages connections between two or more computers.

Compact keyboard A keyboard with reduced-size keys or reduced spacing between keys.

Compiler A program that translates programs written in a high-level language into machine language. A compiler is dedicated to a single programming language, such as BASIC or Pascal, and translates the entire program before execution begins. Contrast with *Interpreter*.

Composition The selection of type sizes and styles and the positioning of type on a page.

Computed field A file field that is based on the values of other fields.

Computer An information-handling device.

Computer conferencing Communication among groups of people through electronic mail.

Computer crime The unauthorized use of computer systems, including software or data, for unlawful purposes.

Computer equity Equal opportunity for computing for all social groups.

Computer-integrated manufacturing (CIM) A system linking CAD/CAM robots and NC systems through a computerized database that plans, schedules, and controls a manufacturing process.

Computer literacy An understanding of what a computer is and how computers are used; the ability to work with and the ability to evaluate computing's effect on society.

Computer system An interconnected set of devices for entering, sending, and storing data.

Computer vision The processing of visual information by a computer.

Concentrator An "intelligent" multiplexer, which can perform preliminary operations on data before transmission.

Connect time Time logged on to a remote computer.

Context switching Moving from one component in an integrated program to another.

Control key A special key on the keyboard, usually labeled [Ctrl]. Like a shift key, a control key is used in combination with other keys; unlike the shift key, it generates different character codes and is used to give commands.

Control panel A portion of the screen reserved for status and help information.

Control structure Any statement that determines the order in which other program statements are executed. Common control structures include FOR statements (for repeating or looping), IF-THEN-ELSE statements (for making two-way decisions), and CASE statements (for multiple-way decisions).

Control unit (1) The part of the CPU that retrieves and interprets instructions and coordinates their execution. (2) A peripheral device that controls other peripheral devices. For example, a disk control unit might supervise the operation of several disk drives.

Coprocessor chip A special-purpose microprocessor designed to handle specific functions such as floating-point arithmetic or high-speed graphics.

Copyfit To get text to fit within the available area.

Copy-protect To prevent a disk from being copied by a standard disk-copying routine.

Copyright The exclusive right to publish or sell a creative work. Copyrights are the most common legal method of protecting computer programs from unauthorized distribution.

Courseware Programs whose main purpose is teaching.

CP/M Short for *Control Program for Microcomputers*. CP/M is a popular operating system for microcomputers.

CPU See *Central processing unit*.

Cracker A programmer who gains access to a system without authorization.

Crop To trim a graphics image for a better fit or to eliminate unwanted portions.

CRT See *Cathode ray tube*.

CSMA protocol A protocol that controls access to a network's bus. Short for *carrier-sensed multiple-access*.

Cursor An indicator on the screen that shows where things will happen next. The cursor can be an underline (blinking or nonblinking), a rectangle, or even an arrow.

Cursor-movement key   A key that, when pressed, moves the cursor in a designated direction. Cursor-movement keys generally have directional arrows on their keytops, as in [↑], [↓], [←], and [→].

Daisy wheel   The print element of a letter-quality printer. Daisy wheels are made from metal or plastic and have spokes radiating from the center. Each spoke contains a letter, number, or symbol at the end.

✓ **Database**   A logical grouping of one or more data files.

✓ **Database management system (DBMS)**   A set of programs that provide for the input, retrieval, formatting, modification, output, transfer, and maintenance of information in a database.

Data decomposition   A system design method in which the designer partitions the system according to the logical closeness of datagrams and data storage items.

Data dictionary   A list of all the files, fields, attributes, formats, and access rights in a database or of data items in a program.

Data flow diagram   A graphical representation of how data move through an information system.

Data structure   A collection of values that provides a method of organizing data. Some common data structures are arrays, lists, files, and stacks.

Data transfer rate   The rate at which data are transferred from external storage to computer memory or from computer memory to external storage.

✓ **DBMS**   See *Database management system.*

Debugger   A program that aids a programmer in locating and removing the errors in a program.

Decision support system (DSS)   Software that allows managers to deal with unprecedented situations in making business decisions.

Dedicated line   A special telephone line that connects a pair of computers.

Default   The value or setting that a program uses if the user does not specify a value.

Delimiter   A symbol that indicates the end of a command, argument, or parameter. In the command TYPE LETTER.JIM, a space is the delimiter between the command keyword TYPE and its argument, LETTER.JIM.

Democratic team   A software development team structure in which team members share responsibility.

Demodulation   Conversion of an analog signal into a digital signal.

Design walkthrough   An overview of a system design by users, programmers, and consultants.

Desktop publishing   The application of personal computers to the production of near-typeset quality documents.

Device driver   Software that tells an operating system or application program how an add-on device functions.

Device independence   The ability to add an input, output, or storage device to a computer system by modifying only the I/O manager of the operating system, without altering other software.

Dialing directory   A file containing telephone numbers and communications parameters. In conjunction with smart modems, a dialing directory can be used to dial a telephone number and log on to a remote computer almost automatically.

Dialog box A temporary window on the screen that contains a set of choices whenever the executing program needs to collect information from the user.

Digital Characterized by handling and storing data as binary numbers. A digital circuit is either on or off; a digital signal is either present or absent. Contrast with *Analog.*

Digitize To register a visual image or real object in a format that can be processed by the computer. Digitized data are read into the system with graphics input devices, such as pucks or styluses.

Direct-access file A file in which records can be read directly, without reading all intervening records.

Direct-connect modem A modem that plugs directly into a telephone jack to make a direct electrical connection with the telephone system. Contrast with *Acoustic coupler.*

Directory A file that lists the names and locations of all other files on a disk.

Disk drive A device that allows a computer to read or write information on a magnetic disk.

Disk pack See *Removable disk.*

Distributed computing The simultaneous use of independent computers that are linked in a network to work on a common problem. Contrasts with *centralized computing,* in which all jobs are fed into a central mainframe.

Dither To approximate the levels of gray in a photograph with a pattern of white and black spots.

Documentation Any written information that describes hardware or software, including tutorial lessons, reference manuals, pocket reference guides, and so forth.

Domain expert A human expert who contributes to the development of an expert system.

Dot matrix printer An impact printer that forms characters by printing a series of dots. Dot matrix printers are very popular and inexpensive, but unlike letter-quality printers, they do not create characters with smooth, fully formed edges.

Download To send information from a large computer to a smaller one.

Drill-and-practice program Teaching software that reinforces old lessons.

Drum printer A line printer whose characters are positioned around the circumference of a cylinder or drum.

Dumb terminal A terminal that has no processing capabilities of its own.

EBCDIC Short for *Extended Binary Coded Decimal Interchange Code,* a computer code used to represent characters. Used more frequently on mainframe computers.

Editor A program used to write, enter, and edit programs. The major difference between an editor and a word processor is that word processors tend to have more features for fancy printing.

EDVAC The first electronic computer to use a memory-stored program.

Egoless programming A team process that separates the individual programmer's ego from the program being developed.

Electronic funds transfer system (EFTS) A computerized system that processes information about financial transactions and facilitates exchanges of this information.

Electronic mail Messages sent and received by computers.

Electronic publishing Using telecommunications or networking to distribute documents.

Electronic thesaurus A program that lists synonyms for a given word.

Embedded microprocessor A programmable processing circuit built into another device, such as a car or a camera.

Encryption A method of protecting data by scrambling it.

End-user computing The use of special software development tools by noncomputer specialists for business applications.

ENIAC The first general-purpose electronic digital computer, developed at the University of Pennsylvania from 1943 to 1946.

Entry mode The spreadsheet mode that is used to enter new information.

Ergonomics The science of adapting the working environment to suit the worker.

Exception statement A control structure that catches errors or unusual occurrences.

Expansion slot A connector inside a microcomputer where an optional circuit board can be plugged in.

Expert system A computer program that simulates the reasoning process used by a human expert in a certain well-defined field.

Expert system shell The portion of an expert system that remains after all rules and user interfaces have been removed.

External storage Long-term nonvolatile storage that is not part of the central processing unit. Tapes and disks are the most common forms of external storage. It is also called *secondary storage* or *auxiliary storage*.

Fair use A situation in which limited copying of copyrighted material is legal.

Fax *Facs*imile transmission, a method of sending documents through phone lines.

Fiber-optic cable A cable made from strands of glass, which carries data in the form of pulses of light.

Field The part of a record reserved for a particular item or type of data.

File A collection of related records on a tape or a disk.

File allocation table An index to the physical locations assigned to files.

File management system A collection of programs for managing data stored in a single file.

File manager (1) The part of an operating system that is responsible for manipulating files. (2) A file management system.

File server A device in a computer network that controls the hard disk and connects it to the network.

Fixed disk A hard disk in which the disk platter is mounted permanently inside an airtight, factory-sealed unit.

Fixed-width spacing A form of printing that pads out short lines by inserting full-size spaces between words.

Floating-point number A number represented in scientific form. A floating-point number is broken into two parts: the fractional part and the exponent.

Floppy disk A flexible, flat, circular piece of magnetic material for storing information. It is the most common medium for external storage for microcomputers.

Font A set of characters in a particular typeface and size.

Footers Lines of text printed in the bottom margin of a page.

Form A template that indicates both items of data and where they are to be placed. Forms assist in the process of collecting and storing data.

Format (1) The arrangement of data. (2) To prepare a blank disk so that it can be used to store information. Also known as *initializing*.

Format code A word processing code that describes how text will be printed or formatted.

Format rule A spreadsheet rule that tells the program how to display a cell's value.

Forward chaining An inference procedure in which an expert system begins with a specific original statement and searches for routes that lead to one or more conclusions.

Free-form windows A method of presenting windows on the screen that allows them to overlap one another, like objects stacked on top of a desk. Contrast with *Tiled windows*.

Frequency-division multiplexer A multiplexer that divides a high-speed signal into frequency bands. Contrast with *Time-division multiplexer*.

Frequency modulation (FM) A method of analog signaling that encodes data as changes in the frequency of the signal. Frequency modulation is used in FM radio and in some low-speed methods of data transmission over telephone lines.

Front-end computer A small computer that is located between a mainframe and the terminals and other devices needing access to the mainframe. The front-end computer handles communications and error-checking tasks related to routing messages in and out of the mainframe.

Full-duplex A method of transmitting data that allows the simultaneous sending and receiving of data. Contrast with *Half-duplex*.

Functional decomposition A system design method in which the designer partitions the system into functionally related subsystems.

Function key An extra keyboard key that is used for a specific purpose, which depends on the program being executed. The keytops of function keys are frequently labeled [F1], [F2], and so forth.

Gantt chart A visual representation of a project schedule; the columns are time intervals, and the rows correspond to activities.

Gateway A device that allows devices on one network to communicate with those on another network.

Gigabyte A unit of storage of roughly 1 billion characters.

Graphics editor A program for editing pictures. Typical operations include drawing, moving, rotating, and enlarging items on the screen.

Graphics package A program that helps depict ideas through graphs and other types of drawings.

Ground station A station for sending and receiving information via satellite.

Hacker (1) A programmer who works alone and is obsessed with learning about programming and exploring the capabilities of computer systems. (2) A programmer who gains access to a system without authorization. See also *Cracker*.

Half-duplex A method of transmitting data that does not allow data to travel in both directions at once. Contrast with *Full-duplex*.

Halftone An image composed of a pattern of dots.

Handshaking The exchange of data signals that controls the flow of information between two electrical devices.

Hard disk An external storage device that stores data on a quickly spinning rigid disk with a magnetic surface. Hard disks offer a much greater storage capacity and faster access time than floppy disks.

Hardware   The physical devices in a computer system.

Head crash   A collision between a disk drive's read/write head and the surface of the disk.

Headers   Lines printed in the top margin of a page.

Help system   A display of explanatory information in an application program.

Heuristic method   A rule of thumb used to guide a search along those avenues most likely to yield a solution.

Hierarchical database   A database that establishes a top-to-bottom relationship among records, much like that among members of a family on a family tree. Each item has a unique parent or owner but can have many items below it. Contrast with *Network database* and *Relational database*.

Hierarchical decomposition   See *Stepwise refinement*.

High-level language (HLL)   A programming language with Englishlike constructs or mathematical notation that is used to describe a procedure for solving a problem. High-level languages require little or no knowledge of the computer being used.

Horizontal software   Programs designed to serve a wide range of users, who must tailor the programs to their own needs. Examples include word processors and database management systems.

Hypertext   A document retrieval network having full-text files and dynamic indexes for links among documents.

Icon   A picture of an object, such as a printer, trash can, or pad of paper, symbolizing a computer function.

Imaging   Reading, analyzing, and graphically displaying two- or three-dimensional data.

Impact printer   A printer that forms images by bringing paper and ribbon into physical contact.

Indexed file   A collection of two or more closely related files, one of which contains the data; the other files contain indexes to the data file.

Inference engine   A part of an expert system that generates inferences from the system's IF/THEN rules and the facts supplied by the user.

Information center   A department designed to centralize computer purchasing decisions and train end users.

Information utility   A timesharing company that provides a wide range of processing and information retrieval services to customers who access the utility through telecommunications.

Initialize   See *Format*.

Input device   A peripheral that converts information into signals that the CPU can process.

Insert mode   A word processor mode in which new characters are added within the text as they are typed.

Instruction register   The register in the CPU that holds the instruction currently being carried out by the computer.

Instruction set   The set of elemental operations that the circuits of a CPU are capable of performing directly.

Integer   A whole number.

Integrated circuit   An electronic circuit etched on a tiny silicon chip. Integrated circuits replaced transistors in third-generation computers.

Integrated program   A collection of related programs combined in a package that provides a means of transferring data between the programs.

Interactive fiction   A computer game in which the story changes according to the interaction between computer and user.

Interactive system A system in which the computer immediately processes its on-line inputs.

Interface The connection between two data processing elements. For example, the central processing unit is connected to peripheral devices through hardware interfaces, and the control of an accounting program might be governed by a full-screen menu interface.

Interpreter A program that translates and executes a program written in a high-level language. An interpreter translates one line of the source program, then executes that line, then translates the next line, and so on. In contrast, a *compiler* translates the entire source program before execution begins.

Intrinsic function A module supplied along with a programming language's translator to make using the language easier.

I/O device A peripheral that accepts input or provides output.

I/O manager The part of an operating system that coordinates data transferred to and from peripherals.

I/O port A standard interface between the computer and external devices.

ISO layers A standard for describing and categorizing network components.

Job control language (JCL) A special programming language used to give instructions to the operating system and to control when programs run.

Justify To align text. Text that is flush with both the left and right margins is often said to be *justified*.

Kerning Reducing the space between specific letter pairs based on their shape. For example, the pair *To* can be placed more closely together than the pair *Th* because the arm of the *T* fits over the top of the *o*. Kerning is especially important with large type sizes.

Keyboard A typewriterlike input device.

Keyboard macro See *Macro*.

Keyword A word with a special meaning or function in a command.

Kilobit A measure of storage capacity equal to 1,024 bits.

Kilobyte (KB) A measure of storage equal to 1,024 bytes (or characters). Kilobyte can be abbreviated K or KB.

Knowledge base The collection of facts and rules within an expert system's subject area.

Knowledge engineer A computer professional who helps develop an expert system.

Knowledge engineering environment The part of an expert system development package that contains the tools needed to build the system.

LAN See *Local area network*.

Landscape A short and wide page orientation. Contrast with *Portrait*.

Large-scale integrated circuit (LSI) Semiconductor chip technology has progressed rapidly; the number of components per chip has grown by 50 percent annually since 1960. In the 1970s, most chips had between 1,000 and 100,000 components, known as *large-scale integration*. Today's technology produces chips with 100,000 to 10,000,000 components, known as *very large-scale integration*. Further refinements should produce *ultralarge-scale integration* (10 million to 1 billion components) and *gigascale integration* (over 1 billion components).

Laser printer A page printer in which a laser beam traces the image.

Leading The spacing between typeset lines.

Leased line   See *Dedicated line.*

Letter-quality printer   A printer that produces output indistinguishable from that of a good typewriter.

Light pen   A pencil-shaped, light-sensitive device used to select a location on the screen or to read bar codes on paper.

Line printer   A printer that prints an entire line of characters almost simultaneously rather than one character at a time.

Linker program   The part of the compiling process that converts the object program into machine language and combines it with operating system programs.

Liquid crystal display (LCD)   A display used in many portable computers because it is small and flat and requires little power.

Local area network (LAN)   A system of interconnected data processing equipment in a limited physical area.

Local echo   In telecommunications, a process that sends characters typed on the keyboard directly to the screen without waiting for the remote computer to echo the characters.

Local formatting option   A word processing feature that allows the user to adjust the appearance of text within a portion of a document.

Logical schema   (1) A standard way of organizing information into accessible parts. (2) The description of the files, records, fields, and relationships among the data in a database. Contrast with *Physical schema.*

Log off   To tell the computer you are through using it.

Log on   To identify yourself to a multiuser computer system by typing an account number and a password for billing and security purposes.

Low-level language   A programming language that translates one for one into machine instructions.

Machine independence   The ability to move software from one type of computer system to another without reprogramming.

Machine language   The binary code that can be executed directly by the ALU of a CPU. All programs written in high-level languages are translated into machine language before they are executed.

Macro   A single instruction or command that invokes a previously stored sequence of commands.

Mainframe   A large, fast, and expensive multiuser computer.

Main memory   See *Primary memory.*

Management information systems (MIS)   The use of computer and other systems to generate the information needed by management to perform its major functions.

Manual search-and-replace operation   A search-and-replace operation that pauses at each instance before replacing the sought word or phrase.

Mass storage unit   A peripheral that functions as a jukebox for tape cartridges or optical disks. A mass storage unit can automatically load any tape or disk in its library to provide quick access to vast quantities of information.

Megabyte (MB)   A measure of storage roughly equal to 1 million characters, although technically a megabyte is equal to a kilobyte squared, or $2^{20} = 1,045,576$ bytes. Megabyte can be abbreviated M, MB, or meg.

Megahertz (MHz)   One million cycles per second. Megahertz is used to measure a CPU's clock rate.

Membrane keyboard   A keyboard without separate keys, sensitive to touch.

Memory chip   See *Integrated circuit.*

Menu bar   A one- or two-line list of commands displayed on the screen. *Keyword menu bars* list the entire word for each available command. *One-letter menu bars* list only the first letter of each command.

MFLOP   Short for *millions of floating-point operations* per second. Used as a rough measure of a computer's processing speed.

MICR   Short for *magnetic ink character recognition*. MICR devices are used mainly to read the characters on the bottom of bank checks.

Microcomputer (micro)   Any small computer based on a microprocessor.

Microprocessor   A programmable processing circuit built on a single silicon chip.

Microspacing   A form of printing that inserts tiny spaces between letters and words to give text an even, professional appearance. Each character is assigned the same fixed-width field regardless of its shape; only the space between characters is adjusted.

Microwave relay station   A station used to transmit data and voice signals between distant locations.

Minicomputer (mini)   A medium-sized computer that is capable of timesharing and is usually dedicated to specific applications.

MITS Altair 8800   The first microcomputer.

Mode   A program state in which only a restricted set of operations can be performed. For example, in the entry mode of spreadsheet processing it is not possible to do anything other than enter or edit the contents of the active cell.

Modem   A communications device that converts (modulates) the digital pulses generated by computer equipment into analog signals that can be sent over telephone lines. When receiving data, it demodulates the incoming telephone signal to recreate the original digital signal.

Modular decomposition   See *Stepwise refinement.*

Modulation   The conversion of a digital signal into an analog signal.

Module   An identifiable part of a program. Writing programs in modules enables programmers to focus attention on one part of the programming problem at a time.

Monitor   A CRT-based visual display unit. Basically, a monitor is a high-resolution television set without a speaker, channel selector, or radio-frequency receiver. In a *monochrome monitor*, each pixel can glow in only one color; in a *color monitor*, each pixel is three dots—red, green, and blue.

Monochrome monitor   See *Monitor.*

Mouse   A hand-operated pointing device that senses movements as it is dragged across a flat surface and conveys this information to the computer. Most mice also have buttons that can be clicked to signal the computer.

Multiplexer   A communications device that timeshares the communications line by merging data from many users into the same line. See also *Frequency-division multiplexer, Time-division multiplexer.*

Multitasking   The ability of a computer to execute two or more programs simultaneously. For example, a multitasking computer might allow the user to edit a document with a word processing program while it uses a communications program to receive a file from another computer.

Natural-language processing   The study of strategies for computer programs to recognize and understand language in written and spoken form.

Network   A system of machines that are connected electrically and can communicate with one another.

Network database   A database that establishes a many-to-many relationship among records. Contrast with *Hierarchical database* and *Relational database*.

Neural-net computing   Hardware or software systems that organize computer memory as in human brain cells.

Nonimpact printer   A printer which does not need to strike the paper to print an image. Examples include ink-jet, laser, and thermal printers.

Nonprocedural language   A very high-level programming language in which the programmer describes *what* the desired results are but does not need to be concerned about the details of *how* the work is done.

Object program   The machine language version of a source program that is created when the source program is compiled or assembled.

Office automation (OA)   The use of the computer to handle manual methods of recording, filing, and communicating data and information.

Off-screen text formatting   An older method of word processing which relies on a two-step process to enter and print documents. After text and format commands are entered in the same data file, a text formatting program reads the file, strips the format commands from the text, and uses them as instructions for printing the text.

On-line   Under the direct control of the computer.

Operating system   The master set of programs that manage the computer. Among other things, an operating system controls input and output to and from the keyboard, screen, disks, and other peripheral devices; loads and begins the execution of other programs; and manages the storage of data on disks.

Optical character recognition (OCR)   Optical character recognition software converts the binary image of typed text into ASCII characters.

Option switch   A parameter that can be included in a command to override a default value. For example, an option switch might be added to the command to execute a program in order to tell the program to send its output to a file rather than to the printer.

Outline processor   A program with special features for creating and manipulating outlines.

Output device   A peripheral that converts signals from the CPU into another form.

Packet-switching network   A telecommunications network that sends information through the network in the form of units of data called *packets*.

Page break   In word processing, the location where one page ends and another begins.

Page composition program   A program that controls page makeup, assembling elements on a printed page.

Page description language (PDL)   A programming language with specialized instructions for describing how to print a whole page.

Page design   The process of specifying the boundaries of text on a page. Includes choosing margins, headings, footings, and page length.

Page printer   A printer that prints an entire page at a time.

Paragraph reforming   In word processing, rearranging the text in a paragraph so that it fits neatly between the margins.

Parallel processors   Processors that can break down a problem into parts and work on it simultaneously.

Parameter A piece of information that regulates the behavior of a program. For example, the command that tells the operating system how to communicate with a printer might include a parameter specifying the speed at which data are to be transferred.

Parity bit An extra bit that is added to a computer word to detect errors.

Parsing The process of breaking down a sentence or command into its basic units.

Patent The legal protection granted by the Patent Office for exclusive use of an original idea or invention. Patents are rarely granted for programs.

PC-DOS Short for *Personal Computer-Disk Operating System*. IBM's trade name for its version of MS-DOS, an operating system developed and licensed by Microsoft for computers that use Intel microprocessors.

PDP-11 During its day, this minicomputer was the best-selling general-purpose minicomputer ever.

Peripheral An external device connected to the computer, such as input and output devices and external storage units.

Personal computer A small, inexpensive, single-user computer based on a microprocessor.

PERT chart A chart that shows the dependencies among activities in a project.

Physical schema The description of how data are physically stored on a disk. Contrast with *Logical schema*.

Pipelining A processing technique in which several instructions can be moving through parts of the CPU in an assembly-line fashion.

Pitch A type measure of how many characters fit within an inch.

Pixel An acronym for *picture element*. A pixel is the smallest display element on the screen. See also *Monitor*.

Plotter A printerlike output device that produces a hard copy of pictures, drawings, or other graphical information.

Point A measure of type size equal to 1/72 inch.

Point-of-sale (POS) system A computer system that facilitates purchase transactions.

Portability The ease with which a program can be moved from one machine to another.

Port protection device (PPD) A black box between a computer system and incoming telephone lines that protects the system from unauthorized access.

Portrait A tall and narrow page orientation. Contrast with *Landscape*.

Presentation graphics An easy-to-understand, high-quality display of numerical information, such as a bar chart, pie chart, or line graph.

Primary memory The memory capacity of the CPU.

Printer server A device in a network that shares a printer among all users connected to the network.

Print spooling A procedure that enables a computer to print a file and execute another program at the same time.

Productivity software Business application software for microcomputers.

Program A set of instructions that directs a computer for solving a problem.

Program analyzer A program that analyzes another program for anomalies.

Program counter The register in the CPU that holds the address of the next instruction to be executed.

Program generator A translator program that converts nonprocedural information into a procedural program. Program generators often use a question-and-answer dialog to determine what processing is to be done and are limited in the type of application that they can produce.

Program inspection A formal technique in which software requirements, design, or code are examined by a person or group other than the author, to detect flaws.

Programmable automation (PA) The manufacturing uses of robots and numerically controlled (NC) tools.

Programming language A formalized notation that allows algorithms to be represented in a rigorous way.

Program overlay A program module that is moved from external storage into computer memory when it is needed for processing.

Project management program Software that analyzes and displays the activities of production, construction, or development projects.

Prompt A signal from the computer that it expects the user to enter information.

Proportional spacing A form of printing that allocates room for characters based on their width. With proportional spacing, an M is printed in a wider field than an i.

Protected cell A spreadsheet cell that cannot be edited, deleted, or moved.

Protocol A set of rules that controls the interchange of data between independent devices.

Prototype A trial system that simulates the behavior of the real system in order to let users try the system before it is constructed.

Public domain Authorized to be duplicated by others at will.

Puck A very precise, hand-held pointing device with cross-hairs and a magnifying glass; it is used to enter the coordinates of graphical data.

Pull-down menu A second-level menu, or list of commands, that appears from the top of the screen when a command needs to be given and then disappears when the selection has been made.

Query language A programming language for giving commands that search or modify a database.

Question-and-answer facility A part of an expert system that explains the system's reasoning.

Ragged-right margin A right-hand text margin in which the lines are of uneven length.

RAM An acronym for *r*andom-*a*ccess *m*emory. RAM is memory built from silicon chips, which is used to store programs and data temporarily while they are being processed.

Random access The ability to read or write each piece of information in a storage device in approximately the same length of time, regardless of its location. Internal memory and disks are random-access devices.

Range of cells In spreadsheet processing, a rectangular group of worksheet cells treated as one unit.

Raster scan monitor A monitor that creates an image by moving an electron beam horizontally across each line of the screen 15 or more times each second, turning pixels on and off.

Read/write head The part of the tape or disk drive that reads or writes information on magnetic media.

Ready mode The spreadsheet mode that is used to move around the worksheet.

Real number A signed number with a decimal point.

Real time A type of processing that acts on information quickly enough to simulate or keep up with events occurring in the outside world.

Record A collection of related data items treated as a unit. Often a line in a data file is thought of as a record.

Register A special high-speed memory cell located within the microprocessor, where information is held temporarily and is manipulated according to program instructions.

Relational database A database designed in accordance with a set of principles called the *relational model*. A relational database is made up of *relations,* which are tables whose columns and rows correspond to fields and records, respectively.

Relative cell reference In spreadsheet processing, a reference to a location in the worksheet that is interpreted with respect to the formula's current cell location. Contrast with *Absolute cell reference.*

Remote echoing Also called *echoplex.* In telecommunications, a process that verifies the transmission of characters by sending them to a remote computer and back before displaying them on the screen. Contrast with *Local echo.*

Removable disk A hard disk cartridge similar to a floppy disk. Also called *Disk pack.*

Repeating key A keyboard key that generates a constant stream of characters when depressed. The keys on most computer keyboards will repeat after being held down for about a half-second.

Report break A position in a report where one or more fields change value according to some rule. For example, in a sales report, a report break might occur after the list of sales made by each salesperson.

Report generator A program that extracts information from one or more files, manipulates it, and then prints it in a formatted form.

Requirements analysis The process in system analysis that involves studying users' needs to define the system's requirements.

Resident routine A part of an operating system that is loaded into memory when the computer is turned on and remains there during processing. The opposite of a *Transient utility.*

Resolution A measure of the accuracy or fineness of detail in a picture or display device.

RF modulator A device that converts a video signal from a computer into the radio frequency of a television channel. RF modulators are used to attach television sets to home computers to serve as visual display units.

Ring network A network consisting of a cluster of computers connected together by a ring.

Robot A computer fitted with sensing devices and motor assemblies like mechanical arms.

Robotics The branch of artificial intelligence concerned with developing machines that can recognize and respond to changes in the senses.

ROM An abbreviation for *read-only memory.* ROM is a form of nonvolatile internal memory that stores information permanently. Thus, the information in ROM can be read but cannot be changed.

Routine Any program or set of instructions that has general or frequent use.

RS-232 A standard that specifies the voltages and signals used to transmit data across an interface cable. The RS-232 standard is used to connect a wide range of peripheral devices to the I/O ports on computers.

Run-time module   The part of an expert system development package or compiler that must be present to run the completed system.

Salami slicing   Computer crime method in which a program is modified to round down all fractions of a penny and add these amounts to the criminal's account.

Scale   To increase or decrease the size of a picture or graphics image.

Scanner   A light-sensitive device that converts drawings, printed text, or other images into digital form.

Schema   See *Logical schema, Physical schema.*

Screen   A pattern of tiny dots used as shading in a graphic.

Scrolling   The horizontal or vertical movement of information on a screen in order to display additional information.

Search-and-replace operation   A word processor feature that searches for and replaces a word or phrase.

Sector   A pie-shaped wedge of one track of a disk. On most computers, a sector is the smallest unit of information sent between the disk drive and the CPU.

Sequential file   A file whose records can be accessed only sequentially.

Sequential storage   The storage of information so that items must be read or written one after the other; thus, jumping from one item to another is not permitted. Tape is the one most common type of sequential storage. Contrast with *Direct-access file.*

Shareware   Software that permits licensees to share or give away copies so that others can evaluate the program before purchasing. Also called *freeware.*

Shell   See *Command processor.*

Simulation   A program that mimics the principles, causes, and effects found in reality.

Site license   Agreement with a software vendor that allows an unlimited or a specified number of copies at a designated site.

Smart modem   A modem capable of accepting keyboard commands.

Soft space   A character which is temporarily added by a word processor to help format a document. A soft space may be added between the words in a line so that the line ends up flush with the right margin.

Software   The generic term for any program or programs.

Software piracy   The illegal copying of a computer program.

Software tool   A program that helps a programmer write another program.

Solids modeling   Production of three-dimensional images and cross-sections of solids.

Sonic pen   A pencil-shaped device using sound to select a screen location.

Sort field   The field or fields on which a file is sorted. There are both *primary* and *secondary* sort keys. For example, a sales report might be sorted on the customer-name field, which becomes the primary sort key; and all the sales transactions with the same customer name might be sorted by the sales-amount field, which then is the secondary sort key.

Source program   A program written in a high-level language. Source programs must be compiled or interpreted before they can be executed by the computer.

Speech synthesis   The artificial production of sounds resembling human speech.

Spelling checker A program that compares words in a document with its own electronic dictionary of correctly spelled words and displays the words that do not match.

Spreadsheet program An application program that displays and manipulates numbers in an electronic worksheet containing a grid of cells.

Star network A network consisting of a central computer surrounded by one or more satellite computers.

Stepwise refinement The process of breaking major program modules down into lower-level components.

Stored-program computer A machine controlled by software stored within the hardware.

Streaming tape drive A cartridge tape system designed to back up and restore information on hard disks.

Structure chart A chart used to describe the most detailed level of a program.

Structured design A disciplined approach to the design and coding of programs that leads to easily understood and maintainable program code. Structured programs use a restricted set of control structures and fit within a top-down design.

Structured walkthrough A formal review process in which a designer or programmer leads one or more members of the development team through a segment of design or code.

Style sheet A word processing file that contains formatting instructions but not text.

Subroutine A set of instructions that has been taken out and made into a subprogram, which can be executed from any point in a main program. See also *Routine*.

Subschema A description of the part of the logical schema that is relevant to a particular user or program. The subschema may also contain a description of how data should be formatted for presentation to the user.

Supercomputer The fastest class of computers that are generally capable of executing at least 100 million arithmetic operations per second.

Supervisor The part of the operating system that schedules and coordinates the execution of other programs.

Synchronous protocol A communications protocol that sends packets of data at agreed-upon times at a fixed rate.

System (1) A collection of people, machines, and methods organized to accomplish a set of specific functions. (2) An integrated whole composed of diverse structures and subfunctions. (3) A group of subsystems functioning as a unit.

System analyst A person trained in the analysis of complex systems in an organization. A system analyst analyzes the problem and designs new systems.

System disk A disk containing operating system programs.

System software Any program that controls the computer system or helps programmers develop new programs. System software includes the operating system, programming languages, utilities, debuggers, editors, and so forth.

System/360 The first IBM family of computers with memory sizes ranging from 16KB to over 1 megabyte.

Telecommunications Any transmission of information over long distances using electromagnetic signals.

Template In spreadsheet processing, a formatted worksheet that contains all the labels and formulas for an application but does not contain the user's data.

For example, an income tax template might contain labels describing how to fill in the template and formulas for calculating the income tax due, but it would not contain the amount of income and expenses.

Terminal Any device that allows a person to communicate with a computer. A terminal usually includes a keyboard, display screen, and connecting wire.

Terminal emulator A communications program that makes a microcomputer act like a terminal for the purpose of interacting with a remote computer.

Test-data generator A program for producing test data for another program.

Text formatting The process of controlling the appearance of a document so that it will look good on paper.

Tiled windows A screen display divided into nonoverlapping windows. The opposite of *Free-form windows.*

Time-division multiplexer A multiplexer that combines many low-speed channels into one high-speed transmission by interweaving them in time slots. Contrast with *Frequency-division multiplexer.*

Timesharing The simultaneous sharing of a computer's resources by many users.

Toggle switch A switch with two settings. Each time the switch is thrown, it maintains its new setting until it is thrown back again.

Top-down analysis and design A system analysis methodology in which the overall structure of the solution is developed first; each succeeding phase of the analysis is more detailed. Top-down design is one of the chief concepts underlying structured programming.

Touch screen A display unit that can sense where a finger or other object touches its screen.

Touch-tablet A touch-sensitive flat electrical device that transmits to the computer the location of a stylus or pen touching its surface.

Track A concentric circle of a disk on which information is stored.

Trade secret The legal protection of an idea, formula, or other valuable business information because it provides the basis for a competitive advantage in the marketplace.

Transient utility A program that is loaded from a disk into memory only when it is needed. The opposite of a *Resident routine.*

Transistor An electronic device for controlling the flow of electrons in an electrical circuit.

Translator A program for converting other programs from one language to another.

Transparent Word used to describe a program action that occurs automatically and usually without the user's being aware of it. For example, the details of how a file is stored on tracks and sectors are transparent to the user.

Trojan horse A computer crime method in which an unauthorized program is hidden within another.

T-switch An electrical switch that allows the user to change the connections between computing equipment just by turning a dial on the switch. T-switches are useful for sharing infrequently used peripheral devices, such as a letter-quality printer.

Turnkey system A complete system of hardware and software purchased together.

Tutorial A program designed to teach and to adjust the level of difficulty according to the user's level of competence.

Twisted-pair wire Wire used to connect telephones to the central switching station.

Typeover mode A word processor mode in which new characters replace characters already in the text.

UNIVAC I The first commercial computer.

UPC Short for *u*niversal *p*roduct *c*ode. A bar code stamped on products, to be read by laser code readers.

Upload To transfer a file from a small computer to a larger computer.

Upward compatible A piece of hardware is upward compatible if it can do everything the previous model could. System software is upward compatible if it supports all of the application programs available for the previous release.

User interface A protocol for communicating between the computer and the user.

Utility server A device that allows everyone on a network to use several peripheral devices.

Value rule A spreadsheet formula that tells the program how to calculate a cell's value.

Variable An area of memory that has been given a name. The term has the same meaning in programming as in mathematics.

Vector graphics monitor A monitor that generates pictures by drawing numerous straight-line segments (vectors) on the screen.

Vertical software Specialized application software that is designed for a particular discipline or activity. Examples include software that tracks the stock market and medical billing systems.

Very high-level language (VHLL) See *Nonprocedural language.*

Very large-scale integration (VLSI) See *Large-scale integrated circuit.*

Virtual Synonymous with *logical.*

Virtual circuit A temporary connection that links two network devices during data transfer.

Virtual memory A method of simulating a very large primary memory by automatically moving parts of a running program from internal to external memory as the program runs. Thus, if a program needs 10 megabytes of memory to execute, it might be run on a virtual memory computer that has only 2 megabytes of main memory and 100 megabytes of disk storage. Also called *virtual storage.*

Visual display unit Any television-like display unit, such as a CRT or a liquid crystal display, accompanied by a keyboard.

Visual operating system An operating system that relies on icons, selected by a mouse, for giving commands to the computer.

Voice recognition system A system that accepts spoken words as input to an operating program.

Volatile The term used to describe memory devices that lose information if electrical power to the device is interrupted. The internal memory of almost all general-purpose computers is volatile, but special-purpose computers, such as portable computers, sometimes use nonvolatile memory. Memory devices relying on magnetic media (tapes and disks) are nonvolatile.

Wild card character A character used to specify a whole category of items.

Window A region of a screen through which part of a file or some data in memory can be viewed. Some programs allow windows to be split into several parts, called *window panes.*

Word A fixed-length packet of bits that is handled as a unit by the computer.

Word length The number of bits in each memory location or *word* of memory. Early personal computers had a word length of 8 bits, minicomputers typically have 16- or 32-bit words, and mainframe computers have 32 or more bits per word.

Word processor A program to prepare written documents.

Word wrap A common and convenient word processing feature that automatically begins a new line of text whenever the word being entered does not fit within the margins of the current line.

Worksheet The grid of rows and columns used by a spreadsheet program.

Write-protect To prevent magnetic media from being written on. Sometimes this is done physically by removing a tab from a tape case or by covering a notch on a floppy disk jacket.

WYSIWYG Short for *"what you see is what you get,"* a reference to programs that attempt to make the screen look just the way their output will look on paper.

Index

Sort operations, 244
Sort-oriented file manager, 245
Source, The, services offered by, 277
Source data automation, 92
Source program, 408, A12
Space(s), soft, 161
Space exploration, use of computers in, 531
Spacing, 178
Special Interest Group on Computer and Human Interaction (SIGCHI), 482
Speech synthesis, 439
Speed, of communication by modem, 270
Spelling checkers, 189, 191–192
Spreadsheet programs, 17, 197–232
  advanced processing with, 221–231
  automatic vs. manual recalculation in, 208–209
  basic concepts in, 198–202
  basic operations in, 202–221
  building better models with, 213
  commands in, 216–221
  comparison of, 218
  copying in, 212, 214–216
  editing cells in, 209
  entering and editing as, 202–209
  entering formulas in, 205–206
  entering functions in, 207–208
  entering labels and numbers in, 204
  exchanging, cutting and pasting in, 211–212
  formatting in, 219
  formulas in, 203–204, 205–206
  inserting and deleting rows and columns in, 209–211
  labels versus numbers and formulas in, 203–204
  loading, saving and quitting in, 220–221
  menu bars in, 217, 219
  office automation and, 476–477
  PC modeling programs compared with, 222–223
  printing in, 219–220
  revising and rearranging in, 209–216
  specifying ranges of cells in, 206
  types of modes in, 202–203
Staffing, management information systems for, 486

Standalone graphics packages, 308–312
Standard interface, 40
Standards, for graphics, 300–301
Star network, 283
Start bit, 272
Start values, in BASIC, A41
Statements
  in BASIC, A23–A24
  in programming languages, 424
Stepsize values, in BASIC programming, A41
Stepwise refinement, 391
Stop bit, 272
Stop values, in BASIC, A41
Storage. See also Memory
  CPU and, 54–79
  external, see External storage
  mass, 77
  secondary, 30
  sequential, 65
Stored program, 43, 568
Stored-program computer, 43
Strategic compatibility, in system development, 396
Strategic Defense Initiative (SDI), 514–515
  potential for error in, 515
Streaming tape drives, 66
String(s)
  format, A28
  of text, characters and, in information representation, A3–A5
String constant, A21
String variables, in BASIC programs, A22
Structure(s)
  control, 424
  data, 424, 426
  of team, in software development, 396–397
Structured design, 391
Structuredness, of programming language, 420, 421–422
Structured programming, 407, 413–416
  as "divide-and-conquer" approach, 413–414
Structured walkthrough, in software development, 398
Style-checking software, 190–191
Style sheets, 169, 368
  in *Microsoft Word*, 171–173
Subdirectory, 75
Subroutines, 419
Subschemas, in database management systems, 250–252
Subscripts, A49

Subsystems, in system analysis, 379
Successive approximations, 523
Summary reports, management and, 488
Supercomputers, 7, 33, 587
  in scientific applications, 529, 530
Superconductors, 587
Supervisor, as component of operating system, 114–115
Sutherland, Ivan E., 297
Swapping, process of, 59
Symbol, in graphics program, 310
Synchronous protocols, 272
Syntax, of programming language, 420–421
Syntax error, A21
System(s). See also Computer system(s); Expert system(s); Information Systems; Management information systems; Operating system
  bulletin board, 274–275
  in business, 9–11
  components of, 6, 377–379, 395
  database management, comparison of, 260
  for file management, 238–248
  for fingerprint identification, 517
  graphic, for art and animation, 329–330
  key-to-disk, 89
  key-to-tape, 89
  life cycle of, 380–381
  memory, 77–79
  to monitor and enforce house arrest, 518
  security of, 547–550
  timesharing, 35, 47
  transistor, in evolution of computing, 575
  turnkey, 326
  unauthorized use of, 543–545
  uses of, 13–15
  vacuum tube, in evolution of computing, 574
System analysis, 376–403
  components of system in, 377–379
  data flow diagrams in, 386–387
  data gathering and analysis in, 386
  design documentation in, 401
  design report in, 394–395
  feasibility study in, 383–386
  installation, maintenance and retirement in, 401–402

System analysis (*cont.*)
  management and software
      plan in, 399–401
  needs analysis in, 383
  process of, 377–381, 386–
      390
  reasons for change and, 382
  requirements report in, 387–
      390
  software development in,
      396–401
  system development in, 395–
      401
  system investigation in, 382–
      386
  testing methods and, 392–
      394
System analyst, 376
System compatibility, of pro-
      gramming languages, 418–
      419
System design
  design report in, 394–395
  software development tools
      in, 398–399
  in system analysis, 390–395
  walkthroughs and prototypes
      in, 392–394
System development
  purchasing hardware and
      software and, 395–396
  purpose of, 395
  software development and,
      396–401
  in system analysis, 395–401
System disk, 119
System investigation
  feasibility study in, 383–386
  needs analysis in, 383
  reasons for change and, 382
  in system analysis, 382–386
System life cycle, 380
  design phase of, 390–395
  in system analysis, 380–381
Systems approach, 377
  as methodology in system
      analysis, 379–380
System software, 16, 133
System/360 computers, devel-
      opment of, 575–576
System/370 computers, evolu-
      tion of computing and, 571

Tabulating machine, 569
Tactical level, of management,
      487–488
Tandy Corporation, 581
Tape(s)
  as external storage, 65–66
  speed of, in data access, 66
Tape drives, streaming, 66
Target program, 408
Task lighting, 481
Teaching systems, 467, 468

Team structure, in software
      development, 396–397
Technostress, 481
Telecommunications, 265–292
  applications of, 274–277
  hardware for, 267, 269–270
  networks for, 278–292
  protocols for, 271–273
  software for, 270–271
  uses of, 265–266
Templates
  in advanced spreadsheet pro-
      cessing, 221, 223–225
  macros and, 224–225
  protected cells and, 224
Terminal(s), 42
  ASCII, 270
  dumb, 270
  point-of-sale, 91
  video display, 480
Terminal emulator, 270–271
Test-data generator, 399
Text chart, 308
Text editing icon, 368
Text file, 76
Text formatting
  local formatting options in,
      165, 173–180
  off-screen, 152
  page design in, 165–173
  in word processing, 165–180
Text-oriented user interface,
      48
Text processing, in program-
      ming languages, 423–424
Textual interface, 113
THEN clause, in BASIC, A36
Thermal printers, 96
Thesaurus, electronic, in ad-
      vanced word processing,
      192–193
Three-dimensional bar chart,
      308
Tiled windows, 132
Time
  access, 66
  connect, 276
  real, 329
Time-division multiplexer, 281,
      282
Timesharing, 35
  hackers and, 545
  process of, 114
Timesharing systems
  mainframes as, 35
  minicomputers as, 35
Time slices, 35
Toggle switch, 158
Token, 283
Token-passing protocol, in ring
      networks, 283
Tooker, Gary L., 585
Tools
  development, for software,
      398–399

expert system, market for,
      452
information, 16–19
integration of, in program-
      ming, 431–432
machine, numerically con-
      trolled, 492
Top-down analysis and design,
      386
Top-down software design, 391
Topology, of networks, 282–
      285
Touch screen, 87
Touch-tablet, 87
Track, 67
Trade secrets, as software pro-
      tection, 551, 554
Transaction reports, manage-
      ment and, 487
Transducers, 281
Transient utilities, 119
Transistor, A1
Transistor systems, in evolu-
      tion of computing, 575
Translation, of programs, 408–
      410
Translator, 408
Transmissions, 282
  baseband, 282
  broadband, 282
  efficiency of, 281–282
  modes of, 272–273
  point-to-point, 278
Transparency, of virtual mem-
      ory, 59
Transport level, 291
Tree chart, 308
Trespassing, by computer,
      545–547
Trojan horse scheme, 545
Truth tables, A7
T-switch, 282
Tuple, 254
Turnkey system, 326, 395
  corporate electronic publish-
      ing systems as, 358
Turtle, 527
Tutorials, in computer-assisted
      instruction, 521–523
Twain, Mark (Samuel Cle-
      mens), 337
Twisted-pair wire, 280
Two-dimensional arrays, in
      BASIC programming, A52
Type-ahead, 85
Typeover mode, 158
Typesetter, 108
Typing, voice-activated, 592

U.S. Census Bureau, 512–513
Universal Automatic Computer
      (UNIVAC I), 572
Universal product code (UPC),
      91, 498

Unstructured inquiry, 489
Upward compatible, 114
User documentation, in system analysis, 401
User interfaces, 48
  comparison of, 140–141
  in file management systems, 238–240
  friendly, 48
  in system design, 392
  text-oriented, 48
  visual, 48
Utility(ies)
  information, services for, 276–277
  transient, 119
Utility server, 289

Vacuum tube systems, in evolution of computing, 574
Value(s)
  binary, 32
  continuous, 32
  start and stop, in BASIC, A41
  stepsize, in BASIC, A41
Value rule, 199
Variables, A12
  in BASIC, A21–A23
  in Pascal, 412
  recurring, in developing expert system, 456
VAX minicomputers, 577
VDT, *see* Video display terminals
Vector, 103, 322
  as mathematical object, 325
Vector graphics displays, raster scan displays and, 103–104
Vector graphics editors, 316–317, 322, 325
  types of monitors for, 103, 322
  using, 322, 325
Vector graphics method, of generating images, 103–104, 322
Vector images, 299
Ventura Publisher, 149
  in desktop publishing, 367–371
  file storage in, 368
  mode-controlling icons in, 368, 371
  PageMaker and, 368
Vertical software, 47
Very high-level languages (VHLL), 429
Very large-scale integration (VLSI), 576
Video display terminals (VDTs), 480

Video driver, 38
Vinci, Leonardo da, 526
Virtual 86 mode, 579
Virtual circuit, 291
Virtual memory, 59
Visicalc, 581
Visual display unit, 102
Visual interface, 113
Visual operating environment, 297
Visual operating system
  commands in, 130–131
  desk accessories in, 133
  Macintosh system as, 113
  types of, 127–128
  use of, 127–133
  window operations in, 131–132
Visual user interface, 48
VLSI, *see* Very large-scale integration
Voice-activated typing, 592
Voice recognition systems, 439
Volatility, of primary memory, 32

Walkthrough
  prototypes and, in system design, 392–394
  structured, in software development, 398
Warnier-Orr charts, 399–400, 401
Weighted-average functions, 304
Weizenbaum, Joseph, 440, 442
"West Coast companies," in evolution of computing, 573, 574
What You See Is What You Get, *see* WYSIWYG display; WYSIWYG programs; WYSIWYG word processor
WHILE/WEND loops, in BASIC, A46–A47
Wild card characters, 123
Window(s), 128
  chart, 302
  free-form, 131
  resizing, 131, 132
  tiled, 132
  in visual operating system, 131–132
Windowing, 138
Wirth, Niklaus, 421
Word(s)
  as grouping of bits, 33
  in information representation, A5
  length of, 33
  reserved, in BASIC, A20

WordPerfect, 149
Word processing, 146–194
  advanced, 183–193
  basics of, 155–183
  comparing programs for, 147–149
  concepts of, 147–154
  editing document in, 155–165
  electronic thesauruses in, 192–193
  form letters in, 187–189
  micro versus mainframe, 151
  office automation and, 476
  outline processors in, 183–187
  saving and quitting in, 180–183
  spelling checkers in, 189, 191–192
  style-checking software in, 190–191
  text formatting in, 165–180
  typical session of, 150
  understanding screen in, 152–154
Word processor, 17
WordStar, 581
WordStar 2000, 149
Word wrap, 160
Workers, home-based, exploitation of, 24
Working conditions, computerization and, 23
Worksheet, 198
  changing appearance of, in spreadsheet operations, 225–228
  changing column widths in, 225–226
  format rules in, 227
  formatting limitations in, 227–228
  window panes in, 226
Workstation design, ergonomics and, 480–481
Wozniack, Stephen, 581
Write-protection, 64
WYSIWIG (What You See Is What You Get) display, 340, 355
WYSIWIG (What You See Is What You Get) programs, 357–358
WYSIWYG (What You See Is What You Get) word processor, 153

XMODEM, 273
X-MP supercomputer, 5, 587

Zuse, Konrad, 406, 570